M000221625

Public Freedoms in the Islamic State

WORLD THOUGHT IN TRANSLATION

A joint project of Yale University Press and the MacMillan Center for
International and Area Studies at Yale University, World Thought in
Translation makes important works of classical and contemporary political,
philosophical, legal, and social thought from outside the Western tradition
available to English-speaking scholars, students, and general readers. The
translations are annotated and accompanied by critical introductions that
orient readers to the background in which these texts were written, their
initial reception, and their enduring influence within and beyond their own
cultures. World Thought in Translation contributes to the study of religious
and secular intellectual traditions across cultures and civilizations.

Series editors

Stephen Angle
Andrew March
Ian Shapiro

PUBLIC FREEDOMS
IN THE
ISLAMIC STATE

Al-Hurriyyat al-'Amma fi-l-Dawla al-Islamiyya

Rached Ghannouchi

Translated by David L. Johnston

Yale

UNIVERSITY

PRESS

New Haven & London

This publication was made possible in part by a grant from the Carnegie Corporation of New York. The statements made and views expressed are solely the responsibility of the author.

Published with assistance from the Louis Stern Memorial Fund.

Copyright © 2022 by Yale University.

Originally published as *Al-Hurriyyat al-'Amma fi-l-Dawla al-Islamiyya*, third edition, by Markaz al-Naqid al-Thaqafi; Mu'assassa Thaqafiyya Fanniyya Mustaqbila, Damascus, 2008. First edition published by Markaz Dirasat al-Wihda al-'Arabiyya, Beirut, 1993. This translation is based on the third edition.
All rights reserved.

This book may not be reproduced, in whole or in part, including illustrations, in any form (beyond that copying permitted by Sections 107 and 108 of the U.S. Copyright Law and except by reviewers for the public press), without written permission from the publishers.

Yale University Press books may be purchased in quantity for educational, business, or promotional use. For information, please e-mail sales.press@yale.edu (U.S. office) or sales@yaleup.co.uk (U.K. office).

Set in Electra by Westchester Publishing Services.
Printed in the United States of America.

Library of Congress Control Number: 2019941085
ISBN 978-0-300-21152-8 (hardcover: alk. paper)

A catalogue record for this book is available from the British Library.

This paper meets the requirements of ANSI/NISO Z39.48-1992 (Permanence of Paper).

10 9 8 7 6 5 4 3 2 1

CONTENTS

TRANSLATOR'S INTRODUCTION

Here is a great book to understand firsthand twentieth-century Islamic political activism. Whether you are a student for whom this is required reading, a curious reader, or a specialist in this field, there is ample material for reflection here.

Two aspects in particular make this treatise on political theory come alive: a young politician wrote it mostly in jail, where he had been thrown and tortured, *because* of his success in the political arena. Rached Ghannouchi knows the evils of authoritarianism firsthand and, not surprisingly, this question is the book's point of departure—how can we curb the despotism so prevalent in many Muslim nations today?

The second fascinating aspect of this book is its stunning relevance. Starting at least with the 1979 Iranian Revolution, and certainly since the 9/11 attacks on American soil, Islam and Muslims have been the object of Western societies' greatest scorn and prejudice. In fact, a neologism was coined to capture it— Islamophobia. This is a book to break those stereotypes and open bridges of understanding and solidarity.

As a scholar, I have long been interested in the phenomenon of political Islam, and particularly in North Africa, beginning with the nine years I spent in Algeria from 1978 to 1987 (I then spent seven years in Egypt and the West Bank). While a research affiliate at Yale University in the early 2000s, I studied the contemporary legal movement that focuses on the objectives of Shari'a. This led me to do some work on Morocco's Islamic scholar and leading independence politician 'Allal al-Fasi (d. 1974) and then turn my attention to Algeria's influential self-taught philosopher Malik Bennabi (d. 1973) and his influence on Ghannouchi's view of civilization.[1] For me this also raised the question of Islamic activism within the modern nation-state, which, most scholars agree, started with the founding of the first modern, Islamic-inspired mass movement in 1928. This was Egypt's Muslim Brotherhood, which spread to many other nations in various forms since then.[2]

Soon after its "Great Persecution" (*mihna*) in 1954, the Muslim Brotherhood renounced the use of violence in its bid to bring about more authentic Islamic governance in the nations where it was active. To be sure, many offshoots of this movement, including those who assassinated President Anwar Sadat in 1981, adopted the militant reading of the Qur'an advocated by onetime chief Brotherhood propagandist Sayyid Qutb. These activists, harkening back to the medieval Islamic paradigm of a world divided between the Abode of Islam and the Abode of War, are those who have made headlines in the Western news media, from al-Qaeda to the Islamic State, from Boko Haram in Nigeria to Abu Sayyaf in the Philippines.

THE DEBATE ABOUT POLITICAL ISLAM

This naturally raises the question: What is political Islam? To be sure, the word that has come to represent it, "Islamism," has drawn a good deal of controversy among both Muslims themselves and scholars writing about these issues. Richard C. Martin and Abbas Barzegar helpfully brought together arguments on both sides in an edited volume, *Islamism: Contested Perspectives in Political Islam.*[3] To oversimplify, those against the use of the term "Islamism" objected to it being deployed by too many commentators and pundits as a way to reinforce the notion that Islam is violent to the core. On the other side, writers like Stanford political scientist Donald K. Emmerson feel that despite its drawbacks the word "Islamism" is useful in pointing to a range of Islamic political activism in the twentieth and twenty-first centuries.

I too recognize the nefarious use of this term to demonize Islam as a whole (though it does improve on "Islamic fundamentalism"), but I tend to agree with the second group in that it identifies a specific political orientation that expresses itself along a wide spectrum of ideologies and political practices, from the Justice and Development Party (AKP), which has ruled Turkey since 2002 under the banner of a secular constitution, to the various Muslim Brotherhood affiliated or inspired parties in countries like Jordan, Yemen, Indonesia, Malaysia, and elsewhere, to finally the jihadi organizations committed to destroying all the political structures of Muslim-majority nations and then bringing them all together under the banner of a new caliphate. But what is of note here is that the vast majority of Muslim political activists envisage and actually use peaceful means for reaching their goals.

Graham E. Fuller has written several books on this topic, having worked for seventeen years as a high-level CIA operative in the Middle East. He captured well this spectrum of political activism in his 2003 book, *The Future of Political Islam*.[4] There he described Islamism as a belief held by Muslim activists that "Islam as a body of faith has something important to say about how politics and society should be ordered in the contemporary Muslim World and seeks to implement this idea in some fashion."[5]

In his short contribution to Martin and Barzegar's edited volume on Islamism, Fuller writes that "there are perhaps several hundred such movements around the Muslim world, each differing in structure, leadership, ideology, goals, methods, and political and social environment."[6] That is why the term should be seen as neutral, especially with regard to the use of violence.

In this book, Ghannouchi uses a very similar concept in referring to the resurgence of Islamic activism in the 1970s. Martin and Barzegar rightly point out that "Islamism is not a concept derived from traditional Islamic theological discourse . . . In fact, the modern Arabic term for Islamism, *islamiyya*, has been adapted to this usage by contemporary Muslim writers and intellectuals when writing about political Islam."[7] Though Ghannouchi never uses the noun *islamiyya*, he does use the adjective "Islamic" with certain nouns to describe the wider phenomenon of Islamic activism he sometimes calls *al-islam al-siyasi* (political Islam): the Islamic project, the Islamic movements, the Islamic conception, and the like. He specifically refers to *al-islamiyyun* (Islamists) over twenty times in the book. Of course, in those cases he is clearly referring to the activists of this wider movement. Most of those instances occur in chapter 6 where he looks at specific movements in various parts of the world.[8] Here in a section entitled "The Islamic Movement in Egypt" we find Ghannouchi's most succinct definition: "By islamist (or Islamic) movement we mean the organized effort to build upon the foundation of Islamic legitimacy with the goal of constructing the complete Islamic edifice, reasoning that Islam is a religion that establishes a system of life, a global community [umma], and a civilization."[9]

Naturally, Ghannouchi is arguing here that Islamism *is* what Islam has always been—"a religion that establishes a system of life, a global community [umma], and a civilization." But not all Muslims see it that way, and his views have shifted somewhat, as we will see.

Most Muslims worldwide, however pious they might be and however much they want Islamic values to be reflected in their state's functioning, seem just as concerned about more democratic reforms and an improved economic life.[10] Differences within nations should also be added to the differences between nations. For instance, the Gallup organization's most extensive polling (thirty-five Muslim nations over six years, 2001–2007) found an overall desire for increased freedoms, especially in the political realm: "Substantial majorities in nearly all nations surveyed (95% in Burkina Faso, 94% in Egypt, 93% in Iran, and 90% in Indonesia) say that if drafting a constitution for a new country, they would guarantee freedom of speech, defined as 'allowing all citizens to express their opinion on the political, social, and economic issues of the day.'"[11]

However, more differences appear when attitudes toward the Shari'a are queried. Just a few countries had majorities saying that Shari'a should play no role in society, yet majorities in most countries wanted it to be only a source of legislation. And again, only in Afghanistan, Pakistan, Egypt, and Jordan did a majority want Shari'a to be the only source of their nation's laws.[12]

This is not to say that Islamism as a movement is dying out or even waning but only that even allowing for the wide spectrum of views within this current, it is a minority view in most Muslim-majority nations. For a variety of reasons in Egypt, for example, while the Muslim Brotherhood was able to take advantage of the 2011 January 25 Revolution to have itself democratically voted into power, it was not able to hold on to that power, and the Egyptian state repression after the July 2013 coup has been formidable and relentless, to say the least.[13]

THE RELEVANCE OF FRANÇOIS BURGAT'S WORK

The eminent French scholar of political Islam François Burgat appears several times in this book. He interviewed Ghannouchi over the years, and they developed a friendly relationship. More importantly, Burgat has lived in several Muslim nations to do his research, besides the many travels required by various projects along the way: Algeria (1973–1980), Egypt (1989–1993), Yemen (1997–2003), and Lebanon (2008–2013). Besides his intimate knowledge of Arab culture, Islam, and the variety of ways they are lived out in many contexts, Burgat has held on to a consistent thesis that has been borne out by developments over time in this region. As it turns out, Ghannouchi agrees with him on most points.

I am leaning here on Burgat's most recent book, which offers a helpful summary of his work since the 1970s, though not yet available in English, *Comprendre l'islam politique* (*Understanding Political Islam*).[14] His thesis rests on two sides of the same coin: a common Muslim discourse (*un parler musulman commun*) and a diversity of practices (*des agir variés*). So his first quest was to explain the dramatic and ubiquitous resurgence of Islam starting in the 1960s. He was trying to "describe the propensity of large sections of these societies to rehabilitate a lexicon that had remained hidden for a time, both in the social realm and in the push and shove of politics." Islam for him is a *lexicon* easily serviceable for multiple uses, and not a *grammar* with rigid rules. He then explains:

> This lexicon refers to a symbolic and normative universe perceived as native, "manufactured locally," neither imposed from outside by the colonial powers nor from above by the elites. On the heels of colonial domination, the culture of the vanquished, as might be expected, found itself marginalized, "nativized," or reduced to folklore. Its symbolic attributes, now seen as odd, had been de facto forbidden to participate in the production of meaning or in expressing universal values. Cordoned off henceforth in the single role of quaint relics of the past, Islamic culture's symbolic universe will now serve only to underline the humiliating centrality of Western culture.[15]

We are talking about a long process by which Muslim intellectuals and activists set out to conquer the status quo inherited from the colonial period and to bring back and put to work their own authentic Islamic worldview. Note that "the mobilizing virtues" of this newly rediscovered lexicon derive more from its homegrown nature than from its "sacred dimension," adds Burgat.[16] For that reason, it packs so much more power than the imported ideologies in vogue in the early postcolonial era such as Marxism, socialism, or nationalism. In that sense, it is more about identity and authenticity than it is about religion. It has more to do with a struggle to assert independence from a neocolonial cultural invasion made more virulent by the ubiquitous tentacles of a global capitalist monster. Though Ghannouchi is a shaykh (deemed an Islamic scholar and spiritual leader) and his book relies heavily on Qur'anic and hadith quotations to weave a comprehensive theology meant to sustain just governance, his diagnosis of the problem at hand is very much in line with the above analysis.

So is his historical perspective on the roots of political Islam. At least a couple of times in the course of this book you will read about the Islamic reformism (*islah*) pioneered in the nineteenth century by Jamal al-Din al-Afghani (d. 1897), Muhammad 'Abduh (d. 1905), and Rashid Rida (d. 1935). Indeed, 'Abduh was an Islamic scholar who finished his career as Egypt's Grand Mufti, but he shared his mentor al-Afghani's anticolonial activism and his passion to see the worldwide Muslim umma united once again, so as to resist and transcend the colonial divide-and-conquer tactics. For proof you only have to look at 'Abduh's collaborator and disciple Rida, who when he witnessed the dissolution of the Ottoman Caliphate in 1924 wrote a book urgently calling for the establishment of another form of caliphate.

Naturally, Hasan al-Banna's founding of the Egyptian Muslim Brotherhood (1928) marks a watershed of Islamic political activism, but both Burgat and Ghannouchi see it organically growing out of 'Abduh's and Rida's work. After all, Rida knew al-Banna and was likely a mentor to him. But whereas Ghannouchi calls the postcolonial scholars and activists the third generation, Burgat calls the period between 1945 and 1990 the second great period of Islamist mobilization, mostly because now the movement's adversaries are the secular elites who came to power on the coattails of their colonial masters. This is also the period during which Islamist leaders make use of the Islamic lexicon in very diverse ways. In the MENA region (Middle East and North Africa) we witness ex-Baathists and communists following very different trajectories in their embrace of Islamism than those chosen by their colleagues in Sudan, for example, where the political arena was dominated by a variety of Sufi orders. Additionally, Islamists brand the North African secular elites as the stooges of France.

Burgat's third Islamist mobilization begins with the fall of the Iron Curtain and the forceful series of American interventions in Iraq (1991), in Afghanistan (2001) and again through the invasion of Iraq (2003). In this era, Muslim Brotherhood–affiliated parties run for elections and integrate the parliaments of Jordan, Yemen, and Kuwait, but what grabs international attention above all is the spread and internationalizing of radical groups like al-Qaeda and later the rise and fall of the Islamic State in Syria and Iraq.

Two last points in Burgat's analysis bear mentioning here. First, the extreme diversity with which the Islamic lexicon is translated to shape particular ideologies and adapt to local sociopolitical conditions also raises the issue of radicalization. Unlike his French colleague Gilles Kepel, who theorizes that religious radicalization precedes political radicalization, Burgat argues that the opposite is actually the case: "Sectarian radicalization—the adoption of disparaging, even criminalizing categories to label the Other's attachments—is in no way a factor triggering political violence. It is at best a contributing factor or an accessory, and therefore the product more certainly than the cause."[17] In other words, to understand bin Laden, examine his armed struggle against the Soviets in Afghanistan and later the establishment of American military bases in his home country, Saudi Arabia. This also means that to bring peace to these regions, do not think that reforming radical theology will turn activists away from violence: "It is not by reforming religious discourse that one pacifies the region; rather it is by pacifying the region that one can reform the religious discourse."[18]

The second point brings us back to Rached Ghannouchi's own intellectual journey. Theology, as just mentioned, is constructed in specific contexts. After twenty years of exile in the UK, Ghannouchi returned to his home country now turned upside down by the Jasmine Revolution in early 2011. In great contrast to the way he was whisked away from prison in the dead of night in 1987, he returned to a hero's welcome, and his Ennahda Party won 40 percent of the votes cast for the parliamentary elections later that year. Tough times lay ahead, but Ennahda with Ghannouchi at the helm responded to popular demand to step down in 2013 and join other parties in drawing up an amazingly secular and democratic constitution. The next year Ennahda came second in the election and joined the coalition government. Significantly, Ennahda's voluntary stepping down from power halfway through their term enabled the Tunisian National Dialogue Quartet—four civil society organizations, including trade unions and a human rights NGO—to guide the political transition. This garnered international attention, as the Quartet was awarded the Nobel Peace Prize for their work in 2015.

Thus Burgat sees Ennahda as showcasing the diversity of ways in which the Islamic lexicon has been put to use:

> Ostracized by the north and south of the Mediterranean for his "islamism," the Tunisian Rached Ghannouchi leads a party, Ennahda, which participates in a government alongside a party close to the regime that was overthrown in 2011 by the revolutionary wave. After contributing in a decisive way to the adoption of a constitution considered to be the first truly democratic one of the Arab world, those whom several decades of propaganda had convinced the world that if ever they were to win an election they would apply the sinister tactic of "one man, one voice, one time"—those same people, then, humbly submitted to the verdict of electoral defeat. And their Tenth Congress in May 2016 defined a strict division between their religious agenda, now relegated to the heading of referential values, and their political agenda. These "islamists" have therefore given a particularly inclusive reading of the "Muslim discourse" (*parler musulman*).[19]

I have no space to document here the remarkable evolution in Ghannouchi's thought, but Burgat alludes to it: that 2016 Tenth Congress "defined a strict division between their religious agenda, now relegated to the heading of referential values, and their political agenda." Practically, that meant that those Ennahda members who preached in the mosques could no longer run for political posts locally or nationally. Perhaps the clearest statement was made in a *Foreign Policy* piece that began with these words: "In May, the leader of the largest party in Tunisia's parliament made a dramatic announcement. 'There is no longer any justification for political Islam in Tunisia,' said Rached Ghannouchi, explaining why his Ennahda Party decided to distance itself from its Islamist origins and recast itself as a political vehicle for 'Muslim democrats.'"[20]

Had the dream of an Islamic state come and gone? Or were the values of human dignity, equality, justice, and freedom always more important than the label of said state? Or was this a transitional phase when all Tunisians join hands to put their nation back on a democratic track and the specifically Islamic agenda picks up from there? Still, some scholars have been talking about "post-Islamism" for a while now.[21] My sense is that Ghannouchi's conception of Islam's political role has shifted. But that does not diminish the historical importance of the present book. To the contrary, this is arguably the most influential articulation of a mainstream twentieth-century conception of Islam and the state.

MORE BACKGROUND MATERIAL

Two recent books on political Islam bear mention here. The first one was edited by John L. Esposito, Lily Zubaidah Rahim, and Naser Ghobadzadeh, *The Politics of Islamism: Diverging Visions and Trajectories*.[22] Besides the chapters that closely examine the Islamic politics of Turkey, Iran, Malaysia, Jordan, and Hamas in Gaza, you find a cogent and articulate statement about Islam and democracy by the Iranian American philosopher Mohsen Kadivar. I am confident that the Ghannouchi of today would agree with most everything Kadivar writes there as a reformist. Finally, Larbi Sadiki offers a chapter on Tunisia's Ennahda, which will help elucidate the changes Ghannouchi led his party to make on the occasion of its 2016 Tenth Congress.[23]

A compatriot of Burgat, Jocelyne Cesari approaches the question of Islamism as a political scientist.[24] Though she might agree with Burgat's concept of an Islamic lexicon put to various uses according to context, she sees political Islam from a much wider perspective and not simply confined to opposition movements and political parties that emerged since the 1970s in Muslim-majority nations.[25] Rather, political Islam is "a set of multiform and contradictory political identities" that came to light with the emergence of Muslim nation-states in the twentieth century. It is both the foundational culture of those societies entering a new political era and the ideology that led particular states to define and regulate public norms in the territories they now controlled in the name of religion. In most cases, this was a version of "hegemonic Islam," that is, one that absorbed religious authorities and Islamic institutions and imposed certain versions of codified Islamic law so as to impose a uniformity that in turn reinforced the state's legitimacy and power. In her words, "The coterminality of Islam's territory and political power shape the modern political cosmology brought by the nation-state in ways unknown in premodern Muslim empires. It creates a connection between Islam and citizenship by establishing Islam as the parameter of public space for Muslims and non-Muslims, believers and non-believers alike."[26]

The fact that this entailed limits on civil liberties and curbs on human rights is what also provoked opposition from a wider movement that in the name of Islam offered different ideological configurations on this bedrock of traditional Muslim culture. And in the case of the Tunisian Ennahda Party after the Jasmine Revolution of 2011, sharing power with secular parties and working together to solve grave economic and political crises only furthered more soul-searching, and by 2016 it led to a separation between its religious advocacy and activism and its properly political activities. But as Cesari maintains, political Islam will endure for the foreseeable future.

The only full-length treatment of Rached Ghannouchi's biography and thought in English is written by Azzam S. Tamimi, *Rachid Ghannouchi: A Democrat within Islamism.*[27] In the course of translating this book, I posted two trilogies of blog posts on Ghannouchi and related material on my website. These were intended primarily for my students but also directed to a wider audience.[28] Those posts also contain some useful references on recent books that touch on these issues in one way or another.

Please note too that the three appendices serve as primary sources on the evolution of thought and practice within this Tunisian movement: Appendix 1: Founding Declaration of the Islamic Tendency Movement; Appendix 2: Bylaws of the Tunisian Ennahda Movement; Appendix 3: Ghannouchi's Speech at Ennahda's Tenth Party Congress in 2016.

REMARKS ABOUT THE TRANSLATION

The translation is based on the third edition of *Public Freedoms in the Islamic State* (Damascus: Markaz al-Naqid al-Thaqafi; Mu'assassa Thaqafiyya Fanniyya Mustaqbila, 2008) in two volumes.

The Arabic transliteration follows the simplified procedure used for other Arabic books translated in this series: only the hamza (*mu'min*) and ayn (*ma'a*) are marked by an apostrophe in the direction used in Arabic.

Unless otherwise noted, all quotations from the Qur'an are taken from M. A. S. Abdel Haleem's version: *The Qur'an: A New Translation by M. A. S. Abdel Haleem,* Oxford World Classics (Oxford and New York: Oxford University Press, 2008). In a few instances, I have chosen to use the older translation by Yusuf Ali: *The Holy Qur'an: Text, Translation and Commentary by Abdullah Yusuf Ali* (New York: Tahrike Tarsile Qur'an, 1987).

ACKNOWLEDGMENTS

Finally, I want to thank my editor, Andrew March, who encouraged me from beginning to end and skillfully decided on the best, most faithful to the original, text after the corrections and suggestions made on my final wording had been turned in. I am also very grateful to Bill Frucht, Yale University Press's executive editor, who kindly and expertly guided me through many twists and turns over the last six years. Then, after my penultimate draft, three people—all PhDs and bilingual Arabic-English speakers—provided extremely helpful comments and corrections on my translation. I want to express deep gratitude to Intissar Kherigi, Yusra Kherigi, and Mourad Chirchi for these comments and corrections. I take responsibility for any remaining flaws.

PUBLIC FREEDOMS IN THE ISLAMIC STATE

Preface to the Third Edition

Naturally, this book reflects the situation in which it was written, gracious reader, but in this case it is much more extreme, as it reveals the great political crisis that has engulfed the Arab book in general. Sadly, this is just one example among many. That crisis became manifest in the obstacles this book faced, such as the effort to prevent it from being published and then from being distributed. This is not fundamentally about some kind of dangerous content some feared would destroy the status quo or threaten an individual or a group. There is nothing like that in the book.

The proof is that this book was published and distributed by an established academic publishing house, which was never the object of any allegation of "Islamic terrorism." That, of course, is the kind of accusation people belonging to the Islamic current encounter all the time. Another sign pointing to the mainstream nature of its discourse is that it refers to hundreds of writings that are available in markets, bookstores, and the press. So where did this almost constant, implacable opposition to it right from the time of its appearing in 1995 come from? My own nation's state organs made every effort to arrest me, muzzle me, and kill me, as it did with hundreds of thousands of freedom activists of all political persuasions. Somehow God allowed me to escape arrest and the gulag, as He allowed me to leave under the cover of darkness. So I joined the fate of thousands of exiles, some of whom were lost for good in the heart of deserts or in the bellies of sharks. He then enabled the book to find its way to one of the most prestigious Arab academic publishers (Center for the Study of Arab Unity), after all the other publishers, including the Islamic ones, showed great reticence to publish it because of possible repercussions.

All of this began with the book's first appearance in 1993, as the Tunisian state set into motion its determined campaign to block the book's distribution by activating the repressive security apparatuses of the Arab world. These are intimately connected, and no disagreement whatsoever among the rulers, be they kings or presidents, ever dampens the warm relations and unlimited cooperation among them on this level, so that even the collapse of the common institutions that bind them in other areas, like defense, the economy, and diplomacy, has no impact on the institution of interior ministers. That is the only institution of Arab unity whose regular meetings and effectiveness never weaken. This collaboration, moreover, was definitely not to share information or coordinate efforts in order to stop infiltration by Zionists and their allies, let alone to plan a counter-penetration. Rather, this close cooperation was focused on confronting political opposition forces.

In this period following the fall of the Iron Curtain, the Islamists became the enemy.[1] Everyone, locally and internationally, believed they were the danger that had to be faced head-on. Thus no one objected to uniting and coordinating efforts to carry out whatever one was asked to do in this area. There was simply no discussion. Tunisian authorities would issue a request to their foreign colleagues to round up the Islamists and their supporters in their country who had managed to slip through the iron wall. This is how more than a thousand brothers were driven out of the Arab and Islamic lands into exile, and I was one of them.

As I recall these events, I still feel the trauma of it all. The police barged into my hotel room while I was visiting arguably the most influential Arab country. In the middle of the night they escorted me to an isolated prison cell at the airport. Still, I was very happy the next morning when they put me on a plane headed for Europe and not to my own country. The one question I could not put out of my mind during those five hours of travel was this: Where is the "Abode of Islam,"[2] of which the jurists say that it is the land in which a Muslim feels safe in his person, in his religion, in his possessions, and in his honor? How can it be that I have left the heart of Islam's Abode and found myself propelled into the heart of the "Abode of Unbelief," where I experienced the security stipulated by Islamic law in all five of its necessities?[3]

These are concepts that must inevitably be revised. The Abode of Islam is where justice and freedom reign. It is where the human person whom God honored, whether Muslim or not, may enjoy the essential and rightful freedoms, including freedom of conscience and the privilege to practice it without fear. So wherever you are able to enjoy your rights as a dignified human being and thus have the right to safely display the rituals of your religion and your deepest held convictions, there is the Abode of Islam and the Abode of justice and freedom.

Ironically, it was the security cooperation among interior ministers of the "Abode of Islam" that was responsible for expelling over a thousand Islamic activists and those struggling for freedom, of which I was one. This expulsion campaign might have stopped, but instead it dragged on and intensified by making use of the state's security and diplomatic connections and by putting our names on an international list of criminals (Interpol). States have no business doing this to political activists, but our own nations even fabricated charges of theft and murder against us. And to the extent that they certified the truth of these allegations, the expulsion order remained against us, and it included all of our media, economic and intellectual pursuits, and even all of our relationships.

Meanwhile, the Arab security services focused intensely on my book, eager to label it as dangerous. They even went after the publisher (Center for the Study of Arab Unity), which until then had good relations with the Tunisian regime, to the point that Tunisia hosted the founding assembly of the Organization of the Nationalist Conference and has hosted other seminars of theirs since. What is more, the center's books had enjoyed great interest and circulation at Tunisia's book fairs, and its journal had benefited from the Ministry of Culture's funding and encouragement. In any case, it had never been dogged by the suspicion of having committed the sin of the age—that is, subscribing to the ideas of the Islamic movement.

Yet none of that will serve to defend it after its deliberate involvement with the Islamists and its rushing to publish the present book with its logo clearly visible on it. As soon as it came out, the state issued an official statute forbidding the importation of all of the center's books. At the same time, its journal's annual subscriptions were banned. This ban lasted ten years, during which the center suffered losses in the millions. As those losses kept accumulating, the center was finally forced to look for an intermediary. In the end, this led to an agreement by which it pledged to refrain from printing the book or exhibiting it at its book fairs. Meanwhile, the ambassadors of this nation monitored the extent of the center's compliance with this agreement by making sure to visit book fairs and filing reports as a result.

The strangest thing in all of this is that in the first year this agreement was applied, the center's publications were banned from Tunis's international book fair. What is more, the center's president, a well-known Arab personality, landed in Tunis and was detained at the airport for one night before being sent back to his country. The reason was that those monitoring the center discovered the present book's title in the bibliography of one of its books.

Is the book so dangerous as to merit such exhausting efforts and such a large-scale prohibition organized by the organs of a modern state? Or does the danger apply to its author? I think neither question makes sense. I will let the judicious readers ponder and reflect on this issue themselves.

I take this opportunity to offer my gratitude to those who contributed to the preparation and review of this edition, and in particular to the two brothers Dr. Bashir Nafaʿ and Mr. Lutfi Zaytun.

Special and deserved thanks also to ʿAlaʾ al-Din Al Rashi, the young publisher and director of the respected publishing house, who boldly tackled the republishing of this book in its revised third edition, in addition to my other books and publications. To God be all praise first and last!

PREFACE TO THE FIRST EDITION

The subject of public liberties is among the most important topics in constitutional law.[1]

The topic of public liberties concerns those political freedoms that the constitution grants to the citizen and safeguards for him against all manner of infringements on those rights and abuse of power to which he may be exposed, whether from individuals or the state. Equally, these public freedoms point to a collection of fundamental rights, individual and collective, pertaining to the human person and citizen of the state.

Since the human person is a metaphysical being—God Almighty said, "And [God] taught Adam all the names [of things]"[2]—therefore his rights and responsibilities, that is, the laws regulating his relationships and other aspects of his life, cannot be elucidated and grounded except in the wider framework of his understanding of himself, the universe, and life itself. Therefore, the study of public freedoms in Islam requires a grasp of the Islamic view of humanity and freedom.

Also, because human beings are social by nature and to the extent that no value can be attributed to people and their behavior except in the context of an organized social life, the topic of freedom in Islam must be dealt with within the framework of Islam and the state, and basic concepts like *shura* and *bay'a*, and the like.[3]

Since humans—even if they are Muslims—are prone to error, ignorance, and injustice, especially those in power, what basic guarantees does Islam have to offer to guard those public freedoms and to resist injustice in the Islamic state?

These are the three issues this project seeks to elucidate: public freedoms in Islam, the principles of the Islamic state, and the guarantees against injustice in the Islamic state.

THE BOOK'S OUTLINE

The following represent the main sections of this book.

ISLAMIC POLITICAL ORGANIZATION

A study of public freedoms is necessarily connected to a study of political organization from an Islamic perspective. It also requires at the outset presenting Islam's comprehensive blueprint for the life of the human person both as an individual and as a member of society, and linking that blueprint's elements to Islam's creeds, rules, rituals, ethics, and objectives in a way that brooks no division. This is the foundational premise of my research, like an assumption upon which I build, for all scholars of Islamic thought, be they Muslim or non-Muslim, have agreed on it—that is, after the fog that surrounded this topic in the first half of the twentieth century had dissipated, a fog created by the enemies of Islam through hatred and ignorance, and especially those who led the invasion of the Islamic world, from the orientalists to the missionaries. These people were able to influence a number of Muslims and particularly those who submitted to the Western methods of education (even among graduates of religious institutions), even though most of them came back to their senses and later recognized their error.[4]

Perhaps one of the factors that was most effective in turning the tide in the fruitless debate about the authenticity of the state in Islam was the general retreat suffered by pro-Western parties—and especially those beholden to the oppressive police powers—and their repeated defeats in the face of a rapidly growing Islamic revival. Add to that the expansion of the Islamic appeal and its increasing power to unite the thinking and hopes of the masses for the sake of liberation and purification, while facing the Western challenge and resisting the imperialist onslaught with Israel as its vanguard, along with its collaborators in the region. The rise of the Islamic movement was evident in various forms. One was the heroic resistance against the American occupation of Iraq and Afghanistan and the Israeli occupation in Palestine and Lebanon, having done the same thing before with the communist occupation of Afghanistan.

Another sign of Islamic resurgence was the resistance against internal despotism and the demand for social justice, freedom, upholding the Shari'a, and participation in public affairs; the demand to reinforce the authority of civil society, including trade unions, mosques, and organizations of public utility; and finally, the call to reform the organs of the state and establish an Islamic polity, some aspects of which had already begun to appear as an essential foundation in international politics.[5] In this light, concrete proof was a more eloquent re-buttal than any other argument responding to the secularist charges and emphasizing that Islam is both a faith and a system of governance. That would be to empty Islam's message of its substance: to establish justice in the world and to free humanity from tyranny, because Islam is both religion and governance. In other words, Islam is a religion and the state is one of the necessary tools for crafting a project of liberation on the scale of an entire civilization. I say this without ignoring the value of the great and blessed efforts made by Islam's scholars and thinkers to answer the secularist tendency, to refute it with logical arguments, and by highlighting the qualities of Islamic organization and the Islamic state in other domains. In this regard, the efforts of Egypt's scholars, followed by those of Pakistan's scholars, were in the forefront—may God reward them for their service to Islam and its followers!

THE NATURE OF ISLAMIC LAW

With respect to the management of the state, Islam limited itself to laying down a set of rules and stressing a number of objectives, and this with no intention of enacting detailed laws, except within a limited scope. In so doing, it allows Muslims to apply their reason on a broad range of issues and thus to interact with a variety of changing circumstances over time and according to context. This has led to a variety of experiences, perspectives, and interpretations of the law, a fact that explains the many different forms of Islamic rule. The researcher on Islam's teachings regarding political authority must distinguish, in his study of the historical applications of Islamic rules, between the fixed fundamentals based on the Qur'an and Sunna, and the interpretations, conceptions, and applications that arise from the interaction between those fundamentals and a specific context. As for the various experiments with Islamic rule and the legal rulings that accompanied them in the past, their only value is to provide us with enlightening examples we can study today and take into consideration. Conversely, by foundational sources I mean only those rulings that are explicitly and clearly enunciated in the Qur'an and the rulings found in the authentic legal texts of the Sunna,[6] also clear and explicit, and with reliable chains of transmitters.[7]

FLEXIBILITY IN APPLYING ISLAMIC PRINCIPLES TO LOCAL GOVERNANCE

The political expression of Shari'a aims to establish justice and remove injustice, and Islam, as we said, is content for the most part to address the affairs of state through its general principles.[8] Thus it relies upon people's rational ability and establishes their freedom, thereby proving the eternal nature of Islam, its applicability to all times and places, and the confidence in the sound opinions of the believing community and its protection from error. For this reason it was natural for Islam's political expression to be responsive to the political heritage of each human context from which it might draw some benefit, either in its philosophy or in the means it uses that are in harmony with Islam's objectives and values, without contradicting its overall objective to promote justice or any specific rule found in its clear texts.[9]

On the one hand, it is not appropriate for someone studying Islamic political organization to be dazzled by any cultural production he happens to come across, and adopt it indiscriminately with its advantages and shortcomings.[10] Nor is it appropriate, on the other hand, for him to refrain from or refuse to accept any wisdom devised by the human mind, the benefit of which has been proven by human trial and error, so that he treads on the path of those "people of understanding," those "who listen to what is said and follow what is best. These are the ones God has guided; these are the people of understanding."[11] Among the annals of Islamic literature these brilliant and luminous words of the great Salafi[12] scholar Ibn Qayyim al-Jawziyya are often quoted, "The objective of Islamic theories of politics is justice, even if this matter is not covered explicitly in the Qur'an.[13] That is because God sent His messengers and sent down His holy books so that people would act according to righteousness, which is justice, by virtue of which the heavens and the earth are able to function. Whenever the signs of truth appear and become evident, wherever they may be, then that is where God's law and religion are to be found."[14] Then he defined politics as "any action with which people become closer to the good and farthest from evil, even if the Prophet did not model it, nor is it mentioned in the Qur'an; it follows that any method by which justice is furthered is at one with religion." It is good to recall the excellent words of our North African sage Abu al-Walid Ibn Rushd (d. 585 H/1198 CE) as he emphasized the necessity of benefiting from the best human experiments regardless of their religious origins, since wisdom is Shari'a's twin.[15]

If, however, the matter goes beyond forms, means, and modalities, and into the realm of ideas, values, and clear-cut commands, then vigilance and circumspection are warranted, particularly in the context of the weak and vulnerable position our umma occupies. Then, and only then, does Islam urge its followers to differentiate themselves from people of other faiths, with the great Ibn Taymiyya even calling this one of the Shari'a's objectives.[16]

INSPIRATION TAKEN FROM THE TEXT, PAST EXPERIENCE, AND PRESENT REALITIES

As we address the problematic of freedom in the Islamic system of governance, we will endeavor to place each challenge within the context of today's reality; then we will lean on quotations from the sacred texts as well as historical precedents and different perspectives provided by the scholars of Islam and the major schools of thought. In this process, we will give priority to what has been favored by the majority of Muslim thinkers as long as it is supported by evidence and is of proven benefit. Further, we will try to avoid being blind to the Islamic reality in which this discourse is elaborated, as one of the means of changing and reforming that reality and resolving its problems, remembering that the Divine Address always comes as an agent of change, redress, and resolution with regard to the tradition's difficulties.

Our motivation is not mere intellectual curiosity but rather an Islamic revolution that uproots tyranny and subjection from God's earth and conquers for the sake of the oppressed, whether men, women, or youth, so that the tree of freedom and justice flourishes again everywhere, watered as it is by the blood of the martyrs and the ink of the scholars. Moreover, we aim to lay out here the details of what we had previously proclaimed.[17] Now that the Islamic movement has achieved gains at the level of political, social and cultural struggle, it is prepared for the defense of public freedoms and human rights. This movement has prepared itself for a new phase of heroic action and generosity as it embarks on the construction of a new Islamic reality—a project that requires renewed efforts at the conceptual level.

INSPIRATION TAKEN FROM THE AUTHOR'S PRISON EXPERIENCE

This study is not designed to explain the general conception of Islamic political organization. Rather, it seeks to present as clearly as possible how to foster individual and public freedoms and human rights in the Islamic state in a way that reflects the author's years of experience in prison. This is nothing but the author's personal description of the matter, and God alone can give success.

THE REALITY OF THE POLITICAL PROBLEM

By instinct people come together because of their natural inability to live independently. They need others to find food, protection, and ways to improve all aspects of their life. This gathering, however, necessitates an authority that curbs the aggression of some against the others. This is because alongside this human propensity and need to come together there is also a basic tendency toward aggression, selfishness, and overstepping one's boundaries, which has led to the emergence of an authority within the community. Yet is it not possible for this authority to become a real threat to the basic dignity of human life? So how do we find a way to curb injustice?

If then the presence of an authority divides society into ruler and ruled, between one who commands and one who obeys, on what basis does this relationship stand, and to what law does it submit? What is the source for the obligation to obey? And what are its limits?

If one of the authority's objectives is to protect the community from its enemies and to maintain social harmony and cohesion, then how can the unity of the community take place while safeguarding its security without interfering with individual and public rights, given that political authority by its very nature inclines toward expansion and domination? What is the relationship between the private and the public, and how can the individual's private life be protected from the state? "The political problem is the problem of the people facing the state."[18] Such are, in another form, the complexities that arise in political thought, which we will attempt to deal with in the course of the following chapters.

HISTORICAL AND PERSONAL
REALITIES BEHIND THIS BOOK

The issue of public freedoms in the Islamic state was indeed the gravest concern weighing upon me from the time the Islamic movement in Tunisia transitioned from a stage of preaching the basic principles of Islam in the face of the imported culture of late to a stage of wide-scale interaction with the concerns of Tunisian society and Arab society in general—that is, since the end of the seventies. Foremost of those concerns has been the question of freedom, and it remains so. It was obviously necessary for the Islamic movement to offer clear answers to the challenges and objections people were raising against Islamic thought in a country like Tunisia, and by doing so this movement took an active part in the national debates about westernization and culture.

Then came the trial of my first prison term (from 1981 to 1984)—a great gift, actually, in the sense that it uprooted me from the pressure of everyday problems and confronted my worries head-on to find solutions to the challenges ahead once the cries of pain and torture had subsided. I spent two years trying to absorb what reference works I could lay my hands on, in order to progressively develop ideas and clear options about the dilemmas before us. This is how the material of this book came together.

This was when, on the heels of the "bread revolution" of 1984,[1] a political opening came about, and I was released from prison, thus leaving behind a life of meditation and writing in order to throw myself into the activism of leading a movement. I was immediately confronted by a widespread campaign to impugn Islam's ability to organize society, with a strong indictment of its ability to guarantee civic and personal freedoms, like the political and religious rights of minorities and women's rights. People also questioned Islam's capacity to prevent

injustice, as in the case of apostasy and what that means for personal and political liberties.

Thus Islam's potency was questioned and it was represented as a menace
descending upon civilization and threatening people's rights, both individual
and collective, and an insurmountable obstacle on the path of progress for nations seeking to achieve their rights! What is ironic is that after the breakdown
of the communist model, our adversaries—most of them former communists
who used to lose their voice heaping curses and ridicule on Western bourgeois
democracy—focused their efforts on distorting the Islamic project and presenting it as the antithesis of all aspects of the contemporary humanistic heritage,
including democracy, human rights, women's freedom, civil society, and every
kind of artistic creation. Meanwhile, a number of convictions were forming in
my mind and heart. They were so clear to me, distinct and different, and I felt
bound to communicate them to others.

I have come to see clearly that democracy is not a simple concept. Democracy presented concepts related to freedom and the institutions necessary to establish it, thereby achieving a consensus among the people of a particular
nation, and could be described as "acceptable" or the least defective mechanism available. Nevertheless, democracy is far from perfection and the absolute
good. Yet in no way is democracy the enemy of Islam lying in wait, an enemy to
be feared and to confront in battle, as some zealots declare. These victims of
tyranny instead of going to the root of the umma's scourge or to the reason
behind their distress have come to the wrong conclusion. They have shot their
arrows at that which was not their enemy, and therefore adamantly reject democracy, as if it were being forced upon them day and night!

Meanwhile, all that is being offered to them—and imposed on them—is a
despotic state that imprisons them, banishes them, gags them; it's a state pro-
grammed to make war on human dignity. How strange is the predicament of a
group of believers, victims of tyranny, who instead of directing their arrows
toward their enemy set out to discredit democracy and attack it and to declare
with great assurance that it contradicts Islam, that it represents a threat to their
livelihood and their religion. In doing so, they ignore the broad common ground
between democracy and Islamic values and objectives of delegating the management of human affairs to humans themselves ("[those who] conduct their
affairs by mutual consultation").[2] They also ignore the public benefit that
comes from meeting the people's need for freedom, mutual consultation, and
from the mechanisms that will move these two values from the level of theory
to that of practice. This is democracy's greatest achievement, while it simultaneously points to the most noticeable failure in the history of our civilization.

This book is based on the firm conviction that Islam is inherently suitable for people in all times and places because it represents God's last word. It is the religion that reflects human nature [*fitra*] at creation, and thus expresses humanity's desires and its deepest needs. This enables it to encompass every advancement in human knowledge and experience, without rejecting or contradicting this progress in any way but welcoming it. This is what explains its position on modern democratic governance—as a set of practical measures enabling collective decision making to give voice to the widest possible spectrum of opinion and common interests. And we all know that to achieve this is one of Islam's objectives in organizing the public sphere. So where does the claim that these two are essentially contradictory come from?

If people truly seek to understand the respective demands of Islam and democracy, they will agree that there is broad common ground and overlap between them, which appropriately creates a solid foundation for the exchange of benefits and enables coexistence, while at the same time the variance between them and the necessary corrections to be made would also be easy to see. These convictions are the fruit of our meditations over many years, which we have brought with us from our prison cells and put to work as we launched into the daily struggle against the dictatorship, armed only with these two weapons: Islam and democracy.

Fresh out of prison, I had to face several challenges. In order for my daily efforts to be as effective and competent as possible, I had to continually and creatively rethink Islam in parallel with contemporary thought and in interaction with facts on the ground and with what they might entail. This required me to tear myself away from daily tasks so as to unclutter my mind and begin to dust off the prison documents. That would not have been possible had it not been for the clear authoritarian determination to eradicate the early signs of the wave of change and revival arising out of the growing popularity of the Islamic movement. I was advised to go into hiding during the summer of 1986, which turned out to be a precious opportunity—and likely the last—to bring together in writing my ideas, convictions, and experiences around the most pressing issues in Islamic thought that had frequently troubled me. Just like we finish picking the fruit in a garden and the branches become lighter, so I too was unloading some of my own burdens, filled with great joy and happiness. From time to time I had a Sufi experience of "realization," and I felt ready to face death.[3]

I emerged from my prison cell and isolation at peace in my soul, as if I had accomplished a death-defying feat or had rendered annihilation impossible. But it wasn't long before the hand of injustice grabbed me and dragged me back to prison. I refused to offer any compromise on my right to be free, knowing that it was my duty to teach my people and fully participate in the service of the mosque, and that without any permission from the ruler. Since the dictator was determined to do away with me once and for all and thought that imprisonment for life was too light a sentence, he ordered that I be sentenced once again. With only a few days left before the ruler's orders were to be executed, God's will preceded his. In fact, God granted me a new life.

I left the prison in May 1988 with new resolve. I returned to the book once again, looking for a way to present it at the university, since it was originally conceived as a doctoral dissertation at the University of Tunis. But the honeymoon was very short this time, as our hopes for the democratic nature of the new ruler and a reconciliation with him, as was my choice, were quickly dashed. For there was only one school, that of westernization and dictatorship, two different faces of a single reality: violence, hypocrisy, and corruption. Is there any worse violence than to rob a people of their identity? And can this be done without suppressing their political will and irreversibly emptying the state of all its values, leaving only a complex security apparatus in its place bent on oppression and corruption? Our concessions had been of no use, including that of changing our movement's name and imposing on ourselves a kind of flexibility and moderation. We had done so to spare ourselves and the nation a return to confrontation with the regime, as long as the powers-that-be provide the people with the means of economic development and confronting the nation's great challenges.

Nevertheless, the government's entrenched authoritarianism,[4] its desire for power and the reluctance of the ruling party and its allies to compete with a young movement with deep roots in society's consciousness and conversant with the heritage of modernity,[5] incited it to renew its resolve to eradicate the movement. Benefiting from the support of an opportunistic elite and new colonial campaigns against the umma, the government implemented its eradication plan, with great financial support and under a complete media blackout. So when the regime falsified the people's will in the elections (April 1989), we returned to confrontation. But this time I leaned toward emigration, toward the painful road to exile and to its trials and tribulations.

Because our fight in essence was a war of ideas, our movement resolved to keep it that way despite attempts to draw us into acts of violence. We believed that our most effective weapons to confront the project of tyranny and westernization was the power to convince and win over people of goodwill and to mobilize the people's energy in order to build a civilization rooted in an identity in harmony with modernity, through which steadfastness and resistance can be realized. This also meant empowering them to challenge the projects of domination and intellectual conquest, so that these projects are exposed for what they really are. They have no currency in a battle of civilization, except as an instrument of naked power, which the regime puts to use and dedicates to one mission—namely, its own safekeeping and increased efficiency—and which can be summarized in one symbolic term, "the stick."

As I said, our fight is between patriotic choices seeking to preserve our civilization and the forces of international dominion targeting the worldwide Muslim community (umma), our independence, and our resources. In this fight, Islam and its Arabic culture represent the armor of resistance and its fuel, and we must continue the struggle on all fronts, and especially in the intellectual confrontation, which is the vital necessity of both clearing mines and lighting the path. There's no escaping this, and it becomes all the more necessary considering all the trials we face, like the growing intensity of the struggle against the hegemonic projects of the world powers, including Zionism and their local allies, the martyrs who fall, the imprisonment of tens of thousands of those who support Islam and the freedom of their nation, and finally, those who pay the price for their defense of Islam, freedom, and democracy, and their resistance to authoritarianism.[6] These fellow Muslims are determined to keep struggling on behalf of the national liberation movement, as they seek to achieve cultural and economic independence by confronting the strategies of globalization and integration.[7]

Our thinking and ideas, therefore, represent the most important and effective aspect of our fight. We struggle against the backwardness reflected in our society's personality, as it suffers from schizophrenia and feelings of inferiority, and with ignorance, inertia, and the inability to activate people's potential. All this, I believe, drives our umma into a cultural and political decline, which is maintained and reproduced by a political autocracy and its allied political elites on the inside and its international patrons on the outside. Ironically, this is happening despite the fact that democratic reforms and respect for human rights represent the dominant Western ideology in this era, just as the slogan "bringing civilization to the backwards" was the driving slogan in the colonial era. Even if that slogan was useful in demolishing and replacing the communist regimes, to apply it now to the Islamic world and especially to the Arab world is very unlikely to produce the same result—that is, godless, Western liberalism. Instead it would lead to loosening the shackles of Islam, the great giant in chains.

Therefore, it was not surprising when the Western military leadership quickly retreated from its policy of spreading democracy in the Arab world as a means of fighting so-called terrorism, and this right after the dramatic victories of the Islamic movement by way of the ballot box in Morocco, Palestine, Iraq, and Kuwait. So these countries quickly returned to the warm bed of dictatorship in order to regain the comfort of peace and tranquility.

Whatever the case might be, the task of thought is made more urgent day by day by the increasing destructive influence of the winds of cultural globalization over people's senses, tastes, ideas, and way of life. Despite the increasing sophistication of machines, the rising importance of economics, and the role of armies, the future likely belongs to the nations most capable of intellectual innovation and renewal, of persuasion, dialogue, and offering things that benefit mankind; and finally, those most capable of resistance, change, and sacrifice.

This mission of right thinking aimed at confronting the storm is on two levels. On the one hand, it is about widening the scope of dialogue and encounter between our Islamic community's activists and people of goodwill in other nations.[8] Our activists refuse the international and Zionist domination of our resources, our sacred beliefs and values, our ideas, and our souls. Even before that, they refused despotism in our own nation and the assault on human rights, whatever its justification and origin. That is why they must be in dialogue with and encounter those on the outside who support freedom, human rights, and the self-determination of nations, however different their ideologies and religions might be. These people, wherever their location, are our friends today and tomorrow, especially the international movement that is fighting for an alternative global world order based on justice. On the other hand, we must continue working towards elaborating the Islamic project, which incorporates the fruit of human effort across the board. That project must transcend past human failures and defeats, the objectification of humanity and the dismantling of its values in the contemporary civilization and seeks to protect it from being crushed and assimilated. In all of this, our starting point is the principle that all human beings have one origin and one destiny, and that God's mercy for humankind is very wide indeed. We cannot imagine its recovery except through a comprehensive rescue of all of humanity, and that is what Islam represents: "It was only as mercy that We sent you [Prophet] to all people."[9]

The need for this kind of collaboration has grown more urgent, as the international aggression is intensifying. In that light, this project is what is left outside the scope of Western thought. In our small Tunisian context and others like it, we are seeing the application of the double project of drying up the sources of our cultural heritage and its elimination, along with other projects such as enforcing normalization, free trade, and eradicating the pockets of resistance, according to what is possible in each context. Add to all of that the systematic crushing of the inhabitants of occupied Palestine and Iraq, and the devastation of their land, their identity, and their heritage, which is part of a global crusader campaign against "Islamofascism," as George W. Bush put it. This campaign aims to break Islam as an idea, as rituals and institutions, and also as a collection of movements, nations, and minorities. Further, it seeks to crush and eradicate these Muslim societies' defenses so that they submit to the international surgeon's scalpel and his hegemonic plans and accept defeat in the civilizational struggle against the global campaign of imperialism.

It is clear that the modernization project, which is in fact westernization, has failed. Having dismantled society in order to dominate it, it has proven incapable of re-building it and fixing its problems. Therefore, it has resorted to violence and police brutality to counter popular discontent and people's aspirations to a return to their roots. It has now become clear that this project of false modernization has no genuine alternative than the Islamic movement and its allies among the supporters of their identity and democracy and those fighting against the international projects of imperialism and Zionism. In fact, there is no other solution to this dilemma—that is, the rising up of a current of resistance to the projects of hegemony and disintegration—than to encourage those regimes bent on violence and destruction. Short of that, there will be direct military intervention.

Because Islam is what is left by way of civilizational thought outside of the Western perspective after the decline of the communist alternative from Western civilization, the Islamic project does not just represent hope for Arabs and Muslims, but it unifies their ranks, mobilizes their energies in a creative direction, and liberates their will from despotism. It also harnesses their human and spiritual resources to complete the freeing of their wills and the liberation of occupied lands, Palestine in particular, which is their main concern, along with giving support to all the marginalized and oppressed everywhere. In that way it will not surrender to the international hegemony and the subduing of all or most other ideologies.

Thus the revival of Islam as seen from this perspective of human liberation also represents in a fundamental way a hope for non-Muslim peoples, including Western ones—a hope to humanize civilization after its technology and politics have become barbaric in the shadow of the materialist philosophy at the foundation of contemporary civilization.[10] It was that philosophy too that poisoned the roots of the modern Arab revival, rendering it a barren movement from the start.[11] Islam presents itself as a source of hope, healing, and happiness in this world and the next to hundreds of millions of people living in misery and despair, suffering a calamity that sank its teeth into their bones and threw them into the abyss: hunger, disease, deadly sexually transmitted diseases, depression, loneliness, family breakdown, devastating wars and the fear of them, religious and racial discrimination, political despotism, brutal torture, ethnic cleansing, the savage and systematic destruction of the environment, the menace of wars of total destruction, without mentioning the return of colonialism in its most naked and direct forms as a threat to our umma and the free people of the world. The marches of millions of people we have witnessed in dozens of great cities, and especially in the West, against the imperialist hegemony over Iraq and Palestine, as just one part of its global reach—these marches, then, were led by forces opposed to globalization, including leftist and Islamic elements, and they portend a new axis of popular resistance against hegemony and destruction. This is a movement that cuts across all civilizations and religions, and it signals a promising future for humanity.

Our great hope is that this personal and humble effort to surmount a few obstacles on the road to our umma's revival and to rouse placid people to reflection and action will succeed: "I cannot succeed without God's help: I trust in Him, and always turn to Him."[12]

Though what you find in this book is one individual's ideas, orientations, and perspective, its most important ideas are present in the founding declaration of the Movement of the Islamic Tendency in the early 1980s. The launching of this book had been delayed for years, due to the challenges faced, but when it finally appeared, it represented an unusual voice in the Islamic arena, and it provoked antagonism and even the accusation of apostasy. Yet, after the ideas in it began to disseminate, it spread widely in Islamic circles, and not just because it became known, but I will say that it met with a growing acceptance even in moderate secular circles. It represented an important factor of development in the Islamic public sphere, promoting a wise interaction with reality and a search for common ground, and a triumphing of dialogue, cooperation, and progress over confrontation and mutual estrangement. Today this trend unites the widest spectrum of movements, including Islamic youth activities dedicated to a variety of Islamic social work, and the supporters of democratic transformation and of the dialogue between various national ideological currents, instead of fighting one another.

Furthermore, it was not my intention to present a blueprint or program for an Islamic party or Islamic state. That goes further afield than this project. I am not, for example, addressing what is now happening in Tunisia and similar countries. I do not consider the current stage to be one of stability that will allow competition between different alternatives and programs vying for power. This is not a stage wherein a secular state competes against an Islamic one; rather, our whole region is engaged in a liberation struggle against a resurgent colonialism seeking to gain what it has lost. This only makes the role of ideas today that of uncovering enemies masquerading behind nationalism and Arab glory, and even behind Islam while being agents of international forces. The struggle, therefore, is between being or not being, between those who support the project of a falsely modern nation state, which dismantles society in order to dominate it or make it subservient to foreign powers, and those who support the project of a strong civil society, organized and coherent, in which there is respect for human dignity and people use the state as a tool for their development. Finally, it is a state where people put to use political institutions as instruments of emancipation.

At bottom, this is the struggle for a philosophy of politics and civilization between the supporters of the national democratic state, the people's state, the umma's state, and the defenders of the autocratic state, which depends on outside support, the mafia state. It is a struggle between those who want to continue the fight for national liberation leading to full civilizational independence and those who give up and retreat. We are very far from achieving democracy or economic development under current circumstances of fragmentation.[13]

So we set out to build our national democratic state, over which society rules and not the other way around, and which the people appoint in order to protect their rights as citizens and human beings and give them peace of mind about their lives, their futures, and their families. This national democratic state will also allow them to contribute their thinking and work to the benefit of all, so that pockets of freedom, for which everyone must fight, will expand and flourish. Then people will see alternatives, their opportunities to choose freely will multiply as their discernment grows, and through the ballot box power will change hands. Until that happens, there is no room for marginal debates. The priority must be on forming a peaceful coalition of resistance against any power grabs and a determination to extend public liberties.

To reiterate, this is a lofty quest to facilitate dialogue within Islamic circles but also between Muslims and the regional and international realities in the light of the rules of Islam and its objectives. It will be necessary, too, to extend this dialogue beyond that scope and encompass the advocates of freedom everywhere who engage in the fight against dictatorship locally and internationally, including those sincerely following the direction of Islamic thought as it evolves today. This dialogue is about a number of issues and problems that are raised in Islamic circles—and beyond also, because above all they are human problems that transcend ethnicity, religion, and party. This is all the more necessary because of the way the information revolution has changed our world.

To conclude, suffice it for me to light a candle on the path of "Tunisia, the beloved, the martyr," as we call her, victim of a delusional modernity, whose awestruck elites are terrified of the Islamic revival and how it would affect their privileges or allegedly threaten their lifestyle. They dread those calls just as they dreaded preceding calls for change, which they had responded to with great petulance, frightened that they might be deprived of consuming a glass of wine by the side of the road or violating the sacred rules of Ramadan in public. That said, the Islamic project is more important than that, and Arabic literature during the golden eras of Islamic civlization testifies to the baselessness of such fears for personal freedoms.

It would be more than enough for me to bear some honor and responsibility as a member of the community of Arabs, of Muslims, and of humanity as a whole. By so doing, I participate in the smallest way in alleviating the suffering of the world's oppressed by renewing the forces of opposition, by creating dialogue, by implanting the values of freedom, by honoring the human person and elevating his rights, one of which is the fundamental right to share in the authority and trusteeship people have over their rulers. It is the responsibility of all people of virtue to fight against despotism, because tyrants come from every nation and religion. Therein is the root of affliction, its pillar and crown. Islam from the start rejected tyranny, then it opened the door to faith in God and to the esteem of all human beings: "so whoever rejects false gods and believes in God has grasped the firmest hand-hold."[14] For this reason, the most beautiful summary of Islam is this: "a comprehensive revolution of liberation."

Any bit of success I have achieved in this book in revealing a small part of the mercy and justice of Islam and its comprehensive revolution of liberation is by God's grace. If success escaped me, let me just say that I sought the good of my people and the umma and the good of a bewildered and suffering humanity. My only charge to you, my esteemed readers, is to proceed with a positive spirit, one of wisdom and freedom, so as to be included among those "who listen to what is said and follow what is best. These are the ones God has guided; these are the people of understanding."[15] So I distance myself from the start from anything that turns out to be mistaken, whether by proof of revelation or by reason. It was certainly not intended. At the same time, I beg your indulgence for any kind of technical mistakes because of the particular circumstances in which the author found himself. I thank every faithful advice giver and every honest critical reviewer.

I would like to thank all those who helped me with their sound advice and correction, and especially the experts from the Center for the Study of Arab Unity who offered advice and graciously published the book. I mean particularly my brother, friend, and teacher Dr. Muhammad Salim al-'Awwa, and the brethren who kindly accepted to read parts of the book or who reviewed it. Particularly, our esteemed Shaykh Dr. Mahmud Abu Su'ud, and the brother Dr. Ahmad al-Mana'i and the brother Muhammad al-Nuri. To all these I offer my most sincere gratitude and esteem, without forgetting to express my heartfelt thanks and indebtedness to all those who helped me to bring this effort to fruition, and in particular the two brothers Lotfi Zitoun and Mokhtar Badri, and sister Salwa al-Mhiri—all three invested considerable effort and fatigue in this project. May God reward them with His kindness! And to God all favor and grace!

London, 11 December 1992

Part I

Human Rights and Freedoms in Islam

ON THE CONCEPT OF FREEDOM IN THE WEST

There is no place here for a philosophical study of the concept of freedom. This kind of rational inquiry into the nature of freedom in order to prove its existence will likely have no other conclusion than that of denying its existence and calling it an illusion. Just as an investigation into the nature of the human person, his mind or his spirit, will only end up with failure and a fall into confusion and contradiction, it is a futile exercise, because the instruments we use for knowledge are not designed to grasp the essence of things.[1] And even when certain schools of philosophical thought imagine that through philosophy they could obtain positive results in understanding freedom by turning away from a purely rational approach and focusing on states of being and free acts, these philosophies tend to be overcome by a nihilistic spirit, which leads them to posit the free human person as an isolated being, anxious and broken, who sees no other path to freedom but that of shattering all ties and values that bond him to others. As a result, there is no longer any meaning to his free existence but suicide and futility.[2]

That said, research into the concept of freedom quickly left metaphysics and headed toward those areas containing a wider vision, like ethics, law, and politics, and efforts focused on the relationship between the person and the political, social, and economic institutions—that is, the person's set of rights. So the discourse turned to the individual's liberties as a whole and away from the concept of freedom. Freedom became the goal of the struggle waged by oppressed peoples and classes, and people of good conscience, rather than the object of meditation for thinkers, unless they were political and legal thinkers seeking to determine the scope of freedom in their declarations of human rights, in their statutes, and in their discourse on how the state is born. They are the ones who take into account the set of rights and services that must be guaranteed and available to each citizen so that he will be able to achieve his material and spiritual personality and thereby contribute to the management of public affairs and determine his own destiny free from any outside pressure. This is only possible through the citizen's possession of an array of possibilities, powers, and rights, like the right to one's thought, to one's conviction, to expression, association, work, travel, worship, and ownership. These are the rights that you find filling up declarations of human rights from the eighteenth century to our day. The 1948 document about human rights described as "universal" represents the gospel of public freedoms from which the constitutions of our world's nations take inspiration and by which they are adorned. The Universal Declaration of Human Rights (UDHR) binds them together as a testimony of their belonging to the world of liberties and democracy, even if in fact they are steeped in despotism.

For this reason it has been objected that this bundle of rights or freedoms is only formal or "negative" that gives the individual theoretical possibilities but without giving him the means to achieve them or protecting him from injustice. He has the right to think, to express himself, to own property, or to travel at will, but how can he exercise those rights as long as a small minority of citizens— theoretically equal to him in rights—monopolizes culture, wealth, and authority, and in reality, therefore, stands above the rest in every way?

This criticism goes on to undermine these liberties, which it describes as bourgeois and restricted to the privileged class and it reminds us that the origin of the various declarations of human rights was associated with the historical rise of the bourgeoisie and, fundamentally, with the struggle that took place between the new class of merchants and industry leaders on the one hand and the kings, feudal lords, and the church on the other. The interests of the new class harmonized with the appeal to human rights based upon their nature as human beings, free from the authority imposed on them by the king or clergy or whoever, just as they were served by the suppression of the church's authority and the call for national homelands no longer based on religious identity, or even hostile to it.

The interests of the new class were also served by removing the plethora of restrictions on commercial and industrial labor previously imposed by the old classes, a fact that led the famous philosopher Bertrand Russell to define freedom as the absence of obstacles to fulfilling one's desires.[3] The state itself from this perspective, as we shall see, is nothing but an association created by individuals in order to protect these rights and liberties, a fact that leads to defining the issue of freedom in these terms, "to reduce [freedom] to an individualistic perspective that is fundamentally and entirely a negative one; it is the liberal tradition's perspective that can see freedom only in terms of the individual's ability to resist the demands of the community or the possibility to live far from the reach of political authority,"[4] that is, from the reach of injustice.

In fact, to conceive of the free agent as a person without any outside pressure underlines a negative and mechanical definition of individual freedoms. That is because the impediments to free will are not all from the outside; some of them come from the inside—and perhaps the strongest ones—either going back to one's own impulses or whims, or to a lack of consciousness or even knowledge. Further, coercion can take many forms, and it can attain a high degree of precision, cunning, and secrecy in doing its job to such an extent that the victim is unaware of it. This is what exists in both Western and Eastern democratic societies through the control of the state or the capitalist firms over the media and the educational and cultural institutions. This gives them enormous influence over the minds and tastes of the masses, thus guaranteeing security and restricting the political process within a limited elite and circle of interests.

Consider the international campaign these days directed by American institutions and firms—and their followers elsewhere—against the so-called danger of fundamentalism. As they carve and fashion their product—a single picture with precise traits—in order to shape public opinion in the West, and even worldwide, into seeing the Arab and the Muslim as a savage terrorist and a danger to civilization, they provide but one example of the contemporary methods of compulsion exercised by the state, which is supposedly the protector of democracy and human rights. If nothing else, this emphasizes the vacuous formalism, negativity, and emptiness of the rights and freedom enshrined in the Universal Declaration in the absence of a strong and stable theoretical foundation that could sustain the universal establishment of liberties and human rights that are undergirded by legal and social guarantees.

Capitalist regimes and corporations have been forced by their fear of a socialist revolution and pressure from the trade union movement to adorn human rights covenants with a minimum of social guarantees relative to the privileges they enjoy. Still, as long as the balance of power remains the only guarantor of rights and liberties, no matter what the official discourse about natural rights might be, then there is nothing to hinder the retreat from those concessions in a way that will tilt the balance of forces to the advantage of rich predators. That has indeed started to take place, as a result of the retreat of the Marxist tide and weakened influence of trade unions.

The above Marxist critique—although valid in its criticism of the background of western democracy, rights and freedoms—remains a critique based on a destructive and hypocritical approach. This critique of individual rights focuses on their being only a formality, as they were stripped of guarantees for their applicability. The reason is that wealth is monopolized in the hands of capitalists, which means that the state's power is at their service. In the Marxist view, there can be no path to political liberties until private property is dismantled and handed over to the collective entity. This, it is argued, spontaneously causes all factors of oppression to fall away. Subsequently, the state itself crumbles and withers away, since there is no longer any justification for its existence. From the Marxist perspective, this kind of state was only a form of tyranny in the service of private ownership. In reality, what occurred after the realization of the beginning of the dream, the utopia of tearing away of ownership from the hands of the capitalists and feudal lords for the last fifty years, was that even if the Soviets and their like achieved to some extent the feeding of the hungry and a minimum standard of living in the best of cases, the price paid by those peoples in terms of their lives, their freedoms, and their dignity was astronomical.

Moreover, political authority did not disintegrate or gradually disappear. On the contrary, it grew stronger, expanding its power and surrounding the poor individual on every side. How could it not do so, since it had monopolized power and with it the means of violent oppression and influence, whether through political authority, wealth, the media, or even culture itself. This is how the Marxist state was able to find ample room to impose its own definition of freedom, or rather lack of freedom, or despotism.[5] This only proves that the main support for political and social freedoms in both the capitalist and socialist West is not faith in the intrinsic value of the human person, individually or collectively, as the source of rights and liberties. All that has been written on that topic is no more than a romantic dream from the age of the "European Renaissance."

Western thought does not function outside the realm of matter and its movement, which means that this being called "human" is no more than an advanced moment in the flow of material evolution. The human being is a phenomenon, not an essence.[6] As a result, the fundamental—and only—determining factor for freedoms and rights is neither God nor human nature nor eternal truth, as Engels put it, but it is another god called the balance of powers—political power, domination, and wealth. That is the West's object of worship and the source of its values. In vain do the downtrodden and tormented people of the earth try to convince their executioners (who go by several names) to grant them mercy and a bit of justice in the name of the Universal Declaration of Human Rights and the various international covenants and national declarations. In the end, this is only self-deception.

The only path they understand is this: the balance of powers, now tilted to their advantage. Yet the balance can be changed.[7] And this is not to neglect the efforts deployed by Western NGOs and humanitarian agencies on behalf of the victims of oppression; on the contrary, as Muslims we greatly appreciate them, for we and they are engaged in a common front opposing the forces of repression in their countries and ours. That said, their influence in Western contexts is limited, and the balance of power is not in their favor.

Yet even when the Western ruler attributes rights to the human person and defends them even when he convenes assemblies, establishes judicial, administrative, media, and economic institutions to make sure they are applied and even protests their violation, he is in fact for the most part maneuvering. For what he calls "human being" is actually only the "citizen" in the best of instances. In reality, the term hardly applies to anyone outside of the privileged classes. This means that declarations of human rights, which grace the preambles of state constitutions, are rather illusory, since they only apply to the Western citizen at best.

In these texts, the term "human being" is inserted and used in a misleading way unless it is to be qualified as applying only to French, English, or "western" citizens in general. Even this human being has no honor in himself, simply because he is human, but rather that honor comes from his belonging to a particular historical, social, and cultural context—nation, class, or European race. As Muhsin al-Mili put it, "According to western human sciences, the human being is nothing but a social atom, and not a transcendent and unique reality with moral characteristics. The human person has no nature; rather, he has a history, and inside this person there are no stable impulses or drives, except, to be sure, the sexual drive and hunger. Human nature has no primary traits or shared characteristics among its species, because the human person has no 'nature.'"[8]

No matter which person Westerners may be talking about, al-Mili continues, "He's 'unconscious' according to Freud, 'insane' according to Foucault, a product of his context according to the environmentalists, and a product of his group according to the social scientists . . . He's a bundle of social relationships defined by the means of production. Human sciences do not study *the* human being, but they study aspects of him from a particular time period. But the human person as a whole formed of mutually complementary parts is in fact absent in these studies, so we must speak of the absence of the 'human' in the human sciences. Should we speak then of the human sciences or of the non-human sciences?"[9]

The world without God or the world of Prometheus who fights God is the foundation on which the materialist civilization in the West is based. It is as

Garaudy stated, "The world without human being."[10] A good part of the West's literary production, the 1968 youth protests in Paris, the uprisings of black Americans, and the marginalized classes in the suburbs of Paris and London— all of these are merely symptoms of Western humanity's rebellion against this civilization, and it is expected that this crisis will deepen and grow more serious. Thus there remains no foundation upon which to base the covenants of rights and liberties in the West, unless it is a bundle of connections and historical, social, and cultural convergences and interests, perhaps on the basis of class, race, or nation. No matter how these covenants expand and their humanity develops, they will not be able to grow out of their Western orbit, wherein there is no god but matter, no authority but brute force, and wherein the Machiavellian ruler is allowed to use everything, including God and religion, and do all that he can to protect, extend, and consolidate his own power.

Further, the concept of a Judeo-Christian civilization—which is the other face of Western civilization in its conception of humanity, its values, and its freedom— cannot extricate itself from this authoritarian and exploitive framework. It is the civilization of the Israelite who fashions a golden calf in order to worship it, and the civilization of the Emperor Constantine, who embraced Christianity, not to submit to it, but rather to make use of its pagan Greek perspective formulated by a Jew, Paul the Apostle. The church was built on this foundation as an ally to the empire since Constantine, even though later church leaders made an effort to free themselves from the Constantinian heritage, with its legacy of inquisitions and colonialism, and this for the purpose of returning to the spirit of Christ (peace be upon him), the champion of the weak and vulnerable.[11]

Here we have been talking about the general orientation that in no way negates the presence of liberation forces in the West, which fight against the hegemony of the political, military, economic, and media institutions for the sake of a different model of international relations, one based on shared human values. With all that said, the idea of human rights remains an important development in human civilization, the vestige of a religious and humanitarian legacy. Yet within the Western political and economic structures and in the arena of international relations, it barely shines through.

2

THE ISLAMIC PERSPECTIVE ON
FREEDOM AND HUMAN RIGHTS

Since the declarations of human rights and civic freedoms within the framework of materialist philosophy and capitalism were only guaranteed for the bourgeoisie against the feudal lords and the papacy, in the end their illusory nature has become obvious along with their limited effectiveness in checking the greed of the powerful and their continued usurping of the oppressed classes of their own people let alone others, as well as the growing destruction of the world's material, spiritual and social foundations. Then came the various socialist currents aiming to expose their empty rhetoric and emphasize social rights for humanity—while in fact imposing another set of tyrants.[1]

The Islamic conception of freedom does not begin with a human nature from which rights emanate, as it does the Western conception. That is plainly wrong. Rather, the reality that sustains everything in the world is this: God is the Creator of the universe and its King; He is more knowledgeable than His creatures; He is the supreme Legislator, the One who commands, and the only One worthy of our worship, submission, obedience, stewardship, and of our reward and punishment. Among all beings God has entrusted only humans as His deputy on Earth [istikhlāf] by virtue of our intellect and will, with freedom and responsibility, and with the divine method to order their life. Verses in the Qur'an that teach how God has empowered humankind to subject creation to themselves, how He has honored humanity and bestowed on it a great trust, touch on all the above truths.[2] They also certify that all human beings are equal by virtue of their creation, in dignity, and before the law. Furthermore, they urge people to refuse tyranny and to resist it with all means available to them, even to the point of giving their lives as martyrs.

That is the message that Islam's jurists summarized by saying that Islam is a comprehensive revolution of liberation against all the ways humans have subjugated their brethren, either literally or figuratively.[3] One should not understand from the common usage of "freedom" that it is simply about permission to act as one wishes. The logic of truth cannot entertain that the emancipatory message of Islam—brought to humankind from creation by thousands of prophets and messengers, in addition to their successors—would be summarized as God allowing you to do what you desire. God honored you above all other creatures with the gifts of intellect and will, which enable you to do what you wish and bear the responsibility for your actions. But God does not want you to do what you wish nor is He pleased that you do so! No, Islam's conception is quite the opposite. God created you and He forbids you to follow your every ignorant whim, and He commands you to follow—as a conscious decision of your own volition and seeking His obedience and love—the path that pleases Him for your life, the only one in which you will find happiness and fulfillment in this life and the next. But if you turn your back on it, you will find only eternal calamity.

Nevertheless, you are free to respond to the call of reason and the sound nature [*fitra*] you received at creation, so that you believe in your Lord and obey Him, ordering your personal and public life according to His law. You will thereby gain the pleasure and love of your Creator and experience happiness in this life and the next. Or you may turn away from the voice of reason and conscience and follow your baser desires and the temptations of Satan, which will then expose you to your Lord's wrath and unhappiness in this life and the next. As we read in the Qur'an: "Say, 'Now the truth has come from your Lord: let those who wish to believe in it do so, and let those who wish to reject it do so."[4] And also, "Whoever follows my guidance, when it comes to you [people], will not go astray nor fall into misery, but whoever turns away from it will have a life of great hardship. We shall bring him blind to the Assembly on the Day of Resurrection."[5]

Freedom, according to the Islamic worldview, is a trust, a responsibility, an awareness of the truth, and an adherence to it, sincerity in seeking it, and a sacrifice of everything, including oneself, for its sake. Yes, according to its literal meaning, freedom is permission and choice, or simply an instinct, for God equipped us through His creation with the power to do both good and evil and to choose between the two, which was in fact a responsibility. According to the specialists in legal theory, in its ethical and legal meaning freedom means "conformity." Freedom is to exercise our responsibility in a positive way, fulfilling our duty in in a spirit of obedience by following what is commanded and avoiding what is forbidden; and in so doing, we are worthy of the status of God's righteous vicegerents and friends on Earth. All scholars of Islam agree on this meaning of freedom.

Perhaps the best of those modern Islamic[6] thinkers to have brought to light the concept of freedom in Islam have been the following great scholars: the Tunisian Shaykh Muhammad al-Tahir bin 'Ashur, the Moroccan scholar 'Allal al-Fasi, the Sudanese thinker Hasan al-Turabi, the philosopher Muhammad Iqbal, the Algerian thinker Malik bin Nabi, and professor Muhammad Fathi 'Uthman. Professor al-Fasi wrote that freedom is "a legal act, and not a natural right, for humanity could never have attained their freedom unless Divine revelation had taken place . . . Humanity was not created free, but in order to become free," according to the extent of their submission to God's law. Freedom is hard work and struggle in the path of serving God, and not animal-like impulsiveness. Al-Fasi commented on this verse, "Those who disbelieve among the People of the Book and the idolaters were not about to change their ways until they were sent clear evidence."[7] He was amazed that the scholars of Islam did not understand this verse of "clear evidence" to have this subtle meaning—that is, that there is no path to release and liberation except by becoming God's servant. It is the path of religious obligations, which renders freedom a personal achievement, the fruit of which manifests itself in a person's actions springing from a heartfelt submission to one's responsibilities before God. The person worthy of the epithet "free" is the believer in God, and the obligation to follow God's commands is the foundation of freedom and its evidence.[8]

Turabi wrote:

> Freedom is the power of the human person which distinguishes him from any other creature to kneel before God in humble submission and obedience, since there is nothing in his constitution that forces him to believe and there is no authorization for him to force anyone else to believe. Freedom is not an end but a means to worship God. To become God's servant, or slave, does not instill in us a sense of alienation, because the believer serves God out of a motive of love, a desire to honor Him, and an awareness of grace and gratitude. This then makes freedom both the means and the result of worshiping and serving God. Although freedom from a legal perspective is permission, from a religious perspective it is the path of service to God, it is humanity's obligation to free themselves unto God, sincerely choosing one's stances and opinions. This freedom from an Islamic perspective is absolute, in that it is a path that points to infinity . . . And the more a person grows in his sincerity in worshipping God, the more he becomes free from the grip of all other creatures . . . and he realizes a greater measure of human perfection.[9]

Further, Shaykh Abbas Madani has said,[10] "Because it condemns oppression and compulsion, Islam has decreed freedom of choice. Freedom in Islam begins with the necessity of sincere worship of God only, who requires us to refuse submission to anyone else but Him, starting with our own selves when we are tempted to disobey God. Freedom, therefore, begins with the power of self-control over our base desires and commitment to follow God's law, so that a person desires only that which agrees with what is written in that law and no longer needs any external motivation."[11]

As we progress in our understanding of human freedoms or duties in Islamic law, we find that today's Islamic thinkers mostly agree in affirming the judicious nature of the theory laid out by the great scholar al-Shatibi in his treatise on jurisprudence, *al-Muwafaqat* [*The Reconciliations*].[12] The summary to keep in mind is that the goal of Shari'a is to achieve humanity's greatest interests.[13] These he classified into three categories: necessary, need-based, and life-improving. In the first category, he placed the following five objectives of Shari'a: protection of religion, life, mind/intellect, progeny/family, and wealth, based on the consideration that religion only exists for:

- the protection of human life, along with the means to achieve that,
- the protection of the mind and all that entails in terms of education, freedom of thought, and expression,
- the protection of progeny and the necessary right to establish a family, and
- the protection of wealth and what flows from it in terms of economic and social rights.

All of this is "necessary" alongside the human rights required to fulfill the need-based and life-improving objectives, and without forgetting what all of this entails in terms of establishing a political framework for the Muslim community based on the principle that those means without which a duty cannot be fulfilled are themselves a duty, and duties and obligations for Muslims are known in constitutional law as "political freedoms."

To this list several Islamic scholars have added other objectives, like human dignity, freedom, and social justice.[14] For freedom in Islam is not just a person's right but also a duty and God's great gift to him. More, it is one of the essential components of God's honoring him with the Trust which the heavens and the earth refused to assume: "We offered the Trust to the heavens, the earth, and the mountains, but they refused to undertake it and were afraid of it; mankind undertook it."[15] Indeed, this represents a boundless and dynamic energy. And because human rights, freedom, and duties are derived from God's right for humankind to obey Him by virtue of having created them as His vicegerents, with all the obligations this entails, and because they chose to believe in this reality, they will not submit to anyone else but Him, consciously and freely; and they are not free to relinquish that freedom, or waste God's gifts to them, or squander their possessions, because their freedom is God's possession, just as their lives are.

CREED IS THE FOUNDATION FOR HUMAN RIGHTS IN ISLAM

Democracy and human rights in the Western conception are based on the individual person, at least on the surface. Their emergence was associated with the struggle against the Church and the absolute rule of kings in order to restrict their authority or completely take them away and restore them to the people as the sole source of power. This marked the Western state with an individualistic stamp and with a nationalist, secular, and legalistic spirit. The situation in Islamic countries, however, is different, as they did not experience this complete separation between political power and the religious community. Even in periods of oppression, the Shari'a continued to constrain the political ruler in two important areas: the authority to legislate and impose taxes. The ruler could not pass any laws that contravened religious edicts, which meant, for instance, that he had no power to go beyond the rules of *zakat*, something that reduced any animosity between the ruler and the umma, much more so than was ever the case under European absolutist rule—even in its worst instances.[16]

Thus individuals and society did not lose hope in reform or even revolution.[17] Nor did those aspirations transgress the limits of Shari'a, having as its highest model the era of prophethood and the rule of the Rightly Guided Caliphs, which offer the best example of what can be applied at any other time. Indeed, the values and models of reform and revolution were based on Islam and its historical experience worthy of emulation and application. In fact, reformers and thinkers—before the time of colonial hegemony and the influence of the cultural assault on Muslims' lives—in their reforming efforts, only needed to look beyond the dust of experience and application and return to the sources. They had no need to issue covenants of human and citizen rights, as long as their certainty was strong and their conviction rooted in the belief that the ideal image of humanity, both individual and collective, is to be found in the precious Book and in the way Islam was applied during its first era.

However, since the second half of the nineteenth century and since the expansion of the military and ideological assault on the Islamic world impacting its territories, resources, and convictions, Muslims began to look at Westerners with diffidence and caution. They inquired into their sources of power and greatness, trying to draw from them what might bring new life and strength to the emaciated Islamic body. Part of that mission in Egypt, Tunisia, Turkey, and elsewhere was to introduce elements of the Western constitutional, administrative, and judicial systems, believing that to defeat one's enemy requires mimicking his ways,[18] and that one of the most important reasons for the Muslims' backwardness was their lack of attention to human rights.[19]

The nationalist movements that led the fight against the Westerners' assault did so against the backdrop of the umma's fragmentation, engineered by these foreign powers, and the elaboration of a new concept of nation tied to territory and language. Though these movements did gain strength by stirring up religious feelings and by spreading the fear that Islam was under threat, they had no choice but to rely on Western law codes in order to write new statutes and constitutions that defined the nature of political power, institutions, and under their umbrella, the rights of individuals.[20] These, however, had little or no impact, in terms of their actual application, on the task of curbing despotism.

The only motive for the rulers to embark on those constitutional reforms was to please foreign powers, since the people themselves had no say in this. The latter were more inclined to doubt the wisdom of reforms that were dictated by military flotillas and written in an Arabic that had no connection to their history. It was not difficult, therefore, for the so-called "modernist" autocratic ruler who had freed himself from the Shari'a's authority to cancel those aesthetic reforms as soon as foreign pressures dissipated, or even to eviscerate them of any liberational content that might put a limit on his absolute power, which he thoroughly enjoyed.

Further, the stance of emulating formal aspects of the Western model and culture adopted by the elites who led the independence movements can be easily understood. This is not surprising, since most of those elites were educated in Western schools and developed an admiration for the victor's culture. On the other hand, the movement of resistance to the West had never rested on a foundation of true Islamic renewal, which draws from Islamic values of liberation and offers contemporary modes of applying Islamic principles within the context of new realities, since the prevailing impulse of Muslim thinkers was only to defend Islam from the malicious assault to which it was exposed. So the leading elites—I mean those who were sincere, not those who collaborated with the colonial powers—had no choice but to imitate the Western lifestyle and to merely cloak the despotic model they had inherited.

Nevertheless, it must be said that the process of introducing legal reforms and constitutions in the past century in a number of Muslim societies, as in

Egypt, Tunisia, and the capital of the Ottoman Empire, represented the initial and perilous intrusions of Western nations into Muslim societies. The reformers' goal was to limit the ruler's power, but, ironically, it never worked. Actually, what occurred was an economic and cultural infiltration which later developed into direct occupation by Western forces. Still, that penetration continued, widened, and deepened, and the post-independence eras were marked by an autocracy that could not be limited by formal constitutions, because of the legacy of internal decay, immense outside pressures, and the lack of consensus among the elites about how to govern. That was the result of the fissures and polarization caused by the Western cultural invasion—deep rifts between traditionalists and modernists, between those on the right and those on the left. This paralyzed the energy of the masses by confusing them and by leading them away from politics to focus exclusively on their individual, private concerns.

MODERN ISLAMIC THOUGHT

With the movement led by Jamal al-Din al-Afghani, Muhammad 'Abduh, Khayr al-Din al-Khatib al-Tunisi, al-Tha'labi, Rashid Rida, Muhibb al-Din al-Khatib, Shakib al-Din Arsalan, and others like them and after them, Islamic thought, to some extent, succeeded in exposing the Western mode of civilization, distinguishing between which aspects of it were beneficial and which were not, and uncovering aspects of its hypocrisy and despotism. On the other hand, it dispelled allegations against Islam and its civilization by highlighting the Islamic alternative in organizing life for the individual and society. These reformers saw no problem in codifying the Shari'a, considering it an issue of technical jurisprudence, and in accepting democratic instruments of governance in order to institute mutual consultation.[21]

Indeed, they believed that the Islamic state is a civil state in every way, with no connection to a rule of the clergy or a theocratic order. In this legal undertaking, Islamic thinkers elaborated Islamic formulations of human rights and individual and public liberties, highlighting the areas of agreement and disagreement between them and the Western or Universal Declaration of Human Rights. They highlighted that the areas of convergence were wider than areas of divergence, despite the difference in the foundations upon which rights and duties are derived in Islam and the Western system.[22] Whereas Muslim thinkers affirm that faith in God is the foundation and source of rights and duties[23]—because the rights of human beings, their freedoms and duties are corollaries of their understanding of the universe, their place in it, and the goal of their existence—Westerners affirm that these rights and duties are grounded in nature.

It is no wonder that one finds scattered throughout the UDHR the marks of secularism or a human religion based on the primacy and self-sufficiency of humankind in the universe and on people decreeing themselves as the source of every right and legislation, and of deviation of behaviors of individuals, communities, and nations from moral values and noble principles, which seek to curb the tendency toward uncontrolled impulses and arrogance and feelings of supremacy. This is what explains the ambiguity of the UDHR, despite the diverse intellectual and religious backgrounds of those who contributed to its drafting, some of whom were religious people, Muslim and non-Muslim, while others were secular.

This is in contrast to the Islamic understanding, which confirms the link between every ethical value and the source of everything in existence, of life itself, and of its goal and modus operandi. Those values can only be grounded in that source, that is, God—may He be blessed and exalted—who alone is Creator and Owner of all His creatures, the One who defines their way of life (Shari'a). It is based on the belief that human beings are His vicegerents or trustees [his "caliphs"],[24] whom the Creator honored by granting them a mind, a will, and freedom. That is why He sent them messengers, allowing them to discover the way of truth and follow the path of perfection by means of their commitment to the Shari'a or law of God, which He defined in its final form, revealed as it was through the agency of the Arab Prophet Muhammad. This Shari'a is the general framework meant to guide human life individually and collectively, but also carving out for humanity within that framework wide-open spaces for them to exercise their reason and judgment (as expressed by the martyr Muhammad Baqir al-Sadr in his book, *Our Philosophy*). They are thus able to fulfill their vicegerency of God by managing everything within their scope, and thereby joining together in harmony, freedom and commitment, unity and plurality. It also brings together faith in God, with whom humans must be in constant connection, on one hand, and on the other hand, the recognition of the human being's personality, free will, and responsibility for his actions.

Therefore, what Islam rejects is both the idea of humanity's independence and its ability to do without God, which is the essence of Western modernity, and the idea of the ancient Eastern civilizations that humanity extinguishes and annihilates itself in the cosmic truth.[25] The two conceptions meet despite their obvious contradictions in the pseudo-pantheistic philosophy that breaks down the barriers between God, human beings, and nature, and which teaches that ethical values are relative, with everything collapsing into everything.

Thus no barrier is left, and no objective definition of what is right and wrong, of what is a worshiper and what is worshiped. It is absolute moral licentiousness, which in the Islamic civilization found its expression in the writings of the Sufi extremists, like al-Hallaj ("there is nothing in my outer garment but God . . . may I be glorified, may I be glorified!") or Ibn 'Arabi ("My heart is capable of accepting every form"), and in literature with the licentiousness of Abu Nuwas. In Western thought one can see this in partial secularism, the most dangerous version of which is extreme, or what Abdelwahhab el-Mestiri (2002) terms "comprehensive" secularism.[26]

By contrast, from the Islamic perspective, humankind stands out as a unique and honored being who bears the responsibility of directing his own affairs and of marking out his own destiny according to the divine plan for his life, according to the Qur'an, "[Have we not] shown him the two highways?"[27] The human person is also accountable as God's servant, bearer of the Trust. To the extent that his performance is best in fulfilling his obligations—that is, his duties as defined by the Shari'a—and to the extent that his devotion is greatest in serving God, to that extent he will experience the greatest freedom within his own person and with regard to nature and the creatures around him.

For all these reasons, these rights become holy duties, which the servant of God, as vicegerent, cannot neglect or treat lightly. He does not own these rights, but they belong to God—may He be praised—the One Possessor of them, with human beings entrusted with them and thereby required to act within that calling according to the Owner's will. To protect one's life, to provide the necessities required for it to continue, and desisting from ending that life, or demeaning it or impoverishing it, are rather duties. Humans are rewarded for fulfilling them and punished for failing to do so. But these rights are duties enjoined by the Shari'a, just as it means to say no to enslavement; to resist tyrants; and to struggle for the sake of freedom, justice, economic development, and the happiness of humanity.

This is how rights from the Islamic perspective acquire a sanctity and constancy that forbids anyone to tamper with them through relativization, whether it be a political party, or a parliament, or a ruler seeking to establish them or annul them or amend them, and all the more since God is their source. Hence, they represent binding authority that provides guidance to individuals and societies, which in turn, through the renewed effort of legal scholars and according to the geographical context and historical situation, is translated into ways of life, modes of thinking in literature and the arts, and into statutes and specific legal codes.

Then, from another standpoint, defending those rights and deflecting attacks against them is a Shari'a obligation that uses all forms of resistance possible, even to the point of declaring war [*jihad*] and seeking martyrdom, in order to defend them. This level of commitment makes faith in God the best guarantee for the enacting of human rights and the protection of freedoms, because of the elevation of their source above any bias, their universal character, their permanence, their resistance to manipulation and finally the sanctity of defending them.

Certainly, if human experience has confirmed that "a human being cannot live without adopting some deity for himself,"[28] then human rights should be grounded in humanity's Creator:

- This gives them a sanctity that pulls them out of the orbit of a regime's domination or that of a political party that manipulates them at will.[29]
- It renders them a trust "hanging around the neck" of every believer, holding them accountable for their protection, for their establishment in human society, and for resisting the tyrants' violation of them, because that is a religious duty that will be rewarded if fulfilled and punished if neglected.
- It gives them the true dimensions of humanity and thus wards off any discrimination based on race, nationality, and class, since He is "God of the Worlds,"[30] and not of only one nation or umma.
- It reinforces the authority of the law that protects those rights through the authority of the religious conscience represented by the believer's conviction that God is always watching him and holding him accountable.
- It gives them a comprehensive and positive dimension that prevents them from being merely theoretical or partial because God is the Creator of humanity and He alone knows the true needs of His creatures.
- Tying rights to the Divine Legislator is not to enforce the despotism of a theocratic polity, for there is no clergy in Islam to sanction or forbid anything. Rather the One who loosens or binds is God, who shows no partiality and treats all people fairly, for He has no need of anything or anyone in the universe, and thus finds no benefit when He is obeyed and no harm when He is disobeyed. This grants rights an absolute and universal character and enlists every believer to defend them when they are violated, whether the violation is directed toward him personally or toward someone else, whether believer or not. It is a duty to both remove injustice and to achieve righteousness. For Islam is an intellectual, spiritual, and

social revolution that aims at freeing human societies from tyranny. Belief in God's Oneness, listening to the voice of Truth, and resisting any attempt to subjugate bodies and spirits is also to approve of any revolution that puts an end to domination over people's minds and persons, even in the name of religion. Islam can only be at the forefront of those fighting theocratic rule, no matter what its sources might be. Despotism is despotism, and the worst kind clothes itself in religious garb. We all know that in Islam there is no authority that can claim the right to interpret the sacred texts and to speak in the name of Heaven, for God calls his people to "conduct their affairs by mutual consultation."[31]

THE GENERAL FRAMEWORK FOR
HUMAN RIGHTS IN ISLAM

Humankind in Islam is empowered by God to be His deputy on earth, and within the covenant of that trusteeship—the Islamic Shari'a—comes a set of rights and duties. There is harmony and unity between individual rights and the common good or public interest as every individual right incorporates within it a "right of God," that is, a collective right—which assumes priority every time there is a clash. The statutes of Islam came to safeguard the people's welfare in this life and the next. Those benefits fall under different categories from the essential ones to those that embellish and perfect human life. It is natural that these benefits be considered the general framework within which the behavior of individuals is regulated and freedoms are exercised, both the private and public ones. Research into the objectives of the Shari'a, which was successfully mapped out by the great North African scholar Abu Ishaq al-Shatibi in his masterpiece, *The Reconciliations*, has been widely accepted, as I mentioned above, among contemporary Islamic thinkers as the basis and framework for the theory of human rights and freedoms, both private and public, from an Islamic perspective.[32]

It is known that al-Shatibi, as he examined the general and specific rulings of the Shari'a, developed a theory of public interest [*maslaha 'amma*] which he found to be organized on three levels. He called the first level "the necessary benefits," the absence of which opens the door to corruption and suffering in people's lives. They are five in number: the protection of religion, life, intellect, wealth, and lineage.[33] For these benefits the Shari'a lays out statutes that either establish them or protect them, and it produces other rulings to prevent them from being violated. The second level of benefits he calls "the benefits of need," meaning those that remove difficulty from people's lives, thus mitigating hardship and misery. The third level comprises "the benefits of life embellishment." These are a collection of good customs and noble ethical guidelines such as giving attention to beauty and kind service. Here, the ordering of the levels is important, as some are ranked higher than others, which necessitates sacrificing the lower benefits in order to preserve the higher ones in the case of a clash. Rules of modesty, for instance, coming from the lowest level of benefits, will have to be waived in case of a threat against religion or life. A person has to uncover for a medical examination or for surgery to be performed. In similar fashion, if one's life or personal integrity are under threat, it may be necessary to make an exception to the normal rules of modesty. The protection of wealth or one's personal possessions is also one of the Shari'a's objectives, though the protection of human lives takes precedence over it, and in case of necessity saving lives means sacrificing one's right to possessions.

That is how one should understand the theory of the Shari'a's purposes and see how it can help a Muslim properly balance his actions and prioritize values like steps on a ladder. He is then able to comprehend Islam's statutes, great and small. This will also give him guidance in managing his freedom and bringing together rights and duties. Contemporary Islamic thinkers and jurists have further developed this theory and have built upon it a jurisprudence of priorities, of checks and balances, and of necessities.

No one can violate these principles as long as his actions fall within the scope of his rights and do not trespass the common good. The theory of freedom in Islam stipulates individual freedom in all things, as long as it does not clash with the right or benefit of the wider community. If it clashes, then it must be adjusted to and limited by the common good.

In this context, I will present a general overview of the individual and general freedoms in Islam in comparison with their counterparts in the well-known covenant the Universal Declaration of Human Rights.

FREEDOM OF CONVICTION AND ITS ROOTS

The aim here is for the individual to freely choose his own belief system without any external pressure. The great legal scholar Shaykh al-Tahir bin 'Ashur argued that freedom of conviction is one of the Shari'a's fundamental principles and forbids any form of compulsion. At the same time, it spares no effort to highlight the necessity of presenting the truth, of establishing the creed with certainty, and holding individuals and the community responsible to maintain it and defend it.

Moreover, it forbids subjecting those who have embraced it to persecution, even by resorting to force, and it urges them to make every effort to subvert the evil ploys of their opponents. One of the greatest objectives of jihad has always been to protect the freedom of conscience and religious pluralism and to forbid coercion. As God says in the Qur'an, "those who have been driven unjustly from their homes only for saying, 'Our Lord is God.' If God did not repel some people by means of others, many monasteries, churches, synagogues, and mosques, where God's name is invoked, would have been destroyed."[34]

Many Qur'anic commentaries and books of jurisprudence agree in considering the verse "There is no compulsion in religion"[35] one of the cardinal rules of Islam and one of the great pillars of its tolerance; for this reason, no one is allowed to force anyone to enter this faith, nor is anyone permitted to compel believers to leave it.[36] In order to guarantee the noncompulsion rule, Islam enjoins Muslims to stand up with vigor against those who would try to compel them to leave their religion behind, just as it orders Muslims who call non-Muslims to their faith to do so with wisdom and gentle admonition, so as to show right from wrong.[37]

For God did not build the matter of faith upon compulsion and coercion; rather, He built it upon empowerment and choice. When religion is imposed on people, it becomes invalid, as it makes redundant the choice given to humans, as God says, "let those who wish to believe in it do so, and let those who wish to reject it do so."[38] Al-Razi was also of this opinion.[39] Since a person's conviction is located in the heart, coercion is impossible from the start. Furthermore, it goes against the Islamic doctrine of each person's moral responsibility, which is the charge to undertake the divine Trust.[40] It would contradict a large number of religious texts that emphasize human responsibility, liberty, and free choice. Without these, the uniqueness of humankind and their responsibility would be void and there would be no justification for reward and punishment in the absence of freedom to choose.

There clearly has been controversy on the subject of this great verse being abrogated, as well as other verses that speak of humanity's freedom—and there are more than 150 such verses.[41] This alleged abrogation is a miserable way to rob people of the essence of their identity and their existence, which is freedom. It is also a way to empty the Islamic message of all liberational content, even if these scholars did so as a failed tactic to defend the absolute freedom of God's will. Muslim scholars today have clearly proven the invalidity of the abrogation of all these texts and of fundamental principles of Islam allegedly by the verses on jihad. Some Islamic thinkers, especially contemporary ones, emphasize the primacy of the basic rule that freedom is the origin and foundation of religious conviction, even to the point of arguing that the "no compulsion" verse (Q. 2:256), contrary to the proponents of abrogation who see it as canceled out by the verses of jihad, actually abrogates the verses calling for warfare, because of the command not to force anyone into the fold of Islam.[42]

I believe that the current consensus within Islamic scholarship rejects the exaggeration and extremism in both positions, emphasizing the authenticity of the twin concepts of freedom and jihad and how they are woven into the fabric of the Islamic worldview, which sees freedom as an objective, and jihad as the means to protect it. The freedom of the weak, for the most part, cannot be safeguarded. This is what the author of the Manar journal (or *The Lighthouse Commentary*) pointed out in his commentary on the following verse, "Fight them until there is no more persecution," that is, until faith rests in the heart of the believer, safe from the onslaught of the obstinate opponent.[43] Religion is not secure unless persecution is driven away such that no foe dares to attack its members. This is confirmed by the injustice and persecution that have been and continue to be visited upon Muslims by their opponents. When their power weakens and state fortunes dissipate, these opponents fight them so as to compel them to leave their faith and forbid them from spreading it to others.[44] The contemporary Shi'i scholar Muhammad Husayn Tabataba'i considered the verse "There is no compulsion in religion" to be the most important verse showing that Islam did not spread by the sword and the shedding of blood, nor by compulsion or by force, contrary to what several Muslim and non-Muslim writers have alleged, namely that Islam is the religion of the sword.[45]

Sayyid Qutb's commentary on this verse ("There is no compulsion in religion") was clear and trenchant:

> It makes no sense and there is no rational or moral logic whatsoever that the call of Islam which fought for establishing freedom of conscience, and whose followers themselves were facing terror as a persecuted minority in Mecca by the forces of perdition and *shirk*[46] (who castigated the Muslims for abandoning the religion of their fathers and forefathers, and who spared no effort in persecuting them and violating their right to choose) that such a people would rise up the next day after being given power on the earth to then set themselves up as executioners and murderers so as to impose on people of other religions tyranny and disgrace in order to force them to change their convictions!
>
> How can one imagine this happening? The testimony of history, building on the proofs of revelation and human reason, converges and points to the most important goal of the Islamic struggle as being to break the power of tyrants and end their oppression and violence, while leaving people free to fol-

low their own religious convictions, as long as they make peace with us, and do not force us to leave our religion or conspire with our enemies. In light of that, it is no wonder that Islamic lands were lands of religious freedom, under whose shade the children of many persecuted religious communities took refuge. They had no place to settle, nor could their identity flourish, unless it was under the protective shade of Islam, as was often the case for many Christian and Jewish sects who had taken refuge in the land of Islam. And many of those, still today, are only to be found in Muslim lands, as they were eliminated by the largest Christian denominations in their own lands.[47]

For that reason, it is not surprising that Muslim thinkers considered freedom of thought to be "the first among public freedoms, because it is its cardinal rule and foundation."[48] It is "the first of all human rights."[49]

What, then, are the legal parameters for the freedom of thought in Islamic society?

Equality Is the Rule of Cooperation in Islamic Society

There is no need, according to the perspective presented above, to resort to the use of abrogation in the Qur'an for the verses on freedom that forbid compulsion or for the verses that call for military action. That is because our starting point was the verses that forbid compulsion, since they are directed to everyone, except to those who raise their weapons against Muslims with hostile and unjust intentions and forbid them to call to their faith. In that case, there are grounds—religious persecution—for applying the verses calling for fighting to safeguard the faith; fight until the enemy desists.[50]

That is the context of the verses seemingly calling to fight the pagans or simply "people" in general, but in fact referring to specific groups like the Arab pagans at the time, as is the opinion of some interpreters, or those who attack Muslims, whoever they might be. So there is no ground for forcing religion on people at any time. This is also illustrated for us through the Messenger of God's biography. From various sources we learn that the Prophet established peaceful relations with other religious communities, such as Jews, Christians, and pagan groups among the inhabitants of Medina. All these formed together with the believers a single political entity, within which all enjoyed the rights of citizenship. This imposed duties on them, like defending the city of Medina and refraining from allying themselves with the enemy, as well as rights such as religious freedom and protection by the state.

Alliances and treaties were established between the state of Medina and groups of Arab pagans. These were respected for treachery is not in the nature of Islam.

Similarly, jurists agreed on the validity of granting non-Muslim communities a protected status—that is, the right to citizenship in the Islamic state—but they disagreed as to whom this applied to.[51] Some of them limited these rights to Jews and Christians; others added the Sabaeans and Zoroastrians; others widened the circle to include all who asked for it, even idol worshipers, as is the opinion of the Maliki school of law, as long as they abide by their obligations, just like other citizens.[52] This is because equality is the basic guiding principle in Islamic society for Muslims and non-Muslims alike. Imam 'Ali, the fourth Rightly Guided Caliph, stated in relation to the rights of non-Muslim citizens under his rule, "They were given the *dhimma* (that is, a covenant of protection) so that they have the same rights and duties that we have." The only exceptions are narrow and are mandated by protection of public order, a society's identity, or the general values that guide it. In any case, there is no need to use the expression "people of *dhimma*" in Islamic political thought, since all citizens have been integrated and modern states have been built upon the principle of citizenship—that is, the equality of rights and duties.[53]

Because Islam valued freedom of conscience from the beginning and demonstrated an acceptance of religious pluralism as a result, all the monotheistic faiths and even pagan communities lived side by side in harmony and peace in all Islamic societies throughout Islam's history. This is why Islam's history is mostly free of the ethnic cleansing and genocide that stained the civilization of other nations, both medieval and modern. It is no wonder, therefore, that Islamic lands are home to some of the most ancient synagogues and churches and even pagan temples, which were protected by the statutes of Islam, the religion of tolerance. There was also coexistence between various schools of Islamic law and theology, aside from a few exceptional events like the disagreement over the creation of the Qur'an, since as a rule, theological convictions and the interpretations of sacred texts were the prerogative of society, and the state had no right to interfere with it. When Muslims fought each other, therefore, it was not over religion but political power.[54]

Freedom to Practice One's Religious Rituals

Islam provides for every religious community the right to establish places of worship and follow their own rituals, while respecting public opinion and the general feelings of the majority. This was an application of the principle of religious freedom and the ban on compulsion in religious matters. The caliphs issued stern guidelines to their governors and military leaders to leave worshipers to their worship, and the people of all religious traditions, including pagans, lived together in peace with the Muslims under Islamic rule. However, when the balance of power shifted in favor of non-Muslims, in medieval or modern times, Muslims and their mosques were either persecuted or eradicated in most cases, and we saw what happened recently to the European Muslims of Bosnia and Kosovo and to the Muslims of Chechnya who witnessed wars of ethnic and religious cleansing. We now see the spread of Islamophobia, because these religions have not recognized Islam nor religious pluralism. This is contrary to the religion of Islam, which has established the principle of religious freedom and the plurality of convictions, along with its constant call for the Oneness of God and the refusal to allow any partners alongside Him, and yet without resorting to compulsion.

Freedom of Expression: Defending One's Faith, Calling Others to It, or Critiquing Others' Faith

The prophets (peace be upon them) offered beautiful examples of high-minded dialogue with their adversaries in order to win them over to Islam, to refute opposing arguments, and establish conviction on a firm basis of proof. In the conflicts we face today we need to take inspiration from the debates that Abraham (peace be upon him) had with the oppressor of his land, as well as with his own father. The same applies to the other prophets, down to the Seal of the Prophets, Muhammad, who answered the arguments arrayed against them with a kind and peaceful tone, far from the insults and quarrels that stir up today's political and intellectual debates. This was the spirit that guided the intellectual life that prevailed during the time of the Companions and Followers,[55] and in the centuries of Islam's flourishing when debates took places between various Muslim sects or between Muslims and the followers of other religions, including atheists, within the palaces and mosques. There was no other authority over them but that of convincing arguments and reasonable proofs. This indeed was a clear expression of Islam's tolerance and of the high place accorded to intellect, science, and freedom.

The great Islamic scholar (and martyr) Ismail al-Faruqi (d. 1986), professor of comparative religion at Temple University in the United States, wrote in an important work on the rights of non-Muslims in an Islamic state, arguing that *dhimmis*, or non-Muslim citizens in an Islamic state, had the right to propagate their personal values in the public sphere, on the condition of not violating the general sensibility of Muslims. For him there is no debate about their right to express their opinion in the context of the law to which all submit, without violating the feelings of the majority, which fundamentally respects the right of the minority to express itself. And if it is the Muslim's right—even his duty—to call his non-Muslim compatriot to Islam, it is also the latter's right to do the same on behalf of his faith. If Muslims fear for the faith of their fellow Muslims, there is no way to remedy this, except for Muslims to deepen their own faith or to submit their doubts and questions to their scholars. For with the modern development of the means of communication, it will no longer be possible to hide or to isolate oneself completely. Thus antithetical viewpoints will reach Muslims by any means, and the only means of protection against any discussion is to offer another discussion, this one better, more intelligent, and more cogent.[56]

Abu'l-A'la al-Mawdudi, a pioneer among jurists of contemporary Islamic constitutional law, expressed very clearly the freedom non-Muslims should enjoy in an Islamic state:

> In an Islamic state non-Muslims will have exactly the same freedoms as their Muslim compatriots: freedom of speech, writing, opinion, thought, and of assembly. Conversely, they will have the same restrictions and duties that Muslims have as well. They will also have the right to criticize the government and its employees, including the president himself, within the boundaries defined by the law. They will also have the right to criticize the Islamic faith, just as Muslims have the right to criticize their schools and sects. Muslims should stay within the bounds defined by the law in their criticism, just as non-Muslims should do, and they will have the right to praise their own sects; and if they leave their faith—Muslims, that is—the responsibility for their apostasy, will fall on their shoulders. Non-Muslims should not be held responsible for it. Non-Muslims in the Islamic state shall not be compelled to believe or do anything that goes against their conscience. They will be allowed to behave according to their conscience, as long as it does not violate the laws of the state.[57]

The meaning of all of this is the recognition of cultural pluralism within the Islamic state and the interaction with freedom. The goal is that all participate through their differences in building an Islamic civilization, far from the ideology of hegemony and assimilation as exemplified by Western states.[58]

The Issue of Apostasy

Apostasy is to leave the faith of Islam after having freely and consciously embraced it by denying that which is fixed in Islam, its tenets, rules, and rituals, such as disparaging the status of divinity or prophethood, or permitting that which it has forbidden, rejecting its obligations, and so on.

Many verses in the Qur'an denounce this crime and warn those who commit it of the most severe penalty but without stipulating any punishment in this life. The Sunna, however, speaks of the death penalty, "Whoever changes his religion, kill him!" All the Companions (May God be pleased with them) agreed with the stance of fighting apostates. Nor did the great jurists of Islam disagree with them in considering apostasy a crime. A majority of them believed in the death penalty for apostates, but others differed.

The debate centers on two issues. Is apostasy a political crime in that it represents rebelling against the authority of the state? In that case, the crime is left to the ruler to adjudicate, choosing between an array of discretionary punishments.[59] That is, it is amongst the crimes for which there is no specific, textually-determined punishment. This is the position of many Modernists. If, on the other hand, the crime is doctrinal and religious, it comes under the umbrella of the *hudud* offenses, which fall under "God's rights," in which case the ruler has no jurisdiction in setting a penalty for it.[60] This was the position of the majority of classical scholars. Which type of crime is it?

Put otherwise, does the freedom of thought that Islam guarantees from the beginning to a non-Muslim stay with him after he enters Islam, so that he is not punished if he renounces his new faith, just as he was not blamed for not having faith before he entered Islam?[61]

The First Opinion: A Person Guilty of Apostasy Should Be Killed

A majority of jurists agreed that apostasy should be punishable by death considering this crime as falling under the hudud offenses. Areas of disagreement include whether the accused is given the opportunity to repent or not (some argue that the accused should be killed without having been called to repentance); whether the accused should be given the opportunity to repent once or twice, or three times (the Maliki and Hanafi schools of law) or for a month, or whether a person can forever be called to repentance (as al-Nakha'i said).[62]

They also disagreed with regard to female apostates and whether they should receive the same sanction as their male counterparts, since the rationale behind the death penalty is the changing of one's religion, as is the position of the Shafi'i school of law. Or should the punishment be imprisonment or corporal punishment until she repents? This is based on what was reported regarding the Prophet (peace be upon him; PBUH): "He forbade the killing of slaves, women, and children. And on the day he conquered Mecca, as he witnessed a female corpse, he said, "She should not have been killed in the fighting."[63]

For the advocates of this position, the wisdom of requiring the death penalty for the apostate, though the person who never believed is spared, is that apostasy is an attack of the individual or group against the Muslim community, and thus leaving Islam after deciding to enter it is like impugning the veracity and validity of this religion. This, it is argued, is to expose the religion to attack, which will lead to the decline of the community, and therefore the death penalty for rebellion is appropriate here, so that no one enters the religion without discernment and understanding and thus no one leaves it after conversion. According to this opinion, this is not about compulsion in religion; that would be the case if Muslims were forcing people to leave their faith and embrace Islam.

The Second Opinion: Apostasy Is a Political Crime

Jurists of the first opinion consider that the penalty for apostasy is a *hadd* (singular of hudud) crime—that is, a penalty seen as God's right to assign, which must be enforced with no possibility of pardon or intercession as it poses such a grave danger to society. Still, there is a large contingent among scholars and particularly among contemporary scholars who believe that this confuses apostasy with the political crime of armed insurrection against a legitimate state, whose sanction is best left to the discretion of the head of state or judge. They draw this conclusion from the fact that the Prophet (PBUH) upon entering Mecca (in 630 CE) pardoned a group of people sentenced to death. Among them was 'Abd Allah bin Abi Sarh, who was one of the scribes of the Quran and then left Islam. But while the Prophet refused to pardon others, he accepted 'Uthman's intercession on 'Abd Allah's behalf. This shows that apostasy is a crime subject to discretionary punishment, unlike hadd penalties for which there can be no intercession. In fact, those on whom the Prophet (PBUH) imposed the death penalty were guilty of other crimes that warranted such a penalty which can be considered, in modern terms, war crimes. For example, the caliph 'Umar bin al-Khattab did not impose the death penalty on Abu Shajara but rather banished him. Proponents of this opinion explain that the caliph Abu Bakr killed apostates because they had taken up arms against the Medinan state and thus represented a threat to the nascent Islamic polity. The caliph's actions, then, were political, not religious.[64]

Further, if apostasy were linked to one of the hadd penalties, that fact would not have been hidden from most of the Companions, and Abu Bakr would not have had to invest a lot of effort to successfully convince them of the wisdom of his policy. The advocates of this second opinion further argue that the Prophet's command to kill the apostate and his actual doing so was issued in his capacity as political leader, and not as the transmitter of divine revelation. His protest about the killing of the woman, saying that she was not among the fighters, clearly shows that the legal rationale for killing an apostate is not because he changed his religion but rather because he threatened the public order. This shows that the Prophet (PBUH) punished apostasy when it was part of a political act—armed insurrection, or treason. Thus it is the head of state who is left to determine the penalty in light of the threat this phenomenon poses to the

Islamic political entity—an entity that is quite different from the modern Western political order, in terms of their respective relationships to religion.

From a legal perspective at least, religion in a Western polity is an individual affair with no relation to the public order, an issue that is on par with racial or ethnic issues. Loyalty is to the state and maintaining its secrets. This view fits with Christianity, which left its public affairs to the Emperor Constantine to manage, while contenting itself with personal matters. As for Islam, it is both a belief system and a way of life, which makes any act that undermines the core doctrines of Islam as a whole a potential threat to public order, of which religion is a fundamental foundation, just as there are fundamentals of national identity in modern states, such as language, constitutional principles and liberties in liberal states, or Marxist doctrine in communist states. It follows that the state in Islam had to safeguard religion and maintain it, and to assess the relative danger posed by each revolt rising up within it, in order to address it by appropriate policies.

I lean toward the second view, which was espoused by some of the classical scholars, like al-Sarakhsi and Ibn al-Qayyim. Many modern scholars have taken this view, like the Imam Muhammad 'Abduh, Shaykh 'Abd al-Muta'ali al-Sa'idi, Abd al-Wahhab Khallaf, Abu Zahra, and Shaykh 'Abd al-'Aziz Shawish. Also among constitutional lawyers, we find Fathi 'Uthman, Dr. 'Abd al-Hamid Mutwalli, 'Abd al-Hakim Hasan al-'Ayli, Dr. Hasan al-Turabi, and Dr. Muhammad Salim al-'Awwa. The essence of this opinion is that apostasy has nothing to do with freedom of thought which Islam guarantees. Rather, it is a political issue, in that it seeks to protect Muslims and the institutions of the Islamic state from the disparagement of its enemies. The statements of the Prophet (PBUH) regarding apostasy were in his capacity as political leader. Thus, the penalty for an apostate is at the discretion of the ruler and not a hadd punishment. It is a political crime equivalent in other political systems to an armed rebellion against state authority and an attempt to overthrow it, and response has to be proportionate to the force used in each case and its relative danger to the state.

Certainly, as Dr. al-Hamid Mutwalli has remarked, there is a clear difference between the apostasy of a Christian who embraced Islam in order to marry a Muslim woman and who, after the marriage fell apart, returned to his religion, and the case of people planning, organizing, and preparing to launch an armed attack so as to overthrow the state. One should also differentiate between individuals whose faith has been shaken through unexpected circumstances or by the influence of cultural onslaught—a situation that can be remedied through appropriate means such as awareness-raising, teaching, and development—and an organized and well-planned campaign meant to destroy Islam and the state.

Therefore, scholars will have to examine each case in order to determine the means by which to resolve the issue.

A Word of Caution

When discussing the question of apostasy, it will be useful to pay attention to the debates between the different schools of Islamic law and how they defined the nature of the historical events preceding apostasy. Does apostasy apply to a person who has consciously chosen Islam and then leaves it deliberately? Does this case apply to a child born to believing parents but who when he reaches adulthood chooses a different religion—is he considered an apostate? Can this picture represent the many people who were raised in a Muslim country and inherited from their family decadent and corrupted versions of a religiosity that cannot hope to survive challenges to their faith? Is the term "apostate" appropriate for them? In dealing with similar cases, is the application of the hadd penalty for apostasy called for, as was the opinion of most jurists? Or would a response of a cultural and educational nature be more appropriate?

Concerning Children Born in a Muslim Family

The majority of jurists argued that a child born to Muslim parents is Muslim and that if he reaches the age of reason as an unbeliever, then he is an apostate. Al-Shafi'i argued that a child has no religion and that if he holds to his faith when he reaches maturity and specifically chooses Islam but then rejects it, only then is he an apostate. That is a perspective more in line with the rules of Shari'a (no accountability before maturity). After all, how can one judge the Islam of a child before he has reached maturity, except in some metaphorical sense? Childhood is a stage of education, preparation, and training for the responsibility of following religious principles, yet without being accountable for following it yet. There is no doubt that most of those who have had their faith shaken—in a favorable milieu for communist and secularist parties to emerge—are themselves the victims of a failed education system, a failed traditional education, a rigid Islamic culture, and a mummified and degraded religiosity that a cultural invasion armed with a modern scientific culture, carrying an atheistic worldview hostile to religion. Are not most of them victims of a decadent culture, a sterile education, and a sovereignty relinquished to the foreigner? A judgmental approach is not the way to deal with this generation that has been cut off from its roots by the cultural invasion of the West at a time of cultural stagnation when scholars were preoccupied by trivialities and legalistic squabbles. Instead of playing judge, it is the attitude of the educator or physician that is appropriate.

Indeed, our families, our schools, and our mosques have failed during a long chapter of our history, the negative results and consequences of which are still with us. They failed to fulfill the mission of ensuring cultural continuity between the generations of the umma. That is why God took pleasure in the stunning accomplishments of the Islamic renewal movement in rescuing new generations. We will never be delivered from this rupture by drawing the sword of the law, but rather by a well-thought through strategy to produce once again what the past generations failed to produce—leaders of family clans, scholars, imams, and institutions like schools, the media, and the arts. What we need to produce is a way to educate and enrich culture by liberating Islam from decline and westernization and elaborating a contemporary Islamic culture that actually connects with the present-day concerns of the masses, armed with the inventions of the age, adding to the earth the colors of Heaven, and through which the umma rediscovers its true essence and finds the solution to its problems and its hopes.

That truly is the challenge our generation is called upon to face in order to undo the damage wrought by the new crusaders' campaign which hit the Maghreb particularly hard.[65] In fact, it is the great challenge we dare not lose sight of, distracted as we might be by other causes. Let us prioritize dealing with the mission of the cultural leaders, the scholars and the educators, rather than judges and politicians, for our top priority is fostering civil liberties and freedom of thought; they are the foundation upon which the new construction must begin. True victory can only be found in the fight for cultural authenticity, and the Islamic movement has been able to marginalize the secularist agenda, despite its monopoly on enormous state resources. In the words of Fahmi Huwaydi, "let our entrance into [building an Islamic society] be through the door of freedom and democracy. I believe that to enter that door successfully is the true criterion for determining the authenticity of any political regime that calls itself Islamic. That should dissipate the fears of those of us who consider freedom another face of God's Oneness."[66]

PERSONAL FREEDOM AND THE RIGHT TO GOD'S DIGNIFYING OF THE HUMAN PERSON[67]

Islam did not stop at recognizing human beings' right to life, freedom, and physical integrity, but rather considered these to be sacred duties of the community, based on the principle of the vicegerency and ennoblement of humankind. The human being is appointed as God's vicegererent—that is, His deputy charged with the responsibility to judge among His creatures with justice. Thus anyone who sets out to obey God and judge His creatures aright is God's caliph.[68] God honored humanity in Heaven by mentioning him among the heavenly council, and having the angels, those brought near to God, bow down to him.[69] It is no wonder that God honored humanity with the gifts He granted them—intelligence, will, and rationality, along with their dominion over the earth's resources, and the revelation He sent them as guidance through His messengers and sacred books.[70] Al-Tabari tells of the Prophet (PBUH) saying, "'Nothing on the Last Day will have more honor than the sons of Adam.' Someone asked, 'O Apostle of God, not even the angels?' He said, 'Not even the angels; they have no free will, just like the sun and the moon.'"[71] From God's honoring of the human person flow the sanctity of life—from himself [suicide] or from others: "Do not take life, which God has made sacred, except by right."[72] And "Do not kill each other, for God is merciful to you."[73] Protecting human life includes protection from all that poses a threat to it, like hunger, sickness, homelessness, grinding poverty, being the object of torture, humiliation, marginalization, suspicion, spying, or slander, and other forms of injustice.

Human beings are worthy of honor by virtue of their being human, regardless of nationality, color or creed, or of any social characteristic. This honor accompanies any human being, dead or alive; the self deserves respect in life and in death, as we read in a hadith, "A funeral procession passed in front of the Prophet (PBUH) and he stood up. Someone said, 'The man who died was a Jew.' The Prophet replied, 'Isn't he a soul?'"[74] An assault on a dead man is just as bad as if he had been alive. Also, a person is innocent until proven guilty by an independent court. Torture is absolutely forbidden, as in the hadith, "On the Day of Resurrection God will torture those who torture others on earth." Torture and its absolute prohibition will be discussed further below.

Islam safeguards people's privacy and forbids falsely accusing them or spying on them and considers a person's home as a sacred enclosure: "Do not enter [other people's houses] unless you have been given permission to do so."[75] It protects a person's good reputation as well, prescribing the punishment for false accusation for those who violate people's honor, and forbids prying into their lives and gossiping about them.

The Qur'an offers striking examples of how highly it regards the power of thinking and freedom of expression by calling the mind to reflect on everything and by the examples of beautiful dialogues the prophets engaged in with their people, and sometimes even with their tyrannical rulers. These dialogues brightly highlight the way these prophets relied on the power of the mind to find convincing arguments, as opposed to relying on force, the final weapon despots always resort to when all else fails. Furthermore, the Qur'an quotes in many places the dialogue between God (may He be exalted) and His angels and prophets, which emphasize again and again the sanctity of the freedom of expression and opinion. Thus the dialogue between God (may He be exalted) and His enemy, the cursed devil, in no way suppresses or forbids the latter from putting forward his arguments and defending his viewpoint. Rather, the Qur'an lets us hear very clearly Satan's voice and his arguments in many places.

The value put on the freedom of opinion is seen in the life of the Prophet (PBUH) with his Companions, and how he, the Prophet (PBUH) gifted with revelation, would openly consider opposing viewpoints. He would even encourage his Companions to hold independent opinions and interpretations: "Let none of you become yes-men, who say, 'I stand with the others.'" It is no wonder, then, that the Prophet (PBUH) founded an excellent school to produce great men in all areas of life. This is how in the midst of a barren desert the greatest and most amazing revolution, a revolution in civilization, took off—that is why all the schools of thought and politics in Islam can find one of Muhammad's Companions as an imam full of knowledge and wisdom whose opinion they can build on—people of knowledge and expert legal reasoning, people of war and courage, people of political power and leadership, people of wealth and generosity, people of austerity and asceticism who stand up against luxury, or people of literature and poetry. There were no identical copies or mass-produced models, but they were all unique, while at the same time they all followed the good example, as the Qur'an says, "Truly you are of strong character."[76]

Islam continued to challenge opposing views, calling them to engage in a serious and honest dialogue confident in the power of its logic and the harmony between that logic and human nature, so that if the path is opened between the two sides in an atmosphere of freedom and objectivity, humanity will have no reason not to accept Islam.[77] The Islamic challenge in calling others to debate is eternally expressed in a strong verse in the Qur'an that echoes in the hearts of Muslims, "Say, produce your evidence, if you are telling the truth."[78] In every generation and with the challenge of every tribulation for Muslims extraordinary men emerged who faced the renewed challenges with proof and logic, giving witness to the Truth. In the many debates between the scholars of Islam and the best of other faiths, never was it recorded in history that a Muslim lost in a free debate. The cherished request made by the Prophet (PBUH) in facing those who fiercely opposed him was freedom: "Let me address the people," and the same request is transmitted again and again to those succeeding him in this call. Seldom are they granted this request, but rather are subjected to persecution, repression, and falsified elections under the pretext of refusing to recognize religious parties.

For this reason, it is no wonder that in the shade of this free-thinking life, brought into being by Islamic ideals, all ideas and tendencies have found their way to dialogue, exchange, and creativity. Seeking knowledge in this kind of environment became a duty and right, while scientific research without any limitations took pride of place, as we read in the Qur'an, "Say, look at what is in the heavens and on the earth."[79] Thus Islam does not impose limits on freedom of thought unless absolutely necessary; what is important is that freedom is not used to undermine freedom itself by becoming a means of provoking ethnic or nationalist conflict, or inflaming our baser instincts. This is because freedom is a lofty human value, and it loses its meaning when it is divorced from the values of truth, goodness, beauty, and fairness.

There should be no freedom, therefore, for those who misuse it—the oppressor (who uses it to oppress others) or the mentally ill (who may use it to harm himself or others). As the Qur'an states, "there can be no [further] hostility, except toward aggressors."[80] For freedom's value is renewed to the extent that it endows our lives with strength, peace of mind, stability, faith, justice, and progress.[81]

FREEDOM OF THOUGHT AND EXPRESSION

It is natural for a religion that bestowed humanity with the status of being God's vicegerent on earth by virtue of our intellect, will, and freedom, not to fetter those resources but rather to release them, set them free, and endeavor to spur them on to action and productivity. In doing so, Islam is content to orient and guide, while leaving people to determine their own destiny and shoulder their own responsibility. Islam's respect for humanity and their freedom leads to regarding the use of reason as a duty. And why not, considering that this duty to reason is the basis for our responsibility to make decisions about the most crucial aspects of human destiny, like religious belief with all its implications for our actions, behaviors, and eternal destiny? That is why the Qur'an never tires of repeating its exhortation to reflect, to guide and spur the use of our intellect, and not to follow our own whims or the crowd, discarding individual judgment, merely copying our fathers and forbears. Engaging our intellect means also refusing that which corrodes our minds, like drugs and intoxicants, and keeping our minds from being passive and submitting to different kinds of servitude and control.

Freedom of opinion played an important role in developing Islamic civilization, causing it to flourish, and in calling people to Islam and preserving it.[82] What is more, freedom of opinion contributed enormously to the unity of the Islamic umma, while protecting it from religious wars, genocides, and ethnic cleansing. These occurred in other civilizations because of fanaticism and intolerance, and a monopoly on representing the sacred and speaking in its name, as was the case for Jews and Christians. Meanwhile, Islam has recognized the principle of religious pluralism and made legal reasoning [ijtihad] permissible for any Muslim with sufficient knowledge.

ECONOMIC RIGHTS

The right to property is one of the individual rights found in international covenants on human rights and in many national laws as well. An individual's right of ownership is considered a natural right. Though Islam recognizes this right, it does so in accordance with its own perspective and specific conditions, yet without seeing it as a natural human right, since all sovereignty belongs to God.[83] For everything that pertains to ownership, from the way it is acquired to the way one manages it, to what can be owned and how it ceases to be owned—none of this can happen unless it is done according to the Shari'a. But note that the Western concept of ownership did not arise in Arab and Muslim history until the beginning of the colonial penetration in the nineteenth century, on the basis of a German form of individual ownership, which Karl Marx described as the kind of ownership characteristic of the European civilization. Individual ownership was not considered absolute where owners had the right to dispose of their property as they wished, to inherit it or even destroy it, as is written in the canons of Roman law.

Prior to European influence, the modalities of ownership that were known in Muslim lands arose on the basis of usufruct and trusteeship—mankind's deputyship of God on the earth and its responsibility to develop it and treat it as the bridge crossing over to the next life. For the human right to property is the fruit of people's collective mandate handed to them by God, meaning that the true and original owner is God and that human ownership is a trust or a loan to be used. Humankind may not dispose of this trust unless it is according to the Owner's will; and if anyone misuses this trust, it will be taken away from him.[84] So because rights or Shari'a-stipulated responsibilities take into account the fact that people are by nature social beings and that these rights and duties play out in specific social settings, it is only natural that people see them as social functions[85] that protect the social fabric and contribute to its development, progress, and safety. But if they fall outside this scope and become a factor that upsets society's balance, a destructive element, an impediment, and a source of hatred and strife then society has the right to impose restrictions on these rights such that it brings them back to their original social function.

One of the functions that individual ownership is meant to perform is the distribution of authority in society to all of its members through their possession of a part of the nation's wealth. This is what gives political freedom and deliberative democracy social content, while the concentration of wealth in the hands of a particular social class, or in the hands of the state itself, represents a foundation for tyranny and for the oppression of have-nots by the haves who control their basic needs. This is where zakat intervenes, by defining the minimum one gives as a basic guarantee for political participation, or mutual consultation [*shura*].[86] This is where the Islamic model differs from the one that prevails in the West, whether it be socialism, which aims to strip individuals from owning wealth in order to give a monopoly to the state, or capitalism, which concentrates wealth in the hands of the few.

By contrast, the Islamic model seeks to distribute wealth among the greatest number of people in such a way as to allow all to be owners and, as a result, shareholders in political authority and in its decision-making process. This in turn is what ensures and strengthens their freedom and their ability to exercise oversight over political authorities and society as a whole through "enjoining good and forbidding wrong,"[87] which is a strong pillar of Muslim society. It is no wonder, then, that Islam denounces opulence, extravagance, waste, and the hoarding of wealth, and considers them to be at the root of oppression and unbelief: "Corah was one of Moses' people, but he oppressed them. We had given him such treasures that even their keys would have weighed down a whole company of strong men . . ."[88] And also from the Qur'an: "But man exceeds all bounds when he thinks he is self-sufficient."[89]

Islam also considers the prohibition on concentrating wealth a cornerstone of the principle of economic distribution: "so that [the gains] do not just circulate among those of you who are rich."[90] And without sharing in the ownership of the sources of basic wealth, according to the hadith, "Muslims are partners in three [things]: water, pastures and fire," there would hardly be any meaning to the lofty ideals Islam sets as the foundations of Muslim society: equality, fraternity, justice, mutual consultation, enjoining good, and forbidding evil. Without those, after a superficial coating of slogans and wishes there would be nothing left but oppression of one kind or another.

The right to property is the foundation of an individual's personal drive and the activation of his or her talent since individuals are predisposed to seek the realization of their aspirations and the right to own the fruits of their labor. Utopian ideologies have in vain attempted to deny this natural human disposition, but the laws of human nature forced their project to fail and to recognize once again people's inner impulses and individual ownership. In reality, individual owner-ship is the recognition of a person's right to enjoy the fruit of his effort, unless it conflicts with a collective right or he chooses to waive his right. This is so because even though Islam attributes to the individual the right of ownership by virtue of his being God's trustee, Islam's predominant social orientation requires the pri-oritization of communal interests when they conflict with those of individuals. In this way, Islam calls individuals to exercise their God-given trusteeship within the context of the greater trusteeship—that of society. As we read, "Do not entrust to those who are weak of judgment the property which God has placed in your charge for [their] benefit: but make provision for them from it, clothe them, and speak to them kindly."[91] This is what most contemporary Muslim scholars be-lieve, as they see individual ownership as a communal function, from which the individual benefits and which he disposes of according to the collective interest.[92] This also gives legitimacy to Islamic political authority as it represents the wider society in determining a general social and economic policy that is binding on individual owners, in delimiting ownership, and in nationalizing some resources and interests. This is necessary whenever the social balance is upset, though it should be done without thereby abolishing society's general interest and while remaining within the context of the Islamic constitution, which rules over society as a whole, whether its rulers or its individuals.

Please note here that property rights throughout Islamic history have taken many forms and that individual ownership among Muslims represented a very limited portion of land as a whole. It is beyond the scope of this book to delve into various forms of ownership in detail. Suffice it to affirm here that Islam recognizes the right to individual property within the scope of society's wider in-terests and within the limits of Shari'a, as a corollary of the right to work and to own the fruit of one's labor according to the doctrine of humanity's trusteeship. In this we should not forget that the purpose of ownership is to guard society's balance by seeking to do away with social classes that rise above others because of the wealth they own. Islam strongly condemns any system built upon classes that draw their power from wealth or from tribal, class, ethnic, or racial superiority.

Historical social research leaves no doubt that Muslims never knew the feu-dal system that prevailed in European history but rather experienced several forms of popular ownership that were more widespread than individual and state ownership, a fact that is a source of strength in society. Until 1840, for instance, 75 percent of properties in the Ottoman Empire were owned as endowments, and in Tunisia three-quarters of all properties were religious endowments. Munir Shafiq proposes in order to keep society strong that Muslims should not relinquish all sources of power to the state. Rather, they should restore the comprehensive organization of ownership that was known under various historical forms of Islamic polity, and in priority forms of ownership that were under the administration of associations, trade unions, municipalities, families, and village councils.

To this we might add scientific institutes, research centers, health and media organizations, political parties, and youth clubs, all of which strengthen civil society and increase the health and vitality of the democratic system, and their ability to resist any attempts by the regime to monopolize power. Additionally, they serve to delink society's fate from that of the regime in power, unlike what happened under secularism. In Islamic societies, the community continued to carry out the most important societal functions—education, health care, and poverty alleviation, and this even during the periods of the greatest government corruption. As for today, where the state controls everything and monopolizes all sources of power, society's and the individual's power have been weakened as a result, and their destiny is completely tied to the state, whether to its good or corrupt behavior.

Yet even if Islamic history witnessed feudalism, it is a totally different kind of feudalism from that known in Europe, in that absolute land ownership was God's possession and people had the right of usufruct according to the Shari'a. Even when the state considered itself to have absolute ownership of land, it did so as a representative of the community that had the right to exploit it. As for the lands owned by endowments, the state could never get any portion of them or even exploit them, since they could only be exploited according to the conditions of the trust.

In the Tunisian constitution of 1956, however, the right to ownership appears shrouded in obscurity, like other rights spelled out in that constitution. Experience has shown that this vagueness does not express a desire for flexibility but rather opens the door for the regime to act in oppressive ways and to violate the rights and freedom of its citizens. We read in article 14: "The right to ownership is guaranteed and is practiced within the limits of the law." That is a formulation that can cover a wide range of potentially contradictory economic choices, from the socialist policies of the 1960s to the dominant capitalism of the 1970s.

SOCIAL RIGHTS

Social rights refer to the individual's needs in life and his access to health and social resources. Yet these are not rights that Western constitutions or human rights covenants gave much attention to, except at a later stage as a result of pressure from socialist ideas and mobilization by trade unions, and as a way to keep at bay the spectre of a Marxist revolution. By contrast, we find these rights to be strongly rooted in the Islamic perspective and practice by presenting a model of social relations that achieved equality, justice, and mutual consultation. The most important socio-economic rights stipulated by most constitutions are the right to work and to health, and the right to a dignified standard of living.

The Right to Work

Al-'Aqqad summarizes the social democracy of Islam in one sentence, "Islam prohibits exploitation and sanctifies the right to work; for democracy needs no more than these two rules to guarantee a stable and peaceful society."[93] Islam abolished unlawful gain by way of cheating, stealing, or usury, or through monopolies. It forbade the hoarding of money, so that the means of profit are available to all and lead to fulfilling the function of wealth which is to achieve sufficiency for everyone.[94] Further, Islam sanctifies work, emphasizing its importance and considering it the main source of ownership. The Qur'an tells us, "Travel [the earth's] regions; eat of His provision."[95] Also, "Then when the prayer has ended, disperse in the land and seek out God's bounty."[96] In a hadith we read, "Out of sinful acts there are some that can only be expiated through preoccupation with making a living."[97] Another hadith says: "Whoever revives a barren land, it becomes his." Again, "No one eats better food than that provided by one's own work. The prophet David ate from the work of his own hands."[98] Work is even considered one of the types of jihad in God's path, "If someone strives to provide enough for himself and avoids needing the help of others, it is in the way of God; if someone strives to provide for needy parents or needy children, it is in the way of God; but if someone strives arrogantly and only to multiply his wealth, it is in the path of Satan."[99] The Prophet (PBUH) once reached for the hand of a worker that bore deep scars from his work in order to kiss them to show his appreciation.[100]

Just as Islam urges people to work and stresses its sanctity, it shuns idleness and living at the expense of others, even if this is for the purpose of consecration to prayer and spiritual exercises; it deplores dependence and begging. For honorable work, no matter what kind, brings dignity to the believer, as in the following hadith, "For if one of you takes a rope, goes to the mountain, gathers wood, ties it to his back and sells it in town, and God has provided for him; this is better than to ask people for money, whether people may give it to him or not."[101] How can someone whose soul has imbibed the dignity of Islam accept to hold his hand out to someone who is not his Creator, but is just another human like him when he is physically able to work?

Begging at the doors of mosques and on street corners, while it goes against a Islamic upbringing and teaching, and is a violation of one's human dignity, is not the sole or worst form of individual and collective vagrancy. Earning a living by dishonest means or through debt, whether with an honest intention to repay it or, which is more serious, without it, something that unfortunately happens so very often in our societies is more offensive than the traditional form of begging. The most loathsome form of indebtedness comes when we abandon our dignity and sell our freedom to various non-Muslim countries in the East and West by way of loans and aid packages. It is a form of humiliation that is impossible for someone who has tasted the sweetness of faith to swallow. For young Muslims have been raised on the wisdom taught by their elders from time immemorial, "Debt is worry by night and humiliation by day."

The Prophet (PBUH) wished to teach his people the gravity of incurring debts so much so that when someone died, the Prophet would ask, "Did the man have a debt?" If they answered, "Yes," he would say, "Pray for your companion", while he himself would refuse to join the funeral prayer."[102] His aim was to eliminate any intellectual and educational causes of dependence and to help mobilize Muslim society to be constantly filled with the positive spirit and pride that comes from God's honoring humanity which can only be achieved through hard work. For Islam's call to knowledge and faith goes hand in hand with its call to work hard, hence good works multiplied, at the expense of empty words. Among the sayings of the caliph 'Umar (may God be pleased with him), "May God bless those who reduce their words and increase their actions!"

What is the state's duty with regard to employment? The role of the state from the Islamic perspective is not to guard or police borders or defend class interests. Even more importantly, its basic function is to establish justice, and the simplest definition of justice—without which there can no longer be justice—is to provide for the basic needs of all as a step toward full sufficiency for all, which would include a sustainable level of food production, housing, clothing, and health care. Until that minimum level is achieved, there is no sanctity for private property, and both private and public funds can be used for these purposes, even if this means combatting those who stand in the way, as rebels.[103] The state's first priority is not to give handouts to the needy but rather to provide jobs, either by way of an educational and media effort to remove the psychological barriers and raise the status of work, or by way of providing the professional tools for those who are able. Here we lean on the example of the first head of the Islamic state, the Messenger of God (PBUH), who always exhorted people to work, provided the needy with the tools to do so, then followed up on their activity so as to make sure they were succeeding while relying on themselves. He did not resort to offering them any financial aid, except to those whose disability precluded them from working.

The institution of zakat in itself is one of the most important resources to guarantee a social safety net within the Islamic state, but it is not about distributing financial gifts to the needy whose hands are outstretched all life long. This only happens in a few rare cases. What is offered to them according to their situation and specific needs are the tools needed to create jobs (workshops, factories, a piece of land, seed money for a small business, etc.). A zakat association then undertakes to provide them with the help and guidance needed to establish themselves and join the ranks of those who contribute to the zakat fund.[104]

If work in Islam is what produces wealth, then the model of social relation that its values seek to inculcate, as we already said, is that each person owns his own effort and works on developing what he already owns, whether it be something owned individually or collectively, not just as a paid worker working on someone else's land. Wage labor in Islam is the exception and not the norm, which is that "land belongs to whomever will till it"—a principle that Islam strives to apply.

In this regard, the Prophet's rule in the state of Medina was revolutionary. What stands out if you carefully look into the model of social relations he established is the Islamic plan to eradicate the system of slavery that was written into the statutes of pagan Arabia, and other forms of exploiting the labor of workers, such as usury, monopoly, the self-appropriation of God's land and the forcing of God's creatures to work on it while robbing them of the entire value of their labor. If it were not for the revolution that the Prophet (PBUH) and his successors mounted against this regime, then the emigrants from Mecca and those who followed them among other nations who were attracted to the just rule of Islam would have been transformed into serfs in a feudal state run by the very few.

In the first instance these values were applied knowing full well the depth of the Islamic concept of justice, guaranteed as it was in the Islamic creed ("There is no god but God") and embodied in the economic principle of the Prophet (PBUH): "Whoever owns land must cultivate it or give it to his brother and not rent it" (a sound hadith), and "Whoever cultivates arid land owns it." Strangely, Islamic legal practice by and large has deviated from these principles in distributing land. It focused solely on the incident of Khaybar during which the

Prophet (PBUH) allowed the Jews right after the defeat they experienced on the heels of their act of treason to stay on the land they owned and to cultivate it in exchange for the *kharaj* tax they would pay the state. The jurists gleaned from this event a principle that only applied to this situation and established it as a general principle covering all kinds of leasing, thus going against many clear principles established by the Prophet (PBUH) on the issue of distribution, one of which was that leasing [*ijarah*] was the exception and not the rule. Even though the Maliki and especially Zahiri schools of Islamic law opposed many forms of exploitation like land leases, nevertheless this system found its way among the customs of Islamic lands.

The legal tradition, gave exaggerated attention to the issue of leasing land for agriculture, in a way that did not reflect the existing economic relations. In terms of industry for instance, which was based on small workshops where the number of artisans was small, the latter soon became owners of the workshops, so that you might say that the period of leasing was only a time to practice one's trade and not a permanent situation. Agriculture was based on a principle of collective ownership of public lands or religious endowment or tribal land. In all cases, it was a system of shared ownership and not that of leasing—a system of profit based on working the land directly. As for who controlled land owner-ship, it was for the most part owned collectively by society.

It may be that what gave such importance to work relations based on remu-neration was that Islamic jurisprudence developed not in rural areas but in the cities, where there was a high number of construction workers, or scribes, or domestic servants. These were occupations that were primarily urban and rare in the countryside, where families work for themselves and not for others. But because wage labor, however exceptional it is, cannot be done away with entirely, as some occupations cannot be carried out without it, Islam carefully laid down some rules for it. Specifically, it rolled out a set of ethical principles that kept this relationship between employer and worker balanced and sought to prevent the for-mer exploiting the weaker party and transforming him into a slave.

At the same time, Islam does not rely purely on a system of contractual agree-ments as the sole way to establish justice, though contracts are usually built on consent, and hence both parties are expected to abide by them: "You who believe, fulfill your obligations."[105] That, however, is not an absolute injunction. Social circumstances can significantly deteriorate and put great pressure on one of the parties of the contract so that his free will becomes merely formal and without real meaning. And because Islam did not come to establish merely formal justice but rather insists on a struggle to establish true justice, it disregards those contracts that are unfair to one of the parties. So when there is a lack of balance between the two parties and one party finds himself in a stronger position than the other, it stipulates that it is for the weaker and not stronger party to dictate the terms of the contract. As we read in the Qur'an, "When you contract a debt for a stated term, put it down in writing . . . let the debtor dictate."[106] But if the opposite happens, then the weaker party no longer has to uphold the terms of the contract.[107]

The worker has a right to a job that is both suitable for his skills and provides for his needs. Imam Ibn Hanbal recounted that the Prophet (PBUH) said: "Let anyone who has been appointed in an official position but doesn't have a house, take a house; or doesn't have a wife, marry; or doesn't have a mount ride, take one." This means that jobs should be distributed on the basis of clear guidelines in order to achieve equality, like competence and ability. On the other hand, Islam requires from the worker integrity and thoroughness. As the Prophet (PBUH) said, "God loves when one of you does any job, that he does it with perfection." And Abu Ya'la narrated this sound hadith, "For God prescribed perfection in all things."

Health Care

Health care is one of the social rights of citizens in the Islamic state. The Prophet (PBUH) was very concerned with preventative medicine, from cleanliness and moderation to the avoidance of anything unclean or impure, intoxicants, and all types of waste and excess. He commanded believers to focus on building their strength and turning away from causes of weakness and destruction: "The strong believer is better than the weak one and both are good."[108] The Prophet (PBUH) stressed the importance of exercise, mandated the sick to seek remedies, and warned against obesity and gluttony.[109] He was also lenient in providing exceptions to religious rituals for the sake of people's health,[110] while mandating the state to provide care for those in need, whether Muslim or not. Thus it is not surprising that the Islamic civilization was the first to set up an excellent health care system, complete with hospitals, pharmacies, and laboratories.[111] In the same way, Islam emphasizes the importance of visiting the sick, considering this one of their rights, and the Prophet (PBUH) praised those who call upon the sick."[112]

Founding a Family

Founding a family is a right that stems from the fact that matrimony is a universal law and that, for believers is an act of worship that equals half of all one's religious obligations. It has a significant effect on spouses by providing balance and development in one's personality, just as it is the irreplaceable framework for the safeguarding of our species, for its growth and development.

For that reason, Islam has granted this institution with great protection and defined rights and duties for all parties according to the principles of equality and complementarity. Furthermore, there is no right that is not matched by an equivalent duty, as we read in the Qur'an, "women have [rights] similar to their obligations, according to what is fair."[113]

Marriage is an honored contract, a solemn covenant, and a crucial institution replete with subtle and overlapping relationships, which means it cannot succeed if built upon passing interests and whims. Therefore, marriage in Islam is established on the basis of mutual consent and respect, and upon solid human values like faith, generosity, kindness, patience, love, and justice. At the same time, Islam works to eliminate all considerations of race and class, which constitute barriers between people, hindering them from mutual acquaintance and friendship—all to accomplish the goal of Islam, which is to bring humans closer together, just as they began as one family: "People, be mindful of your Lord, who created you from a single soul."[114] Since marriage occupies such an important place in Islam, marriage is both encouraged and called for in many cases, and the state or simply the Islamic community has a mandate to facilitate it for everyone: "Marry off the single among you, and those of your male and female slaves who are fit [for marriage]. If they are poor, [let this not deter you] God will provide for them from His bounty."[115]

Islam favors marriage at a young age, protecting the energies of the youth from dissipating or being squandered and society from being eaten away by vice. This means that present-day calls to delay marriage are a kind of social corruption and spur to sin and immorality. Islam calls for the multiplication of the human race, as it fulfills the mandate of human trusteeship—civilizing, developing, and populating the earth. Islam opposes calls to limit the human species or abortion purely for economic motives and the desire to monopolize this world at the expense of others. "Do not kill your children for fear of poverty— We shall provide for them and for you—killing them is a great sin."[116]

Muslims have the full right to choose their marriage partners, indeed it is an obligation, for fear of social unrest, following the hadith, "Whoever among you has the means to do so, let him marry." Whereas marriage is a right for each individual, it is the responsibility of society to make it possible for men and women to do so, as we read in the above Qur'anic quote, "Marry off the single among you, and those of your male and female slaves who are fit [for marriage]. If they are poor, God will provide for them from His bounty."[117]

Islamic law makes no restrictions concerning social class, ethnic, or racial considerations for potential marriage partners but only concerning religious convictions, out of concern for the harmony and longevity of the couple on the one hand and to maintain the security and order of an Islamic society on the other.

Inevitably, any such relationship in society has the potential to undermine that foundation or threaten it, and that is why the Shari'a forbids people to marry adulterous people, as well as atheists and those hostile to Islam. Men are given permission to marry chaste women from among the People of the Book who hold to their own ethical standards, a statute which is meant to facilitate the spreading of Islam's light in that community.[118] That said, there is no such permission for Muslim women to marry non-Muslims, be they Jewish or Christian or something else. Islam further regarded care for mothers and children to be an important obligation. Umar Ibn al-Khattab introduced a grant for each newborn child and a maintenance fee for mothers, as required by the Qur'an. This demonstrates the state's duty to provide for mothers and children as foundations of a sound and strong society.

Right to Learning and Education

Islam underscores the importance of science and learning and holds scholars in high esteem. It exhorts the ignorant to study, the knowledgeable to teach, and the state to facilitate the means to achieve this, so we could consider Islam the first school of thought in history to make education obligatory, as in this hadith: "Knowledge is enjoined on all Muslims, male and female."[119] Islamic civilization arose to realize this objective in practice, and historians testify that Cordoba, for instance, was the first city ever to achieve full literacy for everyone.[120] This took place without draining the coffers of the state, for it was Islamic culture that took care of it—a culture that joins knowledge to faith, and this world to the next, and relies upon the principle of human trusteeship—by founding popular educational associations paid for by religious endowments. This granted educational, legislative, and economic institutions independence from the state, making them an integral part of civil society.

Another reason for this is that Islam sees education as being directed to society as a whole, not just children, and that it is not limited to the three skills of reading, writing, and arithmetic but goes beyond that to cover ethics. For knowledge is no good unless it is followed by good works aimed at the development of the individual and society, and the achievement of happiness in this life and the next. It also involves developing the physical and spiritual energies of old and young, men and women, in harmony with the divine path that secures God's favor.[121]

The Right to Social Security

Western constitutions and human rights laws have not guaranteed the right to social security until recently, and only under the pressure of political realities. The Tunisian constitution, for instance, in its first section ("General Laws") does not go beyond the traditional freedoms (freedom of thought, expression, and movement). It adds just a simple statement in the Preamble without truly guaranteeing the social rights of citizens, like the right to education and health care, or the right to employment and starting a family. There is no provision for the person who is unable to work or whose work is insufficient to provide a living wage. The following formulation shows that it is merely a theoretical declaration:

> The republican system is the best guarantor of human rights, the equality of all citizens, for the provision of well-being through economic development, and for using the country's wealth for the benefit of the people, and the best way to nurture and protect families, and secure the right of citizens to employment, health care and education.[122]

This is simply a declaration of the merits of the republican system, not a binding principle. Otherwise these rights would have been mentioned alongside other rights and liberties in the section on general principles. By contrast, today Western constitutions and declarations of human rights, in addition to the constitutions of socialist nations, clearly guarantee those rights. As we read in the Universal Declaration of Human Rights,

> Everyone has the right to a standard of living adequate for the health and well-being of himself and of his family, including food, clothing, housing and medical care and necessary social services, and the right to security in the event of unemployment, sickness, disability, widowhood, old age or other lack of livelihood in circumstances beyond his control.[123]

In any case, these current declarations—much more the product of political pressures, as I said, than out of conviction regarding human dignity—were very late in recognizing these rights both in theory and practice, compared to Islam's position from its outset. Islam established a society on the basis of brotherhood, equality, and justice, and all that entails in terms of solidarity, mutual assistance, and altruism: "The believers are brothers."[124] Also this hadith: "The Muslim is another Muslim's brother—he doesn't wrong him, betray him, or abandon him." In *The Ornament*, Ibn Hazm comments on this sound hadith, saying, "He who leaves his brother to go hungry or naked, and has the means to feed him or clothe him, has betrayed him." Brotherhood is not simply about beautiful sentiments; rather it is a covenant of mutual solidarity, assistance, and cooperation.

Brotherhood is also a contract in which the umma is the main party, represented on several interconnected levels, beginning with the family. The members of a family are enjoined to help one another through mechanisms such as inheritance, the will, and alimony: "Relatives have a prior claim over one another."[125] The next level in this duty of care are neighbors: The Qur'an exhorts Muslims to take care of "neighbours who are close, and neighbours who are strangers."[126] Also these hadiths: "Gabriel continued to advise me to treat neighbors well until I thought he would make them my heirs" and "A man is not a believer who fills his stomach while his neighbour is hungry." The next level covers the people in your district and then society as a whole—for which one is responsible, through the duty of zakat, which is binding, followed by charity, "Over your money, there are other rights (for the needy) apart from zakat." In a sound hadith, the Prophet (PBUH) acting in his capacity as a political leader pointed to an example of how a small society of believers should deal with economic crises: "Blessed be the people of the al-Ash'ari tribe, when they lost men in the raids or when food became scarce in Medina, they would put all they had in one piece of cloth and divide it evenly between themselves." The way in which the Prophet (PBUH) describes these people shows how much he approves of these actions, and expresses his desire that Muslims, and indeed all of humanity, would imitate them in embodying brotherhood in rising above selfishness and overcoming crises.

Yet the Prophet (PBUH) as leader also went beyond merely praising such behavior by issuing a direct and public obligation "Whoever has an extra mount should offer it to him who is without; and whoever has a surplus of wealth, let him pass it on to the one who has none." Abu Sa'id al-Khudri, who narrated the hadith, stated that the Prophet (PBUH) enumerated all kinds of wealth, so that the companions understood that they had no right to a surplus of any form of wealth. Thus, in our modern times, Muslims should consider this applicable to any surplus in the form of houses, cars, factories, agricultural land, and so on, so that we come to realize that none of us has a right to excess wealth. The Prophet (PBUH) said, "Whoever has land, let him cultivate it, or give it to his brother; if the latter refuses, let him keep it uncultivated," but do not let him keep it for more than three years, since "Rights over uncultivated land lapse beyond three [years]," as it says in another hadith.

The Prophet's successors were filled with the same social and humanitarian spirit, and 'Umar bin al-Khattab barred those who participated in the conquest from turning into feudal lords. For that reason, he prohibited the distribution of the conquered lands among them and declared them the property of all Muslims until the Day of Judgment. Nevertheless, he discovered near the end of his rule that economic inequalities still existed despite this, and he was determined to address them. He said, "Had I known in the beginning what I now know, I would have taken the excess wealth among the rich and divided it among the poor emigrants from Mecca to Medina." The fourth caliph 'Ali's revolutionary rule also offered a clear vision for dealing with poverty. For him it was the fruit of the selfishness of the wealthy: "The poor are hungry only because the rich are depriving them of their rights."[127]

However, the influence of the Persian and Roman civilizations, which were built upon feudalism and exploitation, obscured the egalitarian and humanitarian values that characterized the Qur'an and Sunna and their exemplary application in the first stages of Islamic civilization. Thus these bright shining values became mixed with the injustices within the surrounding societies, and this influenced Islamic jurisprudence to some extent.[128] That said, Islamic history is replete with revolutionary reformers who wiped off the dust of the past that had accumulated, reconnected with the pure source of revelation, and released its brilliant light to shine once again. One of the most famous of those reformers is the revolutionary North African jurist Ibn Hazm (d. 1064), known for his literalist reading of the text into the most reactionary and rigid of all Islamic jurists and an adversary of the rights of the oppressed, both men and women.[129]

The critics of Salafism portray Ibn Hazm as one of the most reactionary and rigid Islamic scholars and an adversary of the rights of the oppressed, both men and women. Those who call for liberation from the authority of the texts in the name of reason—which they claim is a condition to progress—argue that a progressive reading of the text and a literal (or *salafi*) approach to the text are diametrically opposed. They pore over Islamic jurisprudence to find proof for their views but can find no more progressive stances on the economy, on women's rights, on freedom of cultural expression and others than those expressed by Ibn Taymiyya, Ibn al-Qayyim—and, of course, Ibn Hazm, who is the undisputed leading voice of the salafi approach.[130]

The truth is that there can be no renewal except through the salafi methodology. By this we mean that there is no renewal that does not start with a pride in the umma's identity as a civilization and complete confidence in its religion and heritage. And since our history grew out of the sacred text, there can be no authentic renewal outside of its orbit and without building upon it. In fact, intellectual renewal in any civilization must be in this sense "salafi"—that is, a return to the roots as a new starting point for the sake of moving beyond the failed present toward a better future. My only note of caution is that "salafiyya" here means attachment to the texts of Islam and its overall objectives in order to confront attempts at fundamentalist secularization and in no way means opposition to renewal or rejection of the principle of the objectives of the shari'a. Though "salafiyya" approaches carry different understandings, what is common to these approaches is affirming the divine revelation—Qur'an and Sunna—as an essential point of reference. That said, there are different kinds of salafiyya.[131] Let us read carefully this clear declaration of social guarantees in Islam, written by the revolutionary salafi Ibn Hazm:

The rich everywhere are duty-bound to care for the poor, and the state must compel them to do so if zakat is not sufficient for them. They must be provided with a minimum of food for their health and with clothing for both winter and summer; and with housing that protects them from the rain and the sun, and allows them to enjoy privacy. Whoever then has means and sees his brother hungry or naked and does not help him, he has undoubtedly not shown mercy.

Ibn Hazm even permits the hungry person to take what is necessary to meet his needs, even by force. He explains,

Whoever is on the verge of dying of thirst, he must take water from wherever he can, even if he has to fight for it. It is not permissible for a Muslim to be forced to eat a dead animal or pork, when he finds excess food available near him, because it is the duty of he who has extra food to share it with the hungry. Therefore, if the one with food shares it as he ought, then the poor man is not forced to eat from a dead animal or pork meat. If not, he must fight for it, and if he is killed (the hungry man), then his killer will be liable to legal retribution [qisas]; if the latter is killed, he is excluded from God's grace, because he barred someone from receiving his right and according to what God said, he is of the "oppressors": "if one of them [two groups of believers fighting] oppresses the other, fight the oppressors until they submit to God's command;" so the one who violates someone's right has oppressed his brother whose right it was.

The great salafi jurist Ibn Taymiyya in his book *Enforcing Morality in Islam (al-Hisba fi-l-Islam)* comes to a similar conclusion: "If it happens that a group is forced to take shelter in someone's home because they have not found another place to stay, that person is obliged to accommodate them. In the same way, if they need to borrow clothes to keep warm or tools to cook, build, or irrigate with, he must offer this free of charge. Or if they need to borrow a bucket to draw water with, or a pot to cook in, or a shovel to dig with, should he rent them out at cost or for free?"[132] Regarding this question, jurists were of two opinions. The more correct opinion is that one ought to provide these things free of charge if one can spare them, as is written in the Qur'an and Sunna, as God (may He be exalted) says, "woe to those who pray but are heedless of their prayer; those who make a show [of their deeds] and withhold [simple] assistance"[133]

The individual's responsibilify toward his brethren applies to the extent that he may be held legally responsible if he fails to meet their needs when he was able to. The Maliki jurist al-Dardir noted, "One becomes liable for failing to help someone in need if one has the power to do so by means of his position, power or wealth, whether their life is in danger or they need money; he then becomes liable to pay blood money [if the person dies], or the sum of money [that was requested]."[134]

Islam is unique in mandating comprehensive social coverage that includes those in debt, so that it pays their debts and alleviates their troubles; for those in slavery, so that they are freed; for travelers and refugees, whatever their state might have been in their land of origin. Islam was also unique in including in state-provided social coverage care for children in need who have no guardians and monitoring the quality of care provided by guardians where they do exist. It also provided for those of marriageable age to be assisted to get married where they had no guardian or financial means. The caliph 'Umar, for example, added to the state granary flour, dates, oil, and everything that hungry people might need.

Evidently, there is a depth and authenticity to Islam's conception and practice of social security. Clearly too, this conception is unique in tying these rights to God's honoring of humankind as His deputies on earth and in terms of the diversity of institutions providing social welfare—from families to neighborhoods, districts, tribes, civil society all the way to the state. This is consistent with Islam's vision of the relationship between the individual and society with the state, as well as with the doctrine of liberation and service to God. This is the foundation of Islam's social understanding, which refuses a situation in which the state is all-powerful and dominates the individual and civil society, so that the destiny of all of society is tied to that institution, or sometimes even to a single individual, where the state is controlled by a tyrant.

Islam seeks, as we shall see, to achieve a large degree of independence for both the individual and civil society from political authorities in the Islamic state; and this, by virtue of the divine honoring of humanity through the rights by which they are endowed and the duties incumbent upon them, which have no authority unless endowed by God. Islam therefore sought to establish popular institutions independent from the state, like the family, the community, one's neighborhood, and educational and religious institutions like the mosque and the many kinds of social institutions that are supported by the public through religious endowments, which ensures that society enjoys a high degree of independence from the government, which is especially important during times of corruption.

The greatest loss suffered as a result of colonialism was the plundering of most social institutions and the destruction of our social fabric. To make things worse, during the era of "independence" the new colonialists inherited and completed the process of plundering. They perfected the domination and conquest of what remained of the social infrastructure, leaving society at the mercy of their whims and inclinations. This dependence meant that if the rulers were good—which was rare—society was secure, and if they were corrupt, society's needs would be left unmet. What is ironic is that while they continue to invent new ways of destroying the social fabric to strengthen their own grip, they are still not ashamed to use what they call "civil society" to cover up the stranglehold they have on the population.

Islam strives to guarantee people's freedom and the integrity of their worship of God. Among the means it chooses to use is the prohibiting of any monopoly of political and financial power exercised by an elite group. To the contrary, it seeks to disseminate that power to the widest possible circle so as to circumscribe the direct intervention of the state to the smallest possible extent. As the Prophet (PBUH) said, "I am the guardian of him who has no guardian," meaning where society falters and where its balance has broken down.

The Iranian constitution is by and large a worthy effort to produce a contemporary Islamic social blueprint. It features the broad outlines of Islamic social guarantees and the paths that clearly lead to their establishment. It differs significantly from Western and Eastern constitutions and those that find inspiration in them. In it we read,[135]

> The economy of the Islamic Republic of Iran, with its objectives of achieving the economic independence of society, uprooting poverty and deprivation, and fulfilling human needs in the process of development while preserving human liberty, is based on the following criteria:
>
> 1. The provision of basic necessities for all citizens: housing, food, clothing, hygiene, medical treatment, education, and the necessary facilities for the establishment of a family;
> 2. Ensuring conditions and opportunities of employment for everyone, with a view to attaining full employment; placing the means of work at the disposal of everyone who is able to work but lacks the means, in the form of cooperatives, through granting interest-free loans or recourse to any other legitimate means that neither results in the concentration or circulation of wealth in the hands of a few individuals or groups, nor turns the government into a major absolute employer . . .

In the Iranian constitution, which represents the most recent expression of a theory of Islamic social policy, we also read,

> [Article 28] Everyone has the right to choose any occupation he wishes, if it is not contrary to Islam and the public interest, and does not infringe on the rights of others. The government has the duty, with due consideration of the needs of society for different kinds of work, to provide every citizen with the opportunity to work, and to create equal conditions for obtaining it.

[Article 29] To benefit from social security with respect to retirement, unemployment, old age, disability, absence of a guardian, and benefits relating to being stranded, accidents, health services, and medical care and treatment, provided through Insurance or other means, is accepted as a universal right. The government must provide the foregoing services and financial support for every individual citizen by drawing, in accordance with the law, on the national revenues and funds obtained through public contributions.

[Article 30] The government must provide all citizens with free education up to secondary school, and must expand free higher education to the extent required by the country for attaining self-sufficiency.

[Article 31] It is the right of every Iranian individual and family to possess housing commensurate with their needs. The government must make land available for the implementation of this article, according priority to those whose need is greatest, in particular the rural population and the workers.[136]

The above clearly reveals the poverty of the Tunisian constitution relative to the breadth and width of social rights in the Islamic perspective as clearly found in the Qur'an, Sunna, and the legal writings of reformers, or their practical applications as in the Iranian constitution. All this leads Tunisians and their counterparts elsewhere to wonder about the brevity of their own constitutions compared to the general march of humanity toward the adoption of the principles of justice and equality. Should we not be ashamed of our hesitation to this day to enact compulsory elementary and secondary education, or affirm the right of every citizen to employment and social security? Instead, the wealthy in our countries, who live in palaces, spend their time criticizing "religious extremism" in order to distract the disenfranchised from the poor suburbs around our cities or the deprived regions to the northwest and south and dissuade them from adopting Islam as a means to recover their usurped rights and violated dignity; of being able to censure their brutal dictators cruel tyrants and provide spaces of security and national solidarity, freedom, integrity, and dignity, so as to release the people's real potential.

The Right to a Fair Trial

Justice in Islam is the universe. It is the order God has chosen for His creation, and for the sake of establishing that order among them He sent His messengers. As we read in the Qur'an, "He has raised up the sky. He has set the balance so that you may not exceed in the balance: weigh with justice and do not fall short in the balance."[137] Justice is an absolute value that cannot be limited by any relationship, religion, or benefit, or by any motive, be it friendship or enmity. The sacred texts speak with one voice on this issue, directing Muslims to initiate a great legal revolution so as to inscribe the law of justice in all manner of human interactions. Moreover, they created a judicial system with high standards for those who held positions within it in terms of knowledge, integrity, and impartiality, and its judges enjoyed high social standing, great learning, and independence.

Not even rulers were immune from the powerful reach of the judiciary during the Prophet's rule in Medina and that of the Rightly Guided Caliphs. Thereafter, naked power sought to exempt rulers from the judges' reach, and especially on issues that threatened these rulers' grip on power. In other domains, however, judges retained the last word, though perhaps in the modern era the judiciary suffered its greatest period of decline under regimes that derived their laws and modes of training of judges from external sources and marginalized the magnificent heritage of Islam in this field. Despite all the assertions about an independent judiciary and the separation of powers, the judiciary has become subservient to executive power, to an unprecedented extent in the history of Islamic civilization, not even witnessed under foreign occupation.

The Right to Safety or Political Asylum

This is the right granted by the Islamic state to any person, regardless of origin or religious affiliation, who comes to Muslims asking to live safely among them. It is the state's duty to guarantee this person's right and to protect him until he decides to return to his homeland or to another place, on the basis of this verse, "If any one of the idolaters should seek your protection [Prophet Muhammad], grant it to him so that he may hear the word of God, then take him to a place safe for him, for they are people who do not know."[138] The commentator Ibn Kathir remarks, "Anyone who comes from the Abode of War into the Abode of Islam, bringing a message, or on a trade mission, seeking to make peace or engage in truce negotiations, or for any other similar reason, and asks the ruler or his deputy for safety, it will be given him as long as he is in danger, and this until he goes back to safety or to his homeland."

Sayyid Qutb wrote, "Any non-Muslim who seeks asylum and safety in the Abode of Islam should be granted it. It is a religion that grants knowledge to those who do not know, and asylum to those who seek it, even those enemies who have raised their weapons against it, transgressed, it or waged war against it."[139]

Indeed, it is in the atmosphere of safety and justice, which is afforded by a Muslim society and offered to those who are persecuted from whatever background or religious affiliation, that opportunities for dialogue and inquiry into the truth of Islam can grow. Thus Islam preceded both theoretically and practically what we know today as political asylum, which has been codified in the United Nations Geneva Convention Relating to the Status of Refugees (1951). Further, it is striking to note that during the age of prosperity among Muslim societies, a great number of cultured foreign elites joined their ranks, as well as religious minorities persecuted by the churches in their own lands. By contrast today, intellectuals and political groups persecuted for their convictions, including Islamic ones, do not head toward Muslim nations but rather toward the West.

This confirms that the most important characteristic of civilization is that it provides room and opportunity for freedom, security, innovation, tolerance, and coexistence amid diversity, regardless of whether it is Muslim or not. On the other hand, the features of underdevelopment are also manifest: narrow-mindedness, absence of tolerance, inability to tolerate or deal with diversity, or coexist with those who are different, whether this applies to Muslims or non-Muslims. Finally, what is even stranger is that developing Muslim nations are not simply content with strangling freedoms and persecuting rights activists within their own borders, but they are incapable of accepting the existence of freedom outside of their realms and pursue those who fled from their repression in ways reminiscent of seventh-century Arabia, when the Meccans chased those Companions of the Prophet (PBUH) who had found refuge in Abyssinia, which was ruled by a just king, according to the Prophet's description. This is the epitome of backwardness.

CONCLUSION

Islam at its core is a mission to establish justice and to free humanity from all forms of tyranny. It is a mission of unrelenting struggle to achieve and protect people's interests, whether those related to their existence or those necessary for their development and civilizational advancement, or those basic necessities, such as the preservation of religion, life, intellect, progeny, and property, and finally those related to justice and liberation. As such, Islam cannot but rejoice and welcome anything that elevates humankind's conscience, since, regardless of any other consideration, it recognizes that all human beings by virtue of their humanity, regardless of any other consideration, have shared and equal rights. This includes dignity and all the rights and liberties that flow from it, as spelled out in the declarations of human rights and related international covenants and charters.

Indeed, Islam celebrates and welcomes this, considering it part of what its message aspires to achieve. Thus, the general relationship is one of harmony between these declarations and covenants and the values and principles of Islam, despite some differences of perspective and outcomes. However, what Islam deplores is the glaring disparity between the beauty of these declarations and the egregious ways in which they are applied. In reality, human rights conventions and international law are not what determine relations between countries and the relationship between rulers and those governed. Rather, these relations are governed by the disregard of laws, the use of any means to achieve ends, opportunism, dishonesty, and the law of the jungle. These are some of the results of the materialistic philosophies that to a large extent mar today's global culture.

Part II

RIGHTS AND POLITICAL FREEDOMS

The meaning of "rights and political freedoms" in its constitutional usage is that the umma (here, "the people") is the source of authority[1] and the bearer of the highest sovereignty in matters of governance, be it through choosing rulers, overseeing them, holding them accountable, or removing and replacing them.[2] Political freedoms are a set of binding rights recognized by the state for its citizens, such as the right to elections, whether direct or indirect, the right to a free press, the right to freedom of assembly, of forming a political party and unionization, and all other peaceful forms of protest and mobilization.[3]

The Universal Declaration of Human Rights—which is the most important contemporary document offering a concise summary of humanity's thinking on rights and liberties and providing a model that nations can use in their constitutions—states that every individual has the right to participate in managing the public affairs of his nation either directly or indirectly by means of representatives that are freely chosen, and to hold any of the public offices available. It also declares that the will of the people is the source of political authority, and that this will is expressed by periodic and genuine elections run by universal and equal suffrage and held by secret vote or by a similar procedure that guarantees free suffrage.[4]

Almost all modern constitutions establish the sovereignty of the people as one of the fundamental principles of democracy, and this authority is practiced by way of elections and referenda, freedom of expression, freedom of the press, freedom of assembly, the freedom to form political and professional associations, and the like. And among the guarantees provided we also find the separation of powers, the independence of the judiciary, and freedom of assembly. In the Preamble to the Tunisian constitution, for instance, we read the declared intent of the people's representatives in the Constitutional Assembly to be "a democracy founded on the sovereignty of the people, and characterized by a stable political system based on separation of powers . . . We proclaim that the republican regime constitutes the best guarantee for the respect of human rights, for the establishment of equality among citizens."[5] Then at the end of the Preamble, we read, "We, the representatives of the free and sovereign Tunisian people do, by the grace of God, proclaim this Constitution."

In what follows, I offer some articles of the Tunisian constitution:

Chapter 1

Article 1: Tunisia is a free, independent and sovereign State. Its religion is Islam, its language is Arabic and its form of government is Republican.

Article 3: Sovereignty belongs to the Tunisian people, who exercise it in accordance with the Constitution.

Article 18: The people shall exercise the legislative power through the Chamber of Deputies . . . The members of the Chamber of Deputies are elected by universal, free and direct suffrage . . .

Article 20: Any citizen is eligible to vote who is at least twenty years old, and holds Tunisian nationality for at least five years.

Article 21: Any voter born to a Tunisian father or mother and who is at least twenty-three years of age on the day he submits his candidacy, is eligible for election to the Chamber of Deputies.

Article 25: Every deputy is the representative of the entire Nation.

Article 28: The Chamber of Deputies and the Chamber of Advisors exercise legislative power. The power to initiate laws is shared equally by the President of the Republic and the members of the Chamber of Deputies. Priority is given to bills submitted by the President of the Republic. The Chamber of Deputies shall sign off on the Bills concerning the budget and their adoption.

Article 32: The President of the Republic shall ratify treaties.

In Chapter 3, the constitution presents the president of the republic as representing executive power:

Article 38: The President of the Republic is the Head of State. His religion shall be Islam.

Article 39: The President of the Republic shall be elected for a term of five years through universal, free, direct and secret ballot.[6]

Article 40: Any Tunisian whose only nationality is Tunisian, who is of Muslim religion and whose father and paternal and maternal grandfather have been of Tunisian nationality without discontinuity, who is at least forty years of age and no more than seventy-five, and enjoys all of his civil and political rights may stand as a candidate for the presidency of the republic.

Article 42: The elected President of the Republic takes, before the Chamber of Deputies and the Chamber of Advisors meeting in common session, the following oath: "I swear by Almighty God to safeguard the independence of the homeland and the integrity of its territory, to respect the Constitution and the law, and watch scrupulously over the interests of the whole Nation."

The constitution also defines the qualifications of the president of the republic:

Article 41: The President of the Republic is the guarantor of national independence, of territorial integrity, and of respect of its constitution. He strives to ensure the proper functioning of constitutional public institutions and assures the continuity of the state. He enjoys judicial immunity in the exercise of his duties. He also enjoys such judicial immunity after the presidential term for all acts executed in fulfillment of his duties.

Article 44: The President of the Republic is the Commander-in-Chief of the Armed Forces.

Article 48: The President of the Republic concludes treaties. He declares war and concludes peace with the approval of the Chamber of Deputies.

Article 49: The President of the Republic directs the general policies of the State, defines its basic orientations, and informs the Chamber of Deputies accordingly (Articles 50, 51, 52).

Article 53: The President of the Republic names the prime minister and the rest of the government's members. He heads the government and dissolves it at will. He has the final say on laws and he has the right to send back to parliament a draft law for a second reading. Once completed, if it is passed by a majority of two-thirds, then he signs it and executes it. If he is temporarily unable to carry out his duties, he may delegate to his prime minister.

Article 57: Should the office of President of the Republic become vacant because of death, resignation, or absolute incapacity, the Constitutional Council meets immediately and declares a definitive vacancy and notifies the Chamber of Deputies and the Chamber of Advisors, which will undertake the president's functions for forty-five days.

Article 58: The government ensures the implementation of the State's general policy according to the orientations defined by the president of the republic, to whom it is responsible (59).

Article 62: When a motion of censure is adopted by an absolute majority of the members of the Chamber of Deputies, the President of the Republic will accept its resignation.

Article 63: If the Chamber of Deputies adopts a second motion of censure by a two-thirds majority of its members, the President of the Republic may either accept the government's resignation or dissolve the Chamber of Deputies.

Chapter 4 of the Tunisian constitution is dedicated to the powers of the judiciary, and we read in Article 64: "Judgments are rendered in the name of the People and carried out in the name of the President of the Republic" and in Article 65: "The judicial branch is independent. In exercising their authority, judges are subject only to the authority of the law." Article 66 reads: "Judges are appointed by Presidential decree on the recommendation of the Higher Judicial Council."

Chapter 8 of the constitution provides for local authorities, namely municipal councils and regional councils.

Chapter 9 states that the Constitutional Council reviews bills proposed by the president to ensure that they align with the constitution and treaties that have been ratified. The opinion of the Constitutional Assembly is binding on all state institutions. It is composed of nine members, four named by the president of the republic, two by the president of the parliament, and the last three are the president of the Court of Cassation, the president of the Administrative Court, and the president of the Court of Auditors.

Chapter 10 defines the procedure for amending the constitution: either the president or a third of members of parliament have the right to request an amendment to the constitution, as long as this does not threaten the republican nature of the state. The president of the republic must then put the amendment to a referendum. Any revision of the constitution must be agreed by two-thirds of parliament.

We alluded in the last chapter to the freedoms contained in the constitution, such as the right to equality among citizens in both rights and responsibilities, and the right to freedom of thought and expression, freedom of the press, of publication and assembly, and the right of association and unionization. That was in the context of presenting a general description of the Tunisian constitution in order to highlight the general structure of a state inspired by contemporary democratic regimes. Thus the fundamental characteristic of a democratic state is political freedom, although the constitution empties this concept of its substance. It does this on the institutional level through the composition of constitutional institutions and, on the legal level, through the setting of restrictions on rights. The constitution states that a right can be restricted through law, which means that laws exceed their main function of regulating access to a right and instead serve to usurp rights entirely.

Instead, the law gives the president and his right hand, the interior minister, free rein in violating people's lives, dignity, and property when the ruler can protect all his deeds with an immunity that lasts throughout his tenure and even extends beyond it. At the same time, when he disposes of financial resources—though mostly hidden from the public—that are close to those enjoyed by absolute monarchs, he accumulates all power in his own hands as the president, unnacountable to anyone.

For all these reasons, unsurprisingly, a coup d'état was the only recourse for solving the political crisis created by Bourguiba's long illness and senility. The constitution had not designed any instrument for addressing such a crisis. The situation today is even worse, with the constitutional amendments that take up more than half the articles in the 2002 constitution. These were passed by means of a referendum that reminds one of communist referenda, since it granted the president unlimited tenure, with the exception of an age limit that could easily be raised at any time. This provoked the most important opposition groups to refuse these amendments and the cavalier way in which they were thrust upon the people. Especially grievous was the electoral law that went into detail regarding the presidential elections, stipulating that he should face nominal competition by imposing conditions on those competing candidates that would change with every round of elections depending on the situation. The farce reached the point that one candidate in the 1999 presidential elections voted for the incumbent himself. Thus, these amendments became the target of jokes as well as emulation by similar rulers, as happened in Egypt under Mubarak.[7]

This is in addition to the constant gap between theory and practice, which means that the principles of political modernity in this constitution are merely ink on paper, similar to other Arab constitutions. Among these principles, you will find the people's sovereignty, elections and political representation, majority rule, the republican presidential model, the separation of powers, civil liberties, including freedom of the press, of association, of unionization, and of local governance via municipalities, and an independent judiciary. However, all these principles together constitute democratic governance only if they are actually respected and not merely taken as a glamorous cover that disguises and falsifies the regime's true nature, which is the corrupt rule of one man who plays with the principles of democratic governance on the surface but at heart is deeply hostile to the principle of the separation of powers and holds all executive powers in his own hands. This gives him free rein to control the Supreme Court, to render judgments in court, to appoint judges, depose them, promote them, and transfer them.

The president also has the power to dissolve parliament. By means of his party, which has been in power since independence, he controls who the candidates for parliament will be, and appoints members of the Council of Advisors and the Constitutional Court. Moreover, he names the Grand Mufti, imams, university deans, and heads of the biggest media organizations and many other bodies. What state institutions are left that he cannot influence? Who can hold him accountable or remove him? There is no meaning left to the idea of "constitution" itself whose essence is to subject the ruler to the authority of the law. This was the idea that the people fought for, as they spilled out into the streets in massive marches while being sprayed by French bullets. Their main slogan was "A Tunisian constitution," and for nearly a century, little of this has been achieved.

The concrete practice of political authority is the real test of a constitution— whether it can guarantee respect for the dignity of the citizen. It has exposed the true nature of this regime, as all international and local human rights organizations have attested, uniting to condemn the regime for subverting the people's will and systematically violating human rights. The regime practiced torture methodically in order to terrorize citizens, staging sham trials to get rid of political opponents, violating freedom of expression and tightening their control over citizens, even in people's private lives, and their choice of clothing.[8] This is all part of a machine to control and dominate, to break down society and weaken its capacity to resist. No wonder Tunisia has "achieved"—according to journalist Hazem Saghia's phrase—the longest reports from Amnesty International.[9]

3

Basic Democratic Principles

Any discussions of political freedoms in the modern era can hardly be separated from democratic systems of government, given that democracy offers the best mechanisms to enable citizens to practice their basic freedoms, including political ones. Put otherwise, it is the least bad form of government, according to one politician who defended it. So what are the basic principles that make a political system democratic? Have they experienced any evolution over time? If so, what are these changes and what factors have brought them about? How might the democratic system be improved? Finally, what are the basic principles of an Islamic political system? These are the points covered in this chapter.

THE BASIC PRINCIPLES OF THE DEMOCRATIC SYSTEM

OVERVIEW

Democratic systems were not constructed by theoreticians, legal specialists, or political scientists; rather, they came out of historical developments over centuries. Many of the principles and values of democracy derive from Europe's political experiments and the evolution of its thought from the Middle Ages to the Renaissance, and from the Renaissance to the Reformation, and from the common heritage of human civilization. Democracy continues to develop, gradually in some cases (as in the United Kingdom) or by fits of revolution (as in France) to become the foundation for a new system that incorporates older elements that agree with its logic.

Democracy has also been influenced by the evolution of science and the growth of production and the invention of more advanced means of transportation, which led to the discovery of new worlds, and with them, the opportunity to accumulate enormous wealth in Europe and shift the balance of global power in its favor. This evolution in Europe's governance systems and means of production were also connected to their encounter with Muslims in the course of their pilgrimages to the Holy Land and the Crusades, which fundamentally transformed their social structure and values. One result from all of this was the emergence of free democratic political systems.[1] In fact, European contact with the Islamic world caused a psychological shock that contributed to awakening it from the slumber of feudalism, the stupor of ecclesiatical religion, and the dictatorship of kings and the aristocracy.

No doubt, Renaissance thinking played a pioneering role in the revolution against the old order and its symbols, institutions, and values. This happened by means of adjustments and compromises between the various classes in conflict in order to prevent recourse to violence and as a way to resolve conflicting interests. Such social struggle was only natural when new classes were calling for changes in their favor—changes that would take away the feudal powers' privileges and overturn the old political structures, values, and philosophy. At the very least this would reduce the kings' power in favor of the new classes traders, merchants, and artisans.

Unsurprisingly, in such a social climate revolutionary slogans began to surface, calling for the end of absolute monarchy, for humanity to be freed from despotism, and for the elites to be stripped of their privileges so that all would be equal. Among other slogans: liberation to affirm the dignity of humankind in the face of ecclesiatical institutions and feudalism; empowerment of the people to be the source of sovereignty instead of kings; pluralism instead of tyranny; and the separation of powers to prevent its concentration in the hands of one person, which inevitably causes tyranny. Therefore, the most important principles that liberal democracy called for were popular sovereignty, elections, the separation of powers, and public freedoms (freedom of expression, of the press, of organized labor, of multiple political parties, etc.). Altogether, they represent the will to empower the ruled with the tools to stand up to the rulers and influence their decisions.

The spirit of liberation, equality, representation, pluralism and competition remained the essential components of Western democracy until the Second World War. Then various economic, technological, political, and social developments converged, bringing changes to the democratic system with its capitalist framework. The role of the state would no longer be neutral in the ongoing social struggle, limiting itself to the defense of the nation's security internally and externally. Rather, it came under the new and growing pressure exerted by trade unions, public opinion, socialist parties, and a number of other organized forces and associations striving to reach a new balance of power with the capitalist class, which was forced to accept the state's active intervention in economic and social life and inclusion of social guarantees to provide an acceptable level of human dignity for the working class. As a result, the democratic system in the West moved beyond the stage of merely formal freedoms as represented in the declarations of human rights, in the principle of popular sovereignty as played out in parliaments and elections, in the right of the majority to rule and the right of the minority to oppose and then transform itself into the majority (thus creating an alternation of power). All of this led to a new relationship between the masses of citizens and the institutions of political power.

In essence, it is a system where the masses have the right to make demands and the state is obligated to answer that call; a system that empowers the people to effectively influence and participate in the affairs of state, and thus to truly take control of their destiny, and not merely to choose representatives. Yet this participation requires the continuous supply of necessary tools to ensure that participation, including economic and social guarantees, which in fact belong to the people by right, and means of communication that are open and renegotiable through public institutions, including the tools of a free media.

The Algerian thinker Malik Bennabi[2] went beyond this as he defined the essence of the democratic system. For him it was a comprehensive educational project that the people needed to embark on psychologically, morally, socially, and politically. Democracy is not merely the process of transferring power to the masses and the declaration that the people, according to the text of the constitution, have become the locus of sovereignty. In Britain, for instance, it is not a constitutional text—which basically is nonexistent—that guarantees the rights and freedoms of the British people; rather, it is the parliamentarian spirit itself that stands as the guarantor of democracy.[3]

Our great scholar Bennabi, descendant of Ibn Khaldun, dove into the European Renaissance, examining the roots of the democratic sensibility that burst forth in the famous declaration of human rights in the United States of America. That was the spiritual and political crowning of the French Revolution, and he found that it originated in the Protestant Reformation and before that in the Renaissance—both movements constituting the main cultural element behind the European identity as expressed in spirituality, art, and intellectual production. In fact, this is what produced the humanist school and its particular esteem for the citizen and human being.[4]

In short, the democratic system is both form and content. Concerning its form, you see it in the principle of popular sovereignty—the people are the source of all political authority that is practiced by means of constitutional mechanisms that vary in their details from country to country. But they all share the principles of equality, elections, separation of powers, political pluralism, freedom of expression, of assembly, and of forming trade unions. They also agree on allowing the majority to govern and the minority to form the opposition, while alternating who is in power. Finally, this evolution eventually led to a consensus around a series of social guarantees for all citizens.

With regard to the substance of the democratic system, it is an affirmation of the intrinsic value of the human being by virtue of which he acquires a set of genuine rights, which guarantee his dignity and right to effectively participate in managing public affairs, and the capacity to pressure those in power and to influence them through the instruments made available to him, including the power to forge his own destiny and protection from despotism and tyranny. In sum, it is the right of those being ruled to choose their government[5] and the latter's accountability to them.

No doubt, the absolute best political system is the one that is built upon the recognition of human dignity and the availability of political and educational mechanisms that secure that dignity, offer guarantees against tyranny, and create a climate most likely to unleash people's natural abilities, foster personal growth, and enable them to share in shaping their future. When this is happening, the gap between ruler and ruled narrows and almost disappears, politically, economically, and culturally, so that the ruler becomes a servant to the people, answerable before the law and an ordinary citizen like others. He is a member of society, albeit like an older sibling, father, or guardian.

This sharing of power in the social and political realms—and not mere representation—is at the heart of this ideal envisaged by the democratic model. In fact, the highest ideal attached to democracy is that the ruled become rulers in order to achieve for themselves and by themselves the goals and objectives they expect.[6] Indeed, the level of popular participation in public affairs is the principal criterion determining to what extent a regime is democratic, and the higher it is, the closer a regime comes to this ideal.

THE STATE ACCORDING TO THE WESTERN PERSPECTIVE

Law and Religion

No research into the history of human societies has indicated the existence of a society in which people did not worship some kind of deity with humble submission, or that one god was not the source of all authority. From that submission to a higher will was born the idea of law. Then that divine will, which was expressed through clergy or religious scholars, became the essence of the law and the source of its binding authority. For in the beginning the first legal rules grew out of religious rules. In every society, in fact, the law emerged in close connection to religion and intermingled with it, to the point that the members of the clergy were also the jurists.[7] As for superstition and acts of sorcery and magic, they emerged in parallel with the true religion that God sent down to the prophets through revelation in order to guide people to the true worship of God. This worship includes humble submission to a set of rules of conduct, which are the main vehicle for leading people out of the sway of their passions and desires and into the submission to a single authority that transcends them—that is, the law of God [the Shari'a].

Nevertheless, in many civilizations religion evolved into an institution that monopolized the sacred texts in the name of the God. Seeing this, kings were quick to exploit the great influence of religious institutions in order to endow their own authority with the aura of holiness and turn their own will into divine will. This naturally produced an overlap between the law's authority and the will of the ruler, who then could say he was the state—"I am the shadow of God on earth"—just as his religious counterpart, the priest, could say "I am religion." Often, then, the two sides would fight in order to claim power and authority for themselves. This was catastrophic for both religion and politics, as grabbing power became the fundamental goal of both sides.

The Contemporary Political Revolution

For this reason, it is no wonder that political revolutions in the West over the last two centuries have centered on liberating the law from the will of the clergy and the authority of kings, as a transition from the rule of the individual to the rule of law. For this they had to strip kings of their sovereignty and power, which they claimed came to them directly from God. Some even claimed to be God themselves, like Pharaoh, who famously stated, "I am your Almighty Lord"—that is, possessor of absolute authority. Nor were Persian or Byzantine and other rulers any humbler in their claims to power, since their will was in every case the law. In prerevolutionary France, for instance, the king would enact laws to regulate the powers of the state, but he remained above those laws, claiming absolute sovereignty.[8] Thus, that was the goal of modern revolutions—limiting the power of kings and clergy, and then transferring that authority to the people or to their representatives, because sovereignty now belongs to the people. Thus, a shift took place from the authority of a single individual (autocracy) to the rule of law. Thus, legality represents, in effect, the pillar of the modern Western state, along with sovereignty.

Legality

The modern Western state's greatest source of pride is that it is subject to the rule of law. That means that government actions submit to fixed and certain regulations, which individuals can enforce by standing before independent judges.[9] This is what is meant by legality, and it is the basis for the functioning of the modern state. The rule of law by definition is political power bound by law,[10] and the authority of law over administrative processes. A closely related word, "legitimacy," has both a positive and negative meaning. Negatively, legitimacy is when the state refrains from any action that is not in harmony with applicable laws. Positively, it is the state's obligation to respect the authority of the law by respecting society's fundamental values and highest goals[11]; it is the state's striving to achieve the common good which leads to people's voluntary acceptance of the laws and statutes of the political order and to be convinced of their just nature and conformity with the needs and values of society.[12]

Sovereignty

One of the main concepts related to the Western state is the idea that the state represents the highest authority, particularly in the legislative domain. There is no power beside or above it.[13] Sovereignty belongs to the ruling authority, whether a person or a body, which holds the power to legislate for society. In light of this power to change laws, that authority is considered the holder of the highest political power in the state, as the supreme legislator.

In the Middle Ages, it was the pope who held this authority in his quality as Christ's deputy, and before this, the Emperor Constantine's will had the force of law. Then the modern state appeared as the heir to that sovereignty, meaning that it held supreme legislative power in two senses: there was no power higher than it, and its authority could not be contested. Its sovereignty is absolute within its borders, as it is the supreme legislator; and outside its borders it is not bound by the laws of any other state in its relation with other nations. In this regard it has the right to declare war, and even annex the territory of the vanquished nation.[14]

The concept of sovereignty is a legal concept, since it is meant to confer legitimacy. The law, after all, is what is issued by the ruler, the possessor of sovereignty, either in person or as a body. It is law by virtue of its being issued by the highest authority. From another standpoint, nothing that is decreed by someone other than the ruler has the force of law. So if the law is that which is issued by the ruler, it is critical to identify who the ruler is. The answer to that can only be derived from a complex set of legal rules, which in themselves need a source of legality, since the purpose of sovereignty is to give the law legitimacy.

Despite this logical conundrum, which is where the theory of sovereignty leads, sovereignty continues to be an acceptable idea to those who use it, as long as it fulfills a practical objective—for the life of the law, as Judge Holmes once said, "The life of the law has not been logic; it has been experience."[15] This concept of the state was long premised on the existence of absolute sovereignty that had no need of legal justification for its rules; and on the necessity of submission to the state, even if its sovereignty could not be established, no matter how much it collided with morality, religion, and the law of justice. This was the concept of state promoted in a great number of writings by Western writers and political theorists, like the Englishman Hobbes, the Italian Machiavelli, and the German Hegel.

Hegel wrote, for example: "The idea that ruled over the history of humanity is that of reason . . . Reason actualized itself progressively in history through the struggle of ideas. The highest level of that actualization is the nation state, which is the incarnation of reason. This is the absolute reality that transcends the reality of citizens, who must totally submit to the higher goals of the state. Thus the conflict among nation states is a necessary phenomenon for the development and freedom of humanity. As for the struggle between the state and the citizen, it is not even conceivable, in that the state is always right since it embodies absolute thought. Its will is the standard measure of morality and its action the balance of truth."[16]

In truth, modern wars between nation-states have been about glory and wealth, even at the expense of justice and freedom. Note the clear link between those wars and this concept of the state—a "god," which derives its legitimacy from its own self-definition as the source of all legality, yet accountable to no one else. Therefore, the representative or representatives of sovereign power are immune from prosecution. Clearly, it was national pride and a deep desire to free themselves from the authority of the church, feudal princes, and despotic kings that led to the great effort Europeans deployed in thought and action in order to establish this new authority endowed with absolute sovereignty— the state. This meant accepting something surrounded by confusion,[17] delusion,[18] and irrationality,[19] which makes the western concept of the state rather supported on an elephant, to use a picture from ancient conceptions of the world.[20]

This conception of the state that was conceived by the luminaries of the Enlightenment, or rather those who were fleeing the tyranny of the church and feudal rulers, was made into the source and objective of all else, refusing any authority higher than itself and needing no justification for its decisions before anyone. Still, its accomplishments are many: it succeeded in establishing the rule of law and using it to limit the actions of rulers, recognizing people's rights and protecting them through the judiciary, a free press, freedoms of expression and assembly, and the separation of powers. Yet in spite of all of this, such a conception of the state also led to horrific wars in which the strong trampled the weak, and to the appearance of fascist, Nazi, and communist dictatorships. This conception of the state was unable to provide a rationale against colonialism: occupation of small nations, the pillaging of their wealth, and even genocide. A great deal of intellectual effort has been required in order to soften this concept of sovereignty and bring it into harmony with new developments such as the emergence of weapons of mass destruction, the communications revolution that has almost erased physical distance, and the emergence of environmental challenges, increasingly complex international relations, and the growth of international law. This has made nations more interdependent, creating a need for greater dialogue and exchange, for the search for peaceful solutions to international conflicts, and for limiting the threat of mass destruction, which in itself is a product of technological development.

In light of this, there was a growing conviction that there was no escape for the human community if it wanted to survive other than by limiting this concept of sovereignty for the sake of a law that is more general and comprehensive—that is, international law and the international covenants on human rights. These, for the most part, are based on the concept of natural law, meaning that human nature is one regardless of time or place, and if we were to examine its depths, we would discover fundamental, objective ethical rules. Natural law, according to its advocates, embodies the central idea of a higher law that regulates positive law and represents an ethical law independent from a nation's law, through which one can ascertain whether that law is oppressive or immoral.[21] Thus, the state should follow the principles of natural law if it is to be legitimate and more just.[22]

The school of natural law emerged in the seventeenth century in Europe from the idea that the individual is prior to and superior to society, which exists to serve the individual, and that by virtue of his humanity he possesses rights that stem from his nature and not from any law of the state. This is because rights precede the existence of the state, and as a result, the state is not allowed to violate them. If it does, it loses people's trust and it gives them the right to regain sovereignty.

To a certain extent natural law emerged from a period when its theoretical foundations were obscure, when it acted as a loose cloak that every clergyman or unjust ruler could put on to grant legitimacy to his orders or prohibitions. It surpassed this phase when it began to be seen as the source of essential democratic rights that constrain the ruler's freedom. These were enshrined in the UDHR and other international human rights covenants, which were then included to differing degrees in most constitutions. This is what gave them supremacy over any law issued by a state and granted permission to the courts to refuse to apply any legislation that contravened these natural rights, like freedom of thought and ownership, and remaining freedoms, both personal and public.

International law found in the concept of natural law a beneficial foundation to defend its own existence, considering that natural law was loftier than all the specifics of each nation, but it created a difficulty for the proponents of the idea of sovereignty as the foundation for the state, since to recognize international law is to acknowledge an authority over and beyond the state, which constrains its legislative will. It also means an obligation to submit to the requirements and rules of international law, something that the advocates of the absolute power of the state refuse. For them, there can be no validity in placing international law above national law. Still, while remaining sovereign, a state can recognize international laws as a set of self-imposed restrictions. It could also consider its sovereignty absolute in areas other than international ones—that is, in affairs concerning its relations with other entities.

Furthermore, the body of international law remains relatively simple and in many instances lacks the power of enforcement. Further, for the implementation of its rulings, as is the case for rulings made by the International Tribunal in The Hague, it needs the states concerned to recognize its jurisdiction.[23] However, whatever the justification might be, or the methods by which the principle of sovereignty—which is the cornerstone of the Western state—is made to accord with the recognition of international human rights covenants, international law and its institutions possess an authority that supersedes that of states and obliges them to conform to its norms when exercising their power. Unavoidably, this has raised some doubts with regard to the principle of absolute sovereignty as the foundation of the modern state. This has opened the way for speaking of limited sovereignty, even if there are various schools of thought regarding its nature, the source of its value, and what entity has the authority to limit that sovereignty, surpass it, and make it conform and submit to its own requirements. Is it "natural law" that has such authority? Or some kind of moral law? Or international human rights covenants, or international law more broadly? Or God's absolute authority of which His eternal revelation speaks?

To conclude, what is evident is that the two foundational principles of the Western state—legality, or the rule of law, and sovereignty of the people are important but not sufficient to constrain human beings' instinct to dominate others and exploit their need to live together in community as social beings. Fundamentally, the rule of law means the state's submission to the law, and the people's sovereignty denotes here the state's supreme authority to legislate. No authority transcends it, it does not submit to any exterior authority and its authority is derived from the people by means of general elections. These two principles form the essence of the Western state. Their establishment represents an important step in affirming the authority of the law and the people's authority above that of the ruler, and in conferring permanent rights to citizens, and thereby giving them the means to resist autocracy. However, the political conundrum remains that these two principles are unable, on their own, to guard against the human tendency toward domination or exploitation of others.

WHERE IS THE DEMOCRATIC SYSTEM IN RELATION TO ITS IDEAL?

By definition, democracy is the rule of the people, which presupposes the equal participation of all individuals in governing. This is difficult at best, not because of a practical impossibility—either because not enough people have the capacity to meaningfully participate, or because too many are stripped of their civil rights—but because even within the circle of politically minded citizens who enjoy all their civil rights there are no agreed-upon criteria to define who these are. In ancient Athens, the number of citizens did not exceed 20,000, while the total population was 320,000, as women, slaves, and foreigners were excluded from political life. For a long time in Britain only the rich could vote, and women only gained the right to vote in 1928. In France it wasn't until 1945, and Switzerland until 1971 that women could vote. Some American states still do not allow black and white citizens to enjoy equal political rights in reality.

Theoretically the power of those voting is the same for all, but in practice we find a whole class of people who exert undue political influence, like those who own big corporations, cultural elites, and the owners of radio and television stations, as well as those who work under them, including directors and managers, journalists, political and cultural pressure groups, and trade unions. Theoretically all their votes are equal to those of the unemployed, or the workers in industry and agriculture, or minorities like African Americans in the United States. These, in fact, are the majority of voters, but in reality they tend to be highly influenced by the upper classes, which makes the definition of democracy as "the rule by the people for the people" an ideal vision impossible to achieve.

Some modern theorists correct this view of democratic rule by stipulating that it is not the rule of the people but rather a pluralistic form of governance led by an elite group of citizens and political leaders, which involves a dialogue—or conflict—between the representatives of different factions and interests. That said, the elites take power through the will of the voting masses, which in fact turns democracy in practice into the rule of the elites in the name of the people.[24] But opponents of the traditional theory of democracy go further than that in their critique, casting doubt on the credibility of the masses' delegation of power to the elites. Is it a conscious and free act of delegation, or is it an ignorant, misled, or involuntary act that more likely in its essence is akin to compulsion and deceit? Western democracies established political equality and eliminated aristocratic privileges, but progressively gave birth to economic inequality which is leading to the creation of a new aristocracy based on the ownership of capital and media monopolies, which then exercise great influence on political parties and public opinion.[25] This makes it possible for the ruling elite to embark on costly wars on behalf of influential people and businesses, despite opposition by millions of citizens.

But does that mean that government ministers, heads of state and parties, and the press are merely puppets in the hands of capitalists, as simplistic Marxist critiques claim? Unfortunately, a good number of Islamists have bought into this view. Maurice Duverger,[26] an influential constitutional law expert and a socialist, refuted this view, arguing that politicians can rely on voters to give them the capacity to resist economic pressures, despite the influence occasioned by these pressures, so that the decisions they make in the end are not dictated by one constituency but rather are taken in the context of a balance between different constituencies. In addition, voters have the opportunity in the next round of elections to punish the elite who previously ignored their voice and replace them with another elite.

Therefore, the democratic model in reality does not represent perfect democracy, but a semi-democracy ("plutodemocracy"), because political power rests partly on the people and partly on money.[27] Other elements in this conflict have appeared, caused by developments in the West. For example, the growing power of federal government has meant the strengthening of central power at the expense of states or provinces and the intensification of conflict between them. The traditional struggle against the king has now turned against the central power of the state in order to guarantee subnational rights, and the traditional theory of the separation of powers has failed to provide a sufficient bulwark against the domination of the central state over the provinces and the executive branch's usurpation of the lion's share of influence at the center.

Yet despite the limited application of the ideals of democracy in allowing the people to govern themselves, the democratic political system, especially after the expansion of social guarantees (before globalization began to eat away at these), maintains a kind of balance between the public opinion of the voting masses and elites and interest groups, although it is often the case that the balance of power favors the latter. Thus an elite often monopolizes political power through its decision making, despite a strong popular movement against it, as happened with the decision to invade Iraq in March 2003 despite broad popular opposition. In the same way, Western nations took a biased position in favor of Zionist injustice toward Palestinians, while public opinion in Europe was increasingly pointing to Israel as the number one obstacle to international peace.

As for the people's democracies founded on Marxist theory, their critique of Western democracy focuses on the fact that they only provide freedoms on paper, while the real influence is exercised by capitalists. So the people will never be granted their rights as long as ownership remains in the hands of a class of capitalists, in whose interests the state will always act. The only path, then, to the freedom of the masses is for them to own the means of production by banning individual ownership.

The problem is that within these "democracies" there is no balance at all, since the people's ownership is in reality the ownership of the single party or the dominant elites within it and sometimes the one man at the top who holds in his hands the keys to everything. This deprives the masses of any means of resisting the state and the party, which have both monopolized all the means of economic, cultural, media, security, and military domination. Despite the constant repetition of empty slogans claiming the empowerment of the people and rights, the people continue to be stripped of even the basic right to protest, strike and assemble, and of any means to pressure rulers besides indifference and lack of productivity, which puts the regime on the path of a slow, inevitable death.

CONCLUSION

The term "democracy," as ʿAbd Allah al-Nafisi has argued, is wide enough to cover a variety of political systems, and elastic to the point of including the people's democracies in the Communist Bloc and the bourgeois democracies in the capitalist camp. In any case, the term is like a coin with two sides:

1. A system of government
2. A collection of institutions, their mission being to carry out two essential functions:
   - First, the ability to gauge the will of the majority as to who will represent them and how they will govern them. This means the freedom to establish political parties, the right to vote in a system of free suffrage,

in which candidates are freely chosen, far from any compulsion or exclusion.

- The provision of suitable means to guarantee that the elected delegates will truly achieve that which the voters have willed, and the power to change them when they have not achieved this. This means the power to monitor government and allow for the alternation of power through peaceful and organized means.[28] There is no doubt that this is considered the greatest outcome of democracy and its core value.

Despite a number of critiques leveled at democracy by focusing on the faults and unjust policies of democratic nations, the model of the democratic regime remains strong. Its appeal largely lies in the defects of competing systems and the lack of an alternative.

Mohammed Abul Qasem Haj Hamad, the author of *The Second Islamic Internationalism*, only saw in democracy a philosophy that grew out of Europe's own struggles, and whose central mission is to keep a lid on its own continuing struggles and prevent them from exploding, simply providing release valves for those tensions. He argues that the conflicts that are now tearing our world apart are nothing but the outcome of that Faustian spirit.[29]

He also argues that no matter how much the scope of popular participation widens, it will never extend beyond national borders, a fact that most certainly ties democracy to nationalism or a form of racism. It is no wonder that you find the oldest contemporary democracies visiting savagery and tyranny on other peoples, and even with respect to the minorities living among them, like African Americans and Muslims. Democracy, in this sense, is not grounded in absolute values but rather on a foundation of the national interest and racism, which in turn produces selfishness, self-gratification, and hegemony in the name of the national interest. According to this logic, people's freedoms and rights are protected for the strongest while the weak are discriminated against. Such a society is unstable, unbalanced, and divided, and even vulnerable to rebellion and violence. Such an environment will persist as long as there is no absolute value that uplifts and guides the human will, be it the will of individuals, a class, a nation. It holds no security for the weak, whether they are a minority within a nation where the will of the majority is sacred and cannot be contested, or another nation lacking the power to stand in the face of its adversary. Therefore, it has no alternative but to submit or be destroyed, which means the survival of the fittest. In other words, might makes right.[30]

Because democracy is a comprehensive idea that can be applied to a wide range of vastly different regimes, it has to be broken down to its basic components in order to apply it to any specific regime. Understanding the nature of any political order requires examining the circumstances that led to its founding and the array of values, ideas, customs, arts, and philosophies adopted by its people that shape their views of humanity and human society. From these stem a combination of behaviors, both individual and collective, produced by values, ideas, customs that define people's relationships with one another and with the "other."

It is not so important to focus on the mechanics of democracies and all their declarations, like the declaration of the people's sovereignty, or human rights, or people's representation in a parliament or a political party, or elections and majority rule. Those democratic practices are widespread and still exist among the worst dictatorships, such as Tunisia. All manner of injustices and cruelties continue to be perpetrated in the name of spreading democracy, from acts of aggression between nations expressed as military occupation or exploitation, to the spreading of immorality and depravity, corruption, and deceit. The effects of colonialism still shape relations between the oldest democracies and weaker nations and especially their former colonies. This can be seen in the penchant for gathering former colonies under a label that reminds them of their colonial past, like the Commonwealth nations or the Francophone nations. Still today, the democratic system allows the passing of laws that allow military occupations, preemptive strikes, and preventive wars, and the destruction of the natural environment in a way that truly threatens all human life.

This is in addition to laws allowing gambling, homosexuality, and same-sex marriage, and modern forms of infanticide (abortion and family planning).[31] Democratic systems still allow the imposition of unfair trade conditions on weaker nations despite their awareness of the tragic conditions these nations endure. Does not the reality of a quarter of humanity suffering from starvation every year with tens of millions dying every year, most of them children, attest to the failure of contemporary democracy, of its legal framework and its humanist intellectual roots to promote a sense of compassion and humanity and to give to human dignity greater priority instead of all the billions spent on national welfare and glory by democracies in the East and the West? Don't the achievements of today's democracies pale in the face of this tragedy— achievements like the freedoms and rights they provide to Western nations? The destiny of humanity should be seen as a whole, and all the more since it is being made so through technological progress and the communications revolution. In such a world, should not acts of aggression even against one person be considered an aggression against all of humanity, something that threatens its security and welfare? Should not humanity rise up as one to put an end to this aggression?

The problem lies not with the mechanisms of democracy: elections, parliaments, majority rule, party pluralism, and freedom of the press. It comes from what is hidden in Western materialist and nationalist political philosophies, which separate the body from the spirit (Descartes's philosophy), then neglect the spirit and bury it, waging a "holy war" in order to replace God with man, so that in the end, the only thing left in the universe and humanity is matter— movement, pleasure, domination and struggle, and the law the powerful dictate. The tragedies produced by humankind are not caused by the democratic system or its well-known mechanisms, which often yield success and constitute a positive instrument to regulate the relationship between rulers and ruled and limit the power of the ruler who arrogantly proclaims like Louis XIV and other contemporary dictators, "I am the party, I am the state!" In this, they reproduce the words of Pharaoh, who declared "I am your Lord, the Almighty!" And in the Qur'an he declares, "I do not show you except what I see."[32] Democracy transfers this power from the individual ruler to an institution grounded in the people's will.

Indeed, it is possible for the democratic system to achieve success in restricting tyranny and exploitation, but only if it is accompanied by a philosophy and humane values that recognize all of humankind's dimensions, including their spiritual and moral dimensions. People are in constant need of their Creator and cannot live independently from Him without undermining their own humanity and nobility. This philosophy must also recognize all the social dimensions of humanity and uphold human dignity, keeping us from falling into either the abyss of despotism or that of enslavement,[33] and that recognizes all human dimensions, whether physical, spiritual, individual, or social.

What is more, however much effort we put into discovering these human dimensions in all religious and philosophical traditions, we will never find as comprehensive a picture of them as offered by Islam, which represents a framework capable of guaranteeing nations the freedom to decide their own destinies and the kind of political system under which they want to live. But that is no reason to dwell on democracy's faults in order to shun it, for that would be to open the door to tyranny. Even a freedom that is scarce and in decline, after all, is still better than autocracy, and a society governed by an imperfect law is better than one whose law is the will of tyrants and their every whim.[34] We Islamists, for instance, categorically refuse the legal opinions [fatwas] of the despotic minority regimes whose disdain for their own people and hypocrisy has reached a point where they have issued fatwas forbidding elections, claiming they are an innovation [bid'a] and an imitation of the West! They deliberately ignore the fact that Islam teaches that wisdom is the believer's most cherished goal, and that God's law is whatever achieves welfare and justice. Democracy, in fact, is an excellent mechanism for the application of shura among the values of Islam, and the main demand of the reformist movement in our region over the last two centuries has been to subject the authority of the ruler to that of the law. This principle, they argued, was the secret of the West's progress and of our decline.

We will see how Islam can adopt the Western democratic system and preserve for Muslims and humanity all of its positive contributions to political thinking, in particular its transformation of the Islamic principle of shura—which means people's participation in government that reflects their will, and oversight over those in power—from general principles into mechanisms for political governance. This is similar to what the Western mind did with our heritage in the fields of engineering and algebra, since it transformed them into tangible technology. This is one of the dimensions of the scientific revolution and the Western genius—that is, the power to transform ideas and values into systems. So will we refuse these technological and political mechanisms merely because they were made in the West? Or should we see these as being grounded in our own ideas that have now been returned to us? Once again, wisdom is the believer's most cherished goal . . . and God's law is where one finds welfare and justice.

Indeed, it is possible for such mechanisms to help give meaning to Islamic political values, which came to establish justice and bring happiness to humanity, like shura, *bay'a* [pledge of allegiance to a ruler], *ijma'* [consensus], the commanding of the good and the forbidding of evil. We can treat democratic mechanisms as we do industrial ones, by considering them part of the human heritage and as being able to function in various cultural contexts and intellectual landscapes. This is not the case with secularism, for example, or discrimination on the basis of national origin, or giving priority to the principle of profit, or hedonism, domination, force, utilitarianism, or the separation between religion and the state and the deification of man. All those values originated within the framework of the democratic system, but they were not a necessary consequence of the system's own logic.

This is the essence of democracy: a set of constructive settlements among elites and commitments—as long as they agree to respect them—to manage public affairs in a way that promotes mutual consultation and democracy, so that decisions affecting all are made only by those truly delegated power by the people, without any one person or group monopolizing the decision-making process. This is not tied to a particular philosophical or religious school but rather a set of rules and practical mechanisms for managing public affairs including:

- sovereignty belongs to the people;
- the equality of all citizens in rights and responsibilities, including the right to participate in public affairs;
- state institutions originating in the will of the people expressed through free elections;
- alternation of power on the basis of the majority's right to rule and make decisions, and the right of the minority to political opposition and to seek a path to power through peaceful means;
- freedom of expression;
- a judiciary whose procedures and verdicts are both just and independent;
- finally, the separation of powers.

There is nothing here, as we shall see, that necessarily contradicts Islamic values; rather, these values find in the democratic political system the best means available until today, of spurring the development of science and knowledge. These ideals can thus be fleshed out, brought down from the ideational level and applied to our human reality.

In the same way, this beneficial and effective democratic apparatus finds in the values of Islam a philosophy of life, the universe, and humanity, which becomes its best fuel and energy, providing the power to guide it. Islam can also help it avoid errors and the tragic pitfalls that often accompany the contemporary democratic system. In fact, this apparatus seems to have left God behind because of the particular characteristics that it acquired in Western nations at its inception. And even if it boasts Christian political parties, that hardly seems to have any effect on its policies in terms of reining in a capitalism that seeks to usurp the state for its own financial gains, even at the price of starving hundreds of millions of people, exacerbating climate change and causing hurricanes and other destructive catastrophes; waging colonial wars, impoverishing humanity, spreading immorality and deadly epidemics; causing the disintegration of the family and of social relations, thrusting individuals into dangerous isolation; and the oppression of the weak by the strong. Add to all of this the fact that the developing world, including the Islamic world, continues to be submerged in chaos, despotism, poverty, and systematic destruction of people, nature and heritage.

Where the democratic apparatus has functioned within the framework of Christian values, it has produced Christian democracies; where it has functioned within the framework of a socialist philosophy, it produced socialist democracies; if in the framework of Jewish values, a Jewish democracy; and where in a Buddhist and Hindu context, it produced the greatest democracies, like those of India and Japan. So is it impossible for it to function within the framework of Islamic values and produce an Islamic democracy? We support that perspective and see in it a great good, and not just for the Muslim world but for all of humanity. Indeed, we have seen that under the umbrella of Islamic governance, if a nation sets aside democratic mechanisms, as is the case in Sudan and Afghanistan, it will be produce harm rather than benefit for Islam, as we see happening in those two places today. Even an Islamic regime that excludes democratic procedures and institutions is one that offers no sufficient guarantees. The "Islamic alternative" should not be cut off from the heritage of contemporary civilization, but rather an extension of it, one that preserves the best of that heritage and transcends its destructive flaws. Indeed, this is the path of development (to build on what is good and correct what is not),[35] as was the tradition of the Prophet (PBUH) when he completed the work of the prophets before him, may God's prayers be upon all of them! As we read in the hadith, "I was sent to perfect the highest moral values."[36]

4

THE BASIC PRINCIPLES OF ISLAMIC GOVERNANCE

ISLAM'S VIEW OF POLITICAL AUTHORITY

No one who studies Islam with pure motives and a zeal for truth and who has gained sufficient knowledge of the sciences of Islam and its historical trajectory will have the least doubt about Islam's particular nature as a comprehensive blueprint for life. A true perspective on Islam, as Muhammad Iqbal emphasized, essentially reveals it to be both "religion," as seen from one angle, and "state," as seen from another.[1] None of the ancients broke away from that consensus, except one of the Mu'tazilite scholars and one of the branches of the Kharijites.[2] These believed that establishing the imam or caliph, or the Islamic state, was not a religious duty but an objective recognized by the Shari'a that should be applied when the need arises; yet if justice can be achieved without establishing some political authority, then it is not needed.

In the modern era, with the impact of Western domination over Muslim lands, the principle of the separation between religion and state became dominant within the educational institutions founded by the colonizers, in which the holding of Islam and its political orientation as responsible for their society's decline was a central tenet. But even in the traditional Islamic schools one could find advocates for this secular perspective, like the Egyptian professor writing in the first quarter of the twentieth century 'Ali 'Abd al-Raziq, whose book *Islam and the Foundations of Political Power* is well known. A heated debate arose regarding his assertion that Islam did not have any concept of state, that Muhammad (PBUH), just as the prophets who preceded him, was only a proclaimer of God's message, and that what was invented after that with regard to the caliphate was only something necessitated by the circumstances of that particular time but with no connection to religion per se and certainly not mandated by it.[3] Scores of thinkers and Islamic sciences experts pored over the book, some supporting and defending it, while others, after evaluating it, critiqued, or denounced it. But it was not long before all the commotion about the book began to fade, and it began to lose its luster after a ferocious campaign against both book and author launched by the official religious institutions, along with the thinkers and members of the reform movement. All this took place at a time when Western aggression had been able to destroy what was left of the Ottoman Empire.

Islamic reformist thinkers did not just critique 'Abd al-Raziq's book but intensified their efforts to write about the Islamic political system and showcase its unique characteristics. Further, they founded Islamic movements and political parties that called for the rebuilding of the caliphate and the establishment of Islamic governance. This Islamic activism in Egypt since the 1920s and what followed in its wake in most parts of the Islamic world have been influenced to various degrees—and still today—by the conflict that broke out in the 1920s between secular movements (including the liberal, Marxist, and national wings) and Islamic movements. The former took inspiration from 'Ali 'Abd al-Raziq's position, dismantling the Islamic texts in order to strengthen their ties with the West. Secularist regimes are the fruit of that perspective.[4] As for Islamic movements, they strive amid never-ending opposition and hardship to liberate Islam from secularist attempts to impose such interpretations that go against its monotheistic and comprehensive nature.[5] Those interpretations represent an intense effort to Christianize Islam by emptying it of its legislative, social, and political content, as if it had not been applied over many centuries and transformed into a vast dominion and a flourishing civilization.

Research by Muhammad 'Imara has shown that among the great scholars of that generation of western-influenced thinkers, like 'Ali 'Abd al-Raziq, Taha Husayn, Muhammad Husayn Haykal, and Muhammad Khalid, some of them retracted the views they had been spreading and subsequently announced a change of heart. Nonetheless, the pro-Western current continued and experienced a revival in the following generation, in spite of the alienation they suffered in the face of a rising Islamic movement, which left them with no other support than their access to the corridors of authoritarian regimes and the encouragement of the international community. Among the most prominent leaders and spokespersons of a secularized Islam who used the tools of modern linguistics were the Algerian Mohamed Arkoun, the Egyptian Muhammad Nasir Abu Zayd, and the Tunisian Abdel Majid Charfi. At heart, this struggle pits those who advocate dependence on the West against those who call for the independence of the Arab and Islamic umma, their unity, dignity, and the continuation of the struggle for liberation and independence.

The most important arguments that supporters of a link between Islam and politics put forward are the following.

THE HISTORICAL PROOF

It seems hard to imagine that anyone could deny the reality of the political society that arose in Medina after the Hijra.[6] This was a remarkable body politic, independent as to its territory, its unified laws, and its leadership, its inhabitants tied together by common relations, texts, and goals. Further, this society exercised all the functions of a state, including defense and justice, and the authority to ratify treaties and send out emissaries. No one among those who built this system had any doubt about its nature. Supreme legislative authority belonged to God and His Messenger (the Book and the Sunna), and the other sources of law like *ijtihad*[7] were secondary sources to be used within the frame of reference and supreme legal framework of the Qur'an and Sunna—that is, guided by divine revelation and its objectives.

THE PROOF FROM CONSENSUS [IJMA']

Throughout Islamic history, Islamic scholars and thinkers over the centuries have never called into question the necessity of establishing the Imam or of "Islamic governance" in order to apply the Shari'a and serve the interests of the community [umma], following the rule that that without which one cannot perform one's duty is obligatory.[8] The legal argument was as follows:

1. The umma as a whole is commanded to fulfill the Shari'a, which represents the entire system of Islam chosen by God for human beings.
2. There is no way to establish the Shari'a except in an independent political society on its own territory and under its own legal system and leadership, fully convinced of the Shari'a and its founding principles.
3. Then establishing that system of "Islamic government" is what the Shari'a requires, and the entire umma sins if it does not expend the greatest possible effort and consecrate its property and lives to establish it.

This principle becomes even more certain as we look into the Shari'a, which encompasses all aspects of human life—economic, social, moral, and political, including international relations and punishment. In it we find general commands, like establishing justice, mutual consultation, and equality; we also find detailed statutes giving precise instructions on how to meet the needs of the poor, on the distribution of wealth and the forbidding of its accumulation, and so on. There is a command for rulers to act with justice and mutual consultation; for the umma to listen, obey, and provide good advice; and above all for the good to be commanded and evil forbidden. It also calls for fighting all forms of corruption, defending against external aggression, protecting Islam and defending Muslims, guaranteeing full freedom of choice for people, and providing information on Islam and its message. In it we also find detailed prescriptions about the family, international relations, sanctions and education. How could it occur to an educated person, or a well-intentioned one, that all of this could be accomplished within a political framework built upon hostile or "neutral" principles and goals in its relationship with Islam and with people in leadership who have no commitment to any values? This demonstrates the misleading nature of the arguments put forward by atheists and victims of the Western intellectual assault.[9]

THE SOCIAL FUNCTION OF POLITICAL AUTHORITY IN ISLAM

The necessity of establishing political authority in Islam or for Islam does not mean that there is a direct command in Islam to that effect. But not to do so would do away with a number of Islamic commandments. For as long as social connectivity is necessary for human beings and the advancement of people's lives, people come together to live and an inevitable need arises for an authority that establishes justice among them.

Islam is a path to achieving justice. Either political authority is grounded in the safeguarding of Islamic teachings, their objectives, and their application to all areas, and it is therefore Islamic, or it is grounded in the safeguarding of another legal system, while relegating the Shari'a to the margins, and it is not Islamic. Call it what you wish, but it has no relation to Islam. In the latter case, the system, by its shunning Islam or even fighting it, will—consciously or not—at the very least marginalize it, stand in its way, and create psychological, intellectual, and social environments to restrict it as a prelude to eradicating it. In this case, Islam is either resisted or condemned to disappear. As we read in the Qur'an, "God does not put two hearts within a man's breast."[10] In the same way, social development cannot take place without uniting its intellectual, social, and political frameworks.

Political authority from this perspective, even if it is not an explicit command of Islam, is an essential function for its establishment. It is thus classified within the list of "means" rather than one of the Shari'a's objectives. It also follows that the need for political authority need not have been mentioned in the sacred texts, because it is warranted by the existence of human society. What is important to be mentioned in the texts with care are the fundamental guarantees that must be respected in order for a system of political authority to fulfill its function: the command to establish justice, which includes mutual consultation [shura], equality, distribution of wealth, and preventing corruption in government circles, and the duty on all of society, and on scholars in particular, to hold rulers accountable and to make knowledge available. All of this has one purpose: to produce a watchful and alert public opinion that protects the Shari'a from any violation on the part of rulers and ruled by means of a constant practice of commanding the good and forbidding evil.

Yet all of this must be done without resorting to an institution that speaks in the name of Heaven. Islam has no such thing. Only the people can discharge this function, through scholars ['ulama'] and civil society institutions, like the institution of religious endowments. It is the umma that has been empowered to fulfill the Trust, as the Prophet said in his farewell address, "Let whomever is present inform whomever is absent."[11] There is no infallible institution in Islam after the Qur'an—only the umma, and only if public opinion comes to consensus on a particular issue.[12]

Islam did not need to set out an explicit obligation to establish political authority, because the nature of human society requires the establishment of this function, be it just or unjust, as for other life functions, like eating or drinking, breathing or rest, because people do this naturally. That is why Islam has set a framework for the satisfaction of these physiological needs that contains a number of values and teachings, which enable the carrying out of these functions in a positive way, both protecting human life and enhancing it. Thus, it warns against wastefulness, stinginess, oppression, and hoarding. Islam sets a framework of ethics and etiquette, which adds beauty when we practice these functions.

This view of political authority in Islam as a necessary social function represents a middle position between on the one hand the secular [*laïque*] position of those who deny this function and actively call for its abolition, and thus contradict the norms of religion, society, and the will of the people, and on the other hand a school within Islam that has taken an extreme position—though one can find a spectrum of positions among them. The members of the latter trend consider political authority in Islam a religious function like prayer and fasting that is prescribed in the sacred texts. For them, the Qur'an and Sunna contain a list of those who must govern after the Prophet (PBUH), and to believe in that list is in itself a necessary article of faith—that is, on the same level as the belief in God, in His Messenger, and in the Last Day. Muslims, in their view, should just submit to this list in humble submission and to this system of inherited political succession, even though the advocates for this position disagree among themselves as to who is on that list.[13] Some are carried away by the passion and love for the Prophet's family, giving way to unacceptable emotional positions on this issue. For example, from an authoritative religious source like the Imam Khomeini (May God grant him forgiveness) we read, "Our imams achieved a closeness to God never achieved by a prophet sent by God or an angel."[14]

Certainly truth, balance, and moderation are to be found in the Muslim majority view, throughout Islamic history, stating that political authority is a social function for the preservation of the religious and the worldly, and those who lead it are nothing but state officials and servants of the umma, according to the well-known saying, "Religion is the foundation and the ruler is its guardian."[15] From this perspective, government is a civil authority in every respect, which is no different from contemporary democracies, except where the supremacy of the Shari'a and its rules trump every other authority in those areas. All the rest is made up of those means chosen to improve the fulfillment of this function, and they are repelling injustice and establishing justice according to the requirements of God's law—that is, according to what is written in the texts or according to that which agrees with them or at least does not contradict them.

Islam does not provide a sacred text for every law that people need. As a result, where the Muslim legislator esteems that there is no clear text in the Qur'an and Sunna, he must do his best to issue a ruling that achieves justice and advances the public interest. For wherever you find justice and the public interest, that is divine law, with the proviso that those who establish an Islamic state may not issue any law or regulation that contradicts the Shari'a's definitive rules, though they are very few indeed.

As a reminder, human beings are social by nature, and Islam is a comprehensive way of life. Therefore, an Islamic state is an indispensable means to provide a social environment in which the greatest possible number of citizens can live in spiritual and physical harmony with the laws of nature that God sent down to the Prophet—that is, Islam. For the Islamic state is nothing but a political apparatus meant to fulfill the highest ideals of Islam in producing a people that naturally stands up for goodness, justice, and truth, and stands against falsehood throughout the earth.[16] Setting up such a state will promote the worship of God and closeness to Him through obedience to His commands; it will enhance the performance of good deeds and make the establishment of justice something that people desire and find easy and rewarding. As a result too, the violation of sacred rules, the spreading of evil, and the committing of injustice will become things that are loathed and difficult to engage in, at least on a social level.

One cannot imagine allowing the greatest number of people the chance to realize the highest ideals of Islam like justice, benevolence, and piety without establishing an Islamic political authority and working to establish this authority and thereby defend the societies, households, and lives of Muslims by giving them peace of mind. To think that the umma is well as long as it safeguards certain rituals in daily life[17] would be a deviation from from the unifying essence of Islam, and a Christianization of Islam, moving it away from its message. It would also mean surrender to its enemies and guaranteeing continued defeat, division and subjugation, and of the perpetual loss of Palestine. It would mean leaving Islam to its fate, and refusing to take on the Trust that was given to the umma to "establish religion."[18]

For this reason, there was a rejection of, and even a revolution against, the despotic state that imposed fragmentation, dependence and plunder, and which subjugated the people and eradicated religion, becoming a "new clergy" under the shadow of which the umma has only experienced fragmentation, subjection, and backwardness. Thus, the persistent work of individuals and groups and the marshaling of funds and people for the sake of establishing Islamic governance using legitimate means is a duty and a national, human, and strategic interest. As long as this duty remains unfulfilled, the umma and humankind will be deprived of the blessings of Islam and the fruit of its civilization in this life and the next, that is, justice, freedom, unity, security, and global peace and progress. Moreover, today's Islamic movements with regard to their political and strategic dimensions are nothing but an extension and a new beginning of the liberation and independence movements within our umma, because they seek to achieve that which the previous phase failed to achieve— that is, cultural independence, development, unity, justice, mutual consultation, and the liberation of the territories that still remain occupied, with Palestine at the forefront.

Furthermore, today's Islamic movement at its core stems from the liberation forces that stand against global tyranny, which destroys the the environment and the cultures of nations, while pillaging their resources and killing the spiritual and moral dimensions of the human spirit. The French thinker François

Burgat called this "the voice of the south."[19] In fact, it is the voice of the oppressed and of all people whose conscience is free, whether from the south or from the north.

THE COMPONENTS OF THE ISLAMIC STATE IN MEDINA

The structure of the Islamic state that developed in Medina at the time of the Messenger (PBUH) and the Rightly Guided Caliphs provided all the elements necessary to any state, namely a people [umma], a territory, a political authority, and a legal system. Using precise wording, Medina's constitution or charter [al-sahifa][20] defined the groups that constituted the state—one by one it listed the Muslims, the Jews, and the pagans—all of them forming together a political umma. The document mentions their rights and duties as citizens of the state. Regardless of their different beliefs, they constituted a common Islamic umma in its political dimension. Together they laid the solid foundation of an Islamic civilization in which hundreds of ethnic groups and tribes from different faith traditions gathered in response to the divine call, "People, We created you all from a single man and a single woman, and made you into races and tribes so that you should get to know one another. In God's eyes, the most honoured of you are the ones most mindful of Him: God is all knowing, all aware."[21]

The location of the first Islamic state was Medina, or Yathrib. Its leader clearly demarcated the borders of the state, rendering them inviolable and safe and communicating unambiguously to all those who came in and out that this was a new political entity that had just seen the light of day.[22] The charter also specified the locus of political authority in the Islamic state for the sake of regulating the affairs of the people and the umma. Additionally, it detailed the legal system to which everyone submits, as represented in the Shari'a, which remained the point of reference for every conflict.

The Medina Charter further reinforces the equality of all of the religious groups in the state and their obligation to support each other; to defend as one the state's borders, and thus forbidding loyalty to its enemies; to encourage solidarity within each of the groups and forbid all enmity; and finally, to promote the freedom to follow one's religious tradition and practice its rituals.

Constitutional lawyers who have read this document, one of the Prophet's first achievements, consider this a constitutional precedent without rival in the history of constitutional law and particularly worthy of greater scrutiny and study. The Medina Charter addresses several complex issues, such as that of citizenship in a pluralist society with several schools of thoughts and religious convictions. It responded by conferring to all without exception the right to citizenship and by stating that all residents form "an umma from which no member is excluded," meaning it is the political and civilizational umma whose individuals share a common will to live together in peace, with loyalty to the state and a readiness to defend it—in contrast to confessional nations, such as a Jewish or a Muslim state.

The document clearly took note of all the confessional groups living in Yathrib (Medina) at the time. Had there been other groups with other beliefs present at the time, they too would have been welcomed into this covenant. The Medina Charter created the necessary basis for an open political and civilizational space that would extend around the globe, encompassing without exception all the peoples, civilizations, religions, and tribes it encountered in its path, opening the way for mutual engagement with one another within this space and for joint participation in creating the contours of this new society. Additionally, history did not record any instance of ethnic or religious cleansing during this era, and the protected status of minorities [dhimma] was a privilege granted even to pagans, according to the Andalusian jurist Ibn 'Abd al-Barr.

This points to a clear concept of citizenship in that state, which correlates with a shared territory, the will to live together within it, and the commitment to what all this entails in terms of duties and rights. As for the creedal element, it adds to the state a moral foundation based on a legal philosophy and with a legal system to organize it in practice—that is, the creed of Islam and the Islamic Shari'a. So according to the perspective expressed by the Medina Charter and the Qur'an relative to citizenship in this state, no one can enjoy this right of citizenship unless he lives within its territory, be he Muslim or not. This in no way diminishes the importance of creed and Shari'a in the founding of this state and its organization.

Citizenship is granted to all who request it, for those who enter the state's territory and live by its rules. As for those who refuse this, even if they are Muslims, the state owes them no protection whatsoever, unless they choose to join it. But if they prefer to live outside of its territory, even if they are part of the religious umma, they remain outside the political umma. As God said, "As for those who believed but did not emigrate, you are not responsible for their protection until they have done so. But if they seek help from you against religious persecution, it is your duty to help them, except against people with whom you have a treaty."[23]

The clarity you find in the Charter of Medina refutes the contention of several Western scholars of Islam and that of some of our own constitutional lawyers who have followed them. One of them wrote, "The umma is not a distinct and tangible entity, but rather an obscure concept. For this reason, this umma cannot have a will and cannot express anything directly about itself. In fact, an aristocratic elite that expresses its will and monopolizes the umma's power and knowledge."[24]

FOUNDATIONS OF THE ISLAMIC STATE

Political regimes do not stand out by their institutions and legal systems, which allow them to manage various powers and make decisions—despite their importance—as much as they stand out by their ideas, beliefs, values, and their weightiest legal rules. These constitute the essence of a particular regime, its overall spirit. It is what constitutes the individual personality and social relationships of the regime's founding members and their perspectives on what is just, true and good; on what is unjust, worthless and evil; on what makes this work good or evil, fair or unfair. Moreover, with little effort, it is possible to transplant political institutions from one nation to another. However, to transplant the overall spirit, the thought system, and legislative rules—that is a difficult task, because no regime can ever proceed successfully without a unifying spirit, and that is precisely the cause for the emptiness at the heart of Western institutions. They have failed to contribute outside their own historical and cultural boundaries even the meager fruits produced within that framework.

We emphasized above that democracy, for instance, is not simply a constitutional declaration of human rights, the transfer of power to the people, and the reliance on an electoral system in order to put in place executive and legislative powers. All such declarations can be in place and democracy is still absent! Rather, democracy means giving value to humanity, the universe, and life, a value that is rooted in human dignity and freedom, and that keeps them from falling into the pit of slavery and tyranny.[25] No doubt, the benefits of the democratic system stem from the positive aspects of this humanist conception, which were produced by the philosophies of the Renaissance and Reformation. Its defects lie in its failure to strike a balance within the individual's personality between its spiritual and material aspirations, between the interests of the individual and those of the community, and between the interests of weak nations and those of the strong, and the failure to create peace and cooperation between them instead of exploitation and hegemony.

This can be traced back to the content of these philosophies and Reformation doctrine, which established a separation between mind and spirit, spirit and matter, religion and life, and the distribution of power between God and Caesar. It can also be traced back to an individualistic Enlightenment perspective, which deified reason and created a materialistic and individualistic religion, while unleashing reason from its moorings, in order to explore the horizons and push back the borders of knowledge. Yet in many instances it put this knowledge to satanic uses by satisfying their whims and their greed for domination, and by unleashing their base instincts, without control or inhibition. This can be seen in its Marxist materialist or Nazi forms, which denied God, the church, and freedom so as to put in their place the new gods of production, class, party, leader, and state. A new church was erected—that is, the leadership of the party and a new "pope," the party's leader. In all cases, call him what you will—Napoleon, or Hitler, or Mussolini, or Lenin, or Stalin, or Reagan, or Bush—he is the symbol of supremacy internally and externally and the natural product of a humanity in rebellion against God and seeking to take His place.

In the wake of this philosophy, humankind has experienced a form of happiness that comes from being numb and drunk, so that their state, in fact, is a wretched one. In its shadow a person or a group or even a nation might flourish but hundreds of millions will face suffering. Some paths might find light while many hearts will be filled with darkness and misery. Its planes connect continents, only for its fighter jets and bombs to bring them mayhem and destruction. Indeed, these are the poisonous plants of which the Qur'an speaks, "It is like plants that spring up after the rain: their growth at first delights the sowers, but then you see them wither away, turn yellow, and become stubble. There is a terrible punishment in the afterlife."[26] Or it is like the tree of Zaqqum, the fruit of which multiplies and looks beautiful but only gives to the famished searing pain and misfortune.[27]

The central idea in Western civilization and its governments is that of the human being cut off from God or in rebellion against God, which replaced the core doctrine of the European Middle Ages and Near Eastern civilizations which conceived of man as a mortal being connected to God through his service to the church and the clergy and thus seeking to avoid the life of struggle and toil. By contrast, the central idea in Islamic civilization—including Islamic government, as one of the main instruments used by that civilization—is that of humanity mandated by God to be His deputy. This being is honored with reason, will, freedom, and responsibility. His Creator entrusted him with the mission of cultivating the earth, of discovering its resources, and managing it in such a way as to bring forth goodness, truth, equality, justice, freedom, knowledge, and wealth for the benefit of all, according to the guidance and methods, values and creeds revealed by God's messengers, in order to help and show mercy to this creature, so that as a free agent he would freely choose to follow the ways of God in his life, whereas those ways were realized in all other creatures by force or by instinct.

All this was so that man, through his knowledge, freedom, and hard work, would create harmony in all of creation, a harmony that attributes praise to God and brings about righteousness and the enhancement of human life. Humans thus either become lords over creation, surrendering to the dictates of their passions and to Satan, in which case they are thrown back into the abyss of tyranny or the path of slavery, wandering on the earth corrupted and corrupting, despising and despised, miserable in this world and awaiting a much more severe punishment in the world to come. Or they succeed in this great test and challenge God places before them and they inherit two gardens, as we read in the Qur'an, "For those who fear [the time when they will stand] before their Lord there are two gardens."[28] How great a challenge that will be, and how risky a wager!

The theory of human vicegerency of God, an essential pillar in Islamic political philosophy, includes:

(a) A declaration of God's existence, and that He (may He be exalted) is Lord over all things, King and Ruler, with no successor or associate, and that His law is over every other law.

(b) The human person is an honored creature with intelligence, freedom, responsibility, and a mission.

(c) By virtue of this honor the human person possesses rights that no authority can take away, and religious obligations that cannot be annulled, for these taken together constitute a covenant or a contract: that he worship God, who can have no associate, in accordance with His Shari'a; that if he does that, this human being deserves from his Lord the blessings of His pleasure with him and his own prevailing in this world and the next. *The first axiom* of that contract of vicegerency from a constitutional point of view is that the authority of the Shari'a is exalted above every other authority, because of what it contains in terms of creeds, rituals, and systems, which in fact represent a body of general legal rules along with some more detailed ones. All together they represent "the legal, theological and ethical framework of the Islamic state, which may be summed up in one word, 'text,' that is, the revealed text, both Qur'an and Sunna, definitive in its wording and sure signs from God . . . It is the loftiest constitution of the Islamic state. *The second axiom* of the doctrine of human vicegerency from a constitutional perspective, that is, regarding the general organization of Islamic government, can be summarized by the word 'shura,' based on the following binaries: text and shura, or revelation and reason, or obligation and freedom—'God's Shari'a and consultation of the people'"[29] or in other words, God's authority and the secondary authority of umma, derived from Him. These are the two basic principles upon which the Islamic state is founded, and they are the two necessary fruits stemming from the theory of vicegerency, the main pillar of political doctrine. So, then, what details of constitutional law flow from all the above?

THE PRINCIPLES OF THE ISLAMIC STATE

If the institutions of nations, which flow from their constitutions, share commonalities, they are still different, distinguishable, and even contradictory when it comes to their guiding principles and the goals they seek to reach. We say that the principle of a thing consists of the fundamental rules upon which it stands and from which it will not depart. If that is the case, what are the principles underlying the Islamic state, those on which it must stand, and derogation from which will cause its demise?

We proposed that the modern Western state prides itself on having been the first to free the concept of political rule from despotism by relying on two principles: legality, or the submission of the state to the rule of law; and the sovereignty of the people, or their being considered the source of law. By this process the political authority of society transitioned from a state of raw power to an organized power and from the rule of the individual to the rule of law. Then we used the limited reliability of that assertion as an introduction to the principles and foundations of the Islamic state, which we summarized under the two pillars: text and shura, or God and the umma, or revelation and reason.[30]

THE SACRED TEXTS

What do we mean by "text"? What is the extent of its authority in the Islamic state? What is the position of the umma on this?

We read in the Noble Qur'an, "Whatever you may differ about is for God to judge."[31] "Believers, obey God and the Messenger: do not let your deeds go to waste."[32] "Those who do not judge according to what God has sent down are rejecting [God's teachings]."[33] "By your Lord, they will not be true believers until they let you decide between them in all matters of dispute, and find no resistance in their souls to your decisions, accepting them totally."[34] "Do they want judgement according to the time of pagan ignorance? Is there any better judge than God for those of firm faith?"[35] "You who believe, obey God and the Messenger, and those in authority among you. If you are in dispute over any matter, refer it to God and the Messenger, if you truly believe in God and the Last Day: that is better and fairer in the end."[36]

In the hadith[37] we read, "I have left with you that which, if you hold on to it, you will never lose your way: God's Book and the Prophet's Sunna."[38]

In the hadith we also read, "Let me not find one of you reclining on his couch when confronted with an order of permission or prohibition from me, saying, 'I do not know it; we will only follow what we find in the book of God." And this narration, "Beware! I have been given the Qur'an and something like it, yet the time is coming when a man replete on his couch will say: Keep to the Qur'an; what you find in it to be permissible treat as permissible, and what you find in it to be prohibited treat as prohibited."[39]

In the hadith collections of al-Tirmidhi and al-Darimi, in their chapters on the "Virtues of the Qur'an," we find these narrations from 'Ali bin Abi Talib (May God be pleased with him):

> He said: "I heard God's Messenger say: 'There comes a time of testing.' So I said: "What is the way out from it, O Messenger of God?" He said: "God's book. In it is news that happened before you, and prophecy about what comes after you, and judgment for what happens between you. It is the Criterion without jest. Whoever among the oppressive abandons it, he will be ruined, and whoever seeks guidance from other than it, God will let him go astray. It is the firm rope from God, a wise remembrance, the straight path. People's desires cannot distort it, nor can their tongues twist it, nor can the scholars ever have enough of it. The Qur'an does not become dull from reciting it much, and the amazement of it never wanes. When the *jinn*[40] hear it, they did not hesitate to say about it: 'Truly, we have heard a wonderful Recitation! It guides to the Right Path, and we have believed therein.' Whoever speaks according to it has spoken the truth, and whoever acts according to it finds reward; whoever judges by it he has judged justly, and whoever invites to it, guides his hearers to the straight path."

The evidence in the above texts leads to the certainty that in Islam there are principles regarding governance that are instituted by God, spelled out in the Qur'an and Sunna, and to the certainty that reference and submission to them is the dividing line between faith and disbelief. This comes directly from the Islamic conviction that God created all things, that He is the King of all creation without dispute, and that the human being does not hold the original right over himself or anyone else, but that he is a trustee or deputy of God. Nor is he the possessor of the highest power and authority; rather, he has the right to authority by virtue of the highest legislative authority issued by God.[41]

The human must choose to either worship God in accordance with the covenant of vicegerency found in revelation and then join the ranks of believers, or to refuse to do that and he finds himself among those who stray from God's path, act unjustly, and disbelieve:

> The issue is about faith and disbelief, or Islam and *jahiliyya*,[42] or God's law and human passions. For there is no middle ground on this issue, no truce and no reconciliation. The believers are those who judge by what God has revealed without distorting one letter thereof, and without changing one thing contained therein. The disbelievers and those who commit injustice and immorality are those who do not judge by what God has revealed. So either the rulers completely stand upon God's Shari'a and they are within the circle of faith, or they stand upon another Shari'a, which God has not permitted, and they are the disbelievers, oppressors, and sinners. For rulers and judges either accept God's judgment in their affairs and they are believers. There is no middle ground between this and that. Indeed, God is the Lord of humanity and He knows what is good for them, and He issues His laws so as to achieve their true benefit.[43]

These are the words of Sayyid Qutb, and his was the position of the Kharijites who judged Muslims who committed a grave sin as no longer Muslims but infidels,[44] a view that was opposed by the vast majority of jurists and commentators since then. The great Qur'anic commentator al-Zamakhshari quoted from the Companion Ibn al-'Abbas: "'Whoever rejects God's rule [*hukm*] has disbelieved [*kafara*], and any person in authority who does not rule according to it is unjust and a sinner,' and this is the majority Sunni view."[45] And from another commentator, "The term *kafir* applies to the one who replaces God's command with something God did not reveal. He is guilty of being in error; he is negligent and sinful and will be held accountable for exchanging God's rule for something that is not."[46] This is the case for people who because of their own desires or personal gain deviated from God's rule and decided on a rule that was not God's, though without necessarily rejecting it or despising it, and without preferring someone else's rule. That is a transgression and a sin. According to Shaykh

Tahir Ibn 'Ashur's commentary on these verses,[47] "The greatest sin in this regard is committed by the ruler who forces people to judge by what God has not revealed, though there are different degrees of violation, some of which attain the level of apostasy, if it has to do with despising or giving the lie to God's rule."[48]

BELIEVERS AND UNBELIEVERS: AN OUTDATED DEBATE

We should not give undue attention to the dispute that arose in the period when Islamic society was drifting away from God's guidance on the issue of governance. For we are not dealing with a situation of individual wrongdoing or human frailty, in which a believer still has certainty in God's will but a situation in which that soul, whether by reason of desire, compulsion, or negligence, turns away from God's will. No doubt, this does not prevent a person from still being a believer, since Islam does not address angels but weak human beings full of passions and earthly desires. Yet they are still endowed with the divine breath. For that reason we do not expect people to be perfect and never slip and fall along the path. But here we find ourselves with a much more serious situation—rebellion against the authority of God's Shari'a.

This stems from another vision of the world, humanity, and life, one built on the independence of man from his Creator—the laïque or secular perspective, which sees Islam's Shari'a as something it is not—that is, that it came to fulfill the needs of a particular period and circumstances of the past but that it has now been made obsolete by the evolution of society. According to this secular view, the Shari'a is no longer valid for us, as we have no longer need for it, unless, if God gave us that power, we halt the evolution of modern life and science, or we amend the Shari'a in drastic ways. Then we can leave in it only what we find acceptable! The furthest these people will go in making concessions to Islam is to recognize it as a useful part of their heritage.

These people might even go further and call for new ways to interpret the Qur'an, which end up emptying Islam of all its precepts and in a way Christianizing it, as was the case with Christianity under the Reformation, when it had to submit to modernity and secularism. But all of this stems from the desire to put the Western model on a pedestal, as the model whose brilliant light must be the only reference to establish and build human civilization.

Though the Islamic movements do not object to learning from anything that is useful in any civilization, they insist that this borrowing be done within the framework of Islam as the highest authority, and that all diverging perspectives within the Muslim societies be adjusted in light of this model.[49]

Given such extremist secular positions bent on undermining Islamic values as has never been seen in the history of Islamic schools of thought, it makes no sense to bring up an old controversy, from different times, about the ruling concerning the person who violates the Shariʻa, whether he or she has committed apostasy. It makes no sense to apply these arguments to the political, cultural, and social realities of systems of government and ways of thinking that have their references in the political thought of western societies! What we have before us is a case of alienation, estrangement and a disconnect from reality that some contemporary Muslims—good people—are experiencing.

These good people are trapped in old debates, trying to apply them to a different reality, which seriously distorts their perceptions about Islam, reality, and the approach to reform. This often places them on the same side as the conservative forces holding on to this repressive, servile, and ailing reality, defending it and preventing Islamic teachings from working to weaken these repressive systems, which it is in complete opposition to.

Bringing old debates to bear on new and different realities also creates confusion in people's attitudes and positions toward regimes that are devoid of any popular or religious legitimacy. Thus, they wrongly attribute to the Qurʼanic perspective on government certain concepts like "ulu al-amr" (those vested with authority),[50] and the notion of the people's duty to obey authority, regardless (of the rulers' transgressions) as they are merely sinners . . . !! But the truth is that they have neither popular legitimacy, because of their repressive practices, nor religious legitimacy, because of their hypocrisy. Were they democratic rulers, even if secular, a common ground could be found on the basis of the principle of citizenship. However, the problem with these rulers is deeper, even assuming that it is possible to separate democracy from Islam in a Muslim country.

THE TEXT AS FOUNDATION OF THE STATE'S LEGITIMACY

It is clear, therefore, that the first and fundamental source of legitimacy of any ruler in Islamic political theory is that he completely submit to God's law, without the slightest objection.[51] Al-Isfahani put it this way, "The greatest unbelief is to deny the unity of God, or the Shariʻa, or prophethood."[52] Ibn Hazm, for his part, wrote, "Political power may only be authorized if it is based on what God (may He be exalted) revealed through the tongue of His Messenger (PBUH). That is the truth, and anything outside of that is oppression, injustice, and therefore unlawful power."[53] The Islamic sacred text is both Qurʼan and

Sunna, and as such is the highest power and authority, and the great rule upon which Islamic society rests. Even more, it is the foundational authority established for society, the state, and civilization. From it the Islamic ruler derives his philosophy, his values, his structures, his laws, and his goals and objectives. The text is the supreme ruler, and by it everything is governed. The text is the fixed and unchanging Shari'a. It is not *fiqh* or ijtihad, involving detailed laws. Perfection, one of Shari'a's attributes, is not in the specific injunctions but mostly in its general principles.[54]

The divine text, then, is the community's foundational reality; in fact, it could not survive without it, for it is in fact the one and only sustainer of its existence, and enables the community's enduring survival and legitimacy. The text is the root that gives life to the Islamic community and under the protection of which the umma was established. Moreover, it was on this foundation that conflicts and revolutions took place, given that these divisions, whatever their numbers, were never able to disregard the text, for otherwise Islam itself would have been destroyed, and its umma disintegrated. This is the very reason that Islamic society is still enduring, despite the conflicts that began very early in its history and that touched on issues about which there is no explicit guidance.

From the very beginning, then, the text constituted the foundation for every aspect of the community that emerged in its presence. The text is what holds the community together, what governs it, teaches it, and nurtures it every day, for the benefit of those who gathered around the Prophet of humanity (PBUH).[55]

The authority of the divine text—Qur'an and Sunna—has ruled supreme over all other authorities, whether legislative or executive, and it remains the support for all other authority, and the justification for all obedience sought by a ruler. This was perfectly clear to the Prophet's Companions, who were able to distinguish between his role as God's messenger and his role as ruler who, as a human being, is capable of both good and poor judgment. When people were in doubt about a particular order of his, they would ask him whether it came from revelation in his quality as Messenger of God, or from his own opinion, or personal ijtihad. If it was the first, they would answer, "We have heard and will obey." If it was the second, they would make the effort to examine that opinion, and then lean toward either amending it or following it completely. Indeed, there are many historical allusions to this.[56]

This discernment between revelation as absolute truth, legality, and obedience and that which came from another source was plain to see. It was also obvious to the jurists and thinkers of Islam, who, from the various schools of thought, were unanimous that there could be no ijtihad in the presence of a plain text. They also urged their disciples, as did al-Shafi'i,[57] to evaluate their own writings in the light of the Qur'an and Sunna, and therefore retained that with which they agreed and threw out the rest.[58] Further, it was obvious to both rulers and ruled that the Shari'a rules found in the Qur'an and Sunna constitute the ultimate and immutable reference or, in today's terms, the basic law or constitution.[59] Thus rulers would announce in their inaugural speeches before the umma by way of solemn oath their own submission to the text in every aspect of their behavior; they even pressed the umma to rebel against them if they violated divine guidance. When Abu Bakr received the Muslims' oath of allegiance, he said this in his speech, "O my people, I have been put in charge of you though I am no better than you. If I become weak, correct me; if I do well, support me. Truth is a trust, and lying is treason. The weak among you I see as strong, until I return to them what is rightfully theirs, if God wills. The strong among you I see as weak, until I take from them what rightfully belongs to others, if God wills. No group gives up fighting in God's way, unless God strikes them with poverty. Evil doesn't spread among a people, unless God brings down disaster on all. Obey me as long as I obey God and His Prophet. If I turn away from them, you are not to obey me."[60]

No matter how far political rule deviated in Islamic history, the Islamic Shari'a continued to provide the supreme legitimacy that rulers, jurists, and thinkers needed, whereby they could justify their actions and positions. For this reason, Muslims did not experience a theocratic ruler who announced that he was the will of God incarnate, for they knew full well that God's will was embodied in the Shari'a. That which agrees with it is truth, and that which contradicts it is falsehood. In this respect, the directives of the Prophet to the umma were clear, summarized in this well-known hadith, "Let there be no obedience to a creature in rebellion to the Creator." We also find this statement in many forms, "Let there be no obedience to that which is sinful; only to that which is good."[61] Or this one, "Do not obey one who disobeys God."[62] Or, "Do not obey one who rebels against God."[63] Thus, the Muslim believer is obliged to listen to and obey that which he might either love or hate, but not listen to or obey any order to rebel against God.

Ibn Qayyim commented on this constitutional rule,[64] "This is a fatwa [legal opinion] directed to any political leader ordering his people to disobey God, whoever he might be, with no exceptions."[65] Imam al-Ghazali wrote, "People are not obligated to obey a ruler, unless he calls them to agree with the Shari'a."[66] Ibn Khaldun added this about what orders to apply from unjust rulers, "Know that among the commands of the godless he is to implement only that which accords with the divine law."[67]

All of this definitively refutes that which the adversaries of Islam and the ignorant propagate, like the following: "The Muslim's duty is to obey any ruler who seizes power, whether it be by means sanctioned by Islam or de facto";[68] that obedience to any regime that is established is required and that God sees as legitimate any political power that arises on earth. These people also teach that Muslims are to obey rulers, whether they are just or unjust, for our only responsibility is to God and our only satisfaction is that God will judge them on the Last Day for their evil deeds!

Arnold quotes hadiths that urged people to obey, arguing that without exception they justified obedience to despotic regimes that did not limit the ruler's will in any way.[69] Perhaps the source of the mistake behind such positions is their confusing the theory of Islamic rule found in the Qur'an and Sunna and the consensus of the Muslim scholars derived from these sources on the one hand and on the other hand the actual application of this theory in the Islamic heartlands. This is a confusion between the sources and the kinds of deviation and degeneracy that depart from the textual foundations and take Islam as a means for personal gain, despite the fact that no civilization is exempt from instances of deviation from its ideological foundation, whether religious or simply positive law. Muhammad 'Imara wrote, "Islam, as a divine religion, is an ideal. The way people apply religion, that is 'reality,' and there will always be some distance between reality and ideal. Within this distance, however, hides the impetus that drives humanity to try and go beyond the reality and come closer and closer to the ideal. And if not, within that empty space is a whole agenda of actions for life, and without it, the living grow disheartened."[70]

Both the sacred texts of Islam and its exemplary model application (under the Prophet and the rightly-guided caliphs) eloquently affirm the following realities:

- God (may He be praised) is the possessor of power and the supreme authority in the universe and in the life of society, and His rule no one can question or contest. He is the original Ruler.
- Divine revelation in both Qur'an and Sunna spells out God's sovereignty and supremacy over humankind's existence. It is this revelation that gave birth to the Shari'a—God's Shari'a prevails over all else.
- To establish the Shari'a, an obligation incumbent upon all Muslims, requires organizing the Islamic umma in a politically regulated way,

meaning the Islamic state. Islam is the foundational authority of the umma and the state. Foundationally, the state belongs to the umma and thereby gathers all Muslims, no matter how different their ethnicities, their schools of thought, and their languages. This inclusiveness can also be subsumed under the rule of law, or the Shari'a state, which encompasses the people of other religions, no matter the scope of difference between them and the tradition of Islam. This is what happened under the leadership of the Prophet (PBUH) in the first state and continued throughout the history of Islam.

- If the justification for the existence of Islamic government is the carrying out of the Shari'a, the placing of the Almighty within the course of history, and establishing the divine-human connection, and the coloring of human life with the divine hues, then it deserves obedience on the part of its citizens on only two conditions: insofar as it demonstrates submission and commitment to the Shari'a, and its commands and prohibitions are consistent with those of the Legislator, or at least not in contradiction to them. The Islamic state—whether by virtue of its being a political community which has signed a contract of loyalty and obedience to God ("There is no god but Allah, and Muhammad is His Messenger"), or by virtue of its being an aggregate of executive, legislative, and judicial powers—the Islamic state may not swerve even by a fingertip from the Shari'a framework, for the Shari'a undergirds its constitutional law as the original and founding authority for both community and government.[71] Only the Shari'a can abrogate or amend the Islamic state's constitutional laws, and the legality of the ruler's decrees derive from his submission to them, just as they agree with the Shari'a.

- In this case, the obedience of the Muslim to the government is not obedience to a person in power but rather obedience to He to whom the Shari'a belongs, an obedience that is rewarded for that reason. His refusal to recognize those rules that are in the state's constitution (the Shari'a) is a form of transgression.

- In this way Islam has distinguished between the state and the law and has made the commitment to the statutes of the law the basis for the state's legal basis, while making the ruler, as he makes decisions and administrative rules and as he issues commands, subject to the statutes of the Islamic Shari'a—that is, to the statutes of the law. Thus Islam has removed from people the duty to obey an unjust authority, and the most dangerous kinds of violation of the rule of Shari'a are seen in a ruler who ignores its rules.[72] This religious law only concerns the majority Muslim population; as for the non-Muslim minority of citizens, the Shari'a is nothing more than a civil law set up for the political community.[73] It is possible for the non-Muslim minority in the Muslim state to benefit from specific laws within its own courts, since legal pluralism is an option in this state.

• The state which the Prophet (PBUH) founded in Medina can be considered in the following way from a constitutional viewpoint: "as the oldest example of a state, as a structured form of political organization, in which the principle that the state's legitimacy is grounded in the state's submission to law. This was the case, because the Shari'a injunctions (or the injunctions of the civil law), which find their origin in the Qur'an and Sunna, are injunctions that were issued by an authority higher than the powers of the state."[74]

So Islam's state in Medina was the first state in the history of the world to be based on the principle of legality—that is, the separation between the ruler's will and the higher authority of the law over his own. Still, the state is one thing, and the head of state is another. If, for example, the ruler died, all provincial governors continued to enjoy authority until they were removed by the new head of state through a process that involved no contestation by the Prophet's Companions.[75] This points to the fact that the Islamic Shari'a recognized the true nature of state sovereignty at a time when all other civilizations until the eighteenth century, including the Western civilization, were fighting to separate the will of the ruler from that of the law through successive violent revolutions, seeking above all to achieve the rule of law—that is, the ruler's intentional yielding to the law, either by extending the law from the higher legislative authority or simply by declaring the sovereignty of the law once promulgated. Speaking of the Rightly Guided Caliphs, 'Abd al-Wahhab al-Afandi noted, "They continually emphasized submission of the political authority to the statutes of the civil law without any hesitation. Each citizen would be able to address the ruler and oblige him to obey the law and he would have no recourse but to comply.[76]

• The West struggled for a long time to find fundamental social values that the legal structure of the state must clearly enunciate and respect, but in vain, for the concept of natural law is obscure and the value of the declarations of human rights, because of their formality and their inability to include various dimensions of human life, have remained mere recommendations for the most part. This caused the value of justice, which is the goal of lawmaking, to remain without substance.[77] This has left the legislative process open to abuse as it is subjected to the interests of the strong party in the state—the one that controls the power to legislate. By contrast, the Islamic state benefits from the rich texts of the Shari'a, and especially through their higher objectives, and finds them useful to guide the task of governance and to provide clear criteria for social justice.[78] This is so because if the goal of legislation is to express the values of a just social order, then the criteria for that justice are either put forth by the strongest faction of society and that is called "the rule of nature," or they are put forth by reason—but whose reason?—and that is called "the rule of reason," or they are put forth by the Shari'a and that is the rule of Islam.[79] There is no doubt that God's Shari'a issued by the All-Knowing, the Just and Merciful is the only vehicle worthy of offering humanity clear criteria for justice and a worthy guide for legislators. For a government guided by Islam is not just a rule of law but the rule of a just law. And it is not a majority of the people that has established the foundations of this law, nor a ruling class, nor a faction that can be accused of favoritism. But God is the Lord of all, and human institutions chosen and controlled by the umma implement the Shari'a, explain it, and apply it to changing realities through their detailed legislation. It is the umma that is in charge of them, that gives them their office, keeps watch over them, and deposes them. That is the authority of the umma or her power of consultation [shura].

CONSULTATION [SHURA]: WHAT IS THE UMMA'S POSITION IN THE ISLAMIC STATE?

IN THE QUR'AN

"Obey God and the Messenger, and those in authority among you. If you are in dispute over any matter, refer it to God and the Messenger, if you truly believe in God and the Last Day."[80]

"Be a community that calls for what is good, urges what is right, and forbids what is wrong."[81]

"We offered the Trust to the heavens, the earth, and the mountains, yet they refused to undertake it and were afraid of it; mankind undertook it—they have always been very inept and rash."[82]

"[Those] who conduct their affairs by mutual consultation."[83]

"Consult with them about matters."[84]

"If two groups of the believers fight, you [believers] should try to reconcile them; if one of them oppresses the other, fight the oppressors until they submit to God's command."[85]

"If someone opposes the Messenger, after guidance has been made clear to him, and follows a path other than that of the believers, We shall leave him on his chosen path—We shall burn him in Hell, an evil destination."[86]

IN THE HADITH

"The Messenger of God (PBUH), when he sent Abu Mu'adh to Yemen, said, 'How will you judge when you are confronted with a case?' He answered, 'I will judge by the Book of God.' He asked, 'And if you don't find it in the Book of God?' He answered, 'By the Sunna of God's Messenger.' He asked, 'What if you don't find it in the Sunna of God's Messenger?' He said, 'I will rule with my own opinion and not interpret.' The Messenger of God (PBUH) patted him on the chest and said, 'Praise be to God who grants success to the envoy of God's Messenger and brings satisfaction to, the Messenger of God.'"[87]

"Is not each of you a shepherd accountable for His flock?"[88]

"God's hand is with the community; whoever treats them harshly will go into the Fire."[89]

"Whoever leaves the community by one inch has taken off the noose of Islam from his neck."[90]

"What Muslims see as good is good in God's eyes too."

"You are to care for the great majority of the people."[91]

"Whoever dies and doesn't have on his neck the pledge of allegiance to the ruler [bay'a], has died the death of *jahiliyya*."[92]

INTRODUCTION

If Islamic government is a government by law [Shari'a], if both ruler and ruled submit to its authority, the great and the small, and if the Shari'a at its foundation is a divine product (the divinely revealed texts of the Qur'an and Sunna), what is left for the community of believers to enact in terms of legislation? Some repeat again and again that there is no legislative authority in the Islamic state. Is that correct?[93] What is the position of the umma with regard to political rule? How does she exercise her prerogative?

What is shura? With regard to the Islamic political system, it is the second foundation after the sacred text. By nature it, too, is text: a text about the decisions of the umma, as it executes its delegated authority from God by participating in the affairs of state.[94] This is also among the umma's duties as dictated by the Shari'a, since shura is a landmark for an Islamic state and the Muslim umma. Therefore it is a "consultative state" and a "consultative umma."[95]

Islam stands out because of this original principle and therefore has prescribed it as a general code of conduct for members of society and mode of managing public affairs, so that the great Andalusian commentator al-Qurtubi made it a precondition of the legitimacy of the system of government in these words, "All Islamic scholars agree that a ruler who does not consult them should be deposed."[96]

Humankind has only been able to apply this principle after a bitter struggle over hundreds of years, and the Qur'an introduced this principle into an environment that sanctified force and was characterized by enmity and domination.[97]

Mutual consultation [shura] in Islam is not a specific command within the body of religious injunctions, or a rule based on one or two verses, several hadiths, and everyday realities. Rather, it is one of religion's foundations and one of the requirements of humanity's divine vicegerency—that is, the divine transfer of authority to human beings[98] who received God's covenant to worship Him. This is why shura is the backbone of the umma's authority. It allows her to discharge the function of political power given to her as a trust and to exercise it responsibly by promoting participation and cooperation. God entrusted the umma with this privilege of participating in establishing political systems, enacting laws, overseeing their implementation and enjoying the benefit they provides.

WHAT IS THE SCOPE OF THIS PARTICIPATION?

The sacred text represents the first foundation of the Islamic political, social, and religious system ("O you who believe, obey God, His Messenger and those who are in authority over you"),[99] just as it is the cornerstone of the Islamic state's constitution.[100] Al-Shafi'i went so far as to state that had there only been this verse, it would have been enough to support the Islamic state, for it defines with clarity the source of highest authority in the lives of Muslims, which is God, and that, as a result, one may not obey a creature that commands something in contradiction to God's law. It also clearly teaches that obedience to the Messenger (PBUH) is the practical side of obeying God, even if God is to be obeyed first. God said, "Whoever obeys the Messenger obeys God."[101]

The authority of the umma comes next, though its legal influence may not go against God's plain Shari'a rules in the Qur'an and Sunna, and this goes for anyone who has authority among Muslims, whether religious scholar, governor, political ruler, judge, director, or teacher. To sum up, anyone with responsibility ("Each one of you is a shepherd accountable for the flock") should be obeyed within the domain of his responsibility, as long as he carries out his task with faithfulness within the Shari'a's limits. Any conflict that arises, whether between individuals or institutions, should be referred and submitted to the one decisive authority, the Qur'an and Sunna. They both represent the highest law that governs—on an equal footing—the behavior of political leaders and Muslims in general. They also set the criteria for any new ruling [ijtihad] applying to changing conditions, which must not contradict any explicit and definitive text and must fulfill the Shari'a's objectives and general principles. Every person is equal before God's law, and the fact of referring issues to God and His Messenger no doubt requires the existence of a body able to issue binding decisions and take charge of this process of reference and extrapolation. This body could be a high court composed of the best judges among jurists, as we shall see below.

WHO ARE "THOSE IN AUTHORITY" ("ULUL AL-AMR")?

The above Qur'anic verse ("O you who believe, obey God, His Messenger and those who are in authority over you," Q. 4:59), begins by mentioning the authority of God and His Messenger—and that is an absolute authority, because it is established above the community and the state. The verse then mentions an authority tied to and submitted to the first one. For that reason, the verb "obey" is not used a second time, which underscores that this obedience is not unconditional and not independent from their obedience to God and to His Messenger but a part of it.[102]

Who then are these "people in authority"? Does this concept have a connection with basic political and legislative concepts like "the people of shura," ["ahl al-shura"] "the people of binding authority" ("the people who loosen and bind") ["ahl al-hall wal-'aqd"],[103] the people of "choice" or of "consensus" "ahl al-ikhtiyar", "ahl al-ijma'"? What about the oath of allegiance [bay'a]? And does shura have a connection to the idea of a social contract, or the concept of sovereignty, or the idea of elections, of a ruling party and the opposition, or a multiparty system?

The Companion Ibn 'Abbas and the Follower Mujahid Ibn Jabr (may God be pleased with them) opined that "those in authority" mentioned in that verse were the jurists who excelled in their sound judgment, depth of knowledge, and devotion to religion[104]—and they were the ones who were known for creating new rulings when necessary [ijtihad]. The Muslim jurists later called them "the people of binding authority," who were designated as the community of Muslims in Hudhayfa bin al-Yaman's hadith: "Stay committed to the community of Muslims and their imam."[105] These are the Islamic scholars ('ulama') who were promised by the Prophet that they could never agree on an error ("My umma will not agree on an error"), and if they agree on a ruling, then it becomes part of the Shari'a [ijma', or consensus], and if they agree to pledge their oath to an imam, all Muslims will have to obey him, because the legality of that obedience is derived from the "people of consensus" as one of the Shari'a's sources.[106]

Many commentators on the above verse resolved the issue of the "people of binding authority," like for instance Muhammad 'Abduh in his *Manar* commentary, in the following way: "Scholars have disagreed on the issue of 'those in authority'; some say they are the amirs and others say they are the scholars."[107] But the Shaykh concludes that they are the amirs, the rulers, the military leaders, and all other notables to whom people turn to address their general needs and interests. These are the ones who, when they agree on an injunction or ruling, the people are obliged to obey, on the condition that they are "one of us," that they do not contravene God's law or the Messenger's Sunna—that which is known to be completely reliable[108]—that they be free to decide in their examination of the issue and to give their assent to it once decided, and that what they agree upon among the issues of public interest is truly something over which they have authority to decide. In his words,

> As for the "people of binding authority" among the believers, if they agree on a matter of public interest about which there is no text from the Divine Legislator, they are free to decide on that issue, and not bound in any way, and obedience to them is obligatory. It is correct to say that they are free from error in the context of that consensus, and for that reason the command to obey them was issued without condition.[109]

Again, God's law is found in two sources about which there is no discussion: in His Book and the fixed and decisive Sunna of His Messenger. As for issues of public interest not dealt with in any text, those in authority look into them, because the people trust them for that purpose and follow them. But in that process they are obligated to consult one another in deciding those issues: "they are the people of binding authority."[110]

Rashid Rida noted that the "people of binding authority" for al-Razi were the people of consensus and those equipped to issue new rulings based on their learned opinion and juridical knowledge.[111] He also thought that there must be in the umma men of deep insight, learned opinion, and with the power to apply it to the texts with regard to politics and social interests. These are the people who would be consulted about matters of security and other social and political issues, and who in the Islamic tradition are called the "people of shura" and "people of binding authority," and who in other nations would be called "the people's delegates."[112] According to Islamic law, the oath of allegiance to the caliphs is not legitimate unless these people choose the caliph and willingly pledge their oath to him. The author of *Signposts of the Two Schools* put it this way,

> According to the Arabs' language and in agreement with Islamic custom, the imamate is the ruling authority over the Muslims. By imamate is meant the rule of the imam after the Prophet (PBUH). Over that there is no disagreement between the two schools of Muslims (Sunni and Shi'i). The disagreement is about who are the ones rightly called "those in authority." The school of the Prophet's family (*ahl al-bayt*, may God's peace be upon them) believes that when it was clearly revealed that there should be imams, they must necessarily have been designated by God and an infallible, while the Sunnis [*ahl al-sunna*] believe that the imam is merely the ruler to whom the Muslims pledge their allegiance [bay'a].[113]

Speaking about this verse on "those of authority," Professor 'Allal al-Fasi remarked, "The expression 'refer it to God' means to refer it to His Book, and 'refer it to the Messenger' means to refer it to the Sunna, and 'refer it . . . to those in authority' means to refer it to the consensus of the jurists who have exercised *ijtihad*."[114]

This is how scholarly consensus was practiced in the lives of Muslims in the heartland of Islam. It was considered an instrument crafted for the purpose of implementing mutual consultation in a practical way. That said, the introduction of divergent forms of thought and culture in Muslim societies almost emptied this very important concept of all meaning. In effect, it is similar to the concept of public opinion today both in content and efficacy. But historically, this consensus was merely an assumed ideal, difficult to actually put into practice, and so much so that great scholars like Ibn Hazm denied its validity.

CONSULTATION AND CONSENSUS

'Allal al-Fasi pursues the connection between the idea of consensus and that of "those in authority" in identifying those who hold authority in the Islamic state:

The truth is that the concept of consensus [ijma'] has a long history in Islam, but it was the use of consensus after the Prophet's death (PBUH), in order to choose a caliph and establish a rule of shura that sowed doubts in the minds of the Shia and led eventually to the position of the Mu'tazilites with regard to ijma' and its defense.[115]

When the Prophet (PBUH) died and his instructions as to who should succeed him were not known, this nurtured the Islamic spirit built on mutual consultation among the believers and led the umma to fulfill its duty in maintaining order and protecting the oath of allegiance to the ruler. Knowledgeable believers agreed during the Saqifa meeting to exchange views and arguments.[116] After a while they agreed to pledge their oath of allegiance to Abu Bakr, which led to a consensus of the people on accepting this decision. This is the path of consultation and agreement that Muslims continued to take, as they collected the Qur'an into a book and created all manner of systems and regulations. The matter of consensus continued to play an all-important and constructive role in fulfilling what the Prophet (PBUH) had intended, in harmony with his Shari'a and example. Al-Baghawi (d. 1122) disagreed with Maymun Ibn Mahran (d. 735), saying, "When Abu Bakr was presented with a dispute, he would look into the Qur'an, and if he found that which could settle the issue he would offer his judgment; but if he couldn't find the answer in the Qur'an but knew about God's Messenger's custom on the matter, he would offer his judgment. If he could not, he would go out and ask the Muslims, saying, 'I ran into this or that, do you know if God's Messenger ruled on such a case?' If that too failed, he would gather the leaders and most knowledgeable of the people and consult with them; and if their opinion converged, he would judge on the matter based on that."

And thus we find that ijma' rendered the greatest service to Islam, since it opened the door to the search for new rulings [ijtihad] and shura, and facilitated the continuation of the work that the Prophet (PBUH) had begun.

The first period of Islam, as we have seen, was characterized by mutual consultation in all matters not found in the sacred texts, and the "people of binding authority" participated in establishing the historical and social foundations for ijma' as a source of Islamic law. But when Muslims deviated from the system of a consultative caliphate and borrowed from the Persians a system of dynastic, absolute political power, it created a movement of critical backlash on the part of the jurists and other leaders. In order to protect this nascent absolute rule, rulers found it necessary to put obstacles in the way of this movement, and the idea of consensus as conceived by the early Muslims was one of the casualties. Diverging views emerged, and the concept strayed away from its original meaning.

Since the sixth century of Islam what was referred to as ijma‘ was the agreement of people all over the world, an idea that the early Muslims did not
share and one that had no grounds in the Qur’an and Sunna.

In fact, the concept of ijma‘ refers to the agreement of jurists capable of
ijtihad who consult together on a particular issue not specified in the
Qur’an or Sunna—a process commanded by the Qur’an in these words,
“and consult with them on the issue.” Consensus is not about each jurist
or scholar examining another opinion and then giving his own approval,
nor about us knowing his viewpoint and then rallying people’s opinion
around it. That does not appear to be how the Companions (may God be
pleased with them) understood the agreement that was incumbent upon
them to come to on a particular issue. Clearly Abu Bakr, ‘Umar, ‘Uthman,
and ‘Ali would execute their decisions after consulting with representatives from among the knowledgeable Companions. But they never put off
doing so until they had consulted with others dispersed throughout Muslim lands.

Therefore, ijma‘ truly refers to the agreement of a consultative body established by the caliph in order to decide on a particular issue. If everyone
agrees on a Shari‘a ruling, then there is a consensus and the ruling must be
executed, though it is permitted for a jurist (“one of the people of ijtihad”)
who was not present to offer a dissenting opinion. But Muslims are obliged
to implement whatever this body decides. Unfortunately, Muslims have not
followed through and established this process of consensus in the way the
Islamic principles of consultation and the Prophet’s guidance (PBUH) require. The caliph ‘Ali (may God be pleased with him) once said, “I said, ‘O
Messenger of God, what [should we do] about a matter that is neither mentioned in the Qur’an nor supported by any of your customs [Sunna].’ He
answered, ‘Gather the knowledgeable believers and consult among yourselves, but do not proceed on the basis of just one opinion.’”

Did the Prophet (PBUH) mean that everything should be put on hold until
all the scholars from around the Muslim world can meet and settle the matter? If that were the case, Shari’a would be impossible to implement.

CONSENSUS AND TYRANNY

The despotic rule led consensus away from its original role (or mission) and
turned it into a controversy. Shaykh al-Fasi continues his reflections on consensus, consultation, and democracy:

But it is political despotism that afflicted the Islamic political system and trans-formed progress in developing shura into empty debates about the validity of consensus and the possibility of instituting it or not.

If Muslims had continued along their natural path, a group of sincere jurists capable of ijtihad would have come alongside each of the caliphs, advising him of what he should do and how to adjudicate every legal quandary accord-ing to the requirements that a close reading of the Qur'an and Sunna would provide . . . . Do the circumstances of Muslim nations allow their modern democratic institutions the opportunity to revive Islamic shura and to fulfill the meaning of ijma'?

Or can the concept of consensus be abrogated? The best I can say in summary is that the definitive consensus that has been agreed upon cannot be changed, while a dissenting opinion can be changed. Abu 'Abdallah al-Basri argued that it was permitted to abrogate matters on which there had been a consensus, but that the original consensus remained until there was another one on the same issue.

The best solution is to leave ijma' with its consultative mission among Mus-lims and that they return to it every time a matter arises or an event happens that needs attention.[117]

We find, then, that the Moroccan scholar in highlighting the political dimen-sions of ijma' in a crystal-clear manner agreed with the great scholars of Islam in bringing together and applying the concepts of "those in authority," "the people of shura," and "the people of binding authority." He argued that consen-sus is one of the foundations of Islam and that "those in authority" or "the people of shura" are the Islamic legal scholars and opinion leaders who represent the Islamic umma's leading thinkers. They are even "politicians" in the ideal pic-ture of Islamic governance. And though this is not always the case, they are the ones entrusted with managing the public affairs of the Muslim populace; among them you will find the "amir." Their function, in fact, is to help him to run the affairs of state, either by enacting laws or proffering advice, monitoring, or de-signing public policy. The ruler covenants before them to apply with their help the rulings clearly enunciated in the sacred texts in order to respond to situa-tions that arise, as will be spelled out below, with the understanding that consensus is Islam's system of consultation in matters on which the texts are silent or differ.

Muhammad Yusuf Musa offered a similar opinion, stating that "those of bind-ing authority" are the scholars and intellectuals worthy of trust among various strata of Muslim society. This is not very different from the members of parliament in modern constitutional systems. The representatives are the source of all laws without exception, and similarly in Islam, except in matters clearly stated in the Qur'an or in the Messenger's authoritative Sunna. In those matters "those with binding authority" have the duty to understand the texts and consider the circumstances in which they were revealed. The source of sovereignty is the legislation taken from the Book and the authentic Sunna, if the texts are pertinent to particular issues; and in cases where the texts are silent, that which does not contradict the spirit and objectives of these two sacred sources. Then naturally, sovereignty must have someone to embody it. In this case, we say it is those with "binding authority" delegated to represent the whole umma, so that their decisions and enacted laws—built upon their consensus—are legitimate from a Shari'a standpoint and binding for the whole umma.[118]

THREE TECHNICAL TERMS

For his part, Kamal Abu al-Majd considers that as long as ambiguity surrounds a number of terms relating to shura, there is no hope for anchoring Islamic political thought and extracting it from what some have called "the crisis of Islamic political thought."[119] In his words,

> In books of Islamic political theory and books of Islamic jurisprudence in general, we find three technical terms that need precision and definition. Sometimes the jurists point to the "people of shura," sometimes to "those with binding authority," and sometimes to the "people of ijtihad."
>
> The term that comes with most precision from our perspective is the expression "people of shura," which generally indicates those that the ruler finds useful in seeking advice from on a particular matter, and it is natural that, depending on the issue involved, their description and qualifications may vary. As for the term "those with binding authority," it indicates the amount of social influence a particular group might have, in such a way that their leaning toward an individual, or opinion or decision is enough of a reason to rally others to approve of the person or matter and enlist their support for and submission to a particular legal ruling. As for the term "people of ijtihad," the most logical definition is those who are competent to offer legal advice [fiqh] on a variety of matters. If the issue arising is of a legislative nature, then their qualification is their ability to engage the issue using the highest level of Islamic reasoning [ijtihad] on the basis of the Shari'a, that is, the ability to extract Shari'a rulings from textual indicators along with the research, deduction and knowledge that this requires. And if the issue

presented is of an economic, social, engineering, medical or financial nature, then it is those who are qualified to apply their abilities in solving those matters. And if they have no knowledge in that area, they must responsibly seek advice from those who are competent and follow it.

With respect to ijtihad, as the scholars have truthfully said, it is a domain subject to specialization and division of labor, and he who has not attained the level of ijtihad in some area of knowledge is not allowed to offer any legal opinion on the matter and, naturally, one should not seek out his opinion.

The "people of shura," then, are not a particular and stable group, and definitely not a clearly defined "Islamic" system we can look for in academic books from which we can draw ready-made insights.[120]

So "people of shura" are the "people of binding authority" to which the jurists referred, who carry out the functions of the representative assemblies of the present age, but only within the limits of Shari'a principles.[121]

THE LEGISLATIVE DIMENSION OF SHURA

We have now defined some of the basic terms related to the political concept of mutual consultation or shura. Our task now is to explore in more depth how Islamic governance works in practice, first from the legislative side, and then from a wider political perspective.

WHO PERFORMS THE LEGISLATIVE FUNCTION IN THE ISLAMIC STATE?

If there is a consensus that took place among Muslims that the original or fundamental law is purely God's prerogative (may He be exalted), because He is the possessor of all power,[122] the scholars differed on the derived or secondary legislation [ijtihad] by defining the domain of what is permitted and the rulings based on opinion within the framework of the definitive rulings of the Shari'a and its objectives. They also differed on who had the right to perform this task, whether it was the umma, or an elite group within it, or the scholars who had reached the level of ijtihad, or "those in authority."

The Legislative Assembly:

The opinions we have presented all center around a specialized group of people sometimes called "those of binding authority," or the "people of shura," or "those in authority," or the "people of consensus." Professor 'Abd al-Wahhab Khallaf has brought some precision to this question,

In contemporary constitutional governments those who hold legislative power and enact the laws are the members of parliaments. But in the Islamic state those who hold that power are those capable of ijtihad, or jurists giving fatwas, and their authority does not exceed two functions. The first one concerns matters spelled out in the sacred texts. In those matters, their task is to explain the text and extrapolate the ruling to which it points. As to that which is not spelled out by the texts, their task is to find analogies in the text and deduce its rulings through ijtihad, locating the reason behind the divine rule and explaining it. For the Islamic state has a law, which stands on a divine foundation established by God in His Book and in the words of His Messenger. So where in the law there is an applicable text, it must be followed and there is no room for the Islamic legislators to use ijtihad or extrapolation from the text, since their point of reference for ijtihad and extrapolation is found in the texts of the fundamental law, that is, the unchangeable texts and objectives, which can be used in a constitution, thus taking advantage of the umma's past experience and present conditions, as well as of the experience of other nations.[123]

Professor Khallaf continues his argument:

With its reliance upon the fundamental legal structure set up by God, the Islamic legislative authority could have accomplished much. Had it established a system for electing its members by stipulating preconditions for ijtihad and limiting their numbers; and had the state taken seriously their views on matters of justice and administration, it would have been the best legislative authority of any constitutional government and would have met the needs of Muslims throughout the ages. Unfortunately, the system of legislation became chaotic and people claimed to be capable of ijtihad when they were not, impeding the process of enacting laws and rendering impossible the gathering of competent people and their exchange of views. When the scholars realized the extent of this chaos, they were forced to find a solution, but they fixed it by closing the door of ijtihad, and thereby stopped the process of legislation. As a result, they landed in the evil they tried to avoid and Islamic legislation turned away from people's best interests and needs. Yet all the good was there from the start: the community's ijtihad and crafting of laws, and that was the path taken by the Prophet's Companions and those who followed.[124]

Then Professor Khallaf praises the legacy of the Shura Council in the Umayyad capital of Cordoba.[125] He agrees with many contemporary scholars of Islamic political theory [*al-siyasa al-shar'iyya*] about the call to create a new

form that would give shape to the rule of consensus, so as to practice the collective obligation of ijtihad[126] which fulfills the functions of representative assemblies and embodies the concept of sovereignty or the highest authority in the
Islamic state—that is, having the power to give a decisive word on the umma's
public policies and public interests under the Shari'a's sovereignty. But how
does this assembly come into being? The Shari'a does not prescribe any particular model, but the matter is left to the evolution of time. What we know for
sure is that Muslims fell short of filling the gaps the Legislator had left for
them, leaving the matter to run into chaos, which in turn stalled the objectives
of the Shari'a. There have been many proposals in the modern era to establish
this legislative assembly, including through elections, designation by the head
of state, or by reaching a particular level of knowledge.[127]

IS LEGISLATION THE RIGHT OF THE RULER, THE 'ULAMA', OR THE UMMA'S REPRESENTATIVES?

The legislative function, or the enacting of laws covering new situations, is
one of the most debated topic among Muslims, whether in ancient times or
today[128]: Is it the prerogative of the executive branch as represented in the person holding political power, as the great number of references in the early sources
ascribing to him the rank of *mujtahid* would seem to indicate? Or should it be
that of the Islamic jurists? Or is it the umma's function as she chooses those who
will perform the task of legislators within the parameters of the Shari'a? There
are two main opinions on this.

Only the Shari'a Specialists ('Ulama') Carry Out the Legislative Function

The majority opinion in the course of Islamic history and even today among
those who specialize in Islamic political theory is that legislation on the basis
of ijtihad is limited to the Islamic jurists ('ulama') by reason of their ability to
extract rulings from the texts and that no other popular representatives are
capable of performing this task. Professor Subhi 'Abduh Sa'id opined that
since legislation is the extraction of meanings from the sacred texts, it is not the
business of the people (or the citizens), because an Islamic society is not like
other unbelieving societies, nor can their respective representatives be compared. Rather, such a task should be assigned to experts in the principles and
sources of the divine law.[129]

Some have objected to this argument—despite its cogency—that even though
the Islamic jurists are specialized in the Islamic sources, legislative work is not
always about issuing technical fatwas, or verifying the authenticity of hadiths,

or ascertaining the meaning of a Qur'anic verse. Most of the time, it deals with people's conditions, relations between groups, and the criteria necessary to make informed decisions about these affairs, and it would be unfair for the umma to have one group monopolize political decision making, no matter how much it knows about Islam's sacred texts. If legislative responsibility is restricted to one group, even if they are "the people of ijtihad," in order to design policies for war and peace, the economy, social issues and education, and the like would not be in the public interest. The public interest [al-maslaha al-'amma] is in fact the sphere of ijtihad, since it is the Shari'a's highest objective when the texts are silent. On the one hand, there is an advantage to assigning the function of ijtihad to a class of Islamic jurists, as it will guarantee that the laws and the constitution will harmonize with state policies and its Islamic identity expressed by the people's spirit and heritage, and this in turn will keep that spirit and heritage from being sidelined. Neglecting the religious scholars could lead to alienation and deep conflict, which could open the door to movements of extremism and violence—something in fact that has happened. On the other hand, jurist-led legislation deprives the people of the contribution of other specialists whose skills and knowledge are necessary to make wise decisions about problems that grow increasingly complex today.

What is more, the bundling of legislative powers in the hands of one group creates a monopoly of power, which is the definition of despotism, even if the ones in charge are the most pious and knowledgeable of God's creatures. For limitations of knowledge and insight, weakness and error are all part of the human condition, except for the prophets whom God granted immunity from error. Therefore, the only means to limit the potential fallout from this inherent weakness is to make mutual consultation [shura] legally binding, so as to free public affairs, and especially the political arena, from the domination of one person or one class. This means that to restrict the function of ijtihad to the Islamic jurists is to invite the evil of elite rule, limited political participation, and a monopoly on political power.

Although in our day the practice of Islamic scholars coming together for the purpose of collective decision making—a duty in itself and an alternative to the individual legal decisions made in our past—could limit the potential of authoritarianism, the problem will persist, because these scholars are often removed from the nature of the problems that come up for investigation in an age when issues have become more complex. In fact, it has become almost impossible for people with only one specialty to gain all the knowledge necessary to come to an informed decision about an area outside their specialty. This makes it necessary to rely on the collective decision making of a group with many specialties so they can complement one another, thus creating synergy and cross-fertilization.

Since the time of Shaykh Hasan al-Banna (see *The Treatises of Hasan al-Banna*), the leaders of the contemporary Islamic movement consider the parliamentary system of government the most important institution and the closest to Islam's values, in that the legislative body brings together elite thinkers, politicians, practitioners, and representatives of the main forces in society that form the state. When these people pass a bill that aims for the common good, they truly deserve the title "the people of authority" [ulu al-amr]. And despite the presence of Shari'a specialists within the assemblies, the key is to develop institutions that monitor the constitutionality of other bodies, to guarantee thereby the harmony between law and culture.

The Legislative Function of Ijtihad Is Carried Out by the Ruler

The traditional schools of law stipulated that a ruler must have the ability to engage in ijtihad. Yet even if it was difficult to find a head of state who was also a *mujtahid* [a person exercising ijtihad], he was duty-bound to consult one, as Sa'id writes, "the important goal is to keep legislation out of the hands of those incapable of ijtihad."[130] In Article 39 of the draft constitution that Taqi al-Din al-Nabhani[131] considered to be a suitable model for Islamic governance, we read, "The president of the state is the state, and he possesses all of the state's powers. Among these, he executes Shari'a rulings when he adopts them and they become state laws that must be obeyed and not violated."[132] For this he relied on two arguments. First, the life of the caliphs: "Abu Bakr and 'Umar during their caliphates deduced rulings from the sacred texts on their own and used them to govern their people . . . The caliph would derive a particular ruling from the Shari'a and command the people to apply it. They were committed to applying it, leaving behind their own opinions and interpretations of the texts."

The second thing was this: the Shari'a law required that the ruler's decree be obeyed as an observable action reflecting a person's inner submission to that ruler. The consensus of the Companions was that it was the imam's right to issue particular rulings and to command all Muslims to obey them, even if it went against their own interpretation of the texts [ijtihad]. Among the well-known Shari'a rules is this: "The Sultan has the right to issue as many rules as he finds problems." The caliph commanded people to end conflicts, and the caliph Harun al-Rashid (d. 809) created the taxes advocated in Abu Yusuf's *Kitab al-Kharaj* and ordered his people to apply its rules.[133]

We find in Article 2 in a more precise and clear manner: "The head of state adopts particular Shari'a rulings that he enacts within the constitution and state laws, and each law thus enacted becomes a Shari'a statute itself that must be carried out, and at that moment it carries legal force requiring the full obedience of every individual in that state."[134] As a result, the Shura Council in Nabhani's political model does not have legislative powers, though its Muslim members have the right to discuss legislation enacted by the head of state. Though he listens to them, he is not obliged to follow their opinion.[135]

Critique of the above position: this opinion rests on doubtful and unreliable arguments that lead to a dangerous position, namely the umma being robbed, either as a whole or in represented by its opinion leaders, of its right to legislation. Al-Nabhani relied on historical cases, which he then interpreted in a way that supported his position. These cases, as he saw them, represented a style of lawmaking chosen by Abu Bakr and 'Umar (may God be pleased with them), which consisted of imposing on the Muslims the opinion they had come to through their effort to interpret the texts, despite the fact that these cases do not constitute binding precedents for Muslims. The important point is that each one relied on his opinion to guide his policy. Islamic jurists both ancient and modern have made other decisions in light of these cases that go against what Shaykh Nabhani concluded. In fact, the disagreement revolves around whether or not consultation [shura] is mandatory, and, contrary to Shaykh Nabhani, most experts in the Islamic theory of legitimate governance, including the leaders of modern Islamic movements especially, tend to agree that shura is mandatory for a head of state. We will return to this question later.

As for the second argument, it assumes a quasi-consensus in the age of the Companions that the ruler's decision resolves disagreements and binds the umma. And though one can find some support for this position during the age of the Rightly Guided Caliphs (although its main evidence is historical practice, which is not a grounds for rulings but simply an example that can be taken into account), the real issue lies elsewhere. The question remains—what was the process followed by the ruler in order to arrive at the correct opinion, and issue it as a binding rule? Was there any debate that preceded it or not? And with whom? And is the ruler bound by the outcome of that discussion or not? Thus, Sheikh Nabhani's argument is a sort of proof by affirmation or "assuming the conclusion." So, instead of proving to us that public interest (or good) lies in this ruler-jurits monopolizing decisions in crucial matters concerning the umma, and in excluding from the process other jurists, experts, and representatives of the people—even if he does seek their counsel without committing to the majority opinion among them—instead of doing that, he keeps bringing up vague expres-

sions, like "the ruler's ruling ends all dispute," as if it were among the agreed upon
and generally known teachings. And instead of discussing the question of the ruler
dismissing the views of the experts of the umma in favor of his own, he goes over
and over about the claim—that the umma had agreed that the ruler's decision
ends all disputes. In other words, the people had agreed to relinquish their collective will in favor of the ruler's will.

How can any other conclusion be expected from Shaykh Nabhani, when for
him the state embodies or even merges into the personality of its head and when
the head of state *is* the state? Does this not remind us—even if not in an Islamic
context—of similar expressions given by absolute monarchs during various periods of tyranny: "I am the law," "I am the state"? As for the ruler being a mujtahid, this doesn't give his legal interpretation any preeminence with regard to
truth over the interpretations of others. On what grounds could the view be
justified that the individual ruler's opinion is worth more than that of the body
of jurists engaging in ijtihad as they debate among themselves in the Shura
Council? Also, what about the fact that it is nowadays quite impossible for a
single person (ruler or otherwise) to combine ijtihad competence in all fields? Is
it possible for the umma to entrust her entire destiny to an individual ruler who
relies on his own interpretation of God's law and could not care less about the
collective ijtihad of the chosen jurists and representatives in the Shura Council? And could he find an excuse for that on the basis that if his legal interpretation is correct he will receive two rewards, and otherwise, he goes back to the
simple reward that God promises all mujtahids, since he is rewarded in either
case, according to al-Buti?[136] Do the trust and justice attached to political power
in Islam imply that the ruler deserves a reward, while the people bear the brunt
of his mistakes, and monopoly on decision-making? Is the priority the ruler's reward, or is it about the best interest of the people?[137]

Additionally, the issues needing to be researched are not always Shari'a questions or simply religious, so that only Islamic scholars can pursue them and this
regardless of how necessary one thinks their opinions are to the ruler, if in fact
he listens to them in the first place. For instance, matters of war and peace,
economic development, administrative organization, politics, and health—there
are far too many questions that touch on people's everyday lives about which
these scholars have no particular competence and therefore should not offer
their views, and helpful answers will only be forthcoming from limited groups
of specialists in particular areas. But there are also more general questions that
are in no way technical and that touch on people's conditions and opinions that
cannot be answered by Islamic jurists, specialists in other fields, or scientists, and
are best left to popular leaders, such as party and trade union leaders, chiefs of

religious denominations, or tribes. These may include individuals with little religious knowledge, able to discern only the bare minimum with regard to religious issues.

Yet there are other issues that concern all members of the political community, issues that call for representation, delegation, and broad consultation to include everyone, which would give the final decision greater legitimacy and popular recognition. Generally, such decisions involve vital interests that touch on a people's destiny, such as treaties and important covenants, wars and peace settlements, and the oath of allegiance to the imam or ruler. What justification is there in such cases for excluding the people from exercising the function of consensus [ijma'] in the form of a referendum or a general vote, and the like?

Is that not a direct fulfillment of that unchanging, remarkable Qur'anic verse, which is incumbent upon the Muslim community, "And He commanded shura among them,"[138] and an application of the eloquent rule on the participation of all in public affairs, "And he consulted with them on the matter"?[139] Sura Ta Ha (Q. 20) explains the meaning of mutual consultation in a matter: it is to participate in discussing it, an indication taken from Moses's prayer to God, when he asks him to grant him a helper from his family who could share in his task: "And give me a helper from my family, my brother Aaron—augment my strength through him. Let him share in my task."[140] If that request is granted for the purpose of companionship, it is even more needed in the case of a ruler![141] Certainly the use of shura in the time of the Prophet (PBUH) and of his Rightly Guided successors flourished, with many texts attesting that it was an original source of law in building Islamic government and administration, and that there was no worse trait than the tendency to make decisions on one's own: "Whoever isolates himself, Satan will overpower him."[142] There are many passages giving evidence of the Prophet (PBUH) as ruler and commander giving way to others' opinions for the benefit of the community's consensus. In fact, what distinguishes the past experience of Islamic political rule is the independence of the legislative function from the state, restricting and even forbidding the state from encroaching on people's freedom and thereby oppressing them, as discussed below.[143]

The Umma Is the Source of Legislation

With regard to the legislative dimension of shura, even though original legislation in Islam emanates from God's will as it was revealed in the texts of the Qur'an and Sunna, we have clearly seen also that the umma has been called upon to participate in legislative activity. This is so because the final and eternal nature of the Shari'a means that the Divine text is limited to the delineation of general principles to guide human relations, while offering a bare minimum of detailed rules, except for a few areas like a few texts on punishments for a handful of major crimes and on several family matters, for the purpose of helping to establish a framework for Islamic society. At the same time, then, the Shari'a leaves the bulk of details for creating that framework to the legislative efforts of the umma, taking into account the evolution of society over time. This requires considerable effort, and the consensus [ijma'] of the umma is recognized as one of the sources of the Shari'a, alongside divine revelation. The consensus of the people thus becomes a brilliant demonstration of how the umma, as she finds guidance from God's divine guidance, draws from this light the power to shield herself from error. Yet despite the natural and permanent weakness of human knowledge—"the son of Adam is prone to error," as the hadith goes—the hard work of the umma on the path of God affords her protection from collective error, and elevates what is relative to the rank of absolute.

For consensus in Islam is the ennoblement of the whole of humanity, and recognition of the maturity and responsibility of the human being, even if God seeks to guide his soul with the input of advice and direction.

Indeed, consensus, which is considered one of the Shari'a's sources beside the Qur'an and Sunna, is a manifest call to recognize public opinion, in all its diversity, and to take it into account when legislating.[144] This human element, which entered the Shari'a to become part of, it is not foreign to it either. In fact, it is one of the fruits of its guidance as long as the umma remains pure in her intent and keeps toiling in the way of God. If she does so, then she sees through God's light;[145] her dreams become part of the prophetic legacy,[146] and good is that which she deems good.[147]

This human element, touched by the Divine, is not foreign to the Shari'a; in fact, both are made from the same element. Were not the human faculties breathed into the human being through God's Spirit, and are they not another manifestation of the Shari'a?[148] Doesn't the end of the era of prophethood mean human governance shaped by human beings' intellectual capacities and ability to manage their own lives in light of general principles and rules?[149]

Since in the context of the divine Shari'a and its objectives the umma is granted a strong legislative role, and since *hakimiyya*, or what is called in contemporary constitutional parlance "sovereignty," means basically the authority to legislate, this is a legitimate statement and a natural outcome: it is certain that sovereignty in the Islamic state belongs to the Shari'a and also to the law—both the revealed texts and the rules and statutes enacted by the umma[150] within the framework of the texts and their objectives—so that certain

Islamic thinkers have asserted that Muslims are the first community in history
to say that the people are the source of powers.[151] In the same vein, 'Abbas al-
'Aqqad certified the compatibility of the following two statements—the umma
is the source of sovereignty *and* the Noble Qur'an and the Prophetic Sunna are
the source of legislation. This is so, because it is the umma that understands
and interprets the Book and the Sunna, acting upon them, and looking to its
own circumstances to find areas of application, areas of non-application, and
areas calling for amendments. It is the umma that approves the decrees issued
by the ruler or objects to them, just as the caliph 'Umar suspended the penalty
for stealing during the year of famine.[152]

For the Shari'a is not a set of rigid texts, nor is it something shaped in final
form, nor is it a body of written laws such that there is a law for each act and
situation. Rather, there is still much room for interpretation, definition, addition, and renewal through the use of reason, applied either individually or collectively—in other words, ijtihad. What is more, it recognizes the umma's
personality as expressed in a specific period of time and its public will to enact
laws accordingly. Also, the concept of consensus [ijma'], a distinguishing element of the Islamic Shari'a is that it gives a place in the Islamic political system to the umma and her will, which is higher than that given to the people in
any other democratic system, however complete. Muslims, then, decided long
before Rousseau and similar thinkers wrote about the general will and praised
it, that the people's will is free from error and that it emanates from God's will,
recognizing it as a source of legislation, even if in the end it is grounded in the
Qur'an and Sunna.

From a practical standpoint, this will represents the consensus of the jurists
among the umma's scholars,[153] since consensus for Muslims, as al-'Aqqad noted,
is twofold: elite and public. It is among the elite, in that it is the agreement of
opinion leaders in the Islamic sciences and of "those in authority," or the political leaders; and it is public, in that it is the consensus of all the people, specialists or not, learned or not. The consensus of the Islamic elites is required
for legislative sovereignty; the consensus of the elites and the general public is
required for political sovereignty.[154] Razi, for his part, asserted the following in
his commentary of the verse "Obey God, and obey the Messenger, and those
in authority among you": "God's command of obedience here took the form of
an authoritative affirmation, and from this command we surmise that he who
God commanded us to obey must be free from error, otherwise it would be a
command to commit an act of wrongdoing." Razi means that those free from
error are not individuals within the umma but rather a group that represents it

as "those in authority," those who are the scholars of the umma, capable of extracting rules from the texts. And when they agree on a ruling, it becomes part of the Shari'a.[155] As the Prophet (PBUH) said, "My umma will not agree on an error."

With regard to *the source of legislation:* the most important characteristic of the Islamic civilization is that it is a civilization of legislation and jurisprudence.[156] Its legislative wealth has no equal in other nations or civilizations in terms of solidity, breadth, and diversity. And this is what surprises those unfamiliar with this civilization as they open the door to enter it, believing it to be a civilization built on legal texts sent from Heaven, with a deterministic mindset and a theocratic view of governance, all of which erode the stature of humanity and their role in life. According to that worldview, people find themselves in a self-contained and ready-made world in which to every question there is an answer and to every legislative door corresponds a separate legal code, so that the only thing left to do is to comply. In this scenario there is no need for intellectual effort.

This is a complete myth. For according to Islam, humankind is God's deputy, responsible for developing the earth and fashioning life, existence, and humanity in light of lofty principles and the public interest. Indeed, in light of those principles God gave humanity the mandate to create within each age a new model of civilization, a mandate that allows them to invent an infinity of models for Islamic societies, beginning with the texts and shura.[157] What is strange, however, is that in spite of this treasure trove of laws—which still today sets the Islamic civilization apart—some Muslims are calling for a break with Islam and its legislative heritage and demanding an Islam that is watered down and cut off from the Shari'a due to the influence of external intellectual influence. They forget that "our achievements in jurisprudence will last longer than the splendors of our nations and that of our political and military rulers."[158]

THE LEGAL SCHOOLS, CONSULTATION, AND THE UMMA

The flexibility and comprehensiveness of the Islamic texts and the lofty position they granted to human reason—stimulating it repeatedly and urging it continually to free itself, interrogate the horizons of knowledge and explore the minutiae of things by researching causes and effects. This flexibility, then, opened the way for an extraordinary legislative revolution, and though it sprang from the texts and followed a single path, it branched out in amazing diversity and was able to produce multiple comprehensive legal systems, without even speaking of the many divergent views on specific issues—a diversity that is difficult to even grasp. Two aspects in particular stand out.

Schools of Jurisprudence Are Expressions of Shura

These systems of jurisprudence, even though they were often associated with the name of a prominent jurist, were the fruit of the collective effort of many scholars working together and consulting one another. Malik bin Anas (may God be pleased with him), for example, did not express his own opinion but rather the consensus of the juridical community of Medina and its traditions. His legal opinions were, therefore, built on consultation. Similarly, Abu Hanifa (may God be pleased with him) did not produce legal opinions on his own but worked closely with the leading thinkers of his school, like Abu Yusuf, Zafr, and Muhammad. There was an ongoing dialogue between them, and in that process an opinion emerged. The jurist did not isolate himself in his own thinking and opinion; he participated in discussion with others. The imam as legal scholar did not impose a legal opinion, and the same freedom ought to prevail in politics and government.[159]

The same can be said about the process of articulating new rulings in new settings [ijtihad] among the other schools of Islamic law, for instance that of Ja'far al-Sadiq (may God be pleased with him) or the Ja'fari jurisprudence, or that of 'Abd Allah Ibn Ibad (may God be pleased with him) or the Ibadi jurisprudence. Put more simply, each of these schools traces its identity to one great scholar.[160] Yet though most of these schools are named after one person, the majority opinion in them and the focus of their work are not always those of the founder of the school nor the greatest among the founders. Often it is the opinion of one of his Companions that prevails, either during his time or in the centuries following him. This means that the school's name (pointing to an individual) is just a practical way of identifying it. Thus similar expressions spread within the confines of a school, like the contents of the fatwas in Malik's school and so on— that is, the main focus of their work.

Often the Umma, Rather Than the Ruler, Chooses the Legal School

Even though the number of legal schools that grew up in the framework of the Islamic texts and the consultation of jurists was considerable, legislative authority in the life of Muslims emanated from only a few schools, which issued legal opinions [fatwas], provided guidance and acted as reference points for the courts. Despite the undeniable role rulers played in supporting certain schools over others and imposing them on their people, to exaggerate that factor while ignoring or at least downplaying the will of the people would be misleading. For the historical experience of Muslim societies shows that many rulers failed to impose their own school on their people, as was the case with Isma'ili Shia rulers in North Africa as they tried to substitute their own school for that of Malik. This is close to what the Husaynid Turkish rulers did in Tunisia, trying to impose the Hanafi school of law, but the people continue to safeguard and protect the school they had traditionally chosen, despite the will of the political elites.

There is no denying, then, the role of the people's will in giving the upper hand to a particular school over another due to a certain affinity between the school and the social and psychological disposition of the people.[161] This is still the case, even if the layperson has to follow the jurist, for he has the complete freedom to choose among jurists and schools of law, based on the principle of the plurality of schools and the plurality of interpretations. The consensus of the umma remains important, even if its legislative dimension remained the prerogative of the jurists. This in no way cancels out the umma's role in deciding to accept or reject legal schools. In fact, the authority of public opinion prevails within the framework of the fixed tenets of religion. So there also remains for individuals the freedom to follow or not to follow a particular jurist's fatwa, without it turning into a complete refusal of ijtihad, for that would be considered a rejection of the Shari'a, unless that person were a mujtahid himself.[162] For one should not neglect the exhortations of the Prophet (PBUH) to honor public opinion or "the vast majority."[163]

A POSSIBLE MODEL FOR LEGISLATIVE AUTHORITY IN OUR AGE

A religion that came to accompany humankind's journey on earth, traversing both time and space, is not meant to remain ossified and impervious to developments in methods of sociopolitical organization or people's daily lives—how they make a living and organize administrative procedures, health care, and the like. Islam considers that in these matters its task is to indicate general guidelines and signposts, values and basic criteria that provide guidance, prevent social upheaval and the confusion of values, which make us lose our moral compass and fall into the mire of absolute ethical relativism. Then there would be absolutely no meaning to the discernment between truth and falsehood, right and wrong. Islam, however, once the general ethical framework is in place, leaves it up to people's intellect and experience to fill in the vast empty spaces not covered by the texts with their own creativity.[164] To each person according to his ability and knowledge.

'Ali (may God honor him) is reported to have said, "I said, 'O Messenger of God, if a word from God comes to us, but it is not certain whether it is actually a command or a prohibition, what do you tell us to do?' He said, 'Have the jurists and pious ones consult one another and do not enforce one person's opinion.'"[165] The same position was taken during the era of the Rightly Guided Caliphs, even if they did not make this into a specific institution because Medinan society was small, and leadership emerged naturally through the struggle, so the people of shura were not difficult to identify. The mosque was the assembly room where people exchanged views on problems that arose on various levels. However, the first generation dwindled, and Islam spread throughout God's vast earth, and new cities grew up and competed with Medina, like Basra, Kufa, Damascus, and Cairo—and all of this without there being any organizing and development of the methods of consultation that had been used in the Medinan state. That rapid expansion created instability and anxiety from the time of 'Uthman's caliphate. Then the page was turned after the first four caliphs, so that the rule of shura was upended and became the rule of one despotic ruler monopolizing power without the input of those called for in the Shari'a—the umma and her representatives from among "those in authority." Thus one of the Shari'a's pillars came crashing down, and the journey of grievous division between religion and politics began in the life of Muslims,[166] just as Islamic scholarship was cut off from political practice. So one of the Shari'a's sources, consensus, was disabled in practice, both in its collective and individual expression, and when Muslim leaders stopped using the system of consensus, there was no longer any way to know which issues in reality called for consensus and which ones did not. In fact, after that unfortunate separation many Islamic scholars denied there could be any way to obtain shura; some exaggerated that claim, while on the whole it was denied. The only thing left from that source of Islamic law was a nation's consensus around what school of law to follow.

It was only natural that despotism ended up restricting the scope of consensus and freedom of thought. It also created fear about the fate of Islam, especially after all the internal fighting, external military defeats, injustices, and legislative chaos that befell the umma. Tyranny also increased the conflicts among scholars, making them more conservative and reluctant to innovate, and pushing them in the direction of prohibiting all acts that could themselves potentially lead to a prohibited act.[167] As a result, they became more rigid in their interpretation and limited themselves to what had been passed down to them from their fathers and forebears; "imitation" became the watchword among them, and they called for closing the door of ijtihad.[168] So the umma grew more weak and servile, and her despotic leaders gladly handed her over to foreign invaders. Sadly, she did not awaken until the roar of cannons destroyed her forts and wreaked havoc inside her walls.

At the same time, movements of reform and renewal have emerged to revisit this past, trying to make sense of it, to find solutions to the problems they discovered and meet the challenge of dangers they were now discovering. Governance was the biggest problem they encountered, as despotism reared its ugly head, so the reformers took a good look at it. They realized that they must take responsibility for the weakness and abasement the umma was experiencing, in contrast with the power and progress the Western nations had made because they were able to overcome the will of their absolute kings. Therefore, they needed governing instruments, constitutions, and assemblies. It was not long before the influence of Western culture began to express itself when reformers asked the following questions: Does Islam have a system of governance? What are its characteristics? How is it connected to Western state institutions, like the parliament, for instance? In the end, the reformers all agreed that there surely was an Islamic political theory from the start and that its distinctive features do not stand in the way of a serious engagement with the modern world in a process of give- and-take. This is how the issue of forming government institutions was raised, and in particular, the legislative body.

Constituting a Consultative Body

Muhammad Asad wrote:

Constituting a legislative body in the lives of nations is the most important and sensitive task, and as Muslims, we are bound to fulfill God's command in Scripture to deal with all our public affairs on the basis of consultation [shura]. In doing so, we cannot avoid confronting the fact that the very process of establishing an assembly must be done in a perfectly consultative way. Contemporary societies cannot ascertain public opinion and fulfill the principle of consultation without recourse to general elections, since it is the only means to reveal the voters' desires and offer people their right to choose. The electoral system can accommodate direct or indirect voting, regional divisions or divisions based on percentages and any other details that must be worked out—none of which is opposed by the Shari'a, which left such issues for the umma to decide.[169] What is important here is that elections should be the means for constituting the assembly from its inception, thus satisfying the principle of consultation commanded by God. The next step is for the assembly elected by the people to fulfill its mission of enacting laws, being an assembly representative of all its people, men and women equally.[170]

Khalid Muhammad Khalid maintained that . . .

The modern concept of consultation that Islam has developed is parliamentary democracy . . . in which the people elect representatives to give voice to
their own will and desires. These representatives for me are what the tradition called "those in authority," especially if several people with specialized
abilities are added to the representative assembly, even if co-opted for a limited
period of time.[171]

This is so because Islam, though elections do not figure in the texts, has stipulated that public affairs be conducted according to the consultative method. If
it is not possible for everyone to be involved in every issue, then representation
is necessary—representation by those among the people who are wise and capable leaders, traditionally called "those in authority."[172] Any method is permitted that helps to bring forward those who have the people's trust, and most
electoral methods used today are permissible, except those that use dishonest
and evil means.[173]

Stipulations for Membership in the Legislative Body

We have already noted how the classic books on legitimate Islamic governance
use the following terms interchangeably: "those in authority," "the people of
Shura," and "the people of opinion." To study them, one gets the impression
that from the Islamic perspective the Shura Assembly is a specialized group
composed only of Islamic scholars and jurists who have attained the highest
level, since their function is to derive rules from the sacred texts. This would in
fact require them to be mujtahids [i.e., capable of ijtihad]. The assumption here
is that if state and religion are connected, then the state must be led by clerics,[174]
when in fact from the Islamic view of the state the linking of politics and religious
rules certainly do not lead to the domination of clerics—for those who call
them by that name—over the Islamic state's political life.[175] Then what are the
conditions that must be met with regard to this assembly? Perhaps the most
important Islamic jurist to study the Islamic state and its institutions, including its consultative body, is Abu'l-A'la al-Mawdudi. We will use his writing on
this subject as a foil for our own discussion of this important topic.

Mawdudi sees four conditions that members of the legislative assembly must
meet. What are they, and how should we assess them?

First Condition: Islam

This is based on the Qur'anic verse, "O you who believe, obey God and the
Messenger, and those in authority among you."[176] Therefore, only Muslims who

are convinced about the truth of the Islamic constitution are responsible for running the Islamic state. They believe in the Shari'a revealed in the Islamic texts, and their obedience to "those in authority" presupposes that the latter are Muslims. Shaykh Nabhani, for his part, does not agree with this condition but allows people of the dhimma from among the citizens of the Islamic state to participate.[177]

The Iranian model is instructive here. Nabhani limited the participation of these minorities to lodging complaints within the assembly without giving them the right to participate in public affairs and governance. By contrast, the constitution of the Republic of Iran grants membership in the popular assembly to its non-Muslim citizens, including Zoroastrians, Jews, Assyrian and Chaldean Christians—and on the basis that every minority elects representatives in proportion to its population.[178] Nevertheless, the Iranian constitution forbids enacting any law that goes against the Ja'fari school of jurisprudence, Iran's official school. The Iranian constitution has made this a permanent article—an aspect that should be criticized, because it considerably narrows the potential deliberation of the parliament and deprives it of the opportunity to apply the rich tools of Islamic jurisprudence. Instead, it is the Guardian Council that is responsible for this oversight, with the purpose of protecting the Islamic Shari'a and the constitution. This Council is composed of six jurists expert in the requirements of the present age, so as to make sure the laws passed by the assembly are in harmony with the Islamic Shari'a, and six Islamic lawyers elected from among Iran's Supreme Court. All twelve of these men monitor the compatibility of the laws with the articles of the constitution.[179]

By this means the Islamic constitution is able to guarantee agreement between the principle of general elections, the protection of public order, and the Islamic nature of the state. Some of the constitutions of Arab nations have adopted some changes under pressure from the Islamic renewal movement with the intention of Islamizing legislation and the state. The Egyptian constitution, for instance, after a long battle added to the vaguely worded phrase "The state's religion is Islam" (the traditional wording present in all Arab constitutions) the more specific phrase "The Islamic Shari'a is the fundamental source of legislation." As for the Tunisian constitution, it is still holding on to its original vague expression: "Tunisia is a sovereign nation, its language is Arabic, its religion is Islam." So among the twenty articles that form the second part, "Legislative Authority," we find no religious orientation—something that makes you forget you are in a country where the national identity is primarily tied to the Arabic language and the Islamic religion. Surely this points to the lack of Islamic knowledge or hypocritical attitude among the majority of those who framed this constitution, and it certainly gives the lie to anyone claiming that this constitution is Islamic.[180]

This is why Shaykh al-Shadhili al-Nayfar, in his study of the Tunisian constitution, argued that the sacred texts must be explicitly mentioned in the constitution and that every law that goes against the Shariʿa must be null and void. Any such law has no legal validity and cannot be applied. Yet even if that were to happen, it would still be a far cry from the trenchant and clear wording of the Iranian constitution: "All civil, penal, financial, economic, administrative, cultural, military, political, and other laws and regulations must be based on Islamic criteria. This principle applies absolutely and generally to all articles of the Constitution as well as to all other laws and regulations." Ironically, even the Iraqi constitution that Paul Bremer, the U.S. envoy after the 2003 invasion, drew up had a role for Islam, mostly because of pressure from religious leaders—a greater role, in fact, than it has in the Tunisian constitution and others like it. And this, without mentioning the part allotted to civil and political freedoms. They are there, but like in other Arab constitutions their interpretation and especially their application are elastic and deceptive.

All that said, does the Islamic nature of the state require that the members of its representative assembly be top-level Islamic jurists or even Muslims? Several contemporary Islamic jurists have contended that "those in authority" are not necessarily experts in Islamic law, though some should be present; but there should also be other people respected by their constituencies, such as party and trade union leaders and others who are representative of the umma.[181] They only need to accept the political system—that is, to respect the Islamic nature of the state and not enact legislation that contravenes the sacred texts, something that could be monitored by a constitutional council composed of top-level jurists.

As for non-Muslim citizens of the Islamic state, those who willingly give their complete loyalty to the Islamic state by acknowledging and respecting its Islamic identity, there is no obstacle in granting them positions within the state apparatus, including membership in the Shura Assembly, as they represent a minority within the majority of Muslims. So the condition that "those in authority over you" be Muslims would be qualified to read, "as long as the majority of them are Muslims." This guarantees that the majority of the ruling body will be Muslims and thus prevents the state from being diverted from its original goals—the most important of which is, no doubt, the establishment of the Islamic Shariʿa and the defense of Islam and its dissemination and guarding against injustice and oppression. This is what makes total loyalty of the minority to the Islamic state and to its defense so crucial. The same holds for the body that acts as constitutional watchdog, as it examines each law enacted by the assembly. So it is possible to attach the phrase "those in authority" in the verse, not to the members of the legislative assembly but to the leader with executive power, the emir and his associates who implement Islamic law. This is especially appropriate, since "authority" here comes from the same root as the word "amir," about which we find many prophetic traditions concentrating executive powers in one person and commanding obedience to him—whether he is called amir or imam, as in this hadith, "Whoever obeys me, obeys God; and whoever disobeys me, disobeys God. Whoever obeys the amir, obeys me; and whoever disobeys the amir, disobeys me."[182]

Imam Muslim reports the following hadith on the authority of 'Abd Allah bin 'Umar: "Whoever pledges allegiance to an Imam, giving him the clasp of his hand and the fruit of his heart, he should obey him as long as he can, and if another comes to dispute with him, you should fight him."

Probably, what led most of those who wrote that "those in authority" were members of the "legislative" body—that is, the parliament in today's language, whose members embody the state's sovereignty—was their interpretation of Western political practice, particularly the British parliamentary model; second, they aim to refute the accusation of despotism in the Islamic state; third, they want to resist the authoritarian regimes now in power. In parliamentary systems of government the president or king has less power, in that the parliament fulfills the role of head of state as the highest authority, and this as a result of a long history of struggle in Europe against absolute kings. This model is more suitable, then, for Islamic regimes, in which the "amir" or president holds executive powers and participates with the Shura Assembly in establishing public policies.

Thus there is no prejudice to the Islamic character of the state if the assembly or parliament has non-Muslim members, as long as the assembly and the rest of the state institutions work within the framework of the Shari'a and under the oversight of a body of top-level jurists, which is totally independent from the state and whose mission is to monitor the constitutionality of the laws and the general conduct of the state's institutions and agents. That constitutional council must also coordinate with the organs of the judicial branch of government, with the institutions of Islamic learning, and the bodies that shape public opinion such as mosques, the press, and political parties. That broad-based coordination aims to uphold "the duty to command the good and forbid evil," to strengthen the people's power and prevent tyranny, whether from the state's executive powers or from its consultative bodies. For the state has no authority over legislation or over the people's loyalty to any of the schools of jurisprudence, since God alone is the author of fundamental lawmaking. As for deductive legislation [ijtihad], that is the right of the umma. Every citizen has the right to interpret God's law [ijtihad], and that is an act of delegated consultation [shura].

When it comes to the legislative consulting process aiming to express the umma's consensus on important issues, it is best carried out by a body elected by the people, independent of the state and composed of some of the best Islamic scholars and judges.[183] Since everyone is allowed to gain knowledge of the Shari'a and that privilege is not limited to any class of people, there is no reason why the jurists should be those who rule the Islamic state. There should not be any contradiction between the politics of the state and the rulings of God's law, meaning that managing the affairs of state should be in harmony with those rulings,[184] and that the mission of the body of Islamic scholars ['ulama'] should fulfill the same mission as those specialized in the religious and civil law, which is to protect the constitution. This is also the role of the supreme courts or constitutional assemblies in several nations.

Summary: With regard to the verse that commands obedience to God, obedience to His Messenger and to those Muslims in authority, as long as their orders do not conflict with those of God and His Messenger, we have seen that the condition of rulers being Muslims can apply either to the majority of the assembly's members or to heads of state with executive powers. Either way, from a Shari'a perspective there is no objection to the presence of representatives of non-Muslim minorities in the Islamic state carrying out functions within the Shura assembly. We will come back to this issue, God willing, in more detail, but what is important here is to emphasize that the consultative body in the Islamic state may have minority non-Muslim members and that the majority of its members and its ruler especially guarantee the Islamic character of the state.

Second Condition: Maleness

The second condition is that people's political representatives must be men. This is according to the Islamic constitution as drafted by Abu'l-A'la al-Mawdudi for the state of Pakistan. He refers to the following verse, "Men are the protectors and maintainers of women,"[185] and the following hadith found in al-Bukhari's collection, "A people ruled by a woman will never flourish." These two texts, according to Shaykh Mawdudi, teach that the main offices of the state may not be given to women—be they the presidency, or ministries, or membership in the Shura Assembly, or various administrative posts in the government. Put otherwise, politics and governance do not befit women.[186] The Fatwa Council of al-Azhar University and the Fatwa Council of Kuwait have both emitted the same opinion, even taking away from women the right to vote.[187]

Our dear friend Muhammad 'Abd al-Qadir Abu Faris and a number of colleagues, professors in the Shari'a Division of the University of Jordan, have expressed a similar opinion in a yet unpublished study. They do not see any legitimate political role for women, except that of voting in general elections for fear that their not voting might boost the secular votes. But their only support comes from the above fatwas and the testimony of history: it has not happened in the past.

By way of critique, I was amazed to read the fatwas forbidding women to participate in political life based on the above verse and hadith, so I reviewed all the books of the Islamic tradition I could get my hands on, and especially on the subject of governance according to Islamic law and the research on positions taken by authorities in this area. My astonishment grew, as I was not able to find anything on the topic, other than writings on the office of the imamate, or head of state, in which there was a consensus or near consensus among these scholars about forbidding this office to women based on the above hadith. And this, despite the fact that many scholars gave women the right to be judges, stressing its importance, to the extent that Abu Ya'la Ibn al-Farra' stipulated that the imam "must have the qualities that are necessary for being a judge: freedom, maturity, intelligence, knowledge and justice."[188] And even with regard to the function of head of state, some branches of the Kharijites, like the Shabibiyya, allow a woman to become imam, if she takes charge of their affairs and fights aggressors. They also say that Ghazala Umm Shabib became imam after her son's death.[189] 'A'isha Umm al-Mu'minin[190] played a role in Islamic politics, as she led an armed resistance that included over three thousand soldiers, some of whom were Companions from among the Ten with Glad Tidings of Paradise. As Abu Bakr recalled, she would issue both commands and prohibitions to her followers.[191] She fulfilled the functions of head of state, "addressing gatherings, negotiating, and appointing prayer leaders."[192]

Other women were famous throughout Islamic history for their role in politics, like al-Hurra al-Salihiyya, who ruled several regions of Yemen for over forty years in the sixth century. Likewise, the Qur'an speaks of the grandeur of the Queen of Sheba, who was also the symbol of a leader committed to mutual consultation. It states that she and her council were mutually committed to working together: "I only ever decide on matters in your presence."[193] Those who allowed women to hold the office of imam did so by referring to the majority opinion of Muslims on the equality of the sexes, stating that the above hadith does not have enough legitimacy to impugn that equality, because it is a comment about a particular event. It appears that the Prophet (PBUH) had just received the news that the ruler of Persia had died and that the people had chosen his daughter to succeed him. That king had recently killed the envoy the Prophet (PBUH) had sent him, so he was likely expressing his irritation with the situation and referring only to that specific society. It is no more than a commentary on this event and not material for constitutional law, especially since the jurists have not agreed on the rule that a ruling can be based on generic wording in the revealed text rather than the specific reason or circumstances for the revelation. So that which is expressed in general terms does not mean it is also an injunction applicable to all cases—which means too that this hadith cannot be used as the basis for a general prohibition on women from the office of head of state. Further, the hadith, being weak in terms of its chain of narration, cannot be used as a basis for barring women from holding the highest public office.[194]

Additionally, barring a woman from the position of head of state, not because she is incompetent with regard to her knowledge and experience but only because of her gender, is to defy the general principle of equality among Muslims. Yet this debate would still continue on the theoretical level, for the conflict here is not about the caliphate, which extended its jurisdiction over all Muslims, and from the leadership of which the jurists quoted above use that particular hadith to bar any woman. The imamate has come and gone; the page has been turned. We find ourselves today in front of small political entities—indeed, very small ones, with the highest political office now meaning the head of the executive branch in a country or membership in a representative assembly.

Now for the above-quoted verse, before Mawdudi, scholars of Islamic political theory have never used it as grounds to deny women the right to hold public office, let alone prevent them from any political participation. That is because guardianship [qiwama], if it is taken to mean leadership in the general sense of the term, it would follow that women are denied the right to hold leadership positions at any level, be it in a school, a daycare, a medical clinic, a business, or a factory, where there is even just one man. This is a deviation no Islamic scholar or Qur'anic commentator engaged in, to our knowledge, neither past nor contemporary scholars. Even the author of the well-known modern Qur'an commentary 'Fi Zilal Al-Qur'an,' Sayyid Qutb, despite his Salafi leanings[195] and his penchant for rejecting everything Western, acknowledged in his commentary on this verse that he used to understand it to mean general male leadership over females in all matters, but changed his mind on further reflection, considering that the context of the verse relates to marital disputes, which means that the guardianship referred to is limited to the context of the family.[196] Thus, this is about leadership of a limited scope, in the private sphere.

What's more, it is subject to principles in the revealed texts and the obligation for consultation [shura] within the family. In fact, one of the three instances where consultation is mentioned in the Qur'an is in relation to family relationships, "And if both [parents] decide, by mutual consent and consultation, the couple wish to wean [the child]"[197]

In summary, there is nothing in Islam that supports the view that women should be excluded from public office, be it in the courts or in government. Even assuming that we accept the majority opinion that women should not be heads of state, what justification can they hold onto, those who deny women the right to participate in the administration of public affairs at all levels, including membership in a Shura Council?

This is why we were very pleased to see the boldness with which Muhammad al-Ghazali, the most important Islamic thinker today, confronted the strongholds of the conservative current on the issue of women and in particular in his book *The Prophetic Sunna Between the People of Fiqh and the People of Hadith*.[198] In it, he emphasized the place of women from within the Islamic tradition and removed many of the obstacles and burdens of the past from the path leading to women's full participation in the Islamic renewal movement, so that women are strengthened and protected through Islam and not from it. With regard to their political involvement, he followed the same direction as the one here, but unfortunately his book was not yet published when I was working on this manuscript in the summer of 1986. So we have been very loyal to what we learned in his liberating school.

We also rejoiced in what we learned from the sound and courageous position of our Shaykh Yusuf al-Qaradawi, who added to his past contributions by affirming Islam's defense of women's participation in the public sphere, including in political life, like being a member of parliament, without losing sight of Islamic guidelines of modesty and virtue.

As for those who reject the participation of women in public affairs, they can only find support for this in social customs and traditions. Had they only copied the great forefathers of the golden ages of Islam, when the mind was unfettered and the umma soared, they would have been well guided and have read the masters of all Qur'anic commentators, Ibn Jarir al-Tabari, the Imam Abu Hanifa, and our revolutionary jurist from Andalusia, Ibn Hazm, who supported women's right not only to participate in elections and political parties and hold several governmental positions like secretaries and ministers of state but also to become judges, which is a public office that has similar eligibility standards to that for the position of head of state. If only they had freed themselves from the

traditions of the fathers of the age of rigidity and had extended their view beyond them to the age of the Prophet and his successors (may God's prayers and
peace be upon them), they would have found many examples of women who
not only voiced their opinion on public affairs but who also fought in battles.
They intervened with wise opinions and life-saving solutions as did Umm Salma
in the run up to the Hudaybiyya Treaty, when the Companions upset the Prophet
(PBUH) and disobeyed him. He came to her with a troubled heart, and she indicated to him the way out of the most delicate of all situations a leader can experience with his followers. So did the Prophet (PBUH) object to her intervention,
which proved to be the right policy to follow, or state that politics and governance are off-limits to a woman's contribution, as our Shaykh Mawdudi says?
May God forgive him for that opinion, especially with the backdrop of fourteen
centuries!

Think of 'Abd al-Rahman bin 'Awf, head of the Shura Council, as he was
executing 'Umar bin al-Khattab's mandate to screen one of the six candidates
for the caliphate. Did he not seek advice from everyone in Medina, while even
going to the women's quarters to get their opinion on the best candidate? Did
he not know about the guardianship verse in God's Book and the hadith about
the daughter of the Persian king (Khosrow)? Or was it, in fact, precisely because
he was fully aware of it that he did not neglect the opinion of the women on
this crucial matter? And how could this be otherwise, since the fallout of public
affairs affects everyone, both men and women? And what justification is there
for excluding women when they are just as much human beings made fully accountable by God?

What is reassuring is that neither blind following of the forefathers nor the
reaction against the West pushed the majority of modern scholars of Islamic
political theory toward the position adopted by Shaykh Mawdudi. Rather, they
have decided that the foundation of civil rights is equality between men and
women, except for a few areas dictated by the imperatives of social life. Let it
suffice here to quote these brilliant paragraphs from the scholar and Azhar
Shaykh 'Abd Allah Diraz (may God have mercy on him):

> For the Qur'an establishes the participation of men and women as equals in
> the building of the state and society, with just a few exceptions tied to gender
> specificities. It gives women the same rights as men to engage in social and
> political activities in different forms. Whether these men and women are in
> politics, simple citizens, members of parliament or not, from the comprehen-
> sive nature of this life flows all the goods of public life: people and their vari-
> ous classes are represented, institutions are established and laws enacted,

public affairs and political initiatives are monitored, along with religious, national, military, social and reform organizations.

Saying that the Muslim woman is ignorant and careless, and that her work must be restricted to the house and motherhood, has no basis, for the great majority of men are also ignorant and careless, yet no one says that they should therefore be deprived of their political and social rights. Not every woman is a candidate to seek work and activity in the political and social arenas, but only some individuals put themselves forward to do this, as is the case for men. Nor does it mean that in the end women will leave behind home and motherhood.[199]

We say this by way of discussion, aside from the Qur'anic texts that grant women the same political, social, and civil rights as men and which, in fact, should provide the definitive response on this subject.

If women in the first centuries of Islam were not participating to a great extent in public life, it was because of the nature of social life at the time and has no bearing on Qur'anic rulings and instructions, for God's Book and the authoritative Sunna of His Messenger were the source for the Shari'a and the Islamic regulations for different ages and contexts. The text from both sources declares equality as the rule, unless an exception is specified—and such exceptions should themselves be aimed at achieving equity through equivalent rights and duties for women and men in reality and not simply a formal symmetry.

Despite that, women greatly contributed to the movement of change and building of the Islamic civilization, whether in the Meccan or the Medinan periods, in the period of the Rightly Guided Caliphs or in any other period of its flourishing. Women were present during the most crucial times, like the covenant that first founded the Islamic state and the military expeditions. Ibn Hazm pointed to 'Umar bin al-Khattab's appointment of al-Shifa'[200] as administrator and supervisor of Medina's market, arguing that "it is permitted that women assume positions of authority, except that of head of state."[201] As for Taqi al-Din Nabhani, he declared in his constitution that "every adult citizen of sound mind has the right to be member of the Shura Council, whether man or woman."[202]

Moreover, in the constitution of the Republic of Iran, which can be seen as a product of Islamic revivalist thought both on the level of theory and practice,[203] women occupy an important position, in application of the Qur'anic verse, "The believers, both men and women, support each other; they order what is right and forbid what is wrong."[204] And in Article 21 we read, "The government must ensure the rights of women in all respects, in conformity with Islamic values."

In Article 20 we read, "All citizens of the country, both men and women, equally enjoy the protection of the law and enjoy all human, political, economic, social, and cultural rights, in conformity with Islamic values."[205] It is not surprising that the Iranian constitution accords such a prominent role to women in light of their contribution to the igniting of the revolution and their role in nurturing legions of martyrs. Women, therefore, had their place in the Shura Council, in demonstrations and in every aspect of the struggle. This very participation only served to help women to be even better citizens and mothers, producing future generations.

In that light it is not surprising that the "Jamā'a Islāmiyya" of Pakistan, despite the depth and insight of its great founder and the quality of its leadership, has not been able to appeal to the masses.[206] This is likely to be the case as long as it holds to its conservative position on social issues, and on women in particular, and as long as conservatism prevails in its ranks.[207] And this, to the point that Mawdudi (may God have mercy on him) devoted a book to the veiling of women, in which he desperately defended his position that the *niqab* [full face veil] was the only acceptable apparel for a woman according to Islam, thereby going against the vast majority of Muslim scholars.

By way of summary, you will not find in Islam any justification for excluding half of Muslim society from participation and activism in public life. That this actually took place was an injustice done to Islam before it was an injustice done to women. For to the extent that women's participation increases in the public sphere, to that extent their awareness of the world is expanded and they are able to impact it. And there is no way to achieve this without removing the ideological and practical obstacles in the path of female participation in public affairs, without increasing their knowledge of Islam and the world, and without boosting their own self-confidence in being able to contribute effectively to the making of a generation that leaves behind their petty, private issues and plunges into the challenges facing the umma and humanity as a whole.

So we are for the right of women—which may even rise to the level of an obligation in some circumstances—to participate in political life for the sake of equality and respect for Islamic ethics, because ability and character have nothing to do with gender or color.[208] Reflect on this verse, "People, We created you all from a single man and a single woman, and made you into races and tribes so that you should get to know one another. In God's eyes, the most honoured of you are the ones most mindful of Him: God is all knowing, all aware."[209] How desperately our societies need female leaders on the path of 'A'isha, Khadija, Umm Salama, Fatima, Asma', Khawla, and Zaynab! And where are their daughters with a wide Islamic impact today? We see no problem in setting a quota for female members of the Shura Assembly, if only to encourage them and to highlight examples of women as responsible officials rather than the image of women as objects. Among the greatest objectives of Islam is supporting the downtrodden in order to achieve equality. As God has said, "Why should you not fight in God's cause and for those oppressed men, women and children?"[210]

Third Condition: Maturity and Sound Mind

Those are two self-evident conditions for mere participation in politics, let alone leadership. Yet we should note that in choosing members of the legislative assembly, many constitutions are not satisfied with the age of legal majority but pursue a level of maturity that is not possible to attain under thirty or thereabouts. The Tunisian constitution reads, "Any voter born of a Tunisian father who has completed twenty eight years of age has the right to be candidate for membership in the parliament," while among the Islamic constitutions we have consulted, none have any other limit than the age of maturity or the age of legal competence. This makes sense, since participation in the affairs of state is just one possible responsibility, though more weighty than others; so we consider that limiting the age to that of maturity, or no more than twenty years old, is more in conformity with the general outlook on responsibility in Islam.

Yet in the course of Islamic history men under twenty often shouldered responsibilities that might have been weightier than that of members of parliament, like those who led armies and managed wars—recall Usama Ibn Zayd, Muhammad ibn al-Qasem, Muhammed Fatih (Mehmet the Conqueror) and 'Ali bin Abi Talib. And despite the fact that maturity of experience, exposure to greater learning, and greater control over one's emotions and passions are not usually achieved till later in life, the ability to reach valid judgments is not limited to any particular stage in life. Even more so, dynamism and quickness of mind, and freedom from the rigidity of tradition among youth are necessary elements for discovering new ideas and opinions. History teaches that the Prophet (PBUH) did not neglect to seek advice from young people and to take advantage of their quick minds. During the Banu Mustaliq expedition, he listened to Zayd Ibn Thabit, and he went out to meet the enemy during the Battle of Uhud due to the insistence of young Companions for their opinion was sound, as they made sure the archers held their positions so they could encircle the Quraysh. For that reason the Qur'an exhorted the Prophet (PBUH) to keep listening and persevere in consulting with others. Thus he sought advice on the smallest of issues that concerned the Muslim community and in the most critical trial that it had to face—that is, the incident of the slander [al-ifk] against A'isha, when he sought the advice of Usama and Zayd, just as he often consulted with 'Ali. All of them were young men.

The Caliph 'Umar used to invite young people, like 'Abdallah ibn 'Abbas and 'Abdallah ibn 'Umar, to the meetings of elder Companions, despite some unease on the part of the latter. 'Umar challenged the reluctant elders and emphasized the young men's high levels of understanding and insight, which often exceeded those of elders.[211] So they relented and accepted the membership of young people. That is not surprising, for the transformation that came with Islam was a movement of young people. The Qur'an itself underscores the pioneering role of youth in spreading the message of Islam, just as Abraham destroyed the idols of his clan, and he was only a young man. Moses was also a young man when commanded to call his people to believe: "But no one believed in Moses except a few of his own people."[212]

In the same way, the revolution of Islam, which changed the world through the leadership of the Prophet (PBUH), was nothing if not a movement of young people. They are, in fact, the driving force of every civilizational transformation, so what justification is there to exclude them from the arenas of consultation and leadership?

To sum up, both reason and revelation tell us that adulthood is a sufficient legal condition for membership of the legislative assembly. Certainly, it may be that a small number of very talented young people will be able to win enough public support to win the public vote alongside older candidates. Still, the doors must stay open for new generations to take up positions of leadership. What stands in the way of capable student leaders, for example, being elected to the legislative assembly?

Fourth Condition: Residence in a Muslim Nation

The fourth condition, according to Mawdudi, is to reside in a Muslim-majority nation. We read in the Qur'an: "As for those who believed and did not emigrate, you are not responsible for their protection until they have done so. But if they seek help from you against religious persecution, it is your duty to help them, except against a people with whom you have a treaty."[213] Mawdudi argues that this verse highlights two grounds for citizenship: "Faith, and residence in the House of Islam or emigration to it.[214] If a person is a believer but does not relinquish his ties to the House of Unbelief—that is, he does not emigrate to the House of Islam and make it his home—he is not considered to be a member of the House of Islam."[215]

Also, this verse of the Holy Qur'an gives to the pacts and covenants the Islamic state makes with non-Muslim nations precedence over its obligations toward a group of believers who choose to live in a non-Muslim country. Thus, if the latter are exposed to persecution by those nations, they are entitled to support by the Islamic state only within the limits of the pacts and covenants drawn up between the Islamic state and those non-Muslim nations. This shows clearly the possibility of peaceful relations between Muslim and non-Muslim nations, contrary to the views that extremists spread about the duty of jihad in order to bring down any regime that is not ruled by the Shari'a. Indeed, the Prophet himself (PBUH) made treaties, he and his caliphs, and Muslim rulers during the course of Islamic history, with non-Muslim peoples and non-Muslim states. True, relations of war and raids prevailed on the whole, and they were the rule in the absence of an international law that recognized nations' borders and thereby allowed them to recognize each other. That law condemns hostility if it arises, since it goes against the rule of peaceful relations between states.

In this regard, the Iranian constitution moves in the same direction but goes even further, since it defines the umma for which it establishes the rights and duties to be "the members of the Iranian nation." They are equal in rights and duties, regardless of ethnic group and tribe (Article 19); they are required to protect the integrity of their nation (Article 9); and among the conditions for a candidate to the presidency of the Republic are "to be Iranian by birth and have Iranian nationality" (Article 15) and to take an oath before the Iranian people (Article 21).

However, the values relating to Islamic unity are enshrined in more than one article in the Iranian Constitution, which emphasizes brotherly responsibility toward fellow Muslims (Article 3) and the effort to realize the unity of the Islamic world (Article 11). We hoped that this valuable text would not contain that which damages Islamic unity, like the aforementioned articles, and article (12) which emphasized the state's commitment to a specific juridical school.[216]

Many modern Islamic thinkers have opposed Mawdudi's position on the question of citizenship, based on various grounds, aims, and viewpoints.

In the first group we find those who defend the right of non-Muslims to be citizens of an Islamic state—among them, professor of Shari'a 'Abd al-Karim Zaydan,[217] Professor Fathi 'Uthman,[218] Professor Ismail al-Faruqi,[219] and the journalist and prominent Islamic lawyer Fahmi Huwaydi.[220] These writers put forward arguments to refute the position stipulating that all members of the Shura Assembly had to be Muslims and to defend membership of non-Muslims in it. Their right to citizenship, of course, is the first step in this direction, since this provides the basis for the former.[221] And this is true especially, because the contemporary Islamic state represents a new kind of Islamic legal structure, built not upon the foundation of conquest, which was the case of all Islamic states before they became prey to foreign invaders but on the basis of the struggle for national independence.

In response to colonialism those nations mounted a variety of national resistance movements, in which many groups participated for the sake of nationhood. Some of these were non-Muslim, so that when they achieved victory and foreign occupation ceased, these nationalist coalitions established regional states on a new basis, that of liberation, upon which they built a covenant of citizenship. That is the foundation on which the modern nation-state is built, but we should note that this was a situation that traditional Islamic jurisprudence had not yet encountered. To sum up, legitimacy based on the wars of conquest ended with the fall of the caliphate, and a new legitimacy based on shared citizenship was erected upon its ruins.[222]

The second view rejects Mawdudi's condition of residence in the House of Islam and stresses its refusal to allow geographic criteria to define citizenship, since the unity of the Islamic umma means the unity of the Islamic state.[223] The implication is that Muslims, wherever they may be, are citizens of the Islamic state.[224]

Sadr al-Din al-Qabaniji, for his part, contended that,

Citizenship in modern parlance refers to membership in a nation that is politically independent, that is, a state. It includes rights and duties and from a Western perspective, "the basic duty of citizenship in a state is sincerity and loyalty to the nation." The expectation is that every citizen will put the interests and happiness of his nation above the interests and happiness of any other nation.

Among the most important duties that flow out of this duty are the following: obedience to the nation's laws, paying taxes, and serving in the armed forces when one is called to do so.

The citizen also has basic privileges: the first is his eligibility to participate in the process of decision-making that defines the state's policies when he has reached the age of maturity as defined by that state, and this through various means, like voting and the right to hold public office. Secondly, he has the right to have the state protect his person and possessions inside and outside its borders.[225]

From an Islamic perspective, the Islamic state is broader than the geographical borders of any Muslim-majority nation. Every Muslim is considered citizen in that sense, since he is a member of the Islamic umma, with all the rights and privileges, along with all the duties and responsibilities. Belonging to Islam is the basis of this membership, and every other border besides creed cannot divide Muslims. This also means that the responsibility of the Islamic state covers all Muslims in the world, for they are all under this state's care, no matter the geographical distance that separates them.

And if the state's protection of its citizens is their outstanding right, then it must be clear that the Islamic state according to its ability carries the responsibility to protect all Muslims in the world with the best sort of protection, politically, socially, economically and culturally.[226]

When Qabaniji finds himself confronting Professor Mawdudi's position, he stresses that the Qur'anic verse (Sura 8:72) verse the latter relies on is not useful to argue that emigration is a condition for citizenship but rather that it is a duty. Further, it is not an injunction applying to all, and no one today can insist that all Muslims in the world must emigrate to countries ruled by Islam. In fact, that noble verse provides a specific ruling applicable to particular circumstances and situations.[227]

What is strange, however, is that Qabaniji, despite his opposition to Mawdudi's concept of citizenship, ends up with a narrower definition of the Muslim's right of citizenship in the Islamic state. Thus, his enjoying that right is conditioned upon the Islamic state's agreement to care for the Muslims who are outside of the areas where the Islamic state is established, since citizenship is considered a gift that the state can either grant or take away. Only those whom the state recognizes as its citizens can enjoy the privileges of holding office or protection. As for the others, the state's commitment is only "according to its ability."[228] Thus Qabaniji, despite his critique of Mawdudi, arrives at the same conclusion. He appears to be influenced by the Iranian constitution which he refers to frequently. He vacillates between an idealistic position and a pragmatic one, despite his opposition to the Islamic idealism that insists on refusing any geographical borders between Muslims. He yearns for the unity of the Islamic umma and fights for the edification of a state for the umma and not a state for a people. He takes as his ideal form the Medinan state, which all Muslims were encouraged to join in order to unite and go out into the world. As stated above, however, the foundation for the legality of the Islamic state is different in some ways from its legality when built on conquest.

Although Qabanji's position goes against the idealistic Islamic position, its textual basis is valid and its logical arguments are strong, Islamists should not forget reality and deny that rulings change with the changing times. In what part of the Islamic world, for instance, would there be enough space to accommodate the emigration of all Muslims now dispersed? Is that even possible? And if making it possible remains a duty, is it even beneficial? Suffice it that this emerging Islamic entity opens its doors to all Muslims and that it considers itself responsible for all of them, though with the proviso that it has the ability to do so. On the other hand, all Muslims everywhere must feel responsible for strengthening that nascent state, contribute effectively to the defense of the umma, and work together to move the Islamic state from a regional one to one that is united worldwide, even if in some ways it is a symbolic unity.[229]

To sum up, Imam Mawdudi's position that residence within the boundaries of the state is a condition for enjoying membership in the Shura Assembly makes sense to me, especially when you consider that the work of that assembly is not just technical but fundamentally political and thus requires experiencing what others experience on a daily basis and sharing their concerns—which is impossible for a person living elsewhere to do. Still, we cannot avoid noticing that there is a need to simplify the steps toward citizenship in the Islamic state, so that acquiring citizenship is not easier in non-Muslim countries than it is in Muslim ones, including those that claim to be "Islamic" like Iran and Sudan—not to mention the Arabian Gulf states, where a term has been coined to express the grim reality for the many residents unable to obtain citizenship [*bidun*].[230]

It is obvious that the bulk of emigration continues to be from Muslim to non-Muslim nations, and not only for reasons of employment but also for the sake of greater access to rights and liberties, the rule of law and guarantees of justice. In those non-Muslim democracies, most often citizenship is acquired simply by birth, or in some cases after living there a certain number of years. By contrast, a Muslim immigrant might spend his whole life serving an Arab country, especially the wealthy ones, without ever enjoying, he or his children, even the right of residence. That is a sign of backwardness. Which of the two positions is closer to the values of Islam? I am sorry to say, it is not the position of Muslims.

Clearly, the duty of the Islamic state is to do all it possibly can to remove barriers between Muslims and to struggle to become a safe haven and a helping hand to those oppressed, from whatever faith or ethnic background. It should also become an entrepreneurial zone humming with jobs and projects, experiencing a comprehensive revolution that opens its doors to all Muslim talent wherever it might be found. It should never feel less of a responsibility for all Muslims than the state of Israel feels for the world's Jews.

A nation that identifies itself as Islamic ought to avail itself of the talented Muslims from any country when it comes to governance, even at the highest levels of state institutions such as in the specialized committees of the Shura Assembly. The same applies to other areas of specialty, like the Commission of Jurists who monitor the laws, and the like. However, I consider that in this matter the Iranian constitution is too rigid in its affirmation of the Iranian identity of the state, and the same applies to the political Charter of the Revolution of Liberation in Sudan and the constitutional documents that flowed out of it, all of which overflowed with strong national pride. We can only hope that this nationalist zeal will taper off in time.

It is all the more important, then, that the right to full citizenship be granted to very capable or influential Islamic personalities in the service of the umma, thus breaking down the barriers to nationality and recognizing the global umma. This would also highlight the guidance provided by the ideals of our historic models, according to which the Muslim is the citizen of any Muslim nation he inhabits, in the way that made the great scholar Ibn Khaldun a Tunisian, an Algerian, a Moroccan, an Andalusian, an Egyptian, and a Syrian by virtue of his eminent work as an academic, politician, and diplomat in all of these nations. Was Jamal al-Din al-Afghani an Afghan, or was he Iranian, or Egyptian, or Indian? The Islamic project, then, must free itself as much as possible from regional ghettoes, considering them nations of necessity, imposed on us by outside forces.[231] Even Europeans who forced these entities on us have sought to supersede national borders through regional integration. The future lies in embracing freedom's wide-open spaces and forging a global umma and a global human community as a whole.

Fifth Condition: Knowledge

The fifth condition is knowledge that leads not necessarily to the level of ijtihad but at least to the recognition of the general tenets and principles of Islam—that is, what is necessary to know about the religion, such as the obligatory and the forbidden, and the rules of Islam. It is preferable that some would reach the level of ijtihad, but that is not a necessary condition. One acquires this necessary knowledge through hard work and it is evidenced by good conduct and reputation, or in Islamic juridical terms, justice ['adala]. Essential knowledge includes knowing social realities, like people's livelihoods, their places of work, their opinions, their customs, their cultural heritage. A good working knowledge of people's culture, circumstances, and their values and social etiquette is indispensable for the politician, the people's delegate in an Islamic system.

Sixth Condition: Popular Approval

The sixth condition is people's approval. A political leader or representative should be someone whom people respect and listen to. This could be within their tribe, a village, a trade union, a party, or a religious institution. The tribe was the social unit of the first Islamic society, and it was not long before new groupings either took its place or operated alongside it. Leaders were chosen organically, but in Islam there is nothing to prevent any method for designating them, like voting, for instance, especially since there are many instances of this within the Shari'a and in the traditions of the Prophet (PBUH). When he asked the two dominant tribes of Medina, the Aws and Khazraj, to designate leaders, they voted for twelve leaders according to the numbers in each tribe. Muhammad 'Abduh drew from this the principle of not allowing one person to make decisions for the entire group.[232]

Shaykh Khalid Muhammad Khalid wrote,

> As I see it, the concept of mutual consultation that Islam recommends is parliamentary democracy. That is, that the people elect their representatives in order to fulfill their choices and desires. These representatives must be guardians over the umma's rights before the state. These are, in Qur'anic terms, "those in authority," especially if the assembly includes experts in several areas, even if they are only appointed for a time.[233]

The condition, therefore, is that the delegates be elected by the people. In addition, it may be that the elected body takes stock of gaps in several areas of specialty and names some experts to be advisors to the assembly.

In conclusion, the legislative function in the Islamic state, whether the comprehensive or the Shari'a-related kind, is the responsibility of the people or the umma, which it discharges in the three following ways.

First, directly, either by referendum or by general election. This may be used for issues of vital or strategic importance, such as treaties, conventions, the broad outlines of the public policies of the state, and the public oath of allegiance. With regard to these means, are no valid grounds for excluding all people from participating directly as we see in examples from the Prophet's life, the exemplary caliphs, and many historical examples of this direct consultation. This was characteristic of Islam's beginning, since it was the literal application of the Qur'an's teachings on the obligation of collective participation in the affairs of state, so that shura was transformed into a way of life for Muslims in their relationships; in their civil, political, and economic affairs; in their farms and villages; in the administration of their towns and families; and on every level of social life.

Second, by way of delegation of political decision making. Thus, a consultative body is formed, composed of society's leaders, people of good reputation and beyond reproach, leaders within villages, towns, parties, and trade unions chosen by means of election. Where there are non-Muslim minorities they should be represented in the assembly, as well as specialists in various technical fields.

This body undertakes the task of monitoring and guiding both the government and the people: "Be a community that calls for what is good, urges what is right, and forbids what is wrong."[234] In addition, it draws up public policies and enacts laws within the framework of the Islamic Shari'a.

Third, this consultative function can only be carried out with the presence of a body composed of the greatest scholars of Shariʻa and civil law known for their deep knowledge, piety, and public service, who then fulfill the mission of monitoring the Shura Assembly and guarantee that the assembly does not depart from legality through the laws and policies it issues.[235] It can be considered, then, to be a body that exercises collective ijtihad in every area that touches on religion. This must be a body independent from the state, according to the model of the United States' Supreme Court, or the French State Council [*Conseil d'État*], or the Iranian Guardian Council—a body that makes sure that the decisions made by the Shura Assembly and the other government agencies conform to the constitution and the teachings of Islam.[236]

Important remark: In any form that this might take, it is essential that the goal remains not just decision making by simple majority, but arriving at a consensus or at least something akin to it, because mutual consultation does not aim to tear society apart and establish pluralism but to realize consensus and unity. Mutual consultation, therefore, is simply the means by which consensus is achieved in one way or another. Unity, by contrast, is a precious commodity, which can only be attained and reinforced by recognizing and respecting pluralism, and by providing avenues of dialogue, argument, and negotiation as the only way to settle conflicts between groups and achieve consensus, which is the condition for stability and the rotation of power. Note that the latter must not involve lurching from one extreme to another, for that is what revolutions are. Democratic consultation involves movement within the political spectrum rather than from one extreme to the other. Such is the case today in the rotation of Western political parties in and out of power. However, silencing alternative viewpoints on the grounds of preserving unity is a sure path to disaster and conflict, exposing the nation to the threat of external intervention, as the example of Iraq shows.

THE POLITICAL DIMENSION OF SHURA

So far we have mostly dealt with the legislative dimension of mutual consultation [shura], and particularly as an objective expression of the umma's legislative authority completely independent from the hegemony and influence of the state. We concluded that Islam elevated the status of society by allowing it to participate in exercising sovereignty and rule under the Shariʻa's authority. We also argued that consensus [ijmaʼ], in its advanced state, is the practical application of consultation [shura]. Now we would like to shed more light on the political dimension of consultation by dealing with the following aspects: the emergence of the Islamic state, installing the head of state, and the nature of the contract of the caliphate.

The most important theory that prevails in modern political thinking on the issue of the state's emergence is the principle of power, as embodied in the leader or king. That power is based on both the ability to muster a group identity and pure might, and it establishes itself by defeating a rule that is weaker in both of those dimensions.[237] It must also have an ideology that rallies people around it and mobilizes followers, imposing on them submission to its will by founding a state regime.[238] This is how most states known to our history and that of others as well were founded—through conquest and the imposition of the victor's will through law, legitimacy and sovereignty, with the exception of a few models, including that of the Medina state. Then the power of the victorious state transforms under the circumstances of history to become a kingdom, a military rule, or a presidency.[239]

The theory that came to replace it was the theory of the state as contract, and this because of the hypothesis that human beings lived in a state of nature, which some of its proponents describe as happiness and others as misery, before the emergence of the political state. They then agreed to form an organized society, with civil freedom taking the place of natural freedom. It is this contract that gives birth to the state, a state that comes to serve individuals and guarantee their freedoms, and its leader is no more than the servant of the people and an expression of their will.[240]

Despite the criticism faced by the social contract theory, it remains the most prominent theory to explain the genesis of the state. Its popularity likely derives from its ability to lay the foundations for the concept of democracy and mutual consultation, whereby it is the people who create the state and lay claim to its sovereignty. Thus, a particular regime is called to serve the people and strive to please them, and then to step down from power when it loses popular support. This may be part of the reason why most contemporary Islamists have been drawn to see points of contact and rapprochement between Islam and this theory of contract.

The Imamate [Office of the Head of State] Is a Contract

Perhaps the first person to discover both the closeness and distance of this concept to Islam was the famous Egyptian jurist al-Sanhuri in his doctoral thesis on the caliphate.[241] He argued that the contract of the imamate was a true contract with legally binding conditions, and that its goal was to be the source of the ruler's authority.[242] It is a contract between him and the umma, based on consent—a real contract aiming to grant the caliph the highest authority. As a contract between him and the people, it implies that the caliph's authority has its source in the umma and that Muslims discovered the theory of the people's sovereignty many centuries before the appearance of the social contract theory.

According to Diya' al-Din al-Rayyis, Islamic contractual theory is superior, because the contract mentioned by Rousseau was only theoretical, based on a hypothetical state of nature thought to have existed in the distant past but without any historical proof, whereas the Islamic theory of contract goes back to a firm historical fact—that is, the umma's political experiment during Islam's golden age.[243] This is also confirmed by Muslims' consensus that an essential condition to the contract with the ruler is the consent of the umma. We find this summarized in the jurists' saying, "The imamate is a contract," and the pledge of allegiance [bay'a] is the description or the symbol of this contractual agreement between the imam and the umma. Some Muslim scholars base this on the two Pledges of Allegiance at al-'Aqaba, and especially the second one between the Prophet (PBUH) and the two tribes, the Aws and Khazraj, as they vowed to establish an Islamic polity in Medina. This pledge of allegiance was different from the first one, dubbed "the pledge of the women," for it was not a declaration of faith but a political pledge similar to a military one which agreed to establish a political regime based on a sovereign state.[244] Further, it was clear in Abu Bakr's first Friday sermon that it was the people who installed him, that their obedience to him was premised on his own commitment and submission to the Shari'a, and that they were there to monitor his actions and hold him accountable if he went astray. Thus he did not become imam at the Saqifa meeting, for that was merely to propose him as candidate. He became imam during the public pledge in the mosque.[245]

The three other Rightly Guided Caliphs after him gave expression to the same convictions again and again, and each one received the public pledge from the common people in the mosque. They did not consider any other source to their authority but that emanating from their submission to the Shari'a and the consent they received from the people. Moreover, despite the upheavals that took place over time at the heart of the Islamic polity, its legitimacy remained strong in the minds of ordinary Muslims, and their leaders also knew that this authority emanated from a submission to the constitution (the Shari'a) and from mutual consultation (the public pledge of allegiance). For this reason as well, autocratic kings kept a semblance of the caliphate after its reality had all but disintegrated. Hence, the pledge affirms, even if only symbolically, the political and theological meaning that had settled in the conscience of the umma—that is, that the legitimacy of the imam's power stems from the consent of the people and his representing their will through the pledge made to him by the assembly of "those who loose and bind."[246]

As a result, the imamate is a contract between the umma and the ruler by which the latter pledges to apply the Shari'a, to use his good judgment for the sake of the umma, and to consult with her. For its part, the people commit, if the ruler fulfills his duty, to listen to him and obey him. In the end, it is the umma that is the source of all his powers, and it is sovereign over him. All of this follows according to the constitution's framework (the Shari'a).

There is no lack of opposition to this current of thought that sees covenant (as the pledge of allegiance) as the foundation of the Islamic state, although it has become a central concept in contemporary Islamic political theory and finds wide acceptance among scholars because of its consonance with the prevailing modern theory, and because of its support from many passages of the sacred texts and from past Islamic historical experience. Its centrality also comes from its use as a sharp weapon in the fight against despotic regimes in the Muslim world and against the religious and political remnants of feudalism, just as it becomes at the same time a useful defensive weapon in the struggle against the Western cultural invasion that never tires of describing Islamic rule as theocratic and despotic. So there is no denying that this theory has gained general acceptance among Islamist scholars in particular, and that the most prominent scholars and pioneers like Sanhuri, Diya' al-Din Rayyis, Fathi 'Uthman, Salim al-'Awwa, and those of their ilk have advanced this theory. Nevertheless, others have disagreed with this contractual theory, as explored in further detail below.

The Shi'i Current

This current became prominent through the dazzling victory achieved by its Islamic revolution in Iran against the Pahlavi regime. The Iranian revolutionary discourse had adopted a strategy of uplifting the cries of the downtrodden, their suffering from centuries past, and the aspirations of people steeped in the writings of numerous socially active and pioneering scholars who looked anew to Shi'i thought, dusting off what was no longer of use and offering a new vision of a global Islamic revolution as the only official voice of Islam. At the head of these scholars were the Martyr Sadr, Motahhari, and Shariati.[247] This discourse, then, set in motion a gigantic wave of Shi'i thought that washed over a large number of intellectuals the world over, including Sunni thinkers. And within the flood of excitement about the victories of the revolution, the ideas of these pioneers—and even the Shi'i heritage now dusted off and renewed—found an overwhelming response. In fact, these victories were taking the place of the debris left by melting glaciers that had stood in the way of Shi'i thought, allowing people to remember the past without resistance. These Shi'i reformers also provided truly new additions to our thinking, especially in their criticism of Western thought from an Islamic perspective—which was certainly their clearest and most useful contribution—but also in their brilliant development of Islamic philosophy, where indeed pearls of wisdom are to be found, and finally in the area of economics, where Islamic theory has uncovered numerous benefits.

We should also note that, from the outset of the Iranian revolution in the name of Islam, Shi'ism succeeded in gaining the approval of the wide majority of the umma beyond the Gulf region, and they found their way into the hearts of Sunnis by defending Islam in the face of its enemies and dealing with its most important issues, like the Palestinian question and Islamic unity. Indeed, these were the real issues that always needed to be defended, for the sake of which Muslims must take leadership and be willing to sacrifice, regardless of what school or sect they belong to, and even if they are secular like President Abd al-Nasser. So then, what if they wore turbans, made great sacrifices, and endured many kinds of tribulations as happened when bringing about the revolution, tribulations that the enemies of Islam intentionally visited upon them and continue to do so?

Then the Lebanese Hezbollah came along, an apt name for Shi'ism [the "Party of God"]. They were another example of "lofty," engaged Shi'ism, according to Ali Shariati. They added a new accomplishment and created a breakthrough within the ranks of the umma, even though this gain, first accomplished by the 1979 revolution and then strengthened by Hezbollah, began to diminish and unravel as a result of policies that some Shi'i groups had adopted in Iraq for short-term gain. Indeed, those policies came at the expense of the umma's greater needs and ethical principles, though truthfully they were in response to genuine injustices imposed on them.

Yet despite all these numerous contributions, amazingly, Twelver Shi'i thought has hardly moved forward one inch from its doctrinal foundations in the way it reads history and sees how leadership is tied to the umma, except in its discourse about the rule of the jurisconsult [*wilayat al-faqih*], which is only a temporary condition awaiting the return of the absent and infallible imam.[248] The jurist now effectively the head of state has delegated power but is still like the hidden imam, even if he is not infallible, through his political powers, in his relation to

the umma, and in his position as both religious and political leader. Shi'i political theory continues to be built on the analogy between imamate and prophethood: "For we are convinced that the imamate is like prophethood—the rule of
both figures is the same rule."[249] Therefore, to reject the imamate is heresy, just
as to reject prophethood is heresy, so that to ignore either one is just as bad. But
"the imamate stands out from prophethood, in that it brought forth a message
after the latter had finished its mission; for prophethood has its own grace, and
so does the imamate."[250]

One of the moderate Shi'i scholars, Muhammad Mahdi Shams al-Din, states
that the political leader draws his authority from God by means of the Hidden
Imam, who in turns draws his authority from the Prophet (PBUH), who in turn
draws his authority from God (may His name be exalted).[251]

It may be that after Imam Muhammad Baqir al-Sadr's book *The Vicegerency
of Humanity and the Witness of the Prophets*, his student Sadr al-Din al-
Qabaniji clarified his Shi'i political thought in his own work, *The Political
Methodology of Islam*.[252] For him, the infallible Hidden Imam is still present:
"A religious and political leader to whom the umma turns to solve its religious
and political problems and whose decisions are binding on them in both
cases."[253] In his view too, the umma cannot reach the level of infallibility,
whereas the individual in its midst—the infallible one, "he can reach that
level and his delegate can approach it, but the umma with regard to the leader
has no right to choose the Imam nor any authority over him;[254] for the Imam
has absolute power over his flock;[255] political power is neither in the hands of
the majority of the people nor in the consultative assembly, but only in the
head of state."[256]

Despite this, Qabaniji tries hard to talk about the pledge of allegiance and
the authority of the people in designating the imam and in their legislative role,
but he does not succeed in convincing us in a clear and straightforward way that
a human being, after the era of prophecy has ended, can be the only infallible
or quasi-infallible person, who is the one to fill the position of jurist-ruler, while
the umma as a whole has authority over him, yet is far from being infallible.
How can this be?

One can only comment by saying that the Shia nurture an exaggerated love
for the Prophet's family and that this is their self-defense as a minority. Our
Shi'i brethren cannot on the one hand be pleased with their imams as ordinary
human beings, while on the other giving them a higher status midway between
regular people and the prophets. They even make them out to be higher
than the prophets! This is a form of extremism that cannot be accepted; it is an

exaggeration produced by centuries of blind persecution of great imams from the family of the Prophet (peace be upon them), who exemplified in their own time—just like the contemporary Islamist movement—pure Islamic opposition in the face of corruption and despotism. They spoke out, not on behalf of a sect, as the cliché came to be formed after them, but on behalf of the umma's conscience, which had been plagued by oppressive regimes that had turned against the prophetic legacy, likely because of the destructive legacy of the Persians and Romans, and therefore regressed to pre-Islamic Arabian tribalism.

Truly this movement brought back the role of opposition. Yet historical circumstances kept it from ever succeeding, and in time those pressures molded it into a narrow and radical sect, which elevated its own status to the point of seeing itself above simple humanity and demonizing its opponents. Arguably, it represented the longing of a minority to manage its own survival so as not to be crushed by the majority population and the overbearing state.

Stranger yet is that Shaykh Qabaniji, in dealing with what he calls "Islamic political theory," speaks only of the Shi'i position, and not of all the Shia but only the Twelver Shia, and not even all of them but one sect of them! He confidently claims that there is a consensus of Islam's scholars, and of the imams of Islam, no less! And without even once, by mistake, including the opinion of a scholar from outside his sect or of a different opinion. Nor does he show any humility and submit to academic objectivity—even if he could not bring himself to refer to differing opinions of other Muslim scholars—in the way our predecessors used to when speaking about fellow scholars, referring to them as "our companions" and similar expressions that point to the vast universe of Islam, as wide as God's mercy.

One fears that Qabaniji's deliberate ignoring of other views, and thus their vanishing from the world of thought, might only be a prelude and even preparation for their annihilation in the real world. That is a dangerous methodology, not only because it relentlessly tries to recycle in a new form the old well-known opinions that do not go beyond the concepts of "infallibility" and the Hadith of "the stream" and attack the Companions, [257] but further presents that sectarian theory as the only understanding of Islam, implying the negation of the majority of the umma and its existence. How is that compatible with the call to Islamic brotherhood and the unity of the Muslim world, which constitute the foundation of reformist Shi'ism, the Iranian revolution and their leaders?[258]

Even the leader of the revolution and founder of the state, Imam Khomeini (may God have mercy on him), was not free from this exaggeration, and in his book *The Islamic Government* he wrote a passage, which I thought was a mistake that would be picked up by further editions of the book, but have not seen it removed. He wrote that God had appointed "A Proof of God" [*Hujjat Allah*] to lead the Muslims, and his deeds and words are binding for Muslims who must execute them.[259]

In particular, he wrote, "One of the essential tenets of our school of law teaches that our imams have a status no pious king and no prophet sent by God has ever reached."[260] I am assuming these words are actually in his book and faithfully translated. In this case, there is nothing positive here, except for his admission that this doctrine is particular to his branch of Islam, something that rarely came up in the writings of the great scholar and martyr Baqir al-Sadr and never appeared in his disciple Qabaniji's works. Both of their discourses claim to be inclusive and to be speaking for all of Islam!

I say clearly that the tolerance, even the zeal that many Sunni intellectuals and common Muslims display toward their Twelver Shia brethren, their defense of the Iranian revolution, and their suffering grief and attacks because of that have not been generally reciprocated by their Shia brethren, except for numerous and beautiful words about Islamic unity. Yet in the depth of their souls, the revolution for most of our brethren, it seems, has only increased their conviction that their own reading of Islam and its history is the correct one and that all the others are wrong. It has only increased their disdain as well for the majority of the umma and for the legacy and movements it has produced, and it has strengthened in them the hope that these masses will change their doctrines and embrace the imamate and the notion of infallibility, while cutting their ties to their traditional doctrines and their current leadership. That is a treasonous hope and a desire with no basis in fact, after the umma has spent most of its history living with such pluralism, and I believe that it will continue on the same path. Hence we must get used to accepting a plurality of views and by that means seek to live together in unity on the basis of religious common ground, despite political differences, for the common ground is vast if we give precedence to reason. Also, let them resolve to spread the message of Islam beyond Muslim circles instead of fanning the flames of internal disputes, depending on gaining the trust of the umma by focusing on what is common, while at the same time recognizing a plurality of views.

Can we not return to maturity and free our minds from this idea of monopolizing truth? Can every party stop claiming that they show the way and that only their path is that of Islam? This is the wrong approach intellectually and it is destructive politically as well. And no doubt too at the other extreme you find those who declare the Shia infidels, going beyond the traditional Sunni position that the Shia, whether Twelvers or Zaidis, are Muslims, despite the differences to which they adhere. But dozens of books were written and published, and dozens of conferences were convened in order to anathematize the Shia and condemn the Islamic Republic, as if the Shia were a new discovery and Iran in the days of the Shah was Sunni! How far will the umma be driven by the forces of bigotry on both sides while ignoring the dangers that are descending upon Islam, threatening its very being and its thinking? From a Shari'a viewpoint, we should reject all deviation towards extremism and *takfir* (declaring a fellow Muslim an infidel), and develop the rationale and inclination toward moderation, unity, cooperation, and liberation, and finally narrow the circle of disagreements. We should be training people to live together in the midst of diversity, to constantly practice unity, to develop and widen the circle within which we affirm diversity of opinion and practice, within and outside of our Islamic enclosures.

In conclusion, from the Shi'i perspective, we saw a categorical refusal to accept the idea of a mutual contract as the foundation of the state, because the imamate for them is a divine appointment, and to make light of the Guardian or to oppose him is to disparage God (may He be exalted) or to resist Him, which is as bad as ascribing to Him a partner.[261] Further, though the relationship between the imam and the umma became more equal during the age of occultation, the issues of infallibility and the deputyship of the Hidden Imam continue to weigh heavily on the concept of the ruling imam, because the one who holds effective political power is hidden, while the imam in power speaks in his name. So is it the umma who chooses the jurist to rule over it, as some of the texts of our Shia brethren seem to indicate and the texts of the Iranian constitution? Or is it the imam who, after his election and according to the law, carries full political authority?

The latter seems to be the case, especially since the Hidden Infallible Imam, as they believe, is not hidden from his deputies but is present, meeting their needs and showing the way, and even meeting with them on particular occasions.[262] Shi'i literature speaks of his presence with them in battle, strengthening the believers, restoring broken and severed limbs, and pointing to the delegated imam, so that the latter makes no decision without his permission.[263] But this Shi'i literature, which continues to grow and is promoted by the most prominent Shi'i scholars and the silence of many Shi'i scholars (even though they do not believe in these things), is not the object of a Shi'i consensus. In spite of this, mutual consultation—the very basis and modus operandi of the state— gains new adherents every day both in theory and in practice. But the idea of the governance of the jurist, despite its problematic connection to the notion of infallibility, still represents a step forward in Shi'i thinking and a bridge for dialogue between them and the majority of the umma. One of its effects, after all, was to produce unity in the performance of the Hajj.

The Contract Creates the Ruler and Not Governance as Such

The second group that opposes the theory of a contract begins by refusing the interpretation of the oath of allegiance [bay'a] put forward by the partisans of the contractual theory who say that it is a contract between two parties—the ruler and the people in order to establish an Islamic rule. Such a contract did not exist from the beginning, they argue, since the ruler in the Islamic state is not sovereign but derives his authority from his obedience to God. He is a functionary chosen by the people to serve them, and on that basis there is no social contract between ruler and ruled in the Islamic state. Yet it is a contract of sorts: between ruler and ruled on the one hand, and between them and God on the other. It is considered valid as long as both ruler and ruled follow God's will and His laws, so people must obey the rulers they have chosen; otherwise, their disobedience goes against the Islamic law.[264]

Muhammad 'Ali Danawi writes with more elegance about the difference between the oath of allegiance and a contract:

> The theory of *bay'a* (oath of allegiance to the ruler), which rests on the covenant between political authority and the ruled has introduced some doubts in the minds of many Islamists about the similarity between that and the social contract, the theory that came from Europe. It is a mistake, they say, to posit a covenant made by the Muslims as the origin of their state. The truth is that the Muslims through the oath of allegiance did not covenant to found a state, but covenanted to establish a ruler, and there is a great difference between the two. The state was brought into being by the Qur'anic texts, and not by the consensus of the Muslims—texts which cannot be amended or changed. By simply becoming Muslim, the individual connects the political rule to the texts and submits to the theory of the state without entering into a covenant with others.[265]

To sum up, for Rousseau, the contract creates the state, whereas in Islam according to this view, the contract of bay'a does not create the state, but the sacred texts do. And Muslims are not free as long as they remain Muslim to apply the rulings of the Shari'a or not to obey or disobey them. There is no way to establish the rulings of the Shari'a without organizing a political regime under the leadership that applies the rule of the Shari'a. Therefore, the bay'a creates the ruler and not the political system as such. It creates the means of execution, but not the notion or the institution of the state.

The State Is a Fundamental Need in Human Society

The above position connects to the Shi'i idea of divine designation of the ruler on the topic of the imamate, in the sense that the Shari'a text brought the state into being. So the state is a fundamental need in human society and not a passing idea of our time, as many Western theories posit, whether those that are based on brute power, or those based on a contract, or those based on class conflicts. All of them agree on the possibility of the state or its leadership disappearing, either by lack of power, or a broken covenant, or by class conflict ending with the disappearance of its root cause, namely social inequality resulting from private ownership (according to Marxist assumptions which have not been proven). Behind all of this is the idea that the state is an evil, or just the lesser evil, and that it is an instrument to suppress people's desires.

As a result, in order to bring our theory into harmony with the objectives of Islam and its general rules, we would say that the state is a constant and absolute need since human society entered the phase of conflict and political struggle and that it will last until the end. As long as human society moves toward increasingly developed and complex relationships, the state is a social necessity and a healthy phenomenon within the umma.[266]

In the same vein, Imam 'Ali (may God be pleased with him) offered this pointed answer to the Kharijites who stated, "There is no rule but God's,"[267] saying, "A word of truth used to promote falsehood." Yes, there is no rule but God's, but these people say "There is no command but God's. Yet people have to have a ruler whether he is righteous or corrupt."[268]

There is here a temporal and causal connection between the phenomenon of the state and the phenomenon of prophethood. The period of time during which people's modes of living became more complex, schools of thought began to multiply, and people's interests clashed, after an earlier period when people could manage their affairs peacefully—that was when God sent His prophets. They were the ones to create the state, rendering judgment among the people about their areas of disagreement: "Mankind was a single community, then God sent prophets to bring good news and warning, and with them He sent the Scripture with the Truth, to judge between people in their disagreements."[269]

It is unrealistic, whatever the heights to which humanity might soar, that people will be able to do without a state; as the Qur'an says regarding human nature, "And violent is he in his love of wealth,"[270] for humans remain rash, ignorant, and unjust. Still, even though the policing function of the state is necessary, it is not its basic one. Rather, it has other functions such as education and ethical training and providing spiritual and social spaces that raise people's humanity to infinite levels. These are also the fundamental functions of Islamic leadership.

If the two positions above criticize the contract theory by arguing that it is God's command that brings the state into being and not human choice, they differ after that as to how the imam or head of state emerges. Does he emerge solely by divine appointment, as was the case in the days of the infallible imams? Or does he emerge partially, as is the case during the period of occultation, which is the position of the Twelver Shia? Or does he come forth through the oath of allegiance, as is the consensus of most Muslims?

Discussion on the Nature of Islamic Rule

Islamic thought has clearly come to a consensus about political leadership as a necessary ingredient for human social life, whether righteous or not, as 'Ali (may God be pleased with him) stated. And this rule must be according to the way God created human beings to live together and according to the need for livelihood and security to sustain their life.[271] Islam, with its creeds, rituals, ethics, and rules, cannot be established without a state that stands on its foundations, erects its institutions, and carries its message to the world.[272] None of this is a matter of debate. And with regards to the proponents of the contract theory, their position can in no way be interpreted as supporting the view that establishing a state is an optional or secondary matter, for there is absolute agreement among all about the soundness of the jurisprudential rule: "That without which an obligation cannot be fulfilled is an obligation." And what sound-minded Muslim can claim that to apply the Shari'a is not a duty, or that just a few can fulfill this duty, or that it can be carried out under the authority of a non-Muslim state?

So the very idea of the contract or covenant, then, is that the oath of allegiance is not the origin of the Islamic state or of the idea of the state itself, but it is the means to develop it and give voice to its will. The difference with the other theories has to do with the source of the ruler's authority after he has committed himself to follow the Shari'a. Is that source the umma—that is, the opinion of the vast majority of the Muslims? Or is it God's text (may He be exalted), as the Shia believe? Who is God's vicegerent on earth who is responsible for upholding the Shari'a? Is it the umma, as a community? In that case the ruler is merely an employee tasked with carrying out its will, accountable to it, and his responsibility before God is the same as that of any other Muslim. This is the majority opinion among Muslims. Or is the ruler himself made vicegerent directly by God? In that case he is a guardian of the umma, an intermediary between it and God, and its only path to attaining God's pleasure. This is how a minority of Muslims have understood this issue from a long time ago—that is, the Twelver Shia in the period of the infallible imams. Yet in the period of occultation since then, the umma for everyone is the source of political authority—and praise be to God for that.

Plainly, the two preceding theories behind the genesis of the state have left psychological and social scars both near and far, a fact that left us no choice but to delve into them. We could simply have said with Professor Ahmad al-Baghdadi that the methodology of the Islamic Shari‘a in the political arena does not allow individuals to lose themselves in a maze of theoretical conjecture while seeking to find the origin and nature of the political state, or who has the highest authority in society. Rather, the Shari‘a works directly in service of the state as a practical process within society touching on the relationships between people in their everyday lives.[273] Suffice it for us here to emphasize that the Islamic state is an imperative by virtue of the Shari‘a. It is of vital importance to the umma who is God's vicegerent entrusted with His Shari‘a. Without it there is no way for the umma to fulfill its trust and responsibility. The oath of allegiance, even if it is a necessity in managing the state, is not the source of its existence. Rather, the state finds its existence by virtue of the sacred text and nature, and its will is expressed through mutual consultation [shura]. These facts alone bring the Islamic state into being, both as God's government and the government of the people, the government of the text and shura.[274] As the Qur'an puts it, "a covenant from God and from mankind."[275]

APPOINTMENT OF THE HEAD OF STATE

Among the most important areas related to shura is appointing the head of state. In the era following the Rightly Guided Caliphs, shura was all but emptied of any substance as source for the legitimacy of the ruler's authority. It was turned into a mere formality, with the oath of allegiance often given under the threat of force. Still, given the crucial role of the position of head of state as guardian of the faith as well as worldly affairs, jurists saw it as being very important as embodying the loftiest of Islamic values, especially shura.[276] It was out of the question to exclude it from this vital matter, according to the Qur'an, "they conduct their affairs by mutual consultation."[277]

However, the jurists did not put as much emphasis on organizing the shura institution—such that it would place the authority of both the umma and the Shari‘a above the ruler—as they put on securing the state's stability and continuity in a way that ensured order and prevented chaos and unrest. The latter task was a greater concern considering the domestic conflicts that shook the very fabric of society since early Islam. In fact, they should have confronted the true reason for that violence, which was the absence of political mechanisms to give expression to mutual consultation, and the failure to translate a theoretical concept into a governing institution that would confer or take away legitimacy.

Then if the establishment of the state is a duty, since on it depends the observance of the Shari'a, does the same principle apply to the head of state? Here we quote the Imam 'Ali (may God grant him honor), "People must have an amir, whether just or unjust." And this: "A nation can only be righteous by having righteous rulers; rulers cannot be righteous except through the integrity of their people."

Ibn Khaldun attributes this necessity to the need for a restraining force to prevent people from harming one another, due to their animal instincts of aggression and abuse. So that restraint comes when one of them acquires dominance over them, seizes power and the means of violence, so that he is the only one who can deal aggressively with others where faith and conscience cease to be appropriate restraints.

As for Marxism, it only sees the state as an instrument of oppression at the hand of the class that controls ownership. Engels wrote, "[T]he proletariat (still) needs the state, it does not need it in the interests of freedom but in order to hold down its adversaries." Then, according to Lenin, "And the special apparatus remains. The special instrument of oppression, the state, is a necessary thing."[278]

Generally speaking, Islamists view human nature as a mixture of good and evil hence our inclination to err, and for that reason people need to be well supported and guided by social institutions that increase their capacity for good, improve their character, train them to achieve happiness in this life and the next, and restrain them from going astray. The most important of these institutions is the state.[279]

In any case, there is still agreement among all these theories on the necessity of leadership in human society regardless of motivations or end results. No one deviates from this, apart from small movements in the West and in Muslim-majority nations. We mentioned earlier that according to the Islamic perspective, the need for leadership is not limited to one particular function in order to keep people from harming one another. It is a universal and eternal need that is met by establishing the Shari'a, spreading its goodness to all and increasing brotherhood among humanity, and by providing appropriate spaces to elevate people's humanity in every area. It also fulfills the need to make the world a better place and safeguard religion.

Most Muslims agree that to appoint a caliph to rule over the umma is required both by God and by reason. For this they rely on several arguments, including the consensus of the Companions on the designation of a caliph (or successor) as the Messenger (PBUH) was being buried, the general consensus on the impossibility of obeying the Shari'a without an Islamic state, and the others who believed in the logical (and not religious) imperative of that state. As a result, as Professor 'Abd al-Wahhab Khallaf argued, most Muslim scholars agree that the umma ought to have a supreme leader that all Muslims can support, who will symbolize the umma's unity and enforce its will.[280] God said, "O you who believe, obey God and the Messenger, and those in authority over you."[281] Al-Mawardi said, "He has enjoined you to obey those in authority, the imams who rule over you."[282]

Who Is Entrusted to Install a Head of State?

Al-Mawardi and Ibn al-Farra' contend that two groups are responsible for this. The first is composed of those jurists who are capable of ijtihad and therefore put that capacity to use, while the second is composed of those who meet the conditions for being named imam. The assumption is that a select group among the umma, the 'ulama' capable of ijtihad, is entrusted with upholding the Shari'a. It is for those to choose one of their own for the office of imam over the umma. The umma itself, the one with the highest stake in this process, has no say whatsoever according to this distorted perspective. It has to passively wait for what will be done by a largely obscure, loosely defined entity, the group known as "the people of loosing and binding," "the people of election," or "the people of the Shari'a." This means preventing society from playing its role and handing its fate to the unknown, or, more precisely, to absolute monarchs.

Then came constitutional theorizing, after the deviation took root and people grew accustomed to it. More often than not, it came to justify the status quo through interpretations based on the initial period of direct legislation (in the time of the Prophet).[283] Yet, that was a period when society had a certain dynamism that gave rise to its movement of jihad, just as its tribal-based social structure gave rise to new leaders without the formality of elections, since these people were already well-known inside small communities. Later, however, things changed, and these simple forms of shura were not very effective in managing larger and more complex societies. Tyranny and idleness followed; knowledge became divorced from experience, politics from religion, and scholars from rulers. This led to the appearance of flawed readings of the initial legislation era, that were often mere attempts to find religious grounds to justify the status quo, instead of challenging it. There appeared writings on the question of Islamic governance which either failed to deal with the reality of the day—focusing instead on painting an idealized picture of the Righly Guided Caliphs—or engaged in defending and justifying the said reality. They remained stuck between the idealized model from the past and the reality of corruption around them. Thus, what they saw in the early examples of Islamic rule was merely rule by the elite. And since it was the scholars who were the elite excluded from ruling circles during the time of the Abbasids, and even before and after, it was natural that these works would portray the Rightly Guided Caliph model as one where rule was by an elite of scholars. They overlooked, however, the fact that, contrary to the scholars of the day, the scholars of early Islam only rose to the position of leadership after a long and hard struggle. If fact, if there were elections then like there are today, they would almost certainly have been the ones to win them.

To sum up, the elite of scholars who were excluded from ruling circles were presented as "the people of loosing and binding" or "the people of shura" who have the authority to select the ruler. That was a kind of compensation and revenge against history. It was natural also that the question of the steps for selecting the caliph was reduced to a trivial debate about the minimum number of people required to elect a ruler—five or six, or two or one(!!),[284] as in the case of marriage or business contracts. The oath of allegiance was, then, an oath by this small number of people. In fact, even in this restricted form, the oath of allegiance was no longer the only way to choose a leader, but only one among many different ways including through appointment of a successor, through a will, or by force.

Ibn Khaldun explains the controversy over the number of the "people of loosing and binding" and how it ended up becoming limited to one method, one man handing the contract of caliphate to another in a manner analogous to the *shahada* [declaration of faith].[285] There was no longer a public oath of allegiance, as understood in the early days of Islam, and it was reduced to a simple formality for the naming of a new caliph. Admittedly, it was also a way to keep any member of the nomination council from rebelling. But most of all, it meant that no one among the masses could have any part in pledging allegiance to the caliph.

One man among the jurists of the past, to our knowledge, set out to fight and break the stifling orthodoxy of the centuries and corrected many of these concepts, though his strident calls were carried off by the winds of his time—Taqi al-Din Ibn Taymiyya.[286] This great scholar argued in his short but brilliant book *Islamic Governance* [al-Siyasa al-shari'iyya] that the oath of allegiance [al-bay'a] is the only Islamically legitimate way to install a caliph and that the oath of the "people of loosing and binding" operates only to put forward a candidate.

According to him, it was that oath of allegiance [bay'a] in the Medina mosque that sealed the caliphate of Rightly Guided Caliphs—not the Saqifa oath, nor the designation of 'Umar (the will of 'Uthman in which he declared 'Umar his successor), nor Ibn 'Awf's designation of 'Uthman. This is an important correction to the aberrant historical trajectory that robbed the umma of its role, right, and duty and spread violent conflicts. As usurpers reigned over them, the people resigned themselves to their fate, preferring to live on memories of the past and to dream about the great leader who would return them to their glorious destiny.[287] Meanwhile, whether intentionally or not, the others set out to find arguments to justify the corrupt reality and perpetuate it. Some views attributed to Imam al-Razi point in this direction.[288]

Then, in the modern age, Muslims awoke to the cannons of Western ships demolishing their fortresses, bruising their pride, wiping away the torpor of the centuries, and sweeping away the remnants of their civilization, including the caliphate. And so they began to discuss anew the caliphate, mutual consultation, and the "people of loosing and binding," and then they began to yearn for the past in impassioned and abundant discourse. There was one exception, however, for a current among them began to roll up their sleeves and seriously write about these issues. Among them we find the Imam Muhammad 'Abduh and his disciple Rashid Rida, the pioneers of the modern application of the "people of loosing and binding," or the ruler's contract. They were the first to engage with the thinking of this age and to restore faithfulness and confidence to the umma, for it is entrusted with God's commands. As a result, research took off on the institutions and organizations that are best suited to fulfill this trust in their generation.

In particular, 'Abduh stressed that the "people of loosing and binding" are the popular leaders in the various fields of social activity, and they represent the people, for it is the umma or its representatives (the "people of loosing and binding") who install the caliph. Indeed, the umma holds the right of sovereignty over him and can dissolve his contract when it sees fit.[289]

'Abd al-Qadir al-'Awda was perhaps the deepest and most penetrating religious legal mind of our time. His thought reflected the dazzling light of Islam, and his thoughts poured out so clearly and simply. Al-'Awda, the martyr (may God have mercy on him), wrote in "Establishing the Caliphate Is an Obligation" the following words:

> The Caliphate is considered "a communal obligation" (a legal obligation that must be discharged by the Muslim community as a whole) like jihad and the court system, and when someone worthy of it takes that position, then the duty is fulfilled. But if no one is able to fill that position, Muslims as a whole are guilty of wrongdoing until someone worthy of that position occupies it.
>
> Some argue that the responsibility before God lies with two groups within the Islamic umma: first, "the people of opinion" who should be choosing a

caliph, and second, those who meet the conditions for becoming caliph who should be choosing one of their own to be caliph. In truth, the blame for this disobedience to God's command rests on all Muslims, since they are the addressees of the Shariʿa's discourse and therefore have the duty to enforce it. One of their first duties is to command good and forbid evil, and not one of them is commanded to simply look to himself and to his own affairs, but rather to take part in establishing religion in his own life and in the life of others. If the matter is left only to a group of people, then it is the duty of the whole umma to hold that group accountable to fulfill its duty; otherwise, it shares in this dereliction of duty. For it is the whole umma's duty to dissolve this group if it does not carry out its mission, and to name another group, since it named it in the first place and gave it the responsibility to represent the Islamic community. Therefore, if it does not fulfill its duty, it loses its raison d'être by virtue of committing this act of neglect, and it loses its quality as the people's representatives. The people must then elect a new assembly.[290]

The martyr al-ʿAwda concludes that to install a just ruler is to honor God's command and that it is among the most pressing duties of the umma. He thereby corrects a long trajectory of wrongheaded thinking and practice and returns the umma to its leadership role and effectiveness in building a civilization.[291]

How Does the Umma Fulfill This Duty?

Its only path is to organize its ranks and boldly embark in the struggle against injustice and tyranny. That struggle, in turn, brings forward the assembly of "those who loose and bind" to lead the umma and mobilize it to struggle for the sake of freedom according to the Shariʿa, using the appropriate weapons in the way of God. This battle has a clear goal in mind, which is to establish a Muslim democratic rule over the rubble of absolute and autocratic regimes, secular dictatorships and hegemonic theocracies, and to oppose the remnants of religious theocracy. Yet, if current Islamic democracies have focused on installing a president, that is no weighty matter. Each nation chooses its representatives from among its popular leaders, the "people of loosing and binding," and typically they will come from these three classes:

1. The Islamic jurists capable of ijtihad, upon whom others rely for legal opinions [fatwas] and for deducing new rules when the need arises
2. People of expertise in public affairs

3. People looked up to as leaders, like heads of households, clans or tribal leaders, and organizational leaders, like party heads or trade union general secretaries.[292]

It would be correct to call all these people "those who loose and bind." Constitutional jurists within the modern parliamentary system have organized ways to nominate the members of this assembly through elections and various other methods. Islam has no objection to this, provided that it leads to the choice of "those who loose and bind."[293] The second phase after the selection of the assembly of "those who loose and bind" or the Shura Assembly, is its actual assembling, as happened at the Saqifa house in the first instance, in order to select righteous people for leadership. From there, their mutual consultation would point to one or several candidates—there is no objection in Islamic law to having more than one. Indeed, it is better to have more than one candidate to avoid the subsequent steps of the shura process becoming a mere formality, and the door remains open for other candidates to be proposed from outside the assembly. This is so, because the oath by this assembly is nothing but a nominating process leading to the next phase that the masses take charge of and carry through.

The candidate with the most popular votes wins and proceeds to take the oath of allegiance from the assembly of "those who loose and bind" in a direct way, like the shaking of hands. As for the common people, they give their bay'a, among possible modern procedures, by means of casting their ballot, which represents their covenant to listen to and obey the president within the parameters of the Shari'a. The new leader thus covenants, as the ruler of all the people, to expend the utmost effort to apply the Shari'a, to watch over the interests of the umma, to respect their will, and to safeguard the public and private freedoms and human rights of all citizens. All of these belong to the requirements stipulated by the Shari'a.[294]

This way of installing a ruler has many benefits, one of which is to combine the advantages of the parliamentary and presidential systems. According to the parliamentary system, the prime minister has limited authority by virtue of the fact that his authority emanates from and is limited by parliament, and thus he is continually forced to pay attention to the political elite's problems and try to please them more than caring for the people's problems—and, to be honest, the problems of the elites have no end. For that reason, some have quoted the Imam 'Ali (may God be pleased with him) as saying, "You do not please the masses by pleasing a particular group, but you please everyone by pleasing the masses."[295]

Further, parliamentary systems have experienced instability where the ruling apparatus became paralyzed and a political vacuum came about in several countries, lasting for months on end without a prime minister. As a result, governments can collapse after several months because the prime minister lost the parliament's confidence, as happened in Turkey and Italy.

The parliamentary system, however, and especially in countries where a culture and tradition of centralized one-man rule have taken root, whether it be in the form of a monarchy or a republic, is really the most efficient way to prevent the plague of despotism, which is the origin of every bane in the umma. The widest possible distribution of power and the greatest possible limits to the power of the president or king in favor of governing institutions, central and regional, social or civil, that is the most faithful way to express the Shari'a's objective to make governance a matter of consultation among Muslims ("[those who] conduct their affairs by mutual consultation," Q. 42:38).

A king by nature, as Ibn Khaldun showed, leans toward authoritarianism, and that ingrained tendency must be met with a policy of distributing power in the widest possible fashion. Moreover, despite the overwhelming tendency toward despotism in Islamic governance in the course of history, we may also notice that the individual ruler's power was limited by the Shari'a's authority, by the influence of the scholars and jurists, the authority of civil society, and finally by the power of the provincial authorities, which enjoyed a good deal of independence and rendered the relationship between center and periphery more like a federal system. Nor did the umma suffer from a totalitarian state that extended its tentacles in order to choke society's every initiative until the era of the "modern" state put in place by the forces of occupation.

Qualifications of the Head of State

Islam's jurists invested a great deal of care in describing the desirable characteristics of a ruler, and the picture they often painted of him was an ideal and shining one, almost impossible to find in any one person, but nevertheless a picture that embodied practically the high ideals set by Islam's exemplars, the Messenger and the stars surrounding him in the persons of his Companions (peace be upon them). Yet the condition of perfection landed the political jurists in a quandary, which may have been the reason why the discipline of Islamic governance was so far removed from actual political practice and left buried in books of jurisprudence, knowing that the condition of perfection displaced the principle of shura as an obligation ("consult with them about matters," Q. 3:159), as perfection, seemingly, has no need for consultation.

So what did the jurists cite as qualifications for the imam or ruler?

Islam

This is self-evident in a creedal state, as the Islamic creed calls for the enforcing of its statutes, the service of its umma, and the spreading of its message. Still, this stipulation of a creedal condition for the head of state is not only for an Islamic state, but it is a condition for all heads of state, whether it is spelled out in the constitution or simply an unwritten custom assumed by all the people. This is not to mention Eastern Bloc countries, where the sovereignty of the one party in power is built on the Marxist ideology, and where anyone not holding that creed has no right to share in the government on any level, no matter how low or insignificant. That person even loses his right to life, the right to his name, and even the right to be buried according to his convictions.[296] And how could it be otherwise, when Marxism sees the state as an instrument of violence against its opponents and the dictatorship of the proletariat as the party of greatest heroism and ruthlessness? Lenin interprets the dictatorship of the proletariat in these words, "The concept of dictatorship is political rule that is not limited by any legal restraint, nor opposed by any principle and that rests directly on force."[297]

Speaking about the Marxist Eastern Bloc, with the spirit and the legal structure of its ideological and material oppression—with no curbs on it whatsoever, how possibly could a dissenter have any right to share in its political rule?

Nor will we discuss the practices of Israel or the Indian regime's repression of its Muslim population, especially in Kashmir, or the Russian repression of the Chechens, despite the democratic label people attach to those regimes. There is no restraint to the shedding of Muslim blood under the pretext of fighting terrorism, and this among even the oldest Western democracies, where their customary racist practices against the foreigners in their midst are on display.[298] There, too, they multiply laws restricting freedoms, even to the point of allowing policemen to incarcerate a "suspect" without clear justification or trial for an unspecified duration, and thus robbing the accused of every human right, including immunity from torture. The scandal of internment camps such as Guantanamo and Abu Ghraib only illustrates to what extent human savagery can go when it runs from the law and has no fear of punishment.

From a constitutional and legal viewpoint many of these states do not recognize the right of anyone to become politically active, like for instance in forming a political party or running for high political offices, if a person does not follow the creed of the state. Many republican states do not allow the formation of a party calling for the monarchy, and in France, anyone belonging to the royal family that had ruled before the Revolution was for years barred from any public sector job and from holding any high government post.[299] American political custom, the most prestigious of Western democracies, stipulates that the president come from a particular class known as WASP (White Anglo-Saxon Protestant),[300] and the transfer of power from one party to the other takes place according to the American custom, following which about two thousand high-level government employees hand in their resignations to the new president so that he is able to form his own administration with the maximum amount of harmony and cohesiveness. The new party has adopted a particular set of policies and therefore has the right to rebuild the administration according to that political perspective.[301]

Furthermore, equality by no means entails abandoning the general framework for the way the state is run. No doubt, this framework is different from state to state and according to each state's particular distinctives. What is important is that the essential identity markers must be safeguarded in each state, as they are determinative of its public order, which in turn provides the framework for public freedoms, and those cannot be neglected.[302] Certainly, Islam represents an essential component of the Islamic state, and there should be no tolerance for any practice, whether on the part of an individual or a group, that truly threatens—not "supposedly" threatens—the state. It is thus unsurprising that some constitutions of Muslim countries stipulate that the president be Muslim, on the grounds that a non-Muslim president would pose a direct threat to the identity of that state—that is, to its general framework. If we were able to imagine in a republican regime a president who does not believe in the republican principle but in a monarchical one, or imagine in a socialist regime a president who has no faith in socialism, then we have grasped how obvious the condition of a Muslim president is for an Islamic state.

We find it natural, too, that among Islam's opponents, atheists and secularists do not find this condition convincing, especially among those who do not have the legal background to discern the necessities behind the ideological difference between states, for instance the difference in nature between Islam and Christianity. This is especially true of those who categorically refuse the concept of an Islamic state and who insist on imposing a Christian perspective on Islam and breaking any relation between religion and the state. They keep trying to Christianize Islam or to submit it to the same surgical operations that removed Christianity from the public sphere and opened that space to the absolute relativity of values. What then became absolute was the state's power to legislate laws and values, which are indistinguishable from the interests of the ruling elites and the unbridled pursuit of greed.

It also gave free rein to enacting laws permitting the most grievous pillage of nations' wealth, domestically and internationally, and free rein to people's sexual appetites, thereby destroying the family unit and permitting all manner of immorality, including what is called "same-sex marriage," and—God forbid—even between priests.

Here there is no ground for discussion with secular people who are hostile to Islam or any way to free their thinking from the claws of westernization and the ideas that fill their minds on the topic of the religious state, despite the fact that the Islamic state is not the kind that was known in European history, because the umma in the Islamic conception of the state has sovereignty over the rulers and their policies. Actually, in this and every other respect, this state is completely civil and not religious, as we saw according to Shaykh Muhammad 'Abduh and others.

Additionally, the concept of equality, though it rules out discrimination on the basis of race, color, and economic status, does not rule out the idea of classification or even difference on the basis of achievement, like knowledge, for instance. As we read in the Qur'an, "How can those who know be equal to those who do not know?"[303] Or difference could be on a moral basis, "How could the wicked be equal to the righteous?" or distinctions in other areas.

There is no doubt that religious identity in a Muslim-majority state is based on Islam. It is a state in which the majority of citizens have chosen Islam as their nation's authoritative reference, which in turn is tied to sovereignty and public order in the state. Moreover, it allows specific exceptions to the rule of equality by distinguishing between Muslims and non-Muslims, in relation to particular conditions attached to certain high government offices required by the nature of the state and its general framework.

The Islamic conditions here concern descriptions and qualifications for a few positions in the Islamic state, and one should not see that as prejudice based on religious discrimination, since classifying people is not the same thing as discriminating against them. Classification, then, is not incompatible with equality, but discrimination does go against justice.[304] Why would the Islamic faith not be a precondition for a president when his mission is to establish this faith in all areas of society, to orient the political direction of the state within Islamic parameters, to educate the people about Islam and its development through prayers and sermons offered in mosques, and finally, to project through his own person and practice a model for others to follow?

The Qur'an settled this question, stipulating that the ruler be Muslim, "You who believe, obey God and the Messenger, and those in authority among you,"[305] and that it was the condition for the people's obedience.

It would be a vain and impossible demand to ask a non-Muslim to embrace the dual duty of safeguarding religion and managing worldly affairs—the function of a head of state. So for the sake of logical consistency and clarity we affirm that the head of state must be Muslim. It is also a reasonable statement in view of the fact that the Islamic rule we are advocating is for "Islamic countries," that is, Muslim-majority ones.

From a legal and practical viewpoint—and not just from an Islamic one—the head of an Islamic state must be one who "has achieved good works through his faith," that is, he has a solid knowledge of Islam and practices good deeds. Despite this, many constitutions in Muslim nations have dropped this clause due to certain considerations, like preserving national unity in a religiously diverse society or avoiding bloody civil wars like in Sudan. Thus in the constitution prepared by one of the eminent contemporary Islamic jurists, Hasan al-Turabi, there is no mention of the head of state needing to be Muslim. The reasoning seems to be that the office of ruler is no longer a position of near absolute power as it used to be.[306] Instead, the constitution and the law have put limits on it, and have curbed and distributed powers between various state institutions, so that they monitor one another, and thereby have imposed a process of mutual deliberation in decision making by means of institutions that issue orders and enact laws on the basis of the process of majority rule. This naturally reduces the importance of the leader's creed and its influence on his decisions, as it does also in the case of the judge, whose primary qualification used to be his having attained the level of mujtahid.

Today in a judicial system based on many judges rather than just one, and as a result of the codification of Shari'a, the role of the judge has been narrowed down to applying a limited number of texts to real-life situations. The judge therefore is no longer expected to practice ijtihad, or even to be Muslim, for that matter. He only needs to acquire the necessary legal experience. Yusuf al-Qaradawi relies on the same logic to discuss the views of those who do not allow women to be heads of state. He notes that high public office is no longer a question of unlimited power but has been downsized to a position of institutional and collective leadership. Furthermore, there is no longer a universal caliphate but rather a number of Muslim nations, each one with its own limited institutions. Besides, this was not the context in which the classical jurists formulated their rule about the head of state having to be a mujtahid.[307] That said, the multiplication of "emirates" inside the umma did not transform them into regional nations in the modern sense, but they remained united politically within the umma, though in a looser form[308] like provinces within a federal state.

In any case, the preponderance of evidence favors the position that the head of state, as we said, should have these two qualifications ("he has achieved good works through his faith"): knowledge and righteous deeds.

Only the exceptional cases remain, where extraordinary measures might be taken, like in the Sudanese constitution drawn up by the Islamic-leaning salvation government, which does not require the head of state to be Muslim, as his mission is to preserve the benefit of national unity and avoid civil war, even though the president of Sudan was always a Muslim and continues to be so. The issue was settled at the end of the civil war with the stipulation of a Muslim president for the north since the Muslims were the majority, and a Christian vice president to represent the mostly Christian south.

Knowledge

Books on Islamic governance are not content to stipulate that the ruler be Muslim, but also that he be knowledgeable in his faith and one who practices it well.

Jurists have differed, however, on the level of knowledge required for a ruler. Is it at the level of ijtihad? That is what most of the early jurists believed, while accepting the level of *taqlid* as an exception.[309] Most modern jurists, by contrast, specify that familiarity with the basic tenets of the faith and its general rulings is sufficient, adding "that he must be well educated and acquainted with aspects of contemporary sciences, and if he is not specialized in any one of them, he must know about the history and current affairs of nations, as well as international law."[310]

A Just Character

Knowledge of Islam is not sufficient, whatever its level, but he must also be a man of high moral conviction and character—that is what we mean by "a just character." Al-Khatib al-Baghdadi defined the just man as one "who fulfills his duty and knows the obligation to follow what is commanded, refrain from what is forbidden, stay away from immoral behavior, investigate what is true and honorable in his actions, and guard his tongue by saying only that which honors religion and decency."[311]

In one simple phrase Muhammad Asad summarizes the three conditions above, "he must be a pious Muslim" ("In God's eyes, the most honoured of you are the ones most mindful of Him."),[312] meaning he puts into practice the Qur'an's prescriptions and is proud of Islam and its civilization.

He Must Be of Age, of Sound Mind, and Mature

To have a ruler who is a child or mentally ill will not do, because he is not in a state of responsibility before God. As the Prophet (PBUH) said, "God will not record the deeds of three categories of people: the sleeping, until they wake up; the child, until he grows up; and the mentally afflicted, until they come to their senses."[313] A child's oath of allegiance to a ruler is not valid nor that of a person who is mentally ill.

The condition of attained maturity for the position of caliph is not enough. This critical office requires knowledge, especially of the history of nations, experience, and endurance of people's circumstances; it requires experience in administration, organization, and a sufficient amount of interaction between ruler and ruled. Above all and before all, it requires dependence upon God's help. These qualities as a whole cannot be acquired in childhood or adolescence, and for that reason an orphan's guardian does well not to give back his trust to his protégé simply because he has reached the legal age, but is attentive to his maturity, as we read in the Qur'an, "If you find they have sound judgement, hand over their property to them."[314] And if the condition of legal age is not sufficient for handing over a trust, how could it be so for ruling an entire people?

As for the condition of maturity, it goes without saying that this has nothing to do with reaching the legal age or attaining puberty or the like; it is rather acquired through many years of practice and experience, and this only happens later in life. Thus we can add to the condition of legal age that of maturity, which will not be reached before the age of forty hegiri years,[315] because God (may He be exalted) did not send down His message to our Prophet Muhammad (PBUH) until he had reached that age. Perhaps no one should fill the position of successor to Muhammad (PBUH) until he had reached that minimum age as well.

For the age of forty is considered the age at which a person's character matures and finds stability, in addition to the fact that it is a sufficient period of time to provide a useful examination of a candidate's life and personality. If he succeeded in coming through in a healthy manner the trials and changes of youth, frequented mosques and engaged in social activism, as well as interaction with the masses, then he is worthy of being trusted. A hadith narrated by Ibn 'Abbas says, "I heard the prophet (PBUH) say he was afraid for his umma about 'six things,' one of them being 'political authority in the hands of youth.'"[316]

Competence

Ibn Khaldun wrote that competence is to be bold in setting the limits specified by God's law and bold in going into war; to be wise in these matters and responsible in holding people accountable to them; to understand human relationships well and to be shrewd in every situation; to be strong in one's effort in politics so as to fulfill his duties and protect religion by waging jihad against the enemy, applying God's judgments, and managing people's interests. In Al-Mawardi's view, competence is that which allows one to rule a people and manage their interests; it is the courage and assistance that leads to protect the oath of allegiance to the ruler and to fight the enemy.

Perhaps in our day what is sought by competence here is not so much the ability to wage wars, as that is a specialized skill belonging to certain specialists as in other technical areas; rather it is the ability to lead people and guide them, and a strength of personality that makes a person more impervious to manipulation.[317] The prerequisite of competence also includes the physical capacity to discharge one's responsibilities, and experts could set a threshold for this.

The Issue of Qurayshi Descent as a Condition

Many Muslims in the past believed that the ruler had to descend from the Prophet's tribe, the Quraysh, on the basis of certain hadiths on this matter. Some of them argue that, "'The imams from Quraysh so long as they obey God; when they rule, are just; when they promise, they keep their promise; and when they are asked for mercy, they show mercy.' If those qualities are absent, they no longer have the right to the caliphate."[318] Some of these traditions come in the imperative form: "'Keep to the right course for Quraysh as long as they keep to the right course for you.' and 'Put Quraysh ahead and do not go ahead of it.'"[319] Both of these certify how the umma must respect the right of the Quraysh, if it wants to be obedient to God. Some have criticized these hadiths as weak, as they contradict a key Shari'a rule: equality between believers and the prohibition against discrimination on the basis of ancestry and tribe, while the majority (of scholars) adhered to this position, and a third group reinterpreted these sayings.[320]

Perhaps it is better to elucidate this contested issue by aligning it with the Shari'a's general rules, which call for equality among all and for ending all forms of discrimination that exist on the basis of race, color, tribe, nation, wealth, and social status, so that only faith remains and good works as criteria of distinction among human beings. The one who was most successful in dissipating the confusion surrounding these hadiths, without jumping to the weakness argument, is the prominent scholar 'Abd al-Rahman Ibn Khaldun. He argued that the hadiths about Quraysh had nothing to do with religious instruction granting the Quraysh a special and privileged status, but rather it had to do with a desire to preserve the unity of the Islamic community and the stability of its caliphal system. It is about the caliph coming from a lineage with strong solidarity and group feeling ['asabiyya].[321]

And at a time when the tribe was the basis of the social structure, it was natural that political rule in that context could not be stable without its basis in the strongest tribe, which everyone also saw as its leader. It is also a historical fact that no Arab then would have disputed Qurayshi leadership, so there is no wonder that God's wisdom dictated that the prophet should come from the Quraysh. This was clear in Abu Bakr's speech on the day of the Saqifa meeting in the presence of the Shura Council of Companions, as they were discussing who would succeed the Prophet (PBUH) as caliph. Abu Bakr al-Siddiq reminded them that the Arabs have recognized the authority of no other tribe than the Quraysh. He did not refer to hadiths on the leadership of Quraysh; rather, he made a political speech about the common good, and not one about religion. So the issue of the caliphate was not discussed any further and the imamate stayed with the Quraysh, until they deviated from the Islamic norm. Then, having grown opulent they grew weak, and political rule was passed on to other nations like the Turks, the Berbers, and the Persians, nations with greater cohesion and more power than them. The hadiths about a Qurayshi imamate, therefore, reveal a social custom that needed to be respected—that is, the necessary value of social cohesion in creating and sustaining strong states, which in today's jargon would be the strongest social groupings like the political party and regional blocks.

If you translate this in today's terms, having a non-Qurayshi ruler then would have been like having a ruler today who does not derive his power from a strong party but rather from a coalition of several parties in which his own might even be the weakest, then it will not be long before that power becomes weak and is overrun or resorts to the use of force to remain in power. Strong, stable rule needs to be grounded in a strong form of cohesion ['asabiyya], though the reality and nature of cohesiveness likely differ from one society to another in function of its internal makeup. What is important is to achieve the Shari'a objective: the stability of a regime and its strength, not through repression or terror but rather through its ability to represent the fundamental sectors of society. The goal, therefore, is the degree of representation of a regime, so that it achieves a balance between the requirements of shura [freedom] and the requirements of order.

No doubt, the best means of ensuring the government is representative is through the electoral process, which means, incidentally, that the precondition of belonging to the Quraysh tribe was a political issue, not a permanent religious one. It was a political precondition aimed at achieving a Shari'a benefit, namely the unity of the umma. Its means to achieve that was to ensure that government was based on a strong popular block that could keep conflicts in check, as well as divisions and dispersion, and aim to use force sparingly. Then it could provide the people with prosperity and stability and achieve a necessary consensus.

To conclude, the president of an Islamic state must be a Muslim—except in exceptional circumstances—who uses Islam for the good in his life and in his people's lives, and at least is known for the integrity of his religious convictions, worldview, and moral character; one who loves knowledge and the input of scholars; and is attentive to his religious duties in terms of rituals, obligations, and prohibitions. Finally, he is trustworthy and upright in his actions, and enjoys an outgoing personality and good physical health—all this qualifies him to serve his people and lead them with competence. He should also have attained the age of maturity and stability (around forty years of age), and acquired an experience of life and people. He is relatively well known and has had a good amount of exposure to people's worries and cares. Finally, "the people of loosing and binding" (or the people's representatives) give testimony to his religion, his trustworthiness, and his competence, since he is, after all, the most capable among them. Would it not be wonderful if added to all these qualifications were purity of spirit and illumination of thought to enable him to carry out his mission as teacher, educator, reformer, and pioneer, and to earn the people's approval, or at least, a majority of them?[322]

Questions Related to the Ruler's Investiture

We have said earlier that the ruler is delegated by the umma to enforce the Shari'a, safeguard unity, and spread the message, with the help of the Shura Assembly and also the rest of the people; that the path leading to that representation is the specific oath of allegiance [bay'a] he swears before the Shura Assembly and the public oath of allegiance in which all Muslims participate in all regions of the Islamic world in the case of the political unity of the umma, or those within a particular nation,[323] in the case of a plurality of Muslim nations. The latter is the exceptional case from the theoretical perspective, for the rule is that the umma itself enacts the covenant of the imamate. Are there other ways, then, that this covenant of the imamate can be drawn up?

Designation of a Successor (a Covenant of Guardianship)

Many jurists have argued that the head of state is confirmed through designation by the outgoing president, either blood relative or not. This is the position of all the following schools of Islamic law: Malikis, Shafi'is, Hanbalis, as well some of the Mu'tazilites, Murji'ites, and Kharijites. Thus some of them have declared that this is the consensus of all Muslims on this issue.[324] Ibn Hazm even stated that this contractual method was the best and most suitable, whether the outgoing leader did it in good health or as a sick man or on his deathbed, as the Prophet (PBUH) did with Abu Bakr, as Abu Bakr did with 'Umar, and as Sulayman bin 'Abd al-Malik did with 'Umar bin 'Abd al-'Aziz. In Ibn Hazm's view, it is a method that "ensures continuity of leadership, peace and order for Islam and Muslims, and the prevention of the discord, unrest, and chaos associated with other methods."[325]

If it does happen that a ruler designates a successor, the umma has to comply, just as when Abu Bakr designated 'Umar as his successor, the Companions were unanimous in supporting the arrangement.[326] Their position was based on historical precedents and the consensus that was built around them, as well as the public interest.

Circling Back to the Nature of Islamic Rule

Any observer can see the connection between the decay within our religious heritage and our political thought and would point a finger to these ills that weakened Islamic civilization and caused its decline. Without a comprehensive revolution, therefore, these poisons will continue to flow in the umma's veins, paralyzing its energies, aborting its attempts at liberation, and dashing its dreams of renewal, and there will be no hope for a solid and robust rebuilding of the umma's civilization. Part of the reason is that a good deal of our efforts are wasted, not in resisting the intellectual invasion from the West or in spreading Islam, or in building the institutions of revival, but in reproducing the decline again and again or, at best, seeking to resist this decline by using and reproducing its very own logic.

We hope to write a new history of Islam. Yet, we continue to dip our pens into poisoned inkwells. Some of us are still discussing infallibility and hard at work theorizing about it. Others continue to argue without hesitation that the leader must only seek advice, as shura according to their flawed understanding is only consultative and not binding. Still others shamelessly repeat that the head of state *is* the state (as claimed by Sheikh al-Nabhani in the constitution of Hizb al-Tahrir).[327] It is as if the arguments on which these views are based are of any significance to make them worth considering and discussing. However, what are we to do in the face of the calamities visited upon us by so-called scholarly "consensus" [*ijma'*]? Indeed, according to the "consensus of Muslims," designating a successor or an heir is legitimate, and delegating authority to a legatee is legitimate! In other words, the "consensus" is that we be denied our right and freedom to choose the servant we empower to serve us or the functionary who acts on our behalf and on our terms!"

What will we do, while on the one hand we continue to read Qur'anic verses and hadiths about mutual consultation, and on the other we give credence to this dubious "consensus," not realizing that we have landed in the same pitfalls as the followers of other religions before us who were described thus: "Those who have been charged to obey the Torah, but do not do so, are like asses carrying books."[328] It is so unfortunate to see this decadence after such glorious days. Are we worthy of the legacy of the Rightly Guided Caliphate while we heap upon it the garbage of our decline? Are we not reading its inspiring pages through lenses that are clouded by the ignorance of past centuries? In fact, we have made that prosperous period say the opposite of what its luminous jurisprudence taught about religion and its straightforward political philosophy.

Those who profess devotion to the family of the Prophet (PBUH) distorted the Prophet's teachings by turning his shura system into a mantle that is passed down from father to son like an inheritance. They should be ashamed of ascribing to the purest of families the evil of dynastic rule—because that's what it is, no matter how else they might describe it! As for those who profess devotion to the tradition of the Prophet (PBUH), they too distorted his teachings by failing to distinguish between his capacity as prophet and messenger of God, which is about the permanent and the eternal—and his capacity as political leader— which is about changing circumstances. They mixed up the two, as they did with the hadiths limiting eligibility for the position of Caliph to those from Quraysh which ought to be attributed to his second capacity, that of the political leadership which is by nature changing. How could this be otherwise for a religion that is eternal, one that championed the cause of liberating human beings from all forms of injustice and discrimination? Or was he (PBUH) somehow unable or afraid to say it openly and wait until the last moments before his death to deliver to the umma his wishes regarding his successor? Would it not have made more sense to include that in his farewell pilgrimage sermon: "Abu Bakr is my successor," or "Ali and his progeny"?

And if one of the members of the council that met at the Saqifa had entertained such a reprehensible objection (that the Prophet [PBUH] had designated his cousin 'Ali), would he have hesitated to express it during this heated debate about who was the most worthy to succeed the Prophet (PBUH) because he was either unable or afraid to do so? The case would have been easy to settle had this proof or quasi-proof been available. And does the fact that Abu Bakr was entrusted with this office following nomination by 'Umar and Abu 'Ubayda at the consultative council of Saqifa and accepted this nomination after a heated and thorough discussion, as well as a general pledge of allegiance at the mosque, does that give him an absolute right over it, so that he can hand it over to whomever he wishes, and so that his nomination of 'Umar is seen as binding as some form of inheritance where one would pass on his property to anyone he chooses? Far from it! Even this latter transaction is in fact determined in the Shari'a by specific rules.

Why was there a public oath of allegiance to 'Umar in the mosque? Were the Muslims wasting their time with formalities, or were they aware of establishing

contracts and fulfilling obligations and responsibilities? Did 'Umar feel that
after God he was responsible to those who delegated authority to him as the
contract required? Or did he feel that he was responsible to the umma,
because it had entrusted that responsibility to him and therefore it would
hold him accountable? And if he strayed, would it not hold him to account and
warn him even of the ultimate sanction if need be?

The same applied to the following caliphs and with 'Umar in particular, who
designated six men as potential successors, none of whom were related to him.
These designated Ibn 'Awf to choose among them a candidate. Did Ibn 'Awf
feel that the matter rested with himself, so that he could do as he pleased, even
choosing among his own relatives? Or did he feel that he had been entrusted by
the Muslim community and therefore had to listen to them, men and women,
in order to find their preferred candidate? In the end, when it had become clear
that public opinion was leaning toward 'Uthman, Ibn 'Awf had him come to the
mosque for a public pledge of allegiance. But first, people had the opportunity
to question both 'Uthman and 'Ali in a candid debate that resembles the presidential debates we now watch on television, which are meant to clarify what policies each candidate would follow. Was all this a set of haphazard measures
imposed by circumstance, or were these constitutional rules established by the
earlier generation of Muslims according to an enlightened jurisprudence, but
which later were discarded by their descendants who no longer liked them?
And was this distaste not because they had drunk the nectar of emperors and
the dregs of destructive tribalism, and because the darkness of past centuries
clouded their vision and they could only see in their religion and heritage the
kind of dynastic rule common in their day?

How many times did the insurgents seek to convince 'Ali (may God be
pleased with him) to accept that they hand the caliphate to him, but his answer
was unequivocal: "Those of my ilk only accept a pledge of alligiance at the
mosque." How was it then that later generations deviated from this enlightened
legacy of consultation and invented the ideas of infallibility, the naming of one's
successor, the covenant with one's progeny and relatives, children and the insane? It was simply the custom of the time—to each period its own spirit. By
contrast, Islam was a great leap over the ages, freeing itself from the bondage of
customs and lighting a path for mankind toward shura and democracy. Yet it
wasn't long before the zeal of this spirit cooled down and the power behind this
drive weakened, so that the pattern of governance fell back into its historical
patterns, returning to the imperial spirit, with a few modifications, and dynastic rule, which were both practiced at the time. Then the scholars came along,
imparting religious legitimacy to the spirit of their times—namely, infallibility

of the ruler, inherited rule, and naming successors—and nothing was left of the Rightly Guided Caliph model except the name. By then it had turned into a system of "tyrannical and hereditary kingship," in the words of Ibn Khaldun. This is not to say that the Shari'a was entirely disconnected from state governance and society. Rather, it is that the spirit of the age clouded one of its fundamental dimensions—namely, transferring authority from the heavens to the earth, and from the elites to the people. Bringing those two conditions together would truly portend the dawn of a new age.

In all of this, however, we cannot neglect the negative fallout of the internal conflicts that arose early in the Rightly Guided Caliphate, for these civil wars, which quickly transformed the caliphate into a despotic rule, created great anxiety in the Muslim psyche. As a result, the movement of liberation and renewal in Islamic thought weakened—in fact, it reversed course, and a spirit of conservatism and fear of renewal crept in and took over the minds of most Islamic scholars. Even the many renewal attempts made by the great scholars al-Ghazali, Ibn Taymiyya, Ibn Rushd, Ibn Khaldun, and Ibn Hazm were not exempt from the influence of the spirit of their day, and it often took over and aborted their attempts to renew Islamic thought in this area.

Otherwise, how can one explain the idea of rulers designating their successor in the writing of the revolutionary jurist Ibn Hazm? How did this trusted historian miss the beginning of the disastrous decline, with the designation of rulers that came about with the schismatic ruler Mu'awiya bin Abi Sufyan, who was overcome (may God forgive him) by the lust for power and a spirit of tribalism? He was not content with grabbing political power from its rightful owner, but he continued in his error, determined to pass it on along with his possessions and wealth to his son and his clan. According to a famous story, having gathered a group of candidates to the caliphate from among the second generation of Companions, in front of this large gathering one of his aides stood up and gave a brazen speech, saying, "Here is the caliph!" He was pointing to Mu'awiya. He continued, "And if he dies, then this one," pointing to his corrupt son Yazid. "Whoever refuses, he will get this," pointing to his sword. Then Mu'awiya spoke, "Please be seated, for you speak in the people's name." From that time forth, the history of evil and corruption had begun, by institutionalizing dictatorship, rulers designating their successors, infallible leaders, robbing the umma of its right to choose, and dissipating its energies in bitter feuds on the issue of the caliphate.[329] All this naturally led to our civilization's decline, the onslaught of colonialism, and now the dictatorship of the false modernists.

This account, however, does not mean that the caliphate's history is entirely one of tyranny, for our history contains a mixture of tyranny and shura. Nor does it mean that the political deviance we have known erased altogether the Islamic character of the states that appeared throughout the history of Islamic civilization. In fact, given the general adherence to the preeminence of revelation in culture and legislation, Islamic teachings and values have persisted—even if at a level that was still far from the ideal—especially in individual behavior as well as through the very influential civic institutions. What the umma experienced by losing its input in building the state did not erase the value of its intellectual dynamism during at least the first five centuries of its history, nor the effective and vital role played by its political and civil society in the process, though badly shaken by the upheavals that did take place. Recall that the power of the rulers was limited by the Shari'a, since the 'ulama' through their interpretation of the sacred texts were the holders of legislative authority and prevented the ruler from usurping religion since judicial power was also in their hands independent from the state. For this reason, Islamic society was strong because of its cultural, social, economic, legislative, and judicial institutions, and it enjoyed a great deal of independence from the state. These, however, were the very institutions Western colonialism and its allies targeted for destruction—especially the religious endowments, religious institutes, and the Shari'a courts, the better to impose its supremacy and prevent any rebellion.

In conclusion, there is no possible legitimacy for an Islamic regime worthy of that name unless it is founded on a clear and rigorous system of mutual consultation and a genuine pledge of allegiance that expresses the people's will by means of elections made available in the most honest and transparent manner. Conversely, an Islamic political order loses its legitimacy when it results from mere inheritance, or a coup d'état, or from any kind of blatant or hidden authoritarianism by way of rigged elections, or bullying by foreign powers, or the declaration of a divine mandate imposed on the people, or the ruler's infallibility, or some form of legitimacy based on history, and the like.

There is no theocracy in Islam, just civil rule in every sense, with the people of the nation as the source of its authority, and the only way to bestow authority is the public oath of allegiance, for which a private oath, which is a mere process of nomination, cannot be substituted. The instances of designation during the period of the Rightly Guided Caliphs were only one of the possible means to propose a candidate to the assembly of "those who loose and bind" (Shura Assembly), while the umma could either accept this candidate or contest him by putting forward another candidate, or reject him.[330] That is the ideal representation of the Islamic state—the caliphal state, a state characterized by the Shari'a, a state born of the Text and mutual consultation, the state of the one umma.

Nevertheless, we can imagine lesser forms of legitimacy in exceptional cases, such as where division is imposed on the umma, regional states arise, within the general framework of Shari'a as the ultimate reference. Or maybe a state for the umma as a whole, one that defends its integrity, despite being saddled with a kind of injustice and a lack of mutual consultation. That was what happened in fact after the rule of the Rightly Guided Caliphs until the fall of the last form of caliphate in 1924.

What Is the Nature of the Contract of the Caliphate?

The majority of Islamic jurists contend that the contract of caliphate, or the leadership of the state, is a contract of delegation, or the deputyship of the umma, which holds the highest public authority and the source of political power. For, from a constitutional perspective, all the powers the president enjoys are granted him by the umma, for all the collective obligations, including that of establishing the imamate, are social obligations that at least some members must discharge or else the whole umma is guilty of negligence. And because God knows that not everyone is qualified to fulfill this duty, it is necessary for the umma to delegate some of its own to discharge the duties of the imamate. In so doing, the imams or rulers "represent" the umma, or become its agents.[331] Since the primary sovereignty in the Islamic state is God's will as represented by His Shari'a, then the authority of Islamic society is a trust, that is, delegated to it by God, for it is He who empowers the umma with sovereignty and authority by means of His Shari'a and His deputizing it on the earth.

In the context of that sovereignty, the people possess the authority to delegate to one among them this God-given trust that they cannot fulfill collectively. So his power is restricted, then, by the limits imposed on him by God's law and the will of the people, by the Text and mutual consultation, making it simultaneously, therefore, the government of God and the government of the people, as we read in the Qur'an, "a lifeline from God and from mankind."[332] As such, it is a political rule whose legitimacy both at its establishment and its continuation is dependent on the people's agreement with policies and the way the government conducts the affairs of state. The pledge of allegiance from this perspective is nothing but a contract of delegation, meaning that the ruler has become the umma's agent in enforcing the regulations of God's law, according to what the people of shura have decided, "the people of binding and loosing."

The Noble Qur'an has entrusted the umma with the responsibility to apply its divine law and its stewardship over this state, as these verses make it abundantly clear: "O you who believe, stand out firmly for justice,"[333] and "Be a community that calls for what is good, urges what is right, and forbids what is wrong."[334]

Many other passages too point out clearly that the umma is responsible for upholding Islam and its Shari'a and the common good. It is therefore entrusted
with the highest authority under the Shari'a's protection, along with great
responsibility. It has the right to choose the head of state and the right to
monitor him and all the other political leaders.[335] The scholars of the Islamic
Shari'a define the oath of allegiance to the caliph as a mutual contract, considering it as the actual contract of delegation, just as it is not allowed for anyone
to take on the function of the people's delegate of his own initiative and without permission. Thus no one is allowed, whoever he might be, to fulfill the
functions of a caliph if the umma has not appointed him in the first place.

The caliphate, in the opinion of the jurists therefore, is a contract based on
on choice and acceptance between the umma and the caliph. It is a contract
containing commitments and rights. As for the caliph, he must align his rule
and policies on what the Qur'an and the Sunna require; he must establish justice among people, fight injustice, safeguard religion and obey its rules and
stipulations, and defend the House of Islam. All this he must do with the approval of the people individually and collectively. The umma, for its part, must
maintain obedience and loyalty, as well as the effort to assist the ruler in fulfilling the burden of public governance.

According to Mahmud Hilmi, "When the caliphate was a kind of deputyship
and the rules of trusteeship applied to it, one of the rules was that it could not
be transferred to a descendant; another was that if the caliph was deposed or
died, the governors and ministers were not automatically dismissed because
they and the caliph, as agents, are accountable directly to those who appointed
them, which in this case is the collective body of Muslims. The ministers and
governors are not agents of the caliphs, but agents of the umma."[336]

At the worldly, political level, the authority that was in the hands of the
Prophet (PBUH) was the same as that of any Muslim ruler. After him, it was
entirely a civil authority delegated by the umma, and in no way was it a theocracy, where the ruler receives delegated power from God and is appointed
among the people and for the people as an agent who translates for them, by
his actions, commands, and prohibitions, the will of God. No Muslim believes
this, except for a group among them, and some isolated views scattered here
and there in literary works, figures of speech, and ignorant phrases by certain
kings like this saying from the caliph Mansur: "This wealth is God's wealth, with
which he has entrusted me. By his will he can remove me or strengthen me." A
similar statement made by Mansur's ancestor, Mu'awiya bin Abi Sufyan, drew a
vehement protest from the illustrious Companion Abu Dharr al-Ghifari: "This
wealth is God's wealth." The Companion Abu Dharr sternly informed him that

this wealth belonged to all the Muslims. He was not disagreeing with Mu'awiya that all wealth is God's in the first place, but he was pointing out his wicked ways, for the caliph was taking the people's money as his own. The truth is that God's wealth is entrusted to the umma and that the ruler is only a steward managing it. If he acts foolishly in this and misuses it, then he should be legally reprimanded and the money taken away from him, as God commanded, "Do not entrust your property to the feeble-minded. God has made it a means of support for you."[337] Also, "Do not eat up your property wrongfully, nor use it to bribe judges."[338]

An example of theocratic conceptions of political authority in a non-Shi'i context can be found in a passage I read in al-Qarafi's *al-Furuq*, in which he argues that the ruler rules on behalf of God and a ruling by him is an ordinance from God: "As for the ruler, he is a blessing from God, and it is the will of God that a ruling from him is (as) a command from God Himself (or and God has ordained that his decisions as a ruler are God's own). His ruling is tantamount to the revealed text on the matter in question, for the ruling of the ruler is (in itself) a text from God (may He be exalted) specifically crafted in this form."[339]

The commentator Abu al-Qasim al-Ansari hurried to respond, "What he said about the ruler being God's mouthpiece in his rulings is not correct; perhaps he agrees with God's rulings (may He be exalted) and it would be God's rulings. But maybe his judgments do not agree with God's, and in that case they are not God's, but he will still be excused and rewarded.[340]

Qarafi's opinion flies in the face of the Islamic conception of political rule and ruler, in that it is a civil rule from every angle and subject to good and bad decisions, and that is why mutual consultation is so important. It also plainly contradicts what the Prophet (PBUH) advised one of his leaders when he asked him whether he should hand down to the people God's rulings or his own. The Prophet (PBUH) said, "Hand down your own judgments, for you cannot know whether you have interpreted God's judgments correctly or not." 'Umar once corrected his secretary when he was writing down a ruling. He had written, "This is what God has ruled." "No," said 'Umar, "but write 'this is what 'Umar has ruled.'"

A Muslim ruler is no different from any other Muslim, in that he is prone to error, and that, even if he rises to the level of being able to carry out ijtihad, his interpretations are, like any others, subject to scrutiny via scientific research and deliberation [shura], both public and private. They will be followed or not, depending on the degree of acceptance they find among public opinion and the Shura Assembly, and they can be overruled by the majority, forcing him to comply. The Prophet (PBUH) said to Abu Bakr and 'Umar, "If you both agree on a matter, I shall not go against it." The ruler is no different from other Muslims. For these people chose him, appointed him, and entrusted him to lead them in the light of God's law by enforcing its rulings along with the people of shura. So he has no superiority over the latter or ability to impose his will, except for this political qualification—trusteeship or representation—and the only way to obtain it is through the pledge of allegiance to the ruler [bay'a], or in today's parlance, elections.

It is true that the Messenger (PBUH) in his religious calling was God's mouthpiece—a quality that ended with him as the Seal of the Prophets. That calling had no room for consultation, because in that respect he was infallible. As for his political role as ruler, he earned this position through an oath of allegiance, especially the second Pledge of Aqaba, which became the cornerstone of his rule in Medina. And because the non-Muslim groups in Medina, Jews and polytheists, were not parties to the Pledge of Aqaba, one of his first initiatives as ruler upon his arrival in Yathrib (Medina) was to draw up the *Sahifa*, which functioned as Medina's constitution as a state. Considering the way this document organized relations and rights within a multi-religious, multi-ethnic society, it can, in fact, be said to be the oldest and clearest example of a state constitution and the closest to justice in the history of political thought. The signatures affixed to it by each group represented a contract, or a pledge of allegiance to the new state. Thereby they acknowledged the Prophet (PBUH) as a civil ruler from the standpoint of his political deputyship. Further, that is the power that the umma has inherited from him. Let any of its members who wishes to emulate him do so by means of the pledge of allegiance and fulfill the political function that he fulfilled.[341]

However, is the contract of bay'a, from every angle, a contract of delegation? A branch of Islamic scholars contest this perspective, arguing that the caliph is bound to the high ideals of Islam; therefore, the umma cannot entrust him with anything other than that, whereas the agent is bound to enforce the will of his principal. The umma cannot depose a caliph except for corruption, unbelief, or incapacity, whereas the principal can cancel the contract or simply replace the agent.[342]

To that we might add that the principal stipulates in the contract of trusteeship what the agent's behavior should be as a trustee, while the delegation of authority in the contract of Islamic governance is only partial. That is because the umma does not surrender its responsibility for governance by signing a pledge of allegiance to the ruler but continues to exercise its leadership in other ways—by commanding the good and forbidding evil, for instance—which it exercises in many directions, including that of the president, and by means of consultative organizations, whether public or private, in order to solicit people's opinions, including by way of referenda. The president, therefore, has no duties or powers that were not entrusted to him by the people through their representatives in the Shura Assembly.

In any event, the comparison between the oath of allegiance and the contract of trusteeship (or agency, or deputyship) remains valid, especially in view of the fact that the ruler is certainly not the holder of a prior right, but rather his authority is derived from the umma, which holds the authority based on the primordial covenant of vicegerency of God. This highlights the difference between these three political systems. Notice the place of the people in each one:

Theocracy:	God—the ruler—the umma
Western democracy:	the people—the ruler . . .
Islamic democracy:	God—the umma—the ruler

Despite the commonalities between the systems, the distinctions are evident as well. It is clear that Islamic governance, from the fact that its political authority comes from the umma, is the closest to the democratic system. This has led most prominent Islamic thinkers to link Islam and democracy and to speak of "Islamic democracy," meaning that the Islamic state has no authority but that which is derived from the umma, or the people. Still, the umma's authority is tied to the authority of the Shari'a by a self-imposed attachment after it had accepted God by its own choice as its Lord and Islam as its religion. We saw previously that the democratic system gives absolute authority to the people, a position that may have become outdated now, because the space between nations has shrunk, their interests are interwoven, and there is the ever-present danger of brutally destructive wars. All of this has imposed a limit on the states' nationalist authority and allowed the rise and development of international agencies and institutions and human rights covenants. All of these encroach upon national powers. Moreover, the people's authority stripped of all moral boundaries and human values often hatches the vilest dictatorships, stains the soil with blood, and spreads the mantle of famine and fear over the world, just as many Western liberal, Nazi, and communist states did.

And if there was a need for an authority that surpasses that of individual states, how much more appropriate is it to give full sway to the authority of the "Lord of the Worlds," calling people and nations to drop their tribal, national, and religious prejudices and shun tyranny. Let them remember their original unity and the brotherhood and solidarity it entails: "People, We created you all from a single man and a single woman, and made you into races and tribes so that you should get to know one another. In God's eyes, the most honoured among you are the ones most mindful of Him."[343] As we also saw, the chasm between the source of authority of democratic governance (the people) and that of Islamic governance (God's law) is not so great that it cannot be bridged, since the people [umma] are the only source of the ruler's legitimacy, because they freely chose him.

In order to illustrate this potential common ground, it might be helpful to quote the French political scientist François Burgat on the pillars of Western democracy and how many Western nations rely on ethical principles that transcend mere human will:

> To be more precise, we must realize that Western political philosophy rests on people's absolute freedom to choose the laws by which they are governed; and that Western political practices flow from this theoretical principle as an unconditional criterion in practice. It seems, however, that we must qualify this statement to some extent, starting with the United States ("In God We Trust") and the French Republican system; then continuing with the United Kingdom and West Germany—all these experiments exemplify values that are higher than human will, whether the will of the community or that of the majority. And in a number of these states we still find a clear reference to the divine law [namus].
>
> In the United States, for instance, Germany, the UK, and elsewhere, this reference is fairly similar in its wording, since the international covenants morally bind member states to follow principles known to transcend any parliamentary majority. In fact, the principles of natural law imply that human will is always subject to a number of international frames of reference that in turn are not open to discussion. These principles and laws imply that in order to curb the excesses of the majority one has to accept the existence of original principles coming from a source other than human will. It follows that human will is not the only source capable of moral values. If we were to shrink the Islamic Shari'a into the natural law framework and the general principles contained in Western thought, which are used as a final frame of reference for the values enshrined in international covenants, it would not be impossible to find common ground between the Shari'a and the international democratic framework.
>
> Adel Hussein says as much when he refuses to allow the Islamic frame of reference to be the only one. Need one be reminded that the West German constitution refuses political rights to anyone who does not subscribe to its principles, and that the United States refuses entry to any communists?[344]

Concerning the idea that the umma cannot, after its covenant with the ruler, depose him except in cases of unbelief, corruption, or incapacity, though most

Islamic scholars agree on this, it is not an airtight religious rule, influenced as it is by the customs of the time, and it remains a policy open to other interpretations, depending on whether the Shura Assembly sees it agreeing with the public good or not. We have seen that a genuine election in which the ruler is elected for a term, in a process based on integrity and a plurality of candidates comes closest to fulfilling the objectives of Islam in carrying out the mandate of consultation and accountability and in preventing the evil of authoritarianism, the degeneration of the political system, and the piling up of injustice. All of this could lead to social unrest and civil wars, which can only be avoided by the functioning of consultative and democratic institutions to renew the state's legitimacy, and achieve a rotation of policies and a renewal of generations by continually bringing in younger leaders.

Further, the contract of delegation allows various ways of delegating power, and it may only be a partial delegation and its conditions may vary—a reality that speaks to the nature of the oath of allegiance as a contract entrusting the ruler to enforce the Shari'a and safeguard the people's interests. Just like other contracts, it entails rights and duties for both parties signing it, including the obligation of the ruler to listen carefully to other views by consulting the Shura Assembly or by direct referendum. Other means include the stipulation of the length of his term and whether it can be renewed or not, and requiring adherence to specific forms of consultation that either narrow or widen the ruler's influence.

As a side note here, let it be said that nothing in the Islamic texts or objectives prevents limiting the term of office, subject to renewal by means of elections, for the umma can either renew its confidence in its leadership or withdraw it. The historical precedent of the Rightly Guided Caliphate, which did not limit the caliph's term as long as he fulfilled his functions, only points to the fact that this is permissible but not a requirement. It could be that this lack of term limits was the cause of the tragic great civil war, which began in the old age of the third caliph, without the presence of any text or precedent for him to resign. This may be why some modern jurists like Shaykh Yusuf al-Qaradawi have moved to limit the length of a leader's tenure. We have seen how necessary this is due to the destructive results of despotism visited upon the umma, masquerading under the cloak of religion and even democracy and human rights.[345]

What Are the Rights and Duties of the Head of State?

First, allow me to offer some philosophical thoughts about the state and head of state. Clearly we are here talking about the head of an Islamic state, whether it be one state or a plurality. Though Islam does not accept a separation between religion and the state, it does make a distinction between the unity of the political body [umma] and the state that is an expression of it. This means that the territorial nation-state is in contradiction with Islamic political philosophy and that this artificial entity was forced upon the umma by Western colonialism to bring about and reinforce its weakness because it clashes with its creeds, cultural heritage, interests, and the deep aspirations of its people.

Still, the jurists accepted these separate states as a given within the present reality and interacted with it, hoping it would develop in the direction of the ideal state. In truth, just as every effort to move forward within the context of nation states was failing, so also attempts to impose unity among states in a haphazard way only led to disaster. All this made the demand for democracy part of Islamic demands, with the goal to empower our nations to claim their right to self-determination, break the fetters of dependency and tyranny that enslaved them, and proceed toward unity in a way compatible with their beliefs, their heritage, and their interests. In so doing, there will no longer be a contradiction between the transforming of a regional state into one that transcends it (a caliphate) and its transformation into a democratic state, as the demand for democracy forms an integral part of the demand for identity, social justice, and unity. Every step toward a more democratic state is a step toward the unified state.[346]

We now turn to the duties and rights of one who rules an Islamic state. Jurists specialized in Islamic political theory have made an effort to define these duties and rights, building on the texts of the Qur'an and Sunna, Islam's general objectives, the heritage of Islamic rule, and the consequences of the customs that prevailed in its original environment. However, each jurist is shaped by the spirit of his era, and the needs of his society. There is no wonder, then, that this work revealed commonalities and differences. The two preeminent scholars of Islamic constitutional law of the classical period were al-Mawardi and Abu Ya'la Ibn al-Farra'.

The Ruler's Duties

Here is a summary of what they saw as the ruler's duties:

- Safeguard religion according to its established foundations and the consensus of the umma's pious ancestors [*salaf*] (cultural and general mission)
- Apply the rulings among parties in a dispute, so that justice prevails (mission of court adjudication)
- Protect lives and property, so that people can work and travel freely (security mission)

- Enforce God's penalties [hudud] so that God's prohibitions are respected and people's rights are protected (executing penal laws)
- Fortify the breaches so that no enemy can enter through one of them (defense mission)
- Fight [jihad] those who resist Islam after being called to it until they embrace it or join the ranks of the protected minorities [dhimma] so that God's will is done by manifesting His religion in its entirety (jihad to push back enmity)
- Collect taxes and donations on what is owed without fear or apology (fiscal mission)
- Calculate revenue and what is due in the treasury without over- or underestimating it, and disburse it, neither too early nor too late (achieving social security)
- Secure enough trustees and good counselors, so government work is completed in good order and the funds administered by the trustees are safe (good choice of employees)
- Personally supervise the affairs of state, and maintain an overall perspective that is good for managing the policies affecting the nation and safeguard its religious character (direct supervision of state institutions)[347]

The following was added to this list of duties from another source: "Building up the provinces by maximizing their resources and interests and correcting their weaknesses and policies" (economic development mission).[348]

If you look into the functions of the head of state, you will find them falling into two categories, according to Ibn Khaldun, religious functions (safeguarding religion), like establishing the ritual prayers [salat] ("those who, when We establish them in the land, keep up the prayer"[349]), providing Islamic legal advice, the dispensing of justice, jihad, and hisba (maintaining public law and order, supervising market transactions, etc.); then the political function (achieving the interests of citizens), that is, including tax collection, postal service, policing, and defense.

The caliphate allows the umma to follow the path of the Prophet (PBUH) by safeguarding religion and managing worldly affairs according to the Qur'an, like the above verse and all the verses that command the umma to establish justice and resist oppression, and according to the precepts of the Prophet (PBUH), the most comprehensive of which is his farewell address ("Let him who was a witness among you inform him who was absent").

The umma undertook to fulfill this Trust by putting into action this principle of shura in order to establish a political order that would undertake this task on

its behalf and with its help. Its mission is to safeguard religion and the administration of worldly affairs and to work collectively and cooperatively using the
means that fit the needs of the time, so that the influence of the state is able
to expand and contract as it seeks to accomplish its objectives. In fact, modern
scholars have noticed that many important public utilities of the modern state
have not been mentioned by al-Mawardi, such as education, culture, health
care, and social services,[350] and the provision for a free and dignified life for
every son and daughter of the umma.[351] Notice, too, that none of the early political jurists, as far as we know, made mention of consultation, when discussing
it in terms of its outcome, as a mandatory duty for the ruler to follow. However,
with respect to the mere practice of it, several jurists stated that the continued
legitimacy of the authority of the ruler depends on it. Otherwise, he could be
legally removed from office, as al-Qurtubi wrote in his commentary on the
Quranic shura verse.

All those public services could be listed under the two objectives we mentioned for the Islamic state—safeguarding religion and managing worldly interests (or providing for the benefit of those governed). They could also come under
the heading of establishing justice, as the Qur'an teaches, "if you judge between
people, do so with justice"[352]; "God commands justice."[353] No doubt, whoever
rules according to the Shari'a, rules with justice.

Al-Qasimi summarized the ruler's duties in this way, "Overseeing all the
state's affairs, interior, exterior and military, and if he delegates one of these
functions, he is still responsible for it." One should also note that, even if the
functions of the Islamic state are not constant, as they interact with the needs of
the umma, they either expand or contract, for it is certainly not a totalitarian
state that grows stronger at the expense of society.

To the contrary, the state's tasks were limited, as society came to fulfill most
functions independent of the state, like education, legislation, health care, and
social security, and so it intervenes only when society is not able to. On this
model, then, we must seek to strengthen and expand the role of civil society at
the expense of government, so that it might truly become a servant, a helper, a
provider with limited powers, uncomplicated and flexible.

This does not mean in the least that the umma should shirk its duties on behalf of the poor and marginalized. Rather, even in its weakness it helps them
and intervenes on their behalf by making it a priority to serve them. For establishing justice and repelling injustice is the greatest social objective of the Shari'a,
and at the heart of this enterprise are the individuals and social organizations
that initiate ways to meet those needs and fill the gaps, so as to shrink the intervention of the state in this domain, except in exceptional cases.

The Ruler's Ethical Qualities

As we ponder the crucial nature of this high office and its impact on the umma, it includes an influence on people's lives and on every aspect of their being, even as the Prophet (PBUH) said, "There are two groups, which when they act righteously, the people act righteously; and when they become bad, the people become bad: rulers and scholars." In light of that, there is a wealth of Islamic writings offering the ideal of a model ruler and warning him to remain upright or face God's painful punishment. No doubt, the Qur'an and Sunna have played a big part in this. The Qur'an, especially, is replete with stories about the struggle between prophets and power-hungry rulers like Pharaoh and the kings of Nimrod, while the Sunna praises the righteous and just imams who are the first to stand in the shade of the Almighty and enter into Paradise.[354] The minimum requirement for the ruler, his aides, ministers, governors, ambassadors, and those in public service is that, in addition to their competence, they must be people of integrity and righteousness and do not practice any acts of corruption or deceit.

We will end this section on the duties of the ruler from a constitutional and legal perspective by shedding light on the ethical qualities he should display.

Willingness to Seek Counsel from and Consult with Scholars

This includes Islamic scholars and jurists, people of knowledge and experience in other areas, as he seeks to widen as much as possible his access to useful opinions. First and foremost, he seeks out the opinions of the Shura Assembly, for in that case his role is only to execute what they decide or ask them to reconsider a particular question in light of other sources. But if they insist on their position, his only option is to submit to their decision or resign, and that is in line with the divine command to the Prophet and all rulers after him to follow the rule of mutual consultation, ("Consult with them about matters," Q. 3:159). This puts the ruler who does not consult in a position of infraction and rebellion. We emphasized above Qurtubi's interpretation of that verse, when he said that the leader who does not seek counsel from the 'ulama' must be deposed and that the Prophet (PBUH), more than anyone else, sought counsel from others. In many instances, he sought the advice of his Companions, even when he was forced to go into battle at Uhud and divine revelation came to him in order to explain to him how he should deal with this situation, which had the potential to damage the mission God had given him.[355] He was told not to hold back from consulting with his Companions and by that means to mitigate any evil outcome, as his mission was to go on consulting with them on this matter.

Humility and Refraining from Boasting

We read in the Qur'an, "and lower your wing tenderly over the believers who follow you."[356] Whoever desires to be exalted on earth will be excluded from the bliss of the Hereafter: "We grant the Home in the Hereafter to those who do not seek superiority on earth or spread corruption."[357] The Prophet (PBUH) was the humblest of men, and he would prevent any attempt to exalt him, telling his visitors that he was a poor man and the son of "a woman who ate dried meat." He would prevent people from rising when he entered, saying "Do not rise up like the Persians, who exalt themselves above one another," for pride and greatness are for God alone. Whoever vies with Him for them shall be tormented.[358] He warned against boastfulness, saying[359] "He whose heart contains a grain of pride will not enter Heaven." Therefore, rulers, their aides, and governors ought to be humble and remember that they stand between the hands of God stripped of any vainglory and power—He is the One who questions, "Who has control today?"[360]

Compassion for the Umma

God's Messenger (PBUH) and his successors used to govern the people with gentleness. He said, "God is kind and He loves kindness in all things," and also, "Whenever kindness becomes part of something, it beautifies it. Whenever it is taken from something, it leaves it tarnished."[361] He would appeal to governors in this way, "By God, whoever rules over my people in one matter, if he is kind to them, I will be kind to him."[362] Regarding the Prophet's kindness, when he chose between two options, he would choose the easiest of the two, seeking to "prevent every difficulty and hardship for his umma." We read this about him in the Qur'an: "Your suffering distresses him: he is deeply concerned for you and full of kindness and mercy toward the believers."[363] It is the duty of the leader to be kind with people, as much as he finds a way to do that.

Freedom from the Desire to Take Revenge for Himself and Others and from Hatred of Adversaries

He must not be arrogant and oppressive, remembering that it is not for him to exercise divine judgment, which belongs only to God, the Almighty One. He must also be generous and forgiving. The Qur'an states: "[Those] who restrain their anger and pardon people—God loves those who do good."[364] Also: "Let them pardon and forgive. Do you not wish that God forgive you?" Finally, "Out of mercy from God, you [Prophet] were gentle in your dealings with them—had you been harsh, or hard-hearted, they would have dispersed and left you—so pardon them and ask forgiveness for them. Consult with them about matters."[365]

As narrated by 'A'isha, "God's Messenger (PBUH) would never strike anything with his hand, no woman and no servant, except when he was fighting in God's path; and he never disparaged anyone, nor took revenge from his companion, except when he violated one of God's laws and God would take His revenge."[366]

For that reason, when his enemies came with their heads bowed—those who had expelled him from his home and threatened to kill him—he did not insult anyone, or treat them harshly, but he humbly said, "Go, for you are free," reminding us of the story of Joseph and his response to his brothers in the Qur'an: "You will hear no reproaches today. May God forgive you: He is the most merciful of the merciful."[367]

A Commitment to Truthfulness in Making Promises to His People

"Honor your pledges: you will be questioned about your pledges."[368] Therefore, he must not betray anyone, or deceive, or cheat: "Any servant of God to whom God has entrusted people to his care, the day that he dies, if he has cheated them, God will not let him enter Heaven." Especially as the ruler makes promises not in his name but in that of the state, so the commitment is transferred to his successors. Thus Abu Bakr said after being invested as caliph, "If one of you entered a contract with the Prophet or owes him money, let him pay it to us."

The Ruler Must Not Withdraw from People or Their Needs

The Prophet (PBUH) said, "He whom God entrusts with a matter concerning the Muslims and he distances himself from their need, their want and their poverty, God will distance Himself from his need, his want, and his poverty on the Day of Resurrection.[369] One way to withdraw in this context is to live isolated in huge mansions surrounded by high walls and thousands of armed guards.

A Simple Lifestyle

Asceticism is one of the dispositions a ruler should adopt, which means not competing with others in terms of worldly possessions. That is more upright and proper for him and for his people, so that he will not be preoccupied with the niceties and vanities of this world that distract him from God, and so that he will not lose his strong determination. This also means that he will not raise his family in too much comfort and later despair of their spiritual state in this world and the next as they become a bad example to the umma. Those in power—on all levels in society, including the leaders of Islamic organizations—cannot escape from a call to rigorous self-discipline, for the life of luxury cannot coexist with faith nor does it make strong men and women.

This ascetic disposition in the ruler is also better for his people, because he is an example for them, and they will want to live their lives following in his footsteps. If he focuses on this world and its comforts, then they will compete in that realm too, diving into what is most prized, fighting over it, corrupting one another, and never being satisfied. But if he focuses on the next life, then the mosques fill up and the markets will thrive—the markets of ideas, of spiritual and Qur'anic meditation, of fruitful knowledge, good works and kindness, and jihad: "Let those who strive, strive for this."[370]

A ruler cannot hide his situation from his people for long, nor is it possible for a people to run after luxuries while their rulers are content with a simple lifestyle. Since humanity has seemed condemned to live for centuries with rich and poor side by side, the best system would be one in which the rulers live on par with the poor and all raise their standard of living together. What an outrage it would be to have the richest man also the head of state! Sadly, this is the case for most Muslim-majority nations. Here is a saying of the Prophet (PBUH) to ward off such a fate: "O God grant me life as a poor man, cause me to die as a poor man and resurrect me in the company of the poor."[371]

Commitment to the State's Constitution (Shari'a)

No doubt, that is the upshot of all that has been said previously about the ruler's ethical values. Add to that his humility before God, always seeking His approval so that he becomes one of His devoted worshipers, known among the circles of religious discussion, remembrance [dhikr], and nightly prayers, for if he does not seek help in those areas for himself against the temptations and pitfalls of power, he will be lost. That said, surely it is better before God for a ruler to invest his energy in caring for the weak and promoting justice and the best interest of all as a form of worship than in individual supererogatory spiritual exercises like nightly prayers.

However, the work of the ruler to safeguard religion and manage worldly affairs does not cancel the role of the umma. None of what the ruler's office requires of him negates or diminishes the role of the people, from his management of state institutions to his appointment of aides as ministers, governors, directors, military leaders, ambassadors, and judges and all the oversight and accountability that go with it. To the contrary, he does his very best to improve the state's efficiency and self-sufficiency so that its role is brought down to a minimum. Constricting the tasks of the state is not to turn it into a police state, which prioritizes maintaining security above its other roles and above all the security of the ruler or that of the class or clique from which he draws his power. Rather, circumscribing the state's role is for the sole purpose of keeping the people from becoming overly dependent on it. The state, then, should make every effort to get rid of that dependence and lead people to rely on themselves by encouraging individual and collective initiatives for the public good in all areas, and by releasing the powers of innovation and encouraging initiatives that bring public benefit, and the state should facilitate such actions and not obstruct them.

The Ruler's Rights

The best here is to emphasize what one of the jurists of Islamic political theory wrote. He argued that people should not wait for a ruler to fulfill his duty before giving him his rights, because in that case he would have his hands tied, unable to do anything. In order to find out what those rights are, we turn to the classical jurists in this field as they relied on the Shari'a and the example of the Rightly Guided Caliphs. Al-Mawardi wrote, "If the ruler respects the rights of the umma that we mentioned, he has fulfilled God's right (may He be exalted) on their behalf and against them; as for their duty toward him, there are two: obedience and good counsel."[372] Al-Rayyis put it this way: "As long as the imam respects God's command, rules with justice, and applies the Shari'a's rulings by submitting to them in his work and behavior, remaining faithful to all the duties and conditions he committed to in his swearing in—all of which qualifies him as a just ruler—then the umma owes him two duties: obedience and good counsel. Whoever rises up against him is guilty of treason. He has a right to the nation's wealth according to a moderate standard of living. If he desires a raise, it is for the Shura Assembly to decide, one way or another."

Al-Faruq 'Umar noted that the position of the ruler with regard to the state treasury is like that of the orphan's guardian: "If the guardian is well off, he should abstain from the orphan's property,"[373] that is, his salary should be tied to his need, and if he has other revenue, then he should not get a salary. Others argue that he should be compensated as a Muslim of average income, whatever his financial situation, unless he gives it to charity or refuses it, and what applies to the presidency applies to all state employees. In our estimation, the second opinion is better, because the ruler accepts an administrative job, knowing full well that the option of volunteer work remains open. Also, it is well known that many scholars prefer the first opinion, but the second one is more suitable to a small state closer to the ideal, like that of Medina.

Perhaps it is best to recall the story of the first person to be fully dedicated to leading an Islamic state, Abu Bakr al-Siddiq. It is told that the day after his investiture as caliph he went to the market early in the morning carrying clothing, as was his custom. He was met by 'Umar bin al-Khattab, who asked him what he was doing. Abu Bakr answered, "How else will I feed my family?" 'Umar answered, "Go see Abu 'Ubayda and he will advance you some money."[374] A committee formed around Abu 'Ubayda, and it made him one payment from the willing contributions of the Meccan emigrants. He immediately complained about how little it was (maybe because of inflation), and he asked for an increase and they accepted. That became the rule hereafter.

Nevertheless, Abu Bakr ordered before he died that all of what he had taken as personal salary from the treasury be given back, and in that he remained the caliph who set the ideal for those who followed, the "poor caliphs," like 'Umar and 'Ali. He set another rule, that of refraining from taking a public salary when possible, and we do not know if this was followed by any other caliph than 'Uthman bin 'Affan.[375]

In this context, Ibn Jama'a in his book *Documenting the Regulations Ordering the Life of the People of Islam* has listed eight rights of the ruler:[376]

1. Obedience to him inwardly and outwardly in all that he commands, unless it disobeys God's command, "O you who believe, obey God and the Messenger, and those in authority over you."[377] The phrase "those in authority" refers to the ruler and those he has delegated, according to most commentators. The most reliable interpretation is the following: obedience is in matters that God has commanded [*al-ma'ruf*] and not in matters that violate His law. The obedience that Islam enjoins on the umma's leaders is obedience to the constitution—that is, not obedience to individuals but to God and His Messenger (PBUH). Put otherwise, they are to obey the Shari'a, and if the believer obeys his leaders with this intention within the limits of the Shari'a, he will receive his reward as a true worshiper.

2. Offering good counsel to him, secretly or openly, as the Messenger (PBUH) said, "Religion is good counsel." To whom is this addressed? He answered, "To God, to His Messenger, to the rulers of the Muslims, and to all of them.[378] This presupposes freedom of opinion and expression by way of a free press, mosques, freedom to publish, to meet and form associations and political parties, to hold public conferences, and to organize peaceful marches to demand or to protest something, and the like, but without having to obtain the ruler's permission, since all of that is included in the umma's God-given mission to command the good and forbid what is evil. So there is no need to obtain anyone's permission in the matter.

3. Recognition of his excellent status and the praise that befits his ability, treating him as one ought to, with respect and dignity. Thus the greatest scholars would exalt his status and respond to his request with self-sacrifice and piety, without greed and without treating him as do some so-called ascetics, who lack common courtesy and violate good custom.

4. Alerting him when he is negligent, gently advising him when he errs, while protecting his faith and his honor.

5. Warning him when an enemy seeks to harm him or someone wants to cause him grief, or when there is something he should be afraid of, and the like. Warning him of any threat to his safety is among his foremost rights.
6. Informing him of the progress of those working for him, those he is especially meant to supervise, so that he can personally measure their success.
7. Coming to his aid in carrying the burdens, securing the welfare of the umma and helping him to the best of one's ability, as God said, "Help one another for the sake of righteousness and godliness" (Q. 5:2). And the most deserving is the one who helps those in authority.
8. Seeking to change the hearts of those who dislike him, increasing the love of people for him in a way that benefits the umma.

Perhaps this text, despite some repetition, is the most detailed in its genre on the subject of the ruler's rights, as al-Qasimi has pointed out. Yet these rights as a whole do not depart from what al-Mawardi and Abu Ya'la have written concerning the obedience and good counsel owed to the ruler; these are simply more detailed. All this applies, of course, when the ruler is faithful to his contract of investiture. But what if something goes wrong, either by his fault or from something outside his control? Then what? Should he be removed if he did not cause the problem? How does this work?

The Umma's Right to Depose a Ruler

This is considered to be one of the thorniest questions Islamic political theory has had to deal with both in ancient and modern times, and it points to both the strength and weakness of this theory, as we will see, God willing.

The oversight of the presidency belongs to the umma, for it is the one who makes a political contract with one of its members (the oath of allegiance) according to the specific conditions stipulated therein, like his competency and his commitment to justice and to God's law. Two consequences follow from this: the people's duty to monitor him and the duty to remove him if he plainly departs from his pledge the day he was invested.[379]

The Umma's Duty to Exercise Oversight

There are many indications for this in the Qur'an and Sunna, in the consensus of jurists and precedents in Islamic history. They all turn on this central Islamic principle: commanding good and forbidding evil, which represents the authority that exercises oversight over all branches of government, that is the direct power of the umma; or the power of public opinion through the efforts of individuals or organizations of civil society, the media, mosques, associations and centers, and the like.[380]

In the Noble Qur'an:

- "Be a community that calls for what is good, urges what is right, and forbids what is wrong: those who do this are the successful ones."[381]
- "The believers, both men and women, support each other; they order what is right and forbid what is wrong; they keep up prayer and pay the prescribed alms; they obey God and His Messenger. God will give mercy to such people: God is almighty and wise."[382]
- "Those Children of Israel who defied [God] were rejected through the words of David and Jesus, son of Mary, because they disobeyed, they persistently overstepped the limits, they did not forbid each other to do wrong. How vile their deeds were!"[383]

From the Sunna:

- "Religion is to offer good counsel," The Companions asked, "To whom?" "To God, to his Book, to his Messenger, to the Muslims' rulers, and to all the people."[384]
- It was narrated on the authority of 'Ubada ibn Samit that he said, "We pledged our allegiance to God's Messenger (PBUH) to listen and obey him when it was difficult or easy, pleasant or not, to speak the truth wherever we were, not fearing in doing so anyone but God."[385]
- "Command good and forbid evil, or God might send you a punishment, and you will call on him and you will receive no answer."[386]
- "A man asked the Prophet (PBUH), 'What is the best jihad?' He answered, 'Speaking the truth to an unjust ruler.'"[387]
- "If people see injustice and do not act to correct it, God will punish them."[388]

The jurists' consensus was that the Islamic umma in its entire history has agreed upon the duty of commanding good and forbidding evil on the basis of the Shari'a and of human reason.[389] The Mu'tazilites even counted it as one of the five pillars of religion.

Now from the lives of the caliphs: here in Abu Bakr's first speech as caliph: "I have been put in authority over you and I am not the best of you. So if I do the right thing, then help me and if I do wrong, then stop me . . . Obey me, as long as I point you to God, and if I disobey Him, then you should not obey me . . . If I take the straight path, then follow me, and if I deviate, then set me straight."[390]

Now from a sermon by 'Umar bin al-Khattab: "If you see some transgression in me, set me straight." One of the Muslims asked him, "If we found in you some transgression, we would settle it with our swords." 'Umar answered, "Praise be to God who has placed among the Muslims one who would correct 'Umar by the blade of a sword."[391]

When he encountered much criticism and insult, Caliph 'Uthman set out for the mosque announcing that he was ready to be rebuked and to repent, saying, "If I came down from my pulpit, then let the notables come and give me their opinion; then, by God, if the judgment is that I should become a servant, then I would certainly submit to it."[392] Mutual consultation in itself is only one of the aspects of this mandate to promote good and prohibit evil, as the umma's duty is to safeguard religion and supervise government. Muhammad 'Abduh grounded the need for shura using the verses commanding good and forbidding evil, because that mandate represents the heart of the Islamic umma's mission and the reason for its favor. How could it desist from this calling without incurring God's wrath?[393] And is there any good with more positive impact on the umma than upright governance? Or more despicable damage inflicted on it than by corrupt governance?

One thing that magnifies evil is to commit it at a particular time and place, like committing adultery in the sacred enclosure during the Hajj. Another factor is the status of the one committing the sin, like an Islamic scholar or an imam leading prayer. The worst case is that the umma's imam who had covenanted to protect the Shari'a commits an evil act. How could censuring him not be an even greater and necessary duty and his punishment wiser and greater: "The Master of the Martyrs is Hamza, and a man who stood before his amir, commanding him and forbidding him. Then the amir killed him." That is certainly the best jihad: "The best jihad is a word of truth spoken to an unjust ruler."[394]

For the umma to completely turn away from its obligation to enjoin good and forbid evil, fail to institutionalize it as Westerners did, and become distracted by and committing small acts of transgression, is the direct cause for most of the disasters of tyranny visited upon it, and for the decline, intellectual stagnation, and the defeats incurred at all levels. As Imam Malik said, "There will be no other solution for the umma but that which benefited the first Muslims" in order to bring back its authority by exercising once again its duty to command good and forbid evil, starting with the leaders.

You will recall that the Shari'a's rulings were all given for the purpose of drawing benefit and repelling harm and that the umma appoints the ruler to apply the Shari'a and promote their interests in a just way, so that security and prosperity prevail, and dignity and freedom are experienced by all.[395] Thus if the ruler steps out of the Shari'a's bounds, away from justice and human welfare by trampling on human rights and liberty—for instance by squandering their possessions and engaging in various acts that grievously breach the covenant by which he was appointed—then it is the umma's duty to pressure him by constantly monitoring his acts and policies and by protesting in one way or another so as to keep him from misusing his power. This disavowal of a ruler and this resistance to his swerving from the right course and committing injustice is not the responsibility of just one group among the people, however, but everyone's responsibility, whether individually or by groups.

That responsibility is distributed according to the ability of each group within the umma. The 'ulama' class is called to manifest to the people the kind of Shari'a violations of which the ruler is guilty and to criticize him, whether his infringements are textual or against the consensus of the scholars (if he had offered his own interpretation, ijtihad) which he may not do. The mosque preachers too are responsible for raising awareness against such violations, calling the regime to account and pressuring it to address violations. They must draw attention to the violations of human rights and Shari'a regulations and their dangers. They engage in cultivating a public opinion that is savvy politically and religiously, aware of its context, willing to shoulder with others the task of changing and strengthening the people's resolve to either support the current regime or change it. In this way the umma becomes a strong front taking charge of repelling evil and obliging the ruler to respect the people and the law. And if his own faith does not curb him, fear of the people will.

The people's task of monitoring the ruler should not be limited to individual actions but include the formation of parties and organizations whose first duty is to cooperate in order to help society avoid various evils, for the government is a whole system with its own resources and personnel, hence monitoring it cannot merely be the work of isolated individuals, according to the consensus on this practical issue also found in the Qur'an, "Be a community [group] that calls for what is good, urges what is right, and forbids what is wrong."[396] There is nothing in the Shari'a that prevents the establishment of organizations that will monitor the regime in power, strengthen the authority of the umma, and bolster public opinion. In fact, this may be the direct application of the authority to command good and forbid evil. God willing, we will return to this question, but in the meantime there may be a direct application of the general command to "call for what is good," and no doubt there are degrees in the way this is carried out, from the lesser to the greater.

Ibn Hazm wrote, "If any injustice is committed—even if it is rare for the ruler to be confronted—then if he desists and comes back to the right path and submits to retaliation as set by the Shari'a, then there is no need to depose him. If on the other hand he desists from carrying out any of his duties and shows no intent to do so, then he must be deposed and someone else be appointed in his stead, one who will follow the true path, for no Shari'a injunction must go unheeded and every Muslim has the right to monitor this."

Then, centuries later, Muhammad 'Abduh wrote,

> The caliph is obeyed as long as he follows the authority and path set by the Qur'an and Sunna, while the Muslims keep watch over him. If he swerves from the path over which they appointed him, or makes crooked decisions, they will straighten him out with good counsel and plead with him. He is a civil leader in every way, since according to Islam there is no religious authority other than righteous admonition, drawing people to what is good and driving them away from evil. This is the authority God has entrusted to all Muslims, from the most simple to the most distinguished. Therefore, each and every Muslim must speak out a word of truth to the caliph if he swerves from the straight path or neglects to follow God's way. If he does, he will be rewarded, for he has put up a noble fight ("the best jihad is a word of truth spoken to an unjust ruler").[397]

On the subject of the Shari'a's objectives, the "Shaykh of the two Holy Places," al-Juwayni, had this to say: "If the imam commits an injustice and his guilt is in plain view, and he does not listen to any criticism of his wrongdoing, then the 'people of loosing and binding' must come to agreement about deterring him, even by force of arms and declaring a war, if necessary."[398]

Islam's scholars of the past accomplished noble exploits in countering the injustice and mischief of rulers and they raised the authority of the command to do good and the prohibition of evil above the authority of the rulers, to the point that one scholar dared to put a sultan up for sale.[399]

To sum up, exercising oversight over a ruler must lead to either the latter's return to righteousness after his transgression, demonstrating regret, sorrow, and an attempt to correct what had gone wrong, either by providing redress or compensating the parties harmed by his policies, or it leads to the ruler's submission to the pressure of the masses and their leaders from among the Shura Assembly. Or the ruler may insist on continuing on the same path, which is unlikely, if all methods for advising and opposing him have been used gradually and effectively. It could reach the point of refusing to pay taxes and enforce the ruler's commands, for the Muslim judge is bound to avoid making a decision based on invalid injunctions. As the Qur'an says, "Do they want judgement according to the time of pagan ignorance? Is there any better judge than God for those of firm faith?"[400] And again, "those who do not judge according to what God has sent down are rejecting [God's teachings]."[401]

We must act according to the rule, "no obedience to a creature in rebellion to the Creator . . . obedience is only due in obedience [to the Creator]" and in submission to the higher law—and to the constitution. Today in Muslim countries with constitutions that begin by saying that Islam is the state religion one may also find the addition, even without an explanation in the text, that the Shari'a is the supreme source of legislation. This gives support to the Muslim judge and the state's top officials as they desist from applying any text that contravenes the Shari'a's clear texts. This is in application of the rule to override any law that contradicts the higher law. So the policeman and soldier, the leader, the employee and the taxpayer—all of these apply the principle of rejecting what is evil in their hearts and in their knowledge and actions—"boycotting unjust authority"— by not cooperating with it and not following its commands. If the problem persists, then the degree of resistance has to rise to the launching of peaceful forms of opposition such as calls for strikes, protest marches, and popular mobilization in the face of tyrants, led by elites, the youth, and society as a whole.

What regime in the world can stand while facing these kinds of pressures? Though the scholars developed peaceful means to apply the great Islamic principle of enjoining good and forbidding evil, they did not restrict it to the practice of individuals. That said, these methods were not always effective in ending violations by rulers who had militias, security agents, and money at their disposal. This is precisely what led to solutions involving violence, which for the most part produced disastrous results like the spilling of much blood, financial ruin, and the tearing apart of society. This is perhaps what pushed the majority of Sunnis and Mu'tazilites to close that door completely, relying on a number of texts that teach restraint from the use of force in resisting the oppressive ruler until his unbelief becomes obvious to everyone. The Prophet (PBUH) said, "Whoever sees his amir doing something he disapproves of, he should be patient, for whoever disassociates from the Muslim community even slightly and then dies, it will be a death as in the period of ignorance."[402]

He also said (PBUH), "'There will be after me injustice and matters you will condemn.' They said, 'O Messenger of God, what do you command us to do?' He said, 'Render to them [the rulers] what you owe, and seek from God what is your right.'"[403]

'Awf bin Malik al-Ashja'i reported that God's Messenger (PBUH) said, "The best of your rulers are those whom you love and who love you, those whom you bless and who bless you. The worst of your rulers are those whom you curse and who curse you." We said, "O Messenger of God, should we not resist them?" He replied: "No, not as long as they establish the prayer."[404]

Muhammad Asad had this comment on that hadith: "It is evident that the phrase 'not as long as they establish prayer' does not simply mean setting up imams in mosques or practicing the ritual in itself. It means, according to the content of Sura 2, a full implementation of all that pertains to faith and all action that faith entails."[405]

The Prophet (PBUH) said, "Whoever raises the sword against us is not from us."[406] Muhammad Asad had this interpretation, "What is clear here is that God's Messenger (PBUH) commanded Muslims to refuse executing orders of a government that contradict the Shari'a's texts and to remove a government if its actions reach the level of apostasy." 'Ubada bin al-Samit narrated the following, "We called the Prophet (PBUH) and we gave him our oath of allegiance. And regarding our commitment he said that we had pledged to listen to him and obey him, whether we were full of energy or tired, whether we liked it or not, whether it was hard or easy. He then impressed on us not to fight against the ruler, unless we saw a clear sign of unbelief in him and this was proven to us by God."[407]

If these many hadiths are read as a whole, and not in isolation from the general context of the Qur'an, Sunna, and the lives of the caliphs, they strongly encourage each Muslim to play a positive role in his society, commanding, forbidding, exerting himself and striving, resisting without wavering or losing hope, so that even if he hears the blowing of the last trumpet and he has a fertile palm seedling in his hand to plant the good or to root out evil, he will do it.

Taken together these hadiths and others like them that discourage people from taking up arms against an unjust ruler—some of which command the destruction of swords altogether—should not be read in isolation from the overall spirit that runs through the Shari'a, which seeks to shake the umma into action and enable it to discern the positive and constructive aspects of its history and not focus on the negative and passive ones only. A proper understanding of these texts will lead us to the following conclusions.

First, the social and political context in which the texts that oppose the use of force were revealed was an Islamic context in which some violations had been committed, yet without threatening the overall "political regime," as expressed in modern constitutional terms; that is, none of this threatened the identity of the umma's creedal or political framework, or the state's higher source of legitimacy. The amirs who are spoken of in the texts are all "those in authority over you" and they are our rulers: "whoever noticed something about his amir," "the best of your rulers," "the worst of your rulers." One cannot associate dictatorial, corrupt rulers who ignore the Shari'a and the will of the people, since upon inspection these are more akin to criminal gangs who spill the people's blood. Those we cannot consider to be our rulers or those entrusted with our affairs, otherwise we would have to obey them. Yet the texts clearly agree that there is no obedience to a statute that goes against God's law and no obedience to one who rebels against God. The condemnation (of rebellion) in the above texts is related to action to correct deviations that occur within a political system based on righteousness and justice, even if imperfect—that is, as long as the teachings of Islam, including ruling by justice and consultation are respected. "No obedience to the one who does not consult others," as al-Qurtubi reminded us.[408]

Second, the hadiths that forbid raising the sword against deviant rulers who nevertheless have not reached the level of blatant disbelief or rebellion against the Shari'a, do not cancel out the other degrees of rejection or opposition. They do not call for surrender to an evil status quo but rather enjoin a peaceful jihad—that is, speaking the word of truth to an oppressive ruler and resisting evil, not accepting it, which might lead to this evil becoming institutionalized and permanent. The masses maintain their right to disapprove of him and mobilize public opinion to oppose him.

If the scholars and jurists, especially, make the greatest effort in this direction and the voices of protest begin to converge and grow in strength and intensity against the unjust ruler and it produces a strong popular wave behind the scholars to pressure the unjust, tyrannical ruler to turn away from his path—despite his efforts to mistreat and torment his opponents—this will only strengthen the people's will to stand behind them, take up their call, and rally together against the unjust rulers until they retreat, defeated.

This was the method that Imam Ahmad bin Hanbal chose, according to the stories told about his patience and peaceful resistance, when he stood up to the most powerful state in the world at the time, raising the sword of enjoining good and forbidding evil.[409] He resolutely stayed his course until he was able to move the state away from its theocratic tendencies. The wealthy and cultured elite (allied with the Mu'tazilites) had deceived the rulers and encouraged them to follow this course, determined to assert the state's monopoly over religion and the authority to interpret the sacred texts, which is the prerogative of the umma and its scholars and jurists. Imam Ahmad became determined to engage in a peaceful jihad, the jihad of the word; he persevered on that path despite being subjected to various kinds of cruel punishment. This rallied the people around him, thus forcing the state in the end to give up and retreat from its theocratic course.

We can find a modern Tunisian example of this in the person of Shaykh Muhammad al-Salih al-Nayfar (d. 1993), who launched a campaign against the movement seeking to define the beginning of the lunar months on the basis of calculations and not on the traditional method of visual sighting. His action went against the state's recent decision. Thanks to a persistent popular and peaceful campaign, he was able to bring together over a couple of years, he forced the government to retreat and change its policy—and that regardless of whether this or that position was correct or not.

Then, on October 18, 2005, eight Tunisian lawyers and political activists of all stripes, brought together solely by their opposition to tyranny and their long-ing for freedom, began a hunger strike that lasted over a month. Making good use of an international conference on information technology that was meet-ing in the country at that time, they were able to draw the world's attention to Tunisia's tragic lack of freedoms. In the end, they issued a declaration about the formation of the broadest opposition coalition the country had ever known. The "18th of October Freedom Movement" centered on the following three demands: freedom of expression, freedom of association, and the release of po-litical prisoners. This is another kind of peaceful jihad, among many others.

Indeed, the word that springs from a believer's heart devoted to God is im-bued with such power that it is difficult to resist.[410] One should never underes-timate this weapon or hasten to dismiss it, or portray it as a form of surrender or cowardice.

For the haste to take up arms has often visited on the umma disasters, and some of these calamities have opened breaches in the umma's edifice that will not be filled till the Day of Resurrection, like the armed rebellion against the third caliph, which divided the umma and imposed on it an internal conflict that will go on till the Resurrection. Certainly, it would have been possible for the power of the word to correct that trajectory, even if it took some time. One should not neglect this weapon, therefore, or be quick to set it aside. Then, too, we should understand these texts that call for patience with unjust rulers and for contenting oneself with good advice as the best means to redress violations within the context of a legitimate Islamic order. The only red line is contained in the phrase "only if you see evident disbelief."[411]

Third, if the government rebels against the authority of the Shari'a, stands in its way, distorts it, or goes against what Muslims have agreed upon, and thus betraying the terms of its covenant, if it becomes authoritarian and violates public freedoms and encourages what God has forbidden, then what do we do? On this issue, Muslims agree that in these circumstances the ruler's legitimacy must be denied, since they obey God's precept to command what is right and forbid what is wrong, which also gives them the responsibility to correct the na-tion's trajectory and protect its people's integrity. Only in so doing can they guard themselves from the wrath of God and a disastrous outcome. That is according to what is possible, but Muslims have disagreed about timing and means. Some will only use peaceful means, seeking to avoid violent dissension. These are the majority of Sunni jurists, especially after the first phase of Islamic history. Others believe that the use of force is permissible if one is sure that the conditions for change are present or at the very least that victory is likely attainable. This was the majority opinion among the first few generations of Muslims, although it was also a time when armed insurrections accompanied by much bloodletting and repeated failures to reconcile had a catastrophic impact on the unity and stature of the Muslim community. In reaction to this, the jurists tended to restrict the use of force to the most extreme situations, and in the end this led to the position of Imam al-Ash'ari, which states that it is best to abstain from armed rebellion against the state for fear of civil war, preferring a bad situation to one that is much worse indeed. So Muslims limited themselves to using only peaceful means to deny the legitimacy of an authoritarian ruler.

Others say it is our duty to fight a ruler who judges by what God has not revealed, who declares openly his transgressions and makes them lawful, and who violates public freedoms, like freedom of expression, the independence of the courts, and freedom of association.[412] If that is the case, they argue, then they should be disobeyed, and every member of the umma must work to get rid of him, because his position as head of state is a direct cause of civil war [fitna],[413] and even if that means assassinating him.

This was in fact the opinion of the Kharijites and some of the Mu'tazilites. Ibn Hazm asserted that this was also the Sunni position.[414] It may be that these people find support for their position in the "the counsel of the Prophet" (PBUH), in that he ordered the assassination of some Jewish leaders, like Hay bin al-Akhtab. This, however, falls under a different category: treason. Today's defenders of the thesis that it is legitimate to take up arms against current regimes do so on the basis that they are in rebellion against the rule of the Shari'a and betray the umma and deserve, therefore, to face armed insurrection or the kind of jihad in which various groups have engaged in Egypt, Syria, Algeria, and Saudi Arabia. With time, and as they encountered disastrous results, they discovered that they had hurried to base their positions on premature conclusions on Islamic law and from a misguided understanding of local and international realities. As a result, they brought terrible suffering upon themselves and upon their nations.[415]

For his part, the Shi'i jurist from Iran Ayatollah Muntadhiri (Montazeri) summarizes the method of resisting unjust rule in this way:

If a ruler errs in a way that does not threaten the foundations of the Shari'a and the welfare of Islam and Muslims, and the basis of his work remains the Qur'an and the Sunna, then one should not, rather, one may not rebel against him; he should not be deposed either. Instead, what is called for is good counsel and much persistence. But the situation is different if the ruler has fundamentally deviated from the norms of Islam and justice, if he has made despotism and immorality the basis of his rule, monopolized God's wealth, subjugated His creation, or become a collaborator of colonial powers by executing the orders of unbelievers and foreigners, leading to those foreigners taking control of Muslims' policies, culture and economy; if he has not been dissuaded by means of good counsel and reminders but only becomes more obstinate and arrogant, even if he is obliged to confess his attachment to Islam through his words and even demonstrate his religion by practicing some of its outward signs like the ritual prayer and the Hajj, and throws around Islamic slogans—and we can see most kings and rulers doing this in Muslim countries in our region.

And if it is the government ministers, department heads and functionaries who commit evil, the issue should be brought up with the official who installed them, so that he would be the one to dismiss them if he sees that as the right thing to do.

As for the highest trustee, the head of state, it is permissible, indeed it is dutiful for the people to remove him, even by means of an armed insurrection with careful planning. A strategy must be put in place: from the building of political awareness among the umma, to the formation of parties, associations, committees, to the preparation of forces and materials, either in secret or openly, depending on the conditions and circumstances. Then if the objective is accomplished through public gatherings and demonstrations, so much the better. If not, then the people will resort to force of arms with proper organization and great care to limit the loss of lives and property and to maximize the chances of victory. Clearly, the best is that he is forced to resign; and if the umma is unable to depose him, then his government is no longer legitimate.[416]

Fourth, the issue of numbers—if the ruler needs to be deposed due to his manifest departure from the rule of Shari'a, for dismantling the process of mutual consultation,[417] violating public freedoms, and violating prohibitions in the Shari'a,[418] and if there is a sufficient probability of success (for those who deem this a condition for the legitimacy of rebellion), who has the right to announce the revolution against him seeking to depose him? Are a few individuals or a small group sufficient for the task? The "people of loosing and binding" (that is, the 'ulama,' the leaders of groups and organizations considered important in society) only have the authority to propose him as a candidate, and it is the people who elect him directly, then they are the ones who must announce their accusation against him and their withdrawal of trust in him, and then propose a new candidate for the office of ruler. The important point is that the withdrawal of power from the government does not happen by means of an armed insurrection mounted by a small minority in society so as to preserve the umma's unity. No one individual should have the right to decide when obedience to the ruler is withdrawn as a national and religious duty. That kind of authority can only emanate from society as a whole or from its legal representatives.[419]

To sum up this position, no individual or small grouping or even faction among the Muslims has the right in and of itself to change a head of state without the people's agreement.[420] Rather, the responsibility goes to the popular leaders who in this case must announce publicly the government's loss of legitimacy and a call for civil rebellion, even to the point of a full revolution, if need be. These leaders are the ones to initiate and issue orders, and all the Muslims, standing behind them, submit to their command, so that power is not lost and the situation does not become chaotic.

As soon as the ruler is removed, the group that led the action should turn the decision over to the people to choose their new leader, and assist them in safeguarding religion and managing worldly affairs.[421] According to this opinion, then, to oust someone from power is not the work of a small band but rather an expression of a popular will led by sincere leaders who assume the arduous and risky task of confronting tyranny using the proper and necessary means, including violence if it is used against them. According to this view, not a small isolated group but only the masses may exercise this kind of power against an isolated regime, so as to reduce possible casualties and speed up the transition.[422]

This, then, was a summary of views within the scope of Islamic political thinking on the issue of monitoring political authority for the purpose of reforming it and curbing its injustice in a peaceful way. This should be the first choice, as long as the Shari'a is honored and the state does not commit overt infractions of God's law—that is, obviously colliding with the teachings of Islam, the umma's religion, and the expression of its general will. If the regime commits this infraction, seeks to destroy the foundations of religion and begins to advocate wrongdoing, becomes despotic and eliminates mutual consultation, imposing on them a brutal dictatorship or submitting them to foreign powers, or tampering with people's livelihood, or begins to persecute preachers, people of knowledge and distinction—at this point the necessary conditions for armed insurrection and civil war may be present—as the people involved see it and contrary to the historical consensus of the jurists.

Appraisal of the Principle of Rebelling Against Authority

We already indicated that this issue of rebelling against a head of state is both a point of strength and weakness in Islamic political thinking—how so?

The principle of rebelling against a ruler is a positive aspect of Islamic political thought, in that the Islamic state is a state of law, the authority of the law is higher than that of the ruler, and the umma is charged with monitoring implementation of the law. The ruler, therefore, is only the people's agent charged to enforce that law in conformity with the oath of office—that is what justifies the people's obedience to the ruler. Any partial deviation on his part from the Shari'a or any negligence or violation will be problematic. If, for instance, he commits an injustice that does not threaten the highest legitimacy of the state, then he should be corrected by means of good counsel, admonition, and pressure—even to the point of threats. But if he transgresses that limit and rebels against the Shari'a by going against the people's will and bearing down on his injustice, then they are no longer justified in obeying him. In fact, they are obligated to advise him, warn him, and threaten him; and if he persists in his tyranny and arrogance, then the umma will have no other option but to rise up against him and exercise what is in its power to do in order to set him straight and lead him back to the Shari'a, or to remove him if it is able to do so without a civil war and the nation slipping into chaos, for people cannot do without an authority, be it righteous or not, believing or not. This is overall the position of the majority of Muslim scholars.

The principle of rebelling, then, is a very important principle at the very least because it represents the most pivotal constitutional principles that undergird Islamic rule. It represents the best refutation and silencing of those whose hearts still harbor rancor toward the Islamic social reality while being ignorant of it. They do not hesitate to repeat some of the worthless tenets of orientalism, asserting that Islam's scholars have always taught that obedience to any and every ruler is an absolute rule, whether he is unjust or immoral to whatever extent.[423] If such had been the case—and Islamic theory clearly refutes this—how do you explain from a historical perspective all the successive revolutions that stained the land of Islam and its history with the blood of the martyrs? Were not their leaders mainly preachers and scholars whose souls were purified as they prayed in the mosque and carried out nightly prayers? Was that not the reason for the constant clash between the tyrants of Islam's history and the preachers and reformers? How often did these tyrants lose sleep worrying about a shaykh calling for resistance and rebellion against a tyrannical ruler, and mobilizing the umma in a revolution against them?

Did not the most despotic states curry favor at the doorsteps of Islam and do their utmost to be labeled "Islamic," if only to ensure that people recognize their rule? Indeed, tyrants have tried to subdue and make use of Islam for their own designs, and they still do. But day after day they discover that Islam refuses any manipulation and will refuse anything but uphold its principles and the ultimate word.

The second reality is that the doctrine of overthrowing tyrannical rule also reveals a dangerous weak point in this thinking, consisting in the lack of balance between the means and desired ends. This led to a certain idealism in most writings in the field of Islamic political theory. As a result, the theory is not useful from a practical standpoint and fails to rightly interpret history. Among the many possible examples I could cite are the great ideals of Islam's political system like the oath of allegiance, the command to do good and forbid evil, shura, "the people of loosing and binding," and the leadership of the umma as delegated by God—all of these have mostly remained abstract concepts, and when they were applied, it was only in a piecemeal and superficial manner, for the most part. For if the umma had truly been the source of the ruler's powers—a concept that many still doubt—and if the oath of allegiance [al-bay'a] is no more than a contract of delegation, then how can the people, after they have pledged allegiance to this ruler, truly act to limit the ruler's power and even withdraw it from him as stipulated by the oath of allegiance, when he has monopolized these powers for himself over the people and their resources?

Maybe one could answer that question by stating that the authority rests with "the people of loosing and binding." But who are these people? In Islamic theory the ruler draws his power and influence from the public oath of allegiance, which stipulates submission and obedience to him. But this body, what power does it have left to bind or to loose? And because its role remains obscure, there is a gaping hole in the theory, one through which weakness entered the Rightly Guided Caliphate (the first four caliphs in Medina). Indeed, there only remained a small group from those noble Companions (may God be pleased with them) who considered that only they were "the people of loosing and binding," while disregarding those living in the empire's new cities who had been attracted to Islam by the practice of justice and equality. Thus, now finding themselves marginalized in the political system, the latter marched on Medina and assassinated the caliph while he was reading his copy of the Qur'an. He had refused to submit to the rule they, as revolutionaries, had declared ("the strongest seizes power"), and so they killed him.

So when this group came to swear their allegiance to 'Ali (may God be pleased with him), he refused their allegiance in these words, "The decision is not yours but that of those who emigrated to Medina and their Medinan supporters" (this might also have included those who fought at the Battle of Badr). The second generation was well aware that the concepts of political power must adapt to the evolution of society, and Hasan, the son of Ali, had come with advice about this question for his father, telling him not to accept the caliphate unless he receive delegations from the empire's new cities. However, their coming co-incided with a situation in which the leaders of the Umayyad clan had done everything they could to abort the development of the caliphate by inventing a hybrid Islamic principle that fused Persian absolutism with pre-Islamic tribal rule.

From that day forward the ideal Islamic political practice was severed from its roots in the Rightly Guided Caliphate. It no longer incorporated shura, or de-mocracy, and a rule delegated by the people; it no longer had a parliament, or the Shura Assembly, according to its first form in the Saqifa, and the supremacy of law. This happened only because leaders recoiled from developing the institu-tions of an Islamic state from the Medinan system of the Prophet and the two first caliphs into a system befitting the world power it was becoming, when in fact they could have embodied Islamic political values by learning from the brilliant organization developed by the second caliph, 'Umar, and thus they could have written quite a different history for the Islamic civilization. Then our legacy would not have known the notion of guardianship [wisaya] exercised by the ruler, leaders of the schools of law and the Sufi orders nor would a sect have arisen with a political theory based on an infallible ruler over all. What a true catastrophe it was that our history began with mutual consultation and ended up with infallible rulers, dynasties, and coup d'états! For this only meant one thing: the forced ab-sence and marginalization of the umma. The only true trusteeship should have been that of the umma, over its rulers, the leaders of society, and the world. If there is any infallibility here, it is that of the umma as a whole.

It was not just the Umayyad clan that transformed the caliphate into a rapa-cious kingdom—something that God's Messenger (PBUH), the founder of the re-ligion and the state, had warned about. True, the Umayyads managed to regain the stature they had before the start of Islam. But they were not the principal factor. The main cause is found in the ruling elites themselves, "the people of loosing and binding." These men lacked the courage to continue the task of ijtihad that 'Umar Ibn al-Khattab had initiated on the organizational, administrative, and constitutional levels. He had indeed managed to extend in a creative and productive way the Prophet's (PBUH) work as founder of the state of Medina. His successors should have produced an ambitious organizational structure in view of the fact that their state had become the capital of an empire—a project 'Umar had truly begun to implement. Unfortunately, this project was dropped by his successors. As head of the Shura Council, 'Abd al-Rahman Ibn 'Awf succeeded in imposing a conservative policy at the expense of renewal and ijtihad. The third caliph, 'Uthman, bowed to his wishes, and though 'Ali did not, Ibn 'Awf still got his way.[424]

That was how the innovative administrative work of 'Umar was arrested and set back, aborting Islam's revolution of mutual consultation and equality. One might have expected the project to be furthered by the fourth caliph, 'Ali bin Abi Talib, but the caliphate ended with him because he spent most of his efforts to put out the civil strife under his tenure and to restore the unity of the state. Further, his personality leaned more toward keeping the status quo out of principle. Then, too, it may be that in this he was driven by his great love for and loyalty to the Prophet (PBUH), to his generation and to the exact imprint the Prophet (PBUH) had left on the state of Medina—all of which led him to abstain from developing his amazing legacy and inventing new forms of organization for a world power whose base had dramatically expanded by incorporating entire nations and civilizations. Islam had attracted them in the first place; now the state's task was to inculcate them with its values of social justice and equality.

However, this ideal was not achieved to any great extent in the construction of that state, since the fourth caliph himself did not see these new Muslims who had now become the majority of Islamic society as the basis of his rule's legitimacy. Rather, he continued to see that legitimacy as being limited to the immigrants from Mecca and their Medinan helpers, even though that state's importance had shrunk. So the loss of the Rightly Guided Caliphate can be attributed to the massive disconnect between the actual organization and constitution of the state of Medina and its new social reality that had dramatically evolved into a world empire.

We must also admit that the general political culture of that time, which the emperors promoted, stood in the way of developing the democratic revolution Islam came to produce. That relationship with the notion of absolute, empirical rule evolved from clash to friendly coexistence from the Umayyad dynasty and what followed it until the Ottoman Empire and its even more negative evolution into the contemporary Arab state, in spite of its claims to be modern.

But if you look closely, they are merely new vessels containing for the most part an ancient and putrid drink.

Clearly, the administrative apparatus inherited from the Romans in Damascus and from the Persians in Baghdad, upon which the nascent Islamic Empire of humble origins relied, was a key factor in producing those fateful models of governance, and especially those related to the caliph and his elevation far above his people, almost to the point of deification. This of course was the exact opposite of the Prophet's noble and consultative model of leadership. Yet the books on state administration written by the likes of Ibn al-Muqaffa' and 'Abd al-Hamid al-Katib succeeded in creating a new political culture that was called the "protocols of the sultan" [al-adab al-sultaniyya]. As I said, this was like pouring an old imperial concoction into an Arab-Islamic mold.

You cannot blame Islam for setting out the principles of shura, equality, social justice, enjoining right and forbidding wrong, the infallibility of the umma, the authority of consensus, the role of the scholars, jurists, and opinion leaders. These are principles that enable Islam to be eternal and adapt to new ideas, and beneficial elements from other civilizations. In fact, the blame goes to the Muslims who have been content to draw up an elaborate ideal picture of their amir without finding a way to monitor or replace him. And who judges whether the qualifications for this office have been met or not by this person so that he may become amir? Who steps in as judge when these conditions have not been met? What is this body's job description, and whence does it draw its authority? What are the other institutions that allow the umma to monitor its ruler? What happens when opinions within this body diverge, and when it disagrees with the ruler? Disagreement is a natural human phenomenon, and if the political structure is not designed to deal with it within proper limits and rules, then it can lead to disaster.

Even if modern Islamic political thought continues to be chiefly influenced by the Shari'a policies of the past, I estimate that it is increasingly focusing on solving current problems and offering organizational structures to fit Islamic political values. Nevertheless, the attraction to ancient forms remains prevalent, and in most cases it feels like going backward. Still, there is a renewal current in progress, and this blessed procession continues in the footsteps of the Chosen One (PBUH), 'Umar bin al-Khattab, Ibn Hazm, Ibn Taymiyya, Ibn Rushd, Ibn Khaldun, al-Afghani, Muhammad 'Abduh, Khayr al-Din al-Tunisi, Hasan al-Banna, al-Turabi, and others.

We have already seen examples of this penchant toward developing organizational principles—among others:

- The affirmation that the imamate is a contract, of which the umma is the guarantor.
- An Islamic regime has no legitimacy unless it is founded on a genuine oath of allegiance. This proper oath of allegiance must be carried out in three stages:
  1. *The stage of candidacy*, initiated either by the outgoing caliph, and the candidacy is confirmed by the Shura Assembly, or initiated by the latter.
  2. *The stage of examination* of the various candidates by the Shura Assembly.
  3. *The stage of general election*, during which the people (the umma) have the last say over who is to take office. The one winning the most votes takes the oath of allegiance from the people, pledging to safeguard religion and the administration of worldly affairs, fulfilling some of these conditions:
     a. Executing the stipulations of the Shari'a according to the decisions of the Shura Assembly and with a respect for public and individual freedoms;
     b. Renewal of the offer to serve in various state bodies: the amir, the Shura Assembly, the local assemblies for general elections all serve limited terms according to the principle of the rotation of power in a peaceful way;
     c. Members of the Shura Assembly ("those who loose and bind") derive their authority from the same source from which the amir derives his own (the umma) by way of elections, thereby acquiring the legal authority to officially monitor the government and participate with it in the process of setting public policies. In addition to exercising legislative power in accordance with the highest authority represented by the Shari'a, the assembly has the power to challenge the legitimacy of a head of state if he violates the Shari'a, either because he did not care or because his failure became apparent. A constitutional court may be assembled from among the leading judges and jurists in order to arbitrate the dispute and issue its judgment. Or it may resort to a general referendum;
     d. A head of state may not be the sole legislator on the basis of his interpretation of the texts, even if he is capable of doing so, but he will cooperate with the assembly in the task of legislation. He proposes bills and then discusses them with the assembly, but he may not impose his own interpretation;

e. The Shura Assembly is the political body that is made up of the representatives of the state's provinces and of all its classes without any discrimination on the basis of gender or religion, race or class;

f. An assembly chosen from among the most experienced jurists and scholars may take on the task of monitoring the constitutionality of all the decisions and policies of state legislative and executive bodies. This body could be called the constitutional court ["the assembly of those of opinion and ijtihad"];

g. The parliamentary system is a decentralized form of government. Power is distributed and mutual consultation is practiced in the widest possible form; the greatest possible number of people among the state's population participates in the administration of public affairs; and the power of the extremities and branches grows at the expense of the center. To apply such a model is the most faithful way to embody the highest value of Islamic governance, as it is expressed in this divine exhortation, "[and they] conduct their affairs by mutual consultation"[425]—and that is in *all* "their affairs." This was always the ideal model of the Islamic political experience over the centuries, despite all of its deviations, before the umma suffered Western occupation and its imposition of centralized tyrannical government. Indeed, this muzzled the umma's will and dismantled its institutions, so that it imposed its hegemony upon it, either directly or through its agents, under the guise of deceiving slogans like modernity, fighting terrorism, or spreading the values of democracy and civil society. Yet this Western-centric model is in every way contrary to the values of democracy and civil society, which in fact were much more present before the tribulation of Western invasion and the even worse regimes that came after in terms of autocracy and corruption. There can be no democracy or mutual consultation, or civil society, without the dismantling of the despotic government, our liberation from Western hegemony, and our putting an end to the humiliating state of dislocation imposed on us.

THE ECONOMIC DIMENSION OF SHURA

This section seeks to shed light on the economic and social life of the society of mutual consultation. It aims to highlight its foundations, principles, public policies, and values, though it will not go into more detail than that, as it would then go beyond the scope of this work.

INTRODUCTION

Wealth in Islam, like political rule, ultimately belongs to God. It is a trust given to the community by God, and wealth in the hands of individuals is similar to political power in individual hands. In both cases its spending is done according to the theory of God's deputizing of the community; both the community and the individuals who represent it, therefore, are accountable to Him, either as they spend money or political capital. Further, any spending in either domain that is done outside the limits drawn by the Shari'a or the community's welfare is an infraction, which must be met with good advice and counsel, and if that is refused, the person must be fired and removed, as we read in the Qur'an, "Do not entrust your property to the feeble-minded. God has made it a means of support for you." [426]

Money plays a social function, and therefore the individual is responsible to make use of it, so as to invest it in order to improve his situation with integrity and wisdom, and in service of the community, according to the Qur'an, "They ask you again what they should give: say, 'Give what you can spare,'" [427] which means the community may dispose of the excess wealth of individuals over and above the payment of zakat as appropriate, as the hadith reads, "Wealth is a right only after the zakat has been paid."

Protecting wealth and investing it are objectives spelled out in the Shari'a, for God has not called on us to turn away from this world but rather to take possession of it by developing it and investing in it. [428] That said, this objective comes in a list after the protection of religion and of life—that is, it must be in service of these two other objectives. It is a sin for a person who believes in God and the Last Day to be stingy with his money or his own effort for the sake of protecting religion, or to hold on to his money while people do not have the bare necessities. Nor is he allowed to be lazy or hold back from using his own resources or natural resources, while relying on others.

In fact, Islam abhors the sin of despotism, the monopolizing of political rule over a people, and it certifies that the duty and right to participate ("[they] conduct their affairs by mutual consultation") in determining public affairs should not be something done in isolation from other social duties and choices. This is because mutual consultation is not just a method for managing political affairs; it is meant to be practiced in all spheres of life. It begins with humanity's universal vicegerency of God, then the oneness of humanity's origin and destiny; it also includes the priority of the collective over the individual and the reality of the individual's weakness by himself, yet strong when united with his brother; prone to error by himself, yet well guided through his brother's advice. For social life in the Islamic perspective is like an organism in which each function is tied to every other function. It benefits when all functions do their part and suffers when they do not.

It is unrealistic to imagine that we could have political participation in managing political power, while financial power is in the hands of a few international thieves, in the form of industrial, agricultural, and service sector monopolies. At the social level this would quickly produce two contradictory kinds of development and lifestyles, calling into question any discourse about brotherhood ("The believers are brothers," Q. 49:10), national and religious unity ("[Prophets], this is your community, one community," Q. 21:92), and the unity of humanity as a whole ("[your Lord) who created you from a single soul," Q. 4:1). It would render the practice of mutual consultation in politics in the form of elections or public freedoms a joke, a fraud, and would promote deception by the media in capitalist countries and their structures around the world.

Seriously widening the scope of shura in society would require a widening of people's participation in the financial system and a mutual guarantee of profits and losses. For this, the state's form of political authority must correspond to the way cooperatives are run, in that there is no monopolizing of administrative decisions and no injustice in the distribution of profit and loss.[429]

What an economic philosophy from an Islamic perspective must do is to focus on determining how to change a system in which a handful of thieves profit to the detriment of the environment and the basic needs of the masses. Therefore, it must focus on developing an economic system that achieves the greatest possible benefit of the entire community and all of humanity, while protecting nature and providing adequate sustenance for all in such a way as to reduce the gap between social classes and the members of the worldwide human family. This will deal a mortal blow to the scourge of poverty and to its twin, unbelief,[430] and to the inequality that reigns over regional and international relations because a small class of no more than 2 or 3 percent of the population controls the circulation of money. This fact necessarily produces hatred, fighting, epidemics, environmental degradation, the unraveling of the social fabric, conflicts, and wars between nations.

Capitalist profit should not be the only and highest goal of any Islamic economic and social program that seeks to protect the honor of belonging to Islam and of a commitment to implement its teachings and objectives; that is, if we are to be truly serious in building genuine Islamic, national, and universal brotherhood, it will have to be built upon the sharing of profits and losses, in good times and bad times—another aspect of shura. The Prophet's (PBUH) first objective in Mecca—after his relentless struggle against polytheism—was against

Mecca's rich who ruthlessly exploited the poor. This is because satisfying the material and spiritual needs of humanity is the essence of God's will, and therefore at the heart of Islam.[431]

The first acts of the Prophet (PBUH) as he was establishing the first society built upon mutual consultation were to build a mosque, issue a constitution, and spread mutual affection among the believers. He was pointing to the linkage between the educational and cultural life on the one hand, the political life together with the social and economic life on the other. It was the collective spirit of shura that formed the foundation of all of these aspects for the life of brotherhood, freedom, and justice. For this reason, we must seriously doubt any democratic slogan in the midst of a dangerously tense society in which poverty, despair, unemployment, and sickness stand side by side with shameless luxury and mistreatment of people. From this we understand that any social development built upon this foundation will crumble—inevitably, no matter its other successes—which also means the message of those who call for the rebuilding of society must reflect the holistic nature of Islam and its unity without distinction between the notion of unity [*tawhid*] at the level of faith and justice on the social level, and mutual consultation on the political level. Just as a faith that produces no work is nonsense, so the creed of God's unity that does not result in a society of justice and mutual consultation is also nonsense. This is a society of brotherhood, participation, solidarity, and a sharing of basic necessities: "He set down the earth for His creatures"[432] and "in accordance with (the needs) of those who seek (sustenance),"[433] as in the famous hadith, "People must share three things: water, pasture, and fire, i.e. the basic necessities in life."[434]

Suffice it here to underscore that political participation necessarily requires economic participation. Mutual consultation and justice are the two sides of one coin, which is God's unity [tawhid].[435] Islam's repeated call to individuals to spend on behalf of collective interests as a way of seeking God's pleasure presupposes the necessity of allowing private ownership of wealth. This is why Islam aims to raise everyone's economic status by encouraging people to "cultivate the earth and develop it"[436] in a way that brings about a just distribution of wealth, and not a downward spiral of corruption and poverty.

Within the scope of this book, suffice it to make a few remarks:

Islamist Parties in Their Wider Context

What can Islamists do in the economic realm if they come to power or have the opportunity of sharing it? Do they have realistic solutions for solving the many problems currently found in our economies? Put otherwise, what can the Islamic project add to the economic domain, and what are the possibilities of applying it today? Historically, the issue of an economic program as an answer to this question was tied to the Islamic project that started with the contemporary Islamic revival and in particular in the Arab Islamic world. This issue then became more heated and complicated since Islamists entered the political battleground and grew closer to holding power in many cases. They were asked to produce a detailed economic program, while at the same time neither they nor other sections of the opposition were granted their basic freedoms, not even the right to life.

Compounding the predicament of Islamist parties was the authoritarian regimes' lack of transparency and deliberate obscuring of the actual economic situation—information that is absolutely necessary for any scientific appraisal of the facts and for any proposal of alternatives capable of leading the nation out of its economic stagnation. How can any genuine opposition movement in these dark days and in the shadow of these despotic regimes achieve notable progress in the area of renewal, innovation, and development, while simultaneously keeping their focus on guaranteeing their right to survival, being branded as an outlawed party and being the target of the state's repressive security forces?

However, it is natural for Islamists to be asked to present a clear program to solve the complex economic realities and provide the means to face the dangerous fallout of the suffocating economic crisis. Yet the heart of this constant struggle goes beyond the issue of a program, alternatives, or policies. In its wider context the struggle transcends the economic aspect of the nation's crisis, because this crisis has its origins in the absence of basic freedoms, the domination of a despotic state, and the sidelining of committed political and social forces, excluding them from participating in the repair that is needed and in the collective thinking in the interest of the nation and its future. This is why the opposition generally is closer to a movement of national liberation than it is to political parties that fight for the application of detailed political programs. That is what normally happens in a democratic nation in which the elites have agreed to a reasonable sharing of power on the condition that rights are guaranteed for all citizens and that a peaceful transition of power is allowed to rotate among the various factions.

In the absence of such a consensual political framework because of a prevailing authoritarian current, all the partisans of democratic freedoms struggle against despotism. This is at the heart of the national program, as was the case during resistance against colonial occupation. In those days the struggle focused on a clear mission, that of expelling the foreign powers, and it was not impaired by any fierce and divisive ideological struggles within its ranks.

Therefore, it is not surprising that a common initiative (the 18 October Movement) has emerged in Tunisia composed of parties, NGOs, and personalities representing various tendencies, such as liberals, leftists, and Islamists, all of which subscribe to a national agenda focused on freedom: freedom of expression, freedom of association, and the release of political prisoners. This patriotic front is determined to put off ideological conflicts among them, which have divided the opposition throughout the fifty years (since independence) of despotism.

As a result, the continual controversy over programs and alternatives in the end is nothing more than a dishonest political ploy and a pretext to oust a political contender and a religious adversary from the public sphere. These demands by the state are meaningless, unless there is increased political participation for all members of society, and as long as the doors to public freedoms are blocked, oppression continues, and in fact, the transfer of power, or even the mention of it, is forbidden.

Therefore, talk about an Islamic economic program is not about some metaphysical or magical program project, as some who oppose the Islamic solution insinuate; though from an Islamic point of view the metaphysical dimension is important in bringing about development and creating the needed economic renewal. Nor is this talk about a moral project, despite the role morality plays in the revitalization of societies. Rather, the Islamic economic program we have in mind is a program that transcends the economic sphere completely in order to include all the sectors that surround it and complement it. Here we mean especially the cultural, social, and political sectors, which, when well functioning, produce a favorable economic climate. Our program works in coordination with all these sectors in order to produce solutions that reflect society's identity and its historical and civilizational specificities. It aims to meet its citizens' social needs and provide for their material needs, their cultural advancement, and their national pride.

ECONOMICS AND POLITICS

No one disputes the fact that one cannot separate the economy from its political environment, especially these days. Everyone agrees, too, that economic and political issues are not situated in a vacuum but in the context of social structures and organization that reflect a particular ideology. Thus both the economic and political systems in any human society draw their principles from this ideology, and no system can prosper if it goes against the ideology a people hold dear, whether it's free trade liberalism, Marxist socialism, Islamism, or other set of ideals.

It goes without saying that most governments in the Islamic world are not acquainted with Islamic ideals and that they do not want to be defined by them, as they don't believe in them in the first place. In fact, they strive very hard to erase them and eradicate them from people's hearts. So these states pay no attention to these ideals or at the very least give them only marginal importance. This explains the growing gap between the governing elites and the economy on the one hand and the vast majority of the people on the other, and the latter's growing lack of trust in the state.

FOREIGN INTERFERENCE

In the wake of the continuing dismemberment of our umma imposed by ruthless world powers and what this has meant in terms of subjugation, corruption, and autocracy, it does not seem that the projects of autonomy and development desired by our umma are leading to any prosperous or promising results on the horizon. I say this regardless of the kind of economic method that is followed, for there certainly have been attempts at radical changes in economic policy whether on the right or the left, searching for a way out of the abyss in which we found ourselves. But this has gone nowhere, and the evident results of this experimentation only point to worsening poverty, indebtedness, growing economic inequality, and dependence on outside aid, instead of a growing economic interdependence between nations within the umma. This proves that as long as division persists, there are no serious hopes for our people from any program, and whatever differences there might be between these programs, they are only secondary ones.

TAKING ISLAM INTO ACCOUNT

Islam guided our umma's sociopolitical life throughout its long centuries of flourishing as a civilization and remained the highest source of inspiration for all of its cultural, legislative, and economic norms. It was in its light that societies were founded, markets prospered, and people flourished, seeking prosperity in this world and in the life to come. This is the embodiment of Islam's comprehensive ideal of uniting the material and the spiritual. Even during the centuries of decline, these societies continued to produce what they needed and more, even exporting food to European countries and providing loans to them (Egypt lent to Britain and Algeria to France, in both cases before they were colonized). Islam never lacked in its dynamism during all those centuries before it was brought down by force of arms, pushed aside and replaced by other ideologies. This Islam, nevertheless, remains the most important building block of the umma's identity and the catalyst activating its vital energy, if only it were put to work in development projects as happened in Malaysia's experience.

It was Islam that brought together our umma and fashioned both its consciousness and conscience to this day, and so it is natural for our most capable men to mobilize our peoples for any project of economic development and to reunite their comprehensive identity, which was ripped apart by Westernization, causing the rift between the ruling elites and the masses.

ISLAMISTS AND THE ECONOMY

Generally speaking, the Islamic movement is in the opposition while secular politicians are in power, and therefore it has no responsibility for the crisis situation that prevails to the point that not enough food and armament for defense can be produced, and this constitutes a real menace to national security, for which secular groups are responsible. The Islamic movement is not only in the opposition but most of the time it is targeted by a war that is both international and local. Despite that, however, in situations where it is allowed to catch its breath, it puts forward considerable conributions such as its practices of successful development work and especially by means of its civil society organizations, which have contributed to the advancement of Islamic economic theory. Their achievements have caused this area to blossom to the point that it is now the object of study in many universities, some of which are in the West, like Loughborough University in the UK, where scientific conferences are held and where encyclopedias, journals, and hundreds of books are published on this topic.

Additionally, this theory is translated into economic reality locally and internationally by no less than two hundred Islamic banks that manage hundreds of billions of dollars. They also represent poles of attraction for capital, not just Islamic in origin but non-Islamic as well—that is, when the opportunity is provided for an Islamic financial system to function. This is a system in which financial guarantees are cleansed from the stain of charging interest rates for all transactions, as opposed to the way traditional economies were built on interest. This has led the nation whose economy is ranked third internationally, Great Britain, to open a British Islamic bank, and the major banks worldwide like

Citibank, Barclays Bank, and others to open branches that work within the framework of the Islamic Shari'a.

Further, Islamists were able to lead major professional unions in Egypt, like the doctors' union, the pharmacists' union, the lawyers' union, and others, and they were able to demonstrate outstanding skill in elevating the level of service that those unions provide, which in turn allowed them to win the trust of their members. Had the Muslim Brotherhood not limited their participation to a third, they would have been able to control all of them. And the same applied to their skill in running their schools, which explains the intensity of competition and the demand placed on them.

As for their administration of municipalities and their improvement of them, the Turkish example speaks for itself. For the municipality of Istanbul and Turkey's other large cities, which had suffered from misery and bankruptcy under the administration of secular leaders on the right and the left, Islamist administrations improved their level of service even to the point of single-handedly reaching economic benchmarks never before achieved. They therefore were able to enhance the value of the Turkish currency, which had plummeted, managing to delete six zeros that had been added due to inflation. They also reduced Turkey's foreign loans by a third in three years and did the same thing with inflation and unemployment. There is no other obvious reason for these successes than Islam itself, since it is the only new element in the equation. After all, the Islamists like their secular colleagues studied at the same universities and acquired the same competence in the same sciences, technical disciplines, and modern training, except that they surpassed them in a number of areas.

The first is that their message is closest to the widest sectors of the populace, because they address them with concepts and values deeply rooted in their heritage, whereas when the secular person addresses them, it is as if his message comes from a faraway place. Therefore, it does not do much to stir them from within and thus falls short of the power wielded by the Islamist leader to mobilize and spur them on to achieve the goals he wants them to achieve.

The second factor is that the Islamic activist's behavior inspires more confidence than does his secular counterpart, because he embodies the ideal model that the masses know deep down that a Muslim individual must embody: honoring his parents, relatives, and neighbors; truthful in his dealings with people; self-disciplined, God fearing, and pious. He leads prayers in their mosques, witnesses their funerals and weddings, and they find him at their side when they need advice or when calamities befall them, and much more. All of this comes back to Islam.

The third factor is that Islam makes a difference in a person's spiritual formation and value system. It gives people the power to curb their rush to consume in that it allows no place for obsessive hoarding to grow. Very often the ravenous desire to consume is not content within the limits of the salary made by those working for state institutions but finds ways to reach beyond in order to provide for their personal benefit, for their families and their parties. Islam, by contrast, teaches its own to live with less and to stay within the limits of what is allowed so that God will accept their acts of worship. Thus Islam pulls back the reins on consumerism; it warns of the most grievous punishment for those who practice what is forbidden and thereby becomes a very important factor of social development only available to Islamists. Consider, too, that the means of control found in democratic societies are not fully effective in curbing corruption, the scourge of contemporary regimes. As for the dictatorial regimes, it is only a matter of time before the absence of legal controls in combination with the absence of religious oversight spell the inevitable disaster of collapse.

In light of this, notice the unprecedented success of Shaykh Necmettin Erbakan and his disciples in Turkey in eliminating the scourge of corruption, after rampant corruption had spread among the political class among all its parties, whether this was when they were restoring bankrupt cities or when they were ruling the nation as a whole. In just a few years, they raised individual salaries and brought down the soaring rate of inflation and unemployment. They put Turkey on the path of civilized modernity economically, politically, and legally, and this was a brilliant testimony to the virtues of Islam, which achieved a renewal and rejuvenation of Turkey's aging political class. This is what Islam is producing everywhere today, and this economic program is not just about effective planning; before anything else, it is a cultural, educational, and humanitarian project.

Arab governments are trying to transform themselves—under tremendous foreign pressure—into capitalist free market economies. In Western parlance this means creating a democratic system characterized by the individual's freedom to express his views and to elect his representatives, to freely practice his profession and financial dealings, and to make his own decisions about what to produce and what to consume. Therefore, the first suggestion we make to these governments—and they must do this if they desire any reform—is to think logically and combine economic freedom with political freedom, because without the latter, they will never achieve the economic prosperity they promised their people, even on a modest scale, for freedom cannot be divided.

This is self-evident, something that the nineteenth-century partisans of the liberal school promoted. And this is exactly what the followers of this school say in this century and what Islam had declared in the seventh century. This present discourse has its roots in a moral philosophy that gives precedence to the human person as an individual and a community, in such a way as to strike a balance between his material, spiritual, and moral needs. Thus it considers the individual as part of a family, a community, and a society, and sees his relationship with the environment as a necessary part of his destiny. So a serious development project should not focus exclusively on one aspect like financial gain while ignoring the other dimensions, as the capitalist or socialist models have done and continue to do. But will our governments that want reform actually respond to this? Economic policy, along with planning, legislation, investments, education and vocational training—and perhaps before all that—needs an encouraging political environment, a supportive psychological climate, stable social conditions, and just laws.

This can be summed up by the word "democracy" in its widest and most comprehensive sense. In the same way, therefore, that political life is transparent and clear and every person and every organization and institution has its place, its limits, and its rights, so will be the people's economic life and their productive endeavors.

For this reason we consider that the fundamental condition for the success of economic policies is that an atmosphere of honesty, confidence, security, and calm permeate society as a whole. Of course, this is not enough to produce wheat, or literature, or consumer goods; incentive is also necessary. But on the topic of economic policies, there must be a linking up between the economy and the body of Islamic concepts that frame all the cultural and educational institutions of society and the policies of the state, whether domestic or foreign. Finally, I must reiterate that the ideal economic policy is the one that benefits the greatest number of citizens and is ratified by a majority at the polls in an atmosphere of freedom and transparency. Anything else is a form of oppression by one class and its usurpation of the people's rights and powers, actions that undermine the balance and peace of a society and destroy its institutions and environment, and which potentially can lead a nation into civil war or at least to its brink.

This is precisely what is happening in most Arab countries in the name of structural reform, under pressure from international organizations promoting so-called economic liberalization. These policies are being implemented with Western support for the most dictatorial and corrupt regimes, along with the imposition of states of emergency, openly in some cases, or in disguise, in countries like Egypt, Tunisia, Iraq, and Algeria. Ballot boxes were smashed and with them the winners, like the FIS in Algeria[437] and Ennahda in Tunisia, and along with it civil society organizations, unions, and the media. And all of this was to enact policies that favored the international capitalist system and to break the progress of people's independent economic development, which sought to secure people's freedom and their emancipation from foreign dependence.

Therefore, the first measure a democratic government must take is to give back to society and its citizens their voice, enabling them to truly participate in developing economic life, release their initiative within the framework of Islam's values and social justice, guarantee both collective and individual freedoms, support societies and institutions, and limit the state's hegemony. It must mobilize elements of strength among our nations for the sake of a balanced and independent development within contractual and political structures that give expression to the will and conscience of our umma. This will bring back a balance between the state and society to the latter's advantage; it will fulfill its independence, its self-sufficiency, and its ability to exploit these in most spheres of life.

At that stage economic activity will take off as part of a comprehensive revival that frees both the individual and society from the hegemony of the state and from the insatiable dragon of global capitalism, and this by limiting state intervention while filling the gaps, yet without curbing individual freedoms or the initiatives taken by individuals and groups. By contrast, it seeks to enhance the authority of the umma over its rulers and free it from foreign dependence; to regain its pride and unity; free its lands and its will; come to the aid of victims of injustice and the hungry; and provide healthcare and education—as long as we succeed in gradually shrinking government and our society becomes more independent and self-reliant. For when citizens' basic needs are not fulfilled, private property loses any meaning, as previously mentioned, triggering a situation in which Shari'a penalties [hudud] can be suspended. The priority in the present circumstances is to achieve liberty, justice, unity, and the umma's freedom from occupation and foreign interference.

The caliph 'Umar bin al-Khattab asked one of his local governors as he was leaving,

> "What will you do when you run into a thief?" He answered, "I will cut off his hand." 'Umar replied, "If one of these people comes to me hungry or unemployed, I will cut off your hand. Yes, God has entrusted us leaders with the task of satisfying their hunger, of clothing them, and providing what they need

to work their craft. If we give them these blessings, they will be grateful to us. God created hands to work, but if they don't find work pleasing God, they will turn to illicit work. So let them be busy with obedience before they turn to disobedience."

THE EDUCATIONAL DIMENSION OF SHURA

GENERAL INTRODUCTION

We mentioned earlier that one of the Prophet's (PBUH) first acts was to establish the foundation of the Islamic society in Medina by building a mosque. And this mosque became the first institution and the cornerstone for the building of a new society, the axis around which and from which all the activities and institutions of the newborn society branched out. It was also the center of worship and a school of learning; a political meeting place for mutual consultation and a court of justice; a hall in which to welcome delegations and guests of state; a place where the poor found refuge; a venue for the arts and entertainment; a banquet hall; and even a club for physical and military exercises. It was everything in the life of the new society. This vibrant nucleus was to extend its fruitfulness east and west to the far reaches of the earth, creating in its path civilizations and Islamic societies full of light, overflowing with sciences, knowledge, commerce, and industry, with the mosque as the beating heart of each city.

This continued for many centuries until the forces of occupation were able to deal a heavy blow to the very structure of both the city and the civilization. At the center of this was the marginalization of the mosque, the emptying of its contents, and the stripping of its civilizational and avant-garde role. It then ceased to be a school of learning, a university for the sciences and culture, the first nucleus of the Islamic civilization, solid and productive, producing important additions and amendments to human knowledge. This school was first established in a society that was illiterate, with no contact with science and learning, and it spread its culture to the masses far and wide, making it available to all without cost or huge effort.

Seminars at the mosque were the most suitable format to sow widely the spirit of equality, brotherhood, and mutual consultation, and to provide a space that facilitated dialogue and the exchange of knowledge and opinions. In fact, prayer is what rouses people to unify their ranks and commit to following the imam, listening to him, correcting him when he errs, and parting ways with him when he insists on violating the prescribed path for Islamic prayers. Prayer, therefore, is the embodiment of Islam's consultative and social spirituality, which rests upon an attachment to the Shari'a and to the leadership as long as it follows that path, together with readiness to offer good counsel when mistakes are made and the will to remove him if he remains obstinate.

There was no limit to the productivity of that nucleus of mosque activities in Medina, and before long an army of scholars and leaders came out from it, spreading knowledge, freedom, and justice. That is the way they won people over, not by the sword. And, indeed, as time has shown, the light of knowledge has often proven to be stronger than war, so that the majority of the lands that opened to Islam did so in peace. It is also a fact that where the sword failed, knowledge and light prevailed.

It is worth noting that the lands that were brought into the fold by force left the fold as soon as the balance of powers tilted in favor of the adversary, whereas foreign occupiers were not able to separate from the Muslim world lands that were brought into the fold by invitation [da'wa].

Islam calls people to the faith ("Say: 'Believe in it or do not believe'"),[438] but only by choice. Its message enjoins brotherhood between Muslims and peace-loving people, but Islam is more than a message with two wings, faith and brotherhood; it anchored the societal pillars of faith, brotherhood, tawhid, and unity on the foundations of participation in public affairs ("Consult with them about matters").[439] There should be no tyranny, therefore, nor guardianship but rather wide participation in the blessings of knowledge and culture (according to the hadith, "Seeking knowledge is a duty for all Muslims").[440] Nor should there be any elitism but rather wide participation in the sources of wealth ("money is God's money"), so that if a Muslim cannot afford the basic necessities of life (food, clothing, shelter, etc.), all are obliged to help.

This is the spirit of community implanted by the doctrine of God's unity [tawhid], which continues to struggle to defend the unity of Islamic society and provide a measure of economic equality, even under despotic states. Thus mosques were popular institutions that the people would support by way of endowments [waqf, pl. awqaf], and it was the projects of solidarity like the hospices, Sufi centers and clinics, and other grassroots charitable projects that embodied the spirit of faith and brotherhood, and the sense that each believer is responsible before God to engage in public service—and all this as part of "protecting religion and managing the affairs of this world." This is a communal obligation [fard al-kifaya]. The individual Muslim is freed the responsibility before God if the state fulfills it. If the state fails to discharge the obligation, the responsibility falls on every individual Muslim. Actually, there is an ebb and flow between the individual's responsibility and authority and that of the state, since sovereignty in Islam, or establishing religion and managing the common good is a duty for each Muslim to discharge, to the extent that others fail to fulfill it.[441] What is important here is that the Shari'a is not lost and public interests are not neglected.

AN EDUCATIONAL CRISIS

Education in our Arab-Islamic lands is suffering from an acute crisis, despite the great efforts expended and the considerable sums spent on it. From the signs of division between our current generations, our weakness in confronting the arts of enticement, and especially materialism—all of this represents a real threat to our unity as a people and as nations. As a result, our elites are divided, isolated from the culture of the people and out of touch with their feelings, values and heritage. Further, this has made the official discourse, largely shared by the current elites, move toward greater isolation and westernization, a fact one can also notice in what these elites produce generally, whether in literature, in the media, or in the arts. The more they feel a sense of detachment from the masses, the more they move in the following directions.

Violence

We have witnessed over the past couple of decades a growing reliance on the use of force in dealing with the masses and their aspirations for justice, freedom, unity, and identity.

Deceit

We see a lack of honesty on the part of our leaders, and their conversations are drowning in lies and hypocrisy, while they keep hoping that the people will be deceived by the lie that the elites are truly part of the people and that they share their religious beliefs and their feelings. On official occasions those in power go to the mosques to celebrate religious feasts, even though everyone knows that they do not believe in these rituals. They only practice out of hypocrisy.

Isolation

We are witnessing a consolidation of barriers between the ruling elites and the people, to the point that the masses have little information about these disconnected elites, who live in their own neighborhoods, go to their own markets and schools, and even their own universities. In this their relationship with the populace is quite similar to that of the white minority in apartheid South Africa. It is also similar to the relationship between the Native American tribes and the flocks of white emigrants who took over their lands, killing and impovershing them.

Opportunism and Greed

Further, the tyranny exerted by the spirit of opportunism accompanied by a lack of principles is evident everywhere. One sees this, for instance, in the bond created between the elites produced by the modern state, on one hand, and the regime on the other, which, regardless of the various tendencies among them, is focused in its entirety on personal gain, even at the expense of the ethical values and criteria that they raise as their standard, and at the expense of the interests of the masses. The elites got used to falling in line with whoever was in power and rush headlong to knock at his door. They may even go so far as to sacrifice their pride, their religion, and their national duty, as they compete for closeness to the tyrant. The more they gush about their ideals, the more they are Machiavellian in their actions. Do not be fooled by their expansive claims and their displays of idealism during times of ease, for in tough times their weakness has no bounds. This is because of the philosophy of education they received, which produces a sort of cultural schizophrenia, tearing them between two separate worlds, especially because either by birth or by merit they belong to the affluent part of society, which has mostly cut itself off from the rest.

These elites inherited and became accustomed to the dualism and disconnect between the intellectual life and life as it really is. This led them—most of them—to shift from an elite that carried their people's hope for a more equitable society, for which the people made such great sacrifices, into an obstacle to reform and a bulwark of conservatism and support for the regime. They use the pretext of the absence of an alternative to the regime—as if one can only wait for the alternative to come down from Heaven—or fear of the "fundamentalist" bogeyman. Some of them shy away from political life altogether to justify not assisting the victims of injustice and to avoid the thorny issues of freedom and justice. Such a position may appear ascetic, as the intellectual limits himself to the four walls of his hermit's cell, but that is mostly a deceiving picture, for he is waiting for the opportunity to respond to the first sign from the regime and rush to its service, as this interview with the Tunisian intellectual Khamis al-Shamari expresses so well:

> Intellectuals who think that they are outside the political playing field, who recoil from political involvement and devote themselves to the world of thought, if they sincerely thought about it, ninety-nine percent of them over the past thirty years have resorted to the most opportunistic kind of service to whoever was in power, either directly or indirectly, seeking to maintain or ob-

tain personal benefits through their interaction with the organs of power. Our cultural sphere—and I'm specifically speaking about Tunisia—and intellectual and especially university spheres are full of figures that have been in collusion with the centers of power within the last twenty years at least. In fact, the majority of those who were independent in university circles joined the ruling party after the change of November 7th.[442]

The above testimony by an eminent member of the elite attests that the crisis of our nations, which underwent a process of modernization, is a crisis of the elites whose cultural development represented a complete break with the culture and concerns of the people. They effectively abandoned the role that the scholars had played in traditional Islamic societies, which was to mediate between the authorities and the people, bringing the people's demands or grievances to the attention of the authorities and granting authorities religious legitimacy based on their response to those demands and grievances. As for the modern elite, "the new 'ulama'," the process of modernization cut them off from the people, while the rulers weakened them and gave them the task of defending their policies before the masses in return for benefits they would receive at the expense of the public's vital interests.

Increased Westernization

The elites threw themselves more and more into the arms of the West, seeking protection from the anger of the masses. Thus our disconnected schools bear the most responsibility for the continuing state of despotism in our nations and the disconnection of the elites, making them captives and elements of destruction and disintegration, while at the same time protecting foreign interests.

Falling Educational Levels

Among the signs of the educational crisis on a quantitative level, the most relevant ones are poor attainment rates, and high dropout rates. Out of one hundred students entering elementary school in Tunisia, hardly more than one will pass his baccalaureate (university entrance exam). So there is an army of those expelled, for whom school has crushed their hopes and their families' hopes that they would attain a better life. They have become defeated, forced to stay in the social status they inherited. Now they are vulnerable to desperate measures, like crime, violence, drugs—guaranteed customers of the penal system.

On a qualitative level, whether the issue is connected to the educational level, morals, or the sense of belonging,[443] all of this testifies to the abject failure of the educational system to produce competent individuals with regard to knowledge, morality, religion, and pride in their culture and heritage.

Political Repression

Among the signs of this crisis is the phenomenon of violence in the state's relationship with society. You need only follow the reports of human rights organizations and the deteriorating indicators of development. Among these is the Democracy Index, in which we find Arab countries occupying the lowest tier among nations, including African nations that gained their independence in the last century.[444]

Because of this, as long as we have not settled this question, the question of the kind of individual we want our educational programs to produce, and as long as we have not clearly defined the philosophical frame of reference and the specific perspective to guide future generations, our efforts will be in vain, and we will continue going around and around in empty debates about secondary matters that lead us nowhere. That is what is happening in our cultural and educational circles, where conflicts over these issues become intense, where fighting flares up for days and then dies out without either side convincing the other. What is the most useful language of instruction? Is it Arabic, or French, or English? Should one consider sex education an official subject matter within the curriculum? Is a curriculum that requires religious values and ethics better than a "free" one? Heated debate often flares up about these and other issues, but they never come to a decisive resolution based on a clear philosophy with strong ties to our civilizational identity, one that is hammered out through an in-depth dialogue and public consultation. All these are secondary issues fanning out from one crucial question that must be debated from the start: what is the model of the human being that we wish our educational system to promote? And who can legitimately define that model? Is it the representatives of the people or guardians who impose themselves in the name of modernity and progress, or of religion and authenticity? Once we have agreed on that, an agreement on the means to achieve it will be easy.

SOLUTIONS THAT ONLY DEEPEN THE CRISIS

As part of the plan to force our umma into submission and to prepare its new generations to surrender to the hegemony of Israel and its imperialistic backers, and what that plan entails in terms of eliminating the intellectual and psychological obstacles as well as the political and educational institutions, the question of educational curricula became the center of much attention. The aim was not, of course, to rectify the situation by rooting our educational programs in the soil of Islam as a philosophy, a culture, a system of ethics, a heritage, and a civilization—the intellectual soil from which sprang forth our civilization, our legislation, our standards of morality and taste, an element that was the key to our social cohesion, the light during our dark times, the trigger of our revolts against successive invaders, and the unfailing catalyst in our struggles against the enemies, and in regaining our dignity, our lands, our unity, and our glory. In the language of shura and democracy, it is the religion of the people and the heart of its identity. It is the highest reference for every orientation, legislation, or policy, in line with appropriate constitutional arrangements.

This was not, of course, the motivation behind the renewed interest in education and in its philosophical and cultural underpinnings. Rather, the motivation was to reformulate our educational programs in line with the Camp David Accords, the discussions and appendices of which contained grave recommendations to this effect, the upshot being the elimination from the media and educational curricula of all roots of enmity toward Israel.[445]

The interest was also motivated by international policies relating to the comprehensive "war on terror," this banner under which fleets are deployed and all sorts of policies are adopted, yet, there is extreme care not to give any definition of "terrorism," keeping to certain powers the right to interpret it and turn it in the end into a synonym of Islam or a code name for it. The result was an intensification of the blows directed at Muslims, who were painted as being linked to all the evil in the world and presented as a threat to civilization, to the point where Islam itself became the target, as if it were the source of all that. Some even called for submitting the Noble Qur'an to surgical operations, which they claimed were necessary to rid it of the hidden seeds of terrorism within its pages.

These campaigns, known for their connections to Zionist circles, led a number of Muslim nations, like Egypt and Tunisia, to turn upside down their educational curricula and in particular their teaching of religion and history. They went so far as removing verses and suras mentioning jihad and Israelites from their curricula. Will this continue to evolve until it reaches a point where the Qur'an as we know it is banned from the market and replaced with modified and revised versions of it?

This happened in the context of eliminating obstacles from the path of "normalization" with the Zionist entity, the "war on terror," and the campaign against the Islamic movement, since it was considered the greatest obstacle in the way of normalization and the absorption of our umma within the international market,

with the purpose of discarding our distinctive civilizational identity.[446] Moreover, this campaign went beyond the realm of politics and eliminating the Islamic movement as a political rival and an obstacle to the plan of integration and
normalization, extending to the cultural and educational realms as well.

Perhaps the most advanced manifestation of this comprehensive plan took
place in several North African countries, where programs encouraging the use
of Arabic were halted by government decree and a comprehensive process of re-
thinking educational curricula in light of a new philosophy was begun. This
turned the school into an intellectual and political instrument in a civilizational
struggle between the Islamic civilization represented by the Islamic current,
which sought to defend the national identity, and the current of westernization,
dependence, and despotism, as represented by the corrupted elites.

Ministers of education in several of these countries defined the philosophical and theoretical foundation for all the curricula, starting with religious education curricula. That foundation was the Universal Declaration of Human
Rights and the National Charter, although these regimes do not abide by these
texts themselves in their war against the "fundamentalist" political foe. These
charters overlap with our own values and civilization, although they contain elements that can legitimately be objected to. Placing them as the highest frame of
reference for educational curricula is questionable. This is assuming that it is at
all necessary to have a high frame of reference for curricula that leads to a single,
compulsory program for all schools.

These curricula call Islam into question and purport to excise much of what
is central to it because they consider it incompatible with them. Thus, Jihad is
"violence," and so it is eliminated; Islam's teachings on politics, the economy,
and family law, are presented as totalitarian thought that contradicts the
worldview expressed in these charters, and so they are excluded. Thus, the
school has become an arena for a political and civilizational battle against a
political and civilizational adversary, namely the rising Islamic movement,
and against supporters of democracy in general, as part of a comprehensive
security strategy. Along with the school, the security apparatus, diplomacy, the
media, and the rest of the state apparatus were used and transformed into a
war machine to destroy the culture of the people. And all of this aimed to protect the minorities in power and perpetuate their hegemony and interests under the banner of fighting fundamentalism and terrorism and in defense of
modernity and civil society, as though it is even possible to talk about such
ideals in the absence of real freedom and a state based on the rule of law. This
strategy has its defenders, who then endeavor to export it to Arab Muslim coun-

tries on the basis that it represents an especially successful tactic in fighting the common enemy.

In parallel with this plan that has been activated in most Arab countries with varying rates of intensity and speed, depending on local possibilities, efforts toward normalization with Israel have been quietly making headway, not just by countries surrounding the Zionist entity but by the great majority of Arab and Islamic countries. This was in the context of the broader plan aimed at integrating all these economies into the world market, and it is in this context that the campaign against fundamentalism and against the partisans of freedom, identity, justice, and unity is unfolding.

THE EDUCATIONAL TROJAN HORSE

We are witnessing a dramatic expansion of this plan to tear apart and control our umma, one important element of which is the educational component. The educational curricula changed as the Islamic world fell under the thumb of Western colonialism away from the stage of Islamic teaching—that is, based on the foundations of Islam, the religion of the vast majority of its populations, to a stage of a divided education system. Modern schools appeared alongside Islamic schools, which under the colonizer's supervision began to compete with them; to weaken them; and to work on marginalizing and besieging them with religious, linguistic, legal, and cultural questions. At the same time, society was becoming more Western, while the institution of religious education, despite the progress it had made, was pushed to the margins and stripped of its traditional role of leading society. Graduates of these schools saw their livelihoods dwindle, which in turn caused the exodus of more students to the other schools, even forcing Islamic scholars to send their own children to Western schools. The traditional institutes were marginalized despite the strenuous efforts put forward by the reformers (Muhammad 'Abduh, al-Tahir bin 'Ashur, Ben Badis, 'Allal al-Fasi) to enable them to include contemporary sciences alongside the study of Arabic as language and Islam as a culture.

Still, politics betrayed them, and their hands were tied by outside forces. When the colonizers were forced to leave, they handed over control to the graduates of the schools established during the colonial era or that had fallen under colonial influence. These new leaders' policies reflected a continuation of colonial policies, which they implemented with even greater intensity and efficacy, going even further than colonial authorities had done. They not only marginalized religious education institutes but even shut them down. This happened in Tunisia, where they could do so under the pretext of unifying the educational system, just as they had shut down the Shariʿa courts, which the colonizer had first allowed to function with limited jurisdiction under the pretext of unifying the justice system. But this unification was done on the basis of westernization, not on the basis of Islam and its culture. They also seized the gigantic religious endowments institution [waqf], which provided financial support for Islamic education and was the lifeblood of civil society. When they were not able to do away with the religious schools, they were severely weakened and their graduates marginalized. Most were only preserved in order to use their graduates in the state court system and to defend the state's version of religion against its critics. Thus, by reason of the institutional weakness of these institutes, their graduates were often docile instruments in the hands of the secular state to stand against the opposition, both religious and secular, in order to add religious legitimacy to a rule that lacked any democratic legitimacy.

In fact, educational curricula moved from a stage of hidden secularism to one of outright secularism. By secular here I do not mean the state's neutrality vis-à-vis creeds and religious traditions by leaving society and individuals to make their own decisions, as is the case in most democracies. Nor do I mean the positive neutrality of a state that adopts the religion of the majority of its citizens but allows the rest to freely practice their own beliefs, as is the case in England or Norway, or along with this freedom it gives the majority faith certain advantages, like that of teaching, for instance, as is the case in the United States. I do not mean any of these models when I speak of secularism, but rather the French model, which has most influenced the Arab and Islamic elites, and which came out of the bitter conflict between the ossified religious establishment allied to the feudal system and ignorance. This is a specifically French experience, full of animosity toward religion and wary of any semblance of its return. Only the Marxist model of secularism surpasses the latter in its opposition to religion, as it takes atheism and the eradication of religion as the official doctrine of the state.

The Arab-Islamic model of modernization, inspired by the French experience, displays a good amount of hypocrisy. This is unlike the Turkish model, which shed its animosity toward religion and has given it some space in the context of civil society, thus allowing the growth of a private religious sector. The Tunisian model was influenced by the Turkish one, full of preconceptions and accusations against religion, alleging that it represents an obstacle in the path of progress. At the same time, it, too, is hypocritical in relation to religion. As is the case with other Arab regimes, the fact that they adopt Islam as the religion of state does not mean that they will make it into their highest frame of reference. On the contrary, they use that as a justification for controlling it and manipulating it and forbidding any initiative from civil society to protect it. This is the case in the most extreme secularist models such as France, where nevertheless the church still manages huge social service operations, including schools. And when the socialists in power considered withdrawing public funding for this sector, millions of people protested in the streets, forcing them to reconsider.[447] The aberration of the Tunisian model reached the point of eradicating the Arab-Islamic character of its national identity in order to conform to the French model, imagining that it could achieve progress without democracy or religion! Does this development reflect the expansion of the secular currents in the Arab and Islamic world? Or does it reflect their bankruptcy? And how does this arrogant sense of superiority to the masses and insistence on exercising tutelage over them—even by means of repression—even find justification from a democratic and modern perspective?

PHILOSOPHICAL FOUNDATIONS OF ISLAMIC TEACHING

Educational curricula do not operate in a vacuum. Even though reality is one, just as the laws of the universe are one and reason is one, and all this rests on the unity of the Creator, nevertheless the ways of thinking about the universe, human beings, life, and what people add to that in terms of philosophical, scientific, artistic, ethical opinions, values, customs, and experiences with objective reality—all of this has led humanity to create a multiplicity of different cultures. This has also led to different educational methods and curricula by virtue of the difference between those philosophies, customs, and educational models, since the issue is not one of teaching art, vocations, and knowledge, the content of which is common—or just about—among the peoples and cultures of our day. But the issue is about how one defines the human person. It is about teaching: what kind of values and criteria do we bring to bear on what is right and wrong, beautiful and ugly, advanced and backward, true and false? What kind of civilizational identity are we part of? What kind of model of humanity does it promote? Education was the basis for the renaissance of Japan and Germany, in spite of the mass destruction they experienced, but education in the Arab countries was a cause of unemployment, because right from the beginning it was tied to a government job, so that it soon became a liability to the state, which felt responsible to employ its graduates who needed a job. But because the graduates' training only prepared them to work in that context, the number of employees grew and the number of productive workers diminished.

Education is not crafted in a void but rather in a complex matrix of cultural and economic relations. To forget that matrix and the model of humanity that sustains it, and then to try and borrow a ready-made model from another cultural context—a model that has proven to be useful in producing scientific progress, or economic development, or military supremacy—this is precisely what our own educational systems did, hoping that our schools would reach the same results that the Western educational models did, like reversing the backwardness of our nations. The result, unfortunately, was increased backwardness, for we did not achieve any scientific or economic progress. Today we are more than ever dependent in our basic needs like nutrition, health care, and defense, on foreign aid than were our ancestors in their years of greatest decline; we are less independent as well, as our teaching system has been unable even to hold on to what we inherited by way of morality, religion, family cohesion, and self-reliance.

If we want to build a successful educational model for our umma, which is defined by a reliance on a strong philosophical foundation rooted in solid values, it must also be an introduction to the modern era and a window from which one can see the world; a model that offers its people a common philosophical vision, ethical values, aesthetic tastes, a common civilizational membership one is proud of, life goals, and behavioral norms. It should seek to mobilize its people to reach their own highest objectives and to participate in the making of civilization and humanity's future.

Al-Afghani and subsequent religious reformers considered religion to be the most solid basis for building such a model. Religion means the conviction of the heart, the confession of the tongue, and bodily practice; it is life's anchor and purpose.

Every educational system results from a system of ideas, values, and standards— that is, from religion, whether it is spelled out or kept secret. They were not mistaken, those who called for the secular humanist philosophy, that which is found in the Universal Declaration of Human Rights, to be the philosophical framework of our educational systems. Yet they made one mistake, and that is the intention to mix and reconcile opposites, for to justify secularism and market it to our countries under the thin label of religion is deceitful. What is more, this is promoted by a corrupt minority, foreign in almost every way except its color.

They deal selectively with the Western foundation itself, according to their own whims and interests, at the same time favoring the materialist philosophy over religion as the ultimate frame of reference, and refusing the independence of religious institutions from the state, even insisting on controlling and using them. By doing so, they deny the essence of secularism and democracy—that is, the independence of religion and its institutions from the state, while also insisting on the authority of the minority to rule over the majority through its control of state instruments, including all the schools, mosques, and cultural activities.

This is why these secular educational curricula disguised as Islamic are not truly secular either, because their authors are not philosophers stirred by values of liberation, rationalism, and democracy, values that came with the age of Enlightenment. They are not so much secular as they are politicians using a humanistic philosophy, just as they use the schools, the media, legislation, diplomacy, capital, and the other institutions of the state only as instruments in their war against their civilizational and political adversaries in a desperate attempt to safeguard their material and moral privileges, which they acquired while the people were unaware, and they were acting as agents of foreign interests. These are the people ruling in the name of modernity and fighting fundamentalism, just as the colonizers ruled our people in the name of bringing civilization to backward nations. There is no way out of this quandary, except by fighting to lift this tutelage off our people's backs and then by freeing their will and making it the source of all policy.

THE PRINCIPAL CHARACTERISTICS OF ISLAMIC EDUCATION

The foundation and starting point of an Islamic education is freedom. By freedom we mean release from the bonds that impede or limit people's thinking and movement, actions and decision making on the basis of personal conviction. This freedom is guaranteed in Islam, as we read in the Qur'an, "I created jinn and mankind only to worship me."[448] Freedom is also about a group ruling itself and determining its own destiny.

The freedom that Islam calls for is both an individual and collective responsibility. This is in line with the essential function the Qur'an has laid out for humanity: to be God's deputy on the earth ("I will create a vicegerent on earth"),[449] and consequently produce good deeds and make the world a better place, safeguard human life and guarantee the integrity of the planet, since the earth was made to meet human needs. Thus one of the objectives of education is to teach people how to lead good lives and, moreover, intentionally contribute to society—and all of this within the framework of Islamic values, such that all kinds of human needs are met, both individual and collective, physical, spiritual, intellectual, both this-worldly and other-worldly. There is no way to achieve that except through an educational system that forms a person believing in Islam and practicing its precepts.

This science of Islamic education, therefore, is intimately tied to the fundamentals of Islam—to Islamic theology [*'ilm al-tawhid*], its rituals, the Shari'a and its ethics, and to the sources of these sciences—the Qur'an, the Sunna, the consensus of the scholars, analogical reasoning, and the like. It is also tied to Islamic knowledge in general, and Islam's attitude to knowledge in its various forms, because the function of education is to build the human being through these sciences.

We may summarize the theoretical characteristics of Islamic education by referring to the following points:

1. Islamic education links theoretical and practical education with religious education.
2. The object of Islamic education is the human being, with all this word implies in terms of meanings, perspectives, and attitudes in the light of Islam. This is a holistic, balanced, and moderate education.
3. Among the most important goals of Islamic education is the formation of a good human person, a good society, and a good humanistic civilization.
4. Islamic education must train learners to love knowledge of the world as it is and offer them the means to attain it, apply it, and spread it.
5. It aims to join general education with ethical formation, refinement of the soul, and the teaching of wisdom.
6. Islamic education must include a wide scope of educational responsibilities, both individual and collective, for they reinforce the freedom of the human person and his responsibility toward himself, his Lord, humanity, and the universe.
7. It also insists on the importance of a good example in following the values of Islam, whether it is for parents, teachers, or other people responsible for any of society's educational institutions, as in the hadith, "You are all leaders, and you are all responsible for those you lead."[450] All these people seek to draw nearer to the ideals of Islam, just as did the Prophet (PBUH) and his Companions, "The Messenger of God is an excellent model for those of you who put your hope in God and the Last Day and remember Him often."[451]
8. Islamic education is a continuing education from the cradle to the grave.
9. It is a humanitarian spirit that makes no discrimination between people on the basis of color or race.
10. It is a progressive education, discerning everything that is new and useful within the fixed boundaries of religion.

11. It seeks to develop the human person's good nature at creation [*al-fitra*], to guide it and train it on the basis of this nature's values, such as cleanliness, order, patience, dignity, humility, boldness, courage, zeal, honor, and altruism.[452]

To continue investing in education without agreeing on an educational philosophy that is in harmony with the creeds of Islam and our identity as a civilization is harmful. Rather, that educational philosophy must begin with these two and translate them into a form of behavior that impacts society, into an umma that reflects the Qur'an and the pride of Islam and its faith. In turn this teaching instills its students with the commitment to carry forth this message to the world, full of liberation and justice, at a time when the umma has lost hope in its unity and the liberation of Palestine, and in its ability to begin afresh its civilizational march, regain its unshakable pride, and take up its trust to save a tormented humanity and a civilization that is paralyzed.

Tragically, this umma despairs of being able to control its present situation, since it is in the hands of a leadership bent on secularism, hypocrisy, dictatorship, and fragmentation, a situation that has worsened, from its dependence, foreign debts, and economic decline to the destruction of traditional institutions that have not been replaced with alternatives. It is no wonder that these small entities have only become smaller and that direct colonialism has returned and entered the entire umma under the pressure of the Israeli age—and all this in the shade of continuing political and educational conditions imposed by a minority that has sidelined the majority politically, culturally, and economically.

PROPOSALS

Within the limited scope we have in dealing with this dynamic, strategic, and complicated issue of education, and keeping in mind that we want to reinforce the freedoms for our umma and its march forward, I outline the following ideas.

The Independence of Education and Its Institutions from the State

We must strictly refrain from politicizing educational curricula. This does not mean schools should be neutral with regard to society's pressing concerns, for school was designed to address those concerns. But we should resist bringing schools into these conflicts, the greatest of which is the struggle for political power, as when a minister of education says that his mission is to fight the Islamists.[453]

How, then, after that can they call for a depoliticization of the universities, schools, and mosques? This means that what we are facing here is an illegal use of the educational system and political power. School curricula in the West, according to their tradition, witness no structural changes with the advent of a new minister or even with a change of party at the helm. This was the case in our own civilization at the height of its power and stability. States would come to power, others would leave, and the foundations of teaching at the Zaytuna University, for instance, would stay in place, reinforcing and safeguarding the character of the umma. This means a serious reliance upon the principle that teaching and education must be kept independent from the state. To that effect, here are three more practical remarks.

First, the mission of setting up educational curricula should be carried out by a scientific body independent from the state. Its members are elected among the best scholars, intellectuals, and representatives from the main branches of learning.

Second, once the state's stranglehold on the school system is broken and some basic elements are set, there could be a multiplication of curricula and of sources of supervision over the teaching. This would come through the encouragement of the popular institutions that used to do this at the height of our civilization for the entire educational sector until our occupation at the hands of colonialism and its allies, who took possessions of the schools and of the endowments that funded them. Such endowments used to account for a third of ownership in Tunisia, for instance,[454] thus encouraging the private sector through various means, allowing the state to fund education but without carrying all the weight of its administration.

Third, the goal being the independence of the educational sector, one must seek to shrink the central state's influence in the areas of knowledge, culture, and education, so that it is limited to financial support, guidance, and assistance until society is able to play a greater role itself. The goal is that the state can progressively pull away and leave this role to popular and local institutions and to individual and collective efforts, some on a voluntary basis or in organizations like local municipal councils, religious endowments, teaching unions, writers' syndicates, and alumni associations. The role of the ministry of education will be to coordinate between these various popular bodies, and their relationship to the ministry will be similar to that of the ministry of justice to the courts and its judges in democratic nations. This strategy will progressively reduce the government's role in favor of society's institutions and coordinate the state's pulling back with civil society's expanding role.

Making Full Use of Our Educational Institutions, like Mosques and Schools

Historically, mosques were the womb that gave birth to the civilization of Islam, incarnating its holistic education of both mind and spirit, but they have now been mostly stripped of that educational role, as they are used for small periods of time during the day when they could be put to use from early morning to night, and even during the night hours. They are indeed our open universities, and they have witnessed a time of flourishing in the West within the past few years. Nonetheless, the activation of schools and universities is very limited today, maybe at a third or half capacity if you count the holidays. Is not that impairment of their potential one of the evidences of our backwardness and the main cause for it? Think of how by a more effective use of our educational institutions we could raise the level of enrollment and solve for good the scandal of illiteracy in our Arab-Islamic countries, while cutting down the number of years needed to teach people, perhaps even by half.

Education Adapted to the Needs of Each Student

What we need is an open field on the principle "to each person according to their performance." This opens the path of progress up the ladder of education according to the student's intelligence and effort, instead of forcing on everyone a moderate pace—too fast for the slow learner, who then fails, and frustrating the fervor of the fast one, who then loses heart. What we need is the open school and the open field of study, since what is required to produce a good doctor, for example, is a combination of skills. Why would this achievement be conditioned upon twenty years of study, for instance? Why not leave it an open space, with each person achieving those goals earlier or later? And why require a student to pass through a set of fixed rungs on a ladder, as long as he has acquired the needed experience for a particular vocation? The system should allow that possibility, even if it turns out to be an exception in some cases.

Education and the Economy

It is possible to fix the problem of unemployment for teachers and to alleviate the burden on the state by linking education to the economy, especially pairing vocational instruction with business companies. Thus every company would have a school tied to it, which seeks to prepare its workers at all levels. This allows the company to play an educational role, as it affords its employees the opportunity to practice their vocation as they work. That practice thus becomes productive, instead of having an artificial vocational training program assumed by the state, which then cannot find work for its graduates because they are of no use to the business firms who then turn them down. This is how vocational training was done for our traditional industries long before they were painfully impacted by modernity and its futile dreams of progress through destroying all traditional institutions, as though we were a people without any history.

The Open School Set Up like a Mosque or Association

Alongside schools tied to particular businesses or administrations either run by the state or some other entity, there is also the idea of open schools that focus on broader popular education and the theoretical sciences. People of various ages come to learn in these contexts, depending on their availability, and they request the subject matter they want, choosing from among the teachers for that purpose. At the same time, these centers propose various study circles to them, so that their students can progress according to the speed they choose and according to the instructors' assessment of their progress. It may be that for the sake of broadening people's general knowledge—call it "the people's university"—we can engage existing official educational institutions for this task either in a full-time capacity or for select hours during the day or evening, in the summer or winter, even in public gardens or on the beach or under the shade of a tree. The important thing is to widen the scope of learning, make it more accessible, break down its monopoly, and shatter the traditional molds. We are not just trying to eradicate the scandal of illiteracy but also trying to keep raising the general level of knowledge beyond that of a secondary education diploma.

A Passionate Concern for the Education of Women

Women represent half of society and they raise the other half. How can we achieve a renaissance [*nahda*], in which women do not fully and effectively take part?

Keep Raising the Standard of Instruction

In order to improve the mission of teaching, we have to continually raise the teacher's level at every stage of teaching and in every respect, intellectually, ethically, and financially. They must be held to high ethical ideals, higher than all others except for heads of state, judges, and imams in mosques. The teacher, therefore, should be compensated financially in a way that does not compare to other professions.

Raise the Students' Level of Commitment to Islam

Great care must be taken to raise a generation with the highest level of commitment to Islam and with pride in their belonging to its umma and heritage in a spirit of moderation, far from any extremism and narrowness of mind. They should be taught to shun fanatic attachment to one Islamic school of thought. A Muslim should be raised simultaneously on faith, pride in the greatness of Islam, the unity of God, the unity of the messengers, the unity of the umma and of humankind as a whole, and to hold sacred human dignity and the values of freedom and justice. They must also be brought up to embrace freedom of thought, ijtihad and shura, the love of knowledge, love for knowledgable people, and love for pluralism within the Islamic fold.

As the saying goes, "The believer should seek wisdom wherever he finds it," whether inside and outside his own school or inside and outside the Islamic umma. He should be raised to believe in the unity of the human race, suffering with those who suffer on earth, burning with anger at injustice and against those who perpetrate it, anger at tyranny, racial discrimination, colonial hegemony, Israel's oppression of Palestinians, and disregard for the morality of nations. But he will also have a positive attitude in advocating for the causes of truth, justice, freedom, and human rights wherever they may be found, within the umma or outside of it, and be ready to sacrifice for this cause through his efforts, his money, and his own life as he seeks to please God.

We should consider the commitment to ethical and religious values and everything connected to them to be at the heart of education. It is also important to provide some teaching of our umma's history and greatest challenges, as well as the great problems we face today. We should consider these as the roots of a commonly shared knowledge and a basic goal of all institutions of learning and people of learning, since the goal of teaching is not just passing on knowledge. Even before that it is also forming model people and a model umma, carrying the liberating message of Islam, "[Believers], you are the best community singled out for people: you order what is right, forbid what is wrong,"[455] and "You who believe, be steadfast in your devotion to God and bear witness impartially: do not let hatred of others lead you away from justice, but adhere to justice, for that is closer to consciousness of God."[456]

An Education Rooted in Democracy

If it is true that the neutral school does not exist, then the essential requirement for liberation movements within our umma, of all different tendencies—and especially in this stage of confronting foreign aggression and the intensification of conflict between the elites—is an agreement among these elites on the principle of democratizing education—that is, favoring education for all, without excluding either student or teacher.

Arabic at the Heart of Education

The Arabic language is a tool for thinking, expression, continuity in education, administration, and in our economic, cultural, political, and diplomatic life, because Arabic is not just the language of the Arabs as a people, it also mediates the ultimate call from Heaven to earth and the last word of the messengers' legacy. Arabic is the world's only sacred language, because it is the only one that still contains God's words as they were revealed, and this at a time when all the originals of the sacred books have been lost and when all that is left of them, at best, is a number of translations from other translations, so that a researcher cannot possibly authenticate what is true for lack of an original. This is what makes Arabic more than just the language of the Arabs; it is the language of all Muslims as their medium of access to God's revelation, giving meaning to all who are connected to Islam and its history, to Arabs and to Muslims, or anyone who has an interest in dealing with them.

Arabic would be the best candidate for becoming a world language, were it not for the war against it from inside and outside. But, too, beyond its religious dimension and its richness, flexibility, and amazing aptitude for development, without Arabic, advancement and modernization would not be possible, since thinking cannot take place outside of language. Sadly, our children struggle to get over the language barrier in order to gain knowledge, when they could have gained it directly through Arabic, their mother tongue. Indeed, the current curriculum aims to disperse our energies in every direction, and instead of starting with our own cultural heritage, modernizing it and adapting it, we set out to undermine it and discard it, and search for a solution to our problems outside of it.

However, we must also learn other languages, just as the Qur'an urges us to: "Another of His signs is the creation of the heavens and earth, and the diversity of languages and colours."[457] Still, a foreign language must not be a rival or an alternative to the language of religion and nation, as is the case in most Arab countries, treating Arabic like a second-class citizen or even a foreigner in its own land. By claiming progress sometimes we are only going backward. Such an approach is certainly one of the reasons for wasting energy instead of conserving it, for westernizing and dislocating our citizens instead of rooting them in their own context. This approach also blatantly privileges the urban and privileged elites,[458] and the rule of the minority at the expense of the countryside and the great masses.

Any state that forces its citizens to deal with their own state administration in a foreign language is in no way national or democratic; it is falling back on colonial dynamics under the false appearance of national ones. True, the struggle for independence was tied to a struggle to regain the pillars of a national identity, and especially its language and religion, but in fact this struggle, contrary to expectation in light of its goals, was not able to achieve independence. To the contrary, increasingly grave dangers awaited these nations once colonialism crept back in under the disguise of our own people; put differently, the colonizers became "people of our own race."

So our nations, especially those on the front lines like the North African states, resumed their bitter liberation struggle, including the one facing cultural aggression against the Arabic language, even though the results of his struggle after more than a century have been so meager. Changing the language of instruction to Arabic in Tunisia, for instance, has only gone up to the third grade of elementary school, then it changes back. It is like we take one step forward and then two steps back, because of the forced insertion and integration of our countries into the global market economy. Add to that a dreadful plan to attack the elements of the people's identity—Islam and Arabic—and those who support it, including all those forces of liberation and civil society, like the workers and student unions, and the recognized political forces.

Use of Modern Communication Systems

A good Islamic education today will make use of all current communication media, like the Internet, computers, television, radio, satellites, and the like to spread knowledge and form an Islamic public opinion, popular universities that are also cultural, humanitarian, Arab, and Islamic.

Teach and Make Use of Scientific Knowledge

This knowledge has become more than in any previous time the surest path—and no one can do without it—to guarantee the fight for survival and participation in civilization. For us as a Muslim community, it is a form of worship and knowledge of God. You cannot escape the need to raise the level of mandatory education, from trying to wipe out illiteracy to that of higher education. There is also a need to raise the budget for scientific research above 5 percent of the national budget, to build up the institutions that safeguard our unity, and encourage the private sector, for that is where we have to start if we want a community of researchers and innovators in all areas, including finding a way to bring back those who have emigrated.

Tie University and Research Centers to Economic, Social, and Political Institutions

This is paramount, so that scientists and scholars can decide on every future project, which are then implemented through the work of political and business leaders. Universities then become open and free spaces for communication, research, and dialogue about the nation's and the world's problems, and a place where people practice exercising mutual consultation and democracy.

Adapt Training to the Needs of Each Region

This is an important project to carry out, so that it encourages, firmly grounds, and diversifies the components that form the national character— Arab, Islamic, and human on a large scale, thereby making use of the Qur'an, the hadith, biographies, language and literature, and the great issues concerning the umma and the world. We aspire to form the Muslim person with the following qualities: a person of sound faith practicing the rituals of Islam, following the example of the prophets and messengers (peace be upon them), with a grasp of how Islam organizes all of life and solves the world's problems at their root cause and with moderation; a person who is proud of belonging to the umma of Islam and to his own small nation, loving knowledge and Islam's scholars, seeking truth with humility, rational insight, and a commitment to Islam's ethical values; loving to work and practice its skills, enjoying the good things of life with a penchant for temperance; generous and bold in working for justice and ready to resist evil; a person who does not hesitate to give sacrificially of his money or his life in defense of the truth and in defeating what is false; one who puts loyalty to Islam's umma above all other loyalties, whose heart beats with kindness and compassion for the plight of the downtrodden and oppressed of any background and makes every effort to support their cause. And finally, these individuals will have a strong faith in the values of equality, justice, freedom, mutual consultation, piety, cleanliness, orderliness, human dignity, rational insight, collective work, the authority of the people, the priority and loftiness of the realities taught by revelation. In sum, these are people who feel deeply and delight in the signs of creation and beauty in the heavens and on the earth.

Encourage the Practice of Sports

The goal here is to move the masses from a negative state of simply watching matches to everyone participating. It is also an encouragement to practice individual sports, like wrestling, swimming, javelin or discus throwing, horseback riding, mountain climbing—and all this with an attempt to link sports activities with the greater challenges facing the umma rather than engaging in them as a means to distract people from these challenges, as is often the case today.

Work on Nurturing People's Love for Beauty

There is a great need to nurture a public taste that appreciates beauty, cleanliness, good manners, and art. Along with this is the challenge to progressively rid life of ugly behavior, though without compulsion, through the media, cultural clubs, and the other institutions of the state and society.

Seek to Eradicate Fanaticism

Since education is one of the functions of political parties, they should get rid of tendencies toward fanaticism, narrow and unitary perspectives, personalization of power, authoritarian procedures, remnants of the past, and causes of discrimination and division. Even the Islamic parties, despite their taking on the worries of the umma and their commitment to its unity, have often been afflicted by the same ills that have afflicted the umma generally, among them the illness of isolation. And it is no wonder, since these movements are only plants in the same soil that nourishes the umma and gives rise to its inherited customs and centuries-old backwardness. Still, that was only a small part of their legacy in comparison to the great works of jihad and reform these movements produced. Actually, most of these Islamic movements started as part of the umma's wider reaction to the times and its refusing both stagnation and westernization. They have thus become the hope, the resistance, the yearning for a better future.

It is mostly the colonial context that accounted for the emergence of these movements based on resistance. Thus, it is unsurprising that they adopt a very strict culture of educational and organizational discipline.[459] That is indeed what made most of these movements become extremely restrictive in allowing any freedom within their educational perspective, restricting their teaching to only one perspective that is thought to represent the pure and devout discipline. They are also prone to being closed when it comes to broader general culture and other schools and different viewpoints, and when it comes to restricting the freedom to renew leadership within the movement and to offer one's opinion and debate. All of this has led to many divisions.

We believe it is mandatory for Islamic movements to train individuals on the basis of a comprehensive curriculum open to the views of other schools and intellectual currents, and in the process of mutual consultation in all matters and the free circulation of ideas put forward by means of proof and demonstration. This also ensures that their minds will turn to the real and vast world, with its good and bad, and will be able to find their place in it. From there, they can begin to solve its problems without retreating to an ideal and imaginary "historical narrative," so that when they actually encounter reality they do not experience a collision that splits the movement. For when this free education spreads within the Islamic movements, then dialogue becomes the best path to take into account every tendency, or behavior, or mistake.[460]

Extremism is nothing but the conviction that one possesses absolute truth and the determination to impose it on others.[461] It is present, though often hidden, in the official educational system of these movements, in which Islam is presented as a single, homogenous collection of legal rules and makes no distinction between points of consensus, which are the minority, and the points of difference and ijtihad, which are the majority. The ideas of the movement's founder or main thinker are taught as the only source of truth and as having greater authority than those of Islamic scholars of the past and present, and even over the Qur'an and Sunna, as they do not accept any interpretation of them other than that of their shaykh.

This is how such an organization undertakes to train generations of close-minded people, incapable of dialogue with their environment and with other Muslims other than through violence or declaring them unbelievers [takfir]. Even the shura institutions in these movements are but a reflection of the reality of authoritarianism embodied in the state and in the rest of society's institutions, starting with the family, then the school, and up to the unions and state bureaucracy. In addition, political institutions, whether secular or religious, express the authoritarian character imbedded in our various traditions and oppressive states. So much so that one of the thinkers of the Islamic movement who himself shared a long time in the movement's tribulation, thinking, and research did not hesitate to say this about his own experience: "The parliamentary assemblies in the democratic countries are one hundred times closer to the concept of shura than these dysfunctional assemblies that claim it as the guiding principle of all Islamic organizations." Indeed, he considered this kind of shura when applied to these assemblies as fallacious.[462]

There is no way out of this authoritarianism except by eliminating it at the roots in the school, in educational curricula within parties and society's institutions, starting with an educational philosophy that clearly distinguishes between aspects of definitive truth and aspects of interpretation [ijtihad] and difference, that liberates people's minds from illusions, and releases their energy for dialogue and research. This philosophy will also provide wide open pastures where they can graze to their hearts' content on the broad diversity of views within the Islamic school—and beyond it to other schools of thought, both ancient and modern, and to any thought without restriction, so that our umma regains its membership among those praised by the Qur'an, "[those] who listen to what is said and follow what is best."[463] That means every saying is worth considering, for there is no restriction on thought in Islamic society, and if God is One, the world is characterized by multiplicity and plurality. And if the Qur'an and the Sunna are the highest source of truth, nevertheless what human beings can understand by reading them is always subject to error. From this fact is born the process of interpretation and the reality of the umma—that is, the absence of a church that speaks as if it were divine revelation. The umma, after all, is the only source of legitimacy, and it speaks in the name of truth.

Public Opinion Guarantees Public and Individual Freedoms

If the human being is God's most honored creature and if the science of education is responsible for teaching individuals and nations, then the crafting of education is the noblest of industries, and it should be given the greatest care and funding so that it will continually develop and blossom, for the development of the human person, the umma, and humanity in this life and the next depend on it. Education and culture, that are rooted in freedom and human dignity, and public opinion nourished by these values, are the most solid guarantees for private and public freedoms and for continual progress.

Part III

GUARANTEES AGAINST OPPRESSION, OR PUBLIC FREEDOMS IN THE ISLAMIC SYSTEM

The most important challenge any political theory faces on the issue of political power is how to prevent injustice. How can public freedoms be protected? This is because every human being leans toward the abuse of this power, according to Montesquieu.[1] Power naturally leads to abuse.[2] Often what prevents tyranny is the inability to exercise it. As the Arab poet put it, "It is the weak that do not abuse power."[3] How then to prevent injustice when the ruler disposes of vast amounts of wealth and numbers of agents? Is there any limit to his tyranny?

5

THE CONCEPT OF TYRANNY

There are different schools of thought on the issue of tyranny—how to define and explain it, and how to determine what is "acceptable" in it, and what is unacceptable.

DESPOTISM IN THE MARXIST SCHOOL

In the Marxist school, despotism is only one of many faces of political struggle, and every political struggle is at root an economic issue—that is, the class struggle for control over the forces of production. That class struggle is at the root of all manner of struggles in society, and it will endure, along with its offshoot, political conflict. It will only end when the struggle between those who own and those who do not ends, when private ownership of the means of production is finally abolished. So there is no way to stop that conflict, and in fact, there is no use in doing so.

If we were serious about putting an end to autocracy and ushering in the age of freedom, then we would actually need to intensify this conflict. The class ownership of the nation's resources is responsible for creating the state as an institution in order to assure its continued supremacy and repress its adversaries. Despotism is nothing but an instrument used by a class, through its seizure of the state to exploit another class, and there is no way to eliminate it except by eliminating the exploitation and its instrument, the state. That said, the state cannot be eliminated all of a sudden. Rather, society must go through a transitional phase during which the working class can take over the reins of the state and use it to eliminate its enemies. Engels said, "The proletariat needs the state, not for the sake of freedom, but in order to clamp down on its enemies."[1]

Marxist theory sees the sacred violence that the working class uses to eliminate its enemies as completely justified and calls for its use. Still, despotism is not all condemned from this perspective; what this theory condemns is its use by the bourgeoisie or feudal state. As for the proletarian state, its message and actions represent a progressive struggle.

As long as the state remains in the hands of the proletariat, it has no need to be constrained by any moral standards, since its actions are ethical by definition. For that reason, the supreme authority of the communist state recognizes no oversight over it and is not obligated to submit to any law. The people have no freedom other than abiding by the law, and there is no place for freedom of the press nor for the forming of political parties.

We read in the Soviet paper *Pravda* from November 1927, "Under the dictatorship of the proletariat there can be three or even four parties, but with one condition: one party rules, and the others are in prison. If you do not understand this, then you have not understood one iota about the essence of the proletariat's dictatorship, nor about the essence of the Bolshevik party's dictatorship."[2]

Theoretically in such a regime legitimacy, sovereignty, freedom, and wealth all belong to the people, or at least to the single ruling party. In reality, all power is in the hands of the ruling elite who control the party, the administration, the army, and economic life. The people have no part of that rule; they must be content with the right to life.

What guarantee does this perspective offer for the curbing of despotism when its leaders announce without equivocation that the state exists for only one purpose—to eliminate its opponents by force? In this light, the organs of justice cannot possibly admit to any independence, since their only role is to bring about the socialist transformation of society.[3] Despite this, the heirs of this thinking along with their heritage of tyranny and oppression insist—without any attempt at reviewing that heritage—that they should be seen as models of democracy.

DESPOTISM IN THE WESTERN DEMOCRATIC SCHOOL

According to this school, the human person inclines toward evil as he does toward the good, thus we must take the necessary steps to curb his inclination toward evil. Government's role is to limit this evil tendency in the human soul. Had people been created angels, there would have been no need to establish governments.

But what guarantees that the state will not overstep its mission of establishing justice and turn into a tyrannical and despotic power, as long as it's in the hands of human beings in whose souls evil struggles against good?

If you examine the contemporary political systems that operate within a liberal view of the state, you will easily discover two essential pillars or principles: the principle of legality (or the rule of law) and the principle of the people's sovereignty. Western thinkers see these principles as a safeguard against political despotism and as the fruit of their modern philosophies and culture in the political realm.[4]

We have already demonstrated the inability of the two principles of legitimacy and popular sovereignty[5] and subsidiary public liberties, like freedom of the press, freedom to establish political parties, regulatory bodies, and the separation of powers—the impotence of all these means to curb the power of strong interest groups from pressuring, dominating, corrupting, and forcing the state to void the guarantees that democracy's components offer, and especially how the principle of sovereignty grants the state an aura of sanctity and finality in all that it promulgates, in isolation from any authority above it, whether ethical or religious. All of this erects an insurmountable barrier or even a great contradiction between political life on the one hand and the moral and religious life on the other, and all the more so between public opinion and the decisions made by the ruling elites. The practice of politics often finds no justification or moral foundation, nor are they an expression of public opinion, but only the satisfaction of a ruling elite that resorts to all means of interests, deceitfulness, and lies to and justify their policies and force some approval of them.

This is not unlike the deceitful ways and outright lies the political elites in the United States and Great Britain, two well-established democracies, used to justify the destructive war they waged on Iraq that claimed tens of thousands of lives and cost many billions of dollars—money that could have could have stopped famines and epidemics around the world. Similarly, Western democracies have continued to generously support the occupying Zionist entity, despite public opinion. Add to that the support these democracies give to most repressive regimes that use the most force against their people. These are just some examples of the soft or invisible despotism that is widely practiced by these Western democracies, not to mention the oppression created by the policies of systematic looting that the powerful few carry out against four-fifths of humanity, leaving behind them millions of victims, victims of famines and lethal epidemics, even among their own people.

This is in addition to the conscious destruction by the capitalist enterprise of the environment, to such an extent that the world's most powerful nation, which preaches the gospel of democracy and human rights day in and day out, has refused to sign the Kyoto Protocol that limits the emission of deadly gases which threaten life itself. That, too, is violence, which means that despite the importance of instruments and principles of democracy such as the rule of law, the people's sovereignty, the separation of powers, the rotation of power, and a free press, which have curbed blatant forms of violence, like those committed by dictatorial regimes, they have not curbed and not even lightened—perhaps even exacerbated—the hidden forms of violence because they lack an ethical philosophy and moral foundations.

Naturally this opens the floodgates, allowing the devil to assault, penetrate, and release the vilest tendencies in the human heart in terms of injustice and aggression, and greatly bolster the markets of immorality and corruption, the paying off of people's conscience. It may be that the filthy rich of our day are those who control the great global investments and who for the love of profit poison political and social life through their acts of corruption—just as journalism has become a malleable tool in their hands to raise or bring down whom they wish. In the same way, members of parliament and the rest of the institutions of power, including the opposition, have become a wide playing field for them to exert their influence, and comfortable sofas for them to recline on when and how they desire, forcing people to do their bidding.[6]

John Ziegler said, "The West betrayed the true principles of the Enlightenment civilization, the French Revolution, and human rights, despite the fact that it brags about them night and day. This is when it established a deadly economic system that goes by the name of comprehensive globalization, a system that kills hundreds of thousands of people every day in different parts of the world. It is the empire of shame led by George W. Bush and Putin."[7] What else could be expected in the shade of the new idol, "the state," which enjoys supreme authority and legitimacy? Inevitably, it will bring harm to the people and to the world as a whole: "But man exceeds all bounds when he thinks he is self-sufficient."[8]

PREVENTION OF TYRANNY IN THE ISLAMIC CONCEPTION

So what is the guarantee for preventing injustice in the Islamic conception of the state? The state in the Islamic conception is not a weapon in the hands of a particular class in order to eliminate another class or an opposing current—even if the use of violence to ward off aggression does have its place—nor is it an instrument to bring glory to a people or race or sect at the expense of other nations or races. Rather, Islam views the state as an instrument to instruct, refine, and provide a climate of freedom, justice, and self-purification, which would allow the greatest number of people the opportunity to know God, to worship Him, and manage the resources of this universe in such a way as to help nations get to know one another, cooperate, support one another, and achieve development. Still, what will hinder the Islamic state itself from turning into an instrument of oppression and destruction, which persecutes free people and violates the rights of individuals and nations, as has happened during Islamic history and still happens today. What makes matters worse is when the despotic state claims to do this in God's name or the name of Islam. Are we not vulnerable to a religious dictatorship, an evil from which humanity has suffered and is suffering today?

6

THE BASIC PRINCIPLES FOR COMBATING INJUSTICE IN THE ISLAMIC STATE

We have said human nature is a composite of powerful passions seeking to be satisfied by any means, and at the same time a readiness and longing for nobility of character, fairness, and altruism. But the latter are in dire need of care and training, and of the proper context for these virtues to grow and play their role in regulating those other instincts and passions. This means that we should exclude idealistic and simplistic solutions that claim the power to eliminate the scourge of despotism at its root by external technical means. For as long as human nature and human society remain as they are, there will always be wars, oppression, and various kinds of despotism, so that instead of searching for one cure, we will need an array of tools, which can, if used properly, reduce the amount of oppression of man against man, and most nearly approximate justice and freedom by providing intellectual, educational, legal, and social conditions for their existence. This will have to be in the context of a just law and a just judiciary, before which all are equal. When this happens, however, it will never be more than an approximation that reflects the greatest goal that can be aspired to by political thought since absolute justice cannot be achieved in this life.

So what are the (relative) solutions in Islamic thought that can curb state tyranny, for the benefit of freedom, justice, and the human rights of citizens?

GOD'S SUPREME AUTHORITY AND THE PEOPLE'S OVERSIGHT

We saw previously that it is God's will as expressed in His Shari'a that is the source of legitimacy and supreme authority in the Islamic state, along with its attendant laws, principles, and general objectives. Every state institution, as it issues laws or statutes derived from the Shari'a, must conform to the values and supreme objectives emanating from the Divine Legislation. No one with political authority may depart from God's set limits [hudud], whether in his own actions or in what he commands or forbids. As the Qur'an says, "those who overstep God's limits wrong their own souls."[1]

At the same time, no citizen has the right to obey any legislation, statute, or directive issued by a state authority that contradicts the Shari'a or its objectives. In fact, it is his duty to resist and oppose that law, statute, or directive, if only by noncompliance, since a Muslim's obedience to God and to His Prophet (PBUH) is primary and comes before obedience to the state. Further, God's will is clearly recorded in the revealed texts, to which everyone has access; no one can then assert that he has new revelation from God, which others do not know about. The prophetic period came to an end along with all its directives, ushering in the era of equality—every one is equal, ruler and ruled, in submission to God's will, in acting righteously and resisting any authority that commands wrong. This resistance follows this hadith's directive: "If any one of you sees an evil, let him change it with his hand; and if he is not able to do so, then [let him change it] with his tongue; and if he is not able to do so, then with his heart—and that is the weakest of faith."[2] And thus authority is not absolutely attributed to those in power,[3] for the people's obedience is not to them personally, but it is conditioned upon their commitment to order good and forbid evil according to God's law, and in that case their obedience becomes a form of worship, as they are obeying God. Otherwise, obeying rulers who violate those conditions would be disobedience against God, which will incur His punishment.

Thus the Islamic system is the first to base itself on the rule of law and legitimacy, both of which draw from this double source, Qur'an and Sunna. This implies that for a law to be binding on citizens it is not sufficient that it emanate from a legitimate body—that is, an elected one or even from the people as a whole—but it must also agree with the supreme authority represented by the Shari'a. Otherwise, the believer must not only refrain from applying it, but he must resist and rebel against it, according to his means. For that reason, Islam does not entrust the supervision of the state's laws to a particular body—though that, too, is needed—but rather to the people as a whole, who are the guarantors of God's law. The people are obligated to refrain from obeying that which contradicts the divine law and to initiate a movement of resistance against the unjust regime and to pressure it with all the means at its disposal.

That is how Islam underwrites the people's oversight mission. They are ever vigilant in checking state power and preventing its despotism and ensure its commitment to the Shari'a and its objectives. The greatest of these objectives is justice, which means that the unjust ruler merits no obedience or compliance but rather resistance, as one of the citizens of 'Umar's state put it, "By God, if we see you swerving from God's laws, we will straighten you out, even with our swords." 'Umar had asked the people what they would do if they found him swerving from the truth. That kind of attitude spurred them on to resist tyranny.

If one cannot do that, then let him shout in protest in the presence of the tyrant and join Hamza in paradise ("The best of martyrs was Hamza, who stood up against the amir, telling him what he should and should not do, and was killed for it"). If one cannot do that, then let him be quiet, contenting himself to ignore the unjust order ("and that is the weakest of faith").[4] That said, silence is not a negative attitude; among its possible forms, one can disassociate from the aggressor and boycott them, which is an effective weapon against unjust businesses or hostile nations.

Further, any unjust laws that might be issued by majorities within elected parliaments, in the past or in the future, should be seen as emanating from their own will unrestricted by any moral, religious, or humanitarian consideration. The people can find no legal justification for opposing such laws, and this represents the greatest deficiency in the Western state's edifice, which has found no redress by appealing to natural or international law. Yet the principles of Shari'a as a supreme and unbiased authority offer a satisfactory solution.

THE IMAMATE IS A CONTRACT

As we have seen, Muslims have agreed—apart from the Shia[5]—that the imamate is based on choice and that the relationship between rulers and ruled is defined by a contract, the bay'a, or the oath of allegiance. The West waited for ten centuries while suffering under the rule of the popes and kings who claimed divine rights before opening its mind to this principle in the heat of its struggle with Islam and its own heritage. It was then that its identity emerged, and it began to develop its thought by discovering the deficiencies in its governance and ways of life.

The West, then, stepped over the bridges put in place by the Muslims and learned from their considerable contributions by borrowing from the Greek and Roman civilizations the molds and structures into which their scholars poured various elements of the Islamic civilization. At the same time that Western scholars benefited from these contributions, they poured out their hatred, scorn, and defamation of their Muslim counterparts. One of the concepts that was transmitted over those bridges was this contractual relationship between ruler and ruled, instead of the concept of the ruler as god or, in the best of cases, the rule of the minority, which was all that the West had known hitherto.

It was then that Rousseau, Locke, and Montesquieu established the contractual philosophy of governance, or the social contract, derived from the Islamic legacy. Yet they considered the East to be the source of all despotism poured out into the world where one man directs all things according to his will and inclination without any law or rule, drawing his only power from the fear he creates in those he rules. What is more, they believed despotism is the natural state of affairs in the East, while it was alien to the Western kingdoms.

Paradoxically, it is as if generations of Western founders of European Renaissance and Enlightenment all conspired to incorporate the heritage of the Islamic civilization while at the same time robbing her of any merit, and instead blaming all evil, including despotism, on Islam, when in fact it was Islam that withdrew the right from anyone, or any institution or state, to deification, dictatorship, and absolute rule. No one is "absolute" in that sense but God, and no one on earth after the close of the Prophetic period is worthy of speaking on His behalf (may He be praised). All that is left is the believing community's mutual consultation [shura] and its rule regulated by contract. Indeed, that relationship of contract is very important, as it offers a solid foundation for resisting the autocracy of rulers by defining them as only agents and administrators for the people who established them in their position, employ them to enforce their will, and watch over their interests. If they depart from this function, then it is legitimate to correct them or even remove them.

Allow me to insert here a brief survey of differing opinions among the partisans of political Islam, or Islamists, on the principle of the people's sovereignty. We already alluded to some of these differences. Some defend its Islamic character, saying that Muslims were the first to speak of the people's sovereignty. Some went even further, like Hasan al-Turabi, asserting that the theory of sovereignty in Western thought was borrowed from the concept of God's absolute sovereignty in Islam [hakimiyyat Allah] in Islam.[6] Mawdudi was of the same mind when he wrote, "The principle of the umma's sovereignty, which the Qur'an establishes in the words, 'and consult with them on this issue,' is the principle to which humanism came after a long struggle, and thus it should remain in the shadow of the Islamic state."[7]

The majority of Islamic thinkers have denied this principle, however, considering that sovereignty belongs only to God and to His Shari'a. Another group argues that there is no need for the notion of popular sovereignty in Islamic thought. This is what many constitutional lawyers have said, for instance 'Abd al-Hamid al-Metwalli.[8]

Without denying the importance of this disagreement, however, one aspect of it is merely formal since it concerns the word "sovereignty" itself [*al-siyada*]. Some accept its use, while others refuse it. Still, all agree that no authority can surpass that of the Shari'a. At that level, one can say that the umma or its representatives possess a kind of sovereignty within the limits of the Shari'a, noting that the statement "sovereignty is indivisible" is not generally accepted. As for the remainder of the dispute's logic, it is very important and it centers on the respective roles of the elite and the masses. Those who defend the leadership role of the elites spare no effort to disparage the masses, whether consciously or not, describing them in a way that is passed down in these circles: the rabble, the populace, the common folk. This tendency also finds support by quoting passages in the Qur'an, the Sunna, and the writings of the Companions, which seem to reject the principles of popular sovereignty, general elections, and the public oath of allegiance, even though these are now firmly established in Muslim political practice.

In contrast to this ancient elitist tendency in Islamic political thought, another tendency has appeared, which rejects and refutes the assertions of the former tendency, while defending the right of the vast majority of the public to political authority, material resources, and culture. These scholars assert that "the entrusted umma" represents all Muslims and that no regime can draw its legitimacy from any other source than all of its people. In essence, this is to praise the vast majority of the people; it is to refuse the rule of the elites and their glorification, to call for general elections, and to affirm the sovereignty and infallibility of the umma—that which it sees as good is good. Did not the Prophet (PBUH) take pride in the fact that many more people followed him than followed any of the previous prophets?

No doubt, through their outlook and work, the advocates for both of these paths have made a definite impact on their respective social contexts, whether in a conservative or progressive vein. It is also possible that it was the difference in their psychological models and social conditions that was a factor in their emergence and persistence over time. Moreover, it is too bad that the second tendency produced so few books and that its advocates found their time and energy taken up much more by leading movements than meditating and writing. And this despite the fact that our society needs revolutionary books more than they need cold water in the summer! Indeed, there is much about this tendency supportive of popular legitimacy that is encouraging as well. Under that rubric, however, one must also include a strong foundation for the principle of decision making by the majority, elections, the concept of citizenship, women sharing in leadership, political pluralism, known as democracy—whether the term itself is accepted or rejected, it makes no difference, as long as we can agree on its content.

This latter tendency, I must say, is growing by virtue of the destructive influence of authoritarianism, which has always been the greatest obstacle for the revival of the umma and the development of the Islamic movement. The umma itself is the greatest victim of tyranny, which is like fallen leaves in the autumn leaving behind them social decay, famines, and greater division—despite the influence of the growing movement worldwide demanding democracy and the demise of dictatorships. Still, all of this contributed to the growth of the democratic tendency in the midst of the Islamic movement, which, in regard to its ideology, has seen its books circulate more and more; and in regard to its practice, it has seen its political experiments in power sharing grow in more than one country. In fact, Islamists have proven on a high level their own maturity and their ability to interact with reality side by side with other opposition parties in a constructive and mutually helpful way. It may be that the Islamists' experiments in Jordan, Yemen, Malaysia, Indonesia, and Turkey—even though for a time their efforts in Egypt, Tunisia, and Algeria were quickly aborted—are living proofs of the flexibility of Islamic thought, its compatibility with democracy, and the pluralism of views within its movement.

So regardless of the validity or otherwise of the view of the principle of the people's sovereignty, the Western concept of mutual contract between ruler and ruled is indeed well-established in Islam, as explicitly stated in the Qur'an: "Those who pledge loyalty to you [Prophet] are actually pledging loyalty to God Himself—God's hand is placed on theirs."[9] We also read in the Qur'an, "Prophet, when believing women come and pledge to you that they will not ascribe any partner to God, nor steal, nor commit adultery, nor kill their children, nor lie about who fathered their children, nor disobey you in any righteous thing, then you should accept their pledge of allegiance."[10] The Islamic state grew historically on the basis of oaths of allegiance, just as the rule of rightly guided caliphs was based on real oaths of allegiance. Later on, even though they were most often formalities, they nevertheless established the legitimacy of the state throughout the history of Islamic nations.

The issue here is not merely imagination or hypothesis; rather, it is about sacred texts and historical facts, and its importance is immense from a political perspective, and especially when it comes to checking authoritarianism. This is not the ruler who begins his tenure as a bequest from his predecessor, or by inheritance from his father, or by alleged divine appointment, or by a coup d'état, or by a bogus election in which he was the only candidate and thereby achieved the magic Arab number of 99.99 percent. Rather, he is the one who begins his political tenure with a free oath of allegiance and a contract by which he commits himself to implement the Shari'a, establish justice and mutual consultation, and be vigilant in steering away from rash decisions and oppression. He who pledges all the above in return for the people's obedience is more likely to remain conscious that his continued rule is conditioned upon him respecting his contract and keeping his people's favor. If the condition is not met, the deal falls through; he loses the right to be obeyed, and all means of resistance to him become legal, as long as they aim to remove him from the caliphate, since his remaining in that position becomes illigitimate.

The issue of the bay'a (oath of allegiance) is not a marginal issue in the creed of Islam, and it cannot be reduced to the relationship between the people and the ruler [imam], or between ruler and ruled; instead, it is the building block of Islamic life, beginning with the relationship between the creature and his Creator, which is a contract that gives validity to all other contracts. That is absolutely the most important of all contracts, since through it the believer testifies in all sincerity and in full awareness of his responsibility that God is One. He thereby commits himself to obey Him in every detail of his life and vows to dedicate his life to that purpose. This, then, is with the hope that his Lord will be pleased with him and let him into His paradise. As God said, "God has purchased the persons and possessions of the believers in return for the Garden"[11]

This covenantal relationship, therefore, is the general framework of human relationships, which recognizes humanity's freedom and responsibility. It also leads to the guardianship of the "people of loosing and binding," which is another kind of contract between the people and their representatives. The latter commit to defending the Shari'a and the interests of those they represent. If they depart from this framework, their guardianship becomes null and void, and this does not have to wait until the next round of elections, as is the case with most of the world's parliamentary regimes when a member of parliament receives the necessary votes to win an election and then breaks off his relationship with the voters—or almost—since he has no need for them, though it is thanks to their votes and efforts that he now occupies this seat, yet his arrogance grows, for this delegate became the representative of all the people of his district, while they remain simple citizens in their remote village. So what in all of this will motivate him to leave the bright city lights and travel to meet these people not just to learn about their situation but also to give them an account of what he has accomplished as part of his program to defend their interests? The length of his tenure is still long and there is still plenty of time, such that when the date for fresh elections draws near, he rediscovers the way to that remote village and deceives its people once again with his sweet talk, in order to regain their votes, which once given, cannot be withdrawn until the end of his mandate, regardless of his actions.

Representatives in today's parliaments, for the most part, are often—to various degrees—isolated from the masses. They are busy tending to their own interests, to the opportunities for increased wealth and influence their status might afford them, and preoccupied with business contracts and media companies. But the right way to understand the contract of bay'a, as the great jurist al-Mawardi explained, is to see it as a binding power of agents, meaning that the members of elected assemblies are not the umma's representatives but those who were mandated by the electorate to represent them in a similar way to power of attorney in private law, and are thus obliged to give an account to those who elected them on a regular basis, and can be removed before the end of their term. In effect, this obligation places the assemblies under the supervision of the electorate, and that is the meaning of the term "mandatory representation," something that Western regimes were careful to avoid, so as to assure the independence of the parliaments vis-à-vis their electorates for the full length of their terms.[12] Indeed, mandatory representation is the essence of democracy which is breaking down of the barriers between rulers and ruled, in contrast to the representative assemblies in the West, which for that reason are much more vulnerable to despotism.[13]

ACCESSIBILITY OF THE PEOPLE'S REPRESENTATIVES

Political power offers its holder a set of privileges whether or not he seeks them. Indeed, they do come to him, as many keys opening money and power become his; and those seeking such keys will inevitably push and shove on his doorstep—some trying to secure a right and some seeking to rob others of their rights and find the easiest way to get what they hope for. All of this, however, can only come by means of the ruler's favor, so it is no wonder that gifts and services pile up on his doorstep, that he is lured away from justice, and that all of this inexorably leads to injustice as one group is favored above another. Then his fear of the rights he has usurped or out of a desire for pomp and prominence, he begins to take distance from the people in the way he lives and relates to them. He thereby ensconces himself in the prison of his palace, which is surrounded by walls and guards armed to the teeth, while he surrounds himself with a band of hypocrites rushing to comply with his every whim.

Thus, with the passing of time, the gulf between him and the people, between his life and their life, including their true concerns, keeps widening. His only contact with their concerns comes through many intermediaries whose personal interests inevitably distort those popular concerns. So luxury corrupts his heart, his entourage dulls his mind, and signs of despotism begin to appear in his personality. Perhaps this is why Islam insists on mixing in with the people; on spending time with the poor and desperate; and on the continual interaction between leaders and the people in the mosques, markets, and other places of worship or activity. The Prophet (PBUH) said, "He whom God has entrusted with some leadership over Muslims, if he turns away from their need, their hardship and their poverty, God will ignore his need, hardship and poverty on the Day of Resurrection."[14] No wonder that the Prophet's house, and then that of the caliphs, was adjacent to the mosque, the center of Muslim life, and this was something Muslims understood very well, to the point that they would complain about a leader to the caliph if he kept away from them one day.

THE PRINCIPLE OF THE SEPARATION OF POWERS

One of the most important guarantees for freedom and protection from injustice that Western thought has contributed to humanity is the separation of powers—legislative, executive, and judiciary. This principle, enunciated by the Englishman John Locke and by the Frenchman Montesquieu in his book *The Spirit of the Laws*, found a great reception and thus circulated widely, as it was used as a weapon in the last two centuries to fight the tyranny of the kings who were monopolizing power. The separation of powers was an effective way to curb the despotic behavior of rulers and distribute their power by establishing some as supervisors over the others, based on the principle that power cannot be checked except by an opposing power.

The first modern constitution to incorporate this principle was the French constitution of 1791.[15] It spread quickly after that to the rest of Europe and beyond, especially in the twentieth century,[16] as a tradition, and sometimes under the pretense of modernity and the fighting of autocracy. That principle can be summarized by the following two rules:

(a) A tripartite division of the state's functions: the executive, the legislative, and the judiciary
(b) A separation between the various bodies fulfilling these functions[17]

The true purpose here for the separation is to render these powers equal, parallel, and independent of one another, so that none of them can seize power or exert it independently, and this is achieved by means of establishing cooperation among them and with each one controlling and regulating the others.

This distribution of the powers regulates the ability of each power (the government and the parliament) to stop the other one at the limit of its mandate—that is, to hinder it from misusing its power. As Montesquieu put it, "power holds power in check." In this way we provide a guarantee for individual rights and freedoms within a framework that is free from despotism and tyranny, which could result from the bringing together of all the powers under one hand that enacts the law and executes it, which means that laws could be made to measure to serve particular interests, thus depriving it of the qualities of universality and neutrality. This is also the reasoning behind the separation between the powers of the judiciary and those of the executive, just as this separation also accomplishes a beneficial division of labor.

A DIFFERENCE IN PERSPECTIVE ON THE SEPARATION OF POWERS

Despite the success shown by this principle's diffusion, wide acceptance, and wide application, it is far from enjoying unanimous approval. It has faced numerous criticisms because the nature of power is like an organic whole, and thus it cannot be divided into parts. Rather, according to this view, it must have a single head that decides and executes who carries all responsibility and is accountable for it to the people, and the idea of separation only serves to obstruct its work and diffuse responsibility, as each power places responsibility upon the other.

The president of a state in a presidential system, or the prime minister in a parliamentary system, is by constitutional mandate the first one responsible for the nation's policies—but how could he be saddled with the responsibility for a political or economic or military defeat when he can only enforce the policies set by the parliament? According to this principle of separation under the presidential system, the president's only prerogative is to bring before the parliament a particular proposed policy and defend it. Then when it is time to vote on his proposal, he withdraws, with his future actions being set by the parliament's decision. Does not any member of parliament have more weight than he, even though he is the one who before the people carries the responsibility for that decision, which is in fact made by others? The system of the separation of powers changes the president into a subordinate and a mere tool of execution, a position that is simply unfair, besides the fact that its objective of putting all powers on an equal footing is wishful thinking. Experience has shown that one of the powers dominates the others by assuming leadership of the state, and that is what sovereignty is—something that is indivisible, according to the common definition. In fact, problems in real life often force governments to go beyond the separation principle.[18]

This principle makes it difficult to identify the person who is truly responsible within the state, and its detractors argue that it has exhausted its aims since it has achieved the one aim for which it was posited—to curb the tyranny of the absolute kings. So people used this principle as a means among others in the fight against absolute monarchy.

Some legal scholars, however, argue that these objections apply to an absolute separation of the powers, whereas the separation of powers in itself does not rule out cooperation among them and mutual regulation or supervision.[19] Historically, the powers of the state were divided according to their functions as far back as Plato and Aristotle—the legislative, executive, and judiciary functions. No one disputes the necessity of the judiciary's independence from both rulers and ruled for the sake of justice, even if judges are considered from an administrative angle as a branch of the executive power. Therefore, talk about the separation of powers, whether from its opponents or its supporters, essentially revolves around the relationship between the executive and the legislative branches.[20]

We can classify regimes based on the extent of cooperation between these two powers. If the power scale tips toward the legislative function, then it is a federal system or confederation, as it is in Switzerland. If the scale tips toward the head of state, then it is a presidential system with a strong division between powers, as is the case in the United States. If there is a balance between the two powers and cooperation without one becoming stronger than the other, then it is a parliamentary system, as in the United Kingdom, even if this balance often tilts in favor of the government which emanates from the parliament's majority.

MODELS FOR THE RELATIONSHIP BETWEEN STATE BRANCHES

The American Model

This is seen as the model presidential system with a strict separation of powers. Thus the legislative branch is alone responsible for legislation, and the executive branch does not have the right to propose laws, nor can it present them or discuss them or even be present in the legislature. The president of the republic may not dissolve the parliament or call it into session, unless in state of emergency. On the other hand, executive power is fully in the hands of the president, having been elected directly by the people. In that quality, he freely appoints and dismisses his ministers, who then are directly accountable to him. The legislative branch may not question the ministers or dismiss them, but it may impeach the president when he commits grave crimes, in which case the senate takes up his trial.

The judges, on the other hand, are independent. They are elected and the courts have the right to supervise the laws that are enacted and forbid the application of laws that go against the constitution.

One of the criticisms leveled against this system is that the strict separation of powers leads to a collision between them. Other criticisms include the president's lack of accountability for his administrative mistakes, and the inability of the legislative body to hold him accountable. It could also lead to a form of dictatorship, a fact that has pushed the branches of government to a certain amount of cooperation.[21] Gradually, this can lead to a presidential system that relies on more cooperation between the branches, like in France where the president of the republic can address the constituent assembly, propose and approve laws, and oppose some as well.

In the same way, the parliament may authorize the president to issue decrees that function as laws, or it may choose a successor to the president in the case of vacancy or incapacity, until new elections are held.[22]

The Model of Federalism: Switzerland

The Swiss Confederation was founded in 1847. All the executive and legislative powers are concentrated in the parliament, which elects seven members for a term of four years. These are the ministers who initiate the executive tasks of the state in conformity with the recommendations made by the parliament, which has the authority to remove them and annul their decisions. The parliament also chooses the Federal Supreme Court, appoints the commander of the armed forces, and declares war. The electorate, however, has the power to oppose any of the parliament's decisions, and if a particular number of citizens oppose a certain law, then it must be put to a referendum.

Despite the parliament's authority to remove members of the Federal Council (members of the government of seven), this is not likely to happen in reality because they have been elected among leaders; and though they are elected for four-year terms, those terms are renewable, and some of them can serve as long as twenty-five years and do not answer to the parliament.[23] They wield, therefore, considerable influence.

A criticism made about this government as council (a plural executive) is that its literal application leads to a weakening of the state's executive branch and sometimes to chaos. Further, the concentration of powers into one body, even an elected one, could also lead to a power grab and tyranny, as it is well known that autocracy on the part of a parliament is a greater danger for individual freedoms than that of the tyranny of kings and dictators. This is because it hides behind a perverse mirage of popular sovereignty and the people's will.

The Parliamentary Model: British Democracy

This model stands out for its flexibility and integration between the executive and legislative branches of government, thus allowing for cooperation between them, yet not a merger of the two, as happens with the Swiss model, nor the extreme separation that occurs in the American model. The British model has been evolving for seven centuries since its establishment in 1295.

The parliament is composed of the House of Commons and the House of Lords. The latter chamber's powers are considered mostly symbolic. Only the most powerful parties are represented in parliament, as the majority system adopted by the electoral law ensures that only the two major parties rotate as leaders of parliament—the Conservative Party and the Labour Party. The difference between the two is more cosmetic rather than substantial, with neither one adhering to a true political ideology. They are the two faces of the same pragmatic and democratic trend, so that one taking the other's place does not change the direction of policies very much, and especially with regard to foreign policy, which may not even be mentioned during election campaigns.[24] The activities of the House of Commons are limited to legislation and oversight by means of questions and answers, and offering votes of no confidence in the government.

As for the legislative function, though it falls under the purview of the parliament, it begins within the precincts of government.

Concerning the relationship between the parliament and the crown, it is strong, since sovereignty belongs to the Queen-in-Parliament, as it is often said.[25] Put otherwise, the parliament has no independent legislative authority, since it has no constitutional right to impose its will on the queen, who has the right to oppose its decisions. Thus laws are enacted by order of Her Majesty the Queen and in her name; it is she who opens each session of parliament. In addition, she has the right of pardon, as she is "the source of justice" and "the source of honor" by granting honorific titles and names important leaders to government, military, and diplomatic functions. She is the supreme commander of the armed forces and the nominal head of the Church of England, but in reality this has only symbolic importance.[26]

As for the parliament's relationship with the executive branch, the prime minister is the highest and most influential political official as the leader of the majority party in the House of Commons, though he names someone else to manage the party while he leads government, appointing and dismissing ministers at will. No piece of legislation is brought forward without his consent. He may also seek the dissolution of parliament (without handing in his own resignation) and make urgent decisions without first consulting with his ministers. The prime minister's great influence once prompted one commentator to exclaim, "General elections are in reality about naming a prime minister." Thus the most important limit to his power is public opinion. This was seen most obviously and dramatically in the war against Iraq.

All the ministers belong to one party, the one in the majority, and as a cohesive whole they are expected to show solidarity in the face of parliament. They are usually members of parliament, and there are around twenty members in the cabinet, though that does not include the total number of ministers.[27]

In view of the expanded influence of the cabinet and its head today, it is difficult to say who rules the United Kingdom. Is it the parliament, or the cabinet, or the prime minister?[28] This is a legitimate question, especially since the House of Lords has no influence and the House of Commons usually approves every law put before it.[29] In the opinion of Harold Wilson, it is the cabinet that rules the United Kingdom today, and it may be true that the British system is undergoing a crisis, like most parliamentary systems, with the balance of power tilted toward the executive branch.[30] This means that the separation between the legislative and executive branches is somewhat theoretical, as long as the prime minister benefits from a majority within his party and his party enjoys a majority within parliament.

The Marxist Model: The Soviet Union

There is no room here for a separation of powers, since the unity of the people requires the unity of political authority.[31] The Supreme Soviet assumed the supreme authority of the state as the state's legislative authority, which was composed of the Soviet of the Union and the Soviet of Nationalities, equal in authority, even though the former, by custom, occupied a higher rank and was composed of the highest leaders and functionaries. The two chambers held a joint session after election and elected the executive committee, called the Presidium of the Supreme Soviet. According to the constitution, it was the Supreme

Soviet that cumulated all the political powers and thus was the holder of sovereignty. In practice, it was the Presidium of the Supreme Soviet that held the actual sovereignty of the state, in that it exercised all three of its functions: executive, legislative, and judiciary. This was in application of the principle of unified authority—that is, the unity of class, thought, and work.[32] The Presidium, then, monitors the executive organs of the state and the courts. As such, it is the state's collective overseer, similar to the collective representative government in Switzerland. It is the true head of the state, even though it is elected by the Supreme Soviet, whose influence almost disappears in practice.

Proponents of the Marxist school justify their rejection of the separation of powers by considering it a middle solution called for by circumstances, a result of the historic struggle between the bourgeoisie and the nobility. This principle then transformed into a deceptive phenomenon of pseudo-democracy, hiding from view the capitalist class's monopoly of power and wealth and its influence at a time when the working class had access to neither. What happens, then, in the name of separation of powers, is that in fact the executive power, which represents the bourgeois minority, monopolizes real power, bringing the legislative under its influence.[33]

The Chinese political system is similar to its Marxist counterpart, as a committee elected by the representative body carries out all the state powers, including the role of overseeing the Council of Ministers, appointing and removing top state functionaries, signing treaties, and mobilizing the military.[34] However, the truth is that the body that rules Marxist regimes in reality is the communist party, and its First Secretary in particular.

The Presidential/Parliamentary Model of the French Fifth Republic

The current French constitution (1958) was penned after a series of upheavals within the French state, during which it experimented with all the systems governing pluralistic democracies. Generally speaking, the government is organized around a head of state who determines the main direction of national policies, while the various government bodies function under his leadership.

The people elect the president of the republic directly, which means that he draws his support from the nation as a whole and exercises his authority directly, or by means of the government, by enacting his policies through his prime minister, ministers, and the majority of the parliament. Moreover, his term of office is seven years, which greatly increases the competition for that position. Another means of reinforcing his power when he feels his popular support has increased is to resort to a consultative referendum, which he can then turn into a poll on people's confidence in him.

In the same way, the legislative elections halfway into his tenure also serve to determine his popularity. If they turn out to be a bad surprise for the president and the majority of the parliament is now in the opposition, then the regime goes into a confrontational mode, even though the constitution gives the president the responsibility of ruling between the various government branches (Article 5).

The president in normal circumstances defines and carries out national policies by means of a majority in parliament (while it lasts), since he is the one who appoints the prime minister, even outside of parliament if necessary, and the ministers, while taking the prime minister's suggestions into account. He can force the government to resign, since it is accountable to him, and he holds the necessary power to make all the important decisions of state, whether in domestic or foreign policy. This is possible although he is not accountable to the parliament, though the government itself is responsible before the parliament, pursuant to Article 49 of the constitution. So if the president of the republic loses his majority in parliament, as happened in 1986, the republic finds itself in a very precarious situation.

The prime minister represents the majority in the parliament and therefore leads his government and determines the nation's policies. He has a great deal of influence over his colleagues. What is more, he is the head of the administration, appointing the civil and military functionaries by delegation from the president and exercising final organizational authority, since Article 34 of the constitution has restricted the scope of Parliament's powers. Finally, because of his majority in the parliament, he is able to ensure adoption of the necessary laws so as to implement his policies.

The authority of the president of the republic is extraordinary, though it is conditioned upon his ability to safeguard a cohesive and stable majority within the parliament so as to buttress his power. But if he loses it, then his regime enters a stage of severe uncertainty, and it could lead to unrest and paralysis.

Through its two chambers the parliament exercises its legislative power, and it is composed of the National Assembly and the Senate. The former is the true legislative body with 490 representatives elected for a term of five years by general and direct suffrage over two rounds. By contrast, the Senate has only one hundred members elected for a term of six years. Every candidate seeking election to either of the two chambers must present another person who would replace him in case of death or a conflict of interests. The parliament normally meets in two yearly sessions, one lasting eighty days beginning in October, and the second lasting ninety days beginning in April.

Through a motion of censure passed by the absolute majority of its representatives, the National Assembly may force the government to resign. At the same time, the Fifth Republic has limited the legislative role of the parliament to specific areas, stating simply that it may accomplish its legislative work, whereas before the definition of the law was that it was the purview of the parliament regardless of the issue at hand. Then came Article 34 of the constitution, which spelled out the specific areas in which it could legislate and those in which it could not. That was to reinforce the government's power, since it was now not just able to propose laws in the organizational domain but also independent statutes.

Additionally, the government by virtue of its majority controls the agenda and the ability to raise the issue of parliamentary draft law proposals overstepping the limits of their jurisdiction. And in the case of disagreement, it raises the issue with Constitutional Council, which then decides. This also means that the opposition rarely has the opportunity to propose laws that go against the government's wishes. The government may also impose the original draft of a project it proposed without taking into account the amendments put in by committees, and it may impose an up-or-down vote on a project as a whole so as to block the path for any possible maneuvering or postponement.

Therefore, even though according to the constitution the parliament is the legislative branch, it is the government that fulfills the actual legislative function in coordination with the parliament.

If the government issues a statute in a particular area that the assembly considers under its jurisdiction, its only path forward is for its members to present it as simple citizens to the Council of State (the administrative court), petitioning its objection to this project of law on the basis that it was not under the government's jurisdiction. But usually the affair will not be settled for a long time, and thus in the relationship between the government and the parliament, the balance here tilts toward the government.

Clearly, then, the political system of France's Fifth Republic seems to be a presidential one, since it loses its balance of power in favor of the executive branch, and of the president in particular. This system, however, fails to achieve the necessary stability, coherence, and harmony between its institutions, because of the futile and sometimes dishonest nature of trying to combine a presidential and parliamentary system. This is why many see this political system as muddled and ambiguous, though leaning more toward the presidential system. This is because it places the president of the republic in a higher position since he is not accountable to the parliament and has the right to dissolve it, though he cannot shirk his political responsibility by virtue of his being almost the only true holder of power in the eyes of the electorate who make the final call on his policies by renewing or not his mandate at the polls. That said, if he finds himself in a serious disagreement with the parliament, he can dissolve it. Still, he has to wait a year before dissolving the new parliament, though he may also raise the issue of disagreement with the people through a referendum. All of this reinforces the presidential character of France's Fifth Republic, which still retains the imprint of its strong initial leader, General De Gaulle.

As for public liberties, they are entrusted to many agencies, like the commission for the constitutional oversight of the laws [*Conseil Constitutionnel*], the Council of State [*Conseil d'Etat*]), the political parties, and the press, even though the power of money weighs heavily on all of them. The press is only restricted by its duty to avoid slander and not violate the public norms of society, like not heaping scorn on the president or publishing false reports, which could harm the army or people's trust in general, and the like.

The same goes for political parties and associations, which are free as long as they do not break the law or public norms, undermine the republican system, or engage in violence. They must respect the principles of popular sovereignty (Article 4).

In sum, as opposed to the system of government as council in Switzerland and the regimes in socialist or Marxist countries, though it espouses the principle of the separation of powers like most of the Western regimes, the Fifth Republic political system has endeavored with partial success to bring harmony to the relationship between the legislative and executive branches. This is so, because the balance of power tilts toward the president and creates a dysfunctional political life. Against a backdrop of past experimentation and years of instability, this system reveals a distance between the system's ideal—the separation of powers on the basis of balance and equality—and its practical application, according to which the president's great influence allows him to make the final decision on laws, to submit them to referendum, to dissolve the parliament, and to call for new elections.

We have seen, therefore, that the political systems that adopt the principle of the separation of powers generate, for the most part, inbalances, intrigues, and continual conflict, and end up with a dominant executive branch—even in the case of parliamentary systems.

It is important to note that despite the above-mentioned flaws of the principle of the separation of powers, the importance of this principle can be discerned from its antithesis—merging all powers and entrusting them to one person which leads to unlimited hegemony and eventually authoritarianism. Instead, one could reduce the pressure of separating these powers and achieve a level of cooperation and mutual supervision. However, even if one succeeds at softening this separation principle, it nevertheless carries with its Western origins and the circumstances of its emergence a certain tension that is hard to eliminate. That tension comes from this central idea in Western thought—namely, that democracy cannot be achieved without a society based on pluralism with different and conflicting interests and that the greatest threat to democracy, then, is when a majority is formed that remains constant, resting on a stable foundation. That poses a real danger to equality, especially because that clash between rich and poor, strong and weak, believer and atheist offers a continuous and fertile dynamism for society to prevent a dictatorship of the majority.

As a result, there is no escaping the necessity of muzzling these religious convictions in order to prevent the constant formation of blocks in society. Rather, these must be dismantled so that society remains divided into a large number of parties, interests, and classes,[35] for that is the best guarantee for freedom and democracy—and the separation of powers comes as a legal instrument spawned by the same intellectual tradition. This is seen in the idea of constant conflict which holds that freedoms and rights can only be guaranteed by the tearing apart of society and the establishment of institutions competing with each other and seeking to limit each other's influence; otherwise, they will unite and oppress the people.

Marxism's critique of this separation-of-powers principle, and the political model that it develops, which is based on uniting these powers, is the best propaganda for the separation of powers. However, has the principle of separation—in the places where it has been applied—been able to safeguard the right to equality, to nourish a humanitarian spirit, and to prevent a powerful minority from establishing dictatorship and compromising the interests of the majority, forcing them into wars, usurping their wealth, misleading and misinforming them, and spreading unity in order to control them?

In truth, the Western models, generally speaking, only reflect the conflict latent in their societies, the materialist philosophy, and the philosophy of humanity in rebellion against its Creator. And as long as this state of affairs endures, as long as it lacks a true human content and its solutions are focused on exterior forms of social and political organization, this political problem will never be resolved, whether it decides on separating powers or uniting them, since the issue is more about philosophy than social organization.

So what is the position of Islamic thought on the separation of powers principle?

THE RELATIONSHIPS BETWEEN THE BRANCHES OF THE ISLAMIC STATE

The previous section offered a relatively clear picture of how the relationship between the branches of the Western state is defined and worked out in practice.

To sum up, the separation between these powers is either rigid, as in the case of the presidential system, or it leans toward cooperation, as in the case of the parliamentary system, yet with two possible directions. In the first case, power tilts toward the executive branch represented in the head of state; in the second, it tilts toward the prime minister. Alternatively, the powers are merged, as is the case with a pluralistic Western democracy like Switzerland, whose government is a representative council, or the government is framed ideologically around a party, as is the case in the Marxist regimes. We also mentioned the historical circumstances and some of the cultural values behind this separation-of-powers principle, like the value placed on conflict (or competition).

All of this was a prelude to our discussion of the relationship between the various parts of the state from an Islamic perspective. Clearly, for the Islamic system to remain "Islamic," it can never stray from the principles of tawhid or shura, which leads to the establishment of a common foundation of ideas, values, goals, and interests between individuals and institutions—all of which firmly establish among them brotherhood, cooperation, and mutual affection, while preventing any difference of opinion from becoming a source of conflict, mutual recrimination, and rancor. For the society of believers is one of brotherhood, and it rests upon the pillar of faith and finds support in the brotherhood of citizens and the brotherhood of humankind.

The rule that power can only be checked by another power is valid, yet insufficient to curb people's seeking personal interests or their instincts of opportunism and selfishness—and must be supplemented by intellectual, moral, and creedal principles, which must then be implemented through educational methods. Such an education is rooted in the belief of God's omnipresence and knowledge,[36] which endows the human person with inner restraint and lessens the need for the intervention of this worldly authority in a person's life. Put otherwise, the first guarantee for public liberties in an Islamic society is the fear of God (may He be exalted) in private and in public, a vying with others to please Him and one's preparation to meet Him. It is not primarily the establishment of competing forces in the social and political systems so as to prevent any one force from arbitrarily oppressing others, though that is important, since as it is said, God (may He be exalted) restrains through the political order what He does not restrain through the Qur'an. So the intervention of a just political authority in order to prevent individuals and groups from oppressing others is the exception, not the rule. That is the Islamic paradigm, and not simply a rule that keeps various powers in check, exactly as is the case with international peace, which has no guarantee but a frightening balance between the great powers. In fact, that is an "armed peace."

Individual rights and freedoms, according to the Islamic perspective, have no other source but the Creator and His Shari'a. They have no greater guarantee but the continuing divine presence within people's consciences and lives. Obedience by individuals or by those in authority is then out of obedience to God, love for Him, and fear of His painful punishment. Thus the restraint, as Ibn Khaldun said, must come from within.[37] So if faith's restraining power grows feeble and spiritual formation weakens in people's lives, then public opinion begins to stir, unsheathing the weapon of commanding good and forbidding evil, with no difference between old and young, ruler or ruled, for everyone is everyone else's guardian. As the hadith goes, "You are all shepherds and responsible over your flock."[38]

The mere existence of a legislative or judicial authority is not enough to keep a Muslim head of state from abusing his power, even if they were able to legally play their role of supervising him.[39] Even then, he might succeed in manipulating one of them, or getting one to dominate the other, or in manipulating both of them. This is proven by the fact that the principle of the separation of powers is recognized in most of our countries and written into their constitutions. Nevertheless, the blood of the innocent is spilled with impunity, and oppression and exploitation are rampant, nor has the separation of powers in the most established Western democracies stopped them from orchestrating the subjugation and exploitation of nations and from supporting the rule of tyrants everywhere. And within the West itself, the separation principle did not curb all three branches of the American government from colluding in a long-term campaign to eliminate North America's indigenous peoples. Further, an even more vicious war has been waged against all the elements that bring balance to our environment, to such an extent that it threatens life on this planet. One can find innumerable examples of governments in the East or the West proclaiming the separation of powers as one of the means to curb despotism. Does this mean that the principles and values of Islam forbid this model of separation between powers in the Islamic state?

The Supporters of Separation

We should say from the start that there is nothing explicit in Islam's sacred texts to definitively forbid using the principle of the separation of powers, and for that reason a good number of contemporary Islamic thinkers do not hesitate to affirm this principle. Either using the principle of basic permissibility (that is, the rule that all actions are permitted unless expressly forbidden in the sacred texts), or using the principle of common benefit [*maslaha*], as separation represents one of the guarantees against the concentration of power that usually leads to autocracy and nothing here contradicts the experience we know of politics during the Prophetic or Rightly Guided Caliphs periods, during which the Prophet (PBUH) and his caliphs exercised legislative, judicial, and executive power, with some of them even delegating some of those powers to others—none of this amounts to a faith in the necessity of the separation of powers. Rather, it has more to do with dividing up the workload or separating tasks, something more practical than on the level of principle. In fact, they sought advice from the council of scholars, just as they appointed judges and relied on them.[40] However, after their appointment they remained independent and no one was outside the scope of the judgment, including the caliph himself, for he was accountable before the judges and was treated just like all the other state functionaries. As the exercise of political power became more complicated after the initial period, the ruler distributed the various functions. The Islamic scholars and jurists specialized in the deductive task of enacting new laws in addition to being in charge of the judiciary. The executive powers remained in the hands of the ruler.

Despite the fact that the head of state was responsible for all the branches of government, either by exercising those powers directly or by delegating some to others, this does not mean that the separation of powers should be shunned today when human societies have become so much more complex. In fact, according to many contemporary Islamists, nothing prevents using this principle of separation between the powers as a means to protect civil liberties and guarantee people's rights, which is one of Islam's objectives. There is nothing, then, about this idea that contradicts the basic principles of Islam.[41] Though there is some caution or hesitation about separating the two powers of the legislative and executive branches, there is a consensus here nevertheless on the necessity to keep the judiciary independent in the Islamic state as a monitor extending its supervision over everything. No one is immune from this judiciary's jurisdiction, except in the case when a person refrains from anything forbidden by God.

Still, the defenders of this position go even further, since they affirm not only the permissibility of adopting this principle as an administrative procedure invented by and borrowed from the Western experience, but that it constitutes an original feature of the Islamic state from both a theoretical and a practical viewpoint, to the extent that it would be true to say that Muslims were the first to espouse this principle of separation. This is so, because original legislative power belonged to the Shari'a—that is, revelation in the Qur'an and the Sunna. As for the authority to apply the principles of the sacred texts to reality, this was entrusted to the scholars of Islam and to those capable of ijtihad, who are not under the state's control. The state, therefore, in the area of legislation is merely the enforcer of those laws.

As to the Shura Council, according to this perspective, it is a political assembly that defines the state's general policies, but without any legislative role in the sense of interpreting and applying religious norms [ijtihad]. Thus throughout Islamic history, the state was deprived of legislative power, which placed limits on its power.[42] And even in the model of an elected Shura Council representing various sectors of society exercising a legislative role using ijtihad, it is possible to ascertain its commitment to the supreme authority of the Shari'a by the monitoring function of a constitutional court or a supreme court, which are both staffed by eminent jurists who can determine whether laws conform or not to the constitution.

The Opponents of the Relationship of Separation

The legislative, executive, and judicial functions of the state were clearly delineated during the Prophet's rule and that of the Rightly Guided Caliphs. When someone proposed to the caliph an issue that was not covered in a decisive way by the texts or had to do with finding a political solution to the state's policies, he would consult "the people of loosing and binding" from among the scholarly Companions or those with experience, and discuss the matter further. And if the right solution became clear, he would follow it. When the caliph appointed someone as judge, he would not intervene in his work nor overturn his judgment, since the Shari'a offers no constitutional rule that obliges us to combine in the person of the ruler the functions of chief judge and chief executive of the state.[43] Nevertheless, those who study the period of the Rightly Guided Caliphs discover that the head of state was clearly the one truly responsible for the affairs of state, and that he had to conduct them in consultation with "the people of loosing and binding," since as long as the umma had chosen him to lead it, he was responsible for the totality of public affairs, and for that reason there could be no complete separation within the Islamic state—according to Muhammad Asad—between its legislative and executive functions. This according to him was one of the most important principles that Islam brought to political thought.[44]

If the principle of separation in the Western state has shown some advantages, in that it makes the parliament representative of the people's sovereignty and grants it power to oversee the executive branch, nevertheless this separation often turns into a factor that impedes, obstructs, and slows down the state apparatus, robbing it of flexibility and effectiveness, especially in times of crisis. Islam follows the middle path, as can be seen in the opinion of Professor Asad, when he writes that the president independently leads the executive power and leads the Shura Council or delegates someone to do that. So in our state we avoid the crippling Western duality within the state apparatus, he adds, and we purify our system from the problem of conflict—a central tenet of the Western political thought and practice. We thereby achieve a level of cooperation between the executive and legislative branches through the emir's leadership over the Shura Council, a cooperative relationship that flows out of the principle of God's unity [tawhid].

Moreover, if one studies the Prophet's sayings on the topic of the emirate,[45] a picture emerges of a head of state in whose person is concentrated the ultimate responsibility, and obedience to him is part of obedience to God and His Messenger (PBUH), as long as he remains committed to following the Shari'a, so that the citizen of that state feels no oscillation or duality within the government. Thus there is only one authority that the citizen is called to obey, and he is either called the amir or imam: "He who obeys me, obeys God, and he who rebels against me, rebels against God. And he who obeys the amir, obeys me, and he who rebels against the emir, rebels against me. For the amir is like a shield when they fight, for he protects them."[46] Also, with "Indeed each of you is a shepherd and is responsible over his flock. In the same way the imam is the shepherd with responsibility for his people."[47] And then, "If anyone pledges allegiance to an imam, giving him the grasp of his hand and sincerity of his heart, then he should obey him to the best of his capacity. If another comes to seek his position, strike his neck."[48] In the words of Muhammad Asad:

> The Muslim, therefore, is duty bound to pledge his submission and obedience to his ruler so that he will not die the death of one without faith; he must shake his hand in support and give him his heartfelt allegiance, pledging obedience, help, and the spending of his money and effort in response to his demands. He is also bound to devote himself to God by working under a particular leader. Now, can this leadership—that is, the emirate—be an institution composed of several authorities? Does this Muslim then pledge his allegiance to all of them, dividing his attention among them, so that for legal issues he obeys the Shura Council, and for executive orders he obeys the head of state? Or does he pledge his allegiance to one person who represents the whole institution, over every part of which he is the supreme leader? In fact, the members of all state institutions, including the legislative and judiciary, are bound to pledge to him their allegiance and obedience.[49]

Our umma would find itself in a peculiar situation the case of separation of state powers, especially in the parliamentary system. Because the people elected the amir to manage the state's administration, conversely he will discover that the power of his aides, the ministers, does not emanate from his authority, since they draw it from the legislative body that approved them. On the other hand, he will discover another power completely outside of him, in which he has no part. Its orders and decisions come his way, and he can only obey them. So who is responsible, then, for the top leadership over the affairs of state, and how does this fit in with the model of the amir entrusted with supreme authority, as was expressed in the above hadiths? Will this ever amount to the elements of the pledge of allegiance to the leader thus described—giving the hand of support and the fruit of the heart, the sacrifice of self and wealth, and the most heartfelt obedience within the limits of Shari'a? Will he pledge his allegiance to a person or to an institution, or to a plurality composed of different powers? Do the texts on the emirate clearly direct this allegiance to a person, the head of state, or to his helpers? And how does the Muslim commit himself to that person in submission and obedience, while the latter is also expected to commit to obey another body, the legislative assembly, in which he has no right to participate, if we are talking about the presidential system?

In truth, this perspective does not fit within the Islamic conception of the emirate. It only agrees with a perspective that locates the people's sovereignty within the parliament, so that the head of state in that case does not represent the people but the parliament. Or the president is accountable to the people, but only for the powers over which he has control, a fact that does not fit with the unity of the emirate principle, that is, the unity of the commanding and forbidding function of the state, which guarantees the movement of the state as a whole in the same direction and makes the umma stand before one person, whom it can hold accountable, support, or remove. All others are aides to him. Furthermore, he represents the umma or the people of the state by virtue of being elected by them. In other words, he represents the executive branch through directly overseeing it, and also the legislative branch through his membership in the parliament and his supervision over it, though he is bound to submit to its consensus and majority opinion at the same time.

The Philosophy of Islamic Rule and the Issue of the Separation of Powers

On this topic we will look at three different positions and then offer our own solution to the problem.

Hani Ahmad al-Dardiri's Position

Dardiri deals with the issue of the separation of the powers in his study of the Islamic conception of the state, arguing that the purpose of Islamic rule is to apply the Shari'a, and no problem relative to Islamic government can be solved without this purpose staying at the forefront of one's thinking at all times. This is so, because the organs of the state are nothing but instruments to achieve this purpose. But what does "applying Shari'a" mean? It includes:

- Applying the decisive and incontrovertible texts of proven authenticity and explicit meaning
- Identifying the essence of differences in opinion regarding texts and rulings that do not have conclusive authenticity of understanding
- Following the rule of public benefit [maslaha]

With regard to applying the decisive and incontrovertible texts from the Qur'an or the Sunna, or a matter of consensus that has been consistently reported, like the "eighty" in this verse, "As for those who accuse chaste women of fornication, and they fail to provide four witnesses, strike them eighty times."[50] And like "never" in the following verse, "It is not right for you to offend God's Messenger, just as you should never marry his wives after him."[51] Also, on not equating selling and usury, "God has allowed trade and forbidden usury."[52]

These and similar verses make it incumbent upon the Muslim ruler to apply them without the need to prove public benefit. He should not consult anybody in the matter, as a ruler cannot be considered an Islamic ruler if he refrained from applying these statutes, and needing to justify them or consult over them is akin to justifying God's sovereignty or needing to justify the Islamic testimony. "There is no god but Allah." Indeed, these texts do not need the authority of a "legislative" body but rather await an enforcement authority that believes in them and sets out to apply them with faithfulness and resolve.

Now, about the texts subject to various opinions, whether they are not of conclusively proven authenticity like hadiths with a single chain of narration or without a single explicit meaning, there is a wide scope for investigating, deducing, and exploring how public benefit might apply to them, as long as the goal is not to deny or suspend the texts. Hence, unlike the preceding texts, these texts require both an executive authority and an authority for exercising interpretation [ijtihad] in order to determine the appropriate ruling that achieves public interest. It is also possible to suspend the application of such texts on the basis of public benefit.

Finally, as for the promotion of public benefit, this criterion offers a wide scope for interpretation and ijtihad in a wide range of domains and activities. Examples would be laws to regulate traffic on public roads and the entry and departure of people from one's country. This area needs two agencies—one to determine public utility and the other one seeking to achieve it.

In sum, if the centerpiece of Islamic political philosophy is the application of Shari'a, and if Shari'a is composed of clear and definitive texts, of texts subject to interpretation, and of issues of public interest not specified in the texts; if the clear and definitive texts need only an authority to enforce them, while the issues related to the debatable texts and public utility have to be weighed by another authority that we called "the acceptable authority by Shariʻa standards"— if all those elements are in place, then the lead goes to the enforcing authority as the first political authority, since it is the sole authority concerned with ap- plying the clear texts, while also sharing with the other (interpretive) authority responsibility over the non-conclusive texts.

It follows that according to Dardiri the powers in the Islamic state are two in number: *the executive branch*, which endeavors to apply the clear and definitive texts, as well as the debatable ones and the issues of public interest, whether it be via administrative procedure or via dispute resolution and the judiciary; and a second branch (legislative), which assists in discovering the most appropriate way of interpreting and applying the texts open to discussion and discovering elements of public utility where the texts are silent. Leaning on both of these powers, the Islamic state takes responsibility for safeguarding religious affairs and for managing this-worldly affairs in a way that conforms to the requirements of Divine Law, both with regard to domestic policy and to its commitment to spread Islam internationally, according to Dardiri.[53] And if this endeavor is the state's mission to establish Islam domestically and internationally, then clearly this will to some extent require a rather centralized leadership to enable it to take advantage of opportune times, which might be lost opportunities under the pressure of extended negotiations between the two branches.

It has been said that "only power can check another power."[54] We agree, but if the authority of the caliph and his ministers and his governors swerves from its prescribed path, it can be corrected by the authority in the hands of all Muslims, and those capable of ijtihad can explain the issue to the masses. And if the ca- liph goes astray, the presence of a group that monitors him and takes away some of his privileges in order to hold him in check will never work. By contrast, to have all of public opinion involved in this issue will be very effective, especially if public opinion is the executive and administrative body that the ruler leans upon for his domestic policy, while also being the army used in foreign wars. So if the ruler strays from God's law, then the duty of commanding good and for- bidding evil would at the very least require citizens to refuse to execute orders.

Further, in order to become effective in this task of popular oversight, there is no reason why public opinion cannot arm itself with appropriate con- temporary means of communication and enlist the help of trade unions, and professional and political organizations. It is also possible to limit the ruler's term to a specific limit in order to ensure that the executive authority stays on track. If, then, the ruler errs in a flagrant way, public opinion will depose him by means of the Shura Council, and he will experience a crushing defeat in the next round of elections.

There is nothing strange about this, for if we want to establish a society that is strong and superior to other societies of our time, this will not happen by means of a collection of competing powers. Rather, it will be accomplished by means of a good religious doctrine, a just set of laws, and strong, enlightened public opinion. Yet the consultative process need not become a straitjacket for the caliph and his ministers but rather a support in their task of safeguarding the affairs of religion and managing this-worldly affairs in light of the Shari'a. Thus there is nothing to prevent the assigning to the legislative body the task of enacting laws, so long as it does not stand in the way of its recognizing the somewhat superior authority of the enforcement authority.

Hani al-Dardari ends his discussion of the state powers with this recommendation:

> For the revival of our umma will not happen by adopting political systems that emerged under circumstances that were not in line with our history, and in the end they produced systems that perhaps do not conform to our message in this life of "jihad." I use that expression despite all the efforts of the spiritually defeated and the doctrinally deficient to invent for Muslims a religious message devoid of this jihad for the sake of God[55] . . .
>
> Islam neither imposes a separation nor a merging of political powers into one. Rather, it calls for a blending between the two powers and then cooperation for the aim of raising God's word and the authority of the caliph chosen by the Muslims and to whom they have pledged their allegiance. They have done so because of the conditions approved by Islam so that he may be freed from any fear but the fear of God (may He be praised and exalted) and seek the help of mutual consultation as a weapon for him to wield—and not a weapon against him. Thus he will fulfill the mission of the Islamic state, which is the jihad in God's path.[56]

The Position of the Martyr 'Abd al-Qadir al-'Awda

For him there are five powers (or authorities) in the Islamic state—executive, legislative, judiciary, financial, and that of monitoring and correcting.

Executive authority: In Islam the imam is basically the head of state, the administrator of its affairs, and the first person responsible for its actions. This responsibility has no limits except those set by God's law. The imam, as entrusted with this responsibility in full, lays out the policies of the state, oversees their execution, and has control over all the state's initiatives and outcomes. The imam seeks help from his ministers, but they are accountable to him as his delegates. He appoints them and deposes them at will.

Legislative authority: If the Shari'a has granted the rulers among the umma the right to legislate, it has also commanded them to carefully follow the Shari'a's texts, its general principles, and legislative spirit, which obliges them to engage in two sorts of legislation.

The first kind consists of executive statutes—that is, guaranteeing the enforcement of the Shari'a's texts. This sort of legislation is basically similar to the regulations and decisions made today by ministers within their own area of responsibility.

The second sort consists of organizational statutes, which aim to organize society and protect it. This kind may only be in areas about which the Shari'a is silent and on matters about which there are no specific texts. Still, these statutes must always agree with the Shari'a and its spirit; otherwise, they will be in vain and no one should enforce or obey them. Only the imam has the right to exercise legislative authority with regard to the executive statutes, because they are considered truly executive actions, though clothed in legislative garb.

In other matters, the imam exercises legislative authority in collaboration with the "people of shura." While they are the ones responsible for issuing legislation, the imam remains independent in his executive capacity to enforce it.

Judicial authority: Its mission is to spread justice among the people. Even if the imam appoints judges as the people's delegates since he has been delegated by the people, once they are appointed, they are considered as primarily delegated by the umma. That gives them independent authority emanating from the umma, and no one may question their judgment but God. The imam has no right to pardon crimes the punishment of which are stipulated in the texts, and he himself has the same responsibility as any other citizen before the law, as the Shari'a's punishments [hudud] and anything else in its texts apply to him as well, to which the judges may subject him, on behalf of the umma.

The highest objective of Islam is justice, so there is no reason why we cannot adopt any of the administrative procedures elaborated elsewhere, and in particular those that entail higher conditions of justice in court proceedings, like a trial by jury instead of a decision by one person, which also incorporates the principle of mutual consultation. Another aspect which may be adopted is court rulings on several levels such as trial, appeal, etc. This is instead of the traditional Islamic procedure of an individual judgment and only one level of proceedings. Add to this modern high courts, in which the judges are freely elected with limited terms of service so that they can manage their affairs in complete independence from the executive branch.

Islamic history offers remarkable examples of the fairness of judges, of their neutrality and power. They have the right to monitor the legitimacy of laws that are passed by the consultative bodies and the executive's regulatory statutes.

Financial authority: This is an independent power invented by Islam, as the Prophet himself (PBUH) appointed administrative agents, judges, and civil servants to manage charitable giving [*al-sadaqat*], collecting them from the rich and giving them back to the poor, with the remainder going into the treasury [*bayt al-mal*]. Their influence increased as the state expanded and it began to include the collection of taxes on tribute and booty, land taxes and poll taxes, which they would distribute according to Shari'a stipulations.[57]

The imam as the people's delegate supervises these people's work. He appoints them and dismisses them. Yet they alone were responsible for their work, and no one had authority over them, except for God and the Shari'a texts, and the laws enacted by the legislative bodies.

Monitoring and correcting authority: This is a power given to the umma, since it must supervise the rulers and correct them in its discharging of the duty to command the good and prohibit evil. Indeed, the people are the source of the rulers' power, since they are the people's delegates and are responsible before them. "If I do what is right, help me, and if I stray, correct me," the first caliph said, and such was the attitude of his three successors, as they emphasized the cardinal rule of Islamic polity—namely, rulers are accountable to the umma and its sovereignty over them unfolds under the supreme sovereignty of God.[58]

The Position of Professor Sobhi 'Abduh Sa'id

In his work on state powers, Sobhi 'Abduh Sa'id has emphasized a very strong link between authority and responsibility. There can be no authority or power without responsibility, and no responsibility without authority and power. The Islamic ruler cannot be a mere symbol of the state as is the case of a monarch or a president in parliamentary regimes; nor is he like those heads of state whose constitutions grant them immunity from criminal and civil prosecution. Instead, the ruler from an Islamic perspective rules sovereignly and yet carries the same responsibility as any individual in that state. He holds no immunity nor does he stand above the law.

For that reason, he accumulates all the state functions: legislative [ijtihad], executing policies and running the judiciary branch, except that he does not monopolize those powers without relying on others to assist him, which would lead to autocracy. Rather, he accumulates all the functions of state, taking responsibility for them without monopolizing them, and he delegates the carrying out of those official duties to others who help him, while he monitors their work.

Thus according to Sobhi Abduh, the relationship between the various state bodies in Islam rests on a totally different foundation than that of any other regime. It begins with the comprehensive nature of the ruler's authority and of his responsibility for applying God's law and manifesting His objectives. Moreover, his distribution of these powers among numerous institutions all tasked with the application of God's Shari'a does not mean they are divorced from one another. To the contrary, they all depend on one another, because political rule in Islam is constrained by God's Shari'a and is not autonomous, while in Western nations, where lawmaking is the people's prerogative through their representatives in the legislature, the legislative body naturally rises above all other bodies.[59]

Meanwhile, Islamic political power in all of its institutions is essentially executive by nature. A similar opinion is also held by Shaykh Taqi al-Din al-Nabhani in his constitution:

(Article 29): The head of state is delegated by the umma with the authority to enforce God's Law.

(Article 40): The head of state holds all the state's prerogatives: a) he enacts the Shari'a statutes when he deems them applicable; b) he appoints and dismisses the judges; c) he appoints and dismisses his aides and governors.[60]

Our position is that the debate about the state's power is not about numbers and functions but rather about the relation between the powers. Is the relationship a strict division, as in presidential regimes? Or is the relationship a lighter division and one of cooperation, as happens in parliamentary regimes, along with the supremacy of the legislative bodies from a constitutional viewpoint? Or is the relationship one of merging, as in the politically pluralistic model of executive power (Switzerland) or in the autocratic model (Russia)? As for the independence of the judiciary, that is not a matter up for debate, but rather a principle that needs to be affirmed. Also, there is no immunity for anyone in the Islamic state, rather the affirmation of each person's respect for the law, ruler or ruled.

First, there is no clear and definitive Islamic text to support any of the above choices. This means that this issue is amenable to several interpretations [*ijtihadat*], with the proviso that the supreme legislative authority is God's through the Qur'an and Sunna.

Second, one must keep in mind that whatever the nature of the relationsip between the various powers, be it full separation, partial separation, or merging, the notion of struggle between state powers must be completely set aside in favor of a cooperative, mutually supportive model, which is the model for all human relationships, as we read in the Qu'ran, "Help one another do what is right and good."[61]

Third, one must take into consideration, while trying to answer this question and other matters of constitutional jurisprudence, the status of the community for which one wishes to organize the various powers within the state. Is this status one of stability or not? And is the context in which state duties must be accomplished one of peace or belligerence? For there is no doubt that the need to centralize powers will be much less in a secure, stable community, than in one that is unstable or at war.

Fourth, the principle of separation that is used in the West has to do with whole communities—that is, the state, and not partial communities like political parties, which are bound together by an ideology or methodology, so that there is no place for establishing a distinction between a legislative and an executive branch, since the converse might introduce an element of dissension within a community trying to defend its unified program. What is needed in such a case, instead, is a stratification within the group, with various levels each possessing both legislative and executive duties.[62]

Fifth, although Islamic principles taken as a whole together with Islam's values and historical applications point to a recognition of diversity, as we read in the Qur'an, "But they continue to have their differences, except those on whom your Lord has mercy"[63] and prescribed the principle of mutual consultation to deal with diversity of interpretations within the framework of the Shari'a, nevertheless it strongly refuses and resists the principle of conflict between Muslims as individuals and communities. It calls them to unity on the basis of creed and as social groupings, as we read in the Qur'an, "The believers are brothers,"[64] and the hadith, "People are partners in three things."

Sixth, the same principle enjoins Muslims to gather as one and their leaders to resolutely fight conflict that seeks to impose transgression by force, "if one of the [the two groups] oppresses the other, fight the oppressors until they submit to God's command."[65]

Seventh, though Muslims today are in desperate need to resist political despotism and economic exploitation and to revive the Islamic spirit of mutual consultation so that it becomes a consistent path they follow in their lives, this still has to be accomplished according to Islamic criteria and as an expression of the Islamic spirit, avoiding as much as possible imitating conflicting external influences. In fact, this must be one of the objectives of Islamic constitutional thought—a commitment to preserve the independence of the umma's character and avoid imitating other nations' worldviews with all the different methodologies they entail, except for what is wise, for we are deserving of it.

Nevertheless, the need Muslims have to affirm mutual consultation and fight tyranny should not detract them from their need for unity of stance and for the unity and strength of their leadership, so that it may fulfill all its duties of jihad, instruction, and showing compassion. All this requires a leadership that is quick to respond, effective and flexible in its organization of the state. There is no way this can be achieved with a strict separation of powers within the state, especially when this separation is rejected by Islamic values and objectives, like that of Divine Unity and brotherhood, the oath of allegiance, and the unity of public responsibility.

In fact, when this principle of strict separation between state powers, and especially the extreme kind, contradicts Islamic perspectives and values, such as the legislative body's oath of allegiance and obedience to the emir, for instance, since according to the principle of separation roles are switched and the head of state now becomes answerable to the parliament. Strict separation also contradicts the general oath of obedience between the umma and the leader, since, according to this principle and the resulting strengthening of the legislative body's role, it is the parliament that is granted the state's highest authority and not the amir or head of state. In that case, he becomes answerable to the parliament and not to the people, and the public oath of allegiance loses its constitutional meaning and becomes just a formal ceremony. Thus we end up considering the head of state as a mere symbol of the state's oneness and no longer truly accountable to the people.

Still, there is not one of the Islamic political scholars who has permitted such a Western perspective on the head of the Muslim state, and there is no text revealed by God and no precedent from the time of the Rightly Guided Caliphs to this effect. This problem could be solved, however, if a constitution specified for every state body specific function and powers, then it would swear an oath of allegiance to the umma, whereby it pledges its obedience to God and His Messenger (PBUH), upholds the constitution, respects the people's will, and abides by mutual consultation.

Eighth, the principle of separation of powers is linked in the West to specific historical circumstances—namely, the struggle to limit the tyranny of the kings. And even if in the West a considerable limitation of the powers of kings and rulers for the benefit of the people has been achieved, we should not lay hold of this principle in a mechanical way and declare that it was specific constitutional principles that achieved this, when in fact it goes back essentially to an intellectual revolution that took place over a long period of time and that removed from the Western people's psyche a host of intellectual and psychological obstacles, and helped them regain their confidence as the center of the world and the source of political power.

Yet if specific techniques were enough for limiting despotism, all of the world's nations, most of which have adopted this idea of the separation of powers would have been immune from despotism. But the matter is more complex than that. Conversely if the separation of powers were necessary to counter any level of autocracy, then the Swiss system, for instance, would be rife with despotism since it has no separation which is not the case in reality.

And finally, ninth, as we have said previously, the separation of powers is a theoretical principle, which cannot really be applied, since as soon as work begins within any economic, political, or cultural institution, all the actors start to compete for leadership. Then either one of these forces succeeds in this and becomes the leader, and goes on to lead using a consultative or an autocratic style of leadership; or weakness and instability spreads within the institution, and subsequently it loses momentum and its efforts go to waste through competition and strife.

In fact, so many efforts in the West are wasted by the struggle between the powers, so that countries remain for months and even years without a presidency or ministry. And sometimes as soon as they succeed in finding a solution to their dilemma, government falls apart, because confidence is withdrawn from one of its ministers, or one of the parties in the coalition pulls out.

Western democracy is nothing but an attempt to tame the conflict between powers so that it can be contained without exploding.[66] What is more, Westerners entered a phase after World War II when parliamentary systems mostly gave way to presidential ones, and within several of them the pendulum swung in favor of the executive branch. Moreover, even in parliamentary systems the separation of powers is not strict, and is often merely formal, especially when the government is formed by a majority party whose members are also in the parliament.

Neither should we forget the pluralistic nature of Western regimes, which lessens a great deal the problem of the separation of powers and even turns it into a mere formality in most cases. This is so, because the president in presidential systems, or the prime minister in parliamentary systems, represents the party with a majority in parliament, which means that the parliament acts mostly as a rubber stamp for the projects initiated by the government run by the majority. By contrast, even if the Islamic system of governance recognizes pluralism, it avoids conflict on the level of creed and fundamental interests, because of its unitary religious nature, which favors cooperation and harmony.

By way of summary, even if there are no clear and definitive sacred texts or contemporary political theories to support one position on the issue of the separation of powers, the most appropriate constitutional principle for this issue in an Islamic system is one of flexible separation allowing for cooperation between the various organs of the state and a hierarchy of various levels of responsibility. For the supreme framework both in ideology and values belongs to the Qur'an and Sunna, which are independent from all state institutions and which provide the framework within which Islamic scholars and their institutions can carry out the task of interpreting the texts and applying them to challenges arising [ijtihad]. This produces the cultural foundation within which society operates, along with all the state institutions and, in particular, the consultative assembly.

The result is that this original legislative function is completely independent from the state while ruling over it. As for the judiciary, everyone submits unconditionally to its judgment, including the head of state and his ministers. In the case of conflict between the state powers, the power of the umma, as represented in the Shura Council, the institutions of Islamic scholars, and independent civil society institutions must take precedence, with the objective of lifting up the Word of Truth and justice, supporting victims of injustice, spreading well-being in the world, while banishing oppression and enmity. All of this opens the way for the knowledge of God (may He be praised and exalted) to spread, so that unbelief and transgression will be strongly opposed and held in contempt.

If a conflict arises between the head of state and the Shura Council, over which he presides and the conflict cannot be resolved, then the matter will have to be examined. If the opponents represent a consensus, or near consensus, that is two-thirds of the council and more, he will have to submit to its views, since that consensus represents one of the foundations of Islam. As we read in one of the attested hadiths of the Prophet (PBUH), speaking to Abu Bakr and 'Umar: "If you two agreed on a particular matter, I would not oppose you." If the matter of disagreement was backed by a simple majority, then if the issue is related to technical matters of legislation or something of the kind, it should be presented to a committee with this competence and everyone would have to submit to their decision. If the matter relates to public sovereignty, the president may exercise his right of veto against the council's decision and refuse to implement it.[67]

This means that disagreements about technical issues should be decided by experts, applying what God (may He be exalted) said: "if you do not know, ask people who have knowledge."[68] In other matters the president may oppose a council's decision on an issue about which there is no consensus (consensus being at least two thirds of the council's members). But if there is a consensus, then the president has to apply that decision or put it to the people—who are the ultimate authority—for a referendum, and whichever one of the two, the president or the council, loses in the referendum, he or it has to submit to the people's choice or resign.[69]

To summarize, therefore, the issue of the separation of powers remains open to several views, depending on the public benefit seen by those in authority at every stage of a state's history, as long as the objective of keeping despotism at bay remains in view, as well as safeguarding the umma's unity. So it may be useful to adopt a flexible principle of separation, as is the case in a parliamentary system in which the government and its head are part of the parliament. Given the circumstances of tyranny, the flames of which have seared and continue to painfully sear the umma, we suggest that the Islamic system of governance adopt such a separation so as to put a limit on the absolute ruler and distribute power as much as possible, so that the authority of the umma will prevail.

A PLURALITY OF PARTIES AS A PROTECTION FROM TYRANNY

FROM THE WESTERN LIBERAL PERSPECTIVE

Establishing political pluralism in the form of political parties is an essential guarantee in the Western democratic perspective against despotism, and from another angle it is the natural corollary to the principles of freedom, equality, and the consideration of the individual as the first building block of society with intrinsic value. Citizens who share a common opinion, ideology, or interest have the right to form an association in order to find a path to power or put pressure on the existing one, and they have no right to deprive anyone else of that right.

Western democracy does not accept the principle of a single party, since that is a form of dictatorship.[70] That kind of pluralism is not considered a necessary evil but rather as necessary and a required good in order to prevent hegemony and create a balance between ruler and ruled.

Political parties are the main link between the people and power, because it organizes public opinion, crystallizes people's will, and provides an easy way to

know where it is headed by means of elections, or referenda, or parliamentary debates. This is how parties become a school to teach the masses, to organize them
and help them express their opinion; and also the chief arm of a democratic state
apparatus, a fertile arena, and one of many important topics in constitutional law.

IN THE WESTERN MARXIST PERSPECTIVE

As for the Marxist democracies in the former Soviet Union and those like it,
they see political pluralism as a reflection of a stratified society, as opposed to
one "in which there are no classes, and where no differences remain among
people except unimportant ones, since where there is no class distinction, there
can be no political pluralism."[71]

The Marxist party undertakes the mission to mold the masses and develop them as
well as to watch over the state's institutions. Some Third World nations, as they
are called, or nations of the marginal world, have adopted the single-party system,
while others have adopted the multiparty system.[72] However, you will not find
much difference between the Arab nations, for instance, in terms of the state of
public freedoms, human rights, and the political direction of the state, between
those with multiparty systems (Morocco, Tunisia, Egypt) and those one-party
states such as Tunisia (formerly), Algeria (formerly), Egypt (formerly), Syria, Iraq,
and Yemen (formerly). The same goes for those ruled by clans and tribes. Generally, human rights are deficient and mass participation is very limited in public
decision making, even for major issues defining the state's destiny. The succession of power only occurs upon either death or coup d'état—that is, power continues to be the basis for legitimacy. So politics here oscillate between open or
veiled dictatorships apart from some limited steps in the direction of political
openness in some countries, although not yet established nor reaching the crucial stage, at which a peaceful transition of power comes through the popular
will. And that is precisely the essence of a just system, whether Islamic or not.

CURRENT MUSLIM POSITIONS ON POLITICAL PARTIES

If the principle of shura and its corollaries, the command to do good, the forbidding of evil, and good counsel, represent the basic rule in constructing an Islamic
order, is it not possible that political parties are the most adequate framework for a
believer to practice and strengthen his ability to participate in the public order?

The issue of political organization through the methods of contemporary democracies is not something known in prior Islamic history, with the exception of
the Rightly Guided Caliphate, nor in other civilizations. This is despite the fact

that the rule of shura is rightly considered the essential pillar of legitimate Islamic rule, and that it has no meaning unless the umma is given the right to rule and to offer good counsel and advice. This in itself is an application of the mutual consultation rule and the command to do good and the prohibition of evil. It also builds upon the principle of the sealing of prophethood, which transferred the mission of the establishment of religion, the spreading of justice, and the removal of injustice to the umma as a whole, each member of the umma according to his/her position and capacity.

This is what closes the door to any claim to absolute and infallible power speaking in the name of Heaven and absolute truth, nor any power that robs the people of their authority to free thinking, engaging in independent reasoning [ijtihad], or exercising their command of good and prohibition of evil, whether that absolute authority be an individual, a state, a nation, or an institution. After prophethood was sealed for good, there is no infallible authority possible, except that of the umma itself, as translated in the outcome of the interaction of various opinions and religious interpretations on these issues [ijtihadat]—the never-ceasing dialogue between the clear and definitive sacred texts and the ever-changing realities of life—the only authority is the positions of consensus and general guidelines that result from that process.

It was this interaction, which reached its apex during the ages of Islamic flourishing and then slowed down almost to the point of coming to a halt in the periods of decline, that spawned at the high mark of Islamic civilization an overflowing and multiplication of legal, theological, philosophical, and literary schools, while at the same time witnessing an outpouring of political parties vying for power. This is the fundamental arena for conflict and struggle in Islamic history, and not religious conflict, since Muslims have not fought over religion, since religion was not embodied in an institution as happened with the institution of the church or in a state that replaced the church in the West in the modern era. In Muslim lands, that sphere remained open, despite all those who out of greed for power spared no effort to attract it and instrumentalize it to their own advantage as a way to mobilize the masses against their adversaries and as a way to organize and control.

This open religious perspective, then, offered a range of possibilities to create schools of thought, jurisprudence, and political parties, though they did not take modern forms as we know them today. The recognition of legal pluralism came about with the difference in legal interpretation [ijtihad], and from the sacred text there emerged innumerable legal and theological schools, with all of them recognizing one another. Each one had its founding texts, financial endowments, and institutions of learning, and even its own system of courts within the same state.

This was guaranteed even for non-Muslims, which represented such a high level of tolerance that has hardly ever been reached by the most advanced democracies of our day. The legal systems in some of these democracies cannot even tolerate small differences of dress, let alone laws related to family, education, and arbitration, and other specific needs of a religious minority. All of these differences were permitted in the Islamic state for all religious sects, whether Islamic or not, including outside the people of the book, like the Sabeans, Yazidis, and Zoroastrians.[73] The system of religious communities in the Ottoman state, which was the last example of Islamic rule, was an example demonstrating this tolerance of religious diversity.

We have covered the issue of religious and legal diversity. Now concerning political diversity, this flows from the right to take practical part in governance, giving shura, good counsel, and the command to do good and forbid evil. It may even occupy a higher position than that of a religious obligation for which a believer is accountable. Nevertheless, its practice in an organized systematic way—that is, by means of an officially recognized opposition as is known in contemporary democracies—was not known in our own civilizational practice, or among others for that matter. This is what has led some Muslims to disapprove of parties and consider them as alien baggage forced upon them through Western colonialism and considering it an imitation of occupying infidels and a danger that could divide the Muslim community.

We will summarize here the opinions of contemporary scholars on this issue, since it was not a question of concern to traditional Islamic thought, although Muslim societies witnessed divisions and organized political pluralism. Islamic societies of the past were rich in civil society organizations. Already in the seventh century of its history, Islamic civilization knew professional guilds (trade unions), also called *al-asnaf.* Every professional grouping was composed of a guild under the leadership of a shaykh from among the leading artisans of his craft, whom they chose to monitor the quality of their work, defend the rights of the artisans at all levels, and arbitrate the disputes that arose between customers, apprentices, and artisans of that craft.[74]

As for political groups, they, too, were a known phenomenon in Islamic societies. Islamic culture did not distinguish between religious and political issues, and almost from the start there arose theological divisions, legal schools, and mystical brotherhoods (Sufism), which for the most part contained motivations, goals, and dimensions that were political. One could even argue that they were political programs and projects, all stemming from a common Islamic background and differing from one another in their social methodologies, in the demands of their groups and in their level of knowledge. Shaykh al-Islam Ibn

Taymiyya was asked about a group of people who called themselves a party, had chosen a leader for themselves, and made some particular demands, and he said, "As for the party leader, he is the head of the group that has formed itself into a party. If they have agreed to what God and His Messenger have commanded without adding or subtracting anything, then they are believers with the same rights and obligations. But if they have added or subtracted to that, like blind support of anyone who is a member of their party, whether he is in the right or in the wrong, that is to be divisive, something that God and His Messenger condemn. For they have ordered us to come together and be united, to refrain from discrimination and division, and to cooperate in doing what is good and pleasing to God and not to cooperate in committing evil and transgression."[75]

As we can plainly see, Islamic societies offered a rich tapestry of religious organizations and institutions, which were also quite political for the most part. Put otherwise, the umma did experience division and systematic political pluralism since the Battle of Siffin (657 BCE). Notwithstanding, it will suffice here to offer a collection of views from modern thinkers, because the issue of political parties as such was not of concern to traditional Islamic thought. We know that over the centuries important currents of thought emerged, each one advocating a particular view of religion, history, the role of human beings, and of political power and wealth. The most important of these was the Shi'i movement, the Kharijites, the Mu'tazilites, and the Murji'ites. The rest evolved over time and became known as "the community" [al-jama'a], or the people of the Sunna (hence, Sunnis), or the majority. Despite the relationships of coexistence and dialogue that prevailed most of the time between these groups, these relations were cautious and depended on the balance of power between them. And as soon as a party gathered enough strength to overthrow the current regime—and sometimes without even possessing sufficient strength—it rebelled.

Nevertheless, Islamic society achieved a level of tolerance and peaceful coexistence amid religious and sectarian pluralism, a phenomenon unknown elsewhere at the time and even by contemporary societies. From this we see that Muslim societies were mostly free from religious wars or ethnic cleansing, which by contrast many other societies have experienced. The difference comes from the effect of its creed of tawhid, its belief in the unity of humanity's origins, and its refusal to accept the embodiment of truth in one person, nation, or state. This opened the way for religious pluralism ("Let there be no compulsion in religion," Q. 2:256) and legal pluralism. Further, the doctrine of the seal of prophethood put down every claim to speak in the name of absolute truth, leaving only freedom of opinion and of ijtihad. In fact, the respect shown by Islamic societies for religious and legal freedoms reached such a level that they recognized the rights of religious communities to set up their own courts according to their own religious and sectarian norms, a level of progress that the modern state has barely achieved, since its laws express only its own will and sovereignty.

Nevertheless, the stalling of the movement of creative interpretation [ijtihad], the domination of autocracy and the general spirit that reigned in those centuries, espousing religious—or tribal-based absolute political rule—all these factors had an impact on the backwardness of constitutional thought and the lack of clear vision for the basis of legitimacy in an Islamic state and how that legitimacy may be obtained or lost. Except for the Rightly Guided Caliphate, peaceful alternation of power was not the rule. Reaching power by overcoming rivals was the only basis for power, with the duty of obedience to whomever conquered, as long as he recognized the supremacy of the Shari'a, at least its overt and clear rules. Therefore, this was the age when adventurous individuals and families seized political power, and the masses—the true possessors of political authority—were robbed of their right to regulate public affairs, while often made to be lost and distracted in a maze of superstition and myths, and superficial, marginal concerns.

The abdication of the Muslim intellect from its mission of ijtihad and the umma's relinquishing of its duty to fulfill the trust of ruling, considering that it is the source of political power, necessarily led to the entrenchment of despotism and the elaboration of theories to justify it. In turn, this led to the impairment of the masses' effectiveness and their surrender to decline, rigidity and an aversion to the affairs of state as if they were sullied by the devil's intrusion, or a private matter of no concern to them, all of which in effect is a kind of secularism. Yet at least to some extent the Islamic scholars, in addition to their mission to educate and guide the umma, still had a hand in political rule since their specialty is to interpret the texts and to render judicial verdicts. It was their role that limited somewhat the power of the ruler by confining it to executive activities. That in itself reduced the incidence of deviations and slowed down the process of decline, so that when it reached its lowest ebb and was too exhausted to fight back, the umma fell prey to the wiles of the West. Then came the calls for reform [islah], with the aim of saving the umma from the clutches of despotism, while reformists deemed the root of all evils and the essence of decline, and considered the cure to be freedom and the rule of law rather than the rule of one man or family.

Pioneers of Renaissance and Reform

The first generation of pioneers of the modern Islamic movement beginning in the eighteenth and early nineteenth centuries in the Arabian Peninsula and beyond (Shaykh Ibn 'Abd al-Wahhab, al-Dahlawi, al-Sanusi, al-Mahdi) took upon themselves to reform Islamic beliefs and to liberate minds from superstition and urge them to resist the colonizers' aspirations.[76] They did so far from any Western influence but within the ideology of Salafism,[77] which was developed by Ibn Taymiyya and his disciple Ibn al-Qayyim (d. 1350) and al-Shawkani (d. 1839).

The second generation of pioneers of Islamic reformism during the nineteenth and early twentieth centuries under the leadership of al-Afghani, Muhammad 'Abduh, Rashid Rida, and al-Kawakibi was active during a period when Western hegemony—military, economic, and cultural—was intensifying in Muslim lands. Islam was a direct target of that invasion, so it was natural for these pioneers to respond to the Western aggression and prepare the umma psychologically and politically for resistance. One aspect of this response was passive, in that they refuted Western calumnies against Islam and Islamic civilization and their derision of Islamic political rule, which they branded as despotic and theocratic. But their work also had a positive side in that they offered a vision of Islam that at its very core was tied to the principles of freedom, mutual consultation, social justice, revolution against injustice, enhancement of human dignity, and acclaim for the umma as the ruler's source of authority. They went even further and participated in direct political action by forming political parties and articulating their platforms, as did 'Abduh and al-Afghani, for instance.

If the topic of Islamic statehood was not raised by the first generation of pioneer reformers except in a traditional sense, it was seriously raised and discussed in the second generation as a way to meet the challenges of their time in a modern context, both in terms of new political concepts and terminology. It was necessary to take a deep look at reality to analyze the sickness and its cure, then a deep look at the texts and the Islamic heritage, seeking clues and grounding new legal solutions using modern vocabulary, some of which might not be free from imitation caused by their keen desire to reform Islam and their admiration of the West.

For instance Rifa'a al-Tahtawi (1801–1873) tried to bolster political freedom in our lands by extolling political pluralism and by comparing modern political parties with the early sects of Islam. He wrote, "Religious freedom is freedom of creed, opinion and legal school, as long as it does not overstep the boundaries of religion. This includes the views of the Ash'arites and of the leaders of

Islamic schools of jurisprudence in all their variety and similarly with political parties today.[78]

Al-Kawakibi's (1854–1920) work praised Western accomplishments in developing a higher level of organization for the state so that the division of political parties does not weaken the Western state, and that is because the difference between the parties is similar to the way juristic fundamentals are applied to specific questions.[79]

Among us, the most zealous admirer of the parliamentary system and multi-party politics was Jamal al-Din al-Afghani, who wrote, "You will soon witness, when the Egyptian parliament is constituted, it will no doubt have a similar structure to that of the European parliaments, that is, it will include at the very least a right-leaning and a left-leaning party."[80]

After him, the Imam Muhammad 'Abduh (1849–1905) vociferously defended political pluralism, contending that it would not harm the unity of the umma, because it has not divided the European nations either geographically or politically. The reason is that these nations all share the same goal and realize that there are many paths that will lead to it.

Khayr al-Din al-Tunisi (1820–1890) invested great energy in finding Islamic roots for the Western-inspired Ottoman reforms [*tanzimat*], reasoning that if the umma's latent freedom is activated by means of specific political formations which facilitate engagement in political affairs, it would enable it to speed up the process of development, limit the power of dictatorial regimes, and put an end to the assault of Western civilization that overruns everything in its path.

The European reforms on which Muslims' renaissance depended, according to Khayr al-Din, undoubtedly represented a wider concept than just political parties. Still, they were important to him, because he was motivated by the desire to restrict the power of the kings and establish the freedom of the people.

The third generation of pioneers of the Islamic movement and of the renaissance of the Arabs and Muslims in general was the generation of the first half of the twentieth century. They experienced in their youth the fall of the last symbol of Islamic unity—the Ottoman caliphate—and the successful campaign of destruction waged by Western colonialism, resulting in the malicious fragmentation of the umma. It was natural, then, that their work focused on a fundamental issue—rebuilding the Islamic state—and for that to happen, they had to start working on Muslim unity. In this phase, as a result of the previous efforts of reform and the beginning of Western decline, one branch of the Islamic elites shed their admiration for Western civilization, which had been strong among the previous generation. The convergence of these factors brought a number of leaders who were filled with sadness at the fall of Islamic political authority and were determined to bring it back. Although freedom was a value which these pioneers greatly treasured, especially in light of the tyranny they experienced under colonialism and under their own rulers, they were generally not supportive of political parties.

Listen to one of them, the great reformist scholar of the Algerian revolution Shaykh 'Abd al-Hamid Ben Badis, as he sings the praises of liberty: "Every person's right to freedom is like his right to life, and the extent to which he enjoys life is the extent to which he enjoys freedom. Whoever undermines his freedom, attacks his very life. God's main purpose in sending messengers and His Shari'a was to allow humans to live as free people, so that they would know how to lay hold of what leads to life and freedom, and reap the benefits of that life and that freedom to the greatest possible extent. Islam only spread among nations because they witnessed how it values and, protects life, and how it sees all people as equal, something their kings, priests and monks had not known before."[81]

Despite this, that generation in general never considered a multiparty democracy as the best way to secure freedom, but saw in it "another cause of fragmentation, partisanship, and waste of energy, since the umma needs one party to bring her together as one, in order to confront foreign occupation, achieve its independence and freedom and establishes the foundations of comprehensive internal reform. Once that is achieved, future developments would then determine the appropriate means of organization within the framework of unity that Islam requires."[82] This leads to the following section.

The Position of Imam Hasan al-Banna on a Multiparty System

Despite the Imam al-Banna's assertion above, he often emphasized that organizing political life in its modern form based on the representative, parliamentary system did not contradict Islamic political theory.[83] What is important is the commitment to Islam's rules, respect for the people's will, and the achievement of its unity. Yet despite his adoption of representative government, he refused to consider multiparty politics as a condition and inherent basis for it, asserting that the Western linkage of the two came out of specific historical developments—namely, the combination of Western society's class-based structure and past violent confrontations between the monarchy and the people.[84] As for the Islamic umma, by contrast, God has protected her from that. He writes,

> Yet even within Western regimes, conflicts between parties have not reached the point of threatening national unity, since most of the time you find two main parties succeeding one another in power, whose only disagreements are on secondary issues, unlike several Arab countries which have created too many parties and have suffered greatly as a result.

With regard to Islamic countries, and Egypt in particular, where complete independence has not been achieved, this party system constitutes a grave danger for its future, because parties here have lost their raison d'etre and serve but the personal gain of their leaders. They are therefore devoid of any content or credible platforms, with all of them raising the same slogans, with no other role to play but that of tearing the umma apart. No wonder its wise men came to a consensus on rejecting all of them and the opinion that the only ones benefitting from it are the usurping occupiers. And if disagreement could be acceptable in any country, when it is not destructive, then the land of the Nile River is the most in need of a fullest measure of unity in order to rally its forces for the battle of independence and in the work of internal reform. So why then are its people forced to continue this system of factions they call "political parties" after the failure of reformers to unite them? There is no other alternative than to dissolve all these parties and unite the umma's forces under one party that will work toward achieving its independence and freedom, without dispersing its efforts in conflicts between parties and guarding itself from their wiles.

This problem has reached its zenith, and there is no room left for patience with such a scandalous situation. It calls for swift and decisive change.

Clearly, the imam sees no necessary connection between multiparty politics and mutual deliberation, or freedom of opinion: "There is a difference between freedom of opinion, thought and expression, and the duties of shura and good counsel on the one hand—which is what Islam requires—and fanatic attachment to one's opinion, dividing the community, and a relentless effort to widen a gulf within the umma on the other."

We have expanded on Imam al-Banna's position on political parties and his perspective on the state because of the privileged position the martyred imam occupies in view of his founding leadership of the contemporary Islamic movement, his costly struggle [jihad] and great tribulation in service of the umma. All of this gives great weight to his words for Islamists in general, and for those who belong to the Muslim Brotherhood in particular, or for those who sympathize with them. This has meant that his opinions have been viewed less as interpretations [ijtihadat] of a scholar that were affected by circumstances of time and place and which may contain both true and false elements and more as if they were on par with the fixed and binding texts of the Shari'a, which is against the spirit of the Shari'a and scientific research methods.

In fact, the imam is excessively admired by a whole swath of Islamists, while he is excessively loathed and disdained by secularists, to the point of being accused of collusion with the British occupiers—God forbid![85] In truth, the occupation on the banks of the Suez Canal and the Zionist occupation in Palestine have not been dealt more severe blows than those they received at the hand of the imam's disciples. This is how the truth gets lost in the abyss of bias and injustice; language gets polluted, the tearing apart of the cultural and political elites continues apace, and as a result each country continues along the path laid out for them by the colonizer.

What may be a fair evaluation of Imam al-Banna's position on political parties?

Was it a position specifically tied to the state of occupation Egypt was experiencing at the time? After all, a united popular front is required to confront the colonizer, and nations in this stage of confrontation need to tighten their ranks, even if that sometimes demands taking exceptional measures. Or was his view tied to specific kinds of parties that at the time proved to be empty, having exhausted their aims, which led the Egyptian nation into a terrible crisis and resounding defeats creating an atmosphere ripe for a military takeover? No one cried over their loss, a sure sign they were already spent. Or was the imam's view one built on principle, regardless of the sociopolitical context?

Those who are prejudiced against the Islamists—seeking to undermine them through attacking their symbols affirm the second thesis, on the basis of the words of their most famous figure calling for dissolving the parties since Islam is a call to unity and cooperation, while political parties are a call to partisanship and further fragmentation of society. Thus these opponents argue that the Muslim Brotherhood reaped what they sowed and that they are the last political current that could denounce a police state.

Those who defend the Muslim Brotherhood argue that the demand to dissolve political parties should be seen in the context of the circumstances and particular dynamics in Egypt and of the nature of the dominant parties at that time. This demand had no connection to the theological and legal convictions that guide the Brotherhood, like the centrality of shura and freedom in a Muslim society. Finally, one should not forget the Brotherhood's struggle [jihad] against autocracy within and outside the nation and the role they played in halting the aggression of westernization, in restoring the umma's identity, and mobilizing it to unity and resistance. Unifying the nation's ranks indeed needed to be the priority, as the nation writhed under the yoke of occupation, dislocation, and corruption, rather than glorifying the principle of the right to diversity and pluralism even if that led to partisanship, division, treason, and corruption.

Such was the situation political parties created in Egypt. In truth, these were not genuine parties according to the usual definition used everywhere else in the world, and their worn condition now in Egypt and in many Arab countries is hardly any different from what it was in the 1940s. Their condition is even worse, which indicates the need for a radical change. Those rejected parties therefore are, in the words of Professor Mustafa Muhammad al-Tahhan, nothing more than "artificial quasi-parties that fulfill the personal ambitions of individuals at the expense of the umma, without having any program or methodology of reform—parties that corrupt people's conscience, prevent the common good, destroy moral norms, and that care about nothing else but undermining their rivals."[86]

Indeed, one can find sentences here and there in the writings of the imam that can help us to establish that his exact position on political parties, was linked to specific circumstances and that he was specifically talking about Egyptian parties rather than calling for the absolute banning of all parties. For instance, he commented on political parties in Great Britain and the United States in a language that was not at all critical, since they all agreed on fundamentals and goals and that differed only on secondary issues. His overall argument implies that a multiparty system is acceptable, as long as it doesn't threaten the unity of the umma—that is, it doesn't leave the nation's basic structures open to debate, as he himself writes, "Difference in the Islamic *umma* cannot be conceived on essential matters."[87]

This selective reading of the texts, however, does not prove useful in discerning their overall spirit and structure. This much we should say: what al-Banna said about parties was influenced by Egypt's circumstances and its need for unity in order to resist foreign occupation. Had the imam experienced the circumstances of oppression that followed that period, he would have realized with the other Islamists that a defective freedom, or even partial freedom, is superior to a blind and mute dictatorship, and that a political system relying on legitimacy derived from free elections, no matter how defective that system may be, is better—or rather a lesser evil—than one whose legitimacy relies on brute force—that is, on the declarations of a revolutionary council, as the Islamist thinker Fathi 'Uthman put it.[88]

Put otherwise, we can justify the position of the imam by contextualizing his discourse in particular circumstances so that it is not made into a fixed rule of Islamic political thought. What leader or thinker, after all, no matter his stature, has been able to free himself completely from his nation's context and from the spirit of his times? In his day, the mood of the Third World was about revolting against the liberal camp of the colonizers and being attracted to the socialist, fascist, and communist experiments, which preached rapid development by way of mobilizing the nation around one party in order to confront imperialism and carry out a comprehensive reform project. For that reason, it was not surprising that the revolution happened in line with this orientation and implementing al-Banna's call to dissolve political parties, even if the context had been different at the time.[89]

That said, if you study with an open mind all the texts in context which the imam deals with political parties, you will discover without a shadow of a doubt that a multiparty system—at the very least, with regard to emerging nations—is not permitted and that, though he calls for a representative system, he sees no need for multiple parties. Nor is he calling for the dissolution of decrepit parties in order to be replaced by effective patriotic ones; rather, he is calling for the disbanding of the existing parties and for one party to take their place and unite the nation's political forces. In reality, talk about dissolving parties is somewhat questionable, since in the end the birth and death certificates of parties, or of any other civil society organization, are not decided by any other body than particular nations as a whole, either by accepting them and they live or by rejecting them and they die.

Thus the context and overall spirit of what the imam is refusing—that is, a necessary link between the Islamic shura and a multiparty system—clearly demonstrate the models of state the imam recommends. It is not the theocratic model, because the imam emphasizes the respect for the people's will and the necessity of elections as the means to demonstrate that will. He also underlines the accountability of the ruler before the people in a way that resembles the American presidential model and above all else the commitment to Islam and the unity of the umma.

The imam's discourse on the matter, therefore, even if it is tied to particular circumstances, nevertheless transcends any particular context in order to fall under the rules of an Islamic political order.

Objectivity will not allow the Islamists to abandon Islam's methodology of aiming for justice—as much as possible—in evaluating others far and near. But they can justify the position of the imam by pointing to his country's context and the spirit of his time for prioritizing unity over other values, so that individual positions on issues in particular settings do not become general rules of Islamic thought. My interpretation of the imam's position is reinforced by the general mentality among Islamists, even until recently, and their aversion to multipartyism "and taking their distance from party organizations."[90] Thus al-Banna's successor, Shaykh al-Hudaybi, handed in his resignation when the rest of his leaders submitted a request (September 10, 1952) to the government for their official recognition as a party. That then paved the way leading to the dissolution of the Brotherhood alongside all political parties, but the Brotherhood reemphasized the fact that they were not a political party but a community above all parties. They made the following official declaration on March 27, 1954: "With regard to the multi-party system, which Muhammad Najib had called for, our hope is that corruption will not be introduced by this means once again. For we will not be silenced about this corruption but we strongly support the people's complete freedom, and we will never allow the formation of political parties for the simple reason that we call on all Egyptians to march behind us and follow our example in the service of Islam."[91]

It is not important for us here to know what transpired after the parties were dissolved and the Brotherhood became a "society" again, or that Gamal Abd al-Nasser later legalized their status as society and not a political party, for this was all part of the disagreement at the time between Muhammad Najib and Nasser, according to 'Abd al-Salam.[92] What is important, however, is to highlight the general spirit and prevailing mood of a long period of time among a wide swath of activists influenced by Imam al-Banna and Sayyid Qutb, which was an aversion to political parties and an absolute rejection of the term "political party" being used for their organization. In fact, this feeling of rejection of parties, and a view of the party system as a dishonorable and reprehensible concept, was circulating among the Islamic political culture of the time. Yet this was hardly limited to Islamists; rather, that same feeling against parties, and even stronger, was widespread among the pan-Arabists, the socialists, the communists, and the leadership of the liberation movements. These people were all influenced negatively by a common reaction to the capitalist block, and all of them were attracted to fascist and communist experiments which represented an attractive model to third-world activists of fast development through a state-directed economy.

Perhaps in addition to these circumstances, this view of parties was fed by the concept of "ahzab" parties through the lens of the Prophet's life—particularly the Battle of Ahzab (confederates) and their attendant violence. This is when the unbelieving opponents or "the parties" besieged the first Muslim society in order to annihilate it out of pride in their pagan ways and uniting around their misguidance, as the Qur'an says, "but they have split their community into sects, each rejoicing in their own."[93] This view may also be affected by the negative use of the term "ahzab" in the Qur'an, except for "the party of God": "Truly it is the Party of God that will achieve Felicity."[94] In that context, the confrontation was between God's unity and idolatry, between God's unity, which requires Muslims to unite around truth, and unbelief, along with the fragmentation, the weakness, and pride in misguidance that it entails.[95]

Conversely, in a totally different context, the multiparty system in our day is seen as one of the building blocks of a state built on rule of law, and one of the guarantees of freedom and opposition to despotism—all of which are Islamic objectives. This is therefore a different context related to organizing political life, which is a domain that is different from the domain of religious doctrine, and thus governed by relative truth and public interest rather than the logic of certainty and absolute truth, and the duality of truth and falseness, faith and unbelief, guidance and misguidance. The best way to understand Islamic unity is not as simple unity, but rather unity that is produced by diversity through the interplay between the sacred texts and mutual consultation, or between commitment and freedom. Understand, too, that the Party of God, or the Saved Group, are all Muslim groups, the people of the *qibla*, with all their various schools of thought and sects.[96] They are those who believe in God and in His Prophet (PBUH), in his Book and in the Last Day, who agree on the supreme authority of the Shari'a, however diverse their interpretations of it might be. Those saved people are not a specific single group, no matter how wide you count it, but includes all people of the qibla. Indeed, it is a vast community, as vast as God's mercy. Sharing in the common name of "party" [*hizb*] does not necessarily entail sharing the same connotation, since the contexts are different.[97]

CONTEMPORARY ISLAMIC THOUGHT ON THE MULTIPARTY SYSTEM

The Islamic Movement in Egypt

The Society of Muslim Brothers (or Muslim Brotherhood) is considered the oldest and largest of contemporary Islamist movements and the most influential in contemporary Islam from the standpoint of its ideology and its social program.[98] Its emergence coincided with an extremely important time in history—namely, the fall of the last symbol of the historic Islamic caliphate. This called for a new form of Islamic reform that goes further than the changes that were needed every time the Islamic edifice suffered any defects or cracks, at which time the Islamic scholars would step forward to redress that defect by way of commanding good and forbidding evil. Usually, though, this was the work of an individual scholar. But this time, with the abolition of the caliphate, the building collapsed and the sky seemed to fall on the heads of Muslims. Now they needed a reconstruction project, and it was Hasan al-Banna who declared the birth of the Islamic movement. He declared that Islam was a comprehensive system comprising religion and governance, or, as Tunisian scholar Muhammad al-Tahir Bin Ashur described it, Islam as a religion supported by a system of governance.

By Islamist (or Islamic) movement we mean the organized effort inspired by Islam with the goal of constructing the comprehensive Islamic edifice, reasoning that Islam is a religion that establishes a system of life, a global community [umma], and a civilization.

Shaykh Hasan al-Banna (1906–1949) is not only considered the founder of this movement (1928) and the main architect of its organizational, ideological, and educational edifice, he is also the greatest thinker and reformer of what is known as "political Islam," and even beyond that domain. His movement was able—through its engagement in the liberation struggles against the British in the Suez Canal, against Zionist occupation in Israel, and against internal despotism, and through the emergence of scholars from his movement who are considered among the most important figures of contemporary Islam, such as 'Abd al-Qadir 'Awda, Sayyid Qutb, Muhammad al-Ghazali, Yusuf al-Qaradawi, Sayyid Sabiq, and Mustafa al-Siba'i—to become the most widespread and influential school of thought and action among today's Muslims. Herein lies the importance of their ideological positions since it represents the mainstream trend within contemporary Islamic thought, which one of its most eminent thinkers, Shaykh Yusuf al-Qaradawi, calls "the trend of the middle-path [wasatiyya] in Islam." We could even say that, with a bit of exaggeration no doubt, contemporary Islam is "Brotherhood Islam."

After a series of severe tribulations, the Muslim Brotherhood came back to the political scene, reinserting itself as an unrivaled player. They had understood their lessons and learned from their experience, and with the leadership of one of their pioneers, the very learned 'Umar al-Tilmisani, they were able to resolve the issue of political parties by reinterpreting what al-Banna had said against them and thus to reengage with the reality of Egyptian politics. So they entered into political life, though not as a political party, because they were denied that although they repeatedly applied for that permission once they had organized themselves as a party with a specific platform in 1985, and later in 2007. Before that they had also allied themselves with one of the parties that they had erstwhile campaigned to dissolve—the Wafd Party. Then they formed an alliance with the Socialist Labour Party. Thus they acquired experience in the People's Assembly that was rich in honesty, boldness, and moderation.[99] In so doing, they contributed to speeding up Egypt's movement toward Islam and democracy and creating a major influence in Egyptian political party life, leading to sidelining extreme secularist orientations in favor of the Islamic orientation.

The Brotherhood's influence in Egyptian society, especially in the last round of elections in 2005, reached a point where nobody could doubt that they constituted the greatest power socially and politically in Egypt. They stood as the main force against the organs of the state, which were devoid of the values of truth and justice and only kept in place by the power and readiness to oppress the desire and determination of Egypt's president to pass on control of the state to his heirs regardless of the extent of people's oppositon. As for the secular opposition parties, they were no less bankrupt than the state, standing in as mere ornaments for decoration. Most of them were established to serve the regime as window dressing, while others had become outdated and obsolete, like the Wafd and Tajammu' parties. If old age afflicts the state, as Ibn Khaldun stressed, it cannot be cured, and the same goes for political parties.

This strategy allowed all the Muslim Brotherhood organizations—whether in Jordan, Yemen, Algeria, Kuwait, Sudan, Palestine, Indonesia, or Iraq—to participate in politics of their own countries in an effective and moderate manner. Some of them even won landslide victories, like the one the Hamas movement achieved whose engagement in resistance carried to government, and even combining the two today, as they are engaged in an epic war.

The Muslim Brotherhood was not content with simply embracing democracy, political pluralism, peaceful rotation of power in practice—that is, not simply justifying it as required by necessity and adapting to reality in order to reap its benefits, while waiting for the opportune moment to turn its back to it, as their opponents claim. Instead, they have gone beyond this political practice by establishing an Islamic jurisprudential justification for it, just as the basis for every aspect of the Muslim believer's conduct is to conform to the teaching of Islam and flow out of it.

It is not sufficient, therefore, to practice pluralism when working with trade unions or political parties. It is not sufficient to put forward your candidates and their policy proposals, in order to compete with the other choices, satisfied that the masses will decide on their programs and the people via the ballot boxes, even if the most important and established trade unions like the doctors, engineers, and lawyers unions, and teachers, students, and pharmacy unions declared their support for you because of your diligence, flexibility, integrity, and sacrifices, and because of the programs you executed and services you rendered, which were reinforced by a network of schools, clinics, public benefit programs, and Internet services. And even if, in more than one Arab and Islamic country, you gained the lion's share of popular support and the power to renew the elites, which have become aged, corrupted, and exhausted by political power, all of that would not be enough to vouch for your attachment to democracy unless that peaceful democratic path is demonstrated by forcing civil society and engaging it toward changing the infrastructure and superstructure of the social edifice, based on an intellectual foundation that defends democracy from an Islamic point of view.

Accordingly in this last decade the Muslim Brotherhood has issued a number of important official political documents justifying political pluralism, participation in a government even in the context of a secular state, as well as the political participation of women, peaceful transition of power, human rights, including the rights of non-Muslim minorities in a Muslim state. All this they consider political jurisprudence [*fiqh*] governing and guiding collective political behavior in its relation to the state, and to competing organizations and minorities. These documents were published in a book entitled *Contemporary Political Thought of the Muslim Brotherhood*.[100]

The last of these documents tells of the Muslim Brotherhood's adoption of the project of Arab unity, thus putting an end to the bloody period of struggle between the two factions, the Arab nationalists and the Islamists. Among the fruit this path produced was the opening of a dialogue between these two factions in Cairo in 1989, which led to the formation of the Organization of the Nationalist Islamic Conference in Beirut in 1994, along with the Organization of Arab Political Parties.[101] This also led to many forms of cooperation between the two trends in several countries to confront internal despotism, their common enemy, and to defend free nations and the unity of Arab countries. That collaboration could also be in confronting foreign occupation in Palestine, Iraq, and Lebanon.

With regard to political pluralism, the topic of our discussion, the document defends the choice of pluralism contextualizing it among the grand principles of Islamic politics, including the following: mutual consultation, commanding good and forbidding evil, the umma as having authority over the ruler, the rule of inherent difference among humankind, the general rule of permissibility,[102] the need to learn from the experiences of our umma and those of other nations, and finally the rule of seeking benefit [maslaha] and avoiding harm, including that of despotism. Specifically, we read, "Since correcting and confronting rulers, opposing their whims and their deviant behavior are no longer tasks an individual can take on, then it has become necessary for the bulk of the umma to come together for that purpose."[103]

As support for that position, the document also quotes Shaykh Yusuf al-Qaradawi, one of the main reference points in these documents, in saying that for years he has declared that there is no obstacle from a Shari'a viewpoint in there being more than one party within an Islamic state, since such a prohibition would require an explicit text, whereas no such text exists. Furthermore a plurality of parties might be a necessity in our age as a guarantee against the despotism of one individual or one group and oppressing the rest of the population and the absence of a power to question or oppose that oppression. After all, this is what we learn from reading history and examining reality.[104]

The document concludes with this affirmation: "For these reasons, we believe in multiple political parties in Islamic society and that the state should not impose obstacles to the formation and activity of NGOs and political parties. Indeed, this allows every group to communicate its message and clarify its methodology, as long as the Islamic Shari'a is the nominal constitution and the law that the judiciary applies in complete independence from any other power. For all of this is sufficient to guarantee the well-being of society and to prosecute in accord with the Shari'a anyone who acts against the basic principles about which there is no disagreement among Muslim scholars."[105]

For his part, Shaykh Qaradawi offers two conditions for the formation of legitimate political parties in an Islamic state from a Shari'a perspective. First, that they recognize Islam as doctrine and legal framework [Shari'a] and not to be hostile to it or deny it, even if they have a particular interpretation [ijtihad] in their understanding of it in light of recognized scientific ground rules [*usul*]. Second, that they refrain from working with a faction that opposes Islam and its umma, whatever its name might be. For it is not permitted to create a party that defames any of the heavenly religions in general, and Islam in particular.[106]

The document on political pluralism then concludes by affirming this important finding: "We believe that the plurality of parties in the Islamic society in the same way our forbears incorporated into their own politics an acceptance for the alternation of power among political groups and parties, and that by means of periodic elections."[107]

The document goes even further than this by imposing a limit to the time a president stays in power: "We believe since the president is no more than an agent of the people, the presidential term must be for a limited time and cannot be renewed, except for a limited time, as a guarantee against authoritarianism."[108]

Finally, despite the document's stated condition as a matter of principle that all sides of the political spectrum recognize the sovereignty of the Shari'a, in practice the document defends the right of Islamic parties to enter into coalitions with secular parties in order to avoid a common threat, like a foreign invader; or to achieve a common benefit, like establishing a democratic regime that allows everyone to enjoy the right to choose and the other rights on an equal basis, no matter what the ideology of a person or party might be.[109] This is because the Shari'a is built upon the principle of achieving benefit and avoiding harm.

The Ennahda Movement

This is considered the most prominent and oldest among those representing the Islamic movement in Tunisia, and the first to fully adopt the democratic process and to call for political pluralism, with the inclusion of all political tendencies, no matter their ideological background, as long as they came to that position by way of free conviction.[110]

We read in the founding declaration of the movement that it "rejects au-thoritarianism and monopolization of power, which implies denying a per-son's will, neutralizing a people's vital energy, and leading a nation on the path of violence. By contrast, it affirms the right of all popular forces to exercise their freedom of expression and of assembly, and the rest of their legitimate rights, and to cooperate in this with all other national forces."[111]

The proof they adduce for this is that Islamic diversity, which incorporated within its fold Judaism and Christianity, has sufficient flexibility to enable it to incorporate within its framework the communists and secularists, since, even if some may not be believers, they can't be considered even further than them. Further, they appeal to a very important document for support, since the state of Medina was founded upon it, which is known as the Medina constitution [al-Sahifa], brokered by the Prophet (PBUH) with the people of Medina, including Muslims, Jews, and all those who entered into their covenant. It represented a model, a methodology, and a precedent with signs pointing to a civilization that testifies to the flexibility of the political framework of an Islamic state, as well as to the precedent of Islam and Muslims adopting the principle of citizenship as the basis of a pluralistic state, as attested by Coptic politicians.

This move to inscribe political pluralism that excludes no one within an Islamic democratic perspective encountered and continues to encounter opposition, not just from the autocratic power of the state—that is expected since it is determined to allow only a fine veneer of formal democracy to mask the true nature of its re-gime and is happy to engage in a hypocritical contest with itself, thus garnering over 99 percent of the vote. No wonder it persists in giving only one answer to the repeated demands of the Islamists to be recognized as a political party that works within the legal framework of the state—despite its restrictive and oppressive character—and that answer is the recurrent oppressive operations of the security forces mounted against them since 1981 to this day. Indeed, this is the very same policy followed against every political or social group.

Stranger yet, this pluralist posture by Ennahda, which excludes no one who seeks to spread his idea through legitimate means, meets opponents who in the name of Islam itself reach the point of describing this opinion as political hy-pocrisy, fabricating lies against God and a work of deception. As al-Sawi put it, "Does pluralism afford equal opportunity for all sides involved, in light of what is required by popular choice or not? Does the Islamic state allow Jews, Chris-tians, atheists or pagans to rule? And does it allow their ideology to govern in a Muslim-majority nation?"[112] His answer, of course is a strong negative based on a made-to-measure scenario in order to reject the principle altogether. These people assume the state is Islamic, yet they presume that the majority of the people will cast their votes with a party that is not Islamic and adopt a platform that is anti-Islamic, even though the simplest definition of an Islamic state is a group of people who take Islam as their reference. In fact, political differences are not around this point.

What is more, they proceed to simplify what is complex, and they have no concern for, for instance, Islamic minorities that live under non-Muslim rule, which is the case for more than a third of Muslims today. Should we prohibit them from participating in public affairs, like becoming members of parliament, political parties, and institutions of local politics, and even in the government itself? That would be serving their interests, if only to protect their existence in that context. Nor are they concerned about an Islamic organization in a country, which has a Muslim majority but with a deficient awareness of what Islam means. What, then, should that organization do if people choose a non-Islamic program for their government? And even that is an unlikely scenario, since the ruling secular parties in Muslim lands usually do not rule in a democratic way but rather by imposing their will.[113]

So what does a ruling Islamic party do when it fails to keep its majority in free elections? Should it draw its sword and impose its program by force? Should it stay out of politics, or should it reform itself and continue its course, trying to convince the people of the validity of its project? In any case, the issue is not about what should be, but about an Islamic group facing a reality that is complicated, the mission of which is to achieve what is useful and avoid what is harmful. Should Muslims in all cases take out their weapons to confront a non-Muslim majority or even a Muslim majority which does not approve of their rule? Is not the wiser option to move into the opposition, as long as they enjoy the freedom to propagate their cause [da'wa] and to participate in politics?

Put otherwise, where do the Islamists draw the legitimacy for their rule? Is it simply by virtue of their Islamic character? That is the mentality of guardianship, meaning Shi'i guardianship, which Shia themselves have done away with, at least from a practical standpoint.[114] Or does their legitimacy emanate from their being chosen by the people? If we answer "by choice" and not by "guardianship" is the choice an open one? Or is the choice only in one direction? In the end, the issue is not tied to a particular theory of Islamic rule, since sovereignty [al-hakimiyya] belongs to the umma within a Shari'a framework. Additionally, the rule in ordinary circumstances is that one does not imagine anything but a Muslim rule in a Muslim-majority nation, and therefore the authority of the umma would not declare legal what is forbidden by Islam nor to forbid that which Islam has permitted. Still, its authority to interpret the law [ijtihad] is quite vast in other matters. In essence, the difference revolves around one's theory of political change, on who has political authority and what is the source of the state's legitimacy. If we answer, "the people," then we, as Islamic parties, place ourselves on the same footing as each individual or political tendency; if we give another answer, we will have to define it and articulate it, for there is no virtue in ambiguity.[115]

So what does it mean for the Muslim Brotherhood to accept electoral law in Egypt and elsewhere, and the same for all groups representing mainstream Islamism? And what does it mean for them to accept union laws and the competition within them in reality? Isn't that an acceptance of the principle of alternation of power between communists, secularists, and Christians?

Thus when everyone descends from the ideal world into the real world, they are forced to speak with a different logic, not that of how the world should be, on which everyone agrees, but with the logic of reality—that is, the logic of advantages and disadvantages and the balance of forces. Then they become aware of the urgent need for alliances, even with political and ideological adversaries, in order to defend political freedoms, both individual and collective, and to stand in the face of local and international tyranny, even if that means having to work with others, and even secular parties, for the sake of creating a democratic system that allows freedom for all ideologies, including that of Islam. Then Islamic proponents will be able to express themselves freely, whereas before their word was muzzled, and they will come to be content with the rights provided to them by democracy, which makes them equal to others, including the right to convince the public of their Islamic project which they can then apply to the extent permitted by reality.

I will close my commentary on Ennahda's proposed argument in favor of a pluralism that does not exclude any group of citizens who embrace an idea which they promote through peaceful methods and who adhere to the requirements of loyalty to their country. This proposal at the time of its announcement in the early eighties had attracted strong criticism from some Islamist activists and thinkers. This led some thinkers and leaders like al-Sawi, to seek to calm those who attacked this stance with the following advice: "In many cases those involved in Islamic activism lack an understanding about positions taken by certain leaders who start with the premise that one needs a balance between benefits and losses, and as a result these activists cause a lot of clamor around them, create divisions in our ranks and ignite disputes. They warn about a particular stance one day, and the next day it becomes obvious to them that interest obliges them to adopt the very same stance."

To those at the receiving end of the criticism we give this advice: "They should be patient with the biting criticism that comes their way from some of their brethren who do not perceive the scope of this weighing of benefits and harms, because they are not acquainted with the details, and yet they keep on judging them from a distance. For if they were privy to some of the information that these have at their fingertips, they would take a different position. They must be patient and come to understand that their motive in doing this is a passion for Islam and taking to account those they see as going against what God has prescribed. Much sharpness and vehemence in taking positions may be forgiven if a person's purpose is a good one and his initiative is noble."[116]

They and we have the same rights and responsibilities. Some of the Muslim Brotherhood leaders I often talk to, like Professor Mahdi 'Akif, say this when asked the following question: "Can the Islamic state force people to believe against their conscience?" He said no. Then I asked him this: "If the state has no power over people's convictions and ideas, does it fight citizens or groups who believe an idea and express it, or even organize themselves around it, but without resorting to violence, or insulting anybody or making fun of their faith, or giving their allegiance to external parties that are hostile to the Islamic state?" He answered, "Nothing can be done against them." That answer made me happy.

I was even happier to read in a newspaper representing the voice of free Islamic Egypt al-Shaab (close to the Muslim Brotherhood),[117] a weekly column by Shaykh Mustafa Mashhur, one of the historic pillars of the Muslim Brotherhood and its General Guide's deputy. This article was both clear and definitive on the subject of political pluralism, going beyond most of the liberation theses I had seen in the arena of Islamic politics and proposing a significant contribution. You may call it a political fatwa worthy of great respect, due to its boldness and potential in removing a fundamental obstacle in the path of pluralism in our Arab nation. The obstacle I refer to is the status of non-Muslim minorities: What is their position in an Islamic political system based on pluralism—can they create their own political parties, and in that case, does not this situation threaten national unity? Would it not be more advisable, therefore, to forbid the creation of Islamic parties, so that they do not become an excuse for the formation of Christian ones, for instance? This is the principal argument adduced by secularists against the formation of Islamic parties in a nation with other religious minorities.

This of course is only a pretext to exclude Islam and the party of the majority. The proof of this is that our secularist brethren in nations where there are no other religious minorities, like North Africa, make the same demand—ban

Islamic parties, using the pretext that Islam constitutes our common national heritage, and therefore it is not right for one party to monopolize it. So the condition for forming parties around what people have in common becomes transformed into a reasoning by which common belonging justifies excluding those parties, while the creed of minorities, like that of communism, does not justify their removal but becomes a sufficient justification for their recognition.

Clearly, there is no logic in this reasoning! It is simply promoting the logic of power and hypocrisy. As for Shaykh Mustafa Mashhur, he settles the issue through his fatwa, which opens the way for Christians to join Islamic parties. I quote, "Islam supports pluralism of political parties and freedom of opinion, and it does not force anyone to embrace religion" ("There is no compulsion in religion," Q. 2:256). It sets the parameters of relationships with non-Muslims within the context of justice and security, and enjoying their full rights. "They and we have the same rights and responsibilities," he said.

The Muslim Brotherhood affirm their belief in pluralism and that they have been in existence since 1928 and have never been accused of mistreating any Christian or Jew because of their faith. In fact, they welcome the presence of Christians within their Islamic party, believing that Islam is the strongest guarantee for national unity, quoting what nationalist leader Makram 'Abid said: "I am Christian by faith and Muslim by nationality." They further hold that Islam recognizes the existence of faith and unbelief, as well as coexistence with non-Muslims. Christians have lived and indeed they still live in many Muslim lands in security and tranquility, as Islam protects their rights, their possessions, and their places of worship. The fatwa then adds to this by offering Christians another choice besides that of joining an Islamic party—namely, that they form a Christian party on the basis of citizenship. I quote: "It will never happen that forming an Islamic and a Christian party will spark a confessional conflict or fighting between the two parties, since it is the right of every citizen to think about how to improve his country, solve its problems, and choose a path of reform [islah] he believes in and calls others to join. So why exclude those who see in Islam the solution to all these challenges and problems since Islam is from the Wise and Knowing, and why not allow them to have their own party and a newspaper among the more than five hundred that are recognized?"[118]

That position is what has come out of the experience of the Muslim Brotherhood and their explicit recognition of political pluralism and their allowing non-Muslim minorities the opportunity to join Islamic parties within a Muslim-majority country or to form their own. That is indeed the long-standing certainty that characterizes the Muslim Brothers, which has been confirmed through much testing. Indeed, a significant group among them endured all kinds of torture during twenty years of imprisonment, and this is a testimony to their absolute commitment to a methodology of peaceful change and strong activism within the organizations of civil society, like unions, parties, and charitable societies. This document also reflects a serious step forward on the path of establishing a platform of pluralism within an Islamic context, and thus it sets up new policies for Islamists as they interact with a reality that grows increasingly complicated, like coalitions with non-Islamist parties in order to get rid of a common enemy, for instance, or to achieve a common benefit, like creating a democratic space.

This document, even if it does not proceed with the logic it adopts to its ultimate end—namely, the logic of benefit—which it applies to solve situations that are extremely diverse and complex, and solve them in ways that do not contradict the unchangeable parameters of religion, it does nevertheless represent an important step in helping Islamic political thought to evolve toward accepting complete political pluralism without any guardianship over people's choices. That is in fact the position declared by the Tunisian Islamic movement since 1981, until Shaykh Mustafa Mashhur's fatwa came to confirm it and move it forward—that is, recognizing pluralistic democracy with a single standard based on the rule of common citizenship. This is based on the fact that our modern Islamic societies, unlike those of the past, are not founded on the legitimacy of the rule of conquest, something that granted the Muslim community of the past legitimacy to rule. Now our societies are established on the principle of liberation from foreign aggression, and this liberation is what that grants all of its participants, regardless of their faith, the rights of citizenship on an equal basis.

Now for the second document (the Brotherhood declaration), political pluralism from an Islamic perspective is discussed as a principle and ethical value within the context of difference. To advance its argument it leans on Qur'anic verses that portray pluralism or diversity in God's creation as a sign of divine creativity, and it considers that rejecting diversity leads in most cases to despotism and tyranny. The paper then asserts the need to issue a renewed declaration that goes beyond the works of classical authors and beyond repeating slogans, however sincere they might be. What is required, it says, is to translate these slogans into precise statements that show how they might apply to people's everyday lives.

Then the paper stresses the need of connecting the political jurisprudence of state organization and administration to the achievement of people's benefit and the avoidance of harm. It underscores the fact that the Qur'an and Sunna do not define any particular system of government but put forward Islamic values that should be adhered to such as adopting shura as the path to choose a ruler, equality among all citizens, the principle of commanding the good and forbidding the wrong, and the ruler's accountability to the umma. The paper then asks the following question: How can we embody these values in today's society without declaring that political pluralism is necessary to protect them and apply them, and to guarantee the rights that they entail? In fact, the means to activate these values and to protect the umma from tyranny are manifestly different from age to age and from nation to nation.

The document also certifies that the presence of political parties in the current situation of Muslim societies is necessary to guarantee freedom of opinion and prevent despotism—a despotism that is a reality now in most or all of these countries. I quote, "The document sees no objection to the Islamic state mandating for all parties a commitment to the values of Islam."

Further, the declaration emphasizes the full acceptance on the part of the Muslim Brotherhood of political pluralism by citing texts from the Qur'an and Sunna. It cannot be opposed on the basis that it is an innovation nor is difference necessarily one of opposition, but can rather be a type of specialization or diversity—indeed, pluralism and diversity are a consequence of the right to difference and of human nature. Diversity is also mandated by the rule that the only means by which a duty can be fulfilled is itself a duty, which rules out an Islamic political system in our day that denies people's freedom of opinion—itself an eternal right—or their right to assemble in order to communicate what they see as true, another right, or rather duty, mandated by God. Further, the kind of pluralism that results in a peaceful alternation of power only achieves stability and effective government, to the extent that political movements express the identity of the people and represent their interests. Finally, the need to distinguish between means and ends should not make us afraid of using foreign concepts. Now to summarize the document, I offer these points:

- The Islamic political system recognizes the reality of pluralism within its ranks.
- Its limits are found in the basic values and general objectives of the Shari'a or in what may be called "the rules of public order."
- The procedural means like elections and presenting candidates can be accommodated by the Shari'a's texts, which in no way preclude their development.
- The Islamic movement accepts the principle of the alternation of power.

- Further, those who agree on the issue of multipartyism emphasize the need to link it to the reality of basic values. Thus the Islamic movement must not slip into a duality of values on the basis of some supposed distinction between the promotional stage [da'wa] and the governance stage. Otherwise, one would lose sight of the unity of basic Islamic values.
- Since political pluralism is by nature a civilizational idea of great importance, it should not be restricted to political pluralism but rather diversity must be respected at all other levels of civilization and education, which means the acceptance of the existence and opinion of others who are different.

On that basis, then, and in the context of the bloody struggle that Egypt and Algeria are experiencing, the sparks of which threaten to spread to other Arab countries, which for the most part are victims of the same kind of autocracy, many voices are being raised in favor of granting legal recognition to the Muslim Brotherhood.[119] This request found justification by pointing to the Brotherhood's position on political pluralism, its refusal to resort to violence as a means to seize power, and its insistence on using peaceful democratic means. This is also what their spokesman Shaykh Ma'mun al-Hudaybi declared, or their General Guide himself, Professor Muhammad Hamid Abu al-Nasr, on many occasions. He once said this: "It is the experience of the Muslim Brotherhood that causes them to doubt the intentions of any military rule and continually call for the establishment of a parliamentary system that will embody mutual consultation and respect for human nations and their demands, on the condition that this system emerge in a legitimate way, without the use of pressure or deceit."[120] He also expressed concern about the continuation of violence and the use of terrorism.

How the Islamic Movement Came to Accept Democracy

Despite the power and violence of the drumbeat of war against what was called "fundamentalism" or political Islam as an enemy selected—with lavish support from Zionist, Arab, and western parties, despite their varying aims, as the new danger, as an alternative to a collapsing communism, and despite all the efforts to tie Islam to terrorism, hatred of people's freedoms, civility, democracy, and the West, any close observer will not fail to observe a clear tendency in the vast majority of the Islamic current today toward seeking any opportunities to be active under the law within recognized parties, civil society organizations, and unions. These parties practice democratic tools like dialogue and negotiation, the common interest and seeking elections, respect for the freedom of opinion, and alternation of power. Any observer would also note that whenever the opportunity comes for the Islamic tendency to participate alongside other tendencies in the political arena, it has displayed a high level of respect for democracy, moderation in its demands, and a commitment to mutual understanding of common interests, reaching agreements, and an avoidance of monopolization. The clearest example of this in the Islamic world is that of the Muslim Brotherhood in Jordan.

The Islamic Movement in Jordan

This movement has not seen any significant confrontation with the Hashemite Kingdom of Jordan. Its members are an officially recognized presence in the Jordanian parliament, and in particular as members of the Islamic Work Front, which they formed with a number of independent delegates receiving official state recognition since. Their president, Dr. Ishaq al-Farhan, expressed their objectives in the following words, "the establishment of national unity, consolidation of mutual consultation and democracy, and the defense of freedoms and the rule of law."[121]

The Islamic Movement in Yemen

A sister of the Jordanian Islamic democratic movement, the Yemeni movement developed in parallel with it at the same time. They even began the same way, by participating officially in the legislative organs of state and by involving themselves in social and media activities. The movement later formed a front or an alliance, the Yemeni Coalition for Reform, which today actively participates in legislative elections as one of Yemen's key political movements.

This party achieved remarkable success through its alliance with Yemen's most powerful tribes, thus establishing a solid and necessary foundation for a strong Islamic regime in Yemen that would become a pole of attraction and a sturdy point of departure for Islam in the region. The party is known for its moderation and vigilance over the security and stability of its nation. It has been able to integrate itself and interact with the realities of its society, demonstrating boldness and flexibility, and has shared power in a coalition with the ruling party, fighting with them in the war to defeat the southern forces of secession. Then, as circumstances changed, they entered the opposition in alliance with their erstwhile enemies, the socialists, Shi'ites, and Nasserites, giving testimony to the flexibility and competence of the Islamists.[122]

The Islamic Movement in Kuwait

As for the Islamic movement in Kuwait, it has made a recognized contribution not just in the field of social and media activities but also in the political arena. It began as a recognized current within the Kuwaiti National Assembly. Following the Gulf War, the Islamic tendency constituted itself within three bodies: the Muslim Brotherhood, the Salafis, and the Shia, who entered the last elections with success and have become an essential power in the parliament.

The Islamic Movement in Lebanon

The Lebanese Islamic movement reaped the fruit of its steadfastness, its righteous fight to expel the foreign fleets, and its heroic fight against the Zionist occupier. Thus it operated with great success and ease on the two fronts of military struggle and political engagement within the parliament, after the Shia and Sunni parties achieved decisive victories against the traditional tribal and sectarian structure. As Shaykh Muhammad Husayn Fadlallah, one of the most prominent contemporary Muslim thinkers, noted, this clearly demonstrates the deep-rooted nature of Islamic awareness in Lebanon. And not only Muslims voted for them. Hizbullah successfully created alliances that went beyond the sectarian dimension, giving witness to the Islamists' seriousness on the issues of freedom and social justice.

In fact, the Islamists who embarked on their revolutions against the occupiers or the tyrants from within had no political goals, that is, they were simply helping others,[123] as it happened in most parts of the Islamic world where Muslims fought and others reaped the fruit of their struggle. Hezbollah and the Islamic Group [al-jama'a al-islamiyya] are considered the most important representatives of the Islamic movement in this country, which is small geographically but large in terms of its influence and symbolism. Its importance comes from its pluralism, which made it a unique example in the region, which makes it immune to every individualistic and despotic impulse. Finally, its cultural richness is unparalleled, though not as famous as its remarkable heroism in defeating Zionist aggression in more than one campaign and legendary battle.

The Islamic Movement in Sudan

To the experiences of political participation by contemporary Islamic movements in the Arab homeland we could add that of the Sudanese movement. Its political experience has possibly been the most dramatic in that it adopted a variety of practices. Among them was its substantial political participation as an official party in parliament, then its taking up arms as part of an opposition front against the military regime and then entering into an alliance with it. This was followed by a stint in parliament and in government, but then the Islamic movement mounted a coup d'état in the name of national salvation, which it justified as preemptive in the face of another coup aimed at eradicating them. It ruled by itself for a time. Finally, the military wing overpowered them, and it then ruled by the movement, and the country as a whole witnessed divisions that were akin to civil war, which in turn opened the way to international interventions. All of this happened in the context of a fragile process of nation building headed by an autocratic military regime and then a fragile democratic regime incapable of dealing with problems that represented major challenges, such as security and economic issues.

The Sudanese Islamists felt that a third path had been marked out for them: a mix between a coup and revolution, but ended up failing to confront external plans to undermine the country's unity and fragmenting the country further. Regardless, this is a testimony to the fact that human intelligence, even of Hasan al-Turabi's (d. 2016) brilliance, cannot leap over the realities of stubbornly complex situations.[124]

He had estimated that the military could be used to establish a regime built on shura and democracy and that they would go back to their barracks when asked to do so—something that rarely, if ever, happens. Turabi detailed what happened next in an interview on the Al Jazeera network: "We sent our cadres to the state so that they would reform it, but it ended up absorbing them." In his book *Politics and Governance,* he gave more details, "A coup d'état took place in Sudan and the elaboration of the ideal was delayed. When the ideal [the constitution] was finally elaborated, it had been overtaken by a reality that was in stark contrast to the ideal. The president and his soldiers prevailed, and power was stolen from the people, just as the military has done since the days of Mu'awiya."[125]

The ideal that Turabi pointed to is what he explained in great detail in the aforementioned book and throughout his writings over several decades during which he was one of the pioneers of Islamic renewal in the field of Islamic legal theory [usul al-fiqh] and applied jurisprudence [fiqh], including political jurisprudence, in which the values of freedom and mutual consultation were strongly established as central, political authority goes directly to society, or by means of its representatives. This is captured by another word, consensus [ijma'], which is the highest source of political authority. In his words, "the consensus of all, and not just of the scholars."[126]

Turabi continues to explain the ideal by turning to the notion of freedom, which he expands and grounds in the Qur'anic verse "There is no compulsion in religion" (Q. 2:256). Thus he sees no legal legitimacy in jihad, except that of responding to aggression. As for the one who turns away from Islam without taking up arms against Muslims, there is no compulsion in religion, but the believers' responsibility is to continue to call him back to the faith with good arguments.[127] Regarding freedom of opinion and its derivatives, he writes, "The freedom to differ by adopting a variety of ways of thinking and consequent political pluralism, these are among the foundations of governance and political rule in the Islamic faith."[128] For the divine guidance that it provides indicates that public life is wide in its diversity and accommodating of all kinds of views and groups, as the Qur'an puts it, "Each community has its own direction toward which it turns."[129] For this they have no need for special permission or license from the state authorities, for fear that a ruler might come forth with a heavy hand and not allow those who disagree with him the opportunity to differ and give him advice.

For however much different parties go beyond the truth, end up committing actions prohibited by the Shari'a, or at least declared reprehensible [*makruh*], in addition to what the emir disapproves of, "the shining example of the State of Medina, was a clear example of allowing people who chose unbelief (in word and deed) to express their views freely and to form groups on their basis."[130] Turabi is indeed among a very small minority of modern Islamic thinkers who call for the nurturing of an Islamic society built on the freedoms of thought, expression, and organization, following the Medina model, about which the Qur'an narrates many examples that tells a great deal about the debates between various groups of which the Medinian society was composed. Those debates were not settled by the power of the state but by strength of argument. The problem with this liberational and reformist perspective that Turabi proclaims is that it gets severely undermined by the corresponding implementation in reality. Would this be a way of describing the dilemma: not everything a person hopes for can be attained?

The Islamic Movement in Morocco

One of the oldest in the region, this movement was born under a regime with a peculiar relationship with religion, in that it continually seeks affirmation of its religious legitimacy and from the ruling family's descent from the Prophet Muhammad (PBUH). This combination of the political and religious in the Moroccan nationalist movement such that it had at its helm the enlightened scholar and jurist 'Allal al-Fasi. This movement brought together Salafism (the call to return to the roots) and modernization, between the nationalist struggle for independence and the call for the return of the exiled king. Naturally, all these factors converged to make the Islamic movement's mission very delicate and complex.

For that reason too, it is no wonder that the king, who carried with him all that heritage, as well as diverse culture and experience, was able to marginalize and disperse the Islamic movement to a great extent, a movement that seemed to compete with him over religious legitimacy. He easily succeeded in breaking the first wave led by 'Abd al-Karim Muti', the founder of the Islamic youth movement [al-Shabiba al-Islamiyya], who was affected by the blows directed against him and his movement. Later when a number of groups came out from under the debris and survived the tribulations and the stratagems of the regime with diverse goals and methods, the regime would vary its methods of dealing with them, from oppression to curtailment, without either side coming to direct confrontation this time around. But this was before the large-scale campaign that the monarchy launched against the Salafi groups following the events of September 11, 2001, and the terrorist attacks in Casablanca in 2003. The campaign targeted all, including the Justice and Benevolence organization [Jama'at al-'Adl wa-l-Ihsan], almost encompassing the whole of the Islamic tendency.[131]

This movement's guide, Shaykh Abdessalam Yassine (d. 2012), stands out thanks to his spiritual depth, his cultural breadth, and a sharply critical discourse of state policies. Note, too, that his spiritual leadership recalls the kind of traditional Moroccan leadership that brings together noble lineage and great learning with political headship. There is a kind of balance in preserving both sides of this gamesmanship. The two Moroccan noblemen stay on the brink: neither recognizes the other officially, but nor are they at war—just verbal skirmishes and a cautious coexistence. Nor does the king completely deprive the preacher of any space for action and development, so that he falls into despair or danger, nor does he grant him full freedom that would risk changing the balance of powers.

Despite all this, the preacher remains patient, confident, and steadfastly growing perhaps more than any other party and beyond the scope allowed by the ruler who is ever vigilant to remain in control of the situation. How long can such a perilous path be traveled? Notice that Shaykh Abdessalam Yassine is among the most productive preachers and thinkers in the current Islamic movement if not the most active. He writes in the most eloquent Arabic and French, elucidates the finest intellectual arguments, the innermost reflections of the spirit, and the laws of social and political transformation in this country and the world. He elaborates a vision of Islamic society and of the Islamic movement, not seeing it as a refuge from poverty and despair but in his words: "People do not come to Islam as an alternative solution to social ills, but rather as a response to a call that springs up from the depths of the human soul. I do not know what is this tragedy that makes the Western person lose the human sense that allows him to grasp spiritual things, with nothing left within him but elements of economic, social and political analysis, that is, things connected to this world."[132]

The growing wave of religiosity rising from the mosques, in the words of Shaykh Abdessalam Yassine, "expresses at the same time the rejection of the West and the secular ruler, for the latter is accused of serving the West."[133] And then concerning the mutual recognition between Islamists and government, the sheikh notes that "There have been contacts between the state and our group for the sake of obtaining official recognition as a political party in return for concessions, none of which could be accepted, save the condition of working within the boundaries of current laws. Yet our activists continue to be victims of 'royal hospitality.'" But what were these concessions that asked of Shaykh Abdessalam Yassine more than a commitment to work within the law? Were they linked to a pledge of allegiance to the Commander of the Faithful with no conditions attached? He does not mention that. For when the Brother Guide, as his followers call him, was asked about the evolution of the situation in North Africa, he answered, "Let us say that the procrastination of the Algerian rulers and the shortsightedness of (some) in Tunisia—all of this indicates a future that will not be in the interest of the counterfeit democrats."[134]

Despite the controversy surrounding the guide's thinking and pedagogy, not one person—as far as we know—has engaged in criticism and rebuttal, whether among his secular detractors or among his rivals in the Islamic movement, for the Islamist milieu and non-Islamist too are full of respect for Shaykh Abdessalam, even if they disagree with his educational and organizational methods, which he describes as "prophetic." They, on the other hand, describe his group as Sufi, because of the group's domination by a relationship that is more akin to that between guide and disciple within the organization's structure and methods. They have circulated this understanding in those circles, which seems to have prevented any form of, unification of the Islamic tendency in Morocco. Yet this perspective on him has not opened any other channels—if this is true—than that of joining the ranks of his disciples. Still, Justice and Benevolence seems to be the largest and fastest-spreading current within the Islamic movement in Morocco.

Though the Reform and Tawhid [God's unity] movement's first principles go back to the legacy of the Shabiba movement, its intellectual content and methodology sharply differs, especially as other groups have joined them. They all decided clearly and intentionally on the reformist agenda and accepted the legitimacy of the monarchy as the framework in which they would serve religion and nation.

'Abd al-Ilah Ibn Kiran, amir of the Islamic Group [al-Jama'a al-Islamiyya] for many years rejected belief in the existence of hidden secrets and symbols among the clear teachings of the Qur'an and Sunna. Now concerning the central problematic and thorniest issue—its relationship with the monarchy—whereas Shaykh Yassine stopped in his tracks, Shaykh Abd al-Ilah moved ahead, articulating and justifying his recognition of the king as Ruler of the Faithful and recognizing, too, the legitimacy of his trusteeship, which in turn requires the believers' oath of allegiance. Within that framework he reasoned that that which is corrupted can be reformed, and that which is missing can be added. In so doing, as a movement they can avoid any confrontation with the state that would compromise the future of their movement and their country. This movement succeeded in the challenge it took upon itself in tackling thorny issues avoided by others and treading these unchartered waters.

There is no doubt that this political and ideological boldness gave this organization the opportunity to act with greater freedom, while accumulating both experience and growth. It allowed them to avoid the collision with the regime, which normally comes when the latter doubts any group's allegiance or senses that it has become a competitor, even if it has outlawed any shade of radical discourse in a society seeking purity and principled commitment. Still, in a context where misery prevails for the deprived classes while opulence and corruption prevail among the priviledged few, it is no wonder that radical discourse that rejects flattery and compromise, aspires to lofty values, proclaims a wholesome alternative, and threatens the corrupt has a greater ability to win people's hearts than that of its "reformist" counterpart.

Nevertheless, the Group of Reform and God's Unity has maintained a seemingly stable base around a moderate discourse, a reformist methodology, and remarkable preachers, scholars, thinkers, and politicians. Then, too, it has its own active media and institutions based on mutual consultation, all of which seem to make it more ready than its counterparts to interact with the law of Morocco's political game, however changing the rules of that game may be, however restricted the scope of activity, and however dear the demands of integration.

All in all, this path has given it stable growth, both in quantity and quality, and it has integrated with other groups, then directed some of its members to form a political party, Justice and Development [*al-'Adl wa-l-Tanmiya*], which in short order became the second most powerful party in parliament. Today, as Morocco welcomes a new round of legislative elections, it is the object of careful attention on the part of political observers after an opinion poll has shown this party leading its competitors.

With that said, these two political formations do not make up the full breadth of Morocco's revivalist current, diverse and rich as it is, just as Moroccan civilization itself can boast of a wealth and depth of culture and religiosity. Note that there is another Islamic party that has been officially recognized, the Civilizational Alternative [*al-Badil al-Hadari*].

Morocco is certainly brimming with religious organizations, with most of them active in silence, far from the limelight but still above ground. All of this casts Morocco in a promising light for the future of Islam on its soil. Additionally, many observers see the Justice and Development party as a good candidate for winning the upcoming elections, which would enable it to govern Morocco under the leadership of the "Commander of the Faithful."

Yet, while Morocco has achieved a level of success in providing a good legal framework for religion in a society that is both religious and suffers from extreme class inequalities, this has not prevented the rise of violent groups blown in by the winds of international oppression and domination over the umma, with the collaboration of its rulers. This has opened the door for an increase of calls for violence in the name of Islam, acts of violence that have also found opportunity in a climate of poverty and social corruption, as was the case in Morocco.

Naturally, this calls on Islamic reform organizations to prioritize social issues such as combating poverty, corruption, and the international plundering of the people's resources, so that they find appropriate means to succeed and fulfill the hopes that people have put in them. This would prevent anyone from rejecting or doubting the conclusion of Burgat's research which asserts that: "It is clear that political Islamist activists are those who stand the greatest chance of succeeding him,"[135] that is, the king. Or in other words, it can be said that they represent the opportunity to transform an absolute monarchy into a constitutional one, the supreme authority of which is the law, or the Shari'a, within the framework of a monarchic Muslim democracy, similar to Christian democratic monarchies of Europe.

In general, however, external pressures on the Arab region are greater than on any other region, for strategic reasons tied to its location, to the leadership opportunities it provides for the whole Islamic world, and to its location at the intersection of transport routes between all corners of the world. Add to that list its proximity to Europe and the presence of the Zionist entity, which watches over Western interests and is in turn protected by them. Then you take into account the region's extraordinary natural resources, which make it a reserve of essential sources of energy that keep the industrial world in motion. All of these factors throw this region into a perpetual fear of democratic transformation, because it might quickly upend the balance of powers in the world in favor of the regions' peoples, rather than the dominant global powers. This is what the first genuine elections signaled in Tunisia (1989), in Algeria (1992), and in Palestine (2005) in which the Islamic movement won a majority of votes. And a similar outcome could have resulted in Morocco and Algeria, if this movement had expressed its true weight.

As for the rest of the Islamic world, where the interference of the international system in general is less than it is in the Arab world and where the linguistic barrier allows greater possibilities of secularization, there is a slower and more difficult spread of what is called political Islam. Nevertheless, the Turkish Islamists have been able to express their views through a political party that has shared power more than once.[136] This party was removed from power through the army's intervention more than once and dissolved without its leadership calling for jihad. Instead, they endured the blows and responded by forming a new party.[137] Today they rule over Kemalist Turkey within the structure of an imposed secular constitution, which they continually tame and soften so that it conforms to this ancient Islamic land. In this, they have achieved important and unprecedented results with regard to the economy and to democracy and human rights, and they have returned to the nation's rotten political culture an important measure of ethical improvement. These leaders and those like them are today a force of renewal for the secular elites who had been weakened by the sting of corruption, who exhausted whatever legitimacy they had and then sought to replace it by leaning more and more on the state security apparatus and by seeking to please outside forces by spending the legacy still remaining from the independence era, instead of trying to please the inside forces and finding a mutual settlement.

The Islamic Movement in South Asia

In the same way, the Islamic movement in Pakistan represented by the Jamaat-e-Islami (the Islamic Group) stood by their peaceful democratic methodology established in the early 1940s by their founder, one of the most prominent figures of modern Islam Abu'l-A'la al-Mawdudi. It maintained its peaceful strategy in spite of the severe hardship it faced, and today it leads the opposition as part of a wide coalition in parliament that opposes westernized policies that are subservient to international forces on the verge of tearing apart Pakistan's national fabric, after dragging the army into a war with several of the popular factions in order to please the United States.

Qazi Hussain, amir of the Islamic Group and former leader of the student movement, was able to extract his movement from the narrow elitist milieu in which it had long lived in order to become a grassroots movement that embraces the concerns of the masses. This qualified them to aspire to lead their nation and carry out their mission to save it, in addition to significantly contributing to integrating Pakistan within the fold of the Islamic umma. Thus the Islamic Group under the leadership of Qazi Hussain shed its elitism and dove into the concerns of the masses and the causes of the umma. It has now become a well-recognized and respected reformist force, which leads the opposition in parliament and represents a thorn in the flesh of General Musharraf's Americanization policies in that country.

Malaysia is a complex state with regard to its social, cultural, and religious composition. Muslims make up barely more than 55 percent of the total population, yet the democratic process with a regular alternation of power through elections and ballot boxes has not stopped since the nation became independent in 1957. In contrast to the various experiments of openness and political pluralism in the Arab region, the Malaysian Islamists have never been excluded from the democratic process and electoral competition with the other nationalist parties. In fact, the Islamic Party, for instance, founded in 1953, continued to compete with the United Malays National Organization (UMNO), which was founded in 1946 and through the years has continued to represent the majority block of Muslims.

The Islamic Party's influence was not limited to playing the marginal role of filling in the democratic décor of the state; it joined more than once a ruling coalition in the national state and has ruled several states, such as that of Kelantan in the north of the country. The only determining factor in this experiment was the voices of the voters and their choices as they expressed themselves via the ballot box.

As for the Muslim Youth Movement of Malaysia (ABIM), founded in 1972, during the first stage of its development it experienced harsh repression from the state authorities involving the imprisonment of many members and supporters

with Anwar Ibrahim as their head, the founder and president of the movement. This happened in spite of ABIM never presenting itself as a political
party in the traditional sense. But as an organization it did have a great deal of
influence in most cultural, social, and political circles in Malaysia, an influence that increased considerably when Anwar Ibrahim joined the nationalist
ruling party UMNO and became its number two leader and thus an influential member of the federal government. His star continued to rise until it
seemed that he would become the heir of the UMNO leader, Mahathir bin
Mohamad, but the treacheries of politics quickly overtook him, landed him
in prison, and almost destroyed him. Yet today he remains one of the most
important Islamic personalities destined to lead an Islamic alliance that might
have the opportunity to rule after future elections, if they are able to overcome their differences and propose a political project that also encompasses
non-Muslims.

This is true especially as Malaysia has witnessed a slow process of comprehensive development in harmony with Islamic and democratic values, which
has given it advanced status within the ranks of rising nations in Southeast Asia,
or among the "Asian Tigers," as regional economists call them. Their source of
strength is independence instead of dependence, and political pluralism instead
of oppressive regimes and the corruption that is rampant in the Islamic world.
Add to that the pride in Islam as their cultural and developmental foundation,
instead of westernization. This is what has kept this nation from sinking into
the quicksand of violence despite the dangers and tremors, for the ruling party
has remained committed to keeping its Islamic pride, despite its composite nature ethnically and religiously and the many Islamic organizations working in
broad daylight.

The Justice and Prosperity Party of Indonesia

The Indonesian Islamic movement goes back to the time when it held a leadership role in fighting colonialism and liberating the nation. However, in the
context of the rise of forced secularization and modernization trends and in the
context of the Cold War, this country was subjected to an aggressive wave of
westernization and the imposition of alternate political creeds in alliance with
the communist side, which visited severe persecution upon the Islamic movement. With the passing of the communist choice, the country became vulnerable to other currents and in particular to Christian proselytization, which forced
the Islamic movement underground for a long period until the social and political situation became untenable. Then the Muslim youth became a van-

guard for the forces of change, which toppled the elder doctor Suharto and contributed to the founding of an alternate democratic order, after forming the Justice and Prosperity Party, which is the youngest party yet the fastest-growing one and most attractive to the youth. It has shouldered the mission of renewing the decrepit political elite represented by the three largest parties that preceded it in parliament.

There are many similarities between this party and Morocco's Party of Justice and Development, including their rapid growth, their mission to renew the political elites, and the hopes pinned on each of them to rid the nation of the corruption that had accumulated within the decaying political parties.

It is true that in many places Islamic organizations have sought to work within the legal parameters of the state, even though the latter has leaned toward obstinacy and rejection. In this scenario the Islamic response to state violence has been that of tolerance and patience, waiting for circumstances to change. That is for the majority of cases, but sometimes people lose patience, and some groups declare jihad as a response in kind to violence. This all casts doubt on the claim that the Islamic tendency is a monolith and that violence and the inability to live with others is one of its inherent characteristics.

QUASHED EXPERIMENTS IN PARTICIPATION

The Islamic Movement in Iraq

This movement in its different forms, both Sunni and Shi'i, has known a good deal of activity within the political and social arena, before the rise of the nationalist wave that swept a region influenced by the single party model that was dominant in Nazi Germany and various communist regimes. As soon as the nationalist parties were able to rule by overthrowing the existing governments or by a series of assassinations, they eliminated the weak liberal regimes that existed in the Arab Middle East, while great slogans were multiplied, like freeing Palestine, fighting imperialism, achieving Arab unity, and social justice.

The Islamic current was the greatest victim of this oppression, whether Sunnis or Shia, including the Islamic movement in Egypt, Syria, and Iraq. Here we cite in particular the Islamic Party [*al-Hizb al-Islami*], one of the currents within the Muslim Brotherhood, which during the liberalization period effectively participated in the reform and was known for its leaders who were among the most prominent Islamic scholars, most importantly the late reformist scholar Shaykh al-Sawwaf, who had founded their party, the Islamic thinker Professor 'Abd al-Karim Zaydan and Shaykh Muhammad Ahmad al-Rashid. That party's activity, however, experienced some rigidity after the coming to power of the Baath Party. It seems that this was partly due to the party's withdrawing from the political scene because of the balance of powers, and the party itself was no longer active during the Baath rule in the region, though its thinkers did continue to write, and its journals continued to be published abroad. I have recently read its political program and its practical methodology.

What drew my attention was this manifesto's unshakable faith in the umma's right to be consulted by those in power and choose their leaders, its right to monitor them and replace them if they failed in their duties and to determine the modalities of government. One could also clearly note its recognition of pluralism while respecting Islam's basic doctrine, its faith in dialogue as the path to reach consensus with other political parties and among coalitions, and its conviction about the people's right to rule themselves according to God's law. It also believes that it is in the interest of all segments of Iraqi society to work together in order to develop strong electoral practices, so that they become an ingrained custom that rejects political violence and terrorist attacks inside and outside of Iraq. Specifically, it condemns assassinations, bombings, revenge, and reprisals, because violence leads to a response in kind and an infinite cycle of violence. I quote, "If the ruler does not prevent us from addressing the people, then we do not imagine a need for violence, and in fact, there is no grounds for it in our methodology. We rely on a direct appeal [da'wa] to individuals and the masses, to education and the media, as long as there is freedom."

The Iraqi Islamic Party is almost unique in its clear disavowal of violence, though it does leave the way open to it if the ruler becomes authoritarian and suppresses freedoms. From a practical viewpoint, however, it declared that jihad is reserved for the outside enemy, while forbidding evil is the way to reform conditions on the inside. It states that explicitly, as it is the mainstream Sunni position as well.

Similar to the Islamic Party, a party was formed in the Shi'i context, the Da'wa Party influenced by the Muslim Brotherhood and led by distinguished scholars like the martyr Imam Muhammad Baqir al-Sadr, who enriched the Islamic libraries with remarkable volumes on philosophy, economics, and Qur'anic commentary. That said, Iraqi political despotism and the muzzling of the people's will and the forces of civil society—all of this justified by nationalistic and revolutionary slogans—left no place in Iraq for individual opposition voices, let alone collective ones. In fact, the political oppression grew stronger against the Shiʻi organizations after the launching of the Islamic revolution in Iran and the attempts to export it to the Islamic world and to neighboring countries especially. All of this terrified the regimes in the region and pushed them to increase their repression of political opponents. That repression was no different for any of the opposing groups, except in function of their popular appeal and the danger they posed to the state. Thus repression included the Kurds, the Shia, and the Sunnis.

The oppression of the Kurds and the Shia notably increased during the war that the Baath regime declared against the revolutionary state of Iran, because it feared its spread, and found strong encouragement from neighboring countries and the international community. So the country and in particular Iraq was dragged into an all-consuming fire which continued to expand, ending with the fall of Iraq and its subjugation under the heel of occupation. This occupation was facilitated by the ruler's disconnection and isolation from his people, and was aided by nations in the region and outside parties both Islamic and non-Islamic. In the shade of the occupation, parties are today competing for power, most of them being Islamic, yet within a landscape of total destruction, civil war, and a large-scale fragmentation of the national and religious fabric. Gone, too, is the historical conviviality of a civilization that incorporated diverse religious and ethnic communities. All of this testifies to the horror and scandal of despotism and authoritarianism on the one hand, and on the other hand of the danger and absurdity of trying to heal a nation through a disease: foreign occupation.

The Syrian Islamic Movement

This Syrian movement is considered among the most active and oldest groups in the Arab region. It participated in a remarkable way in many of the nationalist events that took place in the region, including the fight against the Zionist entity at its inception. Then, too, for a short time during the brief democratic interlude, it entered parliament and shared power in the ruling coalition. However, the subsequent deterioration of the situation led to a number of confrontations with the regime, with painful consequences. All attempts to find reconciliation, which would strengthen the region's determination to confront outside intervention and resist external pressure to conform to Israeli conditions, to deprive the Lebanese and Palestinian resistance of its support and dismantle its strategic alliance with the Iranian regime, all such attempts ended in failure.

The Islamic Movement in Tunisia

This is one of the most recent movements of Islamic revivalism, or of what is called political Islam, but also a movement that causes controversy and raises eyebrows—perhaps because of its relatively rapid rise in a nation known for its regime being the most zealous and infatuated with Western modernity, in the sense of putting man in the place of God as the center of the universe under the pretext of saving Tunisia from the winds of the East and from medieval remnants, and as the fastest route to "join the ranks of advanced nations," according to the slogan of the nation's builder, Habib Bourguiba. His staunch refusal to integrate Tunisia within the Arabo-Islamic world was only matched and surpassed by his unflinching determination to annihilate the foundations of the nation's Arabo-Islamic identity, its ideas, language, heritage, and civil society organizations. In contrast, he utilized all the state organs to spread and firmly secure the trappings of Western modernity, though not its essence, which is freedom. This is because the kind of state he established belonged to premodern era, where the absolute ruler embodied the state in his own person and family and held it hostage without any distinction.

You could say that this model brings together the traditional sultanic regime with the fascist model that inspired and attracted the youth of the Third World during the second quarter of the twentieth century, because it seemed to be the fastest way to achieve economic development and modernization by mobilizing all the forces of society into one party and one central government led by the single great leader. But it was a colossal failure, a model incapable of delivering on its promises and one that left behind a bitter harvest. Bourguiba espoused secularism and was enthralled by August Comte and the culture of secular positivism, which was in vogue during the French Third Republic.[138] He saw nothing in religion and anything coming from the Arab Middle East in general but an obstacle in the way of progress toward the ideal model of civilization (the West and France in particular).

So the plan to westernize Tunisia and uproot it from its surroundings, identity, and heritage, and its exploitation was carried out to such a degree using the tools of state and the vast influence of a charismatic historic leader and the lack of awareness and weakness of structures of traditional society's institutions and those in charge of them, that those behind the westernization project and following its path came to realize that the fight had finally ended with the creation of a wholly superficial modernization. It may be that the peculiar nature of the Islamic movement that was born in these adverse circumstances was due to its evolution from the stage of traditional Islamic thought—whether local or imported—inherited into what can be described as "Islamic modernism."[139]

The above-mentioned research by François Burgat successfully demonstrated with regard to Algeria's leaders that they wrongly assessed during a certain period the nature of the opposition that was emerging from the mosques as a reaction to excessive modernization and concluded that it was simply the remnants of a passing world that were bound to wither away in the face of an ascendant modernity.

The initial delay in repressing Islamists was not a collusion with governments to combat leftist trends as conspiracy theorists tried to argue that the Islamic current was merely a tool or stratagem created by those countries against the Left. Even if one assumed that major historical phenomena, like the Islamic awakening, which has perplexed those upholding the current international order and continues to frustrate the designs of imperialism on the rise after the surrender of nations, both large and small, could be simply created by such plots, even those who espouse this conspiratory analysis cannot present any actual facts to substantiate the allegation.[140]

Nevertheless, the state's repression did not delay as soon as the first signs of Islamic critical discourse began to emerge, as its influence grew, and the size of its popular support became clear, especially after their joining with the workers in their fight with the regime, along with the university and secondary students during their uprising (January 1980).[141] Later, the Islamic movement modified its position, in accordance with the new official political discourse, when the regime softened its political stance and announced in April 1981 that it would allow the formation of political parties. The Islamic movement itself on June 6, 1981, declared its desire to work within the law as a political party (the Islamic Tendency Movement) that would commit itself to all the requirements of democratic action, such as the peaceful alternation of power and the recognition of all other parties, including the secular and communist ones, and to compete with all of them at the ballot box.

None of this, however, curbed the ruler's repression. Rather, it increased his anger and his determination to use the stick, launching a series of increasingly violent waves of repression and eradication beginning in the summer of 1981, with some periods of truce in between. This is what transformed the state into a highly complex and savage police apparatus that held the whole nation in its grip, ruined politics and culture, spread corruption and fragmentation as much as it could, taking advantage of international climates that were antagonistic to

Islam and the Arab world by using the pretext of resisting extremism and terrorism. But here it should be noticed that the kinds of repression suffered by the Islamic current, represented by the Islamic Group, then by the Islamic Tendency, then by Ennahda—the chief current—did not push them to radicalism, despite the pressures from within and without to take this direction as a reaction to continuing oppression.

Rather, it was the opposite that took place. For as the tribulation continued, so the movement established on an ever firmer foundation an Islamic intellectual discourse that reaffirmed the necessity and importance of bringing Islam into the present day and the world of modernity, the necessity of complete freedom of thought, the affirmation of the rights and freedoms of human beings, a democratic model of political life—that is, political pluralism that includes all of society's constituents and peaceful transition of power via the ballot box, social justice, and civilizational openness, as expressed in the declaration on the occasion of the founding of the movement for the Islamic Tendency, June 6, 1981, and also in the internal constitution of Ennahda and the movement's other writings.

Thus failed the forces of false modernity allied with the oppressive state, despite their expertise in repression and defamation, to drag Ennahda into violence and to transform its image in the eyes of Tunisians and external public opinion into a terrifying obscurantist force. These pseudo-modernists resorted to repression after they had failed to compete with the Islamic current in the strongholds of modernity like the university and the ballot boxes. In fact, in the 1989 elections, no one who followed the political campaign or seriously studied its unfolding could have failed to see that the movement obtained more than the officially announced 20 percent, although even that official figure would have recognized it as the leader of the opposition. In fact, its forcible exclusion was a blow against the opposition, the destruction of the political process, and the gutting of the constitution and the law of all democratic content. The fact is that it had actually won a comfortable majority, which will be revealed in the future on the basis of official documents. In the same way, it was abundantly clear that the elections of June 1990 in Algeria turned out exactly like those in Tunisia had turned out a year before and that this was the chief reason behind the decision to eliminate both winning parties.

This situation also demonstrates that it will be difficult, if not impossible, for the regime to confront the current of political Islam by legally permissible means and that it will be forced to resort to something other than democratic overture, unless it accepts the principle of a transition of power, which had previously been the policy of this state. Muhammad Surur Zain al-'Abidin put it this way: "It is truly sad that the analyses put forward by most Arab and Western media were content to simply relay the declarations of the Minister of the Interior and thus spoke about a conspiracy to take over the state. But the reliability of this theory about a violent conspiracy hatched by political Islam will not be enough to confer legitimacy on the violence practiced by the regime against its political rival, especially if we take into consideration the fact that it was the regime that no doubt initiated the use of political violence to preempt the result of the elections."[142]

This is especially true since the nation's integration into the international capitalist system required cutting it off from its popular forces which might have opposed this plan or benefited from the anger it would produce. For that reason, the regime resorted to repression and the taming of the workers' union in 1986, and in the following year the process of eliminating Ennahda began. This was the same period during which the country was being prepared for this difficult transformation, and that is when Prime Minister Muhammad Mzali was dismissed, who was known for his Arabist orientation after meeting with the leadership of the Islamic movement. This was the interpretation that the philosopher Roger Garaudy gave concerning the attack on Ennahda during a conference in Paris in 1992.

In the end, instead of electoral victory leading to the doorstep of power, it led the victors in both neighboring countries to prison, exile, torture chambers, death, exile, and other forms of persecution, all the way to sacrificing democracy itself out of fear it would benefit Islamists! But Algeria's plight and the scandal of its pseudo-modernists was unparalleled in its flagrance and horror.

Nonetheless, there is a growing conviction among the democratic secular elites in Tunisia that the fundamentalist fearmongering was nothing but a ruse that the repressive authorities used to silence all democratic demands,[143] in addition to the pilfering of Western aid and the exploitation of Western sympathy, just as Israel does to preserve their favor.

A gruesome bloody decade elapsed before our society regained a bit of its health and ability to grasp the extent of the blow it received and then to prepare to react to the regime's policies. It began with petitions by academics and intellectuals demanding freedom of expression, which then developed into a demand for general amnesty for the thousands of political prisoners, the vast majority of whom were members of Ennahda. These last few years, this evolved into the convening of conferences representing a wide spectrum of political opponents, including Ennahda. In turn, this led to the birth of an opposition front after a growing consensus that it was time to abandon any faith in the regime's authoritarian discourse, to rely on mobilizing a coalition of popular forces, and to march into the street to bring about change.

This grassroots movement culminated in the October 2005 declaration by the major opposition forces—including Ennahda, human rights organizations, and well-known personalities—of the founding of a human rights and freedoms movement that would strive for public freedoms and the release of political prisoners. This declaration represented the beginning of the end not just of the isolation of Ennahda and the death of political life but of the era of one-man one-party rule and its policy of pseudo-modernity or westernization in favor of a new era of freedom, identity, and social justice.

The Islamic Movement in Algeria

The evolution of the Islamic movement in general had often been seen as being characterized by explosive and seemingly unexpected growth based on public opinion inside and outside of the Arab region, and even in the eyes of the secular elites both in power and in the opposition. Nevertheless, the Islamists' landslide victory in the Algerian municipal elections of June 1990, represented as they were by the Islamic Front (FIS) led by Abbas Madani and his deputy Shaykh Ali Belhadj[144] and later in December 1991 in the legislative elections, really seemed as if with one leap they rose from under the ground to reach the sky, and their victory was a huge surprise even to experts on Algerian affairs, history, and dynamics of this great nation.[145]

What is amazing here is that the shock that the secular elites harbored inside and outside Algeria lasted throughout the year between the municipal and legislative elections as they continued to hope that the FIS's initial victory was simply a coincidence or a conspiracy that would never be repeated. Then when the "catastrophe" did happen and Islamists won the second time, the world of false modernity inside and outside Algeria revealed its opportunist side and lack of genuine principles. Thus calls multiplied for help among the "democratic" forces, both national and international, to come to their aid with tanks in order to save the "heritage of modernity," which ironically had first entered the country with tanks. After more than a century and a half of this false modernity's rule, it has demonstrated that it is incapable of surviving without the protection of tanks. As soon as it was left face to face with the native inhabitants and with its Islamist foe (the original and true modernity), it exposed its true nature, its weaknesses and the hollowness of its branded slogans. For these reasons, it resorted to calling on the military for help as it cowers in its shade, so that when tanks proceeded to pulverize the ballot boxes, they exuded happiness and danced for joy.

The story of the Islamic movement in Algeria is not very different from that of its counterparts, in that it went through an incubation phase focusing on religious creed and education. However, it was prolonged in Algeria, because of the autocratic military nature of its state which had inherited the honor of its glorious revolution. It was further abetted by its oil revolution, which helped to calm and anesthetize the people's pains and hide from view the failings of a deceitful modernization process, a dysfunctional economic development, and a corrupt political elite. Algerian society had no other option but to turn to Islam to defend its identity and seek hope, warmth, mercy, and dignity. As it did so, the mosques began to fill up, and the call to renew Islam made an impact, while being nourished by the glories of the revolution and by an educational system that was Arabized to a good extent, which in essence contributed to remedy the rupture effected by colonialism.

So the current of Islamic cultural renewal was reinforced by Algeria's opening—unlike in Tunisia—to the figures and movements of revivalism in the East by means of educational delegations sent from the Middle East and Islamic thought conferences that were held on a regular basis in Algeria. These attracted Algerian youth from all over and even Tunisian youth, and some were broadcast live, and thus the Islamic heritage of the past, which had protected and defended Algeria's identity, interacted with the legacy of its own culture of patriotic self-pride and rupture with and hostility toward the West. That was undoubtedly part of the ideology of independence and the basis for its education (especially under President Boumediene, d. 1978), and that legacy intermingled with the new input of Middle Eastern Islamic culture, together with the state's effort to Arabize education and build mosques in addition to the deep sense of disappointment due to the false modernization campaign that relied on freedom slogans while exercising repression, thus creating a deep sense of failed expectation. While extolling social justice and proclaiming Islam and Arab identity, Algeria's political elites practiced corruption and fast enrichment, engrossed in Western ways and anti-Islamic behavior, while some even spread communism, atheism, and immorality.

With time, the reasons for the people's anger piled up, and the populace finally exploded in the uprising of October 1988, which violently shook up the state to the point of almost bringing it down. This quickly brought to the fore the Islamic faction that was the least organized but the strongest in its affinity with the masses, represented by Dr. Abbassi Madani, Ali Belhadj, and their group. The Islamists took the initiative and rapidly caught the surge of popular anger which initially had no clear political goals and fed them with Islamic slogans. For the first time since the revolution, the religious and political ideas came together clearly and coherently, like the establishment of an Islamic state, the application of Shari'a, and achieving justice.

This new gathering (the Islamic Front, or FIS) attracted the widest swath of angry people and preachers, leaving all the factions of organized Islamic movements relegated to their narrow milieus. After the failure of the dialogue initiated between these movements and the FIS after its municipal elections landslide victory, these groups had to establish political entities, including the Movement of Islamic Society, led by Shaykh Mahfouz Nahnah, and the Movement of Islamic Awakening [*al-Nahda al-Islamiyya*], led by Shaykh Jaballah. However, these two movements did not make great headway relative to the Islamic Front, because of the relative differences between the rather elitist nature of these movements and the mass movement nature of the FIS. The Front's victory marked the beginning of a new era in Algeria, and the beginning of the bloody clashes with the state and the problems it would continue to face with the other Islamic factions, not to mention the extreme secular parties.

As for the National Liberation Front (FLN), it continued to witness a terrible collapse that was only lessened by the democratic principles its leaders continued to profess, as befits its history of armed struggle, unlike the Destour Constitution Party,[146] which continually runs after the favors of those in power and thus sullies its history. As it happened, the army, which had left the seat of political power for a short period, now came back to take hold of the reins of power to protect the benefits it had accumulated over a third of a century of state administration, especially since they found the Islamist discourse unsettling, threatening to hold them accountable.

Meanwhile, the secular elites who were dwarfed by the Islamist wave called on the army for help, thus providing justification for its intervention, especially in light of the calls and slogans that emanated from the demonstration that followed the Islamic Front's victory. They were bolstered by the calls from neighboring states and Arab states who were terrified that the Algerian earthquake would reach them. It was also possible that similar and even stronger calls were coming from Western nations.[147] So justifications for the military intervention poured out, as did the encouragements in the form of declarations, funding, and credits from both democratic and Islamic sources.

The FIS was not saved by the call to calm raised by its young leader Abdelkader Hachani (may God have mercy on him), who took over from Madani and Belhadj, now imprisoned, and perhaps his discourse even further encouraged the army to go forward with its coup against the democratic system. In the same way, Shaykh Abbas Madani did not succeed in his call to the masses to cancel their general strike, which was close to paralyzing the whole country. At a time when the Islamic Front was on the cusp of seizing power on the streets, his call on protesters to end the strike was not rewarded by the army and may have incited them to take over from the protesters who withdrew from the streets and to send him and his companions to the prisons in desert camps.[148]

Nonetheless, the enormous wave that was successfully formed by the popular Islamist discourse later deviated—once the tanks drove into the streets and smashed the ballot boxes. In fact, it was the youth who strayed, full of zeal inherited from their grandfathers and their revolutionary legacy that was exploited by the youth who had participated in the Afghan jihad. So by reason of limited knowledge, these youth failed to understand the difference between the relative success with which the umma had fought the foreign occupier and what it takes to fight the domestic occupier, as represented by the tyrants in our own skin. That is what they mostly failed to do, especially during a period in which the nations of our umma and others like them were nothing but—to a great extent—custodians of the great powers' interests.

No doubt the young people's rushing into the armed struggle gave the army the opportunity to take control of the nation, its people and resources, using the combating terrorism as a justification. They managed to turn the greatest political movement in the country into mere armed gangs who fight the security forces and all who stand with them. In turn, the security forces were able to infiltrate them and amplify their operations through false flag attacks to further tarnish them, when instead they should have committed to a strategy of working through the masses and civil society and put to constructive use the popular discourse and the Algerian Islamic contributions that the Front and its two leaders Madani and Belhadj had combined. That ideology proved that Sunnis too (like their Shia counterparts in Iran) had that rare ability to stir up the masses. That indeed is an astonishingly creative fusion, a joining of activist religion and revolutionary heritage in a great nation in addition to a tragically explosive situation for a people of shattered dreams, yet still awesome in its pride, strength, and heritage.

Meanwhile, the extremism of the Algerian secular elites reached the point of raising slogans against Arab culture and Islam in Algeria.[149] Thus to the first coup d'état against democracy and Islamic rule they added a second one against

Algerian identity and its Arabo-Islamic personality, for which one million Algerians had sacrificed their lives. It was that personality, which was deeply felt by Ben Badis, who then fashioned it and reinforced it. In this fashion, the Islamic struggle stripped radical factions of the secular elites in Arab North Africa of the cloak that had hidden their real nature, to pursue more openly their mission of revenge against Islam and its umma, a mission entrusted to them by the occupation powers.

In contrast to that, Islam subscribes to—despite what is said—the values of humanity's heritage aspiring to liberation, social justice, pluralism, and human rights, and it proves that Islam, thus understood, is our only means to enter the world of true modernity and dignity. In contrast to this increasing reliance on Islam, its responsiveness to the aspirations and hopes of the widest possible cross section of society and its mobilization of crowds of people into its ranks from among the elites and the best minds of various countries, and especially from among those forces who struggle against imperialist injustice and international hegemony, the corrupt secular minorities have increasingly thrown themselves into the arms of the autocratic police state or military regime, which is fast becoming the only source of legitimacy for their power and for the outside support for its fight against Arab and Islamic ideals, in harmony with the imperialist-Zionist strategy, whose leaders' discourse can barely be distinguished from that of the secular minorities.[150]

The huge victory in Algeria won by the Islamists did not incite the youthful leader who replaced Abbas Madani to abandon calm and balance. In fact, Hachani declared after the results of the elections were announced: "The Islamic project is one of well-being and mercy for all Algerians, and the Islamic Front is ready to cooperate with the president of the Republic if he allows the newly elected parliament to do its job. There is no truth to the rumors inside and outside of this country that the Salvation Front will clamp down on political pluralism. To the contrary, it certifies that it will respect the constitution and work within the framework of the law."

Granted that there were other declarations that did not contain this level of moderation and reassurance and can even be seen as inciting fear and anger, nevertheless Islamist discourse remains in a dialectical relationship with its milieu, so that however much the latter is open-minded and calm, the Islamists will aim toward moderation, and peaceful coexistence, and display greater tolerance and commitment to the mechanisms of democracy. However, if their rights are violated and violence is used against them, they remember that their Lord granted them the right of jihad to defend themselves and their religion. Some chose this path, while others have taken refuge in patience and perseverance—and that is the path chosen by the vast majority of Islamists. Both sides within the Islamist current continue their heated debate on the issue, sometimes going beyond debate, with each finding support from the texts, from past Islamic history, and from present realities.

It may be the case that some of the rulers who have resorted to repression in their dealing with the Islamic movement imagine that they have succeeded in eradicating their Islamist rivals. This delusion incites them to sing the praises of this solution and actively work to export it elsewhere but without realizing that the calm they experience is not the fruit of their security measures but rather the result of the Islamic movement's self-control and refusal to compete with them by paying back violence with violence.[151]

What is important to note here is that Algeria has paid and continues to pay an exorbitant price in the currency of its lost children, be they soldiers or Islamist youths, and in the currency of insecurity for its people, economy, and reputation. This is a direct result of trading its ballot boxes for ammunition, and of furthering the interests of an isolated secular minority over the broader interest of the masses. One must not forget the effective role played by Madani and Belhadj's preaching over the course of two years in guiding millions of marginalized youths within the context of the peaceful democratic process, giving them hope for the future without spilling a drop of blood.

How great was the loss for Algerian society and for the democratic process in the whole region! Was it not democracy that lost and the world as a whole when permission was given to the tanks to rumble down into the streets, trampling on the will and hopes of the people, crushing ballot boxes, opening the door to the grimmest scenarios, including civil war? Algeria's true leaders were imprisoned and put away in desert camps, while the security forces and the army should have been taking orders from them. Nevertheless, it appears that we are still in need of a greater jihad, one that focuses on ideas and education, so as to deepen and propagate the values of freedom and respect for people's will, individually and collectively, to reinforce civility and come to a wider consensus on an intellectual, political and civilizational common ground that is broader, clearer, and deeper, one that enables our umma to resist outside pressures, provocations, and "advice."

The Islamic Front has been subjected to a ferocious campaign to eradicate it, to smear its reputation and cause it to swerve from its civil path of serving the masses and become criminal gangs who kill indiscriminately—and all this at the hand of the military, which took advantage of overzealous youth who could not accept the humiliation and usurpation of their rights by force, and without thinking they took to the mountains.

President Bouteflika's project of reconciliation has achieved relative success, since it has redressed many injustices, healed many wounds, opened the way for the release and reintegration into society for over ten thousand prisoners and fighters, and paid reasonable compensation to victims of the massacres. Nevertheless, the original wound has not been cleansed, since the project focused on humanitarian solutions, when in fact the problem was political, caused by the army trampling ballot boxes. Yet the reconciliation project exonerated the army from its original sin—a coup d'état, considering it to be a praiseworthy achievement of the mission of saving the state. In contrast, the victim did not even regain full citizenship rights but was held responsible for the catastrophe that engulfed Algeria. Members of the Islamic Front, then, benefited from a presidential pardon but only regained the right to live, and not their political rights, since the law prohibited the return of the Front, even under a different name, and prohibited its leaders from any kind of political involvement. The reconciliation project, therefore, is like stitching a wound without fully cleaning it.

It should be noted in the Algerian state's treatment of the Islamic movement with all its violence, it was not mindless eradicationist violence that sought to eliminate everybody, as in Tunisia. It reserved its venom for the main Islamic faction (the FIS), allowing space for the other recognized formations like Shaykh Mahfouz Nahnah's party, which took the side of the government and was granted the opportunity to join in its executive and legislative powers. In the same manner, Shaykh Abdullah Jaballah's party[152] eschewed violence but took the path of political opposition. Its relationship with the state oscillated between being ignored, weakened, or divided.

All of this points to a rationalization of violence on the part of the Algerian army as it recognized the depth and breadth of religiosity that was expressing itself across a wide swath of the nation, stretching from the mountains to the Council of Ministers and to the parliament. Even the current prime minister is considered an Islamic figure who was educated at the Zaytuna University.[153] Islam in its most basic popular practice was not targeted by the Algerian state, as is the case in neighboring Tunisia. Surprisingly, perhaps, in the last few years certain strange phenomena have appeared on Algeria's horizon that bespeak a certain admiration for the Tunisian experiment and even a desire to emulate it. These include recruiting the help of those who pioneered the westernization and elimination of sources of religiosity project in Tunisia.

Tajikistan's Islamic Movement

The country of Tajikistan, one of the Islamic republics in the communist empire that crumbled, had a similar experience to that of Algeria. Unlike the rest of the republics, which do not have a Muslim majority and where the West put all its effort into excluding communists and replacing them with democrats, in Tajikistan the West backed the return of the communists with all its force and kept Islam from regaining its political authority, stolen from her during the communist era. Yet Tajikistan was the sole nation in the region to witness a democratic Islamic coalition win elections and attempt to expel the communists. What happened, however, was a general alert among the region's neighboring regimes and also Russia, and they intervened to bring down the elected government and put the communists in power once again. In doing so, they committed a series of atrocities, forcing over a half million people to flee the country as refugees in the harshest possible conditions.

All of this was done with the explicit blessing of the international community to stop the Islamic Renaissance (or Awakening) Party [al-Nahda al-Islamiyya] from merely participating in the government dragging the nation into the furnace of civil war. However, when Russia was reassured that the corrupt communist dictator and his entourage had come back, it intervened again in order to bring back stability through a reconciliation between the Renaissance Party and the state. Still, the overall picture remains bleak. The relationship between the state and resurgent Islam is one of conflict throughout the Islamic republics of that region. They came out from behind the Iron Curtain only to fall in the hands of its successors, some of whom are allied with the United States, and these Muslim-majority nations so far have all been deprived of the blessings of democracy, unlike their counterparts without Muslim majorities.

THE POSITION OF JIHADI ISLAMIC ORGANIZATIONS

These many organizations stand out from each other with respect to their ideological backgrounds and strategic goals. Some are from a Salafi background with only local strategic ambitions, like some of the Algerian organizations and the former Islamic Group [al-Jama'a al-Islamiyya] in Egypt.[154] Some of them are Salafi with strategic goals that are global in scope, the most famous of which is al-Qaeda. Both kinds are opposed to political parties; they oppose democracy and any other form of activism under regimes they consider ungodly [*anzima kafira*]. These cannot be changed except by force. For this reason,

they vehemently criticize all the moderate organizations of the Islamic movement such as the Muslim Brotherhood or its counterparts in Pakistan, Turkey, and so on.

This criticism is due to the differences in methods and perspectives, particularly as some of these armed groups emerged as splinters from the mainstream Islamic movements in the dank prison cells of the revolution and
under the plight of repression. As a reaction, these young men labeled the oppressive regimes "infidel" [kafir] and considered that armed attacks against
them were the only way to restore Islamic legitimacy.[155] Then divergences
with the mainstream movements increased as these groups adopted Salafi
doctrines as these became more widely disseminated in the 1970s and 1980s
(See Ayman al-Zawahiri's "The Muslim, Brotherhood and the Bitter Harvest"). The influence of these organizations continued to expand particularly
during certain periods on the Egyptian streets, as a result of the political and
economic crisis in Egypt, and especially after the government's rush to nor-
malize relations with the Zionist entity, even though it was in defiance of
public opinion.

This was in addition to the lack of any progress in political life and the hypocrisy, corruption, and immorality especially rampant among the political class, to
the point of collaboration with foreigners leaving the people crushed under
the weight of the crisis. In turn, this led many to listen attentively to the radical
religious discourse that offered a simple and daring religious diagnosis to the
putrefied political situation. For instance, one could read the following in a
publication of the Egyptian Islamic Jihad organization: Egypt's current situation can be summarized in four ways: an unbelieving government, a class of
apostates supporting it, a lost people, and confused youth.

For each of these points the document then goes on to provide arguments
that are fairly convincing in an Islamic context. The state, for instance, is
unbelieving [dawla kafira] because it does not judge according to God's laws
and replaces them with mixed and fabricated ones, permitting things that
God forbids and forbidding things God allows, to the extent that the state
protects public prostitution, permits consensual adultery and fornication;
recognizes Israel while forbidding jihad as a means to liberate Palestine; and
abolished jihad as a duty, even though a previous fatwa issued by al-Azhar
University affirmed that anyone who establishes contact with Israel or sells
their land to them is an apostate. Furthermore, the state allows unbelievers
[kuffar] to enter the nations of Islam and establish military bases. The constitution itself entertains no other crimes than those mentioned in the state's
legal codes.

So where is the revealed Text in all of this? The publication goes on to reinforce its argument by noting that the Egyptian judiciary in its famous case on jihad recognized in 1981 that the law and the constitution contradicted the Shari'a. Thus the paper ends its argumentation by citing the fatwa issued by Shaykh Ahmad Shakir, who wrote, "The truth about these positive laws is as plain as day. They are a clear form of unbelief [*kufr*] that is neither hidden nor implicit, and there is no excuse for whoever claims to be Muslim and yet follows them, or submits to them or approves them. Let everyone take heed to this warning." The reason given is that Islam makes God the Legislator, and democracy gives this task to the people.

That much was about the rulers. As for the followers, they are considered apostates, as we read in the Qur'an, "Pharaoh, Haman, and their armies were wrongdoers."[156] The group that aids the rulers shares the same classification, as we also read, "Anyone who takes them as an ally becomes one of them."[157] The notion of "ally" here involves support, and whoever supports the ruler by word and deed comes under this judgment.[158] The late Shaykh Muhammad al-Salih al-Nayfar (may God have mercy upon him) issued a more detailed legal opinion along these lines on the topic of political parties that support rulers who disregard the Shari'a or who mock its rulings and persecute its preachers. He wrote the following about those who call for breaking the sacred law of fasting or to make fun of those fasting or of any other Islamic ritual, "Whoever does that, whether under compulsion or trying to curry the rulers' favor, while he knows they are on the wrong path, then he has disobeyed God [*fasiq*]; as for the one who does this while approving their wrong actions, then he is an apostate [*murtadd*]."[159]

The pamphlet goes on with its diagnosis and, sees in most people a nation that has lost its way, classified into disobedient apostates and Muslims. Those who carry the outward signs of Islam such that they pronounce the two shahadas [the twofold witness, or the first pillar of Islam], practice the ritual prayers, and give the zakat, those are Muslim, whereas we should consider whether those who manifest some sign of unbelief can be excused on the basis of ignorance or of being under compulsion. For we do not judge any individuals in society except when the need arises, such as if they are from among the tyrant's aides or soldiers or if they are calling toward misguidance. As for people in general, their remedy is an Islamic government.

Allow me to quote directly from this publication:

If we say that Muslim youth are confused, we mean that that they are pulled in different directions, while most of them do not know the priorities stipulated by their creed or even the basics of Islamic jurisprudence, while those who do have knowledge remain stagnant, caught as they are between the infinite greatness of God's oneness and the ferocity of ubiquitous evil. Sometimes they step forward, and sometimes backwards; and sometimes they choose paths simply to avoid this immense mission. In other words, they suffer from split personalities.

In truth, God's religion is tawhid, and jihad is the means to attain it. The least acceptable level of jihad is to refrain from seeking the help of those disbelieving rulers and to implore God to destroy them and to help those engaging in this jihad by every possible means.

Despite its brevity, this pamphlet broaches the topic of the Muslim Brotherhood with stinging criticism, beginning with the founding guide Hasan al-Banna, all the way to Shaykh 'Umar al-Tilmisani, and then to his successor, to whom these words are attributed, "We want [the state] to be entirely democratic and inclusive of everyone."[160] In the same way, it takes them to task for resolving to work on changing the social and political reality by democratic means and in particular through the parliament.

An article by Professor 'Abd al-Hamid Matlub, chair of the department of the Islamic Shari'a at the al-Azhar University, follows a very similar orientation: there are no political parties in Islam; the basic truth is that all Muslims are one community, as God Himself has said, "This is your community, one community, and I am your Lord, so serve me."[161] Parties, he continues, only appeared in Islamic history as a result of wars, internal squabbles and behavior contrary to God's law, and al-Andalus [Muslim Spain] was only lost after the appearance of Muslim divisions.

As for Omar 'Abd al-Rahman, guide of the jihad formations [under the Islamic Group, al-Jama'a al-Islamiyya], he denies the permissibility of multiple political parties, even in the purely Islamic context, because there are only two parties, the Party of God and the Party of Satan.[162] That said, he took a different position following the horrible bombing of the World Trade Center in New York (1993), which was blamed on a number of Muslim youth who allegedly visited Shaykh Omar Abdel Rahman's mosque in New Jersey. Since the shaykh was now in the limelight, a journalist from *Newsweek* came to interview him, particularly on the topic of democracy in Islam. One of the questions posed was this: "What position should the West take on vis à vis the Islamic movement? Should the West be afraid of Islam?" He answered, "If the West is serious about using slogans about human rights, freedom, and democracy, then it should not be afraid of Islam, but rather love it, since Islam has built its foundation for 1,400 years on the principles of freedom and democracy. So why is Islam opposed? . . . So why does the West fight the Islamic movements in Algeria, Tunisia, and Egypt? The West is seeking to destroy Muslims all over the world."[163]

Maybe the shaykh was using the word "democracy" in a different way than jihad organizations normally use it—that is, as an expression of unbelief [kufr]—like the Party of Liberation [*Hizb al-Tahrir*], for instance—that is in a context of debate and argument, and in trying to clarify Islamic tenets for someone who is ignorant of them, he brings them closer to his interlocutor by using terms that are familiar to him. In that case, he is not referring to democracy in its usual definition of establishing a political order on the basis of mutual agreement and consensus, rather than individual rule or compulsion but focusing on safeguarding the unity of the community instead of creating inner divisions and struggles, yet without allowing that to happen within the pluralistic framework known in the West.

Jihadi organizations have witnessed an immense expansion, which has led a number of formations to constitute a global front to fight Jews and Christians and those who support them. This front is called al-Qaeda and was led by Osama bin Laden and his deputy Ayman al-Zawahiri, formerly the amir of the Egyptian Islamic Jihad organization. Similar formations in several countries have joined al-Qaeda, and as part of its global jihadi strategy it has carried out a number of attacks in far-flung places, the most famous of which was the September 11, 2001, attacks (the Manhattan Raid [*Ghazwa*], in al-Qaeda parlance), which had the worst possible impact on Islam's image and on Muslims worldwide, linking them to terrorism.

At the same time it put a deadly weapon in the hands of the conversative Zio-Christian alliance that controls American political decisions and in the hands of all the enemies of Islam and Islamists, and especially groups of extreme secularists and proponents of the repressive security approach in Arab and Muslim countries, and in fact throughout the whole world insofar as draconian antiterrorism laws were adopted.[164] Thus the powers of security apparatuses were enhanced, and demands for democracy, human rights, the rule of law, and judicial independence were all set back.

Yet other violent movements evolved in the opposite direction, such as what happened with the Egyptian Islamic Group, which was the most important group in the elaboration of the strategy of jihad in contemporary Islam. Among its members, both those behind bars and those on the outside, a radical self-examination took place, which resulted in refuting the tenets of their methodology based on declaring the regimes in Muslim countries as infidels, including the Egyptian state, and on the God-given duty to overthrow them by force. The leaders of the Islamic Group then apologized to the Egyptian people for their deficient jurisprudence [fiqh] and recognized that Islam's method for reforming the current situation in Egypt was that which had long attracted the consensus of Islamic Sunni scholars, namely, the peaceful method of commanding the good and forbidding evil. In truth, the intelligent Egyptian authorities in this case took notice and at the very least encouraged those taking this path; some they even released from prison and facilitated their civil work through the founding of new organizations. These measures of punishment reduction benefited thousands whose suffering had been appalling.

Meanwhile, other formations of jihadis were flocking to international theaters of jihad where they found encouragement from the capitalist camp, especially in Afghanistan in the fight against the communist government. It was there, after all, where the jihadi school's ideology and practice was first instituted, drawing young men from all corners of the Islamic world. Thus, when the mission of expelling the Soviets from Afghanistan was accomplished—and even their empire collapsed—the graduates of this jihadi school were pursued, and they fanned out in several regions finding new ways to attack and create strife.

So in the wake of this expulsion and the infighting of Afghan groups ending with the rule of the Taliban regime, the Yemeni-Saudi Osama bin Laden and his deputy, the Egyptian jihadi amir al-Zawahiri, founded the World Islamic Front for Jihad against Jews and Crusaders, as mentioned above. That organization represented at the time the most serious threat to the international order, especially after succeeding in delivering a painful blow to its head in 2001. That attack also gave the global leader the long-awaited opportunity to mobilize the nations of the world to join him in the war against Islam and its institutions, even the charitable ones, its preachers, and its minorities, including any power it saw as a rival, and all this under the pretext of a holy war against "terrorism."

Jihad in this context (i.e., for the jihadis) is not merely a tool of defense against an aggressor assaulting the abode of Islam, just as all Muslim countries have done when they were invaded, and as they do today wherever they have been occupied, as in Palestine, Iraq, Lebanon, and Afghanistan. For them jihad is a total war against the other who is not under the rule of Islam in order to compel them to submit, since for these people there is no legitimacy for a state that does not rule according to Islam. From this perspective, founded to some extent on the writings of Sayyid Qutb, Mawdudi, and others who succeeded them, there is no place for political and ideological pluralism within Islamic societies nor is there any for multiple states or civilizations on the outside.

Thus, this ideology was not only a challenge to the global order but also to the Islamic view of freedom and pluralism, on the foundation of which the Islamic societies of the past were established and the nature of all their relationships with other nations was calibrated as long as they were ready to shun animosity and live in harmony, peace, and security with the others, since freedom of belief and conscience, dialogue, peaceful relations, and preventing hostility are the foundation for relations with others. Even though the absence of international law before the modern period made relations of war and force the rule in international relations, Islam presented the concept of the Abode of Islam versus the Abode of War. "Abode of Islam" meant the abode of security or those lands in which the Muslim person felt safe and his possessions and honor were protected— that is, the abode of justice and freedom.

With the advent of the modern era, international relations became regulated (at least in theory) by international law, which stipulated that peace, reciprocal recognition, and cooperation be the basis for international relations and not war, as it had been previously. War was to be the exception and could only be justified in order to repel belligerence. As God says, "Fight in God's cause against those who fight you, but do not overstep the limits. God does not love those who overstep the limits."[165] Some of today's jihadi organizations are an extension of the work and strategy of the nationalist movements that emerged in every Muslim nation to confront foreign occupation. Hamas and Islamic Jihad are two examples of movements that fit that description. They are local organizations founded on a moderate ideology rather than *takfir*,[166] and similar ones are also found in Iraq, Afghanistan, Chechnya, and the Philippines.

THE ISLAMIC MOVEMENT IN SUDAN

Sudan is a modern entity that is not fully formed yet and has been the setting for civil wars since its independence in 1956. As a country, it was one of those creations spawned by the colonial design to divide up the umma. It was through the amazing jihad-inspired struggle against the British occupation at the end of the nineteenth century that it was founded. Then it tossed and turned as the winds swept over the region time and time again, between a military regime, which held sway for most of the period after independence, and a short-lived democratic experiment.

The weakness of a state lacking history and financial resources has given opportunities for separatist tendencies again and again. These tendencies have found outside support, aiming to spread Arab identity and limit Egypt's interference in its affairs. All of this increased the state's weakness, though as a fragile state it has not been able to practice the kind of repression that is so common among the other Arab states, something that has allowed the Sudanese in all their circumstances to hold on to the spontaneity, openness of mind, freedom, and good character, that characterize their culture and traditions. Thus there was freedom for all the ideologies that appeared in the region and easily made their way to Sudan, without significant repression relative to others in the region.

It was only natural that the Islamic current would appear in Sudan early on, influenced as it was by neighboring Egypt, and the thinking of the Muslim Brotherhood found a home there since the early 1950s through a movement involved in both preaching and politics. This movement interacted within a society by nature open-minded and became involved in the concerns and institutions of society, be they political parties or trade unions. This interaction developed in them a school of thought and experience that leaned more toward openness and critical thinking than was the norm for organizations that develop in a repressive political environment that forces them to be secretive. This led them to develop a distinct character that was different from and organizationally separate from the mother organization in Egypt, which eventually caused an organizational split.

Dr. Turabi played a key role in all of these developments as a skilled debater in the forefront of Islamic renewal, be it intellectual ideological, political, or jurisprudential, and a respected academic and jurist as dean of Khartoum's law school and as a seasoned political player in the top rank of Sudan's political elite, holding on to these roles for half a century. Nevertheless, his method of action often landed him in prison, even when he led his entourage to power through a coup, imagining that facts could be skipped over, even by a bright person like himself, assuming he could use the army to risk their own lives to seize power on his behalf, then they would hand it over to him to rule and to send them away whenever he wanted and then restore the government to his model of consultative rule.

However, conflicts exploded and divisions multiplied, all because of the dispute over the Islamic model of governance, which since Mu'awiya's takeover had become unclear and influenced by the model of rule by force.[167] And all this happened in spite of Turabi's energetic critique of this kind of rule and his defense of one based on mutual consultation with the people. Nevertheless, he allowed himself to ride the military steed into power and thereby restore a rule by force, while entertaining the fiction that once you use the army, you can then get rid of it. This reminds us of the sons of Jacob in the Qur'an who justified their crime in the following way: "Kill Joseph or banish him to another land, and your father's attention will be free to turn to you. After that you can be righteous."[168]

The second delusion that overcame Turabi's brilliance was this: his underestimation of the regional and international forces as he was carried by the winds of high hopes, as had happened with revolutionaries before him, to attempt a great leap over the hard facts of reality—the reality of a Sudan torn apart, too weak to be used as a launching pad to export a revolution or threaten other regimes, and especially when it is a nation still in the process of building its own national identity. Add to that an Islamic movement that is only a minority that overthrew the majority, because it lost hope in its direction and despised it, using the modern state's institutions in the areas of security, economics, and education, with the goal of curing it of its illnesses.

These are the same wagers and cures chosen by secular modernists, wagers that had already met with abject failure in what they seek to accomplish. This is because people by nature yearn for freedom and therefore hate even that which is beneficial and good for them if it is imposed on them by force. They might submit to it in a moment of weakness, but they lie in wait for the opportunity to rebel against it. In the same way, the wager of the modern Islamic movement of Sudan does not escape this use of the state as an instrument of change and domination over people. It is the same wager that is used by its communist and nationalist counterparts, who all seem to ignore that a people's identity is more solid than any tactic leveled against it by the state. And even if what Turabi contends is true, there is nothing that gives one group permission to impose its mandate over others, whether using Turabi's justification or another, and especially at the hands of a thinker who devoted his work to defend freedom of thought and conviction and freedom of legal interpretation [ijtihad] and mutual consultation [shura].[169] It is no wonder, then, that his disciples used against him the same logic and weapon—violent regime change. They ended a rich experience that had carried the hopes of many in elaborating a modern Islamic model that would be a positive representation of Islam's defense of freedom and pluralism and not bear witness against it, as was the case.

This project was not without its accomplishments, however, like the signing of a reconciliation agreement with the south and a portion of the west, the beginning of oil production, and the expansion of education to more areas of the country. But what is the value of this reconciliation if it came about through international pressure and not with sincere motives or respect for treaties? What is the value of economic development if it is not based on a theory and practice of freedom, political pluralism, peaceful alternation of government, an independent judiciary, and a free press that protects the nation from exploiting influence or wealth gained illegally? The movement's failure to resolve its internal conflicts democratically does not offer much reassurance about its sincerity in principle, which would protect it from hypocrisy instrumentalism—both of which threaten the splintering of Sudan. If that were to happen, it would be the most flagrant proof of the failure of Sudan's Islamic experiment take place.

Here we notice a stridency in the relations between yesterday's brothers, which resembles the violence of reprisal and revenge, and especially the harshness expressed by the shaykh toward his former disciples, as if he were determined to destroy them, even if that meant destroying the whole project. Even before conflicts broke out, this was my advice to him: it would be wiser for his position to be a judge among his disciples, rising above them rather than being a party of the conflict, and to devote himself to the strategic tasks that would benefit the whole umma, which was something he was the most qualified to do. Sudan's worst problem, was that even if it gained some benefits from the experience of the Islamic movement, it lost the most important ingredient that set it apart from the other Arab countries, that is the state's power was so limited and subtle as to seem inexistent. Unfortunately, through its Islamic rule the state grew some claws, and its security apparatus expanded and became more sophisticated.

Notwithstanding, Sudanese society remains very diverse in its composition and political culture, and once it had taken stock of how its wager to centralize the state and dismantle the traditional pluralistic nature of its society had failed, the government was forced to allow once again the formation of political parties. It officially recognized that diversity and accepted a measure of power and resource sharing. Yet this outcome only came about through fighting and rebellion and hence has exposed the nation to further outside intervention.

THE POSITION OF THINKERS WHO REJECT POLITICAL PARTIES

We will not speak here about groups that refuse political action as a whole. If they consider their refusal a temporary issue of transition, they may be justified in doing so. Yet if they refuse it altogether, they have fallen into a secularist position—that is, one that stipulates a separation between religion and politics. Rather, we are speaking about organizations and thinkers who refuse the label "political party" for their gatherings or who refuse political action in the framework of the rule of law. Even if those individuals and groups are numerous, they are dwindling, to the advantage of the moderate current, the one that promotes political pluralism and participation.

Nevertheless, many Islamic organizations working in the political arena scorn the label of political party for themselves. The great scholar Abu'l-A'la al-Mawdudi himself, although he recognized the right to association within an Islamic political system, argued the following: "A difference in opinions is a fact of human life. Therefore, it is possible for different schools to appear among the umma, which rallies around one principle and one theory. Yet their teachings, in any case, remain fairly close to one another. The Imam 'Ali (may God grant him peace), for instance, recognized the right of the Kharijites to form a group, as long as they did not resort to forcing people or to imposing their views."[170]

And yet he was extremely vigilant about keeping the unity of the umma and the unity of the Shura Council, thus forbidding the council members from joining political parties. He even went further than this in his Islamic constitution and called for doing away with the party system, which defiles the state's government with a kind of partisanship reminiscent of pre-Islamic Arabia. This can lead, he contends, to the possibility of one party seizing power because of its influence and authority and spending the people's money to enrich those who support them to stay in power. Thanks to those people, they can act as they choose, despite the people's efforts to rein them in.[171]

We may not be able to explain the contradiction between Shaykh Mawdudi's call for dissolving the party system—around the same time as Shaykh al-Banna's establishment of his organization—and Mawdudi's establishment of his organization, which, although he did not call it a political party, nevertheless, it took part in several elections and had representatives elected to parliament. Is that not in itself a kind of recognition of a state of affairs, though perhaps not of its legitimacy? But if one has to reckon with the likelihood of this interpretation, can it be endorsed by Islamic ethics? We do not see that possibility. We have witnessed the development of the Muslim Brotherhood over the years and how they came to accept a multiparty system and refuse any difference in methodology whether in power or in the process leading up to it.

As for the Islamist thinkers who refuse the principle of political parties in the Islamic state, although their number is steadily decreasing they do still exist and continue to defend their position. I will only present two proponents here.

Sobhi ʿAbduh Saʿid

In his examination of the first Islamic political experiment, Saʿid concludes that the emergence of parties came as the natural outcome of the Islamic society's straying from the foundations of its political order and falling into the hands of rulers who were not able to stringently follow every requirement of God's Straight Path or in the hands of, apostate rulers. So multipartyism emerged as a sign of society's waywardness. He concludes that shura, as opinion and counter-opinion, remains one of the pillars of Islamic rule and the right of every individual to be expressed on an individual basis without gathering people or rallying them around one principle, because Islam does not recognize the use of political games to reach power. Therefore, this mutual consultation is in no need of political parties, but truly in need of an Islamic education that will help to restore the umma's unity on the basis of its creed such that it knows no other banner than that of its God and no party other than God's party through its divine perspective and faithful understanding.[172]

Kalim Siddiqui

A Pakistani Islamic thinker, Siddiqui wrote a book vehemently attacking what he calls Islamic parties, and especially the Muslim Brotherhood and the Pakistani Jamaat-e-Islami. He blames them for adopting Western thought in their ideology and organization, considering them to have swerved from the Islamic methodology for revolution and leadership and as a result, remain out of touch with the concerns of the masses and unable to mobilize them since they did not implement the prophetic model of leadership and the concept of God's party. Within this current of contemporary Islam—even if it is only a minority—one could include the Salafi groups, both the jihadi ones and the more traditional ones.

To sum up, the political thought that rejects multipartyism, though limited, is still represented within Islamic circles that hold on to traditional concepts of the unity of the umma, which link differences and diversity to dissension and division. In reality, this is a legacy of painful past conflicts in the history of Muslims and of wrongful conceptions of what consensus and unity mean. For them these are the opposite of pluralism and difference. This is also a legacy of interpretations of hadiths, the authenticity of which may be doubtful, like the one that has the Prophet (PBUH) declaring that the umma would be divided into more than seventy sects, all of which lead to hell except for one. Naturally, every group starts with the premise that it is the only one leading to salvation, while all the others lead to certain destruction.

Even if this report turns out to be authentic, the collection of saved individuals is the entire umma—that is, all those who recognize the highest authority of the divine inspiration, even if they differ on their interpretations.[173] There is no doubt that a human relationship built on this kind of premise cannot avoid ending up with the annihilation of one of the two parties, or maybe both of them. This makes coexistence between various Islamic groups challenging, dialogue between brethren difficult, and mutual consultation restricted.

Nevertheless, the Islamic public sphere is witnessing a substantial move toward the acknowledgment of political pluralism, either as a result of bitter experiments with political autocracy, the greatest victims of which are the Islamic movement, or as a result of the global democratic wave and the evolution of Islamic democratic theory. We believe that the repression reigning in the Arab region bears the greatest responsibility for the enduring power of Islamic ultraconservatism. Still, the moderate current is the most influential on the streets of Muslim nations, and it is the voice that attracts the widest range of people.

THE FOURTH GENERATION

The fourth generation of the contemporary Islamic movement has tried to overcome the movement's impediments, while consolidating its achievements over previous generations.[174] These include, on the level of doctrine, rejection of imitation [taqlid] and insistence on the priority of the sacred texts as the highest authority; with regard to politics and social policy, their emphasis on mutual consultation as not only an individual practice but also as the foundation of the state, and on the right to assemble and participate in the political, cultural, and economic life of society. From the first generation, they learned and held on to the purity of its Salafi convictions—that is the emphasis on returning to the sources.[175] From the second they retained the boldness of the Islamic project and its realism in confronting the outside aggressors, and from the third they retained its absolute faith in the validity of Islam as a civilizational alternative to the West while incorporating its positive aspects and faith in the unity of the umma in confronting the Zionist-Western attack.

The emergence of the fourth generation was accompanied by the spectacular decline and dramatic defeats of the secular current, both politically and intellectually. The rout of the Arab regimes in 1967, or the invasion of Beirut in 1982, or the Gulf War of 1990, or the Zionist withdrawal from Lebanon in 2000, and finally the humiliating defeat of the undefeatable army by Hezbollah in 2006 all represented the defeat of all the Arab regimes, whether to the right or to the left, and it signaled the dramatic failure of the renaissance project premised on subservience to the West.

On the other hand, the same period saw the gains of the Islamic current on university campuses, in the centers of learning and symbols of modernity, and in domains of activism; and saw the launching of the Iranian Revolution and in the Afghan military resistance; in the growth of the Islamic movements in Egypt, North Africa, and elsewhere; and finally in the abandoning of many thinkers and activists on the left from their negative perceptions of Islam when they discovered its true nature as it repelled the imperialist aggression against the umma in Palestine and Iraq. These represent some defining moments in the development of this new generation.

This blessed forward march, despite the remaining impediments it suffers from, both on the inside and the vicious attacks leveled against it from the outside, has not ceased to affirm Islam's revolutionary and liberationist dimensions and its eligibility to lead the masses and build its civilization and political rule, and affirm that within a Shari'a framework, it is the people who possess sovereignty and authority, and that no one may impose guardianship over the umma.

The fourth generation also saw a development and reinforcement in the specialty of Islamic studies, whether in the field of personal law or in public law, especially constitutional law. Professor Sanhuri, Diya' al-Din al-Rayyis, and Mawdudi were this generation's pioneers in the specialized study of the Islamic state, along with a number of legal scholars in Egyptian universities and elsewhere. As a result, the disciplines of Islamic politics, Islamic economics, and Islamic administration became common within law schools and departments of economics, political science, and civil administration, disciplines which adopt the methodology of comparative studies placing these side by side with Western theories and concluding on that basis the superiority of Islamic thought and its immense potential to solve today's problems. This is how a sizable number of legal scholars who until the 1970s had been bent on spreading Western political, legal, economic, and administrative theories then transformed into pioneers of Islamic thought who in turn trained a new generation of specialized Islamic thinkers.

The prevailing view of this generation on the topic of political parties is the following:

- They recognized people's inalienable rights, the legitimacy of which derives from God who created humankind.
- Differences of opinion are inherent in the very nature of human beings and recognizing that humans have rights is thus a declaration of their

right to disagree, which implies the right of expression and association
and to command good and forbid evil.[176]

- Though the Shari'a grants the right to differ, it does so on the condition that this not be about religion—that is, about its unchangeable
  foundations—and that this not be at the expense of kindness and brotherly love. Otherwise, it becomes blameworthy and harmful.
- The majority of Muslim thinkers of this generation stress the importance
  of parties in order to develop political participation among the masses,
  to express the will of the people, and to strengthen it so as to confront
  either despotism at home or aggression from abroad.

With regard to that last point, however, they add that this right is granted on
the condition that this freedom not overshadow the umma's creed or threaten
its security or independence. Considering that the Islamic state's foundation and
goal are religious in nature, it emerged thanks to Islam and in order to serve the
Islamic cause and provide for the benefits of those being ruled. For the means
one chooses should not undermine the foundational values. Put otherwise,
the religious quality of this state is different from the religious quality of another state that sees religion only as a personal matter, but rather the Islamic
character is fundamental just like another state may be described as a monarchy or republic or as having a socialist orientation, meaning that those characteristics are part of the fundamental nature of that state. The Islamic state, for its
part, decrees the equality of all its citizens in terms of rights and duties, but it
considers religious identity as a valid basis for discernment in religious matters.
This itself results from the principle of equality, because to impose the requirements of a religion on those who do not believe in it—like the prohibition of
drinking alcohol for non-Muslims in Muslim countries as applied to Muslims—
goes against the norm of equality. In the same way, pledging oath to or entering into a covenant with a nonbeliever in order to protect Islam is also an
injustice, or sanctioning an organization that aims to get rid of the state's
religious identity or one that is based on allegiance to the umma's enemies—
these, too, have nothing to do with justice and equality, but demonstrate injustice against the majority's right. Moreover, they represent an attack on the
identity and national spirit of the people. A nation, after all, is not a collection of individuals who met in a street and were forced to put down rules so
that they could live together peacefully. No, a nation is a moral entity with a
particular identity, which constitutional scholars may call public order.[177]
No nation can enjoy stability without the emergence of a consensus over the
fixed parameters of its creed, identity, or mission, without determining a law

or established facts on the scope of liberty and the means for the alternation of power. Yet none of this prevents the existence of minority groups. In the end, however, a people should not be asked to encourage the emergence of that which threatens their national integrity.

CITIZENSHIP: WHAT IT MEANS FOR THE INDIVIDUAL AND THE STATE

As previously stated, no matter what a person's religious or ethnic background, each person in the Islamic state possesses inalienable rights for leading a dignified life. But he also has the right to choose whether to believe or not in the purposes of the state, in the foundations on which it is built, and in Islam, which is its backbone. If he believes in these, there is nothing that sets him apart from his fellow citizens of the Islamic state, except for his qualifications. He equally enjoys the rights of citizenship, since he, whether Muslim or not, has allegiance to the state, recognizes its legitimacy, and does not threaten its public order either by raising a weapon against it or by allying to its enemies.

The non-Muslim citizen of an Islamic state has the right to preserve his religious and cultural specificities, for instance in what he eats or drinks, or in his marital life.[178] Furthermore, he is excused from some of the duties incumbent upon Muslims, like abstaining from certain prohibitions. Nevertheless, these represent a few exceptions and do not infringe upon the principle of equality, which is the principal value observed by the Islamic state.

We do not know of any state in the past or in the present whose constitution does not lay down, when discussing the rights of citizenship, including public freedoms, such as that of association, some restrictions aimed at protecting the state's integrity, or the freedom of citizens, or the right of majorities to stamp public life with some of their own distinguishing traits. Thus Article 4 in the French constitution enacted in 1958 states that political parties and movements shall contribute to the exercise of suffrage. They shall form and carry out their activities freely. They must respect the principles of national sovereignty and democracy.[179] The present constitution of Egypt stipulates that political parties may not contravene the Islamic Shari'a.

If the Muslim living outside the borders of the state has only the right of being rescued from danger, depending on the actual abilities of the state, the non-Muslim (or dhimmi), beyond the right of being rescued, enjoys the same rights as Muslims citizens.

European historians who have studied the history of the Islamic civilization have been drawn to a phenomenon that has no counterpart in other civilizations—namely, the number of influential non-Muslim officials within the Islamic state apparatus. Adam Metz wrote, for example, "Among some astonishing facts was the great number of non-Muslim employees and regional governors in the Islamic state, and it was often Christians who governed Muslims in Islamic lands and as a result, Muslims complained a great deal about it."[180] History teaches us that the early Muslims of the Abassid Caliphate did not only show Christian and Jewish scholars, great respect, but often entrusted them with grand projects and gave them political appointments. The caliph Harun al-Rashid (ruled 786–809 BCE) even put all of the schools under the supervision of the Christian Yuhanna ibn Masawayh and at other times entrusted Nestorians and Jews with this task.[181] Other caliphs appointed a number of ministers who were Christians and Jews.

And why not, since under the protection of Islam each religious minority within the Islamic state all felt secure regardless of faith, a position that allows for people's respective gifts to be enhanced, for cultures and patrimonies to be revived, and for all to effectively contribute to the creation of an Islamic civilization. As a result, respected Jewish historians admit that the age of Islamic flourishing in Andalusia (Spain), for instance, was also the golden age of Jewish culture. As Simon Doubnov in his "Precis d'histoire juive" wrote that "For the first time, part of the Jewish people enjoyed freedom of thought; during the eleventh and twelfth centuries, the development of Jewish thought in the middle ages reached its peak."[182]

As for the contemporary Western state, for all of its claims of being an egalitarian society free of religious discrimination, millions of its Muslim citizens, despite their contribution to its liberation and economic development, like those in France, for instance, have not yet been able to guarantee even their personal rights, like the right to life and the religious freedom allowing them to build mosques and their women to wear the hijab. There is no need to even talk about their political rights and their ability to hold political office. Among the more than twenty million Muslims in Western Europe, there are still very few deputies, ministers, or ambassadors. The appointment of the only Western Muslim ambassador, His Excellency Murad Hoffman, created quite a stir in Germany when he wrote a book defending Islam (*Islam: The Alternative*), with many calling for his removal from office.[183] And all of this at a time when, without creating any stir or even a problem within the public opinion of the Islamic world, citizens belonging to the Christian minority in Egypt, Iraq, and Syria were appointed to high offices in the state as ambassadors and ministers.

STATUS OF NON-MUSLIM PARTIES IN THE ISLAMIC STATE

If non-Muslims can become citizens of the Muslim state—even pagans or idolaters, according to the Maliki scholar Ibn 'Abd al-Barr—as long as they have declared their allegiance to the Islamic state, do they have the right to form political parties and enter the electoral process in order to gain access to power?

Here we cannot overlook the religious and political nature of the Islamic state. This means that all movements and institutions must submit to the principles and directives of Islam. Non-Muslims have no other recourse but to recognize the role of Islam as the faith of the majority in organizing and orienting public life. They may not create obstacles for the state's proper functioning but may form parties that lobby for rights that are allowed under the Islamic Shari'a, like being elected to the Shura Council and seeking to redress injustices. They may also join Islamic parties.[184]

May they call Muslims to their faith? The majority of Islamic thinkers forbid this, saying that it might lead a Muslim away from his faith and into apostasy. Another school of thought says there is nothing wrong with this. Among these we have mentioned the great scholar Mawdudi and the martyr al-Faruqi. We favor that opinion, on the condition that all follow a proper etiquette when it comes to dialogue. This is because when one recognizes other people's right to their own religion, one must also recognize the right to defend them by showing their advantages as well as the shortcomings they see in other religions. This is at the heart of what it means to propagate one's faith—namely, to win over others by way of showing the advantages in one's discourse, while pointing out the disadvantages of those of others.

There is no fear on the part of the religion of truth that may keep it from engaging in intellectual debates with different materialistic currents and deficient schools in the public sphere, like on television, for example, as was mentioned by Shaykh al-Qaradawi in one of his episodes. If Islam was able to defend itself and its community when they were a vulnerable minority and its adversaries controlled the state's apparatus, how then can we be afraid that it might fail when it has become the faith that shapes public life and the basis of education and legislation?[185]

If there is a danger we might fear for Islam, it would be the twin dangers of rigidity of thinking and the autocracy of political power. As for freedom, it is an unmitigated good, a blessing, and one of Islam's great objectives. When it is denied, the humanity of people is denied, which God's religion condemns as the greatest of all dangers.

Therefore, according to this perspective, it is possible for political parties to be established with various non-Muslim orientations on the condition that they remain loyal to the Islamic state in order to contribute to the project of cooperation among the nations, peoples, religions, and schools of thought—the project of Islamic civilization: "O mankind! We created you from a single (pair) of a male and a female, and made you into nations and tribes, that ye may know each other (not that ye may despise each other)."[186] We believe that this disagreement about the legality of non-Muslim parties within an Islamic state currently has no practical implications, since all secular parties today affirm their allegiance to Islam. And even if they were to rebel against it they would only isolate themselves on the margins, and their existence legally and openly would be less harmful than pushing them underground. Their success will never be better than that of an Islamic or communist party in England or America.

This does not mean that the formation of parties on a non-Muslim basis in the Islamic state is necessarily forbidden, for, on the theoretical level, there is no consensus today on that position. In practice, if such parties are constituted, they will only be marginal groups like those of the extreme left in capitalist societies and similar marginal groups that do not share society's common understanding and are beyond the pale of its consensus. Yet as long as they subscribe to the ethics of dialogue and remain loyal to the state, they have the right to enjoy the protection of the law. Differences of opinion are to be addressed by thinkers and not by the law, since "there is no compulsion in religion" (Q. 2:256). Despite their disagreement with Muslims on issues of faith—that is, the foundations of society—they still have the right to organize as they please so as to guarantee their community's longevity and to defend their own existence. However, they may not aim to change or get rid of the foundations of society. Apostasy itself was only fought against when it transformed into a violent political movement aiming to destroy society's foundations. As for the individual and marginal phenomena, civil society's defenses will deal with them, without having to invoke the authority of the law. In any case, there is no need to confront someone with an idea or opinion except by using the same weapon, just as debates were conducted between Muslims and their adversaries over the finer points of religious belief in the mosques and palaces of past caliphs and sultans. And it never happened that Islam was defeated in a free debate, so there should be no fear that freedom will harm Islam. Rather, its eternal enemy is despotism.

The consolidation of Islamic beliefs and ethics within a society's worldview, like its endorsement of justice and mutual consultation and their establishment as the foundation and goal of the state—all of this establishes among the masses and the elites a common culture and a standard of living that minimizes inequalities. This limits social polarization and facilitates the spread of a spirit of brotherhood ("For the believers are brothers," Q. 49:10) and mutual consultation, and limits causes for mutual recrimination, class warfare, conflict, and tendency for upheaval and instability. It tends to guide society in the direction of consensus.

A society built upon mutual consultation is a society characterized by brotherhood based on common faith, common humanity, and social participation. It is on this common ground of shared beliefs and common interests that the process of consultation or popular democracy takes place. On the basis of this kind of shared worldview, it is possible that popular leaders or the elites may find various ways to achieve these common goals. Some lean toward rigid rules, others toward more flexibility; some lean toward speedy measures, while others favor more gradual approaches; some incline toward extremes, and others toward moderation. A difference of opinion about plans and methods among the elites conceivably leads to different interpretations or different leaders people may rally around while competing to reach the same goals; and thus political parties emerge, though in reality there is only one party, the party of God, the community that will achieve salvation.

This is how mutual consultation took place between different groups among the first Muslim society and its elites (the immigrants from Mecca and their supporters in Medina) before a venerable Companion of the Prophet (PBUH) took over the leadership of the Islamic community. But several years later his discipline and strong purpose faltered, that is the third caliph 'Uthman. Matters were no longer under control and the elites were incapable of developing the institutions of a city-state into those of a global state, which resulted in a tribe monopolizing power and wealth and parties emerging in the shadow of a warped reality. Thus parties continued over time to be marked by a spirit of conflict, struggle, and strife.

Democracy, which is our own product [shura], has been neglected,[187] along with other things the West borrowed from us, such as a mechanism for governance that ensures decision-making is achieved through consultation. Our own principles and inventions are the very ones that we then considered alien and rejected. As Hichem Djaït stated, "We will never operate effectively except in a stable and well-established social environment that defines the norms without which no alternation of power can take place."[188]

If it is true that democracy is the rotation of power among the elites according to the law of the majority, then this rotation takes place "among the elites who are similar intellectually, socially and politically,"[189] which means that this alternation takes place on a cultural and social common ground and consensus. This is confirmed by the rotation of power we have witnessed within the major stable democracies like the United Kingdom and the United States, where power is transferred from one party to another that is so similar that there are no great changes in the foundations and directions of their regimes. But as for those democracies that do not have this common ground, they quickly become unstable, as is the case with Italy, Turkey, and France.

Thus one of France's opposition leaders once complained about this condition from which his country suffers—that is, the lack of common ground for the rotation of power which makes the process of transferring power and electoral contests look like a coup d'état—that is, the change from one opposite to another.[190] Yet there is some exaggeration in the analogy, and it would be wrong to say that the Left that governed France was the opposite of the Right in every aspect. France's basic foreign policies have not changed a great deal since the time of the Revolution; in fact, they have not changed much since the Crusades in the medieval era, particularly with regard to their position on Islam, for instance, which has only seen limited change.

There would be no harm, therefore, in having some marginal parties present in our societies as they are in the West, just as in our own history we had marginal groups that did not integrate with the mainstream current of Islamic society. Thus, for instance, communist parties in Britain and America would be similar to some of the groups of heretics and other small groups in our past which were marginalized by civil society without any need for state intervention. Certainly a communist or secular party in an Islamic society would fare no better than an Islamic party in Britain. Note that among a pool of a million Muslim voters, the Islamic Party received no more than five thousand votes as Muslims themselves gave their votes to others. What has happened is that no sooner did our societies begin to regain their awareness than the secular groups did their utmost to declare their link, however tenuous, to Islam. This shows that this is not a practical problem that needs research in the present circumstances.

WHAT MISSION DO PARTIES HAVE IN THE ISLAMIC STATE?

On the basis of the preceding discussion about the necessary common ground, parties have two missions, one organizational and the other educational.

First, in terms of organization, parties take responsibility for organizing the masses and solving the problem of transferring power which represents the rock against which the process of Islamic shura crashed and fell apart. Because of the simplicity of the desert Arabs and their lack of organizational experience in addition to reigning imperial spirit, the principles of shura and the commanding of good and forbidding of evil remained slogans lacking a system that shapes the people into a powerful force, which will pledge allegiance to a ruler and then stand powerless and paralyzed after handing power to the ruler to use as he wishes. Rather, the people retain sufficient popular power, while remaining also accountable (via parties, associations, mosques, religious endowments, educational establishments, tribes and centers of individual or collective interpretation of Shari'a), so that if the entrusted agent mismanages the power delegated to him, the people may depose him, even by force if necessary.

What happened in the absence of an apparatus to organize the masses and transform them into a body with political authority is that the balance between ruled and ruler was upset. The pledge of allegiance [bay'a] is a contract between two parties meant to create an unequal relationship between them, since by virtue of the contract one of the parties (the amir) takes power or, in other words, gains the right to be obeyed. Meanwhile, the other party, by pledging allegiance, loses all power to force the ruler to pay the price for what he gained, that is, his duty to apply the Shari'a, establish justice and consult. In this case, then, the covenant is neither a covenant of representation or proxy in reality, but rather it is like a sale that is postponed with the promise to pay later. And because one party has more power than the other, it then becomes a sale that is free or rather a form of deceit and usurpation. So what weapon is left for the people when the buyer reneges on his promise to pay the price? In this case, there is nothing left but to take the bold individual stands that strike the usurper with courageous words or plot surprise attacks, or to rely on secret organizations to exploit the sultan's moment of weakness and then pounce on him.

Yet because this is such a costly course of action, which often fails and only leads to harming people and destroying a nation, it was natural that most jurists of the past tended to reject the idea of revolution and lean toward accepting the status quo, even to the point of recognizing hereditary rule or rule by violent takeovers, adopting the saying that "right is on the side of the conqueror."[191] They found comfort and justification for this by keeping away violent unrest [fitna] and by establishing some legitimacy for the state through its application of parts of the Shariʿa, despite the fact that one cannot divide the Shariʿa into parts, or take from any of its components and use it to give legitimacy to any usurper, because this will only lead to more injustices until all is destroyed. And this is exactly what happened. The jurists sacrificed mutual consultation, satisfied that the ruler was establishing the rule of Shariʿa. In the end, the masses were cut off from any political participation, all social activism was frozen, and the umma braced itself to accept domestic despotism, which weakened it and exhausted its strength, and prepared it for foreign hegemony. The great wisdom of the poet endures, "Whoever accepts to be humiliated, humiliation becomes a norm for him."[192]

When one abandons one principle, it only leads to relinquishing all principles and to the loss of the whole religious community and nation. Therefore, though it may not be the only solution to the great problem of abandoning the early practice of shura after the rule of the Rightly Guided caliphs, organizing the masses into political parties formed around specific principles, goals, and interests would have been an ideal solution. That problem is how to transform the masses into a political authority that cannot be usurped after pledging allegiance to a ruler, but rather is safeguarded for them as the power to provide sound counsel, advice, and direction for the ruler when he begins to deviate. If that is not sufficient to persuade him to desist, then that authority of advice then becomes one of pressure and protest. If the ruler persists, he is then deposed by withdrawing confidence from him by the leaders of parties and popular associations, starting with the Shura Council or the "people of loosing and binding." Leaving the people with no mechanisms of redress in the face of organized government only leads to despotism and to emptying the principles of Islamic governance—such as mutual consultation, commanding good and forbidding evil, the pledge of allegiance to the ruler, and the "people of loosing and binding"—of all meaning and substantive content, leaving behind only hollow slogans and empty fortresses.

The above applies to the normal situation when Muslims are the great majority of the population and they are aware of the basic tenets of Islam and its objectives. Then Islam and its culture act as the foundation and framework for political action, with the possibility of marginal groups which only represent the exception that proves the rule. If, however, Muslims are a minority or have little awareness of Islam's objectives and of its political implications, then it would be enough to broker a political arrangement between Islamists and other citizens, by which all commit to be loyal to the state, to reject violence as a means to impose a particular opinion, and to the peaceful transfer of power via the ballot box. The important thing is that there be a consensus within society about public freedoms.

If these liberties are founded on Islamic principles, then this is an Islamic state. When they are not, then let them be formulated on the basis of general humanitarian principles, which would make it a "government of reason"—in Ibn Khaldun's language—or a democratic state, which derives its legitimacy from the people by way of mutual consultation [shura]. This is the middle position between a "natural rule," which derives its legitimacy from force, and the caliphate, the legitimacy of which is the sacred text and mutual consultation. Perhaps the government of reason is the closest position to government based on Shari'a. For the most part, the naïve, childish rejection of democracy on the part of some Islamists are the product of the same conditions that produced communist and nationalist groups, and all the other authoritarian trends which cling to formalities in order to reject the core of democracy. The trenchant remark made by Hichem Djaït applies well to them, while at the same time revealing part of the mentality of Arabs and Muslims, who seek the ideal form of a thing instead of grasping it with all of its advantages and disadvantages, and then fixing it. The same, then, goes for their rejection of democracy because of its advantages and disadvantages. It represents a general inclination to prefer nothing over something that is less than perfect. I do not know whether this is an escape from life as it is, or something more dangerous and insidious, which I cannot define.[193]

Second, concerning the educational role of political parties, in the Islamic perspective they are not just political frameworks meant to solve problems like how to transfer power. Rather, above all they are institutions meant to educate the people by raising their level of awareness, their knowledge and ethics, and prepare them to truly become a people ready to shoulder the message of Islam of affirming the Oneness of God, justice, responsibility, faithfulness, compassion, struggle [jihad], self-sufficiency, and oversight of one's government.

Developing an umma that fits the description in the verse, "the best community raised for humanity,"[194] is not the ruler's mission or that of a state apparatus but rather the mission of an Islamic elite, the scholars and people of ijtihad, whom God has entrusted with the responsibility to interpret His Book, convey its message, and transform the principles of Islam from a book form into an umma.

Translating the Book into an umma is the essence of the 'ulama's mission, which is too great and difficult a mission to be accomplished by individual efforts. In this respect, what happened with regard to the command to do good and refrain from evil is what happened with the command to activate mutual consultation. In both cases, personal effort and individual initiative remained the only means to implement the rule, even though the work of the Muslim scholars to protect the umma from decay was much more important than that of the rulers. In fact, the latter often destroyed that which the former had built.

Nevertheless the 'ulama' instilled a degree of organization, by establishing schools and encouraged the people to establish endowments to support those schools, and thus met many social needs that were neglected by the rulers. Then, too, preachers fanned out across many regions spreading Islam. Yet the degree of organization in their activities remained minimal, except among the Shia. It may be that it was the belief in the continuing legitimacy of the state among most of the Shia scholars that accounts for the superior Shia organization both in the political and social spheres, even though Shi'ism itself started with the principle of absence of legitimacy which Muslims had to regain or wait for the one who would do so. In either case, there had to be some organizing in order to ensure the continuation and spread of the sect and to serve its best interests. This is why the contemporary Islamic organizations did not begin until the fall of the caliphate. It was by nature a revolutionary enterprise, which aimed at reestablishing it, while the work of the scholars before that had been confined to reforming that which had been weakened or corrupted.

If we compare what the Shia, Christian, or Jewish organization accomplished, versus what the Sunni scholars accomplished in terms of maintenance, competition, or dominance, the advantage goes to the former because of the importance it gave to organization, whereas in the latter, organization was lacking or not robust, for the reasons mentioned above.

Political parties as they are conceived in an Islamic society, therefore, are not simply instruments to reach power or means to pressure the ruler. These are the weakest of their roles since these are only important when the need arises— that is, in the case of authoritarianism and abrogation of the political covenant.

When it comes to the important proactive missions, they are about action, not just resistance: action aimed at preparing the umma to carry out its mission to convey the message to and liberate the world's oppressed, shining forth the light of Islam in every corner of the world, and strengthening civil society so it has full guardianship over the state which becomes the servant of the people, not vice versa.[195]

Organizing Islamic society in the form of political, cultural, and social organizations is the best, if not the only, path to strengthen its capacities in confronting state power when it becomes tyrannical, in facilitating political turnover without any turmoil, and in moving it in the direction of self-sufficiency and less reliance upon the state, so that it is not taken hostage by a state that becomes arrogant and despotic. This should not be a state only concerned with the distribution of subsidies and security measures but rather one concerned about its essential functions of serving Islam and supporting the oppressed, as we read in the Qur'an, "those who, when We established them in the land, keep up prayer, pay the prescribed alms, command what is right, and forbid what is wrong: God controls the outcome of all events."[196] When such "parties" emerge in a Muslim society, they do not threaten the umma's unity, but rather they are the means to restore it and preserve it.[197]

This view of parties that is imbued with the spirit of God's unity, justice, and truth cannot turn into obstinacy, arrogance, or rigid partisanship, or a disparagement of the value of brotherhood. For the overarching brotherhood of Islam must not be undermined by the more specific brotherhood of a party. The latter must be in service of the former, and that jurist said it best when he proposed that members of the Shura Council should be free of any fanatical attachment to one's party's positions in the course of mutual consultation. On the contrary, a member of parliament must allow the truth of the Qur'an to determine his positions. In such an assembly it is appropriate to protect and seek to develop brotherhood, even when positions of majority and minority change from day to day, and even in one session.[198]

It seems that those who were wary of party politics in Islamic society had only seen it from a Western perspective. What a difference between one who seeks greatness on this earth and the one who seeks God's face! O God, help us to be among those who seek your pleasure and forgive our failings!

Political parties are not only the principal instruments for the purpose of participation in and alternation of power, but also for creating a special kind of God-fearing politicians. Above all, a party is a mechanism to enable the umma to become self-reliant in securing some of its interests, if not most of them. Islamic governance is built upon mutual consultation, which in turn is about distributing political power and hindering it from being monopolized by an apparatus called "the state." For in Islam there is no state in the Western sense, unless it is simply called "Islam." It is the highest authority, above which there can be no other authority. The ruler is merely an employee of the umma.

Distribution of power does not only mean participating in the discussion of public affairs and decision-making. It is more than that and deeper than that. It is about the formation of civil society, one that does not see its relationship to political authority as that of a body attached to a head, which would mean that its functions are curtailed and even ceased by merely being cut off from the head. Rather, its integrity comes from regular contact between the two parties. However, society must be sufficiently organized and independent to be able to gradually decrease its dependence on the state and increase its ability to resist the state's deviations. Society must therefore organize itself so as to provide most of its vital needs such as education, health care, the economy, defense, social solidarity, and other interests. This will keep the state from becoming over-dominant and authoritarian, when it feels that society is fully dependent on it. Regardless of their view of the state, they will still need it to protect their possessions and their lives. But the feeling of arrogance and scorn for the people must not be allowed to grow among the rulers as soon as they have pledged them their allegiance.

Above all, Islamic parties are organizations for the purpose of educating the masses and preparing them to fulfill their mission, "You order what is right, and forbid what is wrong"[199] and "Be a community that calls for what is good."[200] This kind of umma, therefore, cannot hitch its destiny to any particular ruler. To the contrary, the people have political authority over him. But this will not happen unless they are trained to do so and are able to organize to become self-sufficient. As for the non-Muslims, they are not foreigners but citizens in the Islamic society—citizens, but with a distinction. They are generally in the same category as Muslims, for they have agreed to the overall organization of society and to the way its supreme legitimacy derives from the Shari'a. Thus the state provides for the benefits of all on the basis of equality, according to the hadith, "They have the same rights as we have, and have the same responsibilities as we have."[201] So they are Muslims not by creed but by civilization and the general Islamic order[202] and the spirit of solidarity and loyalty. All of these reflect the nature of citizenship in the Islamic state.

Because parties within the Islamic state have such high callings—organizational, educational, and social—they do not need the ruler's permission to be launched.

Indeed, they are a fulfillment of God's injunction to command what is right and forbid what is wrong, and anything of this sort needs no one's permission,[203] especially since that command to offer advice, criticism, and opposition will be mostly directed toward the ruler. So how can someone be asked to give others permission to advise or criticize him? The same applies to establishing newspapers, just like the writing of books and other means of expression, and the administration of mosques.

OTHER GUARANTEES AGAINST TYRANNY

Among those guarantees, we list the following in summary form.

GOD'S SUPREME SOVEREIGNTY

Since the source of prescriptive legislation and legitimacy is exclusively divine inspiration of the Book and the Sunna, this limits considerably the authority of tyrants whose authority comes from manipulating laws and adapting them to their own whims. We have previously explained how foundational legislation is independent of the state altogether, just as the interpretation of the sacred texts and the legal reasoning [ijtihad], both individual and collective. All of this makes the mission of the Shura Council that of enacting laws and deciding on policies. This limits, for instance, the ruler's financial control over the people since he does not determine the obligatory alms tax (zakat) and the zakat institution remains independent from him.[204]

ISLAMIC EDUCATION

Its goal is to create in the Muslim believer a spirit of freedom and submission to God alone, and one that rejects and resists any authority that elevates itself above God's authority, that causes injustice and tyranny, and that manipulates people's possessions and lives for his own benefit. Thus, history has witnessed the eternal struggle between the prophets and their followers, on the one hand, and the tyrants who monopolized resources and power on the other. The tyrants only perceive the creed of God's unity "as a call to revolution,"[205] and thus do their utmost to stamp out or misrepresent with the Islamic mission.

In order to free the Muslim's conscience from fear, except the fear of God, and inculcate the principles of a faith in the afterlife, social order, justice, and equality, Islamic education does not content itself with simply preaching and counseling. It further provides a system of religious rituals, like prayer, alms-giving, the Hajj pilgrimage, the Ramadan fast, which constitute regular exercises that reinforce these values and transform them into constant behaviors and attitudes.

AN INDEPENDENT JUDICIARY

This particularly applies to special courts, like the court of grievances, which rule on contraventions and transgressions committed by state officials against private individuals. The most competent and strictest of judges were selected for these courts. Today's administrative courts are similar, though their jurisdiction is narrower than the courts of grievances since the latter are responsible for the judgment and its execution.[206] No leader in the government, including the president, possesses any immunity. As stated above, the president is accountable for his actions before the people and the courts as much as any other citizen and will be punished if necessary, for he is subject to all the laws of Islam. The legacy of Islam's justice system, with its independence, fairness and the elevated stature of its judges constitute a source of pride for Islamic civilization. Sadly, it was destroyed by Western occupation and subsequent regimes.

THE PROHIBITION OF TORTURE

What is the position of the Islamic justice system regarding the use of coercion and threat to bring the accused to the point of confessing to crimes? Texts and the rules of judicial procedure are clear in prohibiting this, still, there is some disagreement among scholars in relation to it. As for the texts, they strongly affirm the principle of presumption of innocence; the accused is innocent until proven guilty. In the Qur'an we read, "Believers, if a troublemaker brings you news, check it first, in case you wrong others unwittingly and later regret what you have done."[207] Further, "Believers, avoid making too many assumptions."[208] Then in Sura An-Najm (The Star) we read, ". . . yet, behold, never can surmise take the place of truth."[209] This means that "Suspicion must not be the basis of prosecution of or interrogation of those accused."[210] The Prophet (PBUH) said, "If you only have a suspicion, do not pursue it."[211] He also said (PBUH), "Speculation is the most untruthful form of speech,"[212] which establishes the principle of presumption of innocence. It also establishes the sacred inviolability of people's homes, their dignity, and possessions. They must not be transgressed unless there is definite proof.

But may one seek this proof by means of imprisonment, threats, or torture? There is no justification for this, no matter how strong the suspicion. No one, whether individuals, groups, or states, may have the authority of accusation, however grave the accusation might be, unless they are able to prove it by means of conclusive evidence, following this principle, "The burden of proof is on him who accuses." And if they fail to do so, then the word of the accused stands. Either he pleads guilty and is convicted based on that, or he denies it, and there is nothing against him except to swear an oath of innocence.

However, to force an admission through imprisonment, intimidation, and torture is a blatant infringement of Islam's teaching and the teachings and principles of justice. It is a violation and denial of human dignity. Yet despite strong evidence from the Shari'a and reason on this issue, several prominent jurists have put forward contrary views.

Renowned legal theorist Abu Ishaq al-Shatibi attributed to the Maliki School the permissibility of the use of force in interrogation and to Imam Malik the permissibility of preventive detention. Maliki jurists considered public interest (maslaha)—for example, the recovery of stolen property—as legitimate grounds for the use of force in interrogation where evidence cannot be produced. If one objects, "this opens the door to torturing the innocent," they answer, "Not doing so eliminates the possibility of recovering the property. Moreover, torture rarely falls on the innocent."[213]

As for Ibn Qayyim, he distinguishes between three cases. Where the accused is known for his integrity, the use of force is not permissible, and there is unanimity among scholars about this. If the character of the accused is not known, then detention is permissible until truth is revealed. If he is known for his transgressions, including waylaying and other crimes, then the use of force is permissible to get him to reveal the truth. Ibn al-Qayyim supports his position by an incident in which the Prophet (PBUH) ordered 'Ali (may God be pleased with him) to intercept a woman who was carrying a message to the Quraysh tribe informing them of the Prophet's intention to attack Mecca by surprise. When 'Ali (may God be pleased with him) caught up with her and asked her to surrender the message, she denied she had one. He said to her, "Either you give it to me, or you take off your clothes," so she gave it to him. This is an instance of threat during interrogation. This is as far as the argument gets for these jurists, and it does not amount to reliable evidence.

To claim that this incident is proof for the permissibility of employing torture to extract confession from the accused is a flawed and dangerous argument. In fact, the Prophet (PBUH) was not acting as political leader setting

Shari'a-oriented policies, or as investigating judge. Rather, he was acting as a prophet, whom God had given the certainty about what this woman had done. He was not using a threat to substantiate a suspicion he had, and all 'Ali did was to threaten to carry out a search.

As for al-Shatibi's argument in relation to public interest, it is invalid, because the condition for using public interest [maslaha] is that it does not contradict a clear text. And the texts are all plainly in agreement that conjecture is no way to pass judgment on people and that true public interest is in the respect of peoples's rights and integrity, even if this leads to some criminals escaping justice. That is better than the possibility of subjecting innocent people to ill-treatment. As for the permissibility of detaining the accused, which al-Shatibi attributed to Imam Malik, it has no basis. We read in the *Body of Laws* (*Mudawwana*), which is the most trusted source of Maliki law, "'If he was beaten or threatened, then confessed and dug up the corpse or produced the stolen goods, does the Shari'a penalty apply to him because of his confession or not, considering that he produced the evidence?' He answered, 'No, I would only apply that penalty if he confesses while secure and in no fear of anything.'" This position was shared by Imam Ahmad, Abu Hanifa, and Al-Shafi'i, all of whom held that confession under duress is not admissible as evidence.[214]

Therefore, this takes away the justification a tyrant could use to oppress free people, even though today's tyrants do not need fatwas to turn arbitrary detention, savage torture, and political trials into state policy.[215] The philosophy of human rights in Islam is based on the principle that God has honored the human being, making him His vicegerent on earth, that the prophets were sent to establish justice, break the chains, and free humanity. It rejects aggression of any kind and strongly resists and fights all forms of coercion (used to force confession of a crime), no matter how noble the motive.

The philosophy of human rights in Islam supports all international covenants and the efforts of all humanitarian organizations to put in place the necessary guarantees for human rights and dignity, to uproot torture and all kinds of coercion, intimidation, and violence, regardless of whether the perpetrator is an individual or a group, a believer or a non-believer. Islam's teachings represent a strong foundation in support of the principles and values of human rights, the presumption of innocence, the brotherhood of humankind, and the fight against tyranny and injustice. In fact, these are part of the primary objectives of the Shari'a and are at the heart of the message of Islam. Those who defend them are promised great rewards in this world and the next, and those who violate them are warned about the most grievous punishment in this world and the next. Didn't the Prophet (PBUH) talk about a woman who entered hell because of a cat that she tortured? What if it is a human being that is tortured? Or whole populations? Either directly or by giving support to despotic rulers? How despicably despots have sullied our lives and our religion!

THE AUTHORITY TO SUPERVISE PUBLIC MORALITY (HISBA)

Hisba is one of several aspects of the human vicegerency, and as such, it means the responsibility to command good and forbid evil. This is a collective (or communal) responsibility, which means that every Muslim is entrusted with the duty to uphold religion and to actualize Islamic laws and teachings in his life, and in the lives of others around him, to the best of his ability. However, for the head of state, this is a personal obligation, since it is of the essence of his responsibility as head of state to uphold religion by enforcing its laws and preserving it from corruption, and, as far as people are concerned, to promote their welfare, which includes protecting their rights and preventing injustice against their persons. It is, therefore, incumbent upon him to establish the necessary organs to accomplish this task.

The institution (or the concept) of hisba is a product of the literature on Islamic governance or the administration of the Islamic state. Caliphs used to take personal charge of ordering what is right and prohibiting what is wrong. When society expanded under the Islamic empire, they established the hisba system, which involved learned judges and courageous scholars, expert in people's affairs, walking in the streets and markets, inspecting government institutions and agencies, as well as private shops, urging the good and censuring evil. They acted in this way either if Islam's ethical values were being compromised or if people's interests were being harmed. They were in no way spying upon people but only targeting obvious infractions, whoever might have committed them. The hisba system was considered a way to protect the Shari'a in a society ruled by Islam, and thus it was about administration, though it also included some judicial components, like the power to accuse and the authority to try in court and enforce judgments, similar to a public prosecutor. These powers rest on the need to protect the public rights of society, which in an Islamic society are referred to as God's rights [*huquq Allah*].[216]

Moreover, inspectors do not look into cases that need a witness in court, nor do they initiate legal proceedings on the spot. And since they cannot be denied access anywhere, it is also possible for them to oversee and observe centers of detention, prisons, and the other administrative institutions where state functionaries might commit violations or crimes.

OVERSIGHT BY PUBLIC OPINION

Several contemporary jurists consider public opinion as the fourth power in the Islamic state. In fact, it is the source of all authority within the state, since it is in it that true sovereignty resides. This is because it is first concerned with the message of Shari'a and the one responsible for actualizing it. Yet because as a collective body the people cannot accomplish this, it becomes necessary for them to delegate one of their own and entrust him with the task of establishing the Shari'a under the people's supervision and responsibility. For God deputizes the umma, and it in turn empowers the president to represent her in carrying out the requirements of this trust.

Nevertheless, this second trusteeship in no way negates the first one, for the umma retains the responsibility to supervise her representative, whom it has appointed to fulfill the mission for which all of humanity was created: to worship God by means of applying the dictates of His revealed law in the world.

The umma carries out this supervision individually and collectively, as all are mobilized at all times, privately and in public, to instill faith and Islamic values deep in society's conscience and infuse Islam into all of life. The goal is to do away with wrongful behavior by all possible means, including the media, mosques, public demonstrations, and all other forms of individual and collective action. This deep feeling within the soul of every Muslim is faithful to Islam's message wherever he might be, without fearing any ruler or ruled—as they say, "In revering God there is no fear of people's reproach."[217] Such a believer will give an account to God for the mandate entrusted to him. Wherever he might be, he has a responsibility toward the message of Islam, undeterred by fear of anyone, ruler or ruled, ever conscious that he is accountable before God for this trust. Has he dedicated his life to it, or has he neglected it? Did he live for it and by it, or did he neglect it? This is what gives the Muslim a positive spirit. He knows no weakness or despair in his soul. This is the secret of Islam's resilience despite the corruption of rulers, and this is the motivation to create organizations in the social and political spheres of life, seeking to put into practice God's Word, "help one another to do what is right and good; do not help one another towards sin and hostility."[218]

No doubt Muslims have fallen short in obeying God's call to gather and organize their energies into a force that opposes falsehood and promotes truth. This failure to go beyond individual efforts or mere reliance on the state—which more often than not was a burden and a misfortune for both Islam and society—has weakened the authority of the umma—that is, the authority of public opinion—

and opened the way to abuse and authoritarianism. In an Islamic community that seeks inspiration from the ethical values and creed of Islam and is ruled by a state committed to both Text and shura, there is little chance for injustice and abuse of power to arise. And if they do, it won't be for long, as long as Islamic teachings in relation to legislation, education, and sociopolitical organization remain dynamic and active, and as long as every Muslim cooperates with his brethren so as to activate the sovereignty with which God has entrusted the umma as both individuals and groups. That is the mandate to bring truth and justice to the world, the very mandate for which all past messengers were sent, as we read in the Qur'an, "We sent Our messenger with clear signs, the Scripture and the Balance, so that people could uphold justice: We also sent iron, with its mighty strength and many uses for mankind."[219]

INTERNATIONAL COVENANTS

There is nothing in Islam that forbids the establishment of an international order between nations, civilizations, and religious blocks on the basis of justice and equality, in order to guarantee the freedom of nations and to prevent aggression. The Prophet (PBUH) witnessed such a treaty when he was still young (the Hilf al-Fudul Pact).[220] This was a pact ratified by the tribal leaders in order to prevent injustice and enmity and to support those whose rights had been violated. There has been no objection among Muslims to enter into a similar one. Surely the Hudaybiyya Pact brokered between the Muslims and the pagans of Quraysh (CE 628) was another testimony to Islam's commitment to a just peace, the free circulation of ideas, merchandise, and people; and the reliance on peaceful means of conflict resolution.

Admittedly, Islamic thinkers have differed on their reading of the jihad verses. Are they an exhortation to Muslims to spread Islam, even by force? This was the opinion of some classical as well as modern scholars, including Sayyid Qutb, in a particular interpretation of the jihad verses and the Prophet's life.[221] By contrast, most modern jurists lean toward the position that peace is the rule in the relationship between Muslims and non-Muslims, while jihad is a response to aggression and a means to bring back peace. Here are some relevant verses:

"But if they incline towards peace, you [Prophet] must also incline towards it."[222]

"Fight them until there is no more persecution."[223]

"And He does not forbid you to deal kindly and justly with anyone who has not fought you for your faith or driven you out of your homes: God loves the just."[224]

In light of these verses, we conclude that the Islamic state builds its foreign policy with regard to non-Muslim states so as to guarantee:

- The freedom to call people to Islam, and the principle that Islamic law cannot be subordinated to any other law
- Complete independence, and the non-subordination to any international axes
- Peace and nonaggression
- Cooperation based on justice and mutual respect
- Commitment to treaties and covenants
- The right of self-defense[225]

The distinguished scholar Tahir Ibn 'Ashur noted in his Qur'an commentary *al-Tahrir wa'l-Tanwir* (*Elucidating and Illuminating*) that the verses calling (in their literal meaning) for offensive warfare should either be considered as abrogated by later verses or interpreted in a way that does not contradict the following immutable principles of the religion: "There shall be no coercion in matters of faith;"[226] the rejection of aggression, ". . . but do not commit aggression—for, verily, God does not love aggressors;"[227] faithfulness to pacts and covenants, ". . . And be true to every promise—for, verily, [on Judgment Day] you will be called to account for every promise which you have made!"[228] This opens the door for entering into peace and nonaggression pacts with neutral and friendly nations, for having diplomatic and commercial relations, and even for agreements to fight aggression and injustice anywhere in the world in the manner of the pre-Islamic Hilf al-Fudul Pact.

But for this to happen, the United Nations organization would need to develop into a more just and effective institution, turning its back on the hegemony of particular countries and the use of double standards. Then it would represent another safeguard against injustice and tyranny in our world and a serious and just framework for international peace and cooperation. At the same time, it is a pity and a source of shame and humiliation for the community of the Qur'an that the affairs of world government (the Security Council) are settled in its absence. This situation goes against both religion and honor.

HOW DO WE EXPLAIN INSTANCES OF DESPOTISM IN ISLAMIC HISTORY?

First, no one could claim that Islam justifies despotism, because the struggle for justice and against oppression is a central theme throughout the teachings of

Islam, and this to the point that its jurists stated that where there is justice, there you find God's law.[229]

Second, no one can claim that injustice became a legitimate doctrine for the umma, as it did during the Middle Ages in Europe, where a political philosophy arose whereby the kings and church clerics enjoyed a kind of divinity along with privileges, which put them above the law. Uprisings in the Muslim world were a common occurrence, and this would not have been the case were it not for the endurance of the Islamic ideals of justice, truth, and liberation in the hearts of most Muslims, who were willing to sacrifice their lives and property in order to regain the lost ideal—that is, the age of the Rightly Guided Caliphs. As Mahmud al-Nakuʿ put it: "If we study the history of Islamic society in the Arab world and the history of political power during the time of Umayyads and Abbasids, which represent by far most of that history, we discover that the deviant political behavior did not affect the cultural realm and did not destroy any pillars of the faith. Nor did it deny any of the statutes of the Shariʿa nor diminish their role in society. Nor did it impede the movement of populations and the growth of commerce or the spread of education and professions. This was a period in which civil life was flourishing."[230]

Third, despotism was not the monopoly of the Muslims' history; in fact, thanks to Islam, their share of it was smaller than that of others, for there was no one among them claiming to be God or to speak in His name; and the loss of faith and weakness of their masses never reached the point of having indulgences or tickets to Heaven sold in their markets—as happened in some neighboring markets—nor was the earth and its inhabitants ever considered the ruler's property to rule as he wills.

Even today's pluralistic liberal democracies, though a modicum of rights and liberties is recognized for their citizens, witness acute discrimination and class warfare in their societies, and millions of citizens in model democracies like the United States wander its streets without shelter, living as beggars.[231]

Not to mention the ethnic cleansing and massacres committed against indigenous peoples, whether those in Latin America or those in Africa; or the savage tyranny, wanton destruction, and horrible exploitation that the Europeans visited upon the rest of the earth's peoples since their Renaissance. It is as if they had erected their skyscrapers with the skulls, blood, and wealth of subordinate peoples. This is not surprising, considering the Western concept of the God-state—the state as supreme being, that recognizes no value above its own, or a law other than its own; its actions and righteousness are one, its words are truth itself; legitimacy is what its parliaments enact, what its fleets and secret services enforce, and what its media broadcasts. Force is its very nature, it never leaves it, and no authority surpasses it.

By contrast, the supreme legitimacy of Islam, upon which rests Islamic governance, guards against the state getting out of control and being deified; and ensures that its laws, institutions, and people remain under the authority of the highest law.

Fourth, the history of Islam was not a continuous series of oppressive regimes. On the contrary, there always was a level of connection to Islam, with Shari'a—or certain aspects of it—applied, revered, and relied upon by leaders as a source of legitimacy, whether truthfully or simply as window dressing. In fact, the secular state did not openly rise until the fall of the Ottoman caliphate, when the Western (democratic) powers stormed Islam's abode and ravaged its heritage through corruption, exploitation, and destruction. When Muslims started to rise up and unsheathe their swords to expel the wretched intruders, the Western nations managed by their shrewdness and cunning to install a trove of rulers who remained their loyal clients. No rule was established and no stability was achieved without loyalty to their masters, and they ruled with the vilest sort of repression over peoples who nevertheless were driven by the values of Islam to emancipate themselves.

While in Western history secularism is associated with the freeing of minds, the liberation of people from despots, and the rise of democracy and civil society, in our case it is associated with the hegemony of the authoritarian state over religion, the human mind, culture, the economy, and society. This was a distorted modernity, or rather a secular theocracy.[232]

Fifth, deviation from a principle is not an argument against the principle itself. Islam was not the agent of despotism; rather, it came to smash idols, destroy oppression, and wage war against arrogant leaders, and to bring a revolution to free humanity at every level. In fact, the kind of decline, which happened in several periods of its history, from its just society to tyranny, from its light to a state of darkness—none of that can be attributed to it. The history of Islam is not necessarily that of Muslims, but it is the collection of positions and practices that Muslims have taken up in light of it; all else was the history of pre-Islamic ignorance[233] and Arab tribalism.[234]

Sixth, principles are weighed in the balance of freedom, social justice, equality, and the attitude toward the other. For freedom is the true key of any political system, its foundation, and the criterion of its progress or regression, its goodness or corruption. Based on these considerations, we can say that the record of the relationships Muslims have with people of all persuasions and faiths is the best testimony to the deep humansim of Islam and Muslims, and to the level of respect for human rights during Islamic history. Indeed that history has not registered a single case of ethnic cleansing for a village or city belonging to another religion, like what literally happened and continues to happen at the hands of European peoples. They annihilated the people of Islamic Spain, indigenous peoples of America, and millions of Algerians. Then indirectly they contributed to this by supporting Zionism and the apartheid regime in South Africa, and their agents in all parts of the world.

We have read the testimonies of impartial historians, including Jewish ones, who recognize that the Jewish people in the West did not experience a period of cultural flourishing and security for their lives in medieval times like they did in Islamic lands. European historians often express their admiration for the number of Nestorian and Jewish state employees, including ministers and directors, in a variety of Islamic government posts, even to the point of attracting the envy of Muslims and resentment toward some of the caliphs. Is there anything like this today in Western democracies, in which Muslims dwell by the millions? Are they not given the most menial jobs? Are not their children easy targets of hatred and racial discrimination? So what freedom and what human rights is the West talking about? Still, this limited freedom in the West is the cause of its progress and power, and it is better than the empty slogans mouthed by the theocratic regimes that depend on them. These regimes compete in affirming their legitimacy in the eyes of the West, as they try to outdo one another in trampling democracy and human rights under the guise of fighting extremism. It is as if resisting extremism, or Islam, is the main source of political authority in the Arab world.

Islamic scholars, even if they sometimes feel defeated in their task, still offer this advice to the zealous Muslim youth: "I caution the Muslim youth who believe in Islam not to imagine that the way to guard Islamic precepts is to keep others from expressing their own convictions. The only way to safeguard Islam is by this one power, that is, the power of knowledge and the offer of freedom to different ideas, and then you may confront them openly and clearly."[235] The solution, then, is not to be found just in the books of the past, nor in those of modern times, nor in the programs of this or that party. It will not be found in any one of these sources but in the umma as a whole. Then its forces will converge and intersect, and its energies will be mobilized to bring about the needed renaissance [al-nahda].

This will necessarily require the umma's agreement, as it listens to its elites in an atmosphere of political freedoms, and as it practices mutual consultation or democracy with integrity, sincerity, and truthfulness. The mission of the educated people is to brandish the standard of liberty and to enunciate using strong, objective, and clear language the role that ordinary people play and their right to choose their political leaders. Among the signs of weakness and images of our failure today are the great number of intellectuals who have surrendered to the pressures and enticements of the autocratic regimes, and have invested all their skills to serve them and their policies.

In the end, there is an urgent need, in our quest for the society of freedom, renewal, and unity, of an Islamic thought that establishes these values at the core of our culture and practices and links them to people's religious creed and daily concerns. There is an urgent need for a sort of Hilf al-Fudul Pact, or a contract of honor between all factions of the elites that recognizes as its foundation a shared solidarity. This entails a respect for the will of our peoples, their Islamic identity, and the struggle to tame the state, which has gone wild, so that supremacy is for God's Word, then that of the law and people.

A GENERAL PERSPECTIVE ON ISLAMIC PARTIES

Any observer of the evolution of Islamic movements, regardless of the differences between their situation in Muslim-majority countries, which are the only ones to witness the emergence of Islamic groups that have coming to power as part of their program, will clearly notice that these movements have largely and gradually moved in the direction of consultative and democratic internal structures and toward looking for any opportunity to work within a legal framework and pursuing legal means to reach their objectives. This is in contrast to the style of governance exhibited by Arab regimes, which since the 1950s have been stuck in patterns of centralization, stifling individual freedoms and restricting political participation, whether those influenced by Eastern Europe or those beholden to Western Europe. All of them sought to end the phase of weak liberalism and fragile pluralism that prevailed before the revolutionary phase, which had allowed for a free expression of a wide spectrum of ideas. This was the age of giants in the arts and literature, in intellectual pursuits, the media, and religion.

It was then that a pivotal change took place in the relationship between state and society, as a result of foreign pressure on domestic leaders and, by means of a secular discourse, their own exploitation of the Palestinian cause through grandiose and pompous slogans. Add to that the role of the elites who had grown up under foreign protection and who now continue to protect their interests by widening the gap between rulers and citizens. The state, then, through its discourse and its relations has become estranged from its people and as a result is forcing them into a dilemma. Is this state our state? And are those governing drawing their legitimacy from the people or from foreign powers? On the one hand, it calls itself Islamic, but on the other it forbids Islamic parties and encourages people to violate religious commands like fasting and the prohibition to drink alcohol.

It was only natural for such a state that isolated itself by its discourse and allegiance to rely on a mix of hypocritical policies and violence. Unsurprisingly, with the growing opposition to such a state and the appearance of leaders with limited political appeal, the scales tipped toward state violence. We witnessed wave after wave of popular opposition to the state, from the nationalists to the liberals, from the leftists and trade unions to Islamists, and every time a group of prisoners was released, it was only to give way to the arrest of another group. Often, too, prisons brought them together. When pressure reached its highest level on society and the secular current exhausted most of its aims, some of these very quickly turned from being prisoners into being at the service of their former torturers, praising, advising and defending them.[236]

Therefore, a number of factors were converging at this time: the increasing dependence on the state and subservience to foreign powers, a worsening economic crisis; a state propped up by foreigners continually provoking people's religious and moral sensibilities; the decline of traditional institutions without them being replaced by sustainable alternatives; the unchecked Israeli arrogance; and the growing feeling of a society possessing a glorious civilization, yet now reviled, humiliated, and estranged in these weak and savage entities called "states." All of this converged to produce a passionate trend calling for a return to religion at all levels of society, from its humblest members to its elites. All who possess the least bit of honor can feel this humiliation, and its pressure is greater for those who are most educated and aware of this tragic reality than it is for the other sectors.

THE ISLAMIST MOVEMENT AND VIOLENCE

Violence is the most prominent characteristic of the relationship between society and state, and alienation is the most salient and oppressive kind of violence that the state practices. It is a process of tearing a society away from its roots and its conscience, for the purpose of imposing what goes by "modernity." In reality, this is a dictatorship of the West over our peoples by means of a westernizing class. This westernization, or modernization following the western model, is antithetical to democracy in every possible way.

If even the secular classes feel the oppression of a state ruled by those sharing their ideology because of one faction's insistence on monopolizing power, preeminence, and wealth, then the likelihood of Islamists being subjected to violence is even greater. From this we understand the violence directed by the state against Islamic movements, although they were not the only victims, but they remain far ahead of the rest.

Yet after the spread of democratic ideals in the world, and after certain severe experiences, the Islamist mainstream has been on the whole characterized by refusal to react with violence, insistence on clearly propagating its message, and its remarkable patience, as is the official position of the Muslim Brotherhood, the Jamaat-e-Islami in Pakistan, India, and Bangladesh, the Islamic Party in Malaysia, the Refah Party in Turkey, and Ennahda in Tunisia.[237] This is apart from isolated instances of individual violence here and there, which were often exaggerated in order to eradicate a political rival. This is still the method adopted by the widest spectrum of Islamist groups.

That said, the increasingly harsh measures taken against these movements in several countries could truly be called religious persecution[238]: the blocking of their political action by multiplying unjust laws that exclude Islamic parties and deprive them of their right to being legally recognized and other laws that prohibit any action in the mosques without government authorization. In fact, the restrictions even reached the point of forbidding individual religious practices such as prayer and women wearing the hijab, which could truly be called religious persecution.[239] Religiosity itself can be a factor for refusing people jobs in both the private and public sector, while the state deals with Islamic groups through the secret police, which results in persecution campaigns and harassment, violation of freedoms, and the use of torture.[240] What is more, these regimes routinely manipulate elections, even crushing polling boxes with tanks and punishing the winners—the legitimate rulers—with imprisonment and execution, as was the case in more than one nation. What makes matters worse, and what further provokes Islamists' feeling of persecution and pushes them to react with violence, is the full support of the secular elites, even to the point of descending into the streets to demand the cancellation of elections and chant their contempt for all things Arab and Islamic, as happened in Algeria.[241]

Despite all of this, mainstream Islamism in most Arab nations has armed itself with patience as it seeks any possible legal opening for political action and continues to debate with its secular opponents, those whose occupation is the justification of dictatorship and the exclusion of Islamists, alleging that they are the enemies of democracy—and this despite the fact that there is not one elite faction that could boast of offering a track record or a model of democratic behavior. In fact, most of them had only recently been become hoarse from cheering, and their palms sore from clapping so enthusiastically and singing the praise of one-party regimes.

The Islamist movement is accused by some of wanting to seize power, but if they meant simply seeking to be in government and implement their program, then it is exactly for that purpose that political parties are created. Democracy has no other meaning or greater advantage than being the best way to achieve a peaceful alternation of political power. But if by seizing power, they mean taking control over power by illegal means, like in a coup d'état, then the first people to be targeted by such accusations are the elites who control the state with an iron first, having in the last watch of the night crept into power on the backs of tanks, or to those who falsify election results, refusing to allow an alternation of power.[242] And, as the Islamic thinker Muhammad 'Imara stated, why would Islamists need to seize power by force since they represent the majority—unless the road ahead of them is blocked?

METHODOLOGIES OF ISLAMIST GROUPS

It has become clear that the mainstream of the Islamist movement continues to remain patient in the face of persecution, refusing to respond to the increasing calls to violence from within and without, and that the violent groups, a small minority within the wider Islamist current, did not start out violent but became so in response to state violence perpetrated against them and to a situation in which all political action was blocked. We also saw that these very groups could themselves move gradually toward democracy—even if they refuse to use that term—if the state stops using force and opened the door to freedom. Then if they refused to renounce violence, it would be easier for all, even Islamists, to isolate and condemn them, for every Islamist worthy of that name is ready to condemn the violence of such groups unreservedly. All that is possible if the state were to announce its adoption of the path of democracy without discriminating against anyone and to respect human rights and the people's will, and if it stopped using the security apparatus to control the umma's thinking, its political choices, and its media.

If that is the case, then we should proffer to those Islamic activists who have adopted peaceful means of change the following advice born out of the Islamist movement's experience:[243]

Organizations within the Islamist movement must be models of mutual consultation in the way they formulate policies and issue their decisions. They should not stifle contrary opinions, nor claim to be speaking for Islam.

They should sincerely defend their own freedom and the freedom of others equally.

They should steer away from any violence or shedding of blood, for truth by nature prevails, just as lies and corruption naturally fail in the end. The example of Islamic parties or other groups that used non-state violence shows the meager chances of success of such action. This same conclusion was reached by the great majority of Sunni scholars after a long history of civil strife, which led them to forbid the use of violence by severely restricting its scope and conditions.

They should operate fully openly, even if that means being absent from the political arena and having to limit their action to the cultural and social spheres. A Muslim is not obligated to fulfill all of his duties all the time but only those he is able to fulfill.

They should give priority to society over the state, to ethics over law, to inner reform over external reform.

They should seek to reach the masses rather than the elites and be concerned with people rather than with the party. For to the extent that their worries and concerns are those of the people rather than dwelling on internal party issues, to that extent they will be on the right track. They must think the best of others and not look down on them.

They must strive to widen the circle of dialogue rather than force to deal with the people's problems. They should not monopolize those issues but continually seek to build consensus around them. They must also benefit from other Islamic thinkers and scholars from outside their movement, for the Islamic project is much greater than any one group can tackle.

They must announce a clear position that as a matter of principle promotes respect for the constitution and the law, even if they disagree with specific articles that limit public freedoms, or legitimize authoritarian rule, injustice, or violation of the umma's Shari'a. A state governed by a constitution, even if it is unjust, is a lesser evil than a state governed by one man—even if he claims to work for justice and rule by the Shari'a.

Mutual consultation [shura] is not just a tool to manage the affairs of state and of political parties; it is also a general methodology to be adopted by the umma and should be practiced by all society's components, starting with the family. It behooves the Islamic movement, therefore, to make a significant contribution in this regard through its educational role.

They should refuse to be stuck in rigid patterns of thought and in conformity to one legal school, but rather promote continuous ijtihad and evolution of ideas, develop their political methodology, learning from the experiences of all nations and aiming first and foremost to give the opportunity to create the best conditions for the greatest number of God's servants—for all people are God's servants—to worship Him in freedom, in safety, and in peace, far from all compulsion or coercion, since freedom is the path that leads to paradise.

Islamic groups should give great importance to intellectual labor, for knowledge in Islam comes before action. They should do so by paying attention not just to the technical sciences but also to the humanities, to philosophy, the social sciences, art and literature, and the media, so that they might be able to highlight all the variety and wealth of the religious phenomenon. They must elaborate Islamic foundations of the achievements of human civilization, to which we Muslims have made great contributions, although they came to us from the West wrapped up in colonialism, unbelief, and immorality, so we rejected them. Further, we must firmly establish the oneness of human origin and destiny, and its philosophical, scientific, and religious unity, for Islam is the meeting place for people of intellect and free will from every school and religion, and not a call to war and isolationism.

We must affirm—we, as Islamists, on the basis of Islam and in the interest of the people—our allegiance to multiparty parliamentary democracy, for democracy is the best mechanism we have in order to implement God's Shari'a. As we practice this consultative style of politics, we will be able to further develop this tool and reform it as a tool for governing, drawing its inspiration and programs from Islam as understood and approved by the majority of Muslims. Therefore, to refuse democracy because of its shortcomings, we fear, is like a leap into the unknown and a gratuitous service to dictatorship that is the umma's greatest foe and stumbling block on her path to renewal in addition to the dynamic of thought and action.

What is most puzzling here is that many of those who oppose democracy, some of whom claim to monopolize the Shari'a, when tyranny sinks its teeth into them their only refuge is Western democracies, like the early Muslims who found refuge in the Christian kingdom of Ethiopia. Could our mentality be so primitive as to reject something because it is not perfect, rather than accepting it as it is and then working on improving it, just like the issue of freedom?[244] Truly, we see that many of modernity's ideas and technologies that have destroyed other religions are capable of bringing renewal and spur healthy growth in the Muslim community, as noted by the sociologist Ernest Gellner.[245]

Write I write "embracing the path of democracy"—whether they accept the term or not, I just mean the concept—I do not mean that the Islamic parties use Western governance as a model. In fact, the Western model needs Islam as a moral and philosophical source in order to escape the negative outcomes experienced by previous civilizations. They had no shortage of machines, luxuries, and armies, yet their people's hearts were devoid of meaning; their lives had no purpose, hence they became easy prey to deadly epidemics, and the wrath of God overcame them, and His warning came to pass against those who rebel against His ways.

By contrast, the model of governance, civilization, and values adopted by the Islamic movement is that of the Messenger's state and that of the Rightly Guided Caliphs. All we want is to develop an authentic model of governance, which also includes the experience of modern civilization, though going beyond its foundations and objectives. While this model is able to benefit in some areas of Western philosophy and particularly its organizational tools, no doubt these find their source elsewhere—namely, from the tree that is eternal and whose branches reach into Heaven ("a good tree whose root is firm and whose branches are high in the sky, yielding constant fruit by its Lord's leave").[246] This we can do by recognizing the achievements of modernity in liberating the mind from all hegemony and recognizing humans as the objective of civilization, in freeing the will of nations and granting them sovereignty and control over their rulers by means of elected civic institutions and the priority of civil society over the state. The demands of the independence movement, be it nationalist, socialist, or liberal, for independence, unity, social justice, democracy, human rights, the liberation of Palestine, and resisting dependence on foreign nations, fragmentation, and exploitation are not only legitimate demands; they are also essential and recognized pillars in the Islamic project of civilization and renewal. Supporting these demands does not require deference to Western traditions in a servile manner or being overawed by its accomplishments, nor mobilizing feelings of enmity and prejudice toward the West or displaying a childish disdain for putting to use what the West discovered or its civilization has produced. Finally, this willingness to learn from the West does not imply blindness to the dangers, crises, and injustice also present in their midst. And even if the Islamic project must also include patriotic, nationalistic, and socialist elements, it is not a project about patriotism and nationalism, about an ethnic group or class. It is a humanitarian project, which seeks to save humanity and preserve its achievements on the basis of the creed of God's Oneness.

What the Islamic movement refuses from the West is its racism, its westerncentrism, and its extreme secularist tendency, which colors international and local relations with a bent toward power, exploitation, and unethical behavior. This has led to the destruction of the family, religion, conscience, and the environment, and generated wars, famines, and injustice. It transforms the human person into a beast, and the world into a jungle, while their aspiration was to make a god out of man and establish Heaven on earth!

Another matter worthy of attention by the Islamic movement is spiritual formation, that it seeks to train people such that what motivates them to avoid evil and do good works stems from within, out of respect for God and His law, and in imitation of His Prophet (PBUH), seeking to please God in preparation for meeting Him on the Last Day. In addition, the Islamic community will need to foster inside it and around it a climate of love, mercy, altruism, piety, and an absolute commitment to respect ethical standards and the rituals of Islam. Any complacency in this area, being solely satisfied with the individual's party loyalty, is the beginning of deficiency and a step on the road that leads to secularism, ambivalence, and hypocrisy. By contrast, spiritual training should teach independence of character, initiative, boldness, honor, cleanliness, courage, self-discipline, humility, care for the family, simplicity of lifestyle, and keeping oneself from extremism and intolerance. The umma as a whole must itself be trained to demonstrate the virtues of solidarity, self-reliance, and self-esteem.

The Islamic movement must know that it defends the freedoms of all nations and peoples and their human rights everywhere, and supports the oppressed from any religious background.

We call for the establishment of a wide front and the achievement of major reconciliations within our umma, whether it be between governments and their people or between the various intellectual and political trends so as to be able to resist external plots aimed against it, and to ensure freedoms and human rights.

It is appropriate here to quote the bold words spoken by the nationalist thinker from Lebanon Manh al-Sulh during one of his interventions in the conference organized by the Center for the Study of Arab Unity: "The ruler who does not recognize the Islam of the masses turns into a fascist ruler, whether he intends to or not. It is as if Islam is the factor that determines the democratic character of a ruler and his true popularity. In our countries we have many examples to show that the main bone of contention between the ruler and the people is this very issue. The entry point for democracy in every Arab country is the willingness of the ruler to embrace the people's civilization, that is, its Islamic civilization."[247]

We call for an international democratic front that will stand against dictatorship and the violation of people's freedoms, for the sake of a world in which freedom prevails and benefits and ideas circulate freely and in a just manner.

Islamic groups must reassure the world truthfully, responsibly, and with all clarity that the state ruled by Islamic norms will protect public freedoms and expand them. It will safeguard the values that contemporary civilization has acquired, such as freedom, reason, conscience, open communication and publishing, scientific progress, the flourishing of the arts and creative expression, the freedom of minorities—be they ethnic, religious, or intellectual—and the freedom of women and their dignity.

CONCLUSION: THE ISLAMIST MOVEMENT IS FOR DEMOCRACY, BUT . . .

A summary of what I have been reflecting on, what I have become convinced of, what I have been, for long, working toward achieving and called others to can be most clearly and simply expressed in a quote from a Palestinian writer living in the United States, from a good article he wrote in the newspaper *al-Hayat*:

> Rached Ghannouchi, leader of Ennahda, raised a question that perhaps irritated some Islamists in those days, but today we understand it in the context of reshaping and re-evaluating our positions, since we do not claim by our allegiance to Islam that we are pure and correct in all our views. This was his question: if I present myself, my program, my movement, and "my Islam" to the Tunisian people and they reject me, what will be the result? I will withdraw willingly and continue the fight in the following years focusing on making my case more convincing. I propose myself, and if I am rejected, then I will continue using the usual means to convince people.

> If I believe that the Islamic Shari'a must be applied in totality on the one hand, and I believe in democracy on the other, then there is no contradiction. I present my convictions to the people and they either accept them or reject them. If they reject them, I withdraw into the opposition and I practice other means of persuasion, like education, spiritual training, making use of media and teaching. Then, when I sense that the people have been convinced, I put myself forward for the next round of elections. And even if I do not win, I can go on trying indefinitely, because I believe that democracy is the recognition of everyone; that democracy is about equality and alternation of power, about sharing wealth and giving people the right to economic initiative. Democracy is about the people's right to freely choose between different projects. Democracy is not that you choose those who oppose you, but rather that you pursue dialogue and mutual understanding with them. Like mutual consultation, democracy is not simply a style of governance that allows consensus or the expression of the majority's will; it is also a method of education and a way to tackle extremism through dialogue. Can the contemporary Western powers come to understand this genuine Islamic orientation toward respecting the rules of the democratic process? Or is it as John Esposito remarked: we will encourage a democratic transformation only if in practice this one condition is met, that Islam does not win any elections!

Islam has the power to embrace the democratic process and reform it so it becomes the rule of the people guided by the divine law, especially as there is a clear movement among Islamists toward democracy. And if Western democracy itself has a point of reference which is natural law, as Professor Muhammad 'Imara has declared, we Muslims put the Islamic Shari'a as the point of reference. Islamic democracy gives all the authority to the people on the condition that they do not permit what it forbids or forbid what it permits. Our reality is more complex than that, but it also needs a simpler solution. We need a kind of Hilf al-Fudul Pact, an alliance between all intellectual trends, all agreeing to respect human liberty and the will of our peoples, and do so sincerely. Then we can all rest happily today and tomorrow. If not, it will be like Lebanon's civil war yesterday, and today in Somalia, Afghanistan, Iraq, Algeria, and Egypt, and the rest will share the same fate if they persist on this path. God calls to us all, "My servants, I have forbidden injustice for myself and I have made it forbidden to you, so do not oppress one another."[248]

In the end, there is nothing left for the researcher except to stress that freedom and human rights in Islam are not slogans imposed by external pressures or power equations; they are convictions and religious principles that are taught from childhood. No political party or state enacts them; neither does a particular class or people in order to bolster their privileges. Rather, they are mandatory, sacred laws that the Lord of humanity has laid down for all people, and He calls everyone to put them into practice as duties and not simply rights. He informs humanity that He watches them attentively and will call them to account for those duties. He has urged them to cooperate with one another in various ways, including oversight over one another and setting up a just government, whose only power is that given to it by the people so that it can protect those rights under their authority and supervision.

God has also made the loftiest declaration to humanity, that they are all His creation and that they all come from one origin and are equally honored and urged them to be as He intended—that is, one family that competes in doing good and repelling evil, in discovering the treasures of this universe and using them to fulfill their material and spiritual needs through many sorts of clues He has graciously dispersed through His creation. Some of these are useful for bettering their lives, and others are simply signs of beauty that point to His majesty. Equally, He has forbidden them to arrogantly put anyone down and discriminate against one another on the basis of race, skin color, gender, class, or a claim to piety. For all are brothers and sisters, and thus must get to know and help one another without any injustice, and He granted their minds absolute freedom of conscience and a full responsibility to choose their own destiny.

This humble servant before his Lord cannot but stress his inability to reach, let alone exhaustively comprehend, the depths and treasures of Islam. His aspiration has never been to have the last word on every one of the great problems he has raised; not even for one of them. But it is enough for him to be able to inspire those with more understanding than him and provoke them to progress further in their discovery of reality, which cannot be exhausted, and thus contribute to the discovery of the path to our deliverance and that of all humankind in this world and in the hereafter, for "it may be that one passes on understanding to one who has more understanding than himself."[249]

"And God is all we need, and is the best manager of our affairs."[250]

Summary of Research Findings

Is there a concept of human rights in Islam? And if there is one, what is its philosophical basis? What is the connection between it and the modern declarations of human rights? Is there a foundational conception of the state in Islam, and if so, what is its connection to modern Western conceptions of the state? What are the political, economic, and educational dimensions of mutual consultation [shura]? What are the factors that guarantee freedom and prevent injustice in the Islamic state?

These are the central issues highlighted in this book, and they can be summarized with the following points.

PART I: HUMAN RIGHTS AND FREEDOMS IN ISLAM

Freedom in Islam, both in its culture and in its record as a civilization, despite its shortcomings, was a foundational authentic value, since it is the basis and precondition of the Confession of Faith itself. In fact, before the believer certifies his faith in God's existence and in the truthfulness of the Messenger (PBUH) and his Message, he affirms his own existence as a free, rational being.[1] This is because the "I" in full possession of consciousness, freedom, and will certifies ("I testify") that there is no god but God, and "I" testifies that "Muhammad is God's Messenger." It is this free declaration that gives rise to all the commitments a Muslim makes as long as he continues to enjoy reason, consciousness, and freedom, which constitute the precondition for every obligation, since the acts of the coerced, the insane, and the imitator have no moral or religious value.

Freedom here is not simply license or an existential given, but on the one hand it is a duty, and on the other it is the continuous effort to surpass what is necessary, to strive for the most noble actions and against the forces of evil and ignorance on the outside, in order to lift up the word of truth, justice, and freedom. To the extent that the believer has done this, to that extent he has realized the full potential of his freedom. Thus freedom is the constant effort and daily struggle to embody the high ideals (God's Beautiful Names) everywhere and in every soul. The human person, as several modern philosophers remind us, is not free; rather, he frees himself to the extent that he struggles against the forces of oppression inside and outside of him, and to the extent that he fulfills the high ideals of Islam's ethical constitution, as seen in God's Beautiful Names.

Human rights in Islam are based on its fundamental teaching that human beings carry within them God's favor and are therefore empowered by Him and responsible for managing His creation.[2] This calling imparts both duties and rights on them, which no one has the authority to violate.

Our comparison between the principles of human rights in Islam and modern human rights declarations has highlighted a wide agreement between them, save for a few exceptions. As a result, a Muslim aware of the human person's value in Islam must rejoice to see humanity crafting such an important document that recognizes people's inherent dignity, a dignity both remarkable and above any other consideration. For God said, "We have honored the Children of Adam."[3] Anyone belonging to humanity has human dignity, and the Shari'a came to enjoin the protection of that dignity and to prevent its violation.[4]

The disagreements on secondary issues in some articles of the Universal Declaration of Human Rights in no way invalidate Islam's agreement with its general orientation. Yet there remains a major disagreement on its philosophical foundations, on its motivations and goals, since the declaration and following conventions predominantly rely on a philosophy of natural law (a concept not defined therein), which robs these rights of their depth, teleology, and of the motivation needed to apply them, so that a philosophical discussion about freedom frequently ends up denying there is such a thing. This is in addition to the contrast between theory and practice. This is so, despite the fact that the editors of the declaration and later documents belonged to different schools of thought and different religious traditions.

By contrast, human rights in Islam are considered an integral part of the Shari'a and its objectives, and a fruit of its doctrines and rituals, which gives them the quality of duty, permanence, and principle. The person who acts according to them is rewarded, then, and the one who violates them incurs punishment in this life and the next. This is because protecting the humanity of a person is the highest objective of the Shari'a—that is, protecting his religion, his life, his intellect, his family, his possessions, and the rest of his rights, including his right to justice and freedom.[5] This means that saving the person who is drowning, feeding the hungry, supporting the oppressed, and defending freedom and religion are all religious duties; whereas the Shari'a forbids the following transgressions: aggression, invasion of privacy, corruption, suicide or killing, both being forbidden violence, because the human self—that is, myself and all other "selves"—has divine rights. I do not have the right to take my life or that of others; my duty is to protect them, and the same goes for all rights.

These are some of the human rights guaranteed by Islam:

1. *Freedom of belief:* The study pointed to some possible restrictions on this right, yet in discussing the issue of apostasy, we eliminated the clash between it and the principle of liberty. We concluded that apostasy was a political crime consisting of (armed) insurrection against the community's political authority and that therefore it was up to that authority to specify an appropriate penalty.

2. *Corollary rights of freedom of belief:* Our study discussed these rights and affirmed their importance: freedom of expression and discussion, freedom of religious practice, freedom of thought.

3. *Freedom of the self, or the right to enjoy our God-given dignity or personal integrity:* Our study discussed the topic of violence, torture, and means of compulsion, concluding that they must all be forbidden.

4. *Economic rights:* Our study affirmed the right to own goods on the basis of one's work, and the right of the worker to enjoy the fruit of his labor. It considered ownership a social function of the individual according to his religious conscience and society's political authority within the framework of the community's best interest. If he abuses that privilege, society intervenes as the agent delegated by God, the original Owner, in order to redress that which has been distorted.

5. *Social rights:* Our research certified that work is a religious duty and that the poor have a legitimate claim on a specified part of the wealth owned by the rich, a claim that goes beyond zakat revenues, since no money is strictly one's own as long as there remain people in need, or sick, or uneducated, or unclothed, or homeless. These are rights determined by the community's political authority; and if not, then the needy person, possessor of this right, may seize his share when the state does not give it to him. Among these social rights, we listed the right to education, since it is obligatory, the right to health care, to housing, to clothing, and the right to start a family.

CONCLUSIONS OF PARTS II AND III:
POLITICAL FREEDOMS AND FOUNDATIONS
OF THE DEMOCRATIC SYSTEM

In comparing the fundamental principles of Western democracy with Islamic governance or Islamic democracy, we concluded that the democratic order was both form and substance.

Regarding its form, democracy affirms the principle of popular sovereignty. The people are the source of the government's powers, which is a sovereignty they exercise through various constitutional techniques, the details of which may vary but all of which converge around the principles of equality, elections, the separation of powers, political pluralism, the rights of expression, belief, and forming trade unions, and the majority's right to rule and determine policies, and the minority's right to oppose them, thus enabling the rotation of power by peaceful means. In a later development, it declared an assortment of guarantees for citizens, which after the fall of the socialist camp began to be whittled away by capitalism, since those rights were not protected on the basis of principles but by the balance of political power.

As for democracy's substance, it is fundamentally about freeing the law from the authority of the kings and the clergy, and the transition from one-man rule to the rule of law that expresses the people's will. This in turn ensures that government behavior submits to the law and enables those being ruled to demand in front of independent judges that it be respected. Further, it ensures that laws are enacted according to specific procedures and that government respects the values and fundamental goals of society and expresses its will, broadly speaking. That is what the rule of law means.

The second foundation of the modern Western state is sovereignty, which means that the state possesses the highest authority and that the possessors of that sovereignty are those who hold legislative authority. That authority is absolute inside and outside of the nation's borders, for no one can question the state's authority.

This view of the state represents an important step forward in reinforcing the authority of the law above that of individuals, and affording citizens the tools to put pressure on their rulers. Nevertheless, the political problem about how to curb the human tendency toward authoritarianism still has no solution, for the Western democratic system, though it is defined as the rule of the people, remains far from its ideal, in that despite the fact that all votes are equal in theory, in practice society is divided between those who own the great monopolies and the media and those who are salaried and unemployed—with the latter forming the majority. As a result of this division, this system is characterized by a great deal of formalism, and in practice democracy becomes the rule of a minority in the name of the people but without a real mandate.

In any case, the essence of democracy and its criterion is about the people's political participation and the extent of that participation, regardless of the particular forms it might take. For democracy is not a philosophical theory but an assortment of good and useful procedures, which historically were adopted after violent and bloody revolutions, strenuous intellectual efforts, and the accumulation of successive experiments. These led to negotiating between various elites, taking turns in exerting pressure, making compromises that pleased all the parties in one way or another and gave everyone the opportunity to either rule or be in the opposition with the hope of coming to power later. All of this was an alternative to absolute rule exercised by one party, which pushes the other parties to think about using violent or secretive means in order to seize their share of power and wealth.

Our study also highlighted the contradictions, the ambiguities, and the risks of this concept of the state because of its being rooted in philosophical materialism and in the politics of nationalism. Among its manifestations were devastating wars waged for nationalist and economic reasons, the spread of poverty and deadly plagues, environmental degradation threatening to choke humankind, and the breathtaking evolution of weaponry at the expense of humanitarian relief, the development of natural resources, the protection of the environment, and human solidarity. This led the very conception itself to deteriorate as soon as the balance of power that was maintaining it—trade unions and the presence of the socialist camp—shifted, unleashing military fleets once again imposing hegemony over other nations, trampling on the rule of law, the courts, and human rights.

However, this does not negate or take away from the genuine contribution that Western political thought has made to political thought generally. It represents a very important addition in that it makes a separation between the ruler and the state by denying him any ownership of the state, and in that it makes him into a mere high official at the service of the people. This means that political thought owes its democratic system to the West. Additionally, it emphasized the authority of the people as the foundation of a regime's legitimacy and formulated a mechanism to implement that sovereignty through various means, such as elections, political parties, the separation of powers, and other freedoms. Thus for the first time in history, after the short period of the Rightly Guided Caliphs, a transfer of power was effected by means of a free competition among all, which is the essence of democracy and the decisive sign as to whether it is present or not.

The deficiency in this system, however, cannot be traced to the democratic apparatus itself, like elections, an independent judiciary, and freedom of the press, which rather constitute its genius. Rather, the dysfunction comes from the elements of its materialistic philosophy: its exclusion of God, morality, and religion from the organization of society; the deification of humankind, specifically the productive human and the human as a physical body; the extent to which the state is nationally and ethnically based, such that the national interest, policies, and decisions the state makes have absolute value and justify any behavior, as long as they are taken according to the necessary formal procedures. An example would be the U.S. Congress authorizing the 2003 invasion of Iraq. This is the philosophy that gives the state the undisputed right of expressing the public will, the national interest, and sovereignty, and unlimited power. This has led humanity to catastrophes that perhaps will make life as we know it impossible in the long run.

Nevertheless, we have condemned the way tyrannical regimes exploit the flaws of democracy in order to muzzle the demands of their people for democracy, and especially when this silencing of legitimate demands takes the form of religious fatwas that prohibit elections and other political liberties. This is the height of authoritarianism and hypocrisy. Therefore, in the absence of an Islamic regime or of Islamic democracy, democracy as it is practiced in the West remains the best, or least bad, system available, and a legitimate demand for a Muslim to make and to join with other free citizens in the struggle to attain it, for to achieve something imperfect and then to improve it is better than to lack it altogether.

PART IV: FUNDAMENTAL PRINCIPLES
OF ISLAMIC GOVERNANCE

Here we established that the concept of the state is original and authentic among Islamic political principles, and that political authority is a natural and necessary social need as well as a religious obligation in order to establish Islam. Political authority is not a part of Islam, as the Shia maintain, but an essential function in order to establish it. Further, there is no need to refer to the sacred texts to prove the need to establish the state, but there is a need for guarantees that ensure the state's establishment of justice and preventing it from injustice, for the primary mission of the state is to establish justice, protect religion, and provide a climate that as much as possible enables people to worship God freely and intentionally, in harmony with the law of human nature at creation [*qanun al-fitra*] and with the principles of Islam, and enables them to achieve the highest possible potential of their God-given talents, materially and spiritually, and achieve happiness in this world, while distancing themselves from any kind of coercion.

The main philosophical creed upon which human government is built in Islam includes faith in God, in prophethood, and in the Day of Judgment. More, it teaches that the human person is God's vicegerent, since he was blessed with reason, will, freedom, and responsibility for the purpose of developing the earth and making use of its wealth and resources to establish justice, goodness, and freedom for its people. Revelation from God came to help and guide people in carrying out this divine project, which is to ennoble their material and spiritual life and thus to prepare themselves for the eternal bliss that awaits them as they gain God's favor. For the seal of prophethood and the end of revelation are indeed the sign of humankind's maturity and sovereignty, because all human beings from this perspective are God's stewards and thereby exercise this authority on behalf of Him. Moreover, because God entrusts political authority to humankind collectively, it is not possible for anyone to exercise it directly, and therefore it can only be entrusted by way of a legitimate contract [bay'a], which must be entered into according to the law (the sacred text) under the supervision of the people. For the sacred text (Qur'an and Sunna) and mutual consultation [shura] together constitute the foundational authority of the Islamic state.

THE SACRED TEXT

The first and essential source of the legitimacy of political rule according to Islamic theory is its full and undisputed acceptance of and submission to Islamic law (the Shari'a) without any reservation. For the Text of the Qur'an and Sunna that is definitive by way of transmission and explicit in what it conveys; it is the highest judge and authority. It is the essential foundation upon which Islamic society is built and protected. It is the authority that establishes, guides, and organizes the individual, the community, the state, and an entire civilization. It is on this foundation and within its framework that Muslim reason exercises its potential in different creative domains of its civilization, such as law, theology, philosophy, medicine, astronomy, literature, and language. Even political disputes and conflicts never moved outside of the circle of textual interpretation.

The Text is why Islamic society endures, and mutual consultation is the tool that allows it to be embodied, to develop, and to flourish. This in turn makes clear the distinction—for the most part—between this highest guiding authority (Revelation) and the interpretation and legal decision-making [ijtihad] that draws its strength from the second source, which is mutual consultation in any of its forms—either consensus or the voice of the majority, the individual or collective effort to formulate a legal rule.

It is this authority of the Text best summarized in the hadith, "No obedience to a creature in disobedience to the Creator," which prevented the development of a religious authority in Islam (a church), or the rule of one calling himself "the shadow of God on earth." The door to political opposition and even to revolution remains open and legitimate, whether peaceful or not, anytime flagrant acts of unbelief [kufr] have been committed—that is, a blatant deviation from the foundation of Shari'a (the Text). This is what makes the Islamic state more worthy than any other kind of state to be called "a state of law," a state based on Shari'a.

MUTUAL CONSULTATION

This is the second foundation upon which Islamic government stands, in light of the Qur'an's teaching that the umma is God's vicegerent. It is the entity invested with the right to governance, since the ruler is its agent and employee. Among its duties is to choose him, guide him, reprove him, or even depose him. Mutual consultation [shura] in its political dimension is this exercise of political power, this participation in governance at the level of legislation and execution. Our study has established the authenticity of the concepts of consensus, community, oath of acceptance, those with authority ("the people of loosing and binding"), the command to do good and forbid evil, and the relationship of these concepts to shura, as forms and applications of it in society. However, many factors have caused this shura to devolve to the individual level, instead of being transformed by means of a collective decision-making process into political institutions, which was to a large extent achieved by modern Western thought.

The people mandated to use mutual consultation are in traditional terms "the people of loosing and binding," the body that represents the Islamic community with its coalitions and power centers. The caliph, or imam, or president is no greater than just one of the people as he expresses their will in applying the Shari'a and in safeguarding the public interest in conformity with the orientations laid out by this body, under the supervision of that body and of the people, as well as internal motivation from his own religious conscience. Thus, while according to Islam, the state's original legislation belongs to God in the revealed Text, the umma actively participates in detailed legislation through applying the Shari'a's principles and objectives to the evolving social reality. The practical cases of social reality are unlimited—unlike the texts in the Qur'an and Sunna which mostly deal with general objectives and guidelines, leaving for the umma—which is imbued with the spirit of the Shari'a and committed to it—ample space to understand them, disagree about them, and produce a wealth of interpretations of them by means of its consultative mechanisms, yet without damaging its unity.

As these assemblies commit themselves to these guidelines and objectives, and fixed rulings like those that lay out what is forbidden and what is permitted—including the command to consult with one another ("consult with them about matters," Q. 3:159)—their very act of gathering in submission to the Text grants them protection from agreeing on error. This book has demonstrated that it is not a few members of the umma who are protected from error but rather the umma as a whole in its commitment to the Text and to mutual consultation.

As for the possible legislative formulas, they are all acceptable, for Islam does not reject any novel mechanism that may bring a fuller expression to the people's will within the framework of the highest legal authority, that is, revelation, and stave off any form of despotism. Any method chosen to discover where public opinion is going and the person who will obtain the umma's confidence is permissible. And since there is flexibility in the Islamic Text regarding political and public affairs, we can imagine endless and limitless formulas for applying Islamic shura in molding Islamic societies. What is important is to open up spaces for freedom of thought, whether in the press, mosques and clubs, or literature. This involves the development of institutions that express in organized fashion various currents of public opinion, like central or regional parliaments, local councils, and others which constitute decision-making bodies, and the ruler is required to consult them and is bound by the result of their consultation in every domain.

This is because the command form used in the verse implies the obligation to consult, meaning that if a ruler does not confer with his subjects, he has swerved from God's path and is not worthy to rule over Muslims. Their duty, then, is to depose him, just as the commentator from Islamic Spain al-Qurtubi made clear when he insisted that this was the great fault Pharaoh committed—that is, leading by himself as a tyrant. As Pharaoh says in the Qur'an, "I but point out to you that which I see (myself)."[6]

In our study as well, on the topic of what the jurists stipulated for the members of the consultative body, we affirmed the principle of citizenship as the basis of the rights and duties in the state, according to the Islamic perspective. In a Muslim-majority nation, the majority of the consultative body will be Muslims, but there is no objection to the representation of non-Muslim minorities within it. Their representation constitutes no threat to the state's integrity under Islamic law, as long as the Islamic constitution is respected. That constitution is undoubtedly built on Islamic principles, and it would actually be advisable to set up a constitutional high court composed of top jurists, judges, and lawyers, which would guarantee the constitutionality of the laws, as long as they do not monopolize the interpretation of the sacred texts or claim to speak in their name. For the freedom of legal interpretation [ijtihad] must forever remain.

In our discussion too, in reaction to those who stipulate that members of the consultative body must be male, we sided with those who refrain from that condition on the basis of the rule of equality for public rights. On the topic of the minimum age for candidates, we concluded that the condition of maturity was enough for members of the assembly. As for the necessity of residence within the nation's territory or not, it seemed better to consider it a condition, while moving toward facilitating the process of becoming a citizen, whether the applicant is Muslim or not, and to allow a small percentage of seats in any Islamic parliament to outstanding people who have rendered great service to the Islamic cause, to its people, and humanity in general. This is for the sake of benefiting from their input and relaxing the barriers around the territorial nation-state or a somewhat deficient caliphate, which as such goes against the rule of tawhid. One should not accept such a state except by necessity and as a temporary measure, considering that it represents an anomaly that violates the umma's highest interest and the directions taken by contemporary states toward forming major blocks for the protection of their interests.

The consultative assembly (or Shura Council) undertakes the well-known functions of a parliament, including the legislative one, or in Islamic terms, the interpretive one,[7] since legislation at its core belongs to God (may He be exalted) and which is exercised by the umma as delegated by Him in one of three modes:

- Either directly, which is the rule; by means of a referendum or general elections for vital issues like foreign alignments and important national policies, or the choice of a ruler and members of parliament.
- Through delegation to "the people of loosing and binding," from among whom popular leaders with good reputation and wide experience are added to the consultative body. This body takes up the task of monitoring the government, drawing up policies, and drafting laws. Note that the goal of mutual consultation is not simply finding out the direction willed by the majority but reaching consensus.
- Through the existence of a body of the most prominent scholars of the Shari'a and law, known for being endowed with knowledge, godliness, and service to the umma. This body then fulfills the mission of checking the constitutionality of laws and the collective and individual use of the

Text to craft new laws [ijtihad]. This constitutional court focuses its work on the organs of state and public opinion on issues connected to the Shari'a, though their opinion is not binding on them.

There are several dimensions to mutual consultation in addition to the legislative one which involves the umma in legislation.

Political Consultation

This is represented by the way in which the imamate (or presidency) is considered a contract, which the umma is responsible for initiating and managing, for it has authority and sovereignty over its rulers within the framework of Revelation, the highest legal authority.

There is no caliphate (or presidency) without a genuine oath of allegiance, which is what renders Islamic rule a democratic rule in the full sense of the word. It is also a civil rule from every angle, since neither state nor head of state has any religious privilege. Even if the caliph—that is, the head of state—is qualified to perform ijtihad, his own interpretations have no privilege. For his own ijtihad to be considered legislative material, it must be discussed in public, like everyone else's proposal, and only then will the collective decision make it a law or not. As to how this decision is made, our study leans toward the use of consensus or a simple majority. Finally, the ruler is bound by a decision based on mutual consultation, especially if it approaches the level of consensus, that is, two-thirds of the votes and above.

This book concluded that, according to Islam, the state is a social necessity and a reality supported by the Shari'a. Both necessity and Text require its existence; its will emerges from mutual consultation; therefore, it is a government of both Text and shura. Moreover, the study concluded that the Islamic system of governance should have no hereditary rule, no infallible rulers, no naming of successors in a will, and no deputizing anyone in one's stead. Rather, it is a government based on mutual consultation and only attainable through a public oath of allegiance. The source of its authority is the umma within the framework of the highest legitimacy provided by divine revelation. This is what makes Islamic governance, though it differs from a democratic system, the closest model to it. Citizenship is the principal foundation of the state, and it entails the participation of each citizen in the body politic of the nation but without necessarily sharing the same religious tradition.

In other words, this philosophy allows the possibility of a multiplicity of states in Islam as a result of the multiplicity of political communities, even though this goes against Islam's origins, where we find a unified state, because of the unity of the political and the religious in the Islamic perspective, thus rendering the

Islamic umma a unified political body. Whether this multiplicity of states can be attributed to necessity or to the distances between regions, the "caliphate," by which we mean the unified political framework in which the concept of umma meets the concept of nation and the religious meets the political which is the natural result of the Islamic doctrine of God's oneness [tawhid], nevertheless remains a goal of the umma, which it may not abandon, nor would it be in its interest to do so. Rather, the umma must take gradual steps toward this goal by means of flexible forms of unity.

In this context it is possible to consider the Organization of the Islamic Conference as well as the Arab League as frameworks of unity that need to be developed further so as to attain a higher degree of unity.[8] This is because a situation of isolated fragmented states is an anomaly, which can only be seen as an exception. In this respect, democracy is the transitional means for the nation-state to evolve into the ideological state, the umma's state. Then any step of unity taken by the nation-state is a step in the right direction, that is, toward a democratic state with an Islamic identity, a state based on Revelation and mutual consultation, a unified state, or the umma's state, as opposed to secularism and westernization which are other names for autocracy and division.

For both Revelation and mutual consultation require the establishment of the state and the institutions it entails, like state leadership. In this regard, our study has indicated the permanent need for political leadership, a duty that the umma and its representatives are responsible to discharge.

We also established that, according to the Islamic perspective, a state with a majority of Muslims must not only have a Muslim as president or imam but one who has reached a high level in his faith, and his knowledge of Islam and the condition of his people; being nominally "Muslim" is not sufficient. However, contemporary Muslim thinkers have highlighted the difference between the nature and context of the emergence of the Muslim state historically and the nature and context of the emergence of the modern state. It follows, then, that the state about which the jurists spoke was that of the umma (the caliphate), or the great imamate, and they stipulated that the ruler be capable of ijtihad, therefore granting him great authority, almost to the point of absolute power.[9] By contrast, today we talk about Islamic nations in which the powers are distributed to various branches of government, and the ruler's power is limited by means of institutions held in check by constitutional documents and specific laws. This ensures that decisions are reached through institutions and mutual consultation which may not be overly influenced by the diverse backgrounds of those involved in the decision-making process, whether intellectual, legal, or doctrinal. And the same holds true of the juridical task, for which the jurists required that the legal experts be capable of ijtihad, as in the case of the head of state. This was understandable under the specific circumstances of that time, and in particular when a judge functioned alone, there was a single tier of litigation, and no detailed legal codes, which nowadays make the verdict rather straightforward.

Traditionally, a judge had to be a mujtahid [capable of ijtihad] in order to deduce a ruling on a case from the original sacred texts and from a large body of legal interpretations and precedents, while justice today is rendered mostly collectively and on successive tiers, with the higher courts reviewing decisions made on lower levels. That system today offers more guarantees to arrive at the truth, and in particular by following detailed legal codes, so that the judge does not need to be one of the top-level jurists who can practice ijtihad, since his judgment in this case is not much influenced by his school of jurisprudence, ideology, or religious doctrine—exactly as is the case with the ruler's authority.

Muslim thinkers also highlighted another difference between the historic state in Islam and its contemporary form, which has to do with the circumstances of its foundation. The former derived its legitimacy from conquest, which gave the conquerors and their descendants (the Muslims) privileges within the state that the non-Muslim citizens did not have. One of those privileges was the exercise of power at the highest levels, specifically as ruler or judge. However, that conquest-based state has been brought to an end by foreign occupation since movements formed to resist that occupation were based on nationalism, which entailed the equal participation of all its inhabitants in the nation [*al-watan*] with the same rights and same duties, including the duty to defend it, and later military service.

Here we have a state rising on the basis of a new kind of legitimacy, that of liberation and participation in citizenship, a legitimacy that grants everyone equal rights and duties, and no citizen has more privilege than another. In addition, since decision making in the modern state is made by insitutions on the basis of mutual consultation following regulations and laws in a process that prevents individual control and limits the extent to which doctrines can influence the decision makers. This is what led a number of Islamic constitutional jurists to lift not only the requirement for the ruler or judge to be a mujtahid but also for him to be a Muslim, instead proposing conditions and criteria to which all citizens must submit no matter what their creed, as long as they are versed in Islamic culture and ready to defend it.

Meanwhile, the majority of classical and modern constitutional jurists believed that both ruler and judge should be Muslims, and even mujtahids, while granting non-Muslim citizens the right to exercise other functions beside those two. It is noteworthy that the modern state does not recognize absolute power and that this debate has no practical consequence since the majority of citizens are Muslims. If in a Muslim-majority nation there are two candidates for the presidency and one is Muslim and the other Christian, we would expect the majority to vote for the one who shares their faith, unless he is known to be incompetent or corrupt and the other candidate is known for his integrity and experience in governing the state. In this case the one who has more integrity and competence is the better choice, for justice is the law of the universe and the purpose for which God sent His messengers. Therefore, God will support the state ruled by justice though the ruler is an unbeliever. Conversely, He will not support the oppressive state though the ruler may be a believer. Millions of Muslims have been able to live safely in a just but non-Muslim state, as they can do so in regions where Islamic law is applied though the ruler is not a Muslim (as in Nigeria), but they cannot live safely under oppressive Muslim rulers.

Further, the book detailed the duties of the imam or president in protecting the umma and its religious faith and in abiding by the outcome of consultation with the people, also in safeguarding his rights over them, like their compliance and obedience to him, and offering their counsel. It also touched upon his character—namely, his being a model of piety, of simplicity in his lifestyle, of courage and zeal. Finally, it discussed the duties of the umma toward him—namely, advising and monitoring him and deposing him if he becomes a tyrant.

We also broached the topic of rebellion—the use of force—pointing to the positive indications and strengths surrounding this principle in Islamic thought, as well as its weak points represented by its idealism in not connecting the means to their ends and in holding to tradition while lacking the boldness to craft new political directions by continuing to develop the political legacy of the Rightly Guided Caliphate. Had they done so, Muslims would have invented new institutions to embody the umma's will to use a broad-based consultative system and move shura from the level of moral exhortation to that of a political institution. Things remained as they were, until the West, inspired in part by our legacy, took up this task by developing it and elaborating the mechanisms of democracy.

Mutual Consultation, or Freedom in the Economic Domain

Our study demonstrated that mutual consultation is not only a style of managing political affairs; it is also a way of life that grows out organically from humankind's divine trusteeship and from its common origin and destiny, from the priority of the collective over the individual, though the latter is fundamental, and finally from the consideration that the community is an organic structure with mutually reinforcing functions. It would be an illusion to think you could foster political participation while money continues to be monopolized by an elite class. As God said, "So that they do not just circulate among those of you who are rich."[10] In fact, the condition for widening the circle of consultation is the widening of the circle of ownership and solidarity, even though Islam has acknowledged the right of individual ownership of the means of production and services, but it has emphasized that its function is to benefit society. Thus, to the extent that you widen the circle of owners, to that extent you widen the circle of those who can participate in the process of mutual consultation in politics. The opposite is true as well.

Although Islamic economics which recognizes the right of individual ownership and initiative and the bitter struggle against the monopoly of the few by means of their wealth, whether it was under fascism, communism, or socialism, may seem closer to the liberal market economies, its foundations are different, and so are its ethical parameters and objectives.

Mutual Consultation in the Cultural and Educational Domains

What shura means in the domain of culture and knowledge is to participate in the blessings of knowledge and science. Seeking knowledge in Islam is a duty, making education compulsory. So that people will not be enslaved by a regime that controls their minds—Islam facilitates the means to acquire knowledge, prohibits any suppression of knowledge, and liberates people's minds—it calls for thoughtful reasoning [ijtihad] and forbids anyone, association or individual, from monopolizing those decisions. This is to prevent anyone from claiming to speak in the name of "Islamic truth," and to remove any obstacle in the path of anyone wanting to engage in any kind of research. In contrast mutual consultation becomes practically meaningless in societies where illiteracy is rife and an elite monopolizes the power of knowledge and information; or where there is censorship and restriction of thought, and where certain areas are declared out of bounds. The study considered one of the requirements of mutual consultation to be the expansion of knowledge and information as far and wide as possible, and liberating people's minds from the state's control and limiting the latter's action to setting education curricula. The task of managing cultural organizations such as clubs, mosques, and the media is left to scholars and to organizations of civil society, which must preserve their independence and be run by a process of mutual consultation.

PART III: GUARANTEES FOR PREVENTING INJUSTICE IN THE ISLAMIC STATE

Since political power by nature tends toward abuse, what are the means to keep it from doing so? The state, as far as Marxism is concerned, is simply an instrument to crush its opponents and accomplish its goals. As for the Western democratic state, despite all of its oversight mechanisms, because it rests upon a materialistic philosophy that privileges the values of financial gain, personal gratification, and national pride over the institutions of the state, and because it grants the rich great power over the minds, life, and destiny of people, it is almost as if the state becomes an instrument for them to achieve their own ends, even if the price for doing so is the destruction of moral values, the family, society, the environment, and the world itself.

The goal of the Islamic state, by contrast, is to allow as many people as possible the opportunity to taste freedom, social justice, moral purity, and spiritual and material development, with the overall goal to give everyone the opportunity to know God (may He be exalted) and freely choose to worship Him or freely decide not to do so. As we read in the Qur'an, "Say, 'Now the truth has come from your Lord: let those who wish to believe in it do so, and let those who wish to reject it do so.'"[11] That goal also includes the following objectives: to tap into the resources of this universe and manage them in a way that fosters greater understanding and brotherhood among nations, and that enables them to progress and fully share in the enjoyment of the earth's bounties and the blessings of development.

However, what guarantees the Islamic state from swerving from its rightful course and sliding into oppression? This is a crucial question, especially since it has happened, and many dictatorships continue to commit crimes and acts of terrorism (that is, attacks on innocent people), while justifying their acts in the name of religion, stifling the longings of their people for freedom, democracy, and justice.

1. *Holding that the highest legitimacy within the state belongs to God* (may He be exalted), as represented by His Shari'a, and that the umma is delegated by God in the collective sense, which means that no individual, no organization, and no community can claim this role for themselves. This restrains the legislative power of the state, especially in the financial sector or in the area of human rights, whether related to internal or foreign policies. In the same way, this grants the umma, God's deputy, custodianship over its rulers as a matter of principle and the right and even the religious duty to monitor their behavior.

2. *Holding that the oath of allegiance entered by the head of state, or by the members of the Shura Council, or by any elected body, is a specific contract of delegation.* This gives the one with the original political authority, the one granting the oath of allegiance, or the elector, the

permanent authority to monitor the delegates, to advise them and, if necessary, to protest their policies, for they are the principal's delegates and employees, always accountable and always exposed to the possibility of losing the trust placed in them, and thereby being removed from the office to which they were elected.

3. *Ensuring that the rulers do not remove themselves from the people* and preventing them from combining financial and political power, so that they live like ordinary people in their midst.

4. *Establishing an economic system that prevents the monopolization of wealth,* while acting to distribute it and multiply the number of those who partake in it. Some of the instruments for this purpose are the Islamic system of inheritance and the system of charitable giving (zakat), which allows the umma to rely upon its own resources and frees it from dependence.

5. *Establishing a social system that emphasizes the value of work and recognizes personal property and the right the poor have to a portion of the rich's wealth.* It acknowledges that to organize the investment of zakat monies—which can be considerable if they are well collected and used as they were originally meant, as a kind of social security— contributes to eradicating poverty, increasing the number of people with means, decreasing the number of employees (increased self-employment), strengthening the power of society by enhancing its independence from the state, and to tip the balance in society's favor.

6. *Establishing an educational system that spreads knowledge, facilitates access to it, and reduces the authority of the state over the minds and souls of its people.* To allow mosques to fulfill their educational mission independently of the state is to transform them into universities and centers of popular instruction, which diminishes the state's influence and reduces the latter's burden at the same time. Further, it strengthens civil society by increasing its independence and its stewardship over the state.

7. *Establishing a multiparty system.* For many reasons, there have been tensions between the multiparty system and the Islamic sensibility. One reason was that this system was introduced by the Western colonial powers and that many of these parties were beholden to them. Also, many of those parties engaged in marginal struggles at the expense of the higher interest of the public, to the point that some nations almost disintegrated in the wake of the multiparty system (at least on paper), as was the case with Sudan. But this does not justify curing by means

of the disease—that is, despotism, which is the root of the umma's calamity since the time when the Rightly Guided Caliphate devolved
into a destructive dynasty.

8. *Establishing an administrative system for local politics* (the municipal
councils and the trade unions). These take away most of the central
government's power and put it in the hands of deliberative grassroots
councils. The model of deliberative (shura-based) rule is the closest to
a decentralized one, and we inch closer to it in a direct democracy, in
which the number of individuals involved in governance is increased
to the point where everyone rules. This is no doubt the spirit of the
Qur'anic verse ("and they conduct their affairs by mutual consultation,"
Q. 42:38); that is, everyone participates in managing public affairs.

9. Among the measures taken by some nations in order to prevent despotism and the ruler's expanding his influence is to *enact a law that limits his time in office*—that is, he is elected with the chance of running
for only one or two more terms. But this is what the Arab dictator refuses to do.

10. *Thinking through carefully the issue of non-Muslims' rights in the Islamic state.* Our study affirmed the equality of rights and duties of all
citizens—citizenship is the fundamental rule, and the nature of the
state's creed may not violate it. The tolerance that Muslims demonstrated in their nations and still today has no equal in terms of the
rights that people of other religious traditions enjoyed in their midst.
On this basis we declared the right of non-Muslims to form political
parties as citizens loyal to the state or to join other parties, as well as
their right to use peaceful means to show their opposition in any circumstance. That said, a non-Muslim party in an Islamic state will
likely not be offered the chance to rule by democratic means, as is the
case with the communist party in the United States or the Islamic party
in Britain. Even secular parties today in the Muslim world have been
overshadowed by Islamic activism, and all that remains of their legacy is holding the reins of power, and with the ascendance of the Islamic current it is likely that they will draw closer to Islam and either
identify with it or fade away and disappear. In any case, the Islamic
state does not use violence in order to oppose any group whose only
weapon is ideas in honor of the principle of human dignity and thus
freedom ("There is no compulsion in religion," Q. 2:256). Islam does
not fear ideas, no matter how strange they might be. There is no record throughout history of Islam being defeated in an open debate.

11. Having affirmed the freedom of forming parties and their importance, the book then delineated *the official functions of the Islamic state:*

    a. Organizational: Organizing popular forces so as to reinforce society's power and giving the oath of allegiance and the authority of the umma its credibility; finally, achieving a peaceful transfer of power.

    b. Educational: Helping to embody Islam's values and spread them; strengthening social institutions so as to limit the power and reach of the state.

12. *Forbidding torture.* The philosophy of human rights in Islam refuses any aggression against the human person and any use of coercion, based on Islam's teaching that God honored humanity by making them His representatives on earth and that His messengers were sent to establish justice and liberation for humankind. For those reasons too, Islam enjoins the state to uphold international covenants and other efforts by humanitarian and human rights organizations to protect the physical and moral integrity of humans and to absolutely forbid torturing anyone, whether that person is a believer or unbeliever, whatever the motivation might be.

13. *Taking responsibility for public morality* [hisba]—that is, the institution (or the institutions) that carry out the "command to do good and forbid evil." This institution functions as a branch of the judiciary, and it parallels the people's grassroots efforts to fulfill the mission of fighting injustice. It is led by courageous scholars who monitor government departments and the markets in order to guarantee the adherence to Islamic values and justice in everyday life.

14. *Monitoring by public opinion,* which is the source of political authority by virtue of the people's role as the original exponents of the Shari'a. Islam calls upon the umma to fulfill its duty of public oversight, individually and collectively, through the mosques which are popular institutions over which the state has no control and through the other means of communication such as the press. Their establishment, just like the establishment of political parties, gives voice to public opinion as it fulfills its task of commanding good and forbidding evil. They need no permission from the ruler in order to be established.

    Hence, to the extent that Islam has waged relentless campaigns against tyrants and Pharaohs, and to the extent that it emphasized the importance of freedom, mutual consultation, and justice, it constrained—no, it canceled—the rulers' legislative power; it affirmed the importance of the community as a whole and its responsibility, granting

it the kind of power to guarantee a balance between the umma and
the state but with the advantage going to the umma. This is to the
extent that in exceptional cases, some jurists have permitted the use
of force when peaceful means have failed to repel grievous injustice and
the alternative is civil unrest potentially leading to civil war. That said,
we believe that if the umma uses Islam's peaceful means for resisting
oppression, it will not need to resort to violence, which is always risky.

15. Our study also dealt with *the issue of the separation of powers* as one of
several means to avert injustice. While we affirmed the independence
of the judiciary, with respect to the relationship between the legislative
and executive branches, the Islamic position allows for either separation
or cooperation or a merging of the two powers. The author himself favors
a moderate separation as a way to promote the principle of cooperation.

As for how we should deal with the oppression that is evidenced in
Islamic states of the past while Islam contrasts despotism and injustice
with God's oneness and justice ("attributing partners to Him is a terrible wrong," Q. 31:13), we must recognize that injustice did occur, but
the responsibility for it should not be attributed to Islam but rather to
the spirit of the age. One cannot honestly compare ancient political
entities with those of today; rather, we should make comparisons between contemporary states. Doing this will favor Islamist political experiments, for the history of Islam has known a flourishing of cultural
and civilizational pluralism, of religious and intellectual tolerance.
There were even times of political pluralism in different forms that
were significantly ahead of their time, for no matter what form the
Islamic state took and how despotic it became, from the Prophet's Medinan model to that of the Rightly Guided Caliphs, and until the Ottoman period, the state did not deal with its citizens as individuals, but
rather as different religious communities, sects, tribes, and Sufi brotherhoods. All of this limited the power of the state and opened a space for
the authority of society to the extent of tolerating a pluralism of legal
systems, courts, and schools, corresponding to a pluralism of religions
and legal schools within the one state. Even the largest federal systems
of today have not achieved this kind of pluralism.

This is in contrast to the autocracy practiced by the modern state (or
"the secular mythology") at the expense of our peoples, a state that
protects the interests of foreign cultures, just like its twin, the religious
mythology, controlling all of the powers—a new phenomenon in our

history. Therefore, the stumbling block standing in the way of our umma's renewal [nahda] is despotism, conceptual confusion, and the breakdown between theory and practice in our education. The responsibility of our elites, essentially, is to resist these plagues through mutual solidarity against injustice, by identifying with the people and drawing strength from its values, interests, and aspirations, in order to confront the legacies of the cultural schizophrenia both internal and external and despotism both local and foreign—instead of colluding with foreign powers, sharing the spoils, and prolonging the night of our decline.

Finally we believe the best path, if not the only one, for the awakening of a free umma and for the recovery of a new humanitarian and Islamic civilization that participates in the rescuing of humanity's legacy amid a crumbling civilization and a tormented humanity is to establish a foundation of ethical values such as freedom, the acceptance of the right to be different, pluralism, social justice, and the revolution of the masses by means of nonviolent street actions like strikes and sit-ins. It will be to struggle [jihad] to the point of martyrdom to confront the international forces of hegemony. Consolidating a culture of tolerance, discipline, and a spirit of collective action, but also to cooperate in resisting injustice, oppression wherever it be found, and oppressors whoever they might be. Moreover, this path will cultivate altruism, love of the truth, an impartial search for it, and a harmony between word and deed and most of all, respect the will of the umma, controlling individualistic tendencies to favor the collective interest. It will also involve a sharpening of the aesthetic sense, rooted in our culture and lives, and connecting it to the values and creeds of Islam and the culture of liberation and humanitarianism prevalent today. Finally, two more ways to eliminate or at least limit the plague of authoritarianism is first to elaborate a consensus around these objectives, as a foundation for the political process and a framework for achieving individual and collective freedoms and a peaceful alternation of political power without excluding anyone; and second, to achieve collaboration on these issues. All these efforts would contribute to eliminating or at least limiting the plague of authoritarianism convergence of opinion among Muslims, citizens of a nation, and humanity as a whole by highlighting the common ground and interests among nations and religions on spiritual and humanitarian matters for the sake of peace, cooperation, and development.

FOR POSTERITY, IF WE DO NOT MEET AGAIN

This book sought to demonstrate that Islam came for the good of humanity and that it encompasses all of its accomplishments, like its scientific progress, democracy, and the equal rights of individuals, nations, minorities, and women; and further, that the establishment of its democratic state based on mutual consultation, the state of the umma, fulfills a need for Muslims and for the entire human race as well. This has become an even more pressing need since the earth has been soiled by the blood of innocents, prisons reverberate with the cries of decent citizens and freethinkers, millions have been driven from their homes inside and outside of their countries, and people's conscience and the very fabric of society have been torn to shreds. Nature itself, our collective mother's womb, has been nearly destroyed, and us along with it in an age of science, progress, and human rights.

So wake up, O Muslims, reflect and worship your Lord fully aware. Get to work and unite before it is too late. Be mindful of your responsibility toward Islam, whose image of beauty and mercy has been stained, because of reckless acts committed in its name, acts that provided the opportunity for its most bitter enemies to vilify it and link it to that which we all loathe and fear. This, instead of seeking new friends and allies for it, among what constitutes the majority of humankind, who have been harmed by the model of savage globalization. Islam stands in the very first trenches of the fight against this model, at great cost and achieving remarkable victories, which give hope to downtrodden nations as they resist and overcome. Do justice to Islam, the wrongly maligned faith, O people, for it is a mercy for all of you. As God says, "It was only as a mercy that We sent you [Prophet] to all people."[12]

Yet whatever you do, God's sun will rise again over the whole world, for that is God's promise, "They try to extinguish God's light with their mouths, but God insists on bringing His light to its fullness, even if the disbelievers hate it."[13]

Finally, violence is a social phenomenon before being a religious one—its causes are to be found in the nature of a particular society and the kind of prejudice and inequality that festers within it. They are also to be found in international relations built upon injustice, as the authority of naked power is favored over the authority of truth, to the point where colonialism has returned when we thought it was gone, like what is happening in occupied Palestine, in Iraq, Lebanon, and Afghanistan. On the other hand, the speed of resorting to violence to settle disputes, whether ideological or political, is a sign of backwardness. It is, therefore, the product of a backward society, and it is not limited to one particular group, but exists among those who were raised in the shadow of such a society and absorbed its culture, whether they be Islamists or nationalists or those who claim to abide by democracy and human rights.

This is what makes it necessary for thinkers to examine the roots of backwardness and expose them, and these are to be found in the unjust relations in today's global system and its repercussions on the local level. It is also likely that neither the world of ideas and values nor the current style of education is devoid of these roots of backwardness and authoritarianism. For this reason, there is no guarantee we can prevent despotism by simply establishing Islamic or non-Islamic governance unless we address this model of unjust relations, the plundering and subjugation of the weak by the powerful, without neglecting to craft an educational system based on mutual consultation, the right to difference of opinion, and a spirit of collective solidarity and self-discipline. In addition society must be liberated from the excessive power and control of the state, as should be the case in an Islamic society—that is, to gradually take charge of the sectors of education, health care, legislation, justice, and the economy. Even with regard to the army, the state should not continue to monopolize the means of force and the responsibility to defend the country. This should be the people's mission.

Therefore, it is authoritarianism that is the source of violence and evil, and it is a part of the inequitable relations that rob society of its health, as in the case of Iraq's conflict-ridden society and other societies victimized by despotism. And given the fact that this is a complex phenomenon and considering the multiplicity of factors that contribute to its emergence and spread, it will require a complex strategy to treat it. This will involve intellectual reflection, political will, education, and a concerted effort by all social institutions. Fundamentally, it will require giving up on the idea that one party owns the absolute truth and has the right to impose it upon the whole of society, as is the practice, on the world stage, where a few powerful nations impose their will on the world. They forget, however, the fact that truth and justice are the foundations upon which the universe is built. As the Qur'an says, "God always prevails in His purpose, though most people do not realize it."[14]

Appendix 1

—————————•◆•—————————

FOUNDING DECLARATION OF THE ISLAMIC TENDENCY MOVEMENT

INTRODUCTION

The Arab world, of which we are a part, is witnessing the ugliest forms of theft and exile from its own heritage and interests. This began in the recent past as its decline was wreaking havoc on the soul of our umma, leading it to abandon its mission of leadership and enlightenment. Sometimes this played into the hands of Western colonialism; and sometimes, into the hands of ruling minorities that had betrayed their roots, which led to the clash of our people's aspirations.

During all of these various phases the people's first aspiration was Islam, the fulcrum of our civilizational identity and the nerve of our collective conscience. But it was gradually pushed aside, and at times even more radically in a way that was devoid of guidance and a practical approach to the nature of our society. Yet despite its prominence as a determining factor behind the brilliant aspects of our civilization and our nation's struggle to evict the colonizer, Islam has become—almost—a mere symbol surrounded by dangers, whether on the cultural, the ethical, or the political front. And this is a result of what it was exposed to in this century and the preceding one—namely, the negligence and attack on its norms, its institutions, and its leaders.

Beyond these civilizational facts common to all Islamic nations, Tunisia, despite its being granted independence, experienced from the end of the 1950s and during the next two decades a period of crisis and aggravated social conflict, which blocked the path of holistic development. This situation was the result of one-party rule (the Destour Party), which had gradually ascended to a position of hegemony over the state, its institutions, and popular organizations on the one hand. On the other, it was the result of improvisation and fluctuation of economic and social choices and their dependence on international interests that clashed with our own national interests.

It was in such a climate that the Islamic Tendency was founded in Tunisia in the early 1970s. Many factors had converged to facilitate its appearance and confirm how crucial it was, including its call to consider Islam once again as a system of thought, a culture, and a pattern of behavior, and thus to look again at the role of the mosque. The Tendency also

455

contributed to reviving society's cultural and political life and for the first time injected into it a new spirit that grounded its identity, renewed its sense of the common good, and affirmed pluralism by truly embodying it.

The Islamic Tendency, therefore, demonstrated its embrace of the nation's core identity and its embodiment of people's hopes and aspirations by means of its activities and the many positions it took publicly. As a result, it attracted a wide swath of the poor and needy, the youth, as well as the highly educated. Thus it grew quickly and attracted a lot of attention, while the established political forces and organizations observed it warily. And though the Tendency proceeded calmly and cautiously as it sought the most useful paths leading to development and change, it was soon the target of concerted smear campaigns launched by the regime and the media, both the official and the semiofficial ones. These campaigns reached the point of arbitrary aggression against the Tendency's media apparatus so as to silence its voice. The situation then grew even more repressive, as its cadres were tried in court, and the inquiries and investigations multiplied and intensified. The youth were thrown in prison and detention centers where they were beaten, tortured, and abused.

Yet no one was addressing the causes of our society's backwardness—politically, economically, and culturally—and that frustrated the Islamists who were then all the more motivated to discharge their divine, national, and humanitarian responsibility. So they persevered in their efforts to truly free their nation and help it progress on the basis of Islam and justice, and in the shade of God's straight path.

Some would say that this work is a way to drag religion into the world of politics and that it monopolizes the notion of what is "Islamic" while refusing that it be applied to those who disagree with them. For one thing, this reflects a Christian conception that is alien to our original culture. For another, it demonstrates the modern continuation of the great loss that our umma has suffered since the onslaught of the colonial period.

Yet the movement called the "Islamic Tendency" did not present itself as the official representative of Tunisian Islam, nor does it desire to acquire that title in the future. Rather, the Tendency acknowledges the right of all Tunisians to engage Islam sincerely and responsibly, and for that reason it considers that it, too, has the right to adopt a conception of Islam that is comprehensive. Thus it constitutes an ideological ground, from which a number of different intellectual, political, economic, and social visions fan out. But altogether they define an identity for this movement; they also outline its priorities in terms of strategy in light of sociopolitical developments. In this sense, the Tendency is clear about what it is and what it is not; it knows what it is responsible for and does not feel obligated to engage in all kinds of initiatives and positions taken by other movements here and there, except what they happen to adopt officially. Who knows their true convictions in private, however much members of these movements like to wrap themselves in the garb of religion and raise the banner of Islam?

As a confirmation of this situation on the one hand, and in taking stock of the magnitude of the task and the requirements of this stage of the mission on the other, Islamists must enter a new phase of organization that will allow them to gather their energy, sharpen their awareness as they receive more training, and invest themselves in serving the needs of our people and the umma. This task will have to take place within a movement that continues to refine its goals and adjust its means to impact very specific contexts and train model leaders.

Our hope is that the Islamic Tendency Movement will stand alongside her people in the coming days and contribute in an ever deeper and more comprehensive way, especially as we and the wider Muslim masses face together such oppression and terror.

THE MISSION

This movement works to achieve the following objectives:

1. Reviving Tunisia's Islamic personality so that it recovers its mission as the great foundation of Africa's Islamic civilization and puts a stop to the current state of dependence, westernization, and loss of identity.
2. Defining Islamic thought in light of Islam's ageless foundations and the requirements of a progressive society today, and cleansing this thought from the dregs of the decadent past and the scars of emigration.
3. Enabling the masses to take up again their right to determine their own destiny apart from any inside pressures and outside hegemony.
4. Rebuilding economic life on a humanitarian scale, dividing up the nation's resources in a just manner in light of the Islamic principle, "a man and his hard work, a man and his need" (meaning everyone has the right to enjoy the fruits of their labor within the limits of the common good, and to receive according to their needs in every situation). The objective is to enable the masses to receive their God-given right to earn a living wage, far from any sort of exploitation and the rotation in the powerful orbit of the global economy.
5. Participating in the reviving of Islam's political and civilizational apparatus on all levels, including the local, the Maghreb, the Arab world, and the world at large, so that our nations and all humanity might be rescued from the ills that plague it so frequently: loss of meaning leading to all kinds of mental disorders, social injustice, and hegemony of the great powers.

MEANS TO FULFILL THE MISSION

- Returning life to the mosque as a center for worship and popular mobilization in all areas just like the mosque was in the Prophet's time. This is also an extension of the role played by the great mosque, the Zaytuna Mosque, as it maintained the people's Islamic personality and reinforced the nation's role as a global center that reflected the light of civilization far and wide.
- Activating the intellectual and cultural movement in the following ways: by organizing seminars; encouraging the writing and publishing of books; implanting and crystallizing Islamic values and concepts through literary magazines and publications pertaining to general culture; encouraging scientific research; and finally, supporting a conscientious media so that it becomes an alternative to the flaccid and hypocritical media we now have.

- Supporting the use of Arabic in the areas of education and government administration while being open to the teaching of foreign languages.
- Refusing violence as an instrument of change and managing conflict on the basis of mutual consultation in view of a constructive resolution in the academic, cultural, and political spheres.
- Refusing single party rule, which leads to regimenting people's will, disabling the nation's energy, and pushing the country toward violence. Conversely, it is to proclaim the right for all to exercise their freedom of expression and of assembly, and all the other liberties granted by the Shari'a and their active cooperation in this with all other national forces.
- Highlighting Islamic social concepts in contemporary forms and analyzing Tunisia's economic situation in order to pinpoint signs and causes of injustice and then alternative means to redress that injustice.
- Taking a stand for the oppressed, including workers, farmers, and the rest of the dispossessed in their struggle against the haughty and arrogant.
- Supporting the work of trade unions in order to guarantee their independence and ability to achieve national liberation in all its dimensions, social, political, and cultural.
- Leaning on Islam's holistic perspective with a commitment to political activism far from secularism and opportunism.
- Liberating the Muslim's conscience from finding benefit in Western civilization.
- Revealing and embodying the current perspective on Islamic political rule in a way that puts national issues in their historical, theological, and objective perspective, with an emphasis on the Maghreb, the Arab and Islamic world, and on the world of the oppressed generally.
- Strengthening brotherly relations of cooperation with all Muslims globally: in Tunisia, in the Maghreb, and in the entire Muslim world.
- Supporting and assisting liberation movements globally.

Rached Ghannouchi
Tunis, June 6, 1981

BYLAWS OF THE TUNISIAN ENNAHDA MOVEMENT

In the name of God, the Merciful, the Compassionate

SECTION ONE: ENNAHDA'S FOUNDING AND GOALS

ARTICLE 1

This is the founding legal document of the party named "The Ennahda Movement," which Tunisian citizens have ratified or will ratify because they believe in the goals and statutes enumerated below. Ennahda's founding as a party conforms to the law issued May 3, 1988.

ARTICLE 2: GOALS

The Ennahda Movement strives to achieve the following goals:

In the Political Realm

1. Support the republican system of government and its foundations; keep civil society healthy; and achieve the principles of popular sovereignty and mutual consultation.
2. Elevate liberty as the pivotal value that embodies God's honoring of humankind by supporting public freedoms and human rights and by certifying the independence of the judiciary and neutrality of government administration.
3. Institute a foreign policy based upon the nation's pride, unity, and independence from all foreign influence on all levels; establish international relations in conformity with the principles of positive nonalignment, respect for reciprocity, people's right to self-determination, justice, and equality.
4. Support cooperation and mutual aid between Arab and Muslim regions, and work toward reinforcing their mutual agreements and unity.

5. Spread the spirit of Arab and Islamic unity while raising the fundamental issues concerning the worldwide Muslim community in order to put an end to the state of disharmony and division; to focus our efforts on long-term issues and the struggle to achieve comprehensive unity by supporting sincere steps in this direction and by affirming the great importance of the unity of Muslim North Africa's regions.

6. Struggle for the sake of liberating Palestine, considering that it is a crucial mission and duty as required by the Zionist aggression and colonization. It is now a nation that was planted in the middle of our Arab homeland as an alien entity representing an obstacle to unity, while also symbolizing our worldwide community's fight against its enemies.

7. Support the liberation causes in the Arab homeland and the whole Muslim world; fight the colonial policies and discrimination in Afghanistan, Eritrea, South Africa, and other places, as well as situations of injustice and persecution.

8. Develop cooperation with African nations as a strategic choice for our nation; work on ridding the Mediterranean Basin from the tension stirred up by the hegemonic powers; finally, strive with others to create mutual understanding among nations as a way to foster world peace built on justice.

In the Economic Realm

1. Build a national economy that is both strong and integrated because it is fundamentally based on our own capacities and because it achieves self-sufficiency by meeting our nation's basic needs, by developing a balance between sectors, and by helping to integrate it within the wider North African, Arab, and Islamic world economy.

2. Integrate and balance the nation's various sectors: the specific and the general, and cooperation for the sake of the common good.

3. Emphasize the fact that work is the source of economic profit and the condition for social revitalization. It is both a right and a duty, and a nation's economic life must be built on a humanitarian basis with its resources distributed according to the following principle: "a man and his hard work, a man and his need" (meaning everyone has the right to enjoy the fruits of their labors within the limits of the common good, and to receive according to their needs in every situation). This also means reducing inequalities resulting from exploitation, excessive accumulation, industrial and business monopolies, and other forms of illicit practices.

In the Social Realm

1. Provide social services for everyone by giving them access to what is necessary for a dignified life, according to their right to food, health care, education, housing, and so forth. This also serves to maintain society's cohesion and development; and releases people's spiritual, artistic, and creative potential; and all of this while seeking to balance giving people their rights and challenging them to fulfill their duties.

2. Work to support all nongovernmental organizations; protect their efforts, their unity, and their democratic internal functioning; respect their independence so

that they can express the needs of their constituency, defend their interests, and provide the strength and immunity from any kind of tyranny, no matter its origin.

3. Protect the family, which is the pillar of a healthy society; ensure that family relationships are built upon love, compassion, interdependence, and respect; honor the bond of matrimony; provide the appropriate framework to protect children, from early care to education and preparation for the next step ahead.

4. Promote the status of women and ensure they can play a positive role in the social, cultural, economic, and political arenas in order for them to effectively contribute to society's development without feeling dependent or inferior, but rather able to realize themselves and preserve their dignity above and beyond the manifestations of moral slackness and disintegration.

5. Watch over the youth who are the heartbeat of the Muslim community worldwide; make thoughtful preparation for the mission of renewal [*nahda*] and then build it in harmony with a righteous education; widen the youth's horizons to show them how to participate effectively in the nation's comprehensive development, which will also facilitate their integration in society; finally, facilitate their finding jobs, encourage them to marry, and help to ease the process.

6. Strive to build social relations based on our nation's founding principles by modeling and spreading strong moral values so that a spirit of brotherly love and compassion prevails in our society and that it is protected from corruption.

In the Cultural Realm

1. Seek to implant more thoroughly the Arabic-Islamic identity within our nation, as it is one of the conditions for the renaissance, and one that must take its rightful place as it embodies the requirements of our Constitution and our laws. Moreover, Islam represents ethical values and a civilization, and the Arabic language is the receptacle containing our national culture.

2. Provide the appropriate atmosphere for a comprehensive intellectual and scientific renaissance based on Islam's foundational tenets and the requirements of contemporary life. This is to arrest the process of decline, backwardness, dependence, and westernization, and to accomplish the following: set in motion an intellectual movement, enlighten people's minds, refine their tastes and behaviors, and affirm Tunisia's role in advancing civilization.

3. Make use of the Arabic language and encourage its proficiency in the educational, administrative, and cultural sectors, so that it becomes an instrument of civilizational renaissance that brings together the worldwide Muslim community and guards her from a spirit of defeat, self-deprecation, and closed-mindedness.

4. Supply the necessary conditions to encourage and stimulate scientific research, to revere scientists, researchers, and inventors by instilling faith in the role of knowledge and science in achieving the development of our nation, in consolidating our independence, and in bringing about our intellectual and scientific renaissance so that our people's dynamism is in harmony with the laws of the universe and the best practices of the past.

5. Craft a media policy built on respect for others, freedom of thought and expression, and a growing spirit of creativity and invention; provide the necessary conditions for an independent, impartial, and responsible media that contributes to the nation's progress and bolsters its identity.
6. Encourage literature and the arts, as well as the practice of sports, so that they can play a role in spreading virtuous behavior and call for developing and ensuring healthy bodies. All of this will elevate the life of the spirit and bolster the foundations of our renewal.

SECTION TWO: MEMBERSHIP

ARTICLE 3: CONDITIONS OF MEMBERSHIP

The Ennahda Movement accepts any Tunisian man or woman over eighteen years old who subscribes to the Movement's principles, goals, and strategies, as well as its Bylaws and statutes, and pledges its loyalty and commitment to the plans and decisions issued by its organizational leadership.

ARTICLE 4: MEMBERSHIP DUTIES

Every member of the Movement shall do the following:

1. Call for the achievement of the Movement's objectives as much as is realistically possible.
2. Commit to the goals, decisions, positions, and guidelines issued by the responsible structures of the Movement.
3. Participate in the activities of the Movement and engage with its various bodies and their mutual relations; protect its covenant and serve in the realization of its goals.
4. Systematically take part in the programs that seek to educate and train the members.
5. Pay the monthly fee or other financial contributions as officially scheduled.
6. Display integrity, honorable behavior, and virtuous living.

ARTICLE 5: RIGHTS PERTAINING TO MEMBERSHIP

Each member of the Movement shall enjoy the following rights:

1. To participate in the activities of the Movement, and offer his or her opinions following a democratic process that guides the collection of views and safeguards the unity of the Movement.
2. To share in the taking of responsibility according to what is laid out in the Movement's statutes.

ARTICLE 6: APPLICATION FOR MEMBERSHIP

Each applicant shall follow this procedure:

1. Request membership within the Movement.
2. Obtain the testimony of three members of a cell, which then gives its approval and the recommendation by the cell's secretary.
3. Make a vow to be loyal to the Movement and to obey its leadership; commit to safeguard its trust, strive to fulfill its objectives, and be disciplined in submitting to its organization and methods.
4. Have one's name officially registered as a member.

ARTICLE 7: LOSS OF MEMBERSHIP

The following lose their membership:

• Each applicant that submits a resignation request according to the procedures laid out in the Movement's Bylaws.
• Anyone who expresses his refusal to fulfill the duties explained in section four of the Bylaws.

ARTICLE 8: DEATH OF THE MEMBER

The death of a member, whether he was a founder or not, and whether or not he had submitted his resignation or refusal, does not result in putting an end to the Movement and its work.

ARTICLE 9: THE MOVEMENT'S HEADQUARTERS

They are located in Tunis, Tunisia's capital city.

The address can be changed to any location within the capital's vicinity by decision of the Executive Office, which then will notify the authorities according to the law of the land.

ARTICLE 10: TRAINING THE YOUTH

The Movement will endeavor to train the youth and care for their needs by means of an organization ("The Youth of Ennahda"), which it founded according to the requirements of its internal organization. The Executive Office proposes its creation to the wider Movement and the General Shura Council shall give its approval. The youth organization develops its own membership card.

SECTION THREE: ORGANIZATIONAL STRUCTURE

ARTICLE 11

The Ennahda Movement is composed of the following:

1. General Conference
2. General Shura Council
3. President of the Movement
4. Executive Office
5. Leadership Structures:
    a. Regions
    b. Divisions
    c. Branches
    d. Cells

ARTICLE 12: ACTIVITY OF THE STRUCTURES AND THEIR RELATIONSHIPS TO ONE ANOTHER

The Movement's internal organization defines the various structures, their respective activities and work, and the relationship between all of them.

ARTICLE 13: THE GENERAL CONFERENCE

The General Conference is the Movement's highest authority. It shall meet every three years with a simple majority of its delegates. In the case of a lack of quorum, it shall meet after two weeks with any number of delegates present. The Movement's president and the president of the General Shura Council shall be present.

ARTICLE 14: THE EXTRAORDINARY CONFERENCE

The Extraordinary Conference may only be convened at the request of the following: two-thirds of the General Shura Council members, or the Movement's president, or half of all its adherents. Further, two-thirds of the total delegates must be present. In the case of a lack of quorum, it could meet after two weeks with at least half of all delegates present. And if that quorum is not met, then it could meet after a month with any number of delegates present.

ARTICLE 15: THE GENERAL CONFERENCE'S ORGANIZATION

The General Shura Council shall determine the percentage of representation of the Movement's adherents in the General Conference. In normal circumstances it sets the dates and venue of its convening and establishes its agenda. Finally, it offers a proposal for the composition of the conference's leadership bureau.

ARTICLE 16

The Extraordinary Conference proposes its own convening procedure.

ARTICLE 17: CONVENING PROCEDURE

The Executive Office is responsible for sending out invitations to the delegates no later than two weeks before the General Conference convenes, and they must contain the proposed agenda.

ARTICLE 18: THE GENERAL CONFERENCE'S TASK

1. Discussion of the literary and financial reports.
2. Establishing the Movement's orientations and choices.
3. Reporting on the issues brought to the conference's attention.
4. Designating the president by secret ballot.
5. Voting for two-thirds of the General Shura Council's members.

ARTICLE 19: THE GENERAL CONFERENCE'S DECISIONS

The conference makes decisions by a majority vote of those present.

ARTICLE 20: AMENDING THE BYLAWS

Only the General Conference has the right to amend the Movement's Bylaws at the request of the president or two-thirds of the Conference's delegates, and with the agreement of two-thirds of those present. This is an application of Articles 13 and 14 of these Bylaws.

ARTICLE 21: THE GENERAL SHURA COUNCIL

The General Shura Council represents the highest authority in the Movement among the conference members.

ARTICLE 22: COMPOSITION OF THE GENERAL SHURA COUNCIL

The General Shura Council shall be composed of a number of members determined by its own leadership. Two-thirds of the General Conference members are mandated to vote for the remaining third of adherents, according to Article 23 of these Bylaws.

ARTICLE 23: CONDITIONS FOR MEMBERSHIP IN THE GENERAL SHURA COUNCIL

Any member of the General Shura Council must have been a member of the Movement for at least three years.

ARTICLE 24: PRESIDENT OF THE GENERAL SHURA COUNCIL

The members of the General Shura Council, after it has first been established, shall elect a president whose responsibilities are defined in the Council's rules and procedures.

ARTICLE 25: FUNCTIONS OF THE GENERAL SHURA COUNCIL

The General Shura Council shall carry out the following functions:

1. Ratify the Movement's plans and policies as decided by the General Conference.
2. Ratify the Movement's general budget.
3. Follow up on the work done by the Executive Office in conformity with the internal regulations.
4. Ratify the Movement's educational and cultural curriculum.
5. Ratify the various structures' internal regulations that have been passed on to it by the Executive Office.
6. Propose to the General Conference possible amendments to the Bylaws.
7. Discuss and decide on issues brought to its attention.
8. Look into a request of objection to the Movement's refusal on an issue.

ARTICLE 26: THE RULES OF THE GENERAL SHURA COUNCIL'S PROCEDURE

The General Shura Council's own leadership determines its rules of procedure.

ARTICLE 27: THE MOVEMENT'S PRESIDENT

1. Any candidate for the post of president of the Movement shall fulfill the following conditions:
   a. The candidate must be at least thirty years old.
   b. The candidate must have served in a leadership capacity for at least three years (membership in the General Shura Council, or membership in the Executive Office, or regional supervisor).
2. The General Conference shall vote on the candidates by secret and direct ballot.
3. A vacancy in the Movement's presidency takes place in the following cases:
   a. Death of the president.
   b. The General Shura Council has decided that a president is unable to fulfill his functions.
   c. A president resigns and the General Shura Council accepts the resignation.
4. In the case that the post of president is vacated, it is the responsibility of the General Shura Council to elect a new president (and to define the nature of a presidential vacancy).
5. The president of the Movement begins his full-time mission of serving the Movement immediately after his election, having resigned from any previous job, unless the General Shura Council allows him to do so.

ARTICLE 28: THE PRESIDENT'S JOB DESCRIPTION

1. Form the Movement's bodies and structures according to its Bylaws, its statutes, and internal organization.
2. Lead the Executive Office.
3. Embrace the Movement's leadership role and safeguard its unity.
4. Propose plans and curricula to the Movement.
5. Execute the Movement's policies and decisions according to its statutes.
6. Facilitate the work of the Movement's executive bodies.
7. Represent the Movement in its internal and external relations.
8. Ratify the decisions of the Systems and Discipline Commission.

ARTICLE 29

The president has the right to issue pardons and mitigation of penalties.

ARTICLE 30: THE VICE PRESIDENT

The president chooses a deputy or a vice president.

ARTICLE 31: THE EXECUTIVE OFFICE

The Executive Office shall be composed of:

1. A president who is also the Movement's president.
2. The president's deputy, or the vice president.
3. Members designated by the Office's internal statutes (rules of procedure).

ARTICLE 32: FUNCTIONS OF THE EXECUTIVE OFFICE

1. Execute the decisions of the General Conference and General Shura Council.
2. Establish the General Shura Council's yearly agenda.
3. Develop regulations governing enforcement structures, and present them to the General Shura Council.
4. Propose a general budget and execute it once it has been ratified.
5. Take positions on wider political issues.
6. Preparation of the General Conference according to Articles 13 and 14 of the Bylaws and of the General Shura Council's sessions.

SECTION FOUR: THE SYSTEMS AND DISCIPLINE COMMISSION

ARTICLE 33

It shall be constituted by decision of the president, and according to the requirements of the internal statutes (the Systems and Discipline Commission); it considers infractions that may have been committed by a member, but its decisions will not be enforced except by the president's agreement.

ARTICLE 34

The Commission determines the kind of infractions that merit punishment and the penalties incurred for committing them by referring to precedent.

ARTICLE 35

Each member who decides to leave the Movement shall present his request to the General Shura Council with the possibility of reconsidering his decision a month after presenting said request. The decision of the General Shura Council shall be final, without possible reconsideration.

SECTION FIVE: THE MOVEMENT'S FINANCIAL SUPPORT AND DISBURSEMENT OF EARNINGS

ARTICLE 36

The Movement's financial resources shall consist of the following:

1. Membership fees.
2. Revenue from licensed activities according to the Bylaws, and capital gains from the Movement's properties.
3. Donations and contributions according to the laws in force.

ARTICLE 37: MEMBERSHIP FEES

Every member of the Movement shall pay a monthly membership fee determined by the General Shura Council.

ARTICLE 38: BOOKKEEPING

The Movement's accounts shall be monitored, whether those inside or outside, including movable gains and capital gains stemming from property, and all of this according to the requirements of the law.

TRANSITIONAL PROVISIONS

Article 1: The Movement's Founding Body shall be empowered to supervise the establishment of structures, and this until the convening of the first Conference. If the Conference is convened within two years at the most from the time the Movement has received its official government license, the Founding Body will be dissolved by the Conference.

Article 2: The conditions relative to the seniority of members spelled out in these Bylaws shall not apply, except after the passing of the stipulated time period starting from the date the official government license is issued.

Appendix 3

RACHED GHANNOUCHI'S OPENING SPEECH AT ENNAHDA'S [OR NAHDA'S] TENTH PARTY CONGRESS (2016)

TUNIS, MAY 20, 2016

TRANSLATION BY THE CENTER FOR THE STUDY OF ISLAM AND DEMOCRACY (CSID)[1]

"CARVING A PATH FOR DEMOCRACY AND ISLAM TO COEXIST IN TUNISIA"

In the Name of God, Most Beneficent, Most Merciful. Praise be to God, Lord of the worlds, and prayers and peace be on His Messenger.

Your Excellency, president of the People's Assembly, your excellencies, ministers, members of the diplomatic corps in Tunis, representatives of parties and organizations, dear friends and guests who have honored us by coming from abroad to attend our Congress, dear guests, peace be upon you all.

And I also greet Ennahda's faithful supporters—whether those inside the stadium, or the thousands more outside to whom I apologize—this opening ceremony should have been held in an open space; those who were afraid that this stadium may not be filled are still not familiar with Ennahda.

Ladies and gentlemen, guests and delegates, today we inaugurate, by God's grace, the tenth national party congress of the Ennahda Party, the second national congress after the revolution.

Even during the most difficult periods of secret activity and police harassment under dictatorship, our movement was committed to holding its national congress regularly, as a way of evaluating and reforming its path, reviewing its policies, and renewing its leadership. I do not believe that there is another party in the country, despite the great number of parties, that is holding its tenth party congress—which means that you are the oldest amongst political parties. Our first congress was held in 1979—which means that in a period of around a third of a century, ten congresses were held—that is an average of one congress every less than four years. That is an expression of the fact that Ennahda is run by institutions, by democracy, by consultation—an important Islamic value.

At the beginning of this occasion, we pray for the souls of the martyrs of the revolution and martyrs of the struggle against dictatorship, led by martyrs of the movement, such as student Othman Ben Mahmoud—through whom we salute Tunisia's youth.

We also remember the martyrs of the national army and police, and victims of the war against terrorism, and victims killed by terrorism, led by martyrs Chokri Belaid and Mohamed Brahmi.

We reaffirm to all those that we remain faithful to the martyrs and that their sacrifices will not be in vain.

Our accumulated experience in the war against terrorism has struck fear into the opposite camp, which is now receding at the hands of the successful preemptive operations by our security and military forces. As we reaffirm Ennahda's absolute support for the state in its war against ISIS and takfiri extremists, we say to them that Tunisia, despite all the sacrifices, is stronger than their hatred, and it will, God willing, defeat them. In this regard, the great city of Ben Guerdane set a living and striking example that our people will never be defeated by terrorism. A small city that refused to allow evil terrorists to settle in it—for Tunisia will not allow terrorism to triumph, thanks to its national unity and to the well-established concept of the state in this country—even if they may protest against the state or criticize it, they refuse to move from order to chaos—we salute the Tunisian state.

The path of the revolution, therefore, is one of political successes, reestablishing security, and strengthening international solidarity, culminating in Tunisia being awarded the Nobel Peace Prize to the National Dialogue Quartet. Tunisia remains the shining candle among countries of the Arab Spring, having sparked the revolutions, demonstrating that democracy in the Arab world is possible.

In 2011, the spark was lit. Five ships sailed, carrying the hopes of their peoples for freedom and dignity. However, sadly within two years, storms and hardships surrounded those ships—storms of conspiracies, division, ideological polarization, mutual hatred, exclusion, revenge, assassinations, and terrorism.

Some ships met with destruction; others drowned in coups, civil wars, and chaos. Tunisia's ship was the exception. It was able to overcome the storms of the counterrevolution, chaos, and destruction, thanks to Tunisians adopting the principle of dialogue, acceptance of the other, and avoidance of exclusion and revenge. We were able, by God's grace, to bring Tunisia to the shores of safety.

At the height of the acute crisis of 2013, which threatened to drown Tunisia's ship in the swamps of division, His Excellency President Beji Caid Essebsi invited me to a dialogue, in a historic step. I agreed, and I said to those who criticized me at the time for going to Paris to meet him that I was ready to go anywhere for the sake of Tunisia's interest.

As I renew Ennahda's wholehearted support for the policy of consensus, I say today to those who seek political gain through hostility to Ennahda: Do not divide our country. Our hands are stretched out to everyone; the system of consensus accommodates everyone; Tunisia's ship can only sail safely if it carries all Tunisians.

In this context, I would like to commend members of the outgoing Consultative Council of the party, and Ennahda members of the National Constituent Assembly who facilitated Tunisia's path towards social peace and consensus through their difficult and wise decisions: when they chose to preserve the first article of the constitution of 1959, when they voted against the political exclusion law, and when they approved the national dialogue road map. Thus they proved that Ennahda is a national party that places Tunisia's interest above its own. And when we were discussing stepping down from legitimate elected government, we repeatedly said: We may lose power, but Tunisia will win.

I am full of pride in our sons and daughters who were patient and persevered, and withstood the campaigns of doubt, demonization, and provocation against their party.

At this sensitive juncture, I urge them to continue in the same way, for the most important thing for us, before anything else, is our country's stability and prosperity. We stress that Ennahda will remain a pillar of support for Tunisia's stability. We renew our support for the government of Prime Minister Essid and our commitment to the unity of the governing coalition and to the method of consensus which created the Tunisian exception.

We, in Ennahda, are serious and sincere in our desire to learn from our shortcomings before and after the revolution. We admit them and we humbly address them through reform. In our Congress we have an "evaluation motion"—we are a party that evolves and reforms itself and are not afraid to admit our mistakes.

We are a party that never stopped evolving—from the seventies to this day—from an ideological movement engaged in the struggle for identity—when identity was under threat, to a comprehensive protest movement against an authoritarian regime, to a national democratic party devoted to reform, based on a national reference drawing from the values of Islam, committed to the articles of the constitution and the spirit of our age, thus consolidating the clear and definitive line between Muslim democrats and extremist and violent trends that falsely attribute themselves to Islam.

The specialization and distinction between the political and other religious or social activities is not a sudden decision or a capitulation to temporary pressures, but rather the culmination of a historical evolution in which the political field and the social, cultural, and religious field were distinct in practice in our movement.

We are keen to keep religion far from political struggles and conflicts, and we call for the complete neutrality of mosques away from political disputes and partisan utilization, so that they play a role of unification rather than division.

Yet we are astonished to see the insistence of some to exclude religion from public life, despite the fact that the leaders of the national liberation movement considered religious sentiments to be a catalyst for revolution against occupation—just as today we see the values of Islam as a catalyst for development and promoting work, sacrifice, truthfulness, and integrity, and a positive force in our war against ISIS and extremists and supporting the state's efforts in development. Otherwise, if we do not counter ISIS—which claims to represent Islam—through using Islamic values, how can we counter it? We need scholars who champion Islamic moderation and refute extremism in the name of Islam.

Despotic regimes disfigured Ennahda's relationship with the state, through repression, defamation, and fearmongering. But they have failed, by God's grace, to make the state and Ennahda mutual enemies. Our experience in government after the revolution proves that Ennahda is part of the state and a source of significant support for it. Our leaving government to promote the country's unity proves that we are not power seekers nor after domination or monopoly of power.

The Tunisian state is our ship, which must carry all Tunisian men and women without any exception, exclusion of marginalization.

We ask here: When will attempts to undermine the state stop? And in whose interest are these attempts to weaken it, while it is combating terrorism, the ideology of those who seek anarchist methods to promote breaking the law?

The time has come not only to condemn that behavior but to consider it a crime against the nation, martyrs, and future generations.

Our call for a just state becomes devoid of meaning and value if that state is not also strong, able to apply the law and the constitution, and protect freedoms under the supervision of the legislative and judicial powers, the specialized oversight bodies, civil society, and the media.

Freedom does not mean chaos, just as the state's power does not mean repression and denial of freedoms. It is necessary for the revolution to reinstate the role of our well-established state and of its institutions and members, providing for their needs, adopting incentives that encourage productivity and eliminate the mentality of routine administration, the "come back tomorrow," "no network connection," and "a little something for me."

The dignity of public administration workers is part of the state's dignity, and no economic or social renaissance can take place without a real administrative reform that includes full digitization and elimination of paper administration. When will we be able to have an administration where a businessman or a young entrepreneur can create a company in a few hours instead of wasting his life from one department to another?

While it was one of the gains of the revolution to develop administrative working hours by adopting the five-day week, it is now necessary to accelerate the pace of reform far from slogans and political wrangling.

We are proud of our state, we demand rights from it, and we fulfill our duties towards it. Amongst the prerequisites of reinstating respect for the state is that we announce a war on corruption, and that no one should enjoy impunity that places him above the law.

I say clearly that the Ennahda Party is committed to combating corruption, bribery, tax evasion, and wasting of public wealth. Our call for reconciliation does not mean whitewashing corruption or justifying or re-creating a new system of corruption.

Our aim is to distinguish between the majority of businessmen and the minority implicated in corruption, and giving the latter the opportunity to own up, apologize, and give back that which they acquired illegally. That would help encourage free economic enterprise.

We have stressed our support for the president's economic reconciliation initiative, while we await the discussion of its details at the Assembly of People's Representatives.

I also stress our commitment to the transitional justice process. Furthermore, I call for a comprehensive national reconciliation that turns a new page and prevents the perpetuation of enmity. The comprehensive national reconciliation we all seek is not the initiative of one person or one party, but for a whole country looking forward to the future.

Thus we have said repeatedly, we are for a comprehensive national reconciliation and for cooperation and consensus building with all those who recognize the revolution and its martyrs and respect the constitution, a partnership with all those who regard the revolution as an opportunity for all of us—Islamists, Destourians, leftists, and all intellectual and political trends, so we can all go forward steadily towards a future that is free from grudges and exclusion.

Nor is it a "deal under the table" but rather a national vision of reconciliation between the state and citizens, between the state and deprived regions, between opposing political elites, between the past and the present—because Ennahda is a force of unification not one of division.

This also applies to the way we view our history, not as contradictory phases and figures— rather we see Khaireddine Al-Tunisi, Ahmed Bey, liberator of slaves, Moncef Bey, the late leader Habib Bourguiba, Farhat Hached, Abdelaziz Thaalibi, Salah Ben Youssef, Sheikh Mohamed Taher Ben Achour, and Tahar al-Haddad, God's mercy be upon them all, all those and others, as leading symbols of our dear nation, as sources of inspiration for us all, which must all enjoy our respect. They undoubtedly had their mistakes, but we take the positives and build on them.

Tunisians are tired of politicians bickering on media debates; they are concerned about security, terrorism, the cost of living, economic development, and the struggle of vulnerable groups, the poor and deprived, and marginalized regions. You, Ennahda members and supporters, must not be drawn into the elite's ideological battles but should rather focus on the concerns of fellow citizens. A modern state is not run through ideologies, big slogans, and political wrangling. It is guided by social and economic programs and solutions that provide security and prosperity for all.

Ennahda had evolved from defending identity to ensuring the democratic transition, and today moves on to focus on the economic transition. The new phase is primarily about the economy.

Since liberation from colonization, Tunisia has achieved much in the fields of education, health, women's rights, literacy, and other fields of human development. We embrace and value those achievements. We commit to preserving and developing them, within the framework of the continuity of the state and our pride in the republican system and Tunisian society and its choices, as enshrined in the Tunisian constitution.

I salute Tunisian women, in urban and rural areas, in Tunisia and abroad, in schools, universities and workplaces, in society and at home. Our movement is very proud of the gains and rights achieved by Tunisian women and will continue to support them to guarantee further freedom and advancement in fulfilling their potential and preserving the social fabric and the family as the source of social cohesion and unity.

We, Tunisians, are the product of the struggle of our mothers—Sheikh Abdelfattah Mourou sitting here in front of you is the fruit of a hard-working illiterate woman, who gave Tunisia such a man. My own mother was also illiterate, but while my father merely focused on teaching us the Quran, she insisted on sending me and my brothers to continue our education, and accepted to work in the field with my sisters to give the males— only, unfortunately—the chance to be educated. My own wife, a university graduate, devoted her life to her children's education such that my four daughters obtained their PhDs or master's, as did our two sons, who have masters' in law and economics. I salute Tunisian women, who made this nation an educated developed nation.

I say to young people, torn between ambition and despair, who are disappointed in the outcome of the revolution and the political class: We hear you.

You are the future for which we work. The difficulties you face today must not be a source of pessimism or disengagement from public life. We need to overcome these challenges together, through sincere attachment to the nation, determination, and persistence.

We call on the political elite to think about the youth and to provide them with the space to participate and to assume responsibility. It is high time for a national pact for youth development, so that no young man or woman is left marginalized, with no job, house, or prospects to establish a family.

Education is Tunisians' most valued capital. Today we are required to agree on a national vision for its reform in such a way that guarantees balance between knowledge and ethics and employability. We have to address the dangers in young people's environment: violence, drugs, all the ways to exploit young people's minds through terrorism's evil plots. We have to address how education has become divorced from the job market.

We must break with ad hoc reforms and with the search for quantity without quality. It is necessary to stress that education must be a door to work, not a bridge to unemployment.

No human development can take place without a cultural renaissance, without supporting creativity, without establishing cultural and sports activities in all regions, particularly in marginalized regions and popular urban neighborhoods. We want to see in every popular neighborhood a swimming pool, a sports center, a cultural center.

Strengthening the vocational training system and promoting it and reinstating its value are undoubtedly among the pillars of our reform plan.

The postrevolution state inherited an unemployment rate that was close to 14 percent, according to official statistics in 2011, and the current rate is close to that.

Unemployment is the result of historical accumulations in the fields of education and training, the restriction of economic enterprise by laws that restrict freedom of investment, and by weak infrastructure in most regions of the country, making them unattractive for economic projects.

Overcoming unemployment can only take place within a holistic economic model based on investment, which creates jobs and achieves balanced regional development and eliminates the mentality which eschews entrepreneurship and even the value of work.

We believe in the necessity of implementing the principle of positive discrimination enshrined in the constitution for the benefit of deprived regions. We welcome and support the coming process of decentralization after the local elections, just as we support the right of the regions to a percentage of their natural resources in order to achieve regional development.

As I call upon businessmen to invest, particularly in the inner regions, I stress the necessity to lift all restrictions placed before them in this regard.

I call from this platform for an urgent economic recovery program that prioritizes reactivating obstructed production in certain strategic sectors and implementing stalled public projects. This program must adopt exceptional measures in all fields related to employment, investment, and developing deprived regions. We will need to mobilize internal financial resources and reduce dependence on borrowing from outside sources and thereby encourage national savings, reform taxation and further simplify procedures for creating companies and initiating projects.

It is necessary to seek to implement a major economic project in each priority district over the next five years, to begin to distribute national lands to young entrepreneurs, to launch a legislative and administrative revolution to lift restrictions to investment and entrepreneurship, and to support the government's work through a major economic ministry.

It is also important to stress the need to spread social welfare coverage, particularly for workers in the agricultural field, and to direct subsidies to those who need them, to reinstate the culture of work and the link between fulfilling one's duty and demanding one's right.

As I renew my call for a social truce that preserves the rights of workers and protects economic institutions, I salute the important role played by the Tunisian General Workers' Union; the Union of Industry, Commerce, and Handicrafts; the Union of Agriculture and Fisheries; and all national organizations for their role in development.

Your excellencies, ladies and gentlemen, the revolution gave Tunisians abroad for the first time the right to be part of parliament and to elect their representatives, as an integral component of Tunisia. I call for further support to them as they face a new wave of xenophobia. And I call on them to further strengthen their economic ties to their beloved homeland through increasing transfers and spending their summer holidays in Tunisian hotels, as well as investing, and it is necessary to create incentives for them to do so.

It is important in this regard to support Tunisian diplomacy in its official and cultural dimensions, and economic diplomacy in particular. I stress Ennahda's commitment to supporting the state's foreign policy; and Tunisia's role in spreading peace, consensus, and combating terrorism around the world. As I commend the steps made by our Libyan neighbors towards reconciliation and unity, it is our hope that the Arab world will soon inaugurate an age of peace and comprehensive reconciliation.

We also express our commitment to the Arab Maghreb Union; and we salute our neighbors Algeria, Morocco, Mauritania, and Libya; and renew our commitment to strengthening our relations with our Arab, Muslim, and African neighbors; and our pride in the good relations between Tunisia and Europe, the United States of America, and all countries around the world.

We are proud that the Tunisian experience, which has won international acclaim, has proven that the solution to conflict is consensus building and seeking the foundation for coexistence. We have demonstrated that democracy is possible in the Arab world; and that democracy is the solution to corruption, bribery, despotism, chaos, and terrorism; and that investing in democracy is better and more effective than supporting regressive dictatorships.

The solution is reconciliation between the poor and the rich, between the north and south, between cultures and civilizations, between faiths. Our world needs mutual understanding, peace, solidarity, security, and tolerance.

Your excellencies, ladies and gentlemen, Ennahda's members, with their blood, tears, and sacrifices, have gone through trials and tribulations that taught us courage to admit our errors and review our policies far from any arrogance or egoism.

Self-criticism is a condition for evolution in the modern world, and just as we have practiced it throughout our history, we will consolidate it in our tenth congress, for which Tunisians have many expectations.

The success of this congress is primarily about presenting a renewed united Ennahda that is able to participate in solving Tunisia's problems, a party of national ambition, a party of objective analysis and constructive criticism that gives rise to a democratic alternative, a party that is open to its environment and to all capabilities and potential, a party that is proud of its members—women and men.

Every individual in Ennahda is a story of sacrifice and heroism. Families that have been torn apart and exiled, tens of thousands of prisoners.

Ennahda activists sacrificed a lot for the sake of Tunisia—that is why we regard Ennahda as the shared possession of Tunisia and all Tunisians, before belonging to Ennahda members and supporters. That is what strengthens our conviction that the choice of reform is our path to rising to our people's aspirations, and that partnership and cooperation are our choice. Tunisia cannot be ruled in the coming years by the logic of majority and minority but rather by the logic of consensus and partnership.

Ladies and gentlemen, for many years, I was banned from entering Tunisia. When I used to see Tunis Air flights at any airport around the world, I would dream of returning to my land, dreams that were then very far from reality.

Will I return home one day?

Will I once again meet our sons and daughters scattered between dozens of prisons and places of exile?

Will I ever have the right to walk the streets of my country and congratulate my fellow Tunisians, my friends and family on festivals and Eids?

That dream has become a reality, by God's grace. And it continues to grow inside me day by day, turning from the dream of return to the dream of building a new beginning for Tunisia.

A dream of a better Tunisia—a united Tunisia—a democratic, developed, and inclusive Tunisia.

We must share this dream with all Tunisians, as we look together with optimism, determination, and hope to the future, not towards the past.

It is the Tunisian dream that motivates us to work hard and sacrifice in order to turn the revolution's dreams into reality.

You, Tunisian men and women, are stronger than all difficulties and challenges.

You, grandchildren of Hannibal, Jugurtha, Oqba, Ibn Khaldun, el-Chebbi; children of Carthage, Kairouan, Mehdia, and al-Zaytouna; you are able, God willing, through your unity and solidarity, through your attachment to your beloved country and your belief in yourselves, to achieve what we aspire to, and more—to achieve the Tunisian dream, just as you created, through your consensus, the Tunisian exception; and just as you sparked, with your courage and defiance, the flame of the Arab Spring.

It is time for Tunisia's ship to leave the shore, to sail on its journey towards development and prosperity for all its people.

By God's grace, we inaugurate this congress, and we ask God to guide us to choose what is best for our country and our shared future.

NOTES

TRANSLATOR'S INTRODUCTION

1. David L. Johnston, "'Allal al-Fasi: *Shari'a* as Blueprint for a Righteous Global Citizenship?" in *Shari'a: Islamic Law in the Contemporary Context*, ed. Abbas Madanat and Frank Griffel (Palo Alto, CA: Stanford University Press, 2007), 183–203; "The Fuzzy Boundaries between Reformism and Islamism: Malik Bennabi and Rashid al-Ghannushi on Civilization," *Maghreb Review* 29, no. 1–2 (2004): 123–152.
2. Three recent books on the Muslim Brotherhood stand out: Barry Rubin, ed., *The Muslim Brotherhood: The Organization and Policies of a Global Islamist Movement* (New York: Palgrave Macmillan, 2010); Carrie Rosefsky Wickham, *The Muslim Brotherhood: Evolution of an Islamist Movement*, updated ed. (Princeton, NJ: Princeton University Press, 2015); Khalil al-Anani, *Inside the Muslim Brotherhood: Religion, Identity, and Politics* (Oxford and New York: Oxford University Press, 2016).
3. Richard C. Martin and Abbas Barzegar, eds., *Islamism: Contested Perspectives in Political Islam* (Stanford, CA: Stanford University Press, 2011).
4. Graham E. Fuller, *The Future of Political Islam* (New York: Palgrave Macmillan, 2003).
5. Ibid., xi.
6. Fuller, "The Spectrum of Islamic Politics," in Martin and Barzegar, *Islamism*, 51–56, at 52.
7. Martin and Barzegar, "Introduction: The Debate about Islamism in the Public Sphere," in *Islamism*, 1–13, at 9–10.
8. Interestingly, the word does not appear in the historical background chapter written for the first edition but does appear in the short introduction to the third edition (2008), upon which this translation is based.
9. Chapter 6, 343.
10. See, for instance, the Pew Research Center's 2012 polling of Lebanon, Turkey, Egypt, Tunisia, Jordan, and Pakistan along these lines. Available online, http://www.pewglobal.org/2012/07/10/most-muslims-want-democracy-personal-freedoms-and-islam-in-political-life/.

11. John L. Esposito and Dalia Mogahed, *Who Speaks for Islam? What a Billion Muslims Really Think* (New York: Gallup, 2007), 47.

12. Ibid., 48.

13. On this, see, for instance, the updated edition with a new foreword of Carrie Rosefsky Wickham's excellent book, *The Muslim Brotherhood: Evolution of an Islamist Movement* (Princeton, NJ: Princeton University Press, 2015).

14. François Burgat, *Comprendre l'islam politique: une trajectoire de recherche sur l'altérité islamiste, 1973–2016* (*Understanding Political Islam: A Research Trajectory on Islamist Otherness*) (Paris: Éditions La Découverte, 2016).

15. Ibid., 7. Burgat's concept of Islamic lexicon is comparable to anthropologist Talal Asad's thesis that a comprehensive anthropology of Islam can only be founded on the notion of Islam's "discursive tradition." See, for instance, his *Genealogies of Power: Discipline and Reasons of Power in Christianity and Islam* (Baltimore: Johns Hopkins University Press, 1993).

16. Burgat, *Comprendre l'islam politique*, 8.

17. Ibid., 13.

18. Ibid.

19. Ibid., 11–12. See also Nathan J. Brown's *Arguing Islam after the Revival of Arab Politics* (Oxford and New York: Oxford University Press, 2017), which resulted from several visits to the region after the 2011 uprisings as a political scientist specialized in Islam. It is a fascinating account of the various debates in many countries of the region but offers precious little insight into Tunisia's Ennahda, except for one helpful look at its strategy with regard to the drawing up of the new constitution (166–168).

20. Karina Piser, "The Mainstreaming of Tunisia's Islamists," *Foreign Policy* (August 7, 2016), available online, http://foreignpolicy.com/2016/08/07/the-mainstreaming-of-tunisias-islamists/.

21. See, for instance, Asef Bayat, ed., *Post-Islamism: The Changing Faces of Political Islam* (Oxford and New York: Oxford University Press, 2013); Yadullah Shahibzadeh, *Islamism and Post-Islamism in Iran: An Intellectual History* (New York: Palgrave Macmillan, 2016).

22. John L. Esposito, Lily Zubaidah Rahim, and Naser Ghobadzadeh, eds., *The Politics of Islamism: Diverging Visions and Trajectories* (New York: Palgrave Macmillan, 2018).

23. Larbi Sadiki, "Tunisia's Ennahda: Islamists Turning the Learning Curve of Democracy and Civic Habituation," in Esposito, Rahim, and Ghobadzadeh, *The Politics of Islamism*, 127–158.

24. Cesari holds academic appointments on four continents. From her Harvard Divinity School page we read, "Jocelyne Cesari holds the Chair of Religion and Politics at the University of Birmingham, UK. She is senior research fellow at Georgetown University's Berkley Center on Religion, Peace and World Affairs and at the Institute for Religion, Politics and Society at the Australian Catholic University. She teaches on contemporary Islam and politics at the Harvard Divinity School and directs the Harvard interfaculty program 'Islam in the West.'"

25. Cesari, *What Is Political Islam?* (New York: Palgrave Macmillan, 2017).

26. Ibid., 192.

27. Azzam S. Tamimi, *Rachid Ghannouchi: A Democrat within Islamism* (Oxford and New York: Oxford University Press, 2001).

28. The first trilogy: "The Mid-20th-Century Rise of Islamism in the Maghreb," http:// www.humantrustees.org/blogs/religion-and-human-rights/item/143-ghannouchi-1; "Ghannouchi: Improbable Trajectory," http://www.humantrustees.org/blogs/religion -and-human-rights/item/145-ghannouchi-2; "Ghannouchi: Shari'a, Trusteeship, and Human Rights," http://www.humantrustees.org/blogs/religion-and-human-rights /item/148-ghannouchi-3. The second trilogy: "The Impossible Islamic State? (1)," http://www.humantrustees.org/blogs/religion-and-human-rights/item/151-impossible -state-1; "The Impossible Islamic State? (2)," http://www.humantrustees.org/blogs /religion-and-human-rights/item/152-impossible-state-2; "The Impossible Islamic State? (3)," http://www.humantrustees.org/blogs/religion-and-human-rights/item/154 -impossible-state-3. The last one details the changes of perspective already apparent in a paper Ghannouchi delivered at a 2012 conference in Alexandria, Egypt, on the theme of "Religion and State," and offers a short commentary on the keynote speech he delivered to Ennahda's Tenth Congress (appendix 3).

PREFACE TO THE THIRD EDITION

1. [Translator's note] The word "Islamists" here translates the Arabic *islamiyyun*. It seldom appears in the book, but Ghannouchi often refers to these political activists within the "Islamic movement," or involved in the "Islamic project." Islamism is generally used to refer to the twentieth-century effort to bring Islamic values and symbols into the political life of the modern nation-state, starting with the Muslim Brotherhood (founded in 1928) and expressed by a variety of movements, including peaceful ones like the party founded by Ghannouchi in the 1980s, the ruling AKP Party in Turkey, or the ideology that defines the Islamic Republic of Iran, or violent ones like the Salafi-jihadi current typified by al-Qaeda and ISIS.

2. [Translator's note] In classical Islamic jurisprudence (*fiqh*), which emerged at the height of Muslim imperial power, the world was divided between the Abode of Islam and the Abode of War. In the modern period, this attitude changed with the shifting geopolitical realities. The more common distinction today is the one reflected here: the Abode of Islam and the Abode of Unbelief (*kufr*). But as you can surmise from Ghannouchi's text, this distinction for Muslims is much more than just academic. He is here genuinely distressed and baffled at being sent into exile.

3. [Translator's note] Ghannouchi is alluding to the highest level of the Shari'a's objectives, the so-called five necessities: preservation of life, religion, mind, family (or honor), and possessions.

PREFACE TO THE FIRST EDITION

1. 'Abd al-Wahhab al-Kayali et al., eds., *Encyclopedia of Politics* (*Mawsu'a al-siyasa*), vol. 2 (Beirut: Mu'assasa al-'Arabiyya li-l-Dirasat wa-l-Nashr, 1989), 242.

2. Q. 2:31.

3. [Translator's note] The first word, *shura*, means "mutual consultation," and though it is only mentioned once in the Qur'an (42:38), it has come to symbolize divine approval for deliberative democracy for many Muslims today. The second word is *bay'a*, meaning a "pledge of allegiance" to a ruler. Ghannouchi will come back to these terms in detail.

4. Among those who denounced their former writings influenced by the West, one can cite Muhammad Husayn Haykal and Khalid Muhammad Khalid, who publicly announced his repentance with a courage worthy of other reformist thinkers like himself. After naming some of the Western influences that had led him into error, he declared, "Islam is a faith that impacts political organization and it may be that we will not find a religion or theory whose very nature demands the values of a state as is the case with Islam." Khalid Muhammad Khalid, "Introduction," *The State According to Islam (al-Dawla hasab al-islam)* (Cairo: Dar al-Thabit, 1981), 24.

   Muhammad 'Imara has documented how the leaders of the Egyptian secularist movement came back on their positions with repentance and regret. Among those he mentioned was the Shaykh 'Ali 'Abd al-Raziq who had adopted secularism in 1925 and who in 1951 came back to announce his repentance in an article that was published in the journal *Siyasa* (April/May 1951). On this, see Muhammad 'Imara's book, *Islam and Politics (al-Islam wa-l-siyasa)* (Damascus: Markaz al-Rayya li-l-Tanmiyya al-Fikriyya, 2005).

   You can find the full text in Imara's book, as well as Taha Husayn's retraction of his secularist views after defending 'Ali 'Abd al-Raziq. While he was a member of the constitutional committee in 1953, he said, "The constitution must never put forward any law that contradicts the Qur'an." In the same way, Muhammad Hussein Haykel changed his mind and sincerely repented, defending in one of his books the belief that Islam is both religion and state (*al-Islam din wa-dawla*); see Muhammad Husayn Haykel, *The Life of Muhammad (Hayyat Muhammad)* (Cairo: Dar al-Ma'arif, 1965), and *The Status of Divine Inspiration (Manzil al-wahi)* (Cairo: Dar al-Ma'arif, 1937). Muhammad 'Imara himself changed his mind and became one of the staunchest defenders of Islam and its state in the face of secularism. In fact, we expect huge secularist about-faces and returns to Islam after the fall of communism and the ascendance of Islam more than at any time in the past, because it is a power of resistance in the face of internal corruption and evil plots on the outside.

5. One reads in the founding declaration of Tunisia's Islamic Tendency Movement in June 1981 that one of the missions of this movement was to aid in the revival of Islam's political and civilizational embodiment, and one of the means to reach this objective was "the crystallization and incarnation of a contemporary form of Islamic governance."

6. [Translator's note] The Sunna, the second sacred text of Islam, is a collection of the sayings and acts of the Prophet Muhammad. There are six compilations that are considered the most reliable, with at least three others from which scholars often cite. The basic building block is the individual saying or story (*hadith*), which is preceded by a chain of transmitters going backward from generation to generation to the orig-

inal transmitter, one of the Prophet's Companions. Historically, the reliability of each chain of transmission has been the main criterion for determining the authenticity of a particular hadith.

7. The great Egyptian constitutional scholar 'Abd al-Hamid Mutawalli stipulated the condition that there be more than one narrator for any hadith to be used in his constitutional research. See his book, *The Crisis of Islamic Political Thought in Egypt: Its Manifestations, Causes, and Solution* (*Azmat al-fikr al-siyasi al-islami fi Masr al-hadith: madhahiruha, asbabuha, 'ilajuha*) (Cairo and Alexandria: al-Maktab al-Masri al-Hadith lil-Tiba'a wa-l-Nashr, 1970).

8. [Translator's note] The word here is *kulliyyat*, literally "the comprehensive norms" as opposed to the specific or partial rules (*juz'iyyat*). This is traditional nomenclature in Islamic law, but which has become more prominent in the recent focus on the Shari'a's objectives.

9. [Translator's note] In the Qur'an, this would apply to its explicitly legal verses (between 5 and 10 percent of the six thousand or so, depending on the authorities you consult). In the Sunna, each hadith is probed as to its verbal clarity and the reliability of its chain of transmitters.

10. [Translator's note] My preference, naturally, would be to use gender-neutral pronouns as opposed to the author's use of the masculine for people in general (here: "he happens to come across"). I do this throughout the text, if only to preserve the 1980s settings of the original text, which the author kept in this third edition. Additionally, this practice tends to remain in Arabic writing to this day.

11. Q. 39:18.

12. [Translator's note] The word "Salafi" comes from the Arabic *salaf*, meaning in the Islamic context "the righteous forbears." The term was first used by Muhammad 'Abduh (d. 1905) in the modern period, who as a great reformist thinker used it to emphasize the authentic nature of his teaching—that is, he was being faithful to the teaching of the Prophet's Companions and to the great luminaries of the Islamic tradition in its classical period. By contrast, today it is used about the ultraconservative Muslims who pride themselves in strictly following the Prophet Muhammad's words and deeds. This movement tends to emphasize the Sunna much more than other Muslims do and follow it very literally. It has many parallels to the puritanical Wahhabi doctrine from Saudi Arabia, though the two movements should be kept separate. See, for instance, Roel Meijer, ed., *Global Salafism: Islam's New Religious Movement* (Oxford and New York: Oxford University Press, 2009).

13. [Translator's note] I have translated this simple expression differently (*siyasa shar'iyya*: literally, "politics according to the Shari'a") because at least since al-Marwardi's (d. 1058) classic text dealing with Islam and the state this had become a subdiscipline in the Islamic sciences. Ibn Taymiyya (d. 1328) and his disciple Ibn Qayyim (d. 1350) both wrote a good deal on this topic. But as I explained in the introduction, Islamism or twentieth-century political Islam is a modern phenomenon, mostly because of how differently the modern nation-state functions. As a result, there is no simple way to translate this expression here.

14. Ibn 'Abdallah Muhammad bin Abi Bakr bin Qayyim al-Jawziyya, *The Paths of Rulership in God-Ordained Politics* (*al-Turuq al-hukmiyya fi-l-siyasa al-shar'iyya*), Muhammad Hamid al-Faqi, ed. (Beirut: Dar al-Kitab al-'Ilmiyya, n.d.), 15–16.

15. See the famous work by Abu al-Walid Muhammad bin Ahmad bin Rushd al-Qurtubi, *The Philosophy of Averroës: Outlining the Message and Discerning between the Shari'a and the Wisdom in Connection: Discovering the Ways and Reasons behind God's Laws and the Rules of Religion* (*Falsafat Ibn Rushd: fasl al-maqal wa-taqrir ma bayn al-shari'a wa-l-hikma fi-l-ittisal: al-kashf 'an manahij al-adilla fi 'aqa'id al-milla*), Mustafa 'Abd al-Jawad 'Imran, ed. (Cairo: al-Maktaba al-Tijariyya al-Mahmudiyya, 1968); and Muhammad al-Fadil bin 'Ashur, *The Spirit of Islamic Civilization* (*Ruh al-hidara al-Islamiyya*) (Washington, DC: al-Ma'had al-'Alami al-Islami, n.d.), 28.

    I do not concede as does this great scholar that this prohibition is an absolute one, but only in cases that contradict our Shari'a. Otherwise, we would fall into difficulty, and even an impossible situation.

16. The great Islamic scholar Ibn Taymiyya (d. 782 H/1328 CE) said, "The Divine Legislator commanded us to always think differently from non-Muslims. Even if their difference is good, God still intended us to be different; it is clear that the very fact that they are different is willed by God." See Taqi al-Din Ahmad bin Abd al-Halim bin Taymiyya al-Harrani, *Following the Straight Path unlike the Denizens of Hell* (*Iqtida' al-sirat al-mustaqim mukhalafatan ashab al-jahim*) (Cairo: n.p., 1969), 57–59.

17. This was the purpose of the Founding Declaration of the Islamic Tendency Movement (June 1981)—to mobilize support for awakening of Islam's embodiment in politics and civilization, and one of the means to achieve that goal was the crystallization of a contemporary image of Islamic governance.

18. Al-Kiyali et al., *The Encyclopedia of Politics*, 2.

HISTORICAL AND PERSONAL REALITIES BEHIND THIS BOOK

1. [Translator's note] In 1983, the International Monetary Fund (IMF) forced Tunisia (still under the rule of strongman Habib Bourguiba) to raise the price of bread and semolina, sparking a series of riots the following year—hence, the "bread revolution." Ghannouchi's party, the Islamic Tendency Movement (MTI), gained much greater popularity in this period. This was the first time Ghannouchi and his colleagues were released from prison.

2. Q. 42:38.

3. [Translator's note] As a devotee (*murid*) in the mystical branch of Islam (Sufism), one experiences a dying to one's self (fana') and the realization that one has become one with God, the Absolute.

4. [Translator's note] Ghannouchi means by this that those holding the reins of power in Tunisia (as elsewhere) had little popular legitimacy. President Habib Bourguiba and Zine El Abidine Ben Ali after him used the army and security apparatus to stay

in power, despite the broad popular appeal of the main opposition party, the Islamic Tendency Movement (MTI).

5. For a useful study of the Islamic movement, see Muhammad 'Abd al-Baqi al-Harmasi, "al-Islam al-ihtijaji fi Tunis" ("Protest Islam in Tunisia"), a paper presented at a conference ("Contemporary Islamic Movements in the Arab World") sponsored by the Office of Alternative Arab Futures, Social, Political and Cultural Currents (Beirut: Markaz Dirasat al-Wihda al-'Arabiyya, 1987); Francois Burgat, "al-Islam al-siyasi: sawt al-janub" ("Political Islam: Voices from the South"), trans. Lorene Zakri (Cairo: Dar al-Alam al-Thalath, 1992); and 'Abd al-Latif al-Harmasi, "Jama'at al-Islam al-siyasi fi al-maghrib al-'arabi" ("Political Islam Organizations in the Arab Maghreb"), *al-Mawqif* 1 (July/August 1992).

6. [Translator's note] The reference here is to the first Gulf War (though some historians call the Iran-Iraq War the first and this the second one) during which the United States and a large number of international allies ousted Saddam Hussein from Kuwait. Ghannouchi here sides with the majority of Arabs at the time in defending Saddam Hussein, who was seen as the victim of Western aggression.

7. In a 1992 lecture the French thinker Roger Garaudy delivered in Paris during a conference in solidarity with the victims of state oppression in Tunisia, he declared that there was no escaping the systematic aggression that the Ennahda movement and the Workers Union were experiencing, because it was part of a plan to integrate Tunisia with the imperialist economy.

8. [Translator's note] For the word "activists" Ghannouchi chose a military term (*kata'ib*), literally "troops" or "battalions." Interestingly, this was a word also used by Maronite Christians in the Lebanese civil war (1975–1990). The Phalangists were both a political party and an armed militia.

9. Q. 21:107.

10. [Translator's note] The word "revival" at the beginning of the sentence is the same word used for the political party Ghannouchi cofounded and over which he now presides (*al-Nahda*).

11. [Translator's note] "Arab revival": again, this is another modern use of the word *nahda*, only here it refers to the intellectual and cultural renaissance movement in the Arabic-speaking Middle East in the nineteenth and early twentieth centuries. It was sparked by the contact many Arab intellectuals had with their European counterparts, yet it was also a movement that prided itself on its own independence and cultural distinctiveness. Particularly in Lebanon and Syria, this cultural revival was spearheaded by Christians such as Butrus al-Bustani, who created the first modern Arabic encyclopedia. During this time also a number of Islamic reformers appeared, the two most famous being Jamal al-Din al-Afghani (d. 1897) and Muhammad Abduh (d. 1905). But the term *nahda* here mostly refers to the literary effervescence of those years, including new developments of Arab poetry, novels, and literary criticism, a movement that clearly showed signs of secularism and a departure from conservative Arab-Islamic tradition.

12. Q. 11:88.

13. On this, one may consult the books of Professor Munir Shafiq.

14. Q. 2:256. The word translated here as "false gods" is literally "tyranny" (*taghut*). Perhaps the most read translation in English, the one by Abdullah Yusuf Ali, renders it as "Evil."

15. Q. 39:18.

1. ON THE CONCEPT OF FREEDOM IN THE WEST

1. The writings of German philosopher Kant demonstrated this, and long before him those of Ibn Khaldun, which showed that human reason could not grasp the essence of things. They both called for reason to restrict itself to the sensible world. See Immanuel Kant, *Critique de la raison pure* (*Critique of Pure Reason*), preface by Charles Serrus (Paris: Presses Universitaires de France, 1971), and Abu Zayd 'Abd al-Rahman bin Muhammad bin Khaldun, *The Lessons and the Record of the Origins and Experiences of the Arabs, Persians and Berbers and the Contemporary Powers Ruling Them: Ibn Khaldun's Introduction* (*al-'Ibar wa-diwan al-mubtada' wa-l-khabar fi ayam al-'arab wa-l-'ajam wa-l-barbar wa-man 'asirahum min dhawi al-sultan al-akbar: muqaddimat Ibn Khaldun*), 7 vols. (Beirut: Dar al-Kitab al-Lubnani, 1956–1959).

2. The atheist existentialism of Sartre and Camus is the best example of this nihilistic freedom. The great philosopher Roger Garaudy wisely analyzed the phenomenon of loneliness that the contemporary human being experiences in these words, "Individuals in our European societies are condemned to lonely lives cut off from other people and that loneliness has continued to grow since the age of the conquerors until the present decline of the isolated masses due to the expansion of competing ideologies." See Roger Garaudy, *The Promises of Islam* (*Wu'ud al-islam*) (Beirut: Dar al-'Ilmiyya, n.d.).

3. 'Abd al-Wahhab al-Kiyali et al., *Encyclopedia of Politics* (Beirut: al-Mu'assasa al-'Arabiyya li-l-Dirasat wa-l-Nashr, 1979), 244.

4. Jean-William Lapierre, *Political Power* (*al-Sulta al-siyasiyya*), original French title, *Vivre sans état? Essai sur le pouvoir politique et l'innovation sociale* (*To Live without a State? An Essay on Political Power and Social Innovation*), trans. Elias Hanna Elias, Vol. 3 (Paris and Beirut: Manshurat 'Awidat, 1983), 103.

5. Satan threatened Adam and his progeny in this Qur'anic *sura*: "I will surely bring his descendants under my sway—all but a few!" (Q. 17:62). We read the following in a commentary: "I will dominate them by seduction." See Muhammad Hasan al-Humsi, *Commentary and Explanation of the Qur'an's Vocabulary* (*Tafsir wa-bayan mufradat al-qur'an*) (Beirut: Mu'assasat al-Iman, 1998), 289.

6. See the excellent and unhurried study by Muhsin al-Mili on Western thought, *Secularism or the Philosophy of the Death of Man* (*al-'Ilmaniyya aw falsafat mawt al-insan*) (Carthage, Tunisia: Matba'a Tunis, 1986).

7. The West's objective should be seen through the lens of its materialist philosophy, which spawns two phenomena: first, relationships built on power, self-interest, and

material comfort; second, an international order built on hegemony, plundering the goods of the weak, and destroying their cultures. Western nations are by no means excluded from this, for they are the first victims of this philosophy, these values, these organizations, and oppressive corporations.

8. al-Mili, *Secularism*, 134–138.

9. Ibid.

10. From this pagan dualism came the break between religion and politics that the Roman Church decided, so as to grant Caesar absolute authority to manage public affairs independently from God's authority in exchange for the privileges he granted to the clergy. See one of Garaudy's excellent books, *Wu'ud al-islam* (*The Promises of Islam*), 81.

11. On this, see Mustafa Khalidi and 'Umar Farukh, *Evangelization and Colonialism in the Arab Countries* (*al-Tabshir wa-l-isti'mar fi-l-bilad al-'arabiyy*a) (Beirut: Manshurat al-Maktabat al-'Ilmiyya wa-Matba'atuha, 1953).

2. THE ISLAMIC PERSPECTIVE ON FREEDOM AND HUMAN RIGHTS

1. Hasan Turabi, from a speech on "Freedom and Unity" (Khartoum, Sudan: Student Union of Khartoum University, n.d.). [Translator's note] Hasan al-Turabi (d. 2016) was one of the most influential politicians in recent Sudanese history. Trained in the Islamic sciences, he then studied in Britain and earned a PhD at the Sorbonne in Paris. Early associated with the Egyptian Muslim Brotherhood, he founded the National Islamic Front (NIF), which mostly ruled from 1989 to 2001.

2. [Translator's note] The divine Trust (*amana*) offered to humanity comes from Q. 33:72, "We offered the Trust to the heavens, the earth, and the mountains, yet they refused to undertake it and were afraid of it; mankind undertook it—they have always been very inept and rash."

3. Perhaps the first one to define Islam in this way was Mawdudi [founder of the Jamaat-e-Islami movement in Pakistan, d. 1979] and the martyr Sayyid Qutb, who followed his teaching [Egyptian Muslim Brotherhood, d. 1966].

4. Q. 18:29.

5. Q. 20:123–124.

6. [Translator's note] As mentioned in my introduction, the adjective *islami/islamiyyun* as used today is the exact equivalent of the English "Islamists," meaning contemporary Muslim thinkers or activists who want to see Islamic norms (however defined, and to whatever extent) embodied in the public sphere and especially in the political realm. Ghannouchi's list here is actually quite diverse, and certainly not all fit into the category of advocates for political Islam.

7. Q. 98:1.

8. 'Allal al-Fasi, *The Objectives of the Islamic Shari'a and Its Noble Values* (*Maqasid al-Shari'a al-Islamiyya wa-makarimuha*) (Rabat, Morocco: Matba'a al-Risala, 1979), 247.

9. Turabi, "Freedom and Unity."

10. [Translator's note] Born in 1931, Shaykh Madani co-founded the Algerian Islamic Salvation Front (FIS) in 1989, which dominated the municipal elections that year and was poised to win the parliamentary elections in 1991, but then the army stepped in and canceled the elections, triggering a brutal civil war for most of that decade.

11. [Translator's note] No reference given.

12. Abu Ishaq Ibrahim bin Musa al-Shatibi, *The Agreements on the Foundations of Shari'a (al-Muwafaqat fi usul al-Shari'a)*, vol. 2 (Beirut: Dar al-Ma'rifa, n.d.), 5.

13. [Translator's note] I have translated *masalih* (sing. *maslaha*) as "goods" here; this word is the cornerstone of the *maqasid al-Shari'a* movement in Islamic law today. Literally, it means "interest" or "benefit," but it also has the connotation of "common good" or "public utility." This will come up again and again in the book.

14. Ibn 'Ashur, *The Objectives of the Islamic Shari'a (Maqasid al-Shari'a al-islamiyya)* (Tunis: al-Dar al-Tunisiyya li-l-Nashr, 1978).

15. Q. 33:72.

16. [Translator's note] The *zakat* is one of the five so-called pillars of Islam, namely the mandatory yearly distribution of 2.5 percent of one's net worth to the poor and other charitable causes.

17. [Translator's note] Ghannouchi is likely referring to the modern "reformers" of the nineteenth and early twentieth century Jamal al-Din al-Afghani, Muhammad 'Abduh, and Rashid Rida, among others. In his dedication, he also included the Ottoman-Tunisian minister of state, who wrote the first Tunisian constitution in 1861, Khayr al-Din al-Tunisi (d. 1890). Ghannouchi also chooses to include all the twentieth-century Islamists, from the founder of the Muslim Brotherhood, Hasan al-Banna, to the founder of its equivalent in South Asia, Mawlana Abu'l-A'la al-Mawdudi, as well as the more radical Sayyid Qutb, though he remains very eclectic and includes some more moderate or even liberal Muslims like Muhammad Iqbal in British India (d. 1938). The "Revolution" is the Iranian Revolution of 1979, again a sign of Ghannouchi's irenic and conciliatory spirit as a Sunni Muslim (Iran is the most populous Shia-majority nation).

18. Khayr al-Din al-Tunisi, *The Surest Path to Knowledge Regarding the Condition of Countries (Aqwam al-masalik fi ma'rifat ahwal al-mamalik)*, ed. Mansaf al-Shanuqi (Tunis: al-Dar al-Tunisiyya li-l-Nashr, 1982), 27.

19. From the collection of poems by the poet [Shaykh Mahmud] Qabadu on "The Surest Path," 284. [Translator's note] Qabadu was a reformist cleric and professor at the Zaytuna University in Tunis and a personal friend of Khayr al-Din. The two collaborated a good deal and in particular for the framing of the 1861 constitution, the first in the Arab world.

20. [Translator's note] The Arabic word *dustur* (plural *dasatir*) can also mean "constitution," but here it refers more generally to statutes and legal rules. The Shari'a historically was never codified in the modern sense. Classical Islamic states of various kinds were weak in constitutional law and generally had two parallel judicial systems, Shari'a courts staffed by the *'ulama'* (Islamic scholars, most of whom were also ju-

rists) primarily dealing with family status law and some cases of criminal law, and the *madhalim* courts ("complaints" courts) staffed by jurists appointed by the state. Yet the 'ulama' always maintained a certain distance from political power and represented, as such, a buffer against it. Only in the modern period, with the advent of the nation-state in which political power is uniquely concentrated in the state, did Muslim states codify laws for their use in national legislatures.

21. [Translator's note] "Mutual consultation" translates the word *shura*, which will come up very often in this book.

22. See, for instance, the Universal Islamic Declaration of Human Rights (Paris: Islamic Council, 1981); see also the final document of the Conference on Human Rights in Islam, Kuwait, December 1980.

23. Ahmad al-Katib, *The Instruments of Unity and Freedom in Islam (Aliyya al-wihda wa-l-hurriyya fi-l-islam)* (US: n.p., 1984), 119.

24. [Translator's note] A central pillar of Ghannouchi's political theory is the idea that mankind is, individually and collectively, God's "caliph" (*khalifa*) on earth. Derived from a number of Qur'anic verses, particularly 2:30, many modern Muslim thinkers have stressed that political authority and ethical responsibility on earth have been conveyed directly by God to mankind, and thus no other authorities (rulers or scholars, for example) exercise power unless it has been directly delegated to them by the people. Depending on whether the emphasis is on responsibility and custodianship on the one hand, or power and authority on the other, the idea of the "universal caliphate" is rendered in this translation as "deputyship," "vicegerency," "stewardship," "trusteeship," or even "caliphate." On the role of this concept in modern Islamic thought, particularly in grounding a political theology of popular sovereignty, and with a special focus on the place of this concept in Ghannouchi's thought, see Andrew F. March, *The Caliphate of Man: Popular Sovereignty in Modern Islamic Thought* (Cambridge, MA: Belknap Press, 2019).

25. [Translator's note] Author's emphasis.

26. See the works of 'Abd al-Wahhab al-Masiri (often: Messiri in English), and in particular his *Encyclopedia on Secularism and Judaism*; also his abbreviated article in the Islamic journal *al-Ma'rifa* 5 (1996), entitled, "Western Thought: A Critical Project" (*"al-Fikr al-gharbi: mashru' waraqa naqdiyya"*); finally, his book on partial secularism and comprehensive secularism [no details given].

27. Q. 90:10, Yusuf Ali, *The Holy Qur'an: Text, Translation and Commentary by Abdullah Yusuf Ali* (New York: Tahrike Tarsile Qur'an, 1987).

28. Fathi 'Uthman, *Foundations of Islamic Political Thought (Usul al-fikr al-siyasi al-islami)* (Beirut: Mu'assasa al-Risala, 1984), 149.

29. One notices with regard to the various methods of oppression used by Arab regimes that along with mounting oppression and violation of freedoms and human rights, these Arab regimes compete in their propaganda about the values of democracy and human rights and in their creation of ministries and organizations for human rights, pitting them against the original ones, as has happened in Tunisia and elsewhere. It is as if the declaration of war against extremism, the profusion of words about de-

mocracy and human rights, and their organizing elections in which only the dictator participates are enough to justify their oppressive tactics, their monopolizing of power, and their destruction of civil society organizations. These are merely face-saving nods to Western democratic practices, which are a way for Arab regimes to maintain the support of Western powers, while in fact they are the worst violators of human rights.

30. [Translator's note] An expression repeated seventeen times a day in Muslim ritual prayer from the Qur'an's Surat al-Fatiha (first sura, or chapter): "Praise belongs to God, Lord of the Worlds, the Lord of Mercy, the Giver of Mercy, Master of the Day of Judgment" (Q. 1: 2–4).

31. Q. 42:38.

32. I have in my hands three important contemporary volumes dealing with the questions of rights and public liberties in Islam in the context of the objectives (*maqasid*) found in al-Shatibi: 'Allal al-Fasi's *The Objectives of the Islamic Shari'a and Its Noble Ethics*; 'Abd al-Hakim Hasan al-'Ayli's *Public Freedoms* (*al-Hurriyyat al-'amma*); finally, Muhammad Fathi 'Uthman's *The Philosophy of Freedom in Islam* (*Falsafat al-hurriyya fi-l-islam*).

33. [Translator's note] The last one, "lineage," is sometimes called "progeny" (so the protection of family) and sometimes either added or used instead of this, "honor."

34. Q. 22:40.

35. Q. 2: 256.

36. [Translator's note] The Arabic word translated as "jurisprudence" is *fiqh*, which designates the body of law developed by the five main schools of Islamic law, as opposed to "God's will as revealed to humanity in the Qur'an and Sunna," which would be the closest definition of Shari'a. Ghannouchi, admittedly, like other Muslim writers, is not entirely consistent about this distinction. As a shortcut perhaps, he will occasionally write "the Shari'a" says this or that, when it might be the consensus of the schools of law (*madhahib*). After all, the sacred texts have to be interpreted by human readers.

37. Muhammad 'Abduh and Muhammad Rashid Rida, *The Lighthouse Commentary* (*Tafsir al-Manar*) (Cairo: Matba'at al-Manar, 1956); Muhammad al-Tahir bin 'Ashur, *Liberation and Enlightenment* (*al-Tahrir wa-t-Tanwir*) (Tunis: al-Dar al-Tunisiyya li-l-Nashr, n.d.).

38. Q. 18:29.

39. Fakhr al-Din Muhammad bin 'Umar al-Razi, *The Great Commentary: Keys to the Unseen* (*al-Tafsir al-kabir: mafatih al-ghayb*), vol. 7 (Beirut: Dar al-Kitab al-'Ilmiyya, 1955), 15–16.

40. [Translator's note] This is a reference to Q. 33:72: "We offered the Trust to the heavens, the earth, and the mountains, yet they refused to undertake it and were afraid of it; mankind undertook it—they have always been very inept and rash." In contemporary Islamic thinking, the Trust is usually connected to the trusteeship of humanity, as expressed in Q. 2:30, "[Prophet], when your Lord told the angels, 'I am putting a successor [deputy, trustee] on earth,' they said, 'How can You put someone

there who will cause damage and bloodshed, when we celebrate Your praise and proclaim Your holiness?' but He said, 'I know things you do not.'" For a comprehensive treatment of this issue of human trusteeship or vicegerency, see David L. Johnston, *Earth, Empire and Sacred Text: Muslims and Christians as Trustees of Creation* (London: Equinox, 2010).

41. [Translator's note] By "abrogation" Ghannouchi is referring to the debates within classical Islam about which verses were canceled out (or abrogated, in Arabic, *al-nasikh* or "the abrogating" and *al-mansukh*, "the abrogated") by subsequent revelation. The classic example is that of wine. At first, Muslims are forbidden to pray under the influence of alcohol (Q. 4:43). Then, a later revelation tells them that although wine has some benefits, its evil outweighs its good (Q. 2:219). Finally, intoxicants are outright forbidden, along with gambling and the use of arrows for making a decision (Q. 5:90). The classical consensus of all Islamic schools of law was that the verses calling believers to use force in fighting unbelievers (the so-called jihad verses) came last in time and therefore abrogate all the verses that call for peaceful resolution of conflicts and for a spreading of the faith in a courteous and friendly manner. See, for instance, Rudolf Peters, *Jihad in Classical and Modern Islam: A Reader*, Princeton Series on the Middle East, ed. Bernard Lewis and Heath W. Lowry (Princeton, NJ: Markus Wiener, 1996). Peters shows from a series of authoritative texts how the consensus changed in the modern period, as Ghannouchi says here.

42. Ibn 'Ashur, *Liberation and Enlightenment*, vol. 3, 26.

43. 'Abduh and Rida, *The Lighthouse Commentary*, vol. 3, 439.

44. United Nations reports indicate that a majority of the world's refugees are Muslims, in spite of the fact that they only represent one-fifth of the world population. And has the world ever seen a tragedy like that of the Palestinians and Bosnians?

45. Sayyid Muhammad Husayn Tabataba'i, *The Balance in Understanding the Qur'an* (*al-Mizan fi Tafsir al-Qur'an*) (Beirut: Mu'assasa al-A'lami, 1972).

46. [Translator's note] The word *shirk* literally means "associating," from the idea of pagans who associate partners with God, whether other gods, persons, or forces of nature. Because in Islam the unity and oneness of God is the primary truth about Him, there is no greater sin than to commit *shirk*.

47. Sayyid Qutb, *In the Shade of the Qur'an*, 9 vols (Beirut and Cairo: Dar al-Shuruq, 1992), vol. 1, n. p.

48. Muhsin al-Mili, *Secularism or the Philosophy of the Death of Man* (*al-'Ilmaniyya aw falsafat mawt al-insan*) (Carthage, Tunisia: Matba'a Tunis, 1986), 38.

49. Qutb, *In the Shade of the Qur'an*, vol. 1.

50. al-Mili, *Secularism*, 391.

51. [Translator's note] The expression "protected status" translates one word in Arabic, *al-dhimma*, a term in Islamic law granting certain rights to religious minorities like Jews and Christians as "the protected people" (*ahl al-dhimma*).

52. The opponents of Islam know very little about it, and their exploitation of this debated concept of *dhimma* has reached a high water mark. Western orientalist scholars allege that the dhimmis were second-class citizens at best and lacked

many basic rights. In this campaign of disinformation, Westerners agree with Arab scholars like Majid Khadduri in his book, *War and Peace in the Law of Islam (al-Silm wa-l-harb fi Shari'at al-islam)* (Beirut: al-Dar al-Muttahida li-l-Nashr, 1973), 237.

Concerning the position of the Maliki school on the issue of "the people of *dhimma*," see Abu 'Umar Yusuf bin 'Abd Allah bin 'Abd al-Birr, *The Comprehensive Collection of Maliki Medinan Jurisprudence (al-Kafi fi fiqh ahl al-madina al-Maliki)*, vol. 1, ed. Muhammad Ahmad Walad Maddi al-Muristani (Riyadh: Maktabat Riyad, 1977), 479.

53. See Rached al-Ghannouchi, *Rights of Citizenship: Status of Non-Muslims in the Islamic State (Huquq al-Muwatana: mawqi' ghayr al-muslim fi al-dawla al-islamiyya)* (Tunis: Dar al-Sahwa, 1988).

On the same topic, the following books have similar titles: Abu al-A'la al-Mawdudi, *Rights of the Protected Minority in the Islamic State (Huquq ahl al-dhimma fi al-dawla al-islamiyya)* (Beirut: Dar al-Fikr, n.d.); 'Abd al-Karim Zaydan, *The Protected Minority (Ahlu-l-Dhimma)* (Beirut: Mu'assassa al-Risala, n.d.); Salim al-'Awwa, *Rights of the Protected Minority (Huquq ahl al-dhimma)* (n.p., n.d.); Yusuf al-Qaradawi, *Non-Muslims in Islamic Society (Ghayr al-muslimim fi-l-mujtama' al-islami)* (Cairo: Maktabat Wahba, 1977).

54. [Translator's note] Islam's rationalists, the Mu'tazilite school, feared that an eternal Qur'an would threaten the oneness of God. If the divine speech, one of God's attributes, was eternal, then it would be on par with God himself, and thus would introduce some kind of division within the Godhead, similar to Jesus as God's Word in Christianity. This was the position the Abbasid caliph al-Ma'mun declared to be official Sunni doctrine in 827, and he instituted a kind of inquisition *(mihna)* to force all scholars and jurists to toe the official line. This was reversed some twenty years later by the caliph al-Mutawakkil.

55. [Translator's note] That is, during the first two generations of Muslims.

56. Ismail al-Faruqi, "Rights of Non-Muslims in the Islamic State" ("*Huquq ghayr al-muslimim ii al-dawla al-islamiyya*"), *al-Muslim al-Mu'asir* 26 (1981).

57. Abu al-A'la Mawdudi, *Islamic Theories and Discourse and Guidance on Politics, Law and Constitution (Nadhariyyat al-Islam wa-hadith fi al-siyasa wa-l-qanun wa-l-dustur)* (Beirut and Damascus: Dar al-Fikr, 1964), 361.

58. According to Archbishop George Khidr, "I am in the heart of this civilization that flourished with the start of Islam and blossomed under its watch." See George Khidr, "Arab Christianity and the West" ("*al-Masihiyya al-'arabiyya wa-l-gharb*"), *al-Hiwar* 1, 2 (Summer 1986). Wajih Kuthrani, *Lebanon's Cultural Issue: Political Discourse and History (al-Mas'ala al-thaqafiyya fi lubnan: al-khitab al-siyasi wa-l-tarikh)* (Beirut: Manshurat Bahsun li-l-Thaqafa, 1984).

59. [Translator's note] "Imam" refers here to the leader of the state, but it is a contested term. It was often used interchangeably with "caliph" during the first few centuries of Islam, but because the term "imam" came to embody such specific meanings for the Shi'i community, it is more controversial today.

60. [Translator's note] Literally, *hudud* means "limits," or the divine limits given for punishing deviant human behavior—behavior that specifically violates "God's rights." And, importantly, the penalties for these crimes are specified in the Qur'an and the Sunna. In classical Islamic law, these include sexual offenses (adultery, fornication, homosexuality, or accusing someone of these without producing four credible eye witnesses), apostasy, consumption of intoxicants, theft, and armed robbery.

61. Muhammad Salim al-Razuri, *Public Freedoms in Islam* (*al-Hurriyyat al-'amma fi-l-islam*) (Cairo: Mu'assasa Shabab al-Jami'a, n.d.), 95.

62. al-Qama bin Qays al-Nakha'i was considered one of the best scholars of the Followers generation (second generation of Muslims).

63. Narrated by Malik in his *The Great Body of Laws* (*al-Mudawwana al-Kubra*).

64. [Translator's note] Three out of four of the "Rightly Guided Caliphs," Muhammad's successors in Medina (632–665) are mentioned in this paragraph.

65. [Translator's note] "Maghreb" is the Arabic word for "west," but here it refers to North Africa, which was colonized by the French. Ghannouchi and other Muslim leaders and intellectuals see Western colonialism and the continued interference of these powers in the postcolonial world as the new manifestations of a Christian crusading spirit.

66. Fahmi Huwaydi, *al-Majalla* (no title, n.d.).

67. [Translator's note] Literally, "freedom of the self and right to the divine honoring of the human person."

68. Islamic Council of the United Kingdom, "The Universal Islamic Declaration of Human Rights" (London, 1981).

69. [Translator's note] This is a reference to Q. 2:34, where we read that after Adam had, upon God's bidding, told the angels "the nature of all things," they bowed down to him, "[b]ut not Iblis [Satan], who refused and was arrogant." Especially in the modern commentaries, Adam's being named by God as His trustee or deputy and his ability to "give the names of all things" (verse 30), is seen as applying to the whole human race, as Ghannouchi puts it here. So the angels' bow was to humanity as a whole.

70. 'Uthman, *Foundations*, 137.

71. Ibn Kathir, as quoted in ibid., 198.

72. Q. 17:33.

73. Q. 4:29.

74. Quoted in 'Uthman, *Foundations*.

75. Q. 24:28.

76. Q. 68:4.

77. [Translator's note] I am translating *al-fitra al-bashariyya* as "human nature," but this might be misleading to the non-Muslim. The term is an Islamic theological term, found only once in the Qur'an (30:30) but full of significance for Muslims. It certainly should be connected to the trusteeship of humanity and the profound dignity given to humanity at creation. But it is also a statement of difference in dialogue with

Christians. Humankind's fitra from the time of creation is pure and is in no way sullied by any kind of "original sin."

78. Q. 2:111.

79. Q. 10:101.

80. Q. 2:193.

81. Muhammad Husayn Fadlallah, "The Concept of Freedom in Islam" (n.p., n.d.). [Translator's note] Fadlallah was a great Shi'i scholar, often seen as the spiritual father of the Lebanese Hezbullah movement; d. 2010.

82. 'Abd al-Majid al-Najjar, *Freedom of Opinion and its Role in the Islamic Civilization* (*Hurriyat al-ra'y wa-dawruha fi-l-hadara al-islamiyya*) (n.p., n.d.), 64; al-Fasi, *The Objectives of the Islamic Shari'a*, 258.

83. al-Najjar, *Freedom of Opinion*, 64.

84. al-Fasi, *The Objectives*, 258.

85. Mustafa Kamal Wasfi, *Ownership in Islam* (*al-Milkiyya fi-l-islam*) (Rabat, Morocco: Wizarat al-Awqaf wa-l-Shu'un al-Islamiyya, n. d.), 73.

86. [Translator's note] Zakat is one of Islam's five pillars, and it consists of giving alms yearly to the poor (and other charitable causes, including the spreading of Islam) representing 2.5 percent of one's net worth.

87. [Translator's note] An oft-repeated Qur'anic expression (e.g., Q. 3:104, 110; 7:157; 9:71).

88. Q. 28:76.

89. Q. 96:6–7.

90. Q. 59:7.

91. Q. 4:5.

92. Some of the most learned among them being Sayyid Qutb, Mustafa Siba'i, Abu Zahra, 'Abd al-Qadir 'Awda, 'Allal al-Fasi, al-Bahi al-Khawli, Mustafa Kamal Wasfi, Malik bin Nabi, Munir Shafiq, and many others. This wide current of thought was preceded by Abu al-A'la al-Mawdudi, 'Abd al-Salam al-'Ibadi, and Salih Karkar. See Salih Karkar, *The Theory of Value* (*Nadhariyya al-Qima*) (Carthage, Tunisia: Matba'a Tunis, 1986).

93. 'Abbas Mahmud al-'Aqqad, *Democracy in Islam* (*al-Dimuqratiyya fi-l-islam*) (Cairo: Dar al-Ma'arif, 1971), 62.

94. [Translator's note] According to a majority of Muslim scholars today, what the Qur'an is forbidding as "usury" (*riba*) is not a bank charging a fee for financial transactions (which Islamic banks also charge), but their charging exorbitant and exploitive interest rates, which as "usury" is also forbidden in the Torah.

95. Q. 67:15.

96. Q. 62:10.

97. As narrated by al-Tabari.

98. Found in the collection of Bukhari.

99. As narrated by al-Tabari.

100. Muhammad al-Ghazali, *Islam and the Ways of Socialism* (*al-Islam wa-l-manahij al-ishtirakiyya*), 2nd ed. (Cairo: Nahdat Misr li-l-Tiba'a wa-l-Nashr wa-l-Tawzi', 2005).

101. Found in the collection of Bukhari.

102. [Translator's note] No reference given.

103. Abu Muhammad 'Ali bin Ahmad bin Hazm, *The Ornament* (*al-Muhalla*) (Tehran: n.p., n.d.).

104. For this, see the judicious study, a truly substantive contribution to Islamic thought, Yusuf al-Qaradawi, *The Jurisprudence of Zakat* (*Fiqh al-zakat*), 6th ed. (Beirut: Mu'assasa al-Risala, 1989); and Mahmud Abu Su'ud, *The Contemporary Jurisprudence of Zakat* (*Fiqh al-zakat al-mu'asir*) (Kuwait: Dar al-Qalam, n.d.).

105. Q. 5:1.

106. Q. 2:282.

107. This verse provides a strong foundation for contracts in an Islamic society, just as it represents a cardinal rule upon which we can base the work of trade unions in their struggle against the owners who arm themselves from a theoretical point of view with the principle that people are free to enter into contracts or not—a principle that becomes void of content unless the conditions of the contract stipulate the mutual equivalence of both parties. It would be better to begin this subject with the above quoted verse from the second sura, as did the martyr 'Abd al-Qadir 'Awda in his book, *The Islamic Criminal Legislation in Comparison with Positive Law* (*al-Tashri' al-jana'i al-islami muqaranan bi-l-qanun al-wad'i*), vol. 1 (Alexandria: Dar Nashr al-Thaqafa, 1949).

108. This was narrated by al-Hakim. [Translator's note] A tenth-century hadith scholar from Persia, whose full name is Muhammad bin 'Abdullah al-Hakim.

109. Among the best books published on this topic in Tunisia, see al-Tahir al-Gharbi, *Nutritional Systems in Islam* (*Nudhum al-taghdhiyya fi-l-islam*) (Tunis: n.p., n.d.).

110. [Translator's note] Like during the Ramadan fast, pregnant mothers, the sick, and those traveling were exempt from fasting and were able to make it up later.

111. There is much evidence of this in the time of the Prophet (PBUH), of his Rightly Guided successors, and beyond as well. See Mustafa al-Siba'i, *Among the Wonders of our Civilization* (*Min rawa'i' hadaratina*) (Beirut: al-Maktab al-Islami, n.d.).

112. Found in the collection of Bukhari.

113. Q. 2:228.

114. Q. 4:1.

115. Q. 24:32.

116. Q. 17:31. See how al-Mawdudi used this verse to touch on birth control and explain why it must be forbidden: *Fikrat tahdid al-nasl wa-l-dawla al-islamiyya* (The Idea of Birth Control and the Islamic State) (Beirut: Dar al-Fikr, 1977). See also the resolutions made by the Islamic conferences that prohibited this kind of policy and considered them a Zionist-imperialist plan to stop the spread of Islam. In particular, note the fatwa issued by the great shaykh Ibn 'Ashur on this same topic published by the Kuwaiti journal *al-Mujtama'*, in which he forbids this evil policy.

117. Q. 24:32.

118. The expression "chaste women" means women who consider adultery and fornication filthy and shrink back from them because such behavior offends their honor. As for the woman who commits sexual sin, or who if she refrains from it does not see it

as reprehensible, she is no wife for a Muslim, whether she is Muslim or an unbeliever. The European Council for Fatwa and Research makes an exception for the woman who converts to Islam but whose husband keeps his own religion. She is allowed to remain in that marriage so that she can guide him to the truth and protect the family's integrity—that is, if the husband does not show open hostility to Islam.

119. Found in the collection of Ibn Majah.

120. Sigrid Hunke, "The Arabs' Sun Shines on the West" ("*Shams al-'arab tasta'u 'ala-l-gharb*") in *Rabita al-'Alam al-'Arabi* 10, no. 8 (November 1972).

121. See, for example, Abu 'Abd Allah Muhammd bin Abi Bakr bin Qayyim al-Jawziyya, *A Gift to the Beloved on the Rulings of the Newborn (Tuhfat al-mawdud bi-l-ahkam al-mawlud)* (Mumbai, India: al-Jami'a al-Hindiyya al-'Arabiyya, 1961); Abu al-Faraj 'Abd al-Rahman bin 'Ali bin al-Jawzi, *Heartfelt Advice to a Son (Liftat al-kabid fi-l-nasihat al-walad)*, with commentary by Marwan Qabbani (Beirut: al-Kitab al-Islami, 1982).

122. Constitution of the Republic of Tunisia (Tunis: al-Matba'a al-Rasmiyya, n.d.), Preamble. [Translator's note] The 2014 Tunisian Constitution is available online. Articles 38 to 40 very explicitly guarantee the rights to health care, education, and work, https://www.constituteproject.org/constitution/Tunisia_2014.pdf.

123. UDHR, Article 25 (1); quoted in 'Uthman, *Foundations*, 492.

124. Q. 59:10.

125. Q. 8:75.

126. Q. 4:36, Yusuf Ali.

127. [Translator's note] Neither this hadith nor the ones preceding it were given any reference.

128. [Translator's note] I am translating *jahiliyya* as "ignorance" here, but the reader must know that there is a much wider context to this word's meaning. From the time Islamic history started to be written down in the second and third Islamic centuries, *jahiliyya* came to denote the contrast between the light of the Islamic revelation and the darkness that preceded it in the mostly pagan Arabia of the seventh century. That is the meaning here.

129. [Translator's note] The word *salafiyya* here refers to a conservative understanding of the texts; that is, an attempt to go back to the sources of Islam by way of reforming what one considers to be today's deviations from that original message. The first great modern reformer was Muhammad 'Abduh (d. 1905), who first used the adjective *salafi* in our era. Though he became Egypt's Grand Mufti (the highest official position for an Islamic scholar/jurist), he was clearly a reformer who believed that many Islamic beliefs and practices needed to be updated in light of the changing times. This is in contrast to the use of the word "salafi" today, very much an ultraconservative and puritanical movement within Islam; see, for instance, Roel Meijer, ed., *Global Salafism: Islam's New Religious Movement* (Oxford: Oxford University Press, 2009).

For Ghannouchi, writing in his prison cell in the 1980s, salafism was still a positive label and his own use of reason in interpreting the texts is similar to the way 'Abduh used the term.

130. See, for example, Munir Shaqiq, *Scientific Theses* (*Utruhat ʿilmiyya*) (Tunis: Dar al-Buraq, n.d.); Muhsin al-Mili, *The Phenomenon of the Islamic Left* (*Dhahirat al-yasar al-islamiyya*) (Carthage, Tunisia: Matbaʿa Tunis, 1985).

131. ʿAbd Allah bin Kiran writes, "Wahhabism is none other than one kind of *salafiyya*; but for us, *salafiyya* is an objective reading of Islam's sacred texts." Quoted in François Burgat, *Islamism in North Africa: The Voice from the South* (*L'Islamisme au Maghreb: la voix du sud*) (Paris: Karthala, 1988), 33.

132. [Translator's note] No more reference provided.

133. Q. 107:4–7.

134. Ahmad bin Muhammad al-Dardir, *The Great Explanation of the Precious Content* (*al-Sharh al-kabir ʿala-l-matn al-khalil*); and ʿUthman, *Foundations*, 300.

135. The English translation is available online at this official Iranian website: https://www.constituteproject.org/constitution/Iran_1989.pdf.

136. On the Iranian constitution, see the excellent study by Muhammad ʿAli al-Taskhiri, *About the Islamic Constitution* (*Hawl al-dustur al-islami*) (Tehran: Munadhdhama al-Iʿla al-Islami, 1987); Muhammad Salim al-ʿAwa, *On the Political Organization of the Islamic State* (*Fi nidham al-siyasi li-dawla al-islamiyya*) (Cairo and Beirut: Dar al-Shuruq, 1989).

137. Q. 55:7–9.

138. Q. 9:6.

139. [Translator's note] No reference given for this quote and the preceding one.

PART II RIGHTS AND POLITICAL FREEDOMS

1. [Translator's note] Or "authorities," meaning, legislative, executive, and judicial powers.

2. ʿAli ʿAbd al-Wahid Wafi, *Human Rights in Islam* (*Huquq al-insan fi-l-islam*), 4 vols., rev. ed. (Cairo: Dar Nahdat Misr, 1967).

3. ʿAbd al-Hadi Abu Talib, *Authoritative Reference for Constitutional Law and Political Institutions* (*al-Marjiʿ fi-l-qanun al-dusturi wa-l-muʾassasat al-siyasiyya*), vol. 2 (Casablanca, Morocco: Dar al-Kitab, 1980), 146.

4. Fathi ʿUthman, *Foundations of Islamic Political Thought* (*Usul al-fikr al-siyasi al-islami*), vol. 2 (Beirut: Muʾassasat al-Risala, 1984), 243.

5. [Translator's note] This is from the 1959 Tunisian constitution, available online in English at unpan1.un.org/intradoc/groups/public/documents/un-dpadm/unpan042351.pdf. Where there are differences, I have followed the author's version. It can be confusing, as it was amended in 1999 and in 2002. Tunisia now has a completely new constitution as of 2014.

6. Some of these provisions have been amended after the coup against Bourguiba by Zine el Abeddine Ben Ali. The position of vice president was abolished, presidential powers were expanded, and the prime minister's powers were added. In practice, there was also a return to presidency for life.

7. See "Mubarak's superficial, Tunisia-style, reforms" (Islahat Mubarak "nos kom" ala al-tarika al-tunisiya), alarabnews.com, n.d.

8. There was the administrative statute known as number 108, which forbade the modest Islamic dress.
9. See "Amnesty International Report 2006—Tunisia" (May 23), available online, https://www.refworld.org/docid/447ff7bc7.html.

3. BASIC DEMOCRATIC PRINCIPLES

1. Maurice Duverger, *Political Institutions and Constitutional Law (Institutions politiques et droit constitutionnel)* (Paris: Presses Universitaires de France, 1980), 43.
2. [Translators' note] Bennabi's more than thirty books were mostly written in French, so it makes sense to keep his name in its French spelling, just as we do for Ghannouchi. As mentioned in the introduction, Bennabi was Ghannouchi's foremost mentor from the start.
3. Malik Bennabi, *Islam and Democracy (al-Islam wa-l-dimuqratiyya)*, trans. Rached Ghannouchi and Najib al-Rihan (Carthage, Tunisia: Matba'a Tunis, 1983), 14–15.
4. Ibid.
5. 'Abbas Mahmud al-Aqqad, *Democracy in Islam (al-Dimuqratiyya fi-l-islam)* (Cairo: Dar al-Ma'arif, 1971), 25.
6. Abd al-Hadi Abu Talib, *Authoritative Reference on Constitutional Law and Political Institutions (al-Marja' fi-l-qanun al-dusturi wa-l-mu'assasat al-siyasiyya)* (Casablanca, Morocco: Dar al-Kitab, 1980), 30.
7. 'Allal al-Fasi, *The Objectives of the Islamic Shari'a and Its Noble Virtues (Maqasid al-Shari'a al-islamiyya wa-makarimuha)* (Rabat, Morocco: Matba'a al-Risala, 1979), 18–19.
8. Mahmud Helmi, *The Islamic Political System Compared to Contemporary Systems (Nidham al-Hukm al-islami muqaranan bi-l-nudhum al-mu'asira)*, vol. 2 (Cairo: Dar al-Fikr al-'Arabi, 1973), 116.
9. Muhammad Taha Badawi, "A Study of the Islamic Political System" ("Ba'th fi-l-nidham al-siyasi al-islami"), in *Methods of the Orientalists (Manahij al-mustashriqin)* (Cairo: Jami'a al-Duwal al-'Arabiyya, n.d.), 112; Burhan Ghalyun, *The State and Religion (al-Dawla wa-l-din)* (Beirut: al-Mu'assasa al-'Arabiyya li-l-Dirasat wa-l-Nashr, 1991), 32.
10. *The Idea of Law (Fikrat Qanun)*, trans. Salim al-Suwis, ed. Salim Basisu, 'Alam al-Ma'rifa Series, 47 (Kuwait: al-Majlis al-Watani li-l-Thaqafa wa-l-funun wa-l-Adab, n. d.), 40.
11. Ibid.
12. 'Abd al-Wahhab al-Kiyali et al., eds. *The Encyclopedia of Politics (Mawsu'at al-siyasa)*, vol. 3 (Beirut: al-Mu'assasa al-'Arabiyya li-l-Dirasat wa-l-Nashr, 1979), 451.
13. 'Abd al-Hamid al-Mutawalli, *Constitutional Law and the Political Systems (al-Qanun al-dusturi wa-l-andhima al-siyasiyya)*, vol. 1 (Cairo: n.p., n.d.), 135.
14. Dennis Lloyd, *The Idea of Law (Fikrat al-qanun)*, trans. Salim al-Suwis (Kuwait: National Council for Culture, Arts, and Literature, n.d.), 204–208. Fred Donner has this to say about the term "state": "A general and abstract term, which becomes even more obscure when we try to meditate on it or reflect on it with more precision." See

Fred Donner, "The Formation of the Islamic State" (*"Takwin al-dawla al-islamiyya"*), *Ijtihad* 4, no. 13 (Fall 1991).

15. [Translator's note] He is likely referring to Oliver Wendell Holmes Jr., the U.S. Supreme Court justice who wrote a book entitled *The Common Law* (1881).

16. Lloyd, *The Idea of Law*, 242.

17. Ibid., 14–15. The state is an elusive concept, torn between the power seized by an individual and the legitimacy of an order founded on law. The French jurist Georges Burdeau sarcastically asks, "Who can claim to have truly seen the state?" See Georges Burdeau, *The State* (*L'État*) (Paris: Éditions du Seuil, 1992), 13.

18. Rousseau in his heroic work on the foundation of the state establishes its legitimacy and nature by imagining a stage in which people lived in a state of nature—that is, spontaneous individuals—but whose free will leads them to create a common life in which each one gives up some of their natural freedom for the sake of life in society. This naturally requires the presence of law and political authority, both expressing the general will of the citizens. But the Enlightenment thinkers refused the idea of a social contract and saw it as a result of wishful thinking and imagination. See Lloyd, *The Idea of Law*, 239.

19. Dennis Lloyd writes, "Thus we find ourselves entangled in a vicious circle, since sovereignty confers on the law its legality, but then the law conforms to the will of the ruler. Despite this lack of logic, the idea is acceptable as a means of constructing the state." *The Idea of Law*, 210.

20. Ibid., 231.

21. Ibid., 138–157.

22. Sulayman al-Tamawi, *A Digest of Political Organization and Administration* (*al-Wajiz fi-l-nitham al-hukm wa-l-idara*) (Cairo: n.p., n.d.), 35.

23. This was tied to the era of the Cold War when the UN Security Council was paralyzed in its ability to apply international law. Now its authority has become a global government whose will completely surpasses national wills and an effective principle of intervention within national borders. This of course makes the idea of the state's absolute authority even more illusory, as it allows for an authority that transcends its own authority and national laws.

24. 'Abd al-Hadi Abu Talib, *Authoritative Reference on Constitutional Law and Political Institutions* (*al-Maraji' fi-l-qanun al-dusturi wa-l-mu'assassat al-siyasiyya*) (Casablanca, Morocco: Dar al-Kitab, 1980), 34.

25. Duverger, *Political Institutions and Constitutional Law* (*Institutions politiques et droit constitutionnel*) (Paris: Presses Universitaires de France, 1973), 56.

26. [Translator's note] Maurice Duverger (d. 2014) was a French jurist and sociologist, best known for Duverger's Law, which says that proportional representation favors a multiparty system, while plurality rule tends to favor a two-party system.

27. Duverger, *Political Institutions and Constitutional Law*, 54.

28. 'Abd Allah Fahd al-Nafisi, "About Islam and Democracy" (*"Hawl al-islam wa-l-dimuqratiyya"*), *al-Mujtama'a* 8 (December 13, 1983).

29. Muhammad Abu al-Qasim Hajj Hamad, *The Second Islamic Internationalism* (*al-'Alamiyya al-islamiyya al-thaniyya*) (Beirut: Dar al-Masira, 1979), 210.

30. The philosophy of Darwin, Hegel, and Nietzsche is clear about justifying and legislating for the benefit of the strong to the detriment of the weak. Examples of this include the black and indigenous peoples of the United States, North Africans in France, and the organized ethnic cleansing endured by the peoples of Palestine and Bosnia at the hands of regimes that claim to be democratic or supported by democratic regimes. This is the inhumane side of Western democracy, but what stands out in the end is that there is a kind of defective democracy, or one that suffers a kind of deep dysfunction. In any case, it is a thousand times better in its dealing with nations than the despotism that is destroying several Arab nations, where the state has transformed into what can only be described as a repressive, complex, and terrifying apparatus.

31. [Translator's note] The Qur'an expressly forbids a practice of the time, the burying alive of female infants (81:8).

32. Q. 49:29.

33. Bennabi, "Islam and Democracy."

34. For more on this, see Fathi 'Uthman, *Islamic Thought and Development* (*al-Fikr al-islami wa-l-tatawwur*) (Beirut: Dar al-Qalam, 1961); and Abu Zayd 'Abd al-Rahman Ibn Khaldun, *Ibn Khaldun's Introduction* (*Muqaddimat Ibn Khaldun*). Ibn Khaldun put political systems into three categories: a natural government (that is, rule by the strongest); a government based on reason and led by the wise; a government based on God's law or deputized by God. It is possible to insert a democratic rule within the "government by reason" category.

35. Rached Ghannouchi, *Articles* (*Maqallat*) (Paris: Dar al-Karwan, 1984).

36. Narrated by Malik b. Anas in his *Muwatta*.

4. THE BASIC PRINCIPLES OF ISLAMIC GOVERNANCE

1. Muhammad Iqbal, *The Renewal of Religious Thought in Islam* (*Tajdid al-takfir al-dini fi-l-islam*), trans. 'Abbas Mahmud, ed. 'Abd al-'Aziz al-Maghari and Mahdi 'Allam (Beirut: Dar Asiyya, 1985).

2. [Translator's note] The Mu'tazilites (or *mu'tazila*) were a rationalist school of law and theology that reached the peak of its influence in the ninth century but gradually declined thereafter. The puritanical Kharijites (or *khawarij*) were an early splinter group that waged war on the caliphate. Ghannouchi is likely referring to the Ibadi sect (who do not see themselves as Kharijites, but who are often identified with them, though they are moderate and nonviolent), which is represented today in Oman, Algeria, Tunisia, and Libya.

3. 'Ali 'Abd al-Raziq, *Islam and the Foundations of Political Power: A Study and Documents by Muhammad 'Imara* (*al-Islam wa-usul al-hukm: dirasa wa-watha'iq bi qalam Muhammad 'Imara*), 2nd ed. (Beirut: al-Mu'assasa al-'Arabiyya li-l-Dirasat wa-l-Nashr, 1988); Muhammad 'Imara, *The Struggle for Islam and the Foundations of Political Power* (*Ma'rakat al-islam wa- usul al-hukm*) (Cairo: Dar al-Shuruq, 1989).

4. [Translator's note] Ghannouchi's adjective here [*la'ikiyya*] is a transliteration of the French *laïque*, which reflects France's specific brand of muscular republicanism and its desire to rid the public sphere of all religious symbols, like its ban of the *hijab* in

public spaces and the total ban of the *niqab* (full veil) in public. But his use of the word here is to denote all secular regimes, even those like Egypt, which while paying lip service to the Shari'a as a key source of law are not true Islamic states. Then, too, his use of the term reflects Tunisia's colonial past.

5. [Translator's note] I used "strict monotheistic perspective" to translate Islam's "*tawhidic* spirit." The word *tawhid*, literally meaning "unification," refers to Islam's central declaration that God is One and that the greatest sin is to attribute partners to Him (*shirk*). From an Islamist perspective, to separate politics from religion is to undercut God's all-encompassing rule, and therefore to exclude God from the political arena is tantamount to deifying human politics, thereby committing the sin of *shirk*. It is not surprising that Ghannouchi added "comprehensive" in the third edition of this book: "Islam's *tawhidic* and comprehensive spirit."

6. [Translator's note] The Hijra is the "emigration" of the persecuted Muslims from Mecca to Medina in 622, the beginning of the Islamic calendar.

7. [Translator's note] This is a technical term in Islamic law referring to the effort made by the highest-ranking jurists to craft new legal rules covering new circumstances on the basis of the sacred texts and the juridical methods established before them.

8. [Translator's note] In ordinary Sunni parlance, an imam is the leader of a local mosque, literally, the "one who prays *in front of* the others." In this context Ghannouchi uses it as a synonym of ruler, sultan ("one with political authority"), or caliph, and because of that I capitalize it here. This usage goes back to the Islamic legal texts from the eleventh century on, which dealt with constitutional law.

9. The great scholar Abu al-Hasan al-Nadawi wrote a pamphlet on this topic, entitled *Abu Bakr's War against Apostasy (Ridda wa-la Aba Bakr laha)* (Tunis: n.p., n.d.), in which he writes the following: "As is well known, many of the apostates did not object to Islamic doctrine or its rituals, but rather to its sociopolitical dimension, and in particular they refused to submit to the central authority by having to pay *zakat* taxes. Even 'Umar bin al-Khattab was confused about the order to kill them, as long as they believed the doctrine and practiced the ritual prayers—and this, in spite of Abu Bakr's very clear vision: *zakat* like *salat* (ritual prayers) is commanded in the texts—to deny one is to deny the other. He said, 'By God, I will fight anyone who differentiates between prayer and *zakat*.'" By this he condemned the first 'secular' armed rebellion movement that sought to impose its opinion by force. Thus in fighting the apostates Abu Bakr was not fighting an intellectual current he might have faced. Rather, he was doing battle with an armed rebellion against the authority set up by the Shari'a, a movement that was betting on division and darkness and seeking to return to the previous state of ignorance.

10. Q. 33:4.

11. From the earliest biography of the Prophet, *Sirat Ibn Hisham*.

12. [Translator's note] This is a very different conception of *ijma'* ("consensus") from that held historically by the Islamic legal schools. Then it was one of two major "rational" sources of the Shari'a (together with *qiyas*, "analogical reasoning"), but this interpretation was entirely in the hands of highly trained scholars in the Islamic sciences ('*ulama*'). Ghannouchi's reinterpretation of the umma's role, though not revolutionary in more liberal circles, is nevertheless controversial in Islamist ones. Democracy

becomes here a hermeneutical lens through which to rethink traditional Islamic political and legal theory.

13. The Twelver Shia disagree with the Zaydi and Ismaili Shia on the organization of this list and even about the names on it—that is, the list of those entrusted by God to succeed the Prophet (PBUH).

14. [Translator's note] The author had a long footnote here on the Ayatollah Khomeini, leader of the 1979 Iranian Revolution. Ghannouchi argues that the doctrine the Ayatollah invoked, *wilayat al-faqih* ("rule of the jurist"), gives the top Iranian clerics the final say in political affairs. It undercuts the power of the people to determine how the state is run and who runs it. Therefore, it undermines the umma's right to shura, or mutual consultation. This goes back to the Shia idea of the infallibility of the Imams, who in Shi'i terminology are the descendants of 'Ali, the fourth caliph and the Prophet's cousin and son-in-law. Iran is by far the largest Shi'i nation, and like its fellow Shia in neighboring Iraq (60 percent of the population), they are "Twelver" Shia—meaning that they count twelve descendants after 'Ali who inherited his spiritual leadership as the true heir of the Prophet by virtue of being his cousin. These are the "Imams" for the Shia (I capitalize the term to differentiate these Imams from the Sunni term, which mainly designates a leader in a mosque. That being said, the Sunnis in classical Islam also used the word interchangeably for the ruler or head of state. Hence, the term "imamate" you will encounter later in the chapter.

15. The imam, even if he is called "caliph," holds an office with no special aura, for it is the umma as a whole that carries the sanctity of the Prophet's mantle of leadership and the legitimacy of the highest political establishment. See Ridwan al-Sayyid, "A Vision of the Caliphate and Building the State in Islam" (*"Ru'yat al-khilafa wa-bunyat al-dawla fi-l-islam"*), *al-Ijtihad* 4, no. 13 (Fall 1991). See the following books on politics for a definition of the imamate by al-Mawardi, Ibn Ya'la, Ibn Taymiyya among the ancients, and those by recent authors like 'Abd al-Qadir 'Awda, Diya' al-Din al-Rayyis, Fathi 'Uthman, Muhammad Salim al-'Awwa, Mawdudi, and others. Ghazali (d. 1111) wrote, "Religion is the foundation and the ruler is its guardian, and that which has no foundation is destroyed, while that which has no guardian is scandalous" (quoted from Abu Hamid Muhammad bin Ahmad al-Ghazali, *Reviving the Sciences of Religion (Ihya' 'ulum al-din)*, 4 vols., vol. 1 (Cairo: al-Maktaba al-Tijariyya al-Kubra, n.d.), 16.

16. See Muhammad Asad, *Islam's Methods of Government (Manahij al-islam fi-l-hukm)*, trans. Mansur Mahmud Madi (Beirut: Dar al-'Ilm li-l-Malayin, 1975), 70–72.

17. The Islamic community's impotence has become obvious in the shadow of the secular nations that sow division in the face of Muslim suffering in Bosnia, Burma, Somalia, and Palestine.

18. Q. 42:13. [Translator's note] My translation. Yusuf Ali has "that ye should remain steadfast in Religion," and "Uphold the faith." *The Holy Qur'an: Text, Translation and Commentary by Abdullah Yusuf Ali* (New York: Tahrike Tarsile Qur'an, 1987). My more literal rendering of the phrase, I believe, better captures the Islamist interpretation.

19. [Translator's note] Ghannouchi read this in French: François Burgat, *L'islamism au Maghreb: La voix du Sud* (Paris: Payot, 2008).

20. [Translator's note] The Charter of Medina was a short document of confederation drawn up in the beginning of Muhammad's coming to Medina at the invitation of the two main tribes, the Aws and Khazraj, who after decades of rivalries and conflicts realized their need for a skilled arbitrator to rule the oasis. To complicate the picture, Medina also had three Jewish tribes. The charter, which is echoed in the famous biography of Muhammad by Ibn Ishaq, later revised and completed by Ibn Hisham (*al-Sira al-nabawiyya*), granted pagans and Jews freedom of religion on the condition that they submitted to the political rule of Muhammad as both prophet and statesman.

21. Q. 49:13.

22. See the political documents in Muhammad Hamid Allah, A *Collection of Political Documents from the Time of the Prophet and the Rightly-Guided Caliphs* (*Majmu'at al-watha'iq al-siyasiyya li-l-fiahd al-nabawi wa-l-khilafa al-rashidiyya*), 3rd expanded and annotated ed. (Beirut: Dar al-Irshad, 1969); and Ma'ruf al-Dawalibi, "The State and Political Authority in Islam" ("*al-Dawla wa-l-sulta fi-l-islam*"), a paper presented at "Moral and Political Vision of Islam" (a UNESCO conference, n.d.).

    Ibn Hisham (d. 833) provided the text of the charter in his biography. See Abu Muhammad 'Abd al-Malik bin Hisham, *The Biography of the Prophet* (*al-Sira al-nabawiyya*) (Beirut: Dar al-Fikr, n.d.).

23. Q. 8:72. See for the commentary on this verse, Abul A'la Mawdudi, *Towards Understanding the Qur'an*, vol. 3, trans. and ed. by Zafar Ishaq Ansari (Markfield, UK: Islamic Foundation, 2007), 172.

24. Quoted in al-Dawalibi, *The State and Political Authority in Islam*, 8. His rebuttal of 'Iyyad bin 'Ashur's views was also a rebuttal of the position espoused by Jewish scholar of Islam, William Zartman, in the following passage: "Professor 'Iyyad bin 'Ashur from Tunisia spoke after William Zartman and I thought I would find in his words a correction of what Zartman had declared, but there he was, drinking from the same cup."

25. Malik Bennabi, *Islam and Democracy* (*al-Islam wa-l-dimuqratiyya*), trans. Rached Ghannouchi and Naguib al-Rihan (Carthage, Tunisia: Matba'a Tunis, 1983.

26. Q. 57:20.

27. [Translator's note] The Qur'an mentions it in several places as a tree in hell. For instance, "The tree of Zaqqum will be food for the sinners: [hot] as molten metal, it boils in their bellies like seething water" (Q. 44:44–46).

28. Q. 55:46.

29. Fahmi Huwaydi, *The Qur'an and Political Authority* (*al-Qur'an wa-l-sultan*) (Cairo and Beirut: Dar al-Shuruq, n.d.); 'Abd al-Majid al-Najjar, *The Human Vicegerency: Between Reason and the People* (*Khilafat al-insan bayna al-'aql wa-l-nas*) (Beirut: Dar al-Gharb al-Islami, 1988).

30. The martyr 'Abd al-Qadir 'Awda wrote, "The only system of governance Islam knows is based upon two pillars. The first is obedience to God and the avoidance of doing

anything He has prohibited; and the second is shura, that is, the Qur'anic command that there be shura [mutual consultation] among the people. And if governance rests upon those two pillars, then it is pure Islamic governance. Let it then be called: the caliphate, the imamate, the kingdom—all of these designations are equivalent. But if it rests upon other pillars, then it is not Islamic." See 'Abd al-Qadir 'Awda, *Islam and Our Legal Realities (al-Islam wa-awda'una al-qanuniyya)* (Cairo: n.p., n.d.), 77.

31. Q. 42:10.

32. Q. 47:33.

33. Q. 5:44.

34. Q. 4:65.

35. Q. 5:50.

36. Q. 4:59.

37. [Translator's note] Just a reminder for the uninitiated: a "hadith" is actually one report by a Companion of Muhammad, or one of the Followers of the next generation, on what the Prophet said or did—from a phrase to several pages at the most, and then transmitted as an unbroken chain by trustworthy persons in each succeeding generation up to the second or even third century of Islam. With time, as many reports were seen to have been fabricated to bolster one or another position being debated in the Muslim community, critical techniques were developed to sift out the spurious from the authentic, with some in between. There are six main collections that are prized among Sunnis, then up to five more with lesser authority, starting with Imam Malik's *Muwatta* (see next note). Sunna is the name for all these collections of hadiths (the Prophet's godly "example"), but "hadith" here for Ghannouchi, like many others, stands in for "Sunna."

38. Abu 'Abd Allah Malik bin Amru bin Anas, *The Well-Trodden Path (al-Muwatta)* (Beirut: Dar al-Fikr, n.d.).

39. Both narrations are found in Abu Dawud's collection.

40. [Translator's note] The *jinn* are invisible creatures referred to in the Qur'an. Some are good and some bad, but some have also become Muslim by hearing the beauty of the recited Qur'an.

41. Sobhi 'Abduh Sa'id, *Political Authority and Its Foundations in the Islamic System (al-Hukm wa-usul al-hukm fi-l-nidham al-islami)* (Cairo: Jami'at al-Qahira, 1985), 70–71.

42. [Translator's note] *Jahiliyya* refers to the "age of ignorance," a label that Muslim scholars have given to the pre-Islamic society of Arabia.

43. Sayyid Qutb, *In the Shade of the Qur'an (Fi dhilal al-Qur'an)*, 9th ed., vol. 2 (Cairo and Beirut: Dar al-Shuruq, 1980), 888.

44. [Translator's note] The word here for "infidels" or "unbelievers" is *kafir*, and, consequently, the action of declaring a fellow Muslim *kafir* is *takfir*. See the Amman Message for perhaps the greatest consensus ever among Muslims on the forbidding of *takfir*, on the definition of who is a Muslim, and on who is qualified to give a legal opinion (*fatwa*): http://ammanmessage.com/.

45. al-Zamakhshari, *The Revealer (al-Kashshaf)*, vol. 2 (Beirut: Dar Ihya' al-Turath al-'Arabi, n.d.).

46. Wahba al-Zuhayli, *The Illuminating Commentary (al-Tafsir al-munir)* (Dar al-Fikr, 1990), 206–207.

47. [Translator's note] He is referring to Q. 5:48 and parallels, "So judge between them by what Allah has revealed" (Yusuf Ali).

48. Tahir Ibn 'Ashur, *Liberation and Illumination in the Commentary of the Generous Qur'an (al-Tahrir wa-l-tanwir fi-l-tafsir al-qur'an al-karim)*, vol. 7 (Tunis: al-Dar al-Tunisiyya li-l-Nashr, n.d.), 212.

49. The former Tunisian minister of education, Muhammad Charfi, was clear in the press conference in which he laid the foundations for the various curricula and the religious education curriculum in particular. He emphasized the National Charter and the Universal Declaration of Human Rights as the highest authority, even concerning what to add or take out in religion itself. Jihad is about violence, which contradicts the call to peace, so it must be deleted from the curriculum, as well as the sections on Islamic governance, Islamic economics, Islamic family status law, and Islamic criminal law. All of these contravene the above-mentioned authorities and are merely signs of fundamentalism and extremism! So how could they be included in official curricula? See the Tunisian press from 1989–1990.

50. [Translator's note] The author is referring to the theme of submission to those placed in authority, as in Q. 4:59 ("obey the Messenger and those in authority among you").

51. I am speaking here about the Islamic legal perspective on political power and not simply about the general political legitimacy of a state. That legitimacy might only have to do with a political authority's enjoyment of public approval or with the people's expression of their desire for and enjoyment of their best interests. This type of secular democratic rule could be included under the great Ibn Khaldun's category of "rational governance."

52. Abu al-Qasim al-Husayn bin Muhammad al-Raghib al-Isfahani, *The Difficult Vocabulary of the Qur'an (al-Mufradat fi gharib al-qur'an)* (Cairo: al-Babi, 1926).

53. Ibn Hazm, *The Book Embellished by Its Sources (Kitab al-Mahalla bi-l-athar)* (Tehran: n.p., n.d.), issue no. 1774.

54. Zayd bin 'Ali al-Wazir, *Correction of the Path (Tashih al-Masar)* (London: Yemeni Heritage and Research Center, 1992), 204.

55. Ridwan al-Sayyid, *The Umma, Community and Authority: Studies in Arab and Islamic Political Thinking (al-Umma wa-l-jama'a wa-l-sulta: dirasat fi-l-fikr al-siyasi al-'arabi al-islami)* (Cairo: Dar Iqra', 1984), 9–11.

56. See the Prophet's biography by Ibn Hisham, *Sirat Ibn Hisham*.

57. [Translator's note] Abu 'Abdallah Muhammad bin Idris al-Shafi'i (d. 820), later considered the founder of the Shafi'i school of Islamic law, was the first great systematizer and theoretician of Islamic law.

58. The innovative Shaykh Nasir al-Din al-Albani penned a monograph on this topic. See Nasir al-Din al-Albani, *The Characteristics of the Prophet's Prayer (Sifat salat al-nabi)* (Beirut: al-Maktab al-Islami, n.d.).

59. Sa'id, *Political Authority*, 181.

60. Ibn Hisham, *Sirat Ibn Hisham*.

61. Found in Bukhari's collection.
62. Ibid.
63. Found in Ahmad bin Hanbal's collection.
64. [Translator's note] A faithful disciple of Ibn Taymiyya's, Ibn Qayyim al-Jawziyya (d. 1350) was a prolific Sunni (of the Hanbali school) jurist and theologian from Damascus.
65. Abu 'Abdallah Muhammad bin Abi Bakr bin Qayyim al-Jawziyya, *Information for Those Who Write on Behalf of the Lord of the Worlds* (*I'lam al-muwaqqifiin 'an rabbi al-'alamin*) (Cairo: Dar al-Tiba'a al-Minbariyya, 1968).
66. Abu Hamid Muhammad bin Ahmad al-Ghazali, *Hidden Acts of Infamy* (*Fada'i' al-batiniyya*), edited and presented by 'Abd al-Rahman al-Badawi (Cairo: Dar al-Qawmiyya, 1964).
67. Abu Zayd 'Abd al-Rahman bin Muhammad bin Khaldun, *The Lessons and the Record of the Origins and Experiences of the Arabs, Persians and Berbers and the Contemporary Powers Ruling Them: Ibn Khaldun's Introduction* (*al-'Ibar wa-diwan al-mubtada' wa-l-khabar fi ayam al-'arab wa-l-'ajam wa-l-barbar wa-man 'asirahum min dhawi al-sultan al-akbar: muqaddimat Ibn Khaldun*), 7 vols. (Beirut: Dar al-Kitab al-Lubnani, 1956–1959).
68. Santalanu, quoted in Muhammad Diya' al-Rayyis, *Islamic Political Theories* (*al-Nadhariyyat al-siyasiyya al-islamiyya*), 4th ed. (Cairo: Dar al-Ma'arif, 1966), 361.
69. Arnold, quoted in ibid., 320–321. [Translator's note] The author is likely referring to the British orientalist Sir Thomas Walker Arnold (d. 1930) who taught for many years in British India.
70. Muhammad 'Imara, *Hayat* (no. 1086), n.d.
71. Western constitutional law considers the people or nation as the original and founding authority that uphold the constitution, whether directly or indirectly, and as a result, only it can initiate or amend constitutional rules. See Isma'il al-Ghazali, *Constitutional Law and Political Organization* (*al-Qanun al-dusturi wa-l-nidham al-siyasi*) (Cairo: Dar al-Thaqafa al-Jami'iyya, 1989), 39.
72. Muhammad Taha Badawi, *Law and the State* (*al-Qanun wa-l-dawla*), 15; quoted in Muhammad Salim al-'Awwa, *On the Political Organization of the Islamic State* (*Fi-l-nidham al-siyasi li-l-dawla al-islamiyya*) (Cairo and Beirut: Dar al-Shuruq, 1989), 23.
73. See below more details related to the civil rights of non-Muslims in the Islamic state. [Translator's note] The words for law are clearly demarcated in Arabic. The religious law is Shari'a (either *Shari'a* or *shar'*), while the civil law of the state is *qanun*.
74. Al-'Awwa, *On the Political Organization of the Islamic State*, 22–23.
75. *Encyclopedia of Consensus* (*Mawsu'at al-Ijma'*), entry no. 34, quoted in Sa'di Abu Habib, *A Study in the Methodology of Political Islam* (*Dirasa fi minhaj al-islam al-siyasi*) (Beirut: n.p., n.d.), 15.
76. 'Abd al-Wahhab al-Aftidi, *al-Quds* (opinion page), no. 1081.
77. Abu Habib, *A Study*, 15.
78. The Moroccan jurist 'Allal al-Fasi argued that the ground rule that guided him and pointed to that which needed to be included in the laws was also that ideal value that humanity from time immemorial has sought to discover—that is, justice. Un-

fortunately, it has remained elusive. So what is justice? And are we on the path that leads to its discovery, or are we dealing with a justice that is better labeled "injustice"? See 'Allal al-Fasi, *The Objectives of the Islamic Shari'a and Its Noble Virtues (Maqasid al-Shari'a al-islamiyya wa-makarimuha)* (Rabat, Morocco: Matba'a al-Risala, 1979), 41.

79. Ibn Khaldun, *Muqaddima*. Using this Khaldunian nomenclature may allow us to categorize the Western state under "rational governance," while "natural domination" applies globally to several third-world regimes in which law is synonymous with the ruler's will. And because this will is despotic, limited in scope, and unstable, that is why these nations have those same characteristics. To describe such a common state today as one ruled by law is so far from reality, just as it is to call its society a "civil society," when in fact it is in a state of resignation and suffocation and is looking for a chance to rebel and break its chains! Shaykh Mahdi Shams al-Din has strong views on this, like the following, "For all Muslims, the principle of shura in public affairs is the most important of all political and constitutional principles, whether among the Shia during the age of their infallible imam's absence, or among the Sunnis or other Muslims since the death of the Prophet (PBUH) . . . There can be no legitimacy in any political regime—or for any fallible ruler—and there can be no legitimacy in any behavior in public affairs without it being grounded in shura." See Muhammad Mahdi Shams al-Din, *Concerning Islamic Political Society (Fi-l-ijtima' al-siyasi al-islami)* (Beirut: al-Mu'assasa al-Jami'iyya li-l-Dirasat wa-l-Nashr, n.d.), 107.

80. Q. 4:59.

81. Q. 3:104.

82. Q. 33:72.

83. Q. 42:38. [Translator's note] That is the only instance of the word *shura* in the Qur'an.

84. Q. 3:159. [Translator's note] "Consult" is the verb *shawara*, from the same root as shura.

85. Q. 49:9.

86. Q. 4:115.

87. Narrated by Abu Hurayra in the collections of al-Tirmidhi and Abu Dawud.

88. Narrated by Abu Hurayra in the collections of Bukhari and Muslim.

89. Narrated by 'Abd Allah bin 'Umar in al-Tirmidhi.

90. Found in the collection of Abu Dawud and in Ahmad's *Musnad*.

91. No reference given for the last two hadiths.

92. Muhyi al-Din Abu Zakariyya Yahya bin Sharaf al-Nawawi, *The Gardens of the Righteous (Riyad al-Salihin)*, ed. Muhammad Nasir al-Din al-Albani, 2nd ed., vol. 1 (Beirut: Dar al-Nafa'is, 1974), 63. [Translator's note] As a reminder, *jahiliyya*, according to Muslim tradition, is the general state of pagan Arabia before the emergence of Islam. Literally, it means "a state of ignorance."

93. The orientalist Bernard Lewis wrote, "For the Muslim, there is no legislative authority besides the Shari'a. God only is the source of legislation." Lewis, *How Europe Discovered Islam (Comment l'Europe a découvert l'islam)* (Paris: La Découverte, 1984), 225.

94. 'Abd al-Hamid Isma'il al-Ansari, *al-Shura and Its Impact on Democracy* (*al-Shura wa-atharuha fi-l-dimuqratiyya*) (Khartoum, Sudan: Student Union of the University of Khartoum, n.d.), 7.

95. Abu Habib, *A Study*, 599.

96. al-Qurtubi, *A Comprehensive Collection of Qur'anic Injunctions* (*al-Jami' li-l-ahkam al-qur'an*) 3rd ed., vol. 4 (Beirut: Dar al-Kitab al-'Arabi, 1948), 249.

97. Zafir al-Qasimi wrote, "It may be that the researcher in the history of civilizations would be pleased to read books on the sources of Shari'a and to see how shura emerged from within Islam—a surprising appearance in contrast to other nations among which it appeared as the result of a long conflict and a struggle between the rulers and their people." See Zafir al-Qasimi, *Political Organization within the Shari'a and Islamic History* (*Nidham al-hukm fi-l-Shari'a wa-l-tarikh al-islami*), 4th ed., vol. 1 (Beirut: Dar al-Nafa'is, 1974), 63.

 Mutual consultation (shura) in Islam did not result from a need stirred up by the circumstances of the society in which the Prophet was living in the Arabian Peninsula, but rather it came about through divine revelation that came down upon his heart (PBUH). See ibid., 66.

98. Hasan al-Turabi, "al-Shura and Democracy: Characteristics of the Expression and Its Concept" (*al-Shura wa-l-dimuqratiyya: ishkalat al-mustalih wa-l-mafhum*), *Al Mustaqbal Al Arabi* 8, no. 75 (May 1985), 14; Ahmad Kamal Abu al-Majd, *Dialogue, Not Confrontation: Studies on Islam and the Present Age* (*Hiwar, la muwajaha: dirasat hawl al-islam wa-l-'asr*) (Cairo: Dar al-Shuruq, 1988), 105.

99. Q. 4:105.

100. Abu'l A'la Mawdudi, *The Islamic Government* (*al-Hukuma al-islamiyya*) (Beirut: Dar al-Fikr, 1977), 74.

101. Q. 4:80.

102. Ibn Qayyim al-Jawziyya, *Information*, vol. 1, 39.

103. [Translator's note] Literally, "the people who loose and bind," referring to a category of leaders in medieval Islamic political theory who could elect or depose caliphs, though in practice most rulers designated their successors.

104. Al-Qasimi, *Political Organization*, 235.

105. Narrated by Hudhayfa in Imam Muslim's collection.

106. Sa'id Ramadan al-Buti, as quoted in Qasimi, *Political Organization*, 235–237.

107. [Translator's note] The term "amir" is virtually synonymous with "sultan" or simply "political ruler."

108. [Translator's note] Because of the proliferation of hadiths in the second and third century of Islam, the scholars devised a methodology to sift out the weak from the strong ones, the fabricated from the authentic ones. The term used here is *tawatur*, pointing to their method of transmission and thereby making them the absolutely most reliable hadiths.

109. Muhammad 'Abduh and Muhammad Rashid Rida, *The Lighthouse Qur'anic Commentary* (*Tafsir al-Manar*), vol. 5 (Cairo: Matba'at al-Manar, 1956), 181 et passim.

110. Ibid.

111. [Translator's note] The "new rulings" translates "people who use *ijtihad* in order to produce rulings."

112. 'Abduh and Rida, *The Lighthouse Qur'anic Commentary*, vol. 3, 11.

113. Murtada al-'Askari, *Signposts of the Two Schools (Ma'alim al-Madrasatayn)*, vol. 1 (Tehran: Mu'assasat al-Ba'tha, 1991), 227.

114. al-Fasi, *The Objectives*, 80.

115. [Translator's note] Islam's rationalists, the Mu'tazilites, who were influential from the eighth to the tenth centuries, sided with the Shia in impugning the character of Muhammad's first three successors, or caliphs (for the Shia, 'Ali, the Prophet's cousin and son-in-law, was the only legitimate successor, or imam). So both groups devalued the concept of consensus as a valid source of Islamic law.

116. [Translator's note] This was a building in Medina where the Muslim notables gathered upon hearing that Muhammad had died, and after much discussion decided to pledge their allegiance to Abu Bakr. The party of 'Ali (later turning into the Shi'i branch of Islam) accused these leaders of taking advantage of 'Ali's absence due to his mourning and family obligations after his cousin's death.

117. al-Fasi, *Objectives*, 115–118, author's emphasis.

118. Muhammad Yusuf Musa, *The System of Political Organization in Islam (Nidham al hukm fi-l-islam)*, 2nd ed. (Cairo: Dar al-Kitab al-'Arabi, 1963), 81–83.

119. 'Abd al-Hamid Metwalli, *The Crisis of Islamic Political Thought in the Modern Age: Its Manifestations, Causes and Cures (Azmat al-Fikr al-siyasi al-islami fi-l-'asr al-hadith: madhahiruha, asbabuha, 'ilajuha)* (Cairo and Alexandria: al-Maktab al-Masri al-Hadith li-l-Tiba'a wa-l-Nashr, 1970).

120. Ahmad Kamal Abu al-Majd, "Freedom" ("*al-Hurriyya*"), *al-'Arabi*, 104–105.

121. Fathi 'Uthman, "The People of Loosing and Binding: Who Are They? And What Are Their Functions?" ("*Ahl al-hall wa-l-'aqd: man hum? Wa ma hiyya wadhifatuhum?*") *Al-'Arabi* 260 (July 1980).

122. Al-Ghazali wrote, "There is no judgment and no command that is not God's. As for the Prophet (PBUH), the sultan, the lord, the father and the husband, if they command or enjoin something, there is nothing binding in what they enjoin, except that which God (may He be exalted) enjoins them to obey. And if there is an obligation to obey God and the one who enjoins obedience to Him, then that obedience must be a free response to God and in the end not imposed by force; otherwise it is of no value." See Abu Hamid Muhammad bin Ahmad al-Ghazali, *The Essence of the Theory of Islamic Jurisprudence (al-Mustasfa min 'ilm al-usul)*, vol. 1 (Cairo: n.p., n.d.), 23.

123. 'Abd al-Wahhab Khallaf, *The Politics of Shari'a or the Islamic State's System in Constitutional, Foreign and Financial Matters (al-Siyasa al-shar'iyya aw nidham al-dawla al-islamiyya fi shu'un al-dusturiyya wa-l-kharijiyya wa-l-maliyya)* (Cairo: al-Matba'a al-Salafiyya, 1931), 44–45.

124. Khallaf, *The Politics of Shari'a*, 47–48.

125. Ibid., 48. For more information on the Shura Council of Cordoba, consult history books, starting with Ibn Khaldun's *Muqaddima*, 208; and Ya'qub Muhammad

al-Maliji, *The Principle of Shura in Islam* (*Mabda' al-shura fi-l-islam*) (Alexandria: n.p., n.d.), 173.

126. Muslims practiced this style of legislation from the very beginning of the Rightly Guided Caliphs in Medina, starting with Abu Bakr al-Siddiq. See Muhammad al-Khidr al-Hussayn al-Khidri, *History of Islamic Legislation* (*Tarikh al-tashri' al-islami*) (Cairo: n.p., n.d.), 107. Shaltut sees collective ijtihad as the picture that best fits the basic requirement of public lawmaking. See Mahmud Shaltut, *Islam Is a Creed and a Shari'a* (*al-Islam 'Aqida wa-Shari'a*) (Beirut: Dar al-Shuruq, n.d.), 567.

127. Hazi Ahmad al-Dardiri, *Legislation between the Islamic and the Constitutional Versions* (*al-Tashri' bayn al-fikrayn al-islami wa-l-dusturi*) (Cairo: al-Hay'a al-Misriyya al-'Amma li-l-Kitab, n.d.), 81–85.

128. [Translator's note] The phrase "or the enacting of laws covering new situations" is a paraphrase explaining the author's adjective *ijtihadi*. In classical Islam, only the highest level of jurists specialized in the Islamic sciences could perform ijtihad. In practice, however, this never included affairs of state (hence, the mostly theoretical discipline of *siyasa shar'iyya* or "governance according to the Shari'a") and rulers would often have their own parallel courts.

129. This is an expression Sobhi 'Abduh Sa'id uses in contrast to "innovative legislation"—hence his previous contrast between divine legislation as an expression of "elemental legislation" and legislation derived from the indications of the texts and the hard work of ijtihad.

130. Sa'id, *Political Authority*, 146–147.

131. [Translator's note] Al-Nabhani (d. 1977) was a Palestinian jurist from Jerusalem who founded the Party of Liberation (*Hizb al-Tahrir*) in 1953. He taught that much of the sorry state of Islamic countries can be traced to the abolition of the caliphate in 1924 and that the solution was its reestablishment. His Islamist movement is still present in many parts of the world today.

132. Taqi al-Din al-Nabhani, *The Organization of Political Rule in Islam* (*Nidham al-hukm fi-l-islam*) 5th ed. (Jerusalem: Manshurat al-Hizb al-Tahrir, 1953), 57.

133. al-Nabhani, *The Organization*, 74–75. [Translator's note] Abu Yusuf (d. 798) was the caliph's chief judge as well as being the author of many influential works in Hanafi jurisprudence. The *Kitab al-Kharaj*, a book on taxation and finance, is his best-known work.

134. Ibid., 80.

135. Ibid., 84–85.

136. [Translator's note] This is a well-known rule in classical Islamic law. Since the exercise of ijtihad is made by people, who by definition are fallible, then God rewards every mujtahid who invests in all the effort to come to a judgment and doubles that reward if the judgment or ijtihad is correct. But in this view only God knows which judgment is correct, which historically has given Islamic law a good deal of flexibility. Muhammad Sa'id Ramadan al-Buti (d. 2013) was a highly respected Syrian jurist and scholar.

137. Abu al-Majd, "Freedom," 103–104.

138. Q. 42:38, my own translation.
139. Q. 3:159, my own translation.
140. Q. 20:29–32.
141. The top judge Abu-l-Hasan al-Baghdadi pointed to this verse in order to underline the importance of mutual consultation. Quoted in Ya'qub Muhammad al-Malihi, *The Principle of Shura in Islam (Mabda' al-shura fi-l-Islam)* (Alexandria: Manahij al-Mustashriqin; Cairo: Jami'at al-Duwal al-'Arabiyya, n.d.), 87.
142. The imam Muhammad 'Abduh draws from this saying and others like it a Shari'a injunction about impermissibility of "the individual's behavior determining that of the community."
143. Tawfiq al-Shawi, *The Jurisprudence of Consultation and Advice Seeking (Fiqh al-shura wa-l-istishara)* (al-Mansura, Egypt: Dar al-Wafa', 1992), 788.
144. 'Abd al-Karim al-Khatib, *The Caliphate and the Imamate, Religion and Politics: A Comparative Study of Governance and Government (al-Khilafa wa-l-imama, diyana wa-siyasa: dirasa muqarana li-l-hukm wa-l-hukuma)* (Beirut: Dar al-Ma'rifa, 1975), 297.
145. Cf. this authentic hadith: "And my servant continues to draw near to me through works beyond the call of duty so that I will love him. And when I love him, I am the hearing with which he hears, the seeing with which he sees, the hand with which he strikes, and the foot with which he walks. When he asks for something, I grant it to him, and when he asks me for refuge, I grant it to him."
146. Cf. this hadith in the Bukhari collection: "'Nothing is left of prophethood but glad tidings.' They said, 'What glad tidings?' He answered (PBUH), 'Good dreams.'"
147. Cf. the hadith, "What the believers see as good is good in God's eyes."
148. "The unity of religion and reason is a basic tenet of Islamic thought" [no source given].
149. See Iqbal, *The Renewal*; Ghannouchi, *The Islamic Movement and Modernity (al-Haraka al-islamiyya wa-l-tahdith)* (Khartoum, Sudan: Ittihad Tullab Jami'at al-Khartum, 1980), 100.
150. Abu Habib, *A Study*, 100.
151. Al-Shaykh Bakhit, quoted in Ra'fat 'Uthman, *The State in Islam (al-Dawla fi-l-islam)* (n.p., n.d.), 380.
152. 'Abbas Mahmud al-'Aqqad, *Democracy in Islam (al-Dimuqratiyya fi-l-islam)* (Cairo: Dar al-Ma'arif, 1971).
153. Muhammad Diya' al-Din Al-Rayyis, *Islamic Political Theories (Nadhariyyat siyasi-yya islamiyya)* (Cairo: Dar al-Ma'arif, 1966), 380.
154. al-'Aqqad, *Democracy*, 45–46.
155. Fakh al-Din Muhammad bin 'Umar al-Razi, *The Great Commentary: The Keys to the Unknown (al-Tafsir al-kabir: mafatih al-ghayb)*, vol. 3 (Beirut: Dar al-Kutub al-'Ilmiyya, 1955), 357.
    Among the finer distinctions between the Sunnis and the Shia is that the Shi'i doctrine of the infallible imam's occultation allows the umma to come together on a theory of the state, the role of the scholars and public opinion about legislation and the exercise of sovereignty in light of the Qur'an's directives, an issue that dominated the conflict between the two communities over the centuries. It was the Sunni

jurists, however, who had the great merit of defending the freedom of choosing one's leader. See al-Shawi, *The Jurisprudence*, 377.

156. Muhammad 'Abid al-Jabiri, *Takwin al-'aql al-'arabi: naqd al-'aql al-'arabi (The Formation of the Arab Mind: Critique of the Arab Mind)*, 3rd ed. (Beirut: Markaz Dirasat al-Wihda, 1988).

157. Sayyid Qutb, *Toward an Islamic Society (Nahwa mujtama' islami)* (Cairo and Beirut: Dar al-Shuruq, 1980).

158. Al-Shawi, *The Jurisprudence*, 28.

159. Al-Turabi, *Characteristics*.

160. [Translator's note] Ghannouchi is being very open-minded here. Beside the Shi'i school of jurisprudence (Ja'fari), he includes the Ibadi school, or the remnants of the Kharijite movement today.

161. For one interpretation of the Maliki school of law in the Maghreb, see 'Allal al-Fasi, *Self Criticism (al-Naqd al-Dhati)*, 2nd ed. (Carthage, Tunisia: Dar al-Fikr al-Maghribi, n.d.). The present author has also completed a study of North Africa's Islamic civilization (manuscript). See also 'Abd al-Majid al-Najjar, *The Mahdi Ibn Tumart (al-Mahdi Ibn Tumart)* (Beirut: Dar al-Gharb al-Islami, n.d.).

162. Al-Shawi, *The Jurisprudence*, 152.

163. See the hadith "Follow the vast majority" in Ibn Maja's collection, narrated by 'Abd Allah bin 'Umar. This is similar to what we find in Ibn Hanbal's collection, narrated by Mu'adh bin Jabal: "Pay attention to the community and the common people."

164. [Translator's note] I use "creativity" here to translate *ijtihad*. Notice how Ghannouchi, in line with much contemporary Islamic thought, uses this technical legal term from the classical period in a much broader sense. This is part of his argument to limit the role of the traditional 'ulama' in today's nation-states.

165. Hadith narrated by al-Tabarani.

166. See Sayyid Qutb, *Hadha-l-din (This Religion)*, 9th ed. (Cairo and Beirut: Dar al-Shuruq, 1987), chapter entitled "The Grievous Shaking Off" ("al-Fisam al-naqid").

   The deviation, however, was limited to the political state but did not reach the domain of jurisprudence and legislation, which thankfully remained independent and off-limits to the state's authority. This is a right granted by God to the umma that it exercises through its jurists.

167. [Translator's note] The expression "blocking the means" (*sadd al-dhara'i'*) was one of the mechanisms of classical Islamic law. When a particular action was declared forbidden, in order to keep people from even being tempted by that sinful action, jurists thought it expedient to forbid acts that might lead up to it. This is a very similar reasoning to that of Rabbinic law, which added a number of prohibitions in the Mishnah and then the Talmud as a way to "put a hedge around the law."

168. [Translator's note] The author is about to say that the jurist "closed the door of ijtihad," a common saying within juridical circles in Islam, though it has been contested of late. Somewhere around the eleventh or twelfth century, schools of Islamic law were well established, and scholars felt that with many volumes of jurisprudence produced in each one of them, most everything in human society was covered by law—hence, no more need for innovation, just the need to hold on to the accumu-

lated wisdom of the past. The word used for that conservative mindset is *taqlid* ("imitation").

169. [Translator's note] Muhammad Asad, *Principles of State and Government in Islam* (*Manhaj al-islam fi-l-hukm*), trans. Mansur Muhammad Madi (Beirut: Dar al-'Ilm li-l-Malayin, 1975), 90. [Translator's note] Muhammad Asad (d. 1992) was born Leopold Weiss, an Austrian Jew who converted to Islam, worked as a journalist, and was close to Ibn Saud, Saudi Arabia's first king. He later established himself in Pakistan, where he became a close friend of philosopher Muhammad Iqbal. He is best remembered in the Muslim community for his books, including the one cited here, *The Principles of State and Government in Islam* (1961); others include *The Message of the Qur'an* (1980) and his best-selling autobiography, *The Road to Mecca* (1964).

170. Asad, *Principles of State*, 89.

171. Khalid Muhammad Khalid, *The State in Islam* (*al-Dawla fi-l-islam*) (Cairo: Dar Thabit, 1981).

172. [Translator's note] As a reminder, literally, "those who loose and bind."

173. Abu al-A'la al-Mawdudi, *Composing the Islamic Constitution* (*Tadwin al-dustur al-islami*) (Damascus: Dar al-Fikr, n.d.), 85.

174. 'Abd al-Hamid Metwalli, *Principles of Islamic Governance* (*Mabadi' nidham al-hukl fi-l-islam*) (Alexandria: Mansha'a al-Ma'arif, 1978), 107.

175. Al-'Awwa, *On the Political Organization*, 104.

176. Q. 4:59.

177. [Translator's note] These are the so-called *dhimmis* or non-Muslims (mostly from the "people of the book," i.e., Jews and Christians, and later Zoroastrians and others) who were "protected" minorities, yet whose rights do not amount to anything close to contemporary civil rights.

178. Taqi al-Din al-Nabhani, *Islam's Political Organization* (*Nidham al-islami al-siyasi*) (Jerusalem: Matba'a Dayr al-Siryan, 1952), 44.

179. Cf. constitution of the Republic of Iran, Arabic translation (Tehran: Mu'assasa al-Shahid, 1980).

180. For a look at the work of the constitutional assembly, see Conference on Constitutional Law, held in the Law School of Tunis, 1984.

181. 'Abd al-Rahman 'Azzam, *The Eternal Message* (*al-Risala al-khalida*) (Cairo: Dar al-Shuruq, 1978), 279. It may be that in this matter he is a follower of Muhammad 'Abduh and his school of thought. For an interpretation of the above verse, see 'Abduh and Rida's *The Lighthouse Qur'anic Commentary*.

182. This hadith is found in both al-Bukhari's and Muslim's collections.

183. On the issue of independence from the state, see al-Shawi, *The Jurisprudence*, 433.

184. Al-'Awwa, *On the Political Organization*, 287.

185. Q. 4:34, Yusuf Ali. [Translator's note] Yusuf Ali offers two words in English for the Arabic *qawamun* (literally, "guardians"). He rephrases it to say, "Husbands should take good care of their wives."

186. Mawdudi, *Composing*, 84–88.

187. You can find this in the booklet *Legal Opinions about Rulings on Women* (*Fatawa fi ahkam al-nisa'*) (Cairo: al-Azhar, n.d.).

188. Abu al-Hasan 'Ali bin Muhammad al-Mawardi, *The Rules for Heads of State and the Religious Government Offices* (*al-Ahkam al-sultaniyya wa-l-wilayat al-diniyya*), 2nd ed. (Cairo: Maktab Mustafa al-Babi al-Halabi, 1966).

189. Taj al-Din Abu al-Fath Muhammad ibn 'Abd al-Karim al-Shahrastani, *The Book of Sects and Creeds* (*al-Milal wa-l-Nihal*), ed. Albir Nasri Nadir (Beirut: Dar al-Mashriq, 1970), 75–76.

190. [Translator's note] She was the youngest of Muhammad's wives and a famous transmitter of hadiths.

191. *Commentary on the Nahj* (*Sharh al-Nahj*). [Translator's note: "Nahj" is short for a thirteenth-century Shi'i collection of sermons and speeches attributed to the fourth caliph 'Ali; the commentary is similar to the one by Muhammad 'Abduh, vol. 2, 81, quoted in al-Fasi, *The Objectives*, 347.

192. *Sharh al-Nahj*, vol. 2, 81, quoted in al-Fasi, *The Objectives*, 346–347.

193. Q. 27:32.

194. The doubtful nature of the hadith comes from its transmission from Abu Bakra (may God be pleased with him). Even though he is one of the honorable Companions within the Muslim conquering army, he was once punished for false testimony, as he himself admitted. Scholars disagree on the acceptability of a narration made by a repentant felon. Still, Abu Bakra's reputation was not restored even though restoration after moral failing is a condition for accepting a narrator for the scholars of hadith. Despite Abu Bakra's hadiths being in Bukhari's collection and that he is trusted and quoted as an impeccable source, nonetheless legitimate religious rulings and especially those related to the Islamic state must not be built upon a doubtful source, no matter the strength or weakness of the content's credibility.

195. [Translator's note] Though the modern reform movement and especially its standard bearer Muhammad 'Abduh saw itself as a "Salafi" movement (going back to the teaching of the "righteous forbears," the *salaf*), one should not confuse it with the new and distinct ultraconservative movement calling itself Salafi, which has emerged since the 1970s, often closely associated with Wahhabism, Saudi Arabia's official ideology. For a view on its origins, ideology, and great diversity, see Roel Meijer's edited book, *Global Salafism: Islam's New Religious Movement* (Oxford and New York: Oxford University Press, 2009). Ghannouchi is here pointing to Sayyid Qutb and his enormously popular Qur'anic commentary, *In the Shade of the Qur'an*. Qutb is in fact one of the prime influences on the contemporary Salafi movement, and particularly its extremist minority often called "Salafi-jihadi," which includes organizations like al-Qaeda and ISIS.

196. Qutb, *Fi Dhilal*, vol. 3.

197. Q. 2:233.

198. See previous note.

199. 'Abd Allah Diraz, *The Qur'an's Declaration of Ethics* (*Dustur al-akhlaq fi-l-qur'an*), quoted in al-Qasimi, *The System of Government in the Shari'a and Islamic History* (*Nidham al-hukm fi-l-Shari'a wa-l-tarikh al-islami*), 343.

200. [Translator's note] Al-Shifa' bint 'Abdullah was a capable Meccan woman at the time, able to read and write.

201. Ibn Hazm, *The Book Embellished*.
202. al-Nabhani, *The Organization of Political Rule*, 54.
203. Muhammad 'Ali al-Taskhiri, *About the Islamic Constitution* (*Hawl al-Dustur al-islami*), 2nd ed. (Tehran: Munadhdhama al-I'lam al-Islami, 1987).
204. Q. 9:71.
205. The constitution of the Islamic Republic of Iran. See also the important work by Ayatollah Muntadhiri, which does not include the conditions we noted for the councilor: Ayatollah Muhammad Husayn al-Muntadhiri, *Studies in the Rule of the Jurist and Political Jurisprudence* (*Dirasat fi wilayat al-faqih wa-fiqh al-dawla*), 2nd ed. (Beirut: al-Dar al-Islamiyya, 1988).
206. [Translator's note] The author is referring to the Jamaat-e-Islami, the Islamist organization founded in Lahore in 1941 by Abu al-A'la al-Mawdudi, still active today in Pakistan and Bangladesh.
207. Maybe it is witnessing the beginning of a wave of popular growth under its new leader, Shaykh al-Qadi Husayn, who leads the student branch of the organization. As a result, the Islamic movement came out of its cocoon of elitism and left behind some of its extreme conservative positions. It came down into the streets and continues to widen its appeal, encompassing the more knowledge-based Deobandi movement, as well as other Sufi and popular groups. It has even widened its perspective so as to cooperate with secular parties to form a common opposition block in the face of a military regime tied to Zionism. This united opposition is a very powerful force in the parliament, as well as in the streets through massive demonstrations—an opposition that has prepared itself carefully in order to become an alternative in the near future.
208. See Ghannouchi, *The Veil* (*al-Hijab*) (Lahore, Pakistan: Dar al-'Uruba, n.d.). I have traveled through many Pakistani cities, and I have enjoyed seeing the pride displayed by the women in their national culture as demonstrated in their modest apparel, though with a touch of art and beauty, and their refusal to be dragged along by decadent Western fashions. It is a style that needs only slight changes so as to become truly Islamic. That said, I hardly saw any of the fully veiled women that Mawdudi wrote about, except in the "Mutasawwara"—that is, the village where the Jamaat-e-Islami has its headquarters. For this, see Hasan al-Turabi, *Woman between Islam and the Traditions of Society* (*al-Mar'a bayn al-islam wa-l-taqalid al-mujtama'*) (Tunis: Dar al-Raya, 1985); al-Ghazali, *The Prophetic Sunna*; and Rached Ghannouchi, *Woman Between the Qur'an and the Traditions of Society* (*al-Mar'a bayn al-qur'an wa-taqalid al-mujtama'*) (Kuwait: Dar al-Qalam; Tunis: Dar al-Sahwa, 1988).
209. Q. 49:13.
210. Q. 4:75.
211. [Translator's note] "Commander of the Faithful" was the title of 'Umar bin al-Khattab, the second caliph.
212. Q. 10:83.
213. Q. 8:72.
214. [Translator's note] "Abode of Islam" is an important label in classical Islamic texts of jurisprudence. In this perspective, the world is divided between the Abode of Islam

and the Abode of War. Notice that he attenuates the second expression by saying the "Abode of Unbelief." The first expression today means a Muslim-majority nation.

215. Mawdudi, *Composing*, 56–57. See also his commentary on this verse in Mawdudi, *Towards Understanding the Qur'an*. [Translator's note] The author offers no more details, but this book continues to be reprinted in multiple volumes by the Islamic Foundation in Leicestershire, UK.

216. al-Taskhiri, *About the Islamic Constitution*, 80.

217. *Regulations for Religious Minorities and Protected People* (*Ahkam al-dhimmiyyin wa-l-musta'minin*) (Beirut: n.p., 1976).

218. This is from his study on how to revise the laws governing non-Muslims in the journal *al-Bayan* (Beirut, August 1979).

219. Isma'il al-Faruqi, "The Rights of Non-Muslims in the Islamic State" ("*Huquq ghayr al-muslimin fi-l-dawla al-islamiyya*"), *al-Muslim al-Mu'asir* 26, n.d.

220. Fahmi Huwaydi, *Citizens, Not Dhimmis: The Position of Non-Muslims in a Society of Muslims* (*Muwatinun la dhimmiyun: mawqi' ghayr al-muslimin fi mujtama' al-muslimin*) (Cairo and Beirut: Dar al-Shuruq, 1984).

221. Rached Ghannouchi, *Rights of Citizenship: The Status of Non-Muslims in the Islamic State* (*Huquq al-muwatana: mawqi' ghayr al-muslimin fi-l-dawla al-islamiyya*) (Tunis: Dar al-Sahwa, 1988); al-'Awa, *On the Political Organization*.

222. Al-'Awwa, *On the Political Organization*, 257–258.

223. Abu Habib, *The Study*, 525.

224. See, for example, Muhammad Husayn Fadlallah, *The Concept of Freedom in Islam* (*Mafhum al-hurriyya fi-l-islam*). Sayyid Qutb defended the same view before him in his famous phrase, "The nationality of the Muslim is his creed." Qutb, *Signposts along the Way* (*Ma'alim fi-l-tariq*) (Beirut: Dar al-Shuruq, 1973), 80.

225. J. Austin Ranney, *Governing: An Introduction to Political Science*. rev. ed. (Upper Saddle River, NJ: Prentice Hall, 1987), 1, quoted in Sadr al-Din al-Qabaniji, *The Political Methodology of Islam* (*al-madhab al-siyasi fi-l-islam*) (Tehran: Widharat al-Irshad, n.d.), 129–130.

226. Ibid., 130–132.

227. Ibid., 134.

228. Ibid., 135.

229. Al-Shawi, *The Jurisprudence*.

230. [Translator's note] Colloquial Arabic for "without." This is in reference to guest workers from Egypt, South Asia, and elsewhere, who form the large majority of the population but are not allowed to become citizens. Their poor living conditions have been compared to indentured servants.

231. [Translator's note] My expression "imposed on us by outside forces" is literally "imposed on us by iron and fire."

232. 'Abduh and Rida, *The Lighthouse Qur'anic Commentary*.

233. Khalid, *The State in Islam*, 58–59.

234. Q. 3:104.

235. One should note that the absence of such a body negatively affects any effort in these organizations to increase individual rights. This explains why the rights of citizens

found within the constitution, which already downplays what the sacred texts hold up as a standard for an Islamic state, are merely ink on a page.

236. See the chapter "A Contemporary Model of Collective Ijtihad" ("Namudhaj 'asri li-l-ijtihad al-jama'i"), in al-Shawi, The Jurisprudence, 203.

237. [Translator's note] The word translated as "cohesiveness" is specifically taken from Ibn Khaldun's famous The Introduction (al-Muqaddima): 'asabiyya. The idea is that a ruler cannot rule without a strong bond tying together the ruling elite.

238. [Translator's note] The author adds "da'wa" ("a calling," as in calling people to the way of Islam; cf. Q. 16:125 et passim) in parentheses next to "ideology," pointing to the missionary zeal that sparked the early Muslim conquests.

239. Ibn Khaldun, Muqaddima.

240. Cf. al-Turabi, Woman; Muhammad al-Ghazali, Prophetic Sunna; and Ghannouchi, Woman.

241. Muhammad Rashid Rida, The Caliphate (Le Califat) (Paris, n.p., 1926).

242. [Translator's note] Along with the author, I will use "amir," "imam," "caliph," and "ruler" as synonyms throughout this political discussion about state power. I will usually keep umma in the translation, but sometimes translate it as "the people," as that is the role it most plays in this section.

243. al-Rayyis, Islamic Political Theories, 214.

244. al-Fasi, The Objectives, 256.

245. Taqi al-Din Ahmad bin 'Abd al-Halim bin Taymiyya al-Harrani, The Politics Dictated by the Shari'a to Reform the Leader and His People (al-Siyasa al-shar'iyya fi islah al-ra'i wa-l-ra'iyya) (Cairo: n.p., 1969).

246. Imam al-Baqillani said, "The imam becomes imam by virtue of the contract of imamate made with him by the leading Muslims who belong to the 'people of loosing and binding'"; quoted in 'Uthman, Foundations of Islamic Political Thought (Usul al-Fikr al-siyasi al-islami) (Beirut: Mu'assassa al-Risala, 1984), 405.

247. [Translator's note] Ghannouchi is likely referring to the great Shi'i scholar Muhammad Baqir al-Sadr who lived in Najaf, Iraq, and was executed by Saddam Hussein in 1980. The next one is Ayatollah Morteza Motahhari (d. 1979). The last one is Ali Shariati, a sociologist often called the "ideologue of the Iranian Revolution." He died in the UK in 1977, just before the revolution.

248. [Translator's note] The Shia of Iran and Iraq represent the majority of the world's Shia and believe that there were twelve infallible imams descended from the Prophet, starting with 'Ali (hence they are called "Twelvers"). The last one went into occultation (disappeared from this world without dying) in the ninth century and will come back as a messianic figure in the Last Days (al-Mahdi) to rule his people. The Ismailis Shia led by the Aga Khan are called the Seveners and the Zaidis the Fivers.

249. Shi'i Doctrines ('Aqa'id al-imamiyya) [no details given], 74.

250. Abridgement of al-Shafi (Talkhis al-Shafi), quoted in Muhammad 'Imara, "Religion and the State in the Legacy of the Messenger (PBUH)" ("al-Din wa-l-dawla fi injaz al-rasul"), al-Hiwar 1, no. 1 (Spring 1986), 131–132.

251. Muhammad Mahdi Shams al-Din, *Toward the Rule of Islam* (*Ila hukm al-islam*) (Karbala, Iraq: n.p., 1962), 54. [Translator's note] He was an influential Lebanese Shi'i cleric who died in 2001.

252. Muhammad Baqir al-Sadr, *The Vicegerency of Humanity and the Witness of the Prophets: A Study of Islam's Book, Life's Guide* (*Khilafat al-insan wa-shahadat al-anbiya': dirasat min kitab al-islam yaqudu al-hayat*) (Beirut: Dar al-Ta'aruf li-l-Matbu'at, n.d.).

253. al-Qabaniji, *The Political Methodology*, 54.

254. Ibid., 240.

255. Ibid., 241

256. Ibid., 231.

257. [Translator's note] The *Ghadir Khumm* ("Pond of Khumm") hadith has long been disputed between Sunnis and Shia. Both agree that the Prophet on his return from his Farewell Hajj (March 632) had everyone gather at this pond on the way back to Medina, and he made his Farewell speech, saying his life on earth was at its end. At one point, he raises 'Ali's hand and says, "Whomever I am his *mawla*, this 'Ali is his *mawla*." One of the leading Companions of the Prophet, 'Uthman said, "O son of Abu Talib, you have become the *mawla* of every male and every female believer, morning and evening, congratulations!" Part of the disagreement is on the way *mawla* is used here. Its meaning ranges widely from "leader" to "patron" to "client" and even "partner" and "friend." The Shia see this as Muhammad clearly designating his successor, while the Sunnis see it only as an appeal to respect his family.

258. This extreme methodology entrenched in certain schools of thought and in a narrow view of Islam is not present—thank God!—among the leading scholars who despite holding on to their school's views move in the wider circles of Islam. See, for instance, Ayatollah Muhammad Husayn al-Tabataba'i, *The Balance in Interpreting the Qur'an* (*al-Mizan fi tafsir al-qur'an*) (Beirut: Mu'assasat al-A'lami, 1972); and Muntadhiri, *Studies*.

259. Ruhollah Musavi Khomeini, *The Islamic Government* (*al-Hukuma al-islamiyya*) (Beirut: Mu'assasa al-A'lami, 1969), 78.

260. Ibid., 52.

261. This is from the Imam al-Sadiq (may God be pleased with him), as reported by the Shi'i scholars; quoted in Qabaniji, *The Political Methodology*, 206.

262. Ibid., 232.

263. See, for instance, the newspaper *al-'Ahd*, which is published by Hezbollah in Lebanon.

264. Ahmad Madhhar, "A Study on Democracy" (*Dirasa hawl al-dimuqratiyya*), *al-Mabahith* 41 (March–June 1986).

265. Muhammad 'Ali Danawi, *The Concept and the Experiment* (*al-Mafhum wa-l-tajriba*) (Tripoli, Lebanon: Dar al-Iman, 1980), 67–68.

266. Al-Qabaniji, *The Political Methodology*, 76. The origin of this idea goes back to the martyr Muhammad Baqir al-Sadr.

267. [Translator's note] This is not an exact quotation, but the closest wording would be Q. 6:57, "Judgement is for God alone" (cf. also Q. 12:40, 67; 40:12). The Arabic word

translated here as "rule" (*hukm*) can also mean "judgment," as in a judge's decision. This is also the same root for the word "government" (*hukuma*).

268. Al-Sharif al-Rida, *The Way of Eloquence* (*Nahj al-balagha*), with commentary by Muhammad 'Abduh (Beirut: Maktabat al-Andalus, 1954), 18.

269. Q. 2:213. For an interpretation of this verse, see Muhammad Baqir al-Sadr, *The Vice-gerency.*

270. Q. 100:7, Yusuf Ali.

271. Ibn Khaldun, *Muqaddima.*

272. Yusuf al-Qaradawi, *The Islamic Solution Is an Obligation and Necessity* (*al-hall al-islami farida wa-darura*) (Beirut: Mu'assasa al-Risala, 1974).

273. Ahmad al-Baghdadi, "The Concept of Politics in Islamic Society from the Perspective of the Islamic Shari'a" ("*Mafhum al-siyasa fi-l-mujtama' al-islami min mandhur al-Shari'a al-islamiyya*"), *al-Mabahith* 41 (January–March 1986).

274. Shaykh al-Suhani wrote, "The Islamic government in the presence of the Imam (infallible) is a divine and protected government, and when it is impossible to reach him, it is a mixture of divine sovereignty and popular sovereignty . . . It is divine, on the one hand, since legislation comes from God originally and it is popular in the sense that the ruler is elected and the rest of the instruments of state are delegated to the people," Ja'far al-Suhani, *Characteristics of the Islamic Government* (*Ma'alim al-hukuma al-islamiyya*) (Beirut: Dar al-Adwa', 1984), 246.

275. Q. 3:112.

276. [Translator's note] This is a well-known hadith, though not found in the authoritative collections.

277. Q. 42:38.

278. Vladimir Ilyich Lenin, *Selections* (*Mukhtarat*), vol. 2, *The State and the Revolution* (*al-Dawla wa-l-thawra*) (Moscow: Dar al-Taqaddum, 1968), 285.

279. The vast majority of the Mu'tazilites and some of those who supported the Kharijite views deviated from the consensus on establishing the imam over the umma. That view has faded, however, as they were saying that establishing the caliphate was not a duty but what was incumbent upon the umma in application of the Shari'a. For them, if the umma is able to set up a just system in which the Shari'a is put in practice without the imam, then to install him is not mandatory but simply permissible. See Abu Muhammad 'Ali bin Ahmad bin Hazm, *The Criterion for Discerning Sects, Passions and Creeds* (*al-Fasl fi-l-milal wa-l-ahwa' wa-l-nihal*), vol. 4 (Cairo: n.p., 1964), 84.

280. 'Abd al-Wahhab Khallaf, *Shari'a Politics or the Islamic Organization of the State: Its Constitution, Foreign Policies, and Economy* (*al-Siyasa al-shar'iyya aw-nidham al-dawla al-islamiyya fi shu'un al-dusturiyya wa-l-kharijiyya wa-l-maliyya*) (Beirut: Dar al-Ma'rifa, 1932).

281. Q. 4:59.

282. al-Mawardi, *The Ordinances of Government*, quoted in Abu al-Hussayn Muhammad bin Muhammad Abu Ya'la al-Farra', *The Ordinances of Government* (*al-Ahkam al-sultaniyya*) (Cairo: Matba'a al-Babi al-Halabi, 1966), 3.

283. [Translator's note] Here the author is using the expression "age of legislation" to refer to the Prophet's rule in Medina followed by the four "Rightly Guided Caliphs."

284. Al-Mawardi noted that most scholars of the umma believed that the caliph is legally elected by a five-member council, or that one person decides on the contract with the approval of the four others, though some believe that three members choose one of the three. See al-Mawardi, *The Rules for Heads of State*, 33.

285. [Translator's note] This is the "Testimony," the first pillar of Islam, as one Muslim (or new convert) pronounces the words of the Testimony to another: "There is no god but God [Allah] and Muhammad is His Messenger."

286. [Translator's note] Often given the honorific title of "Shaykh al-Islam" today, Ibn Taymiyya (d. 1328) was a controversial yet also prolific and influential jurist, theologian, and logician.

287. Muhammad 'Abduh, *Islam and Christianity: With Knowledge and Civility (al-Islam wa-l-nasraniyya ma'a-l-'ilm wa-l-madaniyya)*, 2nd ed. (Cairo: Matba'at Majallat al-Manar, 1905).

288. Al-Taftarani leaned on al-Razi to show that the umma holds supreme political authority, and it is she that removes the imam, by canceling his contract, since she was its initiator in the first place; quoted in al-Rayyis, *Islamic Political Theories*, 217.

289. 'Abduh, *Islam and Christianity*.

290. al-'Awda, *Islam and Our Political Context (al-Islam wa-awda'una al-siyasiyya)* (Cairo: Dar al-Kitab al-'Arabi, 1951), 103–104.

291. Ibid. Most Islamic political jurists of late have taken the same tack, and among them 'Abd al-Hakim Hasan al-'Ayli, who sees the oath of allegiance to the ruler as the right of the umma, who then puts it to use by means of individuals in all corners of the Islamic state. The experience with "the people of loosing and binding" is nothing but a nominating process carried out by a body of experts in the Qur'an and Sunna and in the best interests of the Muslim population. See 'Abd al-Hakim Hasan al-'Ayli, *Public Freedoms in the Thought and Political Organization of Islam (al-Hurriyat al-'amma fi-l-fikr wa-l-nidham al-siyasi fi-l-islam)* (n.p., n.d.), 229.

292. Hasan al-Banna, *Collected Letters of the Imam and Martyr Hasan al-Banna (Majmu'at rasa'il al-imam al-shahid Hasan al-Banna)* (Beirut: Dar al-Qalam, n.d.), 377.

293. We have already covered the qualifications of the members of the assembly of "those who loose and bind," or the Shura Council (or Assembly).

294. The installation of the head of state is explained by al-Nabhani in his constitution.

295. This saying is quoted in 'Abd al-Salam Dawud al-'Iyadi, *Ownership in the Islamic Shari'a (al-Mulkiyya fi-l-Shari'a al-islamiyya)* (Amman, Jordan: Maktabat al-Aqsa, n.d.).

296. We should maybe return to the various international human rights NGOs and their examination of the crimes committed by the Marxist regime in Bulgaria against Muslims, for instance, or by the Serbian regime, in addition to the bloody crimes committed by the communist, Buddhist, Christian, and Jewish regimes, as well as the Western colonial states and their defenders in the Arab and Muslim nations.

297. Lenin, *Complete Works (al-Mu'allafat al-kamila)* vol. 1 [n.p., n.d.], 31.

298. This happens almost every day for those populations of North Africa who have chosen the tribulation of emigration to France (the land of revolution, the land of liberty, equality, and fraternity), yet without one of them losing heart. The story of the three veiled young women and the brouhaha created around them would not have been unusual had the affair not gone to the supreme court, which ruled that the school had the freedom to decide the fate of the girls. This was a scandalous affront to freedom and democracy in France—even if the State Council finally overturned the decision.

299. ʿAbd al-Hadi Abu Talib, *Compendium on Constitutional Law and Political Institutions (al-Marjaʿ fi-l-qanun al-dusturi wa-l-muʾassasat al-siyasiyya)* (Casablanca, Morocco: Dar al-Kitab, 1980).

300. The American presidency rarely departs from this description.

301. Huwaydi, *Citizens*, 104–105.

302. In a chapter entitled "Shackles on the Freedom of Thought," al-ʿAyli writes, "The shackles on the public freedoms are determined by looking at the meaning of the idea of public order that different political regimes have adopted. Public order refers to a set of fundamental benefits, or a set of essential pillars upon which that order's community and identity is built, so that no one imagines this identity enduring in a sound manner without being firmly established on those pillars. That said, considering the difference between political regimes, the idea of public order changes in its content from one community to another." al-ʿAyli, *The Public Freedoms*, 472–473.

303. Q. 39:9.

304. Huwaydi, *Citizens*, 155.

305. Q. 4:59.

306. al-Turabi, *Characteristics*.

307. Ibid.

308. [Translator's note] An emirate is led by an amir, a word the author uses as synonymous with imam (imamate) or caliph (caliphate)—all pointing to a distinctive form of Islamic state.

309. [Translator's note] The word *taqlid* is used in opposition to ijtihad, meaning "following the precedents of one's school of jurisprudence."

310. Al-ʿAwda, *Islam*, 111.

311. Al-Khatib al-Baghdadi, *The Compendium of Knowledge on the Science of Hadith Transmission (al-Kifaya fi maʿrifat usul ʿilm al-riwaya)*, 80; quoted in al-Mawardi, *The Ordinances of Government*, 87.

312. Q. 49:13.

313. [Translator's note] Narration found in the collections of Abu Dawud and Ibn Maja.

314. Q. 4:6.

315. [Translator's note] That would be about thirty-eight and a half years according to the Gregorian calendar.

316. Narration found in the collections of Ahmad bin Hanbal and al-Tabarani.

317. Al-ʿAwda, *Islam*, 112; al-Mawardi, *The Ordinances of Government*, 96.

318. Narration found in al-Bukhari's collection.

319. Al-'Awda, *Islam*, 117.

320. The Imam Muqbali opines that this hadith is only about what will happen. The Imam al-Jalal contends that it is a report about what is and not about what should be. Both are quoted in Zayd bin 'Ali al-Wazir, *Correction* (*Tashih*) (London: Markaz al-Turath wa-l-Buhuth al-Yamani), 74. Ibn Khaldun, *Muqaddima*.

321. [Translator's note] That Arabic word summarizes one of the seminal ideas of this fourteenth-century political and sociological observer, Ibn Khaldun. On the basis of his participation in half a dozen regimes in the MENA region and his observation of many others, he theorized that the successful ruler had to have a strong support base. These people were cohesive as a group and strongly loyal to him. This is *'asabiyya*. This kind of analysis has made him a popular author in modern times and contributed to his reputation as the forerunner of modern historiography and sociology.

322. Our Moroccan preacher, activist, and brother Shaykh Abdessalam Yassine said, "Our amir is a man blessed with success and luminosity." Cf. Yassine, *Islam Tomorrow* (*al-Islam ghadan*) (Casablanca, Morocco: n.p., n.d.), 908.

323. Abu Talib, *Compendium*, 232.

324. Sa'di Abu Jib, *A Study of the Methodology of Political Islam* (*Dirasa fi manhaj al-islam al-siyasi*) (Beirut: n.p., n.d.), 245.

325. Ibn Hazm, *Discerning between Religions, Divisions, and Sects* (*al-Fasl fi-l-milal wa-l-ahwa' wa-l-nihal*), vol. 4 (Cairo: n.p., 1964), 169.

326. 'Abd al-Qadir bin Tahir al-Baghdadi, *The Fundamentals of Religion* (*Usul al-din*), 3rd ed. (Beirut: Dar al-Kitab al-'Ilmiyya, 1981), 285.

327. al-Nabhani, *The Organization*.

328. Q. 62:5.

329. Cf. 'Abd Allah Fahd al-Nafisi, *When Islam Rules* (*'Indama yahkum al-islam*) (Tunis: al-Ma'rifa, 1981). The caliphate was saved from disaster only when regimes repudiated the monarchical system and its fateful use of naming one's successors and the covenant of political rule.

330. Cf. Muhammad 'Imara, "The State's Dual Character: Islamic and Civil," *al-Jihad al-Islami* 56 (July 1987).

331. Rays, *Islamic Political Theories*, 222.

332. Q. 3:112. [Translator's note] Ghannouchi had a parenthetical phrase in the text drawing from this verse, which cannot be translated literally ("from the cord of God and the cord of men"). The context is that the Muslim community is in danger from the machinations of the "people of the book," and, quoting from the rest of the verse, "unless they hold fast to a lifeline from God and from mankind, they are overshadowed by vulnerability wherever they are found." Yusuf Ali sees here the picture of a tent and its cords well fastened, which in turn points to the idea of covenant: "Shame is pitched over them (like a tent) wherever they are found, except when under a covenant (of protection) from God and from men." Q. 4:135, Yusuf Ali.

333. Q. 4:135, Yusuf Ali.

334. Q. 3:104.

335. Musa, *The System of Political Organization*, 78.

336. Mahmud Hilmi, *The Islamic System of Governance Compared to Contemporary Regimes (Nidham al-hukm al-islami muqaranan bi-l-nudhum al-mu'asira)*, 2nd ed. (Cairo: Dar al-Fikr al-'Arabi, 1973), 95–96.

337. Q. 4:5.

338. Q. 2:188.

339. Shihab al-Din Ahmad bin Idris al-Qarafi, *Cases of Legal Difference (al-Furuq)*, vol. 2 (Tunis: al-Matba'a al-Tunissiyya, 1884), 105–106.

340. Abu al-Qasim al-Ansari, *Sunrise Pearls on the Lights of Legal Difference (Adrar al-shuruq 'ala anwar al-furuq)*, quoted in the margin in ibid.

341. Regarding the source of these documents, see Hamid Allah, *Collection of Political Documents of the Prophetic Era and the Rightly-Guided Caliphate (Majmu'at al-watha'iq al-siyasiyya li-l-'ahd al-nabawi wa-l-khilafa al-rashida)*, 3 vols., expanded and revised edition (Beirut: Dar al-Irshad, 1969).

342. al-'Ayli, *The Public Freedoms*, 230–231.

343. Q. 49:13.

344. François Burgat, *Political Islam: The Voice from the South (al-Islam al-siyasi: sawt al-janub)*, trans. Lorène Dhikra (Cairo: Dar al-'Alam al-Thalith, 1992), 145–147.

345. Cf. al-Qaradawi, *The Islamic Solution: Obligation and Necessity (al-Hall al-islami: farida wa-darura)* (Beirut: Mu'assassa al-Risala, 1977).

346. Cf. "The Shari'a Source of the Islamic State: A Dialogue between a Number of Thinkers" ("*Masdar shar'iyya al-dawla al-islamiyya: hiwar ma'a majmu'a min al-mufakkirin*"), *al-Sharq al-Awsat* (May 25, 1992).

347. Abu Ya'la al-Farra', *The Rules for Heads of State*, 51.

348. Al-Mawardi, *The Proper Way to Manage this World and Religion (Adab al-dunya wa-l-din)* (Beirut: Dar Iqra', 1985), 116.

349. Q. 22:41.

350. Al-Qasimi, *Political Organization*, 354.

351. Musa, *The System of Political Organization*, 74–79.

352. Q. 4:58.

353. Q. 16:90.

354. This is the hadith of the seven whom God covered with his shade on the Day of Resurrection, the first of which is "Imam Adel," which is considered authentic. Also the hadith, "The Justice Makers at God's Right Hand."

355. [Translator's note] The Battle of Uhud was in 625 when a large contingent from Mecca laid siege to Medina, seeking revenge from their defeat the year before at the Battle of Badr.

356. Q. 26:215.

357. Q. 28:83.

358. Found in Muslim's collection.

359. Ibid.

360. Q. 40:16.

361. Found in Muslim's collection.

362. Ibid.
363. Q. 9:128.
364. Q. 4:134.
365. Q. 3:159.
366. Found in Muslim's collection.
367. Q. 12:92.
368. Q. 17:34.
369. Found in the collections of Abu Dawud and al-Tirmidhi.
370. Q. 83:26.
371. Found in the collection of al-Tirmidhi, no. 1376.
372. Al-Mawardi, *The Ordinances of Government*, 51.
373. Q. 4:6.
374. That is, he will determine your salary, for he is responsible for the state treasury [*bayt al-mal*].
375. See al-Qasimi, *Political Organization*, 355–356. Those in our country who call for more modern ways should be ashamed of themselves. Not one member of parliament, or journalist, or preacher, or TV announcer dares to discuss openly the president's budget, especially since they have seen it multiply by five in just a few years! Forget the countries of feudalism in which no one dares to question the origin of wealth. Do they not have enough calamities without making fun of the Shari'a, the caliphate, and the danger of fundamentalism?
376. Ibn Jama'a, *Documenting the Regulations Ordering the Life of the People of Islam (Tahrir al-ahkam fi-l-tadbir ahl al-islam)*, ed. Fuad 'Abd al-Mun'im Ahmad (Doha: Qatar, Dar al-Thaqafa, 1988).
377. Q. 4:59.
378. Found in Muslim's collection.
379. Consideration of this action can be entrusted to a specialized court of complaints or what we call today the constitutional court. It could be the Shura Assembly that decides to hand such a case to the constitutional court.
380. [Translator's note] Presumably, this "fourth power of the state" is in addition to the state's legislative, executive, and judicial powers.
381. Q. 3:104.
382. Q. 9:71.
383. Q. 5:78–79.
384. Found in Muslim's collection.
385. Found in the collections of Bukhari and Muslim.
386. Narrated by Ibn Hayyan.
387. Al-Nawawi, *The Gardens of the Righteous (Riyad al-Sahihin)*.
388. Quoted by Ibn Hazm in his book *Discerning Between Religions*.
389. Al-'Awwa, *On the Political Organization*, 174.
390. Al-'Ayli, *Public Freedoms*, 234.
391. Sulayman al-Tamawi, *'Umar bin al-Khattab: The Foundations of Politics and Modern Administration ('Umar bin al-Khattab wa-l-usul al-siyasa wa-l-idara al-hadith)*, 2nd ed. (Cairo: Dar al-Fikr al-'Arabi), 281.

392. Al-'Ayli, *Public Freedoms,* 235.

393. Al-'Awda, *Islam,* 12.

394. Both hadiths found in the *Musnad* of Ahmad Ibn Hanbal.

395. On the issue of drawing benefit and repelling harm, see al-Shatibi, *The Reconciliation of the Fundamentals of Islamic Law (Muwafaqat fi usul al-shari'ia),* vol. 2 (Cairo: Dar Ibn 'Affan, 1997), 6.

396. Q. 3:104.

397. Quoted in Al-'Ayli, *Public Freedoms,* 246.

398. [Translator's note] No reference given. Al-Juwayni (d. 1085) was a Persian jurist (Shafi'i) and theologian.

399. This scholar's nickname was "the sultan of '*ulama*'," the Shaykh al-'Izz bin 'Abd al-Salam, who issued a fatwa declaring obedience to one of the Mamluk sultans an infraction of the Shari'a. The Sultan then arrested the scholar and brought him to the market to be sold. He then set him free in order to fulfill the commitments of his oath of office from then on.

400. Q. 5:50.

401. Q. 5:44.

402. Found in Muslim's collection.

403. Ibid.

404. Ibid.

405. Asad, *Islam's Method of Government,* 143.

406. Found in Muslim's collection.

407. Found in the collections of Bukhari and Muslim.

408. [Translator's note] Abu 'Abdullah al-Qurtubi (d. 1273) was one of the great Qur'anic commentators and jurists.

409. [Translator's note] Imam Hanbal (d. 855) is the eponym of the Hanbali school of Islamic law, and he is also famous for bravely resisting what he considered the erroneous doctrines chosen by the caliphs of his time.

410. One could revisit the brilliant article ("the power of the word") in the martyr Sayyid Qutb's book *Islamic Studies (Dirasat islamiyya)* (Beirut: Dar al-Shuruq, 1978).

411. Muhyi al-Din Abu Zakariyya Yahya bin Sharif al-Nawawi, *The Explanation of the Authentic Traditions of Muslim (Sharh Sahih Muslim)* (Cairo: al-Matba'a al-Misriyya, n.d.).

412. Al-Nawawi has this comment on the hadith about "evident disbelief": "Do not oppose or resist rulers, except when you see them committing a particular infraction to God's law. When you see that, oppose it, but to take up arms against them and kill them is forbidden, and it is the consensus of the scholars, even if they are immoral and unjust." His text is pointing to regimes that still respect the Shari'a, even though they commit injustices and grave offenses, because those are the only kinds of regimes he has witnessed.

413. al-Nabhani, *The Organization,* 527.

414. Quoted in al-Rayyis, *Islamic Political Theories,* 351.

415. One should commend some of them for the boldness with which they declared their repentance and regret for the evil incurred by their reactions to injustice. See the

texts written by the Islamic Group (*al-jama'a al-islamiyya*) of Egypt when it revised its policies on the use of violence in 1996.

416. Muntadhiri, *Studies*, vol. 1, 594–595.

417. Al-Qurtubi notes the consensus of the scholars on the issue of deposing a ruler who neglects shura. See al-Qurtubi, *A Comprehensive Collection*, vol. 4, 249.

418. Cf. Shaykh Muhammad al-Salih al-Nayfar's fatwa on the kinds of governments and parties existing today and his appraisal of them.

419. Asad, *Islam's Methods of Government*, 144–145.

420. Sa'id, *Political Authority*, 199–200.

421. In exceptional cases a small faction with the proper abilities assumes the mission to oust and depose the despotic ruler, though without monopolizing power, but giving it back to "those of loosing and binding," who in turn propose candidates to the people so that they may choose new leaders.

422. We will come back to the issue of monitoring the government when we come to the subject of the opposition.

423. Diya' al-Din al-Rayyis offered several examples of inane orientalist statements. See al-Rayyis, *Islamic Political Theories*, 360 ff. [Translator's note] *Orientalism* was the enormously influential book written by Palestinian-American literary theorist Edward Said in 1978. This concept reflects the Western production of knowledge in the social sciences and humanities about the peoples of the Middle East and Muslims in general. Said argued that this "hegemonic discourse" was often more indicative of Western preoccupations and attitudes as colonialists than about the real concerns and realities of the people themselves. Ghannouchi clearly follows al-Rayyis in using this as a pejorative term.

424. [Translator's note] Recall that 'Ali was assassinated only five years into his caliphate (661), and that is when Mu'awiya, then governor of Damascus and member of the Umayyad clan, took over the caliphate, moving his capital from Medina to Damascus.

425. Q. 42:38.

426. Q. 4:5.

427. Q. 2:219.

428. Huwaydi, *The Qur'an*, 225.

429. Al-Turabi, *Shura and Democracy*.

430. [Translator's note] This is the word *kufr*, which occurs several hundred times in the Qur'an and has a range of meaning, from "unbelief" (opposite of faith) to ungratefulness.

431. Cf. al-Faruqi, "The Rights of Non-Muslims in the Islamic State." No doubt, al-Faruqi is not speaking of any satisfaction of needs but of a generous satisfying of everyone's needs. Its importance comes from taking away the anxiety of this world and its struggle and conflict, and from creating a climate conducive to sowing the seeds of brotherhood, compassion, faith, and spiritual, intellectual, and moral development in the widest possible manner.

432. Q. 55:15.

433. Q. 41:10, Yusuf Ali.

434. Found in the *Musnad* of Ibn Hanbal and in Ibn Maja's collection.

435. See the section on "Economic Rights" in Chapter 2 of this book.

436. [Translator's note] Compare this to the popular Jewish motto, *tikkun olam*, "world repair," or more generally, social action for justice. In *Earth, Empire and Sacred Text*, I show that some classical (medieval) Qur'anic commentaries used the expression *'imarat al-ard* ("cultivating the earth," in the sense of "civilizing the earth") to express the scope of God's empowering humanity to be his caliphs, or deputies, on earth (269–317).

437. [Translator's note] The Front Islamique du Salut (Islamic Salvation Front, or FIS) was poised to win the second round of parliamentary elections in December 1991 when the army stepped in, canceled the elections, and declared martial law. This was the beginning of a civil war that lasted most of that decade and killed as many as two hundred thousand people.

438. Q. 17:107.

439. Q. 3:159.

440. Found in Bukhari's collection.

441. [Translator's note] The author uses the same word three times in this sentence (*wilaya*), but it has a range of meanings, especially when translated. Here I use "sovereignty," but I had just used two other English words to render it before ("responsibility" and "authority"). I am trying to express Ghannouchi's concern to strike a balance between individual responsibility and that of the state but with the lion's share on the shoulders of the people. He's a democrat through and through, and he comes to this position partially through his own experience of state repression (this book was mostly written in prison) and partially through his own theological understanding of God's empowerment of human beings as his deputies on earth, and of Muslims in particular as answerable (*mukallafun*, from *taklif*) to God's laws, or His Shari'a.

442. "Dialogue with Khamis al-Shamari" ("*Hiwar ma'a Khamis al-Shamari*"), *Haqa'iq* 382 (no author, n.d.). The context is November 7, 1987, when Zine El Abidine Ben Ali took power in a bloodless coup, the previous leader, Habib Bourguiba, having been declared incompetent.

443. Muhammad Fadil al-Jamali, "The Role of Education and Teaching in Planting National Pride in People's Hearts" ("*Dawr al-tarbiyya wa-l-ta'lim fi ghars al-'izza al-qawmiyya fi-l-nufus*"), *al-Quds* 1140 (n.d.).

444. [Translator's note] You can find the chart he is referring to on the following web page: https://en.wikipedia.org/wiki/Democracy_Index.

445. Appendix 3 of the Camp David Accord stated that educational methods would be formulated in agreement with the texts of the Accord—that is, the removal of obstacles and a full and comprehensive normalization.

446. [Translator's note] The author uses "Zionist entity" instead of "Israel" almost every time This is a reflection of the Arab refusal to recognize the state of Israel because of its dispossession of Palestinians, first in 1948 and then in 1967. Nor were the Arab nations forthcoming in trying to integrate the Palestinian refugees in their midst. Jordan did a bit better than Syria and Lebanon, but then it also made peace with

Israel. These nations watched closely the Oslo Peace Accords of 1993 and what transpired in their wake. The second uprising (Intifada) in 2000 was a clear sign that the two-state solution was no longer on track, yet the Arab League's Peace Initiative of 2002 stated that all twenty-two Arab nations would recognize Israel if she pulled back from the territories she occupied in 1967 and helped to establish a Palestinian state in its place. Though this commitment was reaffirmed in 2007 and 2017, the Israelis—who now have over half a million settlers living in the West Bank—have no intention of dismantling those settlements. Israeli-Palestinian peace is just as distant a possibility now as it was in 1993 when this book came out.

447. See my chapter entitled "The Philosophy of Curricula and the Lost Generation" ("*Baramij al-falsafa wa-jil al-da'i*"), in Rached Ghannouchi, *Articles (Maqalat)* (Paris: Dar al-Qarawan, 1984); and Ghannouchi, "Which Modernity? Our Problem Isn't with Modernity" ("*Ayyatu-l-hadatha? Laysa mushkiluna ma'a-l-hadatha*"), in *Qira'at Siyasiyya* 4 (Fall 1992).

448. Q. 51:56.

449. Q. 2:30, Yusuf Ali.

450. Found in the collections of Bukhari and Muslim.

451. Q. 33:21.

452. 'Abd al-Hadi Abu Talib and 'Ali Abu Laban summarized the objective of Islamic education in two goals:

 1. Teaching the individual about his Lord, so that he worships Him and follows His Shari'a.

 2. Teaching him God's laws in the universe, so that he worships Him and spreads goodness on the earth, enabling its people to follow Islam.

 See al-Hadi and Laban, *Development, between Reality and Futility (al-Tatwir bayn al-haqiqa wa-l-tadlil)* (Cairo: n.p., 1991), 6.

453. See the declaration by Muhammad al-Sharfi, the Tunisian minister of education, made to the journal *Jeune Afrique* (April 1990).

454. Mustafa Karim, *History of Tunisia and its Trade Union Movement (Tarikh Tunis wa-l-haraka al-niqabiyya)* (Tunis: al-Dar al-Tunisiyya li-l-Nashr, n.d.).

455. Q. 3:110.

456. Q. 5:8.

457. Q. 30: 22.

458. Mohamed Mzali, *Tunisia: What Future? (Tunisie: Quel avenir?)* (Paris: Publisud, 1991), 137.

459. [Translator's note] Though some Islamic movements arose to fight the colonial powers militarily (e.g., in 1830s Algeria or 1910s and 1920s Libya), this proved mostly futile from the beginning. The jihad here is a peaceful one, though still militant in its zeal to roll back some of the legal and cultural implications of Western interference with local governance. Paramilitary groups came to the fore starting in the 1970s, some being secular nationalists (like the Palestinian perpetrators of the 1972 Munich massacre at the Olympic Games) and others increasingly Islamists seeking to overthrow "ungodly" regimes (like President Sadat's assassins in 1981). The adjective

jihadi today, even in Arabic, refers to groups like al-Qaeda and ISIS, who use violence to establish what they see as God's rule on earth.

460. We selected that long text from this excellent study, 'Abd al-Majid al-Najjar, *The Role of Freedom of Thought for the Unity among Muslims (Dawr hurriyat al-ra'y fi-l-wihda al-fikriyya bayn al-muslimin)* (Washington, DC: International Institute of Islamic Thought, 1992), 84–85.

461. Roger Garaudy, ed., *Fondamentalismes* (Paris: Pierre Balfont, 1990).

462. Ja'far al-Shaykh Idris, *Contemporary Islamic Organizations: Critical Perspectives (al-Tandhimat al-islammiyya al-mu'asira: nadharat naqdiyya), al-Sahwa al-islamiyya* (India: n.p., n.d.).

463. Q. 39:18.

PART III GUARANTEES AGAINST OPPRESSION, OR PUBLIC FREEDOMS IN THE ISLAMIC SYSTEM

1. Baron de Montesquieu, *The Spirit of the Laws (De l'esprit des lois)* (1748).

2. 'Abd al-Rahman al-Kawakibi, *The Nature of Tyranny and the Struggle against Slavery (taba'i' al-istibdad wa-masari' al-isti'bad)*, 135.

3. 'Umar bin Abi Rabi'a, from a poem that begins thus: "I wish that Hind would fulfill her promise, and be a tyrant only once."

5. THE CONCEPT OF TYRANNY

1. Lenin, *Selected Texts (Mukhtarat)*, vol. 2 (Moscow: Dar al-Taqaddum, 1968), 287.

2. *The Modern Revolutionary Organization (al-Tandhim al-thawri al-hadith)* (n.a., n.p., n.d.), 141, quoted in Sadr al-Din al-Qabaniji, *The Political Methodology of Islam (al-madhab al-siyasi fi-l-islam)* (Tehran: Widharat al-Irshad, n.d.).

3. 'Abd al-Hakim Hasan al-'Ayli, *Public Freedoms in the Thought and Political Organization of Islam (al-Hurriyat al-'amma fi-l-fikr wa-l-nidham al-siyasi fi-l-islam)* (n.p., n.d.), 181.

4. Muhammad Taha Badawi, "Research in the Islamic Political System" ("*Bahth fi-l-nidham al-siyasi al-Islami*"), in *The Methods of the Orientalists (Manahij al-mustashriqin)*, ed. al-Manazama al-'Arabiyya li-l-Tarbiyya wa-l-Thaqafa (Arab Organization for Education and Culture) (Cairo: Jami'at al-Duwal al-'Arabiyya, n.d.), 109.

5. See the section "The State According to the Western Perspective" in chapter 3 of this book. This is something that Italian democracy has discovered in its political life, for instance, from the extraordinary spread of corruption, even to the point where it seems it is the underworld that governs it more than the democratic institutions of the state. This is a dramatic example of what politics can become when it is cut off from morality and religion—in this case, in democratic societies where regulatory bodies are still muzzled. As for our own societies, which are neither religious nor democratic, the calamity is even greater.

6. [Translator's note] The expression I translate as "the filthy rich of our day" is a Qur'anic reference to Qarun, or Korah in the Hebrew Bible, the archetype of the evil rich man.

7. Ziegler quoted in an article by Hisham Salih in *al-Sharq al-Awsat* (March 28, 2006).

8. Q. 96:6–7.

6. THE BASIC PRINCIPLES FOR COMBATING INJUSTICE IN THE ISLAMIC STATE

1. Q. 65:1.

2. A well-attested hadith.

3. Muhammad Taha Badawi, "Research in the Islamic Political System" (*"Bahth fi-l-nidham al-siyasi al-Islami"*), in *The Methods of the Orientalists* (*Manahij al-mustashriqin*) (Cairo: Jami'at al-Duwal al-'Arabiyya, n.d.).

    To take the original legislative power away from the state and entrust it to a just, knowledgeable, and neutral party—that is, God's Shari'a—represents the most important Islamic contribution to the opportunity of protecting peoples from the tyranny of their states. This is so because the state's greatest means of influence and hegemony over its people is the absolute legislative power it wields, which allows it to craft laws that benefit the ruling elites and oppress the forces of change and revolution. This in turn results in the state's ability to harness legislative power in a vital and crucial area—enacting tax law, just as *zakat* legislation with its precise specifications imposes a limit to the influence of the rulers on the ruled. See the important study on this issue: Tawfiq al-Shawi, *The Jurisprudence of Shura and Consultation* (*Fiqh al-shura wa-l-istishara*) (Al Mansura, Egypt: Dar al-Wafa', 1992).

4. Both quotes are from well-known hadiths.

5. At least during the time of the infallible imams; as for the period of their absence (that is, now), the entire umma agrees that the basis for the state's legitimacy is shura.

6. See Hasan al-Turabi, *Shura and Democracy* (*al-Shura wa-l-dimuqratiyya*), 15.

7. Cf. Abu al-A'la al-Mawdudi, *Towards an Islamic Constitution* (*Nahwa al-dustur al-islami*) (Cairo: al-Matba'a al-Salafiyya, 1953).

8. 'Abd al-Hamid al-Metwalli, *The Crisis of Islamic Political Thought in the Modern Age: Its Manifestations, Causes, and Cure* (*Azmat al-fikr al-siyasi al-islami fi-l-'asr al-hadith: madhahiruha, asbabuha, 'ilajuha*) (Cairo and Alexandria: al-Maktab al-Masri al-Hadith li-l-Tiba'a wa-l-Nashr, 1970). See also Badawi, *Research*; Ya'qub Muhammad al-Malliji, *The Principle of Shura in Islam* (*Mabda' al-shura fi-l-islam*) (Alexandria: n.p., n.d.).

9. Q. 48:10.

10. Q. 60:12.

11. Q. 9:111.

12. Article 25 of the Tunisian constitution: "Every member of the House of Representatives is considered a representative of all the people."

13. Badawi, *"Research,"* 130–131.

14. A hadith found in the collections of Abu Dawud and al-Tirmidhi.

15. Those who defend this principle from an Islamic perspective see, perhaps, that Islam and Islamic thought taught and practiced this principle for many centuries until the abolition of the caliphate in the early part of the twentieth century. The original leg-islation came from God, while the detailed legislation [*fiqh*] was the work of the scholars and jurists, who acted as the people's representatives, and the government nothing other than an executive body.

16. We read in the Preamble of the Tunisian constitution, "We, the representatives of the Tunisian people gathered in the national constituent assembly announce the es-tablishment of democracy founded on the people's sovereignty and supported by a stable political system the center of which is the rule of the separation of powers."

17. Hani Ahmad al-Dardiri, *Legislation: Between the Islamic and the Constitutional Ide-als* (*al-Tashri' bayn al-fikrayn al-islami wa-l-dusturi*) (Cairo: al-Hay'a al-Misriyya al-'Amma li-l-Kitab, n.d.), 94.

18. The head of state from the Western perspective is invested with sovereign power, ac-cording to Georges Burdeau's definition. See Burdeau, *Constitutional Law and Po-litical Institutions* (*Droit constitutionnel et institutions politiques*), 19th ed. (Paris: Librairie générale de droit et de jurisprudence, 1980), 27. In the Islamic perspective, he is invested with public guardianship [*wilaya*] over the Muslims—that is, the high-est position of leadership over them. So how does this agree with the presence of an-other authority, besides that of the Shari'a, which is the people who either elevate him or push him aside? How can the people recognize two parallel and equal sover-eigns? So who speaks on behalf of the umma, then, expressing its will and being re-sponsible to it? This is what the opponents of this view put forward.

19. Mahmud Hilmi, *The Islamic System of Government Compared to the Contemporary Political Systems* (*Nidham al-hukm al-islami muqaranan bi-l-nudhum al-mu'asira*), 2nd ed. (Cairo: Dar al-Fikr al-'Arabi, 1973).

20. Ibid., 355.

21. Ibid.

22. al-Tamawi, as quoted in ibid., 361.

23. Ibid.

24. Claude Rillieux, *The Political and Administrative System in Great Britain* (*al-Nidham al-siyasi wa-l-idari fi Britania*), trans. 'Isa 'Usfur (Beirut: Manshurat 'Uwidat, 1983), 19.

25. Dennis Lloyd, *The Idea of Law* (*Fikr al-qanun*), trans. Salim al-Sawis, 'Alam al-Ma'rifa Series 47 (Kuwait: al-Majlis al-Watani li-l-Thaqafa wa-l-Funun wa-l-Adab, n.d.).

26. Rillieux, *The Political and Administrative System*, 35–36.

27. [Translator's note] The Arabic for "cabinet" reflects a common nomenclature out-side the United States: "Council of Ministers."

28. Ibid., 30–31.

29. Ibid., 37.

30. Ibid., 38.

31. 'Abd al-Hamid al-Metwalli, *The Intermediary in Constitutional Law* (*al-Wasit fi-l-qanun al-dusturi*) (Cairo: n.p., n.d.), 211.

32. Ya'qub Muhammad al-Maliji, *The Principle of Shura in Islam (Mabda' al-shura fi-l-islam)* (Alexandria: n.p., n.d.), 255–257.

33. The Soviet Union collapsed and is now past history. We only bring up its political system because of its historical value in pointing out what autocracy can lead to, and no matter how much one embellishes or aggrandizes its structure, or expands on its armies or the spread of its followers, there is no escaping that it is a failed system. This applies to all autocracies, whether the obvious communist kind, or the unacknowledged kind of a democracy ruled by the great capitalist interests and Zionism, as is the case with the American system, which is now leading its people and the world to ruin.

34. Ibid., 265.

35. James Madison, the fourth president of the United States, quoted in Sadr al-Din al-Qabaniji, *The Political Methodology of Islam (al-Madhhab al-siyasi fi-l-islam)* (Tehran: Widharat al-Irshad, n.d.), 146.

36. [Translator's note] Literally, "as in the efficacy of the authority of the beyond [*sultan al-ghayb*] in the world of the *shahada*."

37. Abu Zayd 'Abd al-Rahman bin Muhammad bin Khaldun, *The Lessons and the Record of the Origins and Experiences of the Arabs, Persians and Berbers and the Contemporary Powers Ruling Them: Ibn Khaldun's Muqaddima (al-'Ibar wa-diwan al-mubtada' wa-l-khabar fi ayam al-'arab wa-l-'ajam wa-l-barbar wa-man 'asirahum min dhawi al-sultan al-akbar: muqaddimat Ibn Khaldun)*, 7 vols., vol. 7 (Beirut: Dar al-Kitab al-Lubnani, 1956–1959).

38. Hadith found in Muslim's collection.

39. [Translator's note] Here "Muslim head of state": *imam al-muslimin*.

40. See 'Abd al-Qadir al-'Awda, *Islam and Our Political Context (al-Islam wa-awda'una al-siyasiyya)* (Cairo: Dar al-Kitab al-'Arabi, 1951).

41. 'Abd al-Hakim Hasan al-'Ayli, *Public Freedoms in the Thought and Political Organization of Islam (al-Hurriyat al-'amma fi-l-fikr wa-l-nidham al-siyasi fi-l-islam)* (n.p., n.d.), 580.

42. Cf. Muhammad Salim al-'Awwa, *On the Political Organization of the Islamic State (Fi-l-nidham al-siyasi li-l-dawla al-islamiyya)* (Cairo and Beirut: Dar al-Shuruq, 1989); and Tawfiq al-Shawi, *The Jurisprudence of Consultation and Advice Seeking (Fiqh al-shura wa-l-istishara)* (Al Mansura, Egypt: Dar al-Wafa', 1992).

43. Abu al-A'la al-Mawdudi, *Redacting the Islamic Constitution (Tadwin al-Dustur al-islami)* (Damascus: Dar al-Fikr, n.d.), 39.

44. Muhammad Asad, *Islamic Methods of Government (Manahij al-islam fi-l-hukm)* (Beirut: Dar al-Musayyara, 1979), 101–102.

45. [Translator's note] Again, by way of reminder, the author uses emirate, imamate, and Islamic state as synonyms, having earlier argued that the ideal is a collective state for all Muslims but that these principles still apply to a modern nation-state.

46. Found in both Bukhari's and Muslim's collections.

47. Found in Muslim's collection.

48. Asad, *Islamic Methods*, 115.

49. Ibid.
50. Q. 24:4.
51. Q. 33:53.
52. Q. 2:275.
53. [Translator's note] Literally, "for the *jihad* of *da'wa* on the outside."
54. An expression attributed to Montesquieu.
55. [Translator's note] I have translated this second instance of the word "jihad" as "militancy." Ghannouchi is using jihad in its classical meaning—that is, striving in the way of God by all means necessary. That includes one's personal striving to defeat our base desires in order to follow God's path, spreading the faith among non-Muslims (*da'wa*), establishing Muslim-majority states based on the just laws of Shari'a, and if possible, uniting these nations so as to form a Muslim caliphate. But he strictly follows the modern Islamic consensus on the military side of jihad, in that it is purely defensive. A nation must defend its borders from hostile intruders. Like other mainstream scholars since the nineteenth century, he has repudiated the classical Islamic worldview—that is, the world as divided between the Abode of Islam and the Abode of War and the duty of Muslims to extend their borders by means of war. This is precisely what Sayyid Qutb and the jihadis after him are trying to revive. See, for instance, Mary R. Habeck, *Knowing the Enemy: Jihadist Ideology and the War on Terror* (New Haven and London: Yale University Press, 2006).
56. al-Dardiri, *Legislation*, 106–107.
57. The independence of the financial authority in the Islamic state corresponds to the independence of the central bank from the government's authority in most modern states like Germany. The goal of this financial authority is essentially to collect *zakat* [mandatory Islamic charity and one of Islam's five pillars], the revenues of which are defined in their collection and in their disbursement. This supervision could be done by a body with members from the Islamic scholars class, like deans of universities, members of the financial committee in the Shura Council, and representatives from the most important administrations, so as to ensure that the treasury remains independent from the state authority and can fulfill its functions in a manner that is above board.
58. al-'Awda, *Islam and Our Political Context*, 183 et passim.
59. Sobhi 'Abduh Sa'id, *Political Power and its Foundations in the Islamic System (al-Hukm wa-usul al-hukm fi-l-nidham al-islami)* (Cairo: Jami'at al-Qahira, 1985), 148.
60. Taqi al-Din al-Nabhani, *Islam's Political Organization (Nidham al-islami al-siyasi)* (Jerusalem: Matba'a Dayr al-Siryan, 1952), 87.
61. Q. 5:2.
62. al-Nabhani, *Islam's Political Organization*, 101.
63. Q. 11:118–119.
64. Q. 49:10.
65. Q. 49:9. Perhaps the tragedy of Somalia and before that the catastrophe of Kuwait offer a stark example of the destruction that the umma experiences in the absence of a collective Islamic state, as a people was almost annihilated by civil war and famine.

As a result, the United States had to come in and do what the Islamic state should have done to put an end to civil war and hostility, though it was not done without exacting a price.

66. Muhammad Abu al-Qasim Hajj Hamd, *Islam's Second Globalization (al-ʿAlamiyya al-islamiyya al-thaniya)* (Beirut: Dar al-Masira, 1979).

67. al-Mawdudi, *Redacting the Islamic Constitution.*

68. Q. 21:7.

69. This style of resolving a conflict between the president and the legislative body is similar to what happens in the American system, as mentioned above.

70. ʿAbd al-Hadi Abu Talib, A *Compendium of Constitutional Law and Political Institutions (al-Marjaʿ fi-l-qanun al-dusturi wa-l-muʾassassat al-siyasiyya)* (Casablanca, Morocco: Dar al-Kitab, 1980), 152.

71. Joseph Stalin, as quoted in ibid., 241.

72. On the expression "the marginal world," it was the Egyptian thinker Samir Amin who offered this vision of the world as centered on Europe with the rest at the margins.

73. [Translator's note] I added "People of the Book," as a clarification. The text says, "pagans" (or "idol worshipers"), which is misleading according to classical Islamic law, which only technically protected Jews and Christians, the People of the Book. In practice, at least in certain localities, Zoroastrians, Buddhists, and Hindus were given protected status (*alh al-dhimma*), including the sects the author mentions here.

74. See "Civil Society Organizations in Muslim Societies" (*al-Jamaʿat al-madaniyya fi-l-ijtimaʿ al-islami*), in Ridwan al-Sayyid, *Concepts of Organizations in Islam (Mafahim al-jamaʿat fi-l-islam)* (Beirut: Dar al-Shuruq, 1984), 77.

75. Cf. Ibn Taymiyya, Collection of Letters and Debates (*Majmuʿat al-rasaʾil wa-l-masaʾil*) (n.p., n.d.) 152–153.

76. [Translator's note] Ibn ʿAbd al-Wahhab (d. 1792), a religious reformer, allied himself with a tribal leader, and thus was able to spread his "Wahhabi" teaching to most of the Peninsula in his day. Shah Walli Allah al-Dahlawi (d. 1762) was the most famous Islamic scholar in eighteenth-century India. Sayyid Muhammad Ibn ʿAli al-Sanusi (d. 1859), born in Algeria, founded a Sufi order in Mecca later known as al-Sanusiyya. He was also an Islamic reformer and a leader in the fight against Western colonialism, mostly in Libya, where he fled after being persecuted by the Wahhabis. Muhammad Ahmad Ibn ʿAbd Allah (d. 1885), also a Sufi leader, founded a dynasty in Sudan and proclaimed himself the Mahdi, or the messianic figure of the end times according to Islamic eschatology.

77. [Translator's note] Literally, "the ideology of the righteous forbears," which, as mentioned earlier, was best articulated by Muhammad ʿAbduh (d. 1905) and evolved in the last fourth of the twentieth century into a much more literalistic, puritanical movement that dovetailed with an ascendant Wahhabism, thanks to Saudi petrodollars.

78. Rifaʿa Rafiʿ al-Tahtawi, *Complete Works of Rifaʿa Rafiʿ al-Tahtawi (al-Aʿmal al-kamila li-Rifʿa Rafiʿ al-Tahtawi*, ed. Muhammad ʿImara (Beirut: al-Muʾassassa

al-'Arabiyya li-l-Dirasat wa-l-Nashr, 1973), quoted in al-Nabhani, *Islam's Political Organization*, 27.

79. 'Abd al-Rahman al-Kawakibi, *The Nature of Tyranny and the Struggle against Slavery (Taba'i' al-istibdad wa-masari' al-isti'bad)* (Cairo: al-Maktab al-Tijariyya al-Kubra, 1931), quoted in al-Nabhani, *Islam's Political Organization*, 27.

80. Ibid., 28.

81. 'Abd Allah Sharit, *Problem of Political Rule in the Amir Abd al-Qadir's State and in the Theory of Ibn Badis (Mushkilat al-hukm fi dawlat al-amir 'Abd al-Qadir wa nadhariyyat al-shaykh Ibn Badis)*, quoted in al-'Awwa, *On the Political Organization*, 237.

82. Hasan al-Banna, *The Imam and Martyr Hasan al-Banna: Collected Letters (Majmu'a rasa'il al-imam al-shahid Hasan al-Banna)* (Beirut: Dar al-Qalam, n.d.), 376. [Translator's note] Hasan al-Banna was the founder of the first Muslim mass movement, the Muslim Brotherhood (1928).

83. Ibid., 366.

84. Declaration of the Fifth Conference of the Egyptian Muslim Brotherhood.

85. See, for instance, Rif'at al-Sayyid, *The Muslim Brothers in the Political Game (al-Ikwan al-muslimun fi lu'ba al-siyasiyya)* (Cairo: Dar Samad li-l-Nashr wa-l-Tawzi', 1985), a book about the Imam Banna. This book gives expression to the prejudice and abuse akin to the official position of Marxist, nationalist, and Arab political parties, and even the Tunisian Destour members who adopted this book and republished it by installment in their daily "al-'Amal" during a comprehensive anti-Islamic and anti-opposition campaign. Also similar to Rif'at al-Sayyid's study was Salih 'Issa's introduction to American scholar Richard P. Mitchell's book on the Muslim Brotherhood (*The Society of the Muslim Brothers* [Oxford and New York: Oxford University Press, 1993]). In addition to a method that violates scientific research norms, his approach also represents a great obstacle in the way of dialogue between the secular elites and the Islamic current. There is no alternative to this mean-spirited quarreling but to accept to live together with our differences and to rely on dialogue in order to achieve the lowest common Arab denominator built upon resistance, renaissance, and the transition toward a pluralistic democratic system encompassing everyone.

86. Mustafa Muhammad al-Tahhan, *Activist Thought between Authenticity and Deviation (al-Fikr al-haraki bayn al-asala wa-l-inhiraf)* (Kuwait: Dar al-Watha'iq, n.d.), 122.

87. Message of the Fifth Conference of the Egyptian Muslim Brotherhood (*Risalat al-Mu'tamar al-Khamis li-Ikhwan Masr*).

88. Fathi 'Uthman, *Islamist Thought and Development (al-Fikr al-islami wa-l-tatawwur)* (Beirut: Dar al-Qalam, 1961).

89. [Translator's note] Hasan al-Banna was assassinated by government agents in 1949, and though the organization had to lay low for a time, the leadership allied itself with the Free Officers who fomented the October Revolution of 1952. That collaboration was short lived, however, as the Muslim Brotherhood experienced its greatest crackdown (known by them as the *mihna*, or tribulation) in 1954. Historically, the 2013 military coup, which toppled democratically elected Mohammed Morsi and outlawed the Muslim Brotherhood once again, was possibly an even greater and bloodier

crackdown than that one. In both cases, however, they were beaten down by a military regime.

90. This was one of the Brotherhood's principles, as noted in the proceedings of the Fifth Conference of the Egyptian Muslim Brotherhood.

91. Quoted in Faruq 'Abd al-Salam, *Islam and Political Parties* (*al-Islam wa-l-ahzab al-siyasiyya*) (Cairo: Maktabat Qaliyub, 1978), 10.

92. Ibid., 11. [Translator's note] The veteran general Muhammad Najib was the figurehead leader of the Free Officers' 1952 coup, but from the beginning the younger officer Gamal Abd al-Nasser was the prime mover. Already in 1953 he overcame Najib's objections and banned all political parties, subsuming them under the Liberation Rally. In February 1954, Nasser succeeded in getting Najib's resignation from the Revolutionary Command Council (RCC) and had him put under house arrest.

93. Q. 23:53.

94. Q. 58:22, Yusuf Ali.

95. [Translator's note] The Arabic word I translate here as "idolatry" is *shirk*, literally, association. Here it means "associating partners with God," and therefore one could think of *shirk* as the one unpardonable sin in Islam.

96. [Translator's note] The *qibla* is the direction of prayer (toward Mecca) indicated in the mosque by the niche in the front.

97. [Translator's note] The Qur'anic word for "party of God" is *hizb*, also the same word in modern Arabic for a political party.

98. [Translator's note] In Arabic, the adjective I translate as either "Islamist" or "Islamic" is the same. The masculine plural is different: *islamiyyun* (Islamists). The Muslim Brotherhood is in fact the first Islamist movement. See the introduction for more on Islamism as a modern phenomenon. Though Islam and politics have been intertwined since Muhammad's rule in Medina, this was the first attempt to integrate Islamic values and a distillation of past political models into a modern nation-state context. I will go back and forth between Islamic and Islamist, as Islamists like Ghannouchi strongly believe that this movement is first and foremost "Islamic."

99. For this, see Muhammad al-Tawil, *The Muslim Brotherhood in Parliament* (*al-Ikhwan al-muslimun fi-l-barlaman*) (Cairo: al-Maktab al-Masri al-Hadith, 1992).

100. *Contemporary Political Thought of the Muslim Brotherhood* (*al-Fikr al-siyasi al-mu'asir 'inda-l-ikhwan al-muslimin*) (Kuwait: Maktabat al-Manar al-Islamiyya, 2001).

101. See the documents of that conference published by Markaz Dirasat al-Wihda al-'Arabiyya in Beirut. [Translator's note] The author has provided no other publication details.

102. [Translator's note] In Islamic law, silence of the texts on a particular issue constitutes permission. The assumption is that every action is permitted by God, except when he forbids it.

103. This is on page 131 in the document published by Markaz Dirasat al-Wihda al-'Arabiyya.

104. Ibid., 101.

105. Ibid., 132.

106. Ibid., 101.

107. Ibid., 132.

108. Ibid., 131.

109. Several countries have known a kind of coordination and collaboration among Islamist and secular groups, including Egypt, Syria, Lebanon, and Tunisia.

110. [Translator's note] I will use this (now most common) transliteration of the Arabic al-Nahda ("Renaissance," "Awakening," or "Revival") for the party Ghannouchi co-founded.

111. From the "Founding Declaration of the Islamic Tendency Movement," see appendix 1.

112. Salih al-Sawi, *Political Pluralism in Islam* (*al-Ta'addudiyya al-siyasiyya fi-l-islam*) (Cairo: Dar al-I'lam al-Dawli; Markaz Buhuth Tatbiq al-Shari'a, 1992).

113. As Dr. Najimi remarked in his dialogue with the extremist 'Umar Bakri on the BBC (June 21, 2006).

114. [Translator's note] The author is referring to the official doctrine of the Republic of Iran, the rule of the jurist (*wilayat al-faqih*), according to which the person with the greatest political power is a top cleric.

115. See Rached Ghannouchi, "The Principle behind Islamists Participating in a Non-Muslim Rule" (*Mabda' musharaka al-islamiyyin fi hukm ghayr islami*). This was a paper I presented to a conference on "Participation of Islamists in Political Rule," University of Westminster, London, April 20, 1993.

116. al-Sawi, *Political Pluralism*, 91.

117. al-Sha'ab ("The People").

118. al-Sha'ab (February 2, 1993).

119. Among the vanguard of those who after the fall of communism propose Islam, including its movements and civilization, as the candidate for the new enemy of the West and its civilization are the leaders of the Zionist entity and the groups that support them, especially the United States. At their head you find Bernard Lewis and Samuel Huntington. In this context, the Madrid Conference has given in to this by reconciling with Israel and its Middle East project. See the comments by Hazim Saghiyya in *Hayyat* (April 3, 1993).

120. This is from his response to a question published in the Kuwaiti newspaper *al-Mujtama'* (February 1993).

121. Ishaq al-Farhan, General Secretary of the Front, in a press conference, as reported in *al-Liwa'* (Jordan) (February 24, 1993).

122. [Translator's note] The "Nasserites" refer to those who allied themselves with the pan-Arab and socialist ideology of Egyptian president Gamal Abd al-Nasser.

123. Rached Ghannouchi, *Majallat Filistin al-Muslima* (April 1993).

124. [Translator's note] Born in 1932, Hasan al-Turabi has been the face of Islamist politics in Sudan since he became secretary general of the Sudanese branch of the Muslim Brotherhood in 1964.

125. Turabi, *Politics and Rule: Political Systems between Foundational Rules and the Laws of Reality* (*al-Siyasa wa-l-hukm: al-nudhum al-sultaniyya bayn al-usul wa*

sunan al-waqi') (Beirut: Dar al-Saqi, 2003), 79. [Translator's note] Mu'awiya was the founder of the Umayyad dynasty (660–750) based in Damascus.

126. Ibid.
127. Ibid., 108.
128. Ibid., 125.
129. Q. 2:148.
130. Turabi, *Politics and Rule,* 127.
131. [Translator's footnote] This name can be translated as well as "Justice and Good Works." It was started in the late 1970s by Shaykh Abdessalam Yassine (like for Ghannouchi, the French spelling is the most common).
132. François Burgat, *Political Islam: The Voice of the South (al-Islam al-siyasi: sawt al-janub),* trans. Lorène Dhikra (Cairo: Dar al-'Alam al-Thalath, 1992), 327–391.
133. Ibid.
134. Ibid.
135. Ibid.
136. Muhammad Mustafa al-Tuhan, *The Islamic Movement in Turkey (al-Haraka al-islamiyya fi-Turkiya)* (Western Germany: n.p., n.d.). Despite Turkey's secular framework upheld by the army, the Islamic Refah Party led by Necmettin Erbakan was able to arrive at the threshold of power for the first time since the abolition of the caliphate. The military, however, had him overthrown and his party disbanded, and then arrested him. But this did not stop his disciples from alternative political parties, the most famous of which were the Felicity Party and the Justice and Development Party. The latter was able to win a majority in the elections and rule independently, scoring results never achieved before in the area of freedom and economic development, and in reconciliation between Turkey and its identity and Islamic environment. This is an eloquent tribute to the huge possibilities of development that Islam can bring, if given the opportunity.
137. Ibid.
138. Burgat, *Political Islam,* 157.
139. See, for example, Muhammad Abd al-Baqi al-Harmasi, "Protest Islam in Tunisia" *(al-Islam al-ihtijaji fi-Tunis),* a paper he presented at the conference entitled "The Contemporary Islamic Movement in the Arab Homeland; Bureau of Alternative Arab Futures: Social, Political, and Cultural Directions" *(al-Haraka al-islamiyya al-mu'asira fi-l-watan al-'arabi; maktabat al-mustaqbilat al-'arabiyya al-badila: al-ittijahat al-ijtima'iyya wa-l-siyasiyya wa-l-thaqafiyya)* (Beirut: Markaz Dirasat al-Wihda al-'Arabiyya, 1987). See also 'Abd al-Latif al-Harmasi, "Groups of Political Islam in the Arab Maghreb" *(Jama'at al-islam al-siyasi fi-l-maghrib al-'arabi), al-Mawqif* 1 (July-August 1992). Finally, see the studies of 'Abd al-Zaghil on the same topic and Burgat's book on political Islam, as well as John Esposito, "Islam as Political Power in the North African States" *(al-Islam ka-quwwa siyasiyya fi bilad al-maghrib)* [no more details given].
140. See the work of Mukhtar Badri, *What Is Happening in Tunisia? (Madha yajri fi Tunis?)* (London and Kuwait: al-Markaz al-'Alami li-l-Kitab al-Islami, 1992).

141. See the petition signed by two hundred members of Tunisia's intellectual and political elite on April 9, 1993.

142. Muhammad Surur Zain al-'Abidin, "Message to the Algerian Soldier" (*Risala ila-l-jundi al-jaza'iri*), *Majallat al-Sunna* 23 (May 1993).

143. Again, see the petition signed by Tunisia's intellectual and political elites on April 9, 1993.

144. [Translator's note] This movement was known by its French acronym FIS (Front Islamique du Salut, or Islamic Salvation Front). I will use the French spelling for Madani's and Belhadj's names as I did for Ghannouchi, since they are the most common ones.

145. [Translator's note] The FIS won 48 percent of the popular vote and 188 of the total 231 seats in parliament in the first round of elections. See Wikipedia, "The Islamic Salvation Front," available online at https://en.wikipedia.org/wiki/Islamic_Salvation _Front, and my own entry in the *Encyclopedia of Islam and the Muslim World*, 2nd ed. (New York: Macmillan Reference USA, 2016).

146. [Translator's note] This was the mostly secular party that brought Algeria through the brutal war of independence (1954–1962) and continued over the years to be the sole party in power, as is the case still today.

147. The French newspaper *Le Monde* pondered this question (January 1, 1992), "Will the Army Save Democracy in Algeria?" Thus the French politician Michel Hubert reassured his people that the Algerian army had not yet spoken its word.

148. Cf. Zain al-'Abidin, "Message to the Algerian Soldier."

149. Shaykh 'Abd al-Hamid Ben Badis (d. 1940), founder of the Association of Ulama, was the most influential modern person in shaping Algeria's Arabo-Islamic personality. This poem of his has been on the lips of every Algerian and repeated with conviction: "Algeria's people are Muslim, and belong to the Arab nation."

150. Rached Ghannouchi, "The American Strategy and the Extremist Danger" (*"al-Istratijiyya al-amrikiyya wa-l-khatar al-usuli"*), *al-Fajr* (April 17, 1993).

151. Ghannouchi, "The American Strategy."

152. [Translator's note] This is the Front for Justice and Development Party (FJD).

153. [Translator's note] This is likely Abdelaziz Belkhadem, who was prime minister from 2006 to 2008. The Zaytuna University (or Ez-Zitouna) in downtown Tunis, Tunisia, is the oldest Islamic studies center in North Africa after Cairo's al-Azhar University.

154. [Translator's note] As a reminder, Salafis in this context represents an ultraconservative movement that appeared in the 1970s and shares many commonalities with the Saudi Wahhabis. To this day, most are apolitical and nonviolent.

155. [Translator's note] The word *kafir* means "unbeliever" or "apostate," designating in some cases non-Muslims, but in this context it refers to a regime led by Muslims whom Salafi-jihadis no longer consider worthy of the name "Muslim." By not following God's laws as these jihadis understand them, these Muslim leaders are now considered apostate and by virtue of classical Islamic law could be worthy of the death penalty. The action of calling a fellow Muslim *kafir* is called *takfir*. That this issue is critically important today is demonstrated by the fact that a widest possible consensus

of Muslim leaders and scholars signed a document in 2005 called "The Amman Message" (see the first point on this page, which condemned *takfir* in no uncertain terms: http://ammanmessage.com/).

156. Q. 28:8.

157. Q. 5:51.

158. "The Verification of God's Oneness by Fighting the Tyrants Is a Prophetic Sunna That Cannot Be Changed" (*Tahaqquq al-tawhid bi-jihad al-tawaghit sunnatan rab-baniyya la tatabaddil*). First in a series of pamphlets by the Egyptian jihadis.

159. From a fatwa circulated by Shaykh Muhammad al-Salih al-Nayfar in Tunisia in 1979.

160. Al-'Alam (June 1982).

161. Q. 21:92.

162. Quoted from an article by Hasnin Karum in *al-Quds* 1121.

163. Ibid.

164. [Translator's note] The two nations are Afghanistan and Iraq.

165. Q. 2:190.

166. [Translator's note] Again, calling fellow Muslims infidels (*kuffar*).

167. [Translator's note] Recall the series of battles between 'Ali the fourth caliph and the governor of Damascus, Mu'awiya, who initially lost his bid to grab the caliphate from him but subsequently declared himself caliph. After 'Ali was assassinated in 661, he moved his capital from Medina to Damascus. Mu'awiya was the founder of the first Muslim dynasty, the Umayyads.

168. Q. 12:9.

169. Turabi argued that there was no pluralistic system that could be applied in Sudan, because of its ethnic and religious diversity.

170. Abu al-A'la al-Mawdudi, *The Islamic State* (*al-Hukuma al-islamiyya*) (Beirut: Dar al-Fikr, 1977), 187.

171. al-Mawdudi, *Redacting*, 62.

172. Sa'id, *Political Power*, 141–142.

173. Cf. the author's book *The Debate about Unity and Diversity in Islam* (*Jadaliyyat al-wihda wa-l-ta'addud fi-l-islam*) (n.p., n.d.).

174. Sa'id, *Political Power*, 141–142.

175. [Translator's note] Recall that the first generation of Islamic reformers led by Muhammad 'Abduh were also the first to use the label of Salafis, but this should not be confused with the contemporary Salafis, who go back to the 1970s and have significantly been influenced by Saudi Wahhabism.

176. Cf. the chapter entitled "Difference in the Islamic Shari'a" ("*al-Khilaf fi-l-Shari'a al-islamiyya*") in Abd al-Karim Zaydan, *Collection of Essays on Islamic Jurisprudence* (*Majmu'at buhuth fiqhiyya*) (Baghdad: Maktabat Qadi; Beirut: Mu'assassat al-Risala, 1982), 279.

177. See an interview conducted by the newspaper *al-Ra'y* (Tunis) with Rached Ghannouchi in 1984, and the dialogue that ensued with the journalist Qasi Darwish.

178. The legal interpretation in Sudan went beyond this, giving regions with a majority of Christians the right to self-rule and to disregard the requirements of Shari'a.

179. Pierre Pactet, *The French Political Institutions* (*Les institutions françaises*) (Paris: Presses Universitaires de France, n.d.) [this book has been published in at least eleven editions].

180. Adam Metz, *The Islamic Civilization in the Islamic Fourth Century, or the Renaissance Age* (*al-Hadara al-islamiyya fi-l-qarn al-rabi' al-hijri aw 'asr al-nahda fi-l-islam*), trans. Muhammad 'Abd al-Hadi Abu Zayd, 2nd ed., vol. 1 (Cairo: Maktabat al-Khaniji, 1967), 67, quoted in Hasan al-Zin, *The People of the Book in Islamic Society* (*Ahl al-kitab fi-l-mujtama' al-islami*) (Beirut: n.p., 1986), 109–110.

181. al-Zin, *The People of the Book in Islamic Society.*

182. Quoted in Jean Paul Sartre, *Les Temps Modernes*, no. 252.

183. Murad Hofmann, *Islam: The Alternative* (Beltsville, MD: Amana, 1997).

184. We have previously mentioned Shaykh Mustafa Mashhur's fatwa on the rights of Christians, such as their right to join Islamic parties or form their own.

185. Election realities in Muslim countries like Jordan, Sudan, Tunisia, and Algeria have pointed to the weakening of the forces of atheism and secularism, in spite of the means of communication and resources they possess. What if the emerging and mostly persecuted Islamic movement had in its hands the authority of the state to shape public opinion and affect society? Would any current ruler dare in that case to confront public opinion by announcing his atheism? This shows the extent to which freedom could shape society along the values of Islam. There would only be a few individual and collective cases for civil society to resolve.

186. Q. 49:13, Yusuf Ali.

187. See lecture by Hasan al-'Alakim at the Conference on Islamist Power-Sharing at Westminster University, London, February 20, 1993.

188. Excerpted from Hisham Jaït, "Commentary" (*Ta'qib*) in *The Crisis of Democracy in the Arab Homeland: Research and Discussions of the Intellectual Conference Organized by the Center for Arab Unity* (*Azmat al-dimuqratiyya fi-l-watan al-'arabi: buhuth wa-munaqashat al-nadwa al-fikriyya allati nadhdhamaha Markaz al-Wihda al-'Arabiyya*) (Beirut: Center for Arab Unity, 1984), 55.

189. Ibid., 65.

190. Giscard D'Estaing, *French Democracy* (*Démocracie française*) (Paris: Fayard, 1976).

191. [Translator's note] We would say, "Might makes right."

192. From a verse by the poet al-Mutanabbi. (d. 965). The second half reads, "A wound never hurts a dead man."

193. Cf. Ja'it, "Commentary," 53.

194. Q. 3:110.

195. Rached Ghannouchi, "The People of the State or the State of the People" ("*Sha'ab al-dawla aw dawlat al-sha'ab*"), *al-Fajr* (1991). The newspaper *al-Fajr* was shut down because of this article.

196. Q. 22:41.

197. Pakistan's ruler Zia-ul-Haq declared in the Shura Assembly, whose members had been appointed after a movement of rebellion, that "democracy will better be assured by means of elections without political parties for there is no room for opposition in

an Islamic system of government that seeks unity and stability," *La Presse*, Oct. 23, 1983. His colleagues in the Arab world made similar declarations, saying that the electoral process is un-Islamic, while others recognized it to be good yet went against it in practice.

198. al-Mawdudi, *Redacting*.

199. Q. 3:110.

200. Q. 3:104.

201. [Translator's note] Mariz Tadros writes that this hadith is attested in five hadith collections and refers to the people of *dhimma*—that is, those non-Muslims considered part of the People of the Book and who live in an Islamic state. Yusuf al-Qaradawi quotes this hadith declaring that "Non-Muslims have reached *ijma'* (consensus) from the very first day that they have the same rights and duties as the Muslims." Tadros, *The Muslim Brotherhood in Contemporary Egypt: Democracy Redefined or Confined?* (New York: Routledge, 2012), 100–101.

202. Similar beautiful expressions have influenced our Christian brethren in the Middle East, like Makram 'Abid and several Lebanese scholars.

203. al-'Awa, *On the Political Organization*.

204. [Translator's note] As a reminder, *zakat*, the alms tax, is one of the five pillars of Islam.

205. [Translator's note] No reference given.

206. al-'Ayli, *The Public Freedoms*, 647.

207. Q. 49:6.

208. Q. 49:12.

209. Q. 53:28.

210. Sayyid Qutb, *Fi Zilal al-Qur'an*, vol. 9 (Cairo and Beirut: Dar al-Mashriq, 1980).

211. Found in al-Tabarani's collection.

212. Found in Bukhari's and Muslim's collections. "Opinion" here is often translated as "suspicion."

213. Abu Ishaq Ibrahim bin Musa al-Shatibi, *The Preservation (al-I'tisam)* vol. 2, (Cairo: Dar al-Sha'ab, 1970), 120.

214. Khalil Shabat, in *al-Thaqafa al-Islamiyya* 41 (February 1992).

215. From a press release on human rights by Amnesty International in Tunisia (March 1992).

216. al-'Ayli, *The Public Freedoms*, 647.

217. [Translator's note] This is a common expression that comes from Q. 5:54, "a people whom He will love as they will love Him . . . fighting in the Way of God, and never afraid of the reproaches of such as find fault" (Yusuf Ali).

218. Q. 5:2.

219. Q. 55:25.

220. [Translator's note] This was a solemn (pre-Islamic) agreement between feuding clans in Mecca for the purpose of establishing justice. It also allowed them to widen the scope of their commerce, with Yemen in particular.

221. See Qutb's commentary *Fi Dhilal al-Qur'an* and his interpretation of these verses.

222. Q. 8:61.
223. Q. 2:193.
224. Q. 60:8.
225. Muhammad Mahdi Shams al-Badin, *On a Comprehensive Islamic Politics (Fi-l-ijtima'
    al-siyasi al-islami)* (Beirut: al-Mu'assassa al-Jami'iyya li-l-Dirasat wa-l-Nashr, n.d.),
    131–132.
226. Q. 256.
227. Q. 2:190. Ibn 'Ashur adds this footnote: "The Arabic command *la ta'tadu* is so gen-
    eral that commentators have agreed that it includes prohibition of starting hostili-
    ties, fighting noncombatants, disproportionate response to aggression, etc."
228. Q. 17:34.
229. Abu 'Abd Allah Muhammad bin Abi Bakr bin Qayyim al-Jawziyya, *Informing Those
    Who Write on Behalf of the Lord of the Worlds (I'lam al-muwaqqi'in 'an rabbi al-
    'alamin)* (Cairo: al-Maktab al-Minbariyya, 1968).
230. Mahmud al-Naku', *Political Power and Despotism in the Arab Homeland (al-Sulta wa-
    l-istibdad fi-l-watan al-'arabi)* (London and Beirut: n.p., 1991).
231. The flames sparked by the riots [literally, *intifada*] of Los Angeles and the destruction
    they caused only went out because a state of emergency was declared and a massacre
    took place. [Translator note: Most likely the Rodney King riots of 1992.] This was only
    a small sample of what is going on within the fabric of Western societies in terms of
    oppression and injustice, which makes the blessed Palestinian intifada against the Israeli
    "democracy" look like child's play. See al-Naku', *Political Power and Despotism*, 88.
232. See Rached Ghannouchi, "What Modernity? Our Problem Is Not with Modernity"
    (*Ayyatu hadatha? Laysa mushkilatuna ma'a-l-hadatha*), *Qira'at Siyasiyya* 4 (Fall 1992).
233. [Translator's note] Literally, *jahiliyya* or the traditional Islamic label for the Arabian
    tribal society that preceded Islam and points primarily to "ignorance."
234. On the topic of Islam and *jahiliyya* in the arts, see Muhammad Qutb, *The Way of
    Islamic Art (Minhaj al-fann al-islami)* (Cairo and Beirut: Dar al-Shuruq, 1981), 182.
235. The martyr Ayatollah Morteza Motahhari, as quoted by Salah al-Din al-Jurashi in a
    report on Iran published by the daily *al-Ra'y* (March 31, 1984).
236. An expression used by Tunisian social scientist Khalil al-Zamiti in his critique of a
    leftist group in the journal *Haqa'iq*.
237. Rached Ghannouchi, "The Islamic Movement and Violence" ("*al-Haraka al-islamiyy
    wa-l-'unf*") in the declaration "The Third Anniversary of the Founding of the Islamic
    Union in Tunisia" (*al-Dhikra al-thalith li-inbi'ath haraka al-ittihad al-islami fi Tunis*)
    (June 6, 1984).
238. Salih al-Din Jurashi, "Dialogue with Khamis al-Shamari" ("*Hiwar ma'a Khamis al-
    Shamari*"), *Haqa'iq* 382.
239. This happened in Turkey and Tunisia.
240. Job discrimination for religious reasons happened and continues to happen in most
    Arab countries. On the use of torture, see the reports made by Amnesty International
    regarding Arab countries, like the March 1992 report on what was happening in
    Tunisia.

241. As reported in the newspaper *al-Quds* about a demonstration by the secular parties (March 1993).

242. During the preparation of the National Charter, Mr. Muhammad Sharafi [usually spelled Mohamed Charfi, d. 2008], who was charged with editing the text, refused to add the words "rotation of power," even after it was pointed out to him. The representatives of the ruling party insisted on not adding this scary expression, explaining that democracy did not mean a rotation of power.

243. On Islamic parties, see Tayyib Zayn al-'Abidin's piece in *al-Mustaqbila* 4 (April 1993); and Rached Ghannouchi, "Lessons from the Islamist Movement" ("*Durus min al-haraka al-islamiyya*"), *al-Insan* 9 (December 1992).

244. Recall the remark I have already alluded to by Tunisian historian and thinker Hichem Djaït.

245. Ernest Gellner, *Postmodernism: Reason and Religion* (London: Routledge, 1992).

246. Q. 14:24–25.

247. Manh al-Sulh, "Difference and Complementarity between Arab Nationalism and Islam" ("*al-Tamayuz wa-l-takamul bayn al-qawmiyya al-'arabiyya wa-l-islam*"), paper included in the publication of the conference proceedings *Arab Nationalism and Islam: Research and Discussions of the Conference Organized by the Center for the Study of Arab Unity* (*al-Qawmiyya al-'arabiyya wa-l-islam: buhuth wa-munaqashat al-nadwa al-fikriyya allati nadhdhammaha Markaz Dirasat al-Wihda al-'Arabiyya*), vol. 3 (Beirut: Markaz Dirasat al-Wihda al-'Arabiyya, 1988), 270.

248. A well-known hadith recorded in Muslim's collection, in Nawawi's *Forty Hadiths*, and a *hadith qudsi* [a hadith in which God speaks in the first person].

249. Found in the collections of Ibn Maja and al-Tirmidhi.

250. Found in the collections of al-Bukhari, Muslim, and al-Tirmidhi.

SUMMARY OF RESEARCH FINDINGS

1. [Translator's note] Here the "Confession of Faith" refers to Islam's first pillar, the "testimony" or "witness" [shahada]: "I testify that there is no god but God [Allah] and that Muhammad is God's Messenger."

2. 'Allal al-Fasi, *The Objectives of the Islamic Shari'a and Its Noble Virtues* (*Maqasid al-Shari'a al-islamiyya wa-makarimuha*) (Rabat, Morocco: Matba'a al-Risala, 1979).

3. Q. 17:70.

4. 'Abd al-Majid al-Najjar, *New Dimensions of the Shari'a's Objectives* (*Maqasid al-Shari'a bi-ab'ad jadida*), vol. 1 (Beirut: Dar al-Gharb al-Islami, 2006). [Translator's note] "Humanitarian spirit" here is to render an Arabic word difficult to translate (*insaniyya*).

5. Bin 'Ashur, *The Objectives of the Islamic Shari'a* (*Maqasid al-Shari'a al-islamiyya*), ed. Muhammad Habib Ibn al-Khawja, 3 vols. (Doha, Qatar: Wizarat al-Awqaf wa-al-Shu'un al-Islamiyya, 2015).

6. Q. 40:29, Yusuf Ali.

7. [Translator's note] Literally, the "deductive" one [*al-istinbatiyya*], since this is the verb often used to describe the function of the jurist who "deduces" from the text a ruling that applies to new circumstances under review [ijtihad].

8. [Translator's note] The Organization of the Islamic Conference (OIC) changed its name to the Organization of Islamic Cooperation in 2011 (still OIC).

9. [Translator's note] This is to say that the ruler had to be a jurist of the highest level, something which in practice never happened. This might have been another way for them to say that he needed to lean heavily on the Islamic scholarly class, which often did happen. Rulers needed the 'ulama' to maintain their legitimacy, but that relationship could also be tense at times, depending on the historical context.

10. Q. 59:7. [Translator's note] The context is the following: "Whatever gains God has turned over to His Messenger, kinsfolk, orphans, the needy, the traveler in need—this is so that they do not just circulate among those of you who are rich—so accept whatever the Messenger gives you, and abstain from whatever he forbids you. Be mindful of God: God is severe in punishment."

11. Q. 18:29.

12. Q. 21:107.

13. Q. 9:32.

14. Q. 12:21.

APPENDIX 3

1. Available online, http://d19cgyi5s8w5eh.cloudfront.net/eml/Z3MRep5sSxWcE6LJf AnytA. Thanks to the Center for the Study of Islam and Democracy for permission to reproduce its translation of the speech.

INDEX

Arabic personal names of the premodern era are not inverted. Personal names beginning with the article al- are alphabetized by the part following the article; for example, Abu Hamid al-Ghazali is alphabetized under G as Ghazali, Abu Hamid, al-. Names of organizations beginning with al- are alphabetized by the article; for example, al-Qaeda is alphabetized under A as al-Qaeda.